ETHIOPIAN STUDIES

Dedicated to

WOLF LESLAU

on the occasion of his seventy-fifth birthday
November 14th, 1981
by friends and colleagues

Edited by
Stanislav Segert and András J.E. Bodrogligeti

1983

OTTO HARRASSOWITZ · WIESBADEN

CIP-Kurztitelaufnahme der Deutschen Bibliothek

Ethiopian studies: dedicated to Wolf Leslau
on the occasion of his 75. birthday November 14., 1981
by friends and colleagues /
ed. by Stanislav Segert and András J.E. Bodrogligeti. — Wiesbaden: Harrassowitz, 1983.
  ISBN 3-447-02314-7
NE: Stanislav Segert. [Hrsg.]; Leslau, Wolf: Festschrift.

CONTENTS

LINGUISTICS AND PHILOLOGY

ALPHABET

HISTORY

CONTENTS

ABBREVIATIONS OF PERIODICALS

AAL	Afroasiatic Linguistics
AE	Annales d'Éthiopie
AION	Annali. Istituto Orientale di Napoli
AuÜ	Afrika und Übersee
BSL	Bulletin de la Société de Linguistique
BSOAS	Bulletin of the School of Oriental and African Studies
CIH	Corpus Inscriptionum Himyariticarum (Semiticarum)
C.R.GLECS	Comptes rendus du Groupe Linguistique d'études Chamito-sémitiques
CSCO	Corpus Scriptorum Christianorum Orientalium
EMML	Ethiopian Manuscript Microfilm Library
GLECS	see C.R. GLECS
GSAI	Giornale della Società Asiatica Italiana
IJAL	International Journal of American Linguistics
IOS	Israel Oriental Studies
JA	Journal Asiatique
JAL	Journal of African Languages
JAOS	Journal of the American Oriental Society
JEA	Journal of Egyptian Archaeology
JES	Journal of Ethiopian Studies
MIO	Mitteilungen des Instituts für Orientforschung
MO	Le Monde Oriental
MUSJ	Mélanges de l'Université Saint-Joseph
PO	Patrologia Orientalis
RES	Répertoire d'Épigraphie Sémitique
RRAL	Rendiconti della Reale Accademia dei Lincei
RSE	Rassegna di Studi Etiopici
RSO	Rivista degli Studi Orientali
SBWAW	Sitzungsberichte der Wiener Akademie der Wissenschaften
WZKM	Wiener Zeitschrift für die Kunde des Morgenlandes
ZA	Zeitschrift für Assyriologie
ZÄS	Zeitschrift für ägyptische Sprache und Altertumskunde
ZDMG	Zeitschrift der Deutschen Morgenländischen Gesellschaft
ZfE	Zeitschrift für Ethnologie
ZVORAO	Zapiski Vostochnogo Otdeleniia Rossiiskogo Arkheologicheskogo Obshchestva

PREFACE

On the occasion of the seventy-fifth birthday of Professor Wolf Leslau, the Department of Near Eastern Languages and Cultures at the University of California, Los Angeles, is proud to honor its founder, first chairman, distinguished member, and long-time friend with a volume of studies contributed by his colleagues, friends, and disciples.

Wolf joined UCLA in 1955 as an established scholar with an impressive record of publications and fifteen years of teaching experience in Paris, New York, Addis Ababa, and Waltham, Massachusetts. His achievements were recognized as early as 1946 and 1947, when, twice in succession, he was awarded the fellowship of the John Simon Guggenheim Memorial Foundation.

UCLA has become his permanent home, the focus of his manifold academic activities. Here, in 1958, he established the Department of Near Eastern Languages, later to become known as the Department of Near Eastern Languages and Cultures. For two terms he served as its chairman: in 1958-65 and again in 1974-76. It was largely through his efforts that the department grew from modest beginnings to its present size: 17 professors in seven programs covering all important areas of the Ancient and Modern Near East and Central Asia. He also played a vital role in planning the Center for Near Eastern Studies, that under its first director, Gustave E. von Grunebaum, emerged as one of the leading centers for such studies in the United States. In 1967 he founded the Near Eastern Club (we call it The Leslau Club) that with its informal meetings has become a forum for exchanging ideas and debating scholarly issues.

Wolf's teaching has covered a broad area, from Hebrew to Ethiopic languages and Comparative Semitics. Many students, both graduate and undergraduate, attended his courses. Between 1964 and 1966 he served the country as director of a series of Peace Corps training programs in which about 1,500 volunteers learned Amharic and prepared for their mission to Ethiopia.

His scholarship has earned Wolf many distinctions. He has been awarded two honorary doctorates, one by the University of Judaism, Los Angeles (1961) and another by the Hebrew Union College, Cincinnati and Los Angeles (1963). He is a fellow of both the American Academy of Arts and Sciences and the American Academy of Jewish Research. In 1965 he was elected Faculty Research Lecturer of the University of California. On that occasion he presented a memorable paper, "The Land of Prester John". The same year he also received the International "Haile Sellassie Award for Ethiopian Studies".

Retirement has exempted Wolf from teaching, but it has not slowed his research, as his recent publications demonstrate. While working on a project sponsored by the National Endowment for the Humanities, he finds time to participate actively in the life of the department. His broad experience is so rare.

We are pleased that this volume, so long in planning, has become a reality. Our thanks and appreciation go to the individuals and institutes that have made its publication possible: at UCLA, to Albert A. Barber, Vice Chancellor, Research Programs; Elvin W. Svenson, Vice Chancellor, Institutional Relations; Philip Levine, Dean, Division of Humanities, College of Letters and Science; Speros Vryonis, Director, Richard Hovannisian, Acting Director, Gustave E. von Grunebaum Center for Near Eastern Studies; Michael Lofchie, Director, Center for African Studies; Fredi Chiappelli, Director, Center for Medieval and Renaissance Studies; at the University of Judaism, Los Angeles, to its president, David Lieber.

We are grateful to Monica S. Devens for her meticulous bibliography of Wolf Leslau's works and to Rima Yoohanna, secretary of our department, for help in clerical matters.

We gratefully acknowledge the assistance of Dr. Helmut Petzolt and his co-workers at the publishing house of Otto Harrassowitz, Wiesbaden, as well as the exemplary work of the Imprimerie Orientaliste, Louvain, Belgium.

Stanislav Segert   A. J. E. Bodrogligeti
Professor of Biblical Studies   Professor of Turkic and Iranian, and
and Northwest Semitics   Chairman, Department of Near Eastern
                                          Languages and Cultures

AN ANNOTATED BIBLIOGRAPHY
OF THE WORKS OF WOLF LESLAU

MONICA S. DEVENS
Pomona College

The community of specialists in Ethiopian studies is aware of the pivotal place that Wolf Leslau occupies in the field. The production of this volume alone attests to that fact. The contribution of Wolf Leslau to Semitic and Ethiopic studies has been great, both in quality and quantity. The reader need only glance at the bibliography below to gain an appreciation of this work of forty five years. But despite the breadth of Leslau's endeavours—including even recordings (nos. 276 and 277)!—certain aspects stand out as particularly "Leslav-ian".

First and foremost, one thinks of Wolf Leslau as a comparativist and a lexicographer. The importance of the dictionaries he has produced cannot be overestimated. These are the only modern dictionaries—and, for some languages, the *only* dictionaries—available to us. Of particular importance to the field are the comparative dictionaries (nos. 1, 3, 7, 11, 14, 25 and 39) among which the *Etymological Dictionary of Gurage* (no. 25) stands out as a tour de force. Likewise of importance are the dictionaries of Amharic (nos. 23 and 24), as they are of use to a much wider public, and are the work for which he is known outside the confines of our field.

His comparative work is evidenced through the etymological dictionaries mentioned above as well as through the comparative and etymological studies in connection with Hebrew (nos. 9, 29), Ugaritic (no. 196), and Akkadian (nos. 167, 177 and 200). The Arabist will be interested in his articles on the Arabic loanwords in the various Ethiopian languages (see Index, "Arabic loanwords"). In the field of comparative grammars, mention should be made of his studies on Gafat (no. 7) and on Harari (no. 10).

Looking at Leslau's writings from a different vantage point, one sees that certain languages have particularly engaged him. Here we must give priority to Gurage and Gafat. Indeed Leslau might well be called the "Father of Gurage studies" with some 50 publications on various aspects of these languages and peoples. For the study of Gurage Leslau has been the prime mover, opening up an area which now interests others. On Gafat, however, Leslau has closed the book. His *Étude descriptive et comparative du gafat* (no. 7) contains all the primary data which will ever be available to us as he caught the language on the eve of extinction.

The work on Tigre and Tigrinya is not of the same exclusive nature, but in fact his grammars of these languages (nos. 2, 33 and 37) broke ground as the first solid scientific works available to Ethiopic scholars.

While Wolf Leslau is, of course, a linguist, he has produced much which is anthropological in nature. One must single out in this regard the continuing series *Ethiopians Speak: Studies in Cultural Background* (nos. 17, 18, 20, 26 and 29), and *Gurage Folklore* (no. 27), for here one finds the first published texts in languages and dialects which would otherwise have no legacy of written literature. These texts were composed by native speakers and give unique insight into the daily lives of these peoples. One (no. 18) was so successful that it even appeared in English as a novel.

Wolf Leslau is known outside of the specialized circle of Ethiopian studies for two other achievements: his practical tools for the study of Ethiopian languages and his work on the Falashas. Many people with varied interests wish to learn Amharic; the *Amharic Textbook* (no. 19) and *An Amharic Conversation Book* (no. 15), added to the dictionaries mentioned above (nos. 23 and 24), make this possible. The former (no. 19) is the international student textbook for Amharic. In addition, his many annotated bibliographies (nos. 16, 34, 64, 131, 132, 140, 203 and 211) make the world of Semitic studies readily accessible to a broad audience.

His work on the Falashas came at a time when they were not in the public eye and Leslau did much to bridge the gap between the earliest interest in their history and culture and the prominence in which they now stand. The *Falasha Anthology* (no. 6) opened up the study of this interesting people to students of Judaica as well as others in the fairest and the most objective way possible: by making their own writings available in translation.

The account of Leslau's accomplishments in the field of Ethiopian studies would not be complete without mention of the fact that all of the research discussed above was the result of field work, numerous trips to Ethiopia undertaken over a period of many years beginning with 1946. Anyone who has worked in the field appreciates the difficulties involved and the sacrifices which must be made by the researcher and the researcher's family.

Much of this work makes significant if indirect contribution to general linguistics. Leslau's work has made Ethiopian languages, perhaps more than those of any comparable region of Africa, known to general linguistics, where they serve as a check on theories of language which tend to be based on European and other geographically and politically more important language groups. Many of the articles have dealt with linguistic features interestingly represented in, or specifically characteristic of, Ethiopian languages, e.g. reduplicative morphology (no. 48), metaphors for "rainbow" (no. 121), laryngeal consonants and their reflexes (nos. 147, 207), expressions for "yes" and "no" (no. 168), expressions of future tenses (no. 194), the effect of frequency on phonological change (no. 198), nasalization (no. 205), spirantization (no. 216), influence of substratum languages (nos. 57, 98, 145 and 164), and phonetic adaptation of loanwords (to mention only one, no. 128). Here might be mentioned the linguistic-phonological resource of the "Outline of Gurage phonology" in volume III of the recent *Etymological Dictionary of Gurage* (no. 25), in which a wide range of specific phonological phonemes are catalogued and exemplified in the Gurage languages.

Finally there is the field of Modern South Arabian. This comes last because the present volume is dedicated to Ethiopian studies, but Modern South Arabian should come first in any discussion of Wolf Leslau's scholarly career because it came first chronologically. His first book, published in 1938, was the *Lexique soqotri*. This and some 15 other publications revived a field in which nothing had been produced since the early years of the 20th century.

The annotated bibliography presented here is divided into six categories: books, pamphlets, collections of articles, articles, reviews and recordings. Entries are given chronologically within each category and alphabetically under each year. A subject index follows referring to the consecutive numbering used throughout the bibliography.

Books

1938

1. *Lexique soqotri (sudarabique moderne) avec comparaisons et explications étymologiques.* (Collection de la Société de Linguistique de Paris 41). Paris: Librairie C. Klincksieck. 501 pp.

     Soqotri-French etymological dictionary (pp. 47-446) and French-Soqotri index (pp. 449-491), plus a discussion of Soqotri phonetics (pp. 14-43) and a grammatical sketch (pp. 9-13).

1941

2. *Documents tigrigna (éthiopien septentrional). Grammaire et textes.* (Collection de la Société de Linguistique de Paris 48). Paris: Librairie C. Klincksieck. ix, 388 pp.

Comprehensive grammar (pp. 3-154) and texts (pp. 159-378) with both an interlinear and a free translation.

1945

3. *Gafat Documents: Records of a South-Ethiopic Language. Grammar, text and comparative vocabulary.* (American Oriental Series 28). New Haven: American Oriental Society. 188 p.

> Grammar based on the text of the Song of Songs translated from Amharic at the initiative of James Bruce (pp. 1-99), text of the Song of Songs (pp. 101-138), Gafat-English vocabulary (pp. 139-181) and English-Gafat index (pp. 183-188).

1950

4. *Ethiopic Documents: Gurage.* (Viking Fund Publications in Anthropology 14). New York: Viking Fund. 176 pp., 12 plates.

> Chaha texts (pp. 33-81), folktales (pp. 82-111), songs (pp. 112-126) and proverbs (pp. 127-136) with interlinear and free translations, notes, an outline of Chaha grammar (pp. 12-32) and a Chaha-English glossary (pp. 145-168). See also nos. 85 and 93.

5. *The Fire on the Mountain and other Ethiopian Stories* (with Harold Courlander). New York: Henry Holt and Co. 141 pp.

> Collection of Ethiopian folktales. Translated into Czech, Rumanian and Russian.

1951

6. *Falasha Anthology.* (Yale Judaica Series 6). New Haven: Yale University Press. xliii, 222 pp. Reprinted in paperback in 1969 by Schocken Books, New York.

> Texts in translation with notes (pp. 3-184) plus a lengthy introduction (pp. ix-xliii), a selected bibliography (p. 190), glossary (pp. 191-192), and a list of scriptural references (pp. 193-201). Parts have been reprinted in nos. 89 and 90.

1956

7. *Étude descriptive et comparative du gafat (éthiopien méridional).* (Collection de la Société de Linguistique de Paris 57). Paris: Librairie C. Klincksieck. xx, 277 pp.

> Descriptive and comparative grammar of Ethiopic (pp. 7-168) with a Gafat-French vocabulary (pp. 169-252) and a French-Gafat index (pp. 253-260). The Gafat-French vocabulary is comparative. Gafat was considered extinct and indeed the author found only four speakers of the language.

1957

8. *Coutumes et croyances des falachas (juifs d'Abyssinie)*. (Travaux et mémoires de l'Institut d'Ethnologie 61). Paris: Institut d'Ethnologie. vii, 98 pp.
   Amharic texts with translation and notes.

1958

9. *Ethiopic and South Arabic Contributions to the Hebrew Lexicon*. (University of California Publications in Semitic Philology 20). Berkeley and Los Angeles: University of California Press. 76 pp.
   Addenda to Ludwig Koehler, *Lexicon in Veteris Testamenti Libros*. Includes indices of the languages under discussion.

10. *The Verb in Harari (South Ethiopic)*. (University of California Publications in Semitic Philology 21). Berkeley and Los Angeles: University of California Press. 86 pp.
    Descriptive and comparative study of the Harari verb.

1959

11. *A Dictionary of Moča (Southwestern Ethiopia)*. (University of California Publications in Linguistics 18). Berkeley and Los Angeles: University of California Press. 83 pp.
    Moča-English, English-Moča vocabulary with comparisons to other Cushitic and Semitic Ethiopic languages, plus indices by language of all the words mentioned in the comparisons.

1962

12. *African Proverbs* (compiled together with Charlotte Leslau). Mount Vernon: Peter Pauper Press. 61 pp.
    Proverbs from various African countries.

1963

13. *African Folktales* (edited together with Charlotte Leslau). Mount Vernon: Peter Pauper Press. 62 pp.
    Folktales from various African countries.

14. *Etymological Dictionary of Harari*. (University of California Publications in Near Eastern Studies 1). Berkeley and Los Angeles: University of California Press. xv, 240 pp.

Analysis of the Harari vocabulary (pp. 17-170) giving Ethiopic, Semitic and Cushitic etymologies, with indices of Semitic roots (pp. 171-175) and Arabic loanwords (pp. 176-186), and an English-Harari index (pp. 187-240).

1965

15. *An Amharic Conversation Book.* Wiesbaden: Otto Harrassowitz. 169 pp.

   Collection of dialogues dealing with everyday life in Ethiopia, with translation and notes.

16. *An Annotated Bibliography of the Semitic Languages of Ethiopia.* (Bibliographies of the Near East 1). The Hague: Mouton. 336 pp.

   Entries are given by language and subject within each language, with indices for authors, reviewers, and subjects, the last both general and by individual languages.

17. *Ethiopians Speak: Studies in Cultural Background. Vol. I. Harari.* (University of California Publications in Near Eastern Studies 7). Berkeley and Los Angeles: University of California Press. xii, 262 pp.

   Texts with interlinear and free translations, notes, and an index of Harari terms.

1966

18. *Ethiopians Speak: Studies in Cultural Background. Vol. II. Chaha.* (University of California Publications in Near Eastern Studies 9). Berkeley and Los Angeles: University of California Press. 219 pp.

   Book-length text in Ethiopian script, transcription and translation, with notes. A literary translation of the text was published as *Shinega's Village: Scenes of Ethiopian Life* by Sahle Sellassie, translated by Wolf Leslau (Berkeley and Los Angeles: University of California Press, 1964).

1968

19. *Amharic Textbook.* Berkeley and Los Angeles: University of California Press and Wiesbaden: Otto Harrassowitz. xviii, 675 pp.

   A 50-lesson textbook with exercises, reading texts, Amharic-English and English-Amharic vocabularies, and grammatical tables.

20. *Ethiopians Speak: Studies in Cultural Background. Vol. III. Soddo.* (University of California Publications in Near Eastern Studies 11). Berkeley and Los Angeles: University of California Press. ix, 236 pp.

   Texts with interlinear and free translations, notes, an outline of Soddo grammar, and an index of Soddo terms.

1969

21. *Hebrew Cognates in Amharic.* Wiesbaden: Otto Harrassowitz. 105 pp.
    Amharic-Hebrew index to words of common origin, with a more concise Hebrew-Amharic index and a discussion of the principles involved. The Geez origin of the Amharic roots is indicated throughout.

1970

22. *African Poems and Love Songs* (compiled together with Charlotte Leslau). Mount Vernon: Peter Pauper Press. 62 pp.
    Poems and love songs from various African countries.

1973

23. *English-Amharic Context Dictionary.* Wiesbaden: Otto Harrassowitz. xviii, 1503 pp.
    English-Amharic dictionary illustrating the various meanings of each word by using them in complete sentences.

1976

24. *Concise Amharic Dictionary.* Berkeley and Los Angeles: University of California Press and Otto Harrassowitz: Wiesbaden, xiv, 538 pp.
    Amharic-English (pp. 1-253), English-Amharic (pp. 257-535) dictionary with phonetic transcription.

1979

25. *Etymological Dictionary of Gurage (Ethiopic).* Wiesbaden: Otto Harrassowitz. 3 volumes.
    Volume I (xxix, 1244 pp.) contains individual dictionaries of the twelve Gurage dialects translated into English. The dialects are: Čaha, Endegeň, Ennemor, Eža, Gogot, Gyeto, Masqan, Muher, Selṭi, Soddo, Wolane, and Zway. Volume II (xii, 702 pp.) is an English-Gurage index. Volume III (cvi, 856 pp.), the etymological section, gives all Semitic Ethiopic comparisons, selected Semitic comparisons, and selected Cushitic comparisons with an emphasis on Sidamo. In addition, this volume contains an outline of Gurage phonology (pp. xv-xcii) and indices of Semitic roots (pp. 737-756), Arabic loanwords (pp. 757-761), and Ethiopian roots (pp. 762-854). See also no. 218.

1981

26. *Ethiopians Speak: Studies in Cultural Background. Vol. IV. Muher* (Äthiopistische Forschungen 11). Wiesbaden: Franz Steiner Verlag. ix, 205 pp.

> Outline of Muher grammar (pp. 6-50) plus texts in transcription with both
> interlinear and free translations (pp. 53-183), notes, and a subject index.

1982

27. *Gurage Folklore: Ethiopian Folktales, Proverbs, Beliefs, and Riddles.* (Studien
zur Kulturkunde 63). Wiesbaden: Franz Steiner Verlag. xiv, 327 pp.

> Folktales in Soddo, Eža, Muher and Ennemor (pp. 4-219), folk wisdom in
> Soddo (pp. 220-224), proverbs in Ennemor and Soddo (pp. 225-256),
> superstitions and beliefs in Endegeň (pp. 257-281), and riddles in Endegeň
> and Soddo (pp. 284-317). All have translations, notes and indices.

28. *North Ethiopic and Amharic Cognates in Tigre.* (Supplemento no. 31 agli
Annali 42). Naples: Istituto Orientale di Napoli. 86 pp.

> Suggestions for comparisons between Geez, Tigrinya, Amharic and Tigre
> using Enno Littmann and Maria Höfner's *Wörterbuch der Tigrē*-Sprache as a
> base.

1983

29. *Ethiopians Speak: Studies in Cultural Background. Vol. V. Chaha and
Ennemor.* (Äthiopistische Forschungen 16). Wiesbaden: Franz Steiner
Verlag. ix, 243 pp.

> Brief outline of Chaha and Ennemor (pp. 1-22) with Chaha texts (pp. 25-
> 133) and Ennemor texts (pp. 136-205), notes, and a subject index.

Pamphlets

1956

30. *The Scientific Investigation of the Ethiopic Languages.* An inaugural lecture
delivered at the University College of Addis Ababa on 12 February 1954.
Leiden: E. J. Brill. 31 pp.

> Survey of Semitic Ethiopic with a discussion of the importance of the study
> of Ethiopic. Includes a selected bibliography.

1968

31. *The Land of Prester John: Problems and Challenges.* Faculty Research Lecture, University of California, Los Angeles, December 2, 1965. Los Angeles. 35 pp.

> Problems and challenges encountered by the scholar in the study of Ethiopia.

32. *Three Addresses to His Imperial Majesty, Haile Sellassie First.* Addis Ababa. 19 pp.

> Texts of three speeches in Amharic, with translations, delivered on the occasions of the author's acceptance of the Haile Sellassie Award of Ethiopian Studies, the International Congress of Ethiopian Studies, and Charter Day ceremonies at the University of California at Los Angeles.

Collections of Articles

1945

33. *Short Grammar of Tigré.* New Haven. 66 pp.

> Reprint of nos. 55 and 61. No. 73 is a supplement to this work.

1946

34. *Bibliography of the Semitic Languages of Ethiopia.* New York: New York Public Library. 94 pp.

> Annotated bibliography reprinted with additions and corrections from the *Bulletin of the New York Public Library* 49 (1945):287-302, 375-390, 438-455, 516-529, 597-606. Published in condensed form in no. 64.

1964

35. *Ethiopian Argots.* The Hague: Mouton. 65 pp.

> Collection of four previously published articles (nos. 76, 77, 96, 170) plus a short discussion of common principles.

Articles

1933

36. "Explications et rapprochements à propos de quelques éléments du vocabulaire mehri", *Comptes rendus du groupe linguistique d'études chamito-sémitiques* 1 (1931-34):35

1935

37. "Remarques sur quelques mots du sud-arabique moderne", *Mémoires de la Société de Linguistique de Paris* 23:407-409.

> Discussion of some Modern South Arabic prepositions presenting the evidence of Ethiopic, based on the work by Bittner, *Studien zur Mehri-Sprache in Südarabien.*

1936

38. "Sur le préfix *n-* en soqoṭri", *Comptes rendus du groupe linguistique d'études chamito-sémitiques* 2 (1934-37):45-46.

> Examination of the meaning of this prefix in Soqoṭri and its relationship to the same prefix in the Ethiopian languages and in general Semitic.

1937

39. "Contributions à l'étude du harari", *Journal asiatique* 229:431-479, 529-606.

> Extensive etymological vocabulary along with comments on grammar and the text of the history of Ruth with interlinear and free translations. The vocabulary is taken from the writings of various authors.

40. "Mots amhariques présentant le traitement $k > \check{c}$" (with Marcel Cohen), *Comptes rendus du groupe linguistique d'études chamito-sémitiques* 3 (1937-40):11-12.

41. "Notes sur le tigrigna", *Comptes rendus du groupe linguistique d'études chamito-sémitiques* 3 (1937-40):37-40.

> Phonological and morphological notes on Tigrinya.

42. "Observations sur quelques faits éthiopiens et sudarabiques", *Comptes rendus du groupe linguistique d'études chamito-sémitiques* 3 (1937-40):19-20.

> Phonological, morphological, and lexicographic notes on Ethiopic and Soqoṭri.

43. "Le passif interne en soqoṭri", *Comptes rendus du groupe linguistique d'études chamito-sémitiques* 2 (1934-37):91-92.

> The internal passive is very common in Soqoṭri and is generally of the form *qítel* in the perfect, *iqútol* in the imperfect, and *máqtil* in the passive participle.

44. "Der š-Laut in den modernen südarabischen Sprachen", *Wiener Zeitschrift für die Kunde des Morgenlandes* 44:211-218.

> Discussion of the etymological correspondences of Modern South Arabic š, showing that it generally corresponds to Arabic s and Hebrew š.

45. "Über das *ḫa*-Präfix im Arabischen", *Wiener Zeitschrift für die Kunde des Morgenlandes* 44:219-220.

> Based on the work of W. Vycichl (*WZKM* 43:109), it is shown that the *ḫa*-prefix in Arabic is to be connected to Ethiopic and not to Mehri.

1939

46. "Essai de reconstitution des désinences verbales du tigrigna", *Revue des Études Sémitiques* pp. 70-99.

> Reconstruction of the quantity of the final vowels of the verb based on the presence or absence of gemination in the suffix pronouns. The dialect under discussion is that of Akkele Guzay.

47. "Observations sur quelques dialectes du tigrigna. Dialectes d'Akkele Gouzay, d'Adoua et du Hamasen", *Journal asiatique* 231:61-115.

> Discussion of phonology, grammar, and vocabulary plus texts in the dialects of Adoua and Akkele Gouzay.

48. "Le thème verbal fréquentatif dans les langues éthiopiennes", *Revue des Études Sémitiques* pp. 15-31.

> Discussion of the verbal type *qatāt(t)ala*, with a note on the hypothesis of a reduplicative stem in Epigraphic South Arabic.

1943

49. "South-east Semitic (Ethiopic and South-Arabic)", *Journal of the American Oriental Society* 62:4-14.

> Discussion of the genetic relationship between Ethiopic and South Arabic, including a vocabulary of common roots. Reprinted in *Comparative Semitic Linguistics: A Student's Reader* (ed. M.H. Goshen-Gottstein).

1944

50. "Eugen Mittwoch (1876-1942). Necrology", *Annuaire de l'Institut de Philologie et d'Histoire Orientales et Slaves* 7 (1939-1944):531-532.

51. "The position of Gafat in Ethiopic", *Language* 20:56-65.

> Analysis of Gafat based on documents collected by James Bruce, resulting in the conclusion that Gafat belongs in the Harari-Occidental Guragué group of South Ethiopic. See also no. 86.

52. "Le rapport entre *š* et *h* en sémitique", *Annuaire de l'Institut de Philologie et d'Histoire Orientales et Slaves* 7 (1939-1944):265-272.

> Examination of the question based on data from Modern South Arabian, resulting in the hypothesis that an original phoneme *š* became *h* in some Semitic languages.

53. "Texts on Yemenite folklore", *Proceedings of the American Academy for Jewish Research* 14:221-251.

> Collection of texts in transcription with translation and notes, plus a list of words having special meaning in Yemenite and a list of the Hebrew words in the texts.

54. "Vocabulary common to Akkadian and South-east Semitic (Ethiopic and South-Arabic)", *Journal of the American Oriental Society* 64:53-58.

1945

55. "Grammatical sketches in Tigré (North Ethiopic), dialect of Mensa", *Journal of the American Oriental Society* 65:164-203.

> Study of the parts of speech other than the verb based on the texts published by E. Littmann (see no. 61). Reprinted together with no. 61 as no. 33.

56. "Hebrew elements in the Judeo-Arabic dialect of Fez", *Jewish Quarterly Review*, New Series 36 (1945-46):61-78.

> Discussion of the influence of Hebrew on the phonology, morphology and lexicon of the Judeo-Arabic dialect of Fez based on materials published by L. Brunot and E. Malka, *Textes Judéo-Arabes de Fès.*

57. "The influence of Cushitic on the Semitic languages of Ethiopia: a problem of substratum", *Word* 1:59-82.

> Study of Cushitic influence on the phonology, morphology, syntax and lexicon of Semitic Ethiopic. See also no. 164.

58. "Judeo-Arabic dialects", *Yivo Bletter* 26:58-78.

> Written in Yiddish. Analysis of the Judeo-Arabic dialects of North Africa, Yemen, and Bagdad.

59. "The parts of the body in the Modern South Arabic languages", *Language* 21:230-249.

> The parts of the body in Mehri, Šḥauri, Soqoṭri, Harsusi, and Curia Muria compared with the other Semitic languages. English-South Arabic index, pp. 246-249.

60. "Sur le diminutif verbal en sémitique", *Word* 1:277-280.

> Discussion of verbal forms of the types *qaytala*, *qatayla*, and *qatyala.*

61. "The verb in Tigré (North-Ethiopic): Dialect of Mensa", *Journal of the American Oriental Society* 65:1-26.

> Based on the texts published by E. Littmann, *Publications of the Princeton Expedition to Abyssinia*, Vol. I. Reprinted together with no. 55 as no. 33.

1946

62. "Bibliography of the Modern South Arabic languages", *Bulletin of the New York Public Library* 50:607-633.

> Annotated bibliography with indices by language and by author.

63. "Linguistic observations on a native Yemenite document", *Jewish Quarterly Review*, New Series 36 (1945-46):261-279.

     Additional linguistic observations on the Judeo-Arabic text published by S. D. Goitein, *Travels in Yemen. An account of Joseph Halévy's journey to Najran in the year 1870, written in San'ani by his guide Hayyim Habshush.*

64. "The present state of Ethiopic linguistics", *Journal of Near Eastern Studies* 5:215-229.

     Annotated bibliography condensed from the author's no. 34.

1947

65. "Chansons harari", *Rassegna di Studi Etiopici* 6:130-160.

     Songs with an interlinear translation, a free translation, and notes.

66. "A Falasha religious dispute", *Proceedings of the American Academy for Jewish Research* 16:71-95.

     Falasha text in Geez with translation, notes, short accounts of the dispute as presented by others, and an excursus concerning the question of the Falashas' knowledge of Hebrew.

67. "Four Modern South Arabic languages", *Word* 3:180-203.

     Discussion of the phonology and morphology of Šḥauri, Mehri, Harsusi and Botahari, based on the material collected by Bertram Thomas, "Four Strange Tongues from South Arabia, the Hadara Group", *Proceedings of the British Academy* 23 (1937):231-331.

68. "The position of the dialect of Curia Muria in Modern South Arabic", *Bulletin of the School of Oriental and African Studies, University of London* 12:5-19.

     Establishment of Curia Muria as a Šḥauri dialect based on the vocabulary collected by J. G. Hulton in his "Notice on the Curia Muria Island", *Transactions of the Bombay Geographical Society* 3 (1840):183-197.

1948

69. "Ha-Falashim", *Edoth* 3:26-45.

     Based on a visit made in 1946 and written in Hebrew. No. 75 is the English version of this article.

70. "Mother's Day in Ethiopia", *Journal of American Folklore* 61:392-395.

     Traditional celebration among the Gurage.

71. "Preliminary report on a trip to Ethiopia", *Transactions of the New York Academy of Sciences*, Series 2 10:291-297.

     Based on 9 months spent in Ethiopia in 1946-47.

72. "Le problème de la gémination du verbe tchaha (gouragué)", *Word* 4:42-47.

Discussion of the Chaha verb showing that, while there is no gemination of the 2nd radical, original type B verbs can be spotted by the phonetic quality of their 2nd radical.

73. "Supplementary observations on Tigré grammar", *Journal of the American Oriental Society* 68:127-139.

Supplement to no. 33. The study is based on personal investigation in Keren.

74. "A year of research in Ethiopia", *Word* 4:212-225.

The author spent October, 1946-July, 1947 in Ethiopia.

1949

75. "The Black Jews of Ethiopia: an expedition to the Falashas", *Commentary* 7:216-224.

English version of no. 69. Also published in *Negro Digest*, September, 1949; *Ha-Tsofe* (in Hebrew), October 2, 4, 1949; *Yalkut Ha-Mizrach Ha-Tichon* (in Hebrew) 1 (1949):7-8; *Der Tag* (in Yiddish), August 30-September 4, 1952; and *Évidences* (in French) 6 (1954):28-33.

76. "An Ethiopian argot of people possessed by a spirit", *Africa* 19:204-212.

Discussion of belief in the *zar* and an analysis of the vocabulary used by the *zar*. Reprinted in no. 35 and, in a short version, in no. 125.

77. "An Ethiopian merchants' argot", *Language* 25:22-28.

Analysis of morphological, morphophonemic, and semantic aspects of the merchants' argot of Godjam, with an alphabetical index of words discussed. Reprinted in no. 35.

78. "Ethiopic proverbs of Chaha", *Word* 5:214-223.

Collection of proverbs with a literal translation, a free translation, and notes.

79. "Examen du supposé argobba de Seetzen et de Lefebvre", *Word* 5:46-54.

Analysis of the vocabulary presented by Seetzen and Lefebvre, resulting in the conclusion that their descriptions concern not Argobba, but rather Selṭi-Walani Gurage.

80. "The meaning of *ARAB* in Ethiopia", *The Muslim World* 39:307-308.

Study of the use of *arab* to indicate a foreign or imported object.

81. "Notes de grammaire et d'étymologie éthiopienne", *Word* 5:273-279.

Phonological, morphological, and lexical notes on Semitic Ethiopic.

82. "A parallel to the non-gemination of the Hebrew *R* ", *Journal of Biblical Literature* 68:55-56.

The phenomenon occurs in the Gafat verb.

1950

83. "Ethiopia", *The New International Year Book, Events of 1949*. New York: Dodd, Mead and Co. Pp. 169-170.

84. "Impressions of Ethiopia", *Middle Eastern Affairs* 1:316-320.
    Based on research trips to Ethiopia in 1946-47 and 1950.

85. "Observations on Gurage documents", *Word* 6:234-238.
    Addenda to no. 4.

86. "La position du gafat parmi les langues sémitiques de l'Éthiopie",
    Comptes rendus du groupe linguistique d'études chamito-sémitiques 5:47-48.
    Based on additional data, the author places Gafat in the same group as the
    Gurage dialect of Aymallal, contrary to no. 51.

87. "The religious life of the Falashas", *Yivo Bleter* 34:209-220.
    Written in Yiddish.

88. "A wedding 'law-suit' in Harar (Ethiopia)", *Journal of American Folklore*
    63:363-365.
    Description of an imaginary lawsuit brought during the wedding ceremony.

1951

89. "The Angels bury Moses. A legend of the Falashas", *Commentary*
    12:481-483.
    Reprint of "The Death of Moses" from no. 6.

90. "The Apocalypse of Gorgorios", *Commentary* 12:583-585.
    Reprint of "Apocalypse of Gorgorios" from no. 6.

91. "Archaic features in South Ethiopic", *Journal of the American Oriental
    Society* 71:212-230.
    Examination of phonological and morphological features common to both
    North and South Ethiopic (excluding Amharic), leading to the conclusion
    that North and South Ethiopic may indeed derive from one ancestral
    language. See also no. 192.

92. "Ethiopia", *The New International Year Book, Events of 1950*. New York:
    Dodd, Mead and Co. Pp. 176-178.

93. "Observations on 'Gurage Notes'", *Africa* 21:139-145.
    Reply to a review by E. Ullendorff (*Africa* 20:335-344) of no. 4.

94. "Le type *läbsä* en gouragué", *Rassegna di Studi Etiopici* 10:85-98.
    Examination of the jussive forms in Chaha, Ennemor, Muher and Masqan
    and their similarity to the corresponding Geez forms. See also no. 173,
    189, 221.

1952

95. "Ethiopia", *The New International Year Book, Events of 1951*. New York:
    Dodd, Mead and Co. Pp. 185-187.

96. "An Ethiopian minstrels' argot", *Journal of the American Oriental Society*
    72:102-109.

Analysis of morphological, morphophonemic, and semantic aspects of the minstrels' argot of Godjam and Gondar, with an alphabetical index of words discussed. Reprinted in no. 35.

97. "A footnote on interlingual word taboos", Letter to the Editor, *American Anthropologist* 54:274.

Discussion of Gurage *bädda*.

98. "The influence of Sidamo on the Ethiopic languages of Gurage", *Language* 28:63-81.

Discussion of Sidamo influence in phonology, morphology, syntax and vocabulary.

99. "The languages of Ethiopia", *Ethiopian Student News*, March 1952, pp. 17, 20-22.

100. "Linguistic observations on a Tigre codex", *Rassegna di Studi Etiopici* 11:33-46.

Different interpretation of some passages of Maria Höfner's translation of the *fĕtĕḥ mähäri wä'ädotät*.

101. "Notes on Kambatta of Southern Ethiopia", *Africa* 22:348-359.

Brief outline of Kambatta phonology and morphology. See also no. 114.

102. "Popular interpretations of bird sounds in Ethiopia", *Journal of American Folklore* 65:361-364.

Collection of interpretations of bird sounds in terms of human language in various Ethiopian languages.

103. "Report on a second trip to Ethiopia", *Word* 8:72-79.

The author stayed in Ethiopia from February to July, 1950.

1953

104. "Contemporary Yemenite letters", *The Joshua Starr Memorial Volume; studies in history and philology.* (Jewish Social Studies. Publications 5). New York. Pp. 249-262.

Letters written mostly in Hebrew, partly in Arabic, with translation and linguistic notes.

105. "Ethiopia", *Britannica Junior.* Chicago: Encyclopaedia Britannica, Inc. 3 pp.

106. "Ethiopia", *The New International Year Book, Events of 1952.* New York: Dodd, Mead and Co. Pp. 161-162.

107. "The imperfect in South-east Semitic", *Journal of the American Oriental Society* 73:164-166.

Discussion of the presence or absence of gemination in the 2nd radical of the imperfect of the basic stem in Proto-South-east Semitic.

108. "La réforme de l'alphabet éthiopien", *Rassegna di Studi Etiopici* 12:96-106.

> Review of *Fidälən Maššašal* (Addis Ababa, 1948) plus additional suggestions in connection with the proposed reform of the Ethiopic alphabet.

109. "Suggestions for a phonetic transcription of Ethiopian languages", *New Times and Ethiopia News*, June 6, 1953, pp. 1, 4.

1954

110. "Ethiopia", *The New International Year Book, Events of 1953*. New York: Dodd, Mead and Co. Pp. 152-153.

111. "Les Fallachas", *Évidences*, November, 1954, pp. 28-33.

> Notes on Falasha life based on a visit to their villages.

112. "Le type verbal *qatälä* en éthiopien méridional", *Mélanges de l'Université Saint Joseph* 31:15-95.

> Study of Type C verbs in South Ethiopic excluding Amharic, plus a list of these verbs.

1955

113. "Ethiopia", *The New International Year Book, Events of 1954*. New York: Dodd, Mead and Co. Pp. 148-149.

1956

114. "Additional notes on Kambatta of Southern Ethiopia", *Anthropos* 51:985-993.

> Discussion of various phonological and morphological questions. See also no. 101.

115. "The Arabic loanwords in Gurage (Southern Ethiopia)", *Arabica* 3:266-284.

> Discussion of the phonetic and morphological principles governing the treatment of Arabic loanwords and a list of loanwords by subject.

116. "Arabic loanwords in Harari", *Studi orientalistici in onore di Giorgio Levi Della Vida*. (Pubblicazioni dell'Istituto per l'Oriente 52). Rome: Istituto per l'Oriente. Vol. 2, pp. 14-35.

> Discussion of the phonetic and morphological principles governing the treatment of Arabic loanwords and a list of loanwords by subject.

117. "Arabic loanwords in Tigré", *Word* 12:125-141.

> Discussion of the phonetic and morphological principles governing the

treatment of Arabic loanwords and a list of loanwords by subject. See also no. 220.

118. "Arabic loanwords in Tigrinya", *Journal of the American Oriental Society* 76:204-213.

> Discussion of the phonetic and morphological principles governing the treatment of Arabic loanwords and a list of loanwords by subject.

119. "Ethiopia", *The New International Year Book, Events of 1955.* New York: Dodd, Mead and Co. Pp. 147-149.

120. "The expressions 'under, after' in the Ethiopic languages", *Journal of Near Eastern Studies* 15:241-245.

121. "The rainbow in the Hamito-Semitic languages", *Orbis* 5:478-483.

> Listing of expressions with an index by language.

1957

122. "Arabic loanwords in Amharic", *Bulletin of the School of Oriental and African Studies, University of London* 19:221-244.

> Discussion of the phonetic and morphological principles governing the treatment of Arabic loanwords and a list of loanwords by subject.

123. "Arabic loanwords in Argobba (South Ethiopic)", *Journal of the American Oriental Society* 77:36-39.

> Discussion of the phonetic and morphological principles governing the treatment of Arabic loanwords and an alphabetic list of loanwords.

124. "Ethiopia", *The New International Year Book, Events of 1956.* New York: Dodd, Mead and Co. Pp. 146-147.

125. "Ethiopia's language of the possessed", *Tomorrow* 5:84-88.

> Short version of no. 76.

126. "Une hypothèse sur la forme primitive du type B en amharique", *Word* 13:479-488.

> Discussion of the possibility that the original form of the Amharic type B verb was *fellägä*.

127. "Observations on a comparative phonology of Semitic Ethiopic", *Annales d'Éthiopie* 2:147-166.

> Detailed review of E. Ullendorff, *The Semitic Languages of Ethiopia. A comparative phonology.*

128. "The phonetic treatment of the Arabic loanwords in Ethiopic", *Word* 13:100-123.

> General study based on the material presented by the author in nos. 115, 116, 117, 118, 122, 123 and 134.

129. "The Semitic phonetic system", *Manual of Phonetics.* (ed. L. Kaiser). Amsterdam: North-Holland Publishing Co. Pp. 325-329.

130. "Some mutilated roots in Ethiopic", *Lingua* 6:268-286.
     Investigation of 42 roots in the Ethiopic languages which have radically changed due to phonetic developments.

131. "A supplementary Falasha bibliography", *Studies in Bibliography and Booklore* 3:9-27.
     Annotated bibliography supplementary to A. Z. Aešcoly, "The Falashas: a bibliography", *Kiryath Sepher* 12, 13 (1935-37).

132. "Ten years of Ethiopic linguistics (1946-1956)", *Annales d'Éthiopie* 2:277-318.
     Annotated bibliography. See also no. 140.

133. "To the defense of the Falashas", *Judaism* 6:142-147.
     Reply to an article by D. M. Friedenberg, "The Decline and Fall of the Falashas", *Judaism* 5:239-247.

1958

134. "Arabic loanwords in Geez", *Journal of Semitic Studies* 3:146-168.
     Discussion of the phonetic and morphological principles governing the treatment of Arabic loanwords and a list of loanwords by subject.

135. "The Arabic origin of the Ethiopic *qollē* 'spirit'", *Arabica* 5:194-196.

136. "Ethiopia", *The New International Year Book, Events of 1957*. New York: Dodd, Mead and Co. Pp. 135-136.

137. "The languages of Ethiopia and their geographical distribution", *Ethiopia Observer* 2:116-121.

138. "Moča, a tone language of the Kafa group in South-western Ethiopia", *Africa* 28:135-147.
     Discussion of phonology and morphology.

139. "Observations of a Semitist on recent etymologies proposed by Africanists", *Africa* 28:324-328.
     Response to Joseph Greenberg's *Studies in African Linguistic Classification*.

140. "Report on Ethiopic linguistics 1946-1956", *Journal of Near Eastern Studies* 17:49-55.
     Narrative bibliography according to subject based on no. 132.

1959

141. "An analysis of the Harari vocabulary", *Annales d'Éthiopie* 3:275-298.
     Division of the Harari vocabulary into groups with common origins (Ethiopic, North Ethiopic, South Ethiopic, loanwords, doubtful or unknown etymologies, etc.).

142. "On mule-back through Gurage in Ethiopia" (with S. Chojnacki), *Canadian Geographical Journal* 58:90-99.

> Travelogue which delimits the region of Eža.

143. "The position of Ethiopic in Semitic: Akkadian and Ethiopic", *Akten des 24 internationalen Orientalisten-Kongresses, 1957*. (ed. Herbert Franke). Wiesbaden: Franz Steiner Verlag. Pp. 251-253.

> Examination of the question of the genetic relationship between Akkadian and Ethiopic and a rejection of the theory that they form a dialectal unity in Proto-Semitic. Reprinted in *Comparative Semitic Linguistics: A Student's Reader* (ed. M. H. Goshen-Gottstein).

144. "A preliminary description of Argobba", *Annales d'Éthiopie* 3:251-273.

> Presentation of phonology and morphology, with some syntactic information.

145. "Sidamo features in the South Ethiopic phonology", *Journal of the American Oriental Society* 79:1-7.

146. "Taboo expressions in Ethiopia", *American Anthropologist* 61:105-108.

> Expressions used in particular by the Gurage.

147. "Traces of the laryngeals in the Ethiopic dialect of Ennemor", *Orientalia* 28:257-270.

> Presence of the glottal stop and vowel changes which point to an original laryngeal. See also no. 207.

1960

148. "Echo-words in Ethiopic", *Annales d'Éthiopie* 4:205-238.

> Typology of echo-words in Amharic, Tigrinya, and Tigre, according to types of rhyme, meaning, syllable structure, and initial consonants, including an alphabetical index of the words under discussion.

149. "Gleanings from the Harari vocabulary", *Rassegna di Studi Etiopici* 16:23-37.

> Notes on various morphological, semantic and lexicographical problems based on the material found in no. 14.

150. "Homonyms in Gurage", *Journal of the American Oriental Society* 80:200-217.

> Investigation of the problem of homonyms caused by the reduced phonetic system of Gurage, with an alphabetical list of homonyms discussed.

151. "Local participation in language research", *National Conference on the Teaching of African Languages and Area Studies, March 1960*. Washington, D.C.: Georgetown University Press. Pp. 40-46.

> Describes the sources for linguistic work in Ethiopia. No. 179 is a French translation of this article.

152. "The names of the fingers in Ethiopic", *Orbis* 9:388-397.

153. "Sketches in Ethiopic classification", *Atti del Convegno Internazionale di Studi Etiopici, Roma, 1959*. (Problemi Attuali di Scienza e di Cultura). Rome: Accademia dei Lincei. Pp. 89-107.

> Discussion of the problems of North and South Ethiopic and the positions of Argobba, Zway and Harari.

1961

154. "Ethiopian terminology in Almeida's report on Ethiopia", *Bulletin of the School of Oriental and African Studies, University of London* 24:581-582.

> Addenda to the translation of Almeida's *The history of High Ethiopia or Abassia* by C. F. Beckingham and G. W. B. Huntingford.

155. "The names of the weekdays in Ethiopic", *Journal of Semitic Studies* 6:62-70.

156. "Réflexions à propos du type C en tigrigna", *Bulletin de la Société de Linguistique de Paris* 56:202-211.

> Discussion of the Proto-Ethiopic form of the Type C imperfect in connection with the quantity of the vowels *ä* and *a* in Proto-Ethiopic.

157. "Remarks on the gemination of the Gurage dialect of Azarnat-Mugo", *Bibliotheca Orientalis* 18:19-20.

> Study of unusual gemination in an East Gurage dialect, resulting in the conclusion that it is due to the influence of Endegeň. Based on materials published by A. J. Drewes.

158. "Semitic languages", *Encyclopaedia Britannica*. Chicago: Encyclopaedia Britannica, Inc. 4 pp.

> See also no. 191.

159. "Sur les lettres 'arabes' de l'alphabet éthiopien", *Bulletin de la Société de Linguistique de Paris* 56: xviii-xxi.

> Study of the use of *aräbi* to mean foreign or strange, applied to letters such as *š*, *ž*, etc.

160. "Syriac language", *Encyclopaedia Britannica*. Chicago: Encyclopaedia Britannica, Inc. 2 pp.

161. "Tigre games", *Rassegna di Studi Etiopici* 17:61-68.

> Description of seven games played by boys in the Keren area, with Tigre texts in transcription and translation.

1962

162. "An Ethiopian parallel to Hebrew עלה 'went up country' and ירד 'went down country'", *Zeitschrift für die Alttestamentliche Wissenschaft* 74:322-323.

163. "Ethiopic denominatives with nominal morphemes", *Le Muséon* 75:139-175.

   Typology of denominatives from nouns with prefixed *m*, *t*, or ', suffixed *m*, *t*, *n*, *w*, or *y*, or vocalic suffixes, plus an index by language of all the examples.

164. "The influence of the Cushitic substratum on Semitic Ethiopic re-examined", *Trudy 25 mezhunarodnogo Kongressa vostokovedov, Moscow, 1960.* Moscow: Izdatelstvo Vostochnoi Literary. Vol. I, pp. 387-390.

   Extension of no. 57 based on newly collected data.

165. "A prefix *ḥ* in Egyptian, Modern South Arabian, and Hausa", *Africa* 32:65-68.

   Collection of examples showing non-etymological *ḥ* arranged by subject.

166. "Semitic and Egyptian comparisons", *Journal of Near Eastern Studies* 21:44-49.

   Addenda to work done by A. Ember, F. Calice, and M. Cohen.

167. "Southeast Semitic cognates to the Akkadian vocabulary. I.", *Journal of the American Oriental Society* 82:1-4.

   Addenda to W. von Soden, *Akkadisches Handwörterbuch* for the dictionary entries a-e. See also nos. 177 and 200.

168. "'Yes' and 'no' in the Ethiopian languages", *Language* 38:147-148.

   Discussion of the expression of "yes" and "no" in answer to a negative question.

1963

169. "Harari idioms", *Rassegna di Studi Etiopici* 19:150-154.

   List of idioms compared with the idioms in Amharic, Galla, and Arabic, languages with which Harari is in contact.

1964

170. "An Ethiopian argot of a Gurage secret society", *Journal of African Languages* 3:52-65.

   Analysis of morphological, morphophonemic, and semantic aspects of the secret language of a Gogot *mʷẓyät*, with an alphabetical index of words discussed. Reprinted in no. 35.

171. "A Falasha book of Jewish festivals", *For Max Weinreich on his seventieth birthday.* The Hague: Mouton. Pp. 183-191.

   Concerning a book called *Mekor Mayim ve-Chagim u-Zmanim* translated into Amharic by Yona Bogale.

172. "The farmer in Chaha song", *Africa* 34:230-242.

   Collection of songs with translation and notes.

173. "The jussive in Chaha", *Language* 40:53-57.

> Examination of the three types of jussive in Chaha. See also no. 94, 189, 221.

174. "Linguistic principles of the Ethiopian argots", *Journal of Semitic Studies* 9:58-66.

> Based on the analyses of individual argots published by the author (nos. 76, 77, 96, and 170).

175. "A Monophysite epistle — 'The consolation of the soul'", *Orientalia Christiana Periodica* 30:447-484.

> Text, translation, notes, and summary.

176. "Observations on a study on the Ethiopian quadriradicals", *Rassegna di Studi Etiopici* 20:120-128.

> Detailed review of Murad Kamil, *Beiträge zur Entstehung der vierradikaligen Verben in den gesprochenen semitischen Sprachen.*

177. "Southeast Semitic cognates to the Akkadian vocabulary. II.", *Journal of the American Oriental Society* 84:115-118.

> Addenda to W. von Soden, *Akkadisches Handwörterbuch*, for the dictionary entries g-k. See also nos. 167 and 200.

178. "Toward a history of the Amharic vocabulary", *Journal of Ethiopian Studies* 2:12-20.

> English-Amharic vocabulary comparing modern usage with that presented in C. H. Armbruster, *Initia Amharica*, Part 2, 1910.

1965

179. "À la recherche de matériel linguistique en Éthiopie", *Communications et Rapports du Premier Congrès International de Dialectologie générale, Louvain and Brussels, 1960*. (ed. S. Pop). Louvain: Centre international de dialectologie générale. Vol. III, pp. 241-247.

> French translation of no. 151.

180. "Chaha riddles", *Rassegna di Studi Etiopici* 21:27-93.

> 267 riddles with translation, notes, and index.

181. "Gleanings in Harari grammar I", *Journal of the American Oriental Society* 85:153-159.

> Discussion of certain morphological and syntactic questions in Harari.

1966

182. "An analysis of the Argobba vocabulary", *Journal of African Languages* 5:102-112.

> Division of the Argobba vocabulary into groups of common origins

excluding those identical with Amharic, plus an index of the words discussed.

183. "Characteristics of the Ethiopic language group of Semitic languages", In: *Handbook of African Languages. Linguistic Analyses. The Non-Bantu Languages of North-eastern Africa*. By A. N. Tucker and M. A. Bryan. London: Oxford University Press. Pp. 593-613.

> Discussion of the characteristic features of Ethiopic phonology, morphology and syntax and their relation to the Semitic languages.

184. "The origin of Geez *'awādi* 'herald'", *Journal of Semitic Studies* 11:226-227.

> Response to J. A. Thompson, "Expansions of the עד root", *JSS* 10:226, showing that *'awādi* is to be connected to the root *'wd* (*'* representing a laryngeal) rather than to *'wd*.

185. "A short chronicle on the Gafat", *Rivista degli Studi Orientali* 41:189-198.

> Text in Amharic with translation and notes.

1967

186. "Eža riddles", *Rassegna di Studi Etiopici* 23 (1967-68):43-78.
> 110 riddles with translation, notes, and index.

187. "Hypothesis on a proto-Semitic marker of the imperfect in Gurage", *Journal of Near Eastern Studies* 26:121-125.

> Examination of the auxiliaries of the compound imperfect in Ethiopic, arriving at the conclusion that the auxiliary in Muher, Gogot and Soddo is the proto-Semitic marker of the main imperfect or indicative.

188. "The impersonal in Chaha", *To Honor Roman Jakobson. Essays on the occasion of his seventieth birthday*. The Hague: Mouton. Pp. 1150-1162.

189. "The jussive in Eža", *Journal of Semitic Studies* 12:66-82.

> Examination of the five types of jussive in Eža, with an index of the verbs discussed. See also no. 94, 173, 221.

190. "The pseudo-gerundive in Čaha", *Rassegna di Studi Etiopici* 23 (1967-68):27-42.

> Discussion of the usage and forms of the pseudo-gerundive in the various verbal classes.

191. "Semitic languages", *Encyclopaedia Britannica*. Chicago: Encyclopaedia Britannica, Inc. Vol. 20, pp. 208-211.

> Reprinted in *Comparative Semitic Linguistics: A Student's Reader* (ed. M. H. Goshen-Gottstein). See also no. 158.

1968

192. "An archaic vowel of the jussive in Gurage, Gafat, and Harari",
Orientalia 37:90-93.

> Evidence that the vowel *ä* of the prefix *yä-* of the jussive in Gurage,
> Gafat, and Harari (against the prefix *yǝ-* of the other Ethiopian languages)
> may go back to the Semitic prefix *ya-*.

193. "An Ethiopian parallel to the Arabic expression 'the eye of the hen'",
Arabica 15:316-317.

> The idiom is used in Soddo.

194. "The expression of the future in the Ethiopian languages", *Journal of
African Languages* 7:68-72.

> Discussion of the near and far future in the main affirmative clause.

195. "Is there a Proto-Gurage?", *Proceedings of the International Conference on
Semitic Studies, Jerusalem, 1965*. Jerusalem: Israel Academy of Sciences
and Humanities. Pp. 152-171.

> Investigation of the problem of the classification of the Gurage cluster,
> culminating in the conclusion that they are ultimately of common origin.

196. "Observations on Semitic cognates in Ugaritic", *Orientalia* 37:347-366.

> Addenda to the Semitic (particularly Ethiopic) cognates in Ugaritic
> presented by Cyrus Gordon in his *Ugaritic Textbook*.

197. "*Äsät*, the soul of the Gurage", *Africa* 39:281-290.

> Two texts in Chaha and Eža with an interlinear translation, a free
> translation, and a glossary.

198. "Frequency as determinant of linguistic changes in the Ethiopian
languages", *Word* 25:180-189.

> Demonstration of the effect of normal phonetic changes on frequently
> used words more so than on less frequently used words.

199. "The negative particle *'in* in Arabic and *(')ǝn* in Ethiopic", *Annali.
Istituto Orientale di Napoli* (Nuova Serie) 19:137-145.

> Discussion of the relationship of the negative particles in Arabic, Hebrew,
> and Ethiopic, with an excursus on Amharic *ǝmbǝza(m)*.

200. "Southeast Semitic cognates to the Akkadian vocabulary. III", *Journal
of the American Oriental Society* 89:18-22.

> Addenda to W. von Soden, *Akkadisches Handwörterbuch*, for the dictionary
> entries k-n. See also nos. 167 and 177.

201. "Toward a classification of the Gurage dialects", *Journal of Semitic
Studies* 14:96-109.

> Analysis of the phonology, morphology and vocabulary of Muher,
> Gogot, Masqan and Soddo "in an attempt to establish the relationship
> between Muher, Gogot, and Masqan on the one hand and Muher, Gogot
> (and Masqan), and Soddo on the other".

1970

202. "Classification of the Semitic languages of Ethiopia", *Proceedings of the Third International Conference of Ethiopian Studies, Addis Ababa, 1966.* Addis Ababa: Institute of Ethiopian Studies, Haile Sellassie I University. Vol. II, pp. 5-22.

203. "Ethiopic and South Arabian", *Current Trends in Linguistics.* (ed. Thomas A. Sebeok). The Hague: Mouton. Vol. 6, pp. 467-527.

> Bibliographical review of the work done on Ethiopic and South Arabian, including textbooks, dictionaries, published texts, and specific grammatical problems.

204. "The *ma*-clause in Harari", *Mélanges Marcel Cohen.* (ed. David Cohen). The Hague: Mouton. Pp. 263-273.

> Discussion of the meaning of the *ma*-clause, its agreement in verb form with the principal clause, the structure of successive *ma*- clauses and the subjects of the two clauses.

205. "Nasalization in the East Gurage group of Semitic Ethiopic", *Phonetica* 22:160-169.

> Examination of the question, arriving at the conclusion that nasalization is not dependent on a laryngeal ḥ or ʿ.

1971

206. "The Geez imperfect again", *Proceedings of the Twenty-Seventh International Congress of Orientalists, Ann Arbor, Michigan, 1967.* Wiesbaden: Otto Harrassowitz. Pp. 89-90.

> Proposed explanation of the gemination of the 2nd radical of the North Ethiopic imperfect as resulting from special phonetic conditions.

207. "Traces of laryngeals in the Gurage dialect of Endegeň", *Journal of Near Eastern Studies* 30:218-224.

> Presence of the glottal stop and vocalic changes in quality and quantity point to an original laryngeal. See also no. 147.

208. "The verb forms of the Gurage dialect of Endegeň", *Afrikanische Sprachen und Kulturen — Ein Querschnitt.* (Hamburger Beiträge zur Afrika-Kunde 14). Hamburg: Deutsches Institut für Afrika-Forschung. Pp. 180-187.

> Examination of Type A triradicals.

1974

209. "While working on the English-Amharic context dictionary", *4 Congresso Internazionale di Studi Etiopici, Roma, 1972.* (Problemi Attuali di

Scienza e di Cultura). Rome: Accademia dei Lincei. Vol. II, pp. 203-213.

> Discussion of problems arising during the compilation of a dictionary, including decisions concerning orthography, loanwords and translations.

1975

210. "Amharic parallels to semantic developments in Biblical Hebrew", *Eretz-Israel 12. (Nelson Glueck Memorial Volume)*. Pp. 113-116.

> Words under discussion are listed in alphabetical order in Hebrew.

211. "Ethiopian Studies in the United States since World War II", *Proceedings of the First United States Conference on Ethiopian Studies, 1973*. (ed. Harold Marcus). East Lansing, Michigan: African Studies Center, Michigan State University. Pp. 1-9.

> Includes bibliography.

212. "Taamrat Emanuel's notes of Falasha monks and holy places", *Salo Wittmayer Baron Jubilee Volume on the occasion of his eightieth birthday*. (ed. Saul Lieberman). Jerusalem: American Academy for Jewish Research. Pp. 623-637.

> Annotated edition of Taamrat Emanuel's private notes with commentary.

213. "What is a Semitic Ethiopian language?", *Hamito-Semitica*. (ed. James and Theodora Bynon). The Hague: Mouton. Pp. 129-131.

> Presentation of phonological and morphological features found only in Semitic Ethiopic and not in other Semitic languages.

1976

214. "The triradicals in the Gurage dialect of Endegeň", *Israel Oriental Studies* 6:138-154.

> See also no. 217.

1977

215. "Argobba vocabulary", *Rassegna di Studi Etiopici* 26 (1973-77):21-43.

> Etymological presentation of the Argobba vocabulary.

1978

216. "Spirantization in the Ethiopian languages", *Atti del Secondo Congresso Internazionale di Linguistica Camito-Semitica, Florence, 1974*. (Quaderni di Semitistica 5). (ed. Pelio Fronzaroli). Florence: Istituto di Linguistica e di Lingue Orientali, Università di Firenze. Pp. 175-199.

Re-examination of the question based on new evidence from Harari and Gurage, plus a brief discussion of spirantization in Cushitic.

217. "A supplementary note to the verb in the Gurage dialect of Endegeň", *Israel Oriental Studies* 8:142-143.

Examination of a geminated perfect Type A which is phonetically conditioned. See also no. 214.

1980

218. "Additional Gurage etymologies", *Annali. Istituto Orientale di Napoli* (Nuova Serie) 30:472.

Addenda to no. 25.

219. "Proto-*Sidamo *ẓ", *Afrika und Übersee* 63:119-129.

Re-examination of the discussion presented by Hans-Jürgen Sasse (*Afrika und Übersee* 59 (1975/76):130-142).

1981

220. "Additional Arabic loanwords in Tigre", *Al-Hudhud. Festschrift Maria Höfner zum 80. Geburtstag.* (ed. Roswitha G. Stiegner). Graz: Karl-Franzens-Universität. Pp. 171-198.

A review of principles governing the treatment of Arabic loanwords and a list of loanwords by subject. See also no. 117.

1982

221. "The jussive in the Gurage dialects of Muher and Masqan", *Zeitschrift der Deutschen Morgenländischen Gesellschaft* 132:85-97.

Examination of the three types of jussive in Muher and Masqan, with an index of verbs discussed. See also no. 94, 173, 189.

Reviews

1937

222. Cerulli, E. Studi etiopici. I. La lingua e la storia di Harar. In: *Journal asiatique* 229:654-659.

1939

223. Féghali, M. Proverbes et dictons Syro-Libanais. In: *Revue Scientifique* 5:347-348.
224. Grébaut, S. Catalogue des manuscrits éthiopiens de la collection Griaule. In: *Revue des Études Sémitiques* pp. 103-104.

1943

225. Cohen, M. Nouvelles études d'éthiopien méridional. In: *Journal of the American Oriental Society* 63:292-294.

1944

226. Rossi, E. L'arabo parlato in Ṣanʿa. In: *Journal of the American Oriental Society* 64:88-91.

1948

227. Fleisch, H. Introduction à l'étude des langues sémitiques. In: *Word* 4:230-233.

1949

228. Cohen, M. Essai comparatif sur le vocabulaire du chamito-sémitique. In: *Language* 25:312-316.
229. Conti Rossini, C. Proverbi, tradizioni e canzoni tigrine. In: *Journal of the American Oriental Society* 69:241-246.
230. Höfner, M. Altsüdarabische Grammatik. In: *Journal of the American Oriental Society* 69:97-100.
231. Perham, M. The Government of Ethiopia. In: *The Middle East Journal* 3:474-475.

1950

232. Diringer, D. The Alphabet. In: *Word* 6:89-90.
233. Fevrier, J. G. Histoire de l'alphabet. In: *Word* 6:90-91.

1951

234. Barthélemy, A. Dictionnaire arabe-français. In: *Language* 27:429-431.

235. Brockelmann, C. Abessinische Studien. In: *Journal of the American Oriental Society* 71:275-278.

1953

236. Linguistic Bibliography for the Years 1939-1947, published by the Permanent International Committee of Linguists. In: *Word* 9:167-169.
237. Polotsky, H. J. Notes on Gurage Grammar. In: *Language* 29:100-103.
238. Pritchard, J. B. (ed.) Ancient Near Eastern Texts Relating to the Old Testament. In: *Word* 9:196-197.
239. Sisto Verri. Saggio di comparazione lessicale fra il Cunama e le lingue Bari e Lotuxo. In: *Word* 9:195-196.
240. Talbot, D. A. Contemporary Ethiopia. In: *Middle Eastern Affairs* 4:416.
241. Trimingham, J. S. Islam in Ethiopia. In: *Middle Eastern Affairs* 4:302-303.

1955

242. Gelb, I. J. A Study of Writing In: *Word* 11:280-282.
243. Moorhouse, A. C. The Triumph of the Alphabet. In: *Word* 11:282-283.

1956

244. Sandford, C. The Lion of Judah Hath Prevailed. In: *Middle Eastern Affairs* 7:406-407.
245. University College of Addis Ababa. Bulletin of the Ethnological Society 1, 2. In: *Journal of American Folklore* 69:91-93.

1957

246. Cerulli, E. Peoples of South-West Ethiopia and its Borderland. In: *American Anthropologist* 59:917-918.
247. The Gurages and their Social Life: In: *American Anthropologist* 59:732-733.
248. Rundgren, F. Über Bildungen mit š- und n-t- Demonstrativen im Semitischen. In: *Word* 13:527-529.
249. Tucker, A. N. and M. A. Bryan. The Non-Bantu Languages of Northeastern Africa. In: *American Anthropologist* 59:935-936.

1958

250. Annales d'Éthiopie 1. In: *American Journal of Archaeology* 62:111-112.
251. Strelcyn, S. Kebra Nagast czyli chwała królów Abisynii. In: *Oriens* 11:294.
252. University College of Addis Ababa. Bulletin of the Ethnological Society 3, 4, 5. In: *Journal of American Folklore* 71:96.

1959

253. Crawford, O. G. (ed.) Ethiopian Itineraries ca. 1400-1524. In: *Spaeculum* 34:258-260.
254. Kamil, M. Amharische Kaiserlieder. In: *Journal of Near Eastern Studies* 18:160-161.

1960

255. Diringer, D. The Story of Aleph Beth. In: *Spaeculum* 35:295.
256. Leiris, M. La possession et ses aspects théatraux chez les Éthiopiens de Gondar. In: *Journal of American Folklore* 73:175-176.

1961

257. Hammerschmidt, E. Äthiopische liturgische Texte der Bodleian Library in Oxford. In: *Journal of Semitic Studies* 6:256-258.
258. Hohenberger, J. Semitisches und hamitisches Sprachgut im Masai, mit vergleichendem Wörterbuch. In: *Language* 37:176-179.

1962

259. Beckingham, C. F. and G. W. B. Huntingford. The Prester John of the Indies. In: *Journal of the American Oriental Society* 82:560-561.

1963

260. Simoons, F. J. Northwest Ethiopia. Peoples and Economy. In: *Journal of Semitic Studies* 8:306-308.

1965

261. Jesman, C. The Ethiopian Paradox. In: *Journal of Semitic Studies* 10:141-142.

262. Khater, M. R. The Teaching of Arabic in the Arab World. In: *Linguistics* 16:116.

263. Malaika, N. Grundzüge der Grammatik des arabischen Dialektes von Bagdad. In: *Linguistics* 15:105-108.

1967

264. Grohmann, A. Arabien. In: *Journal of the American Oriental Society* 87:615.

1971

265. van Donzel, E. J. ʿEnbāqom Anqaṣa Amin (La Porte de la Foi). In: *Der Islam* 48:185-186.

266. Hammerschmidt, E. and O. Jäger. Illuminierte äthiopische Handschriften. In: *International Journal of Middle East Studies* 2:190-191.

1973

267. Gamst, F. C. The Qemant: A Pagan-Hebraic Peasantry of Ethiopia. In: *International Journal of Comparative Sociology* 13:239-240.

1974

268. Mantel-Niećko, J. Les verbes du type B/C en amharique. In: *Journal of the American Oriental Society* 94:542-545.

1975

269. Hammerschmidt, E. Äthiopische Handschriften vom Ṭānāsee 1. In: *Wiener Zeitschrift für die Kunde des Morgenlandes* 67:280-282.

1980

270. Bairu Tafla. A Chronicle of Emperor Yohannes IV (1872-89). In: *Wiener Zeitschrift für die Kunde des Morgenlandes* 72:148-151.

271. Hammerschmidt, E. Äthiopische Handschriften vom Ṭānāsee 2. In: *Wiener Zeitschrift für die Kunde des Morgenlandes* 72:147-148.

272. Macomber, W. F. A Catalogue of Ethiopian Manuscripts Microfilmed for the Ethiopian Microfilm Library. Vol. I. In: *Journal of the American Oriental Society* 100:144-146.

273. Strelcyn, S. Catalogue of Ethiopian Manuscripts in the John Rylands University Library of Manchester. In: *Journal of the American Oriental Society* 100:146-147.

1981

274. van Donzel, E. Foreign Relations of Ethiopia 1642-1700. Documents relating to the journeys of Khodja Murad. In: *Wiener Zeitschrift für die Kunde des Morgenlandes* 73:225-228.

275. Macomber, W.F., and Getatchew Haile. A Catalogue of Ethiopian Manuscripts Microfilmed for the Ethiopian Microfilm Library. Vol. II, III, IV. In: *Northeast African Studies* 3:95-99.

Recordings

1950

276. "Religious Music of the Falashas (Jews of Ethiopia)", *Ethnic Folkways Library*. 2 records.

    Contains prayers with responsive reading in Geez and musical accompaniment.

1951

277. "Music of South Arabia", *Ethnic Folkways Library*.

    Documentary recordings from the Western Protectorate and Aden containing different types of songs.

Index

WOLF LESLAU ET LA FRANCE

Maxime Rodinson
École pratique des Hautes Études, Sorbonne, Paris

Comme la plupart des *Festschriften*, celle qui est dédiée à Wolf Leslau contiendra des articles savants et, dans ce cas, surtout linguistiques, que lui offriront des amis et des collègues, en témoignage très mérité d'estime pour son œuvre considérable. Mais, puisqu'on insère aussi parfois dans ces «colliers floraux» (cf. le titre de *Serta Monacensia* donné aux Mélanges offerts à Franz Babinger) ou dans ces «offrandes de fruits variés» (cf. la Παγκαρπεῖα dédiée à Henri Grégoire) un minimum d'éléments biographiques sur la personne honorée, pourquoi ne permettrait-on pas à un très vieil ami de Wolf Leslau d'évoquer quelques souvenirs à son sujet? Et, puisque tout savant est d'abord, malgré tout, un homme, pourquoi ces souvenirs n'échapperaient-ils pas aux sèches données et énumérations de titres de travaux qui sont la spécialité des *Who's Who* et autres *World of Learning*? Rien ne saurait restituer la physionomie profonde et unique d'un homme, mais surtout pas une banque de données.

Je manque d'ailleurs d'un certain nombre de ces données. Mais en presque un demi-siècle, même si les rencontres ont été souvent sporadiques, espacées, on apprend à connaître un homme. La rédaction de cet article m'a poussé à chercher à préciser des événements de la biographie de Leslau que je n'avais connus que de façon floue et sur lesquels ma discrétion et sa pudeur m'avaient poussé à ne pas l'interroger. J'ai fini par faire une véritable enquête pour laquelle j'ai trouvé une documentation non seulement dans les lettres que j'ai conservées, mais dans plusieurs livres et dans la correspondance de Marcel Cohen, notre regretté maître commun. Sa veuve a bien voulu me confier le dossier des lettres échangées avec Leslau ou le concernant, certaines remontant à 1931. Qu'elle en soit ici très sincèrement et affectueusement remerciée.

Le nom de famille de Wolf Leslau indique un lieu de résidence ancien de sa famille. C'est en effet la forme allemande du nom de la ville polonaise de Włocawek sur la Vistule à près de 150 km au Nord-Ouest de Varsovie. Mais Wolf est né en novembre 1906 à Krzepice, en Pologne alors russe, à une trentaine de kilomètres au Nord-Ouest du fameux sanctuaire de Częstochowa et à moins de dix kilomètres de la frontière de la Silésie allemande de cette époque. Dans cette vieille bourgade résidait une nombreuse communauté juive au sein de laquelle il fit ses premiers pas dans l'existence et dans la connaissance. Il fit ses études secondaires à Częstochowa, puis, en 1926, partit pour Vienne. À l'Université de Vienne, il compléta sa connaissance de l'hébreu et aborda l'étude des langues sémitiques. Il obtint enfin un diplôme de l'Hebräisches Pädagogium, une sorte d'école normale qui formait des professeurs d'hébreu. C'est là qu'il rencontra la Viennoise Charlotte Halpern dont le père venait de Galicie et la mère de Bohême. Elle devait devenir la compagne de sa vie.

En 1931, le jeune couple décida de quitter l'Autriche où pourtant Leslau était apprécié par d'éminents professeurs de langues sémitiques. Essentiellement, Wolf avait déjà décidé de se spécialiser dans la branche méridionale de ce groupe linguistique et il savait trouver à Paris la possibilité d'étudier ce domaine non représenté pratiquement à Vienne. Charlotte avait déjà une bonne connaissance du français. Peut-être aussi la situation en Europe centrale et orientale, spécialement pour quiconque était d'origine juive, leur apparaissait-elle déjà menaçante. W. Leslau, en tout cas, écrivit de Vienne à Marcel Cohen dont la réputation de linguiste sémitisant était déjà considérable et qui développait particulièrement l'étude de ces langues méridionales, l'éthiopien et le sudarabique, sur lesquelles il donnait un enseignement. Marcel Cohen lui répondit favorablement, mais en le mettant en garde contre les difficultés qu'il aurait, en France, à assurer son existence quotidienne.

Ces difficultés furent bien plus grandes que le couple ne l'avait imaginé. Les premières années en France furent très difficiles. Malgré l'aide dévouée de Marcel Cohen, Wolf et sa femme eurent le plus grand mal à trouver des sources de revenus qui n'impliquaient pas l'interruption des études. Les lettres de Wolf Leslau à Marcel Cohen durant ces années — d'abord en allemand, puis de plus en plus en français — portent témoignage de multiples démarches pénibles et souvent humiliantes. La grande crise ne facilitait pas les choses et les Français avaient naturellement la priorité. Les conditions de vie assez misérables auxquelles le ménage était réduit, malgré les petites aides et les travaux mal payés qu'il pouvait décrocher çà et là, durent contribuer à aggraver l'état de santé de Wolf dont les poumons furent affectés.

Malgré tout, le couple avait décidé de refaire sa vie en France. Wolf se mit à étudier le français avec l'acharnement qu'il apportait à toutes ses études. Dès 1934, il demandait à être naturalisé français. Les autorités françaises prenaient alors une attitude de plus en plus réticente devant les demandes de cet ordre, étant donné le flot de réfugiés d'Europe centrale et orientale que la venue au pouvoir de Hitler faisait croître de façon considérable. La réponse à la demande de W. Leslau fut un ajournement qui, répété, devait avoir de graves conséquences. Il commençait aussi à travailler pour acquérir des titres universitaires français.

Wolf s'attacha, dès son arrivée à Paris, à utiliser les ressources de la capitale française pour étendre et approfondir les connaissances déjà très poussées qu'il avait dans le domaine de la linguistique sémitique, particulièrement en ce qui concerne les branches les plus méridionales de cette famille de langues. Marcel Cohen qui était son principal protecteur s'intéressait particulièrement à cette zone et l'encouragea dans cette voie. En lui, W. Leslau et sa femme devaient découvrir rapidement un appui infatigable et efficace, un ami à l'indéfectible et loyale fidélité. Pourtant, cette protection, sans laquelle Leslau aurait peut-être été contraint d'abandonner ses ambitions scientifiques (au moins temporairement), avait ses dangers. Si Leslau était résolument éloigné de tout engagement politique, Marcel Cohen, en plus de son activité scientifique, était, depuis 1920, un militant communiste actif. A cette époque, le fait était très rare dans l'enseignement supérieur français et d'autant plus remarqué et réprouvé. M. Cohen prenait grand soin de ne pas laisser interférer ses convictions politiques avec ses travaux, ses rapports avec ses collègues et l'appui qu'il apportait à tous ses élèves méritants. Je l'ai connu, alors qu'il avait vigoureusement pris parti pour l'Ethiopie lors de l'agression italienne de 1935, traiter avec la plus grande correction un jeune fasciste italien vivant en France qui venait à ses cours étudier l'amharique, visiblement pour se préparer à des fonctions dans la nouvelle Afrique orientale italienne. Mais Marcel Cohen n'était pas toujours payé de retour. Et il est probable que, dans certains milieux anticommunistes, ses protégés, quels qu'ils fussent, étaient regardés avec suspicion.

*   *   *

Leslau s'inscrivit donc à l'École nationale des langues orientales vivantes pour les cours d'arabe littéral (classique) et d'amharique (ce dernier était donné précisément par Marcel Cohen). De même, il suivit à la IVe section (sciences historiques et philologiques) de l'École pratique des Hautes Études (à la Sorbonne) les séminaires de William Marçais sur la philologie arabe et de Marcel Cohen sur la philologie éthiopienne et sudarabique[1]. Il dut d'ailleurs s'interrompre pour raison de santé. Heureusement, cette interruption ne fut pas trop longue. Il était dans une phase de pré-tuberculose. Il dut passer quelques mois, au cours du second semestre de 1932 et jusqu'en mars 1933, au sanatorium de Saint Hilaire du Touvet près de Grenoble. Il réussit à y faire un très studieux séjour tout en améliorant radicalement sa santé. Au

---

1 Marcel Cohen écrivait alors sud-arabique en deux mots. Plus tard, pour imprimer un peu plus encore dans l'esprit des lecteurs la notion que le groupe de langues en question ne représentait pas un ensemble de dialectes arabes du Sud de la péninsule, mais une autre branche du sémitique, il prit l'habitude d'écrire «sudarabique» en un seul mot. Lui succédant, j'ai suivi cet usage ainsi que d'autres de ses disciples.

retour, les Cohen intervinrent vigoureusement pour que les Leslau n'aillent pas habiter à Paris dans la chambre qu'ils s'étaient proposés de louer. Le quartier et le logement ne leur paraissaient pas très sains pour un homme tout juste échappé au péril de la tuberculose. La décision d'habiter en banlieue posait des problèmes que les Cohen aidèrent à résoudre. Finalement, le couple Leslau s'installa en effet à Fontenay-aux-Roses, à neuf kilomètres seulement au Sud de Paris, faubourg encore assez aéré à cette date.

Peu à peu, Leslau acquérait les diplômes nécessaires. En 1933, il obtenait à l'École nationale des langues orientales vivantes le diplôme d'arabe littéral et, en 1934, celui d'amharique. Il réussissait à l'examen du certificat d'études supérieures de langues sémitiques anciennes, ce qui devait lui permettre, avec d'autres diplômes, d'obtenir le grade de licencié ès-lettres de l'Université de Paris. Il voyait enfin s'étendre le temps qu'il pouvait consacrer à des travaux de recherche. En novembre 1935, il présentait sous la direction de Marcel Cohen son *Lexique soqoṭri* comme mémoire (on disait alors thèse) pour l'obtention du diplôme de l'École. Sur le rapport favorable d'E. Dhorme et de R. Labat, le 12 janvier 1936, ce travail était accepté et valait à son auteur le titre (très réputé) d'élève titulaire. Il était publié en 1938 dans la collection de la Société de linguistique de Paris.

Marcel Cohen avait l'immense qualité de ne pas ménager sa peine pour aider ceux qu'il estimait mériter cet effort à faire leurs premiers pas dans le monde difficile où doit progresser le chercheur universitaire. Il devait fournir chaque année — comme je le fais encore en tant que son successeur — un rapport sur le sujet de ses cours et sur les élèves qui les avaient suivis. Ces notations, imprimées dans l'*Annuaire* de l'École, pouvaient servir d'attestation des mérites de l'étudiant et l'aider à gravir des échelons. Dès la première année du séjour de W. Leslau à Paris, Marcel Cohen n'oublie pas de noter dans son rapport concernant les cours de l'année académique 1931-1932: «M. W. Leslau, nouveau à l'École, mais sémitisant déjà exercé dont l'intérêt se porte spécialement vers le domaine sud-arabique et éthiopien, a montré de solides connaissances et une utile curiosité. [...] Des lectures d'exercice ont été faites avec M. Leslau, notamment dans le *Kebra Nagast*». Marcel Cohen indique plus loin que W. Leslau a assisté également aux conférences qu'il donnait sur le sudarabique épigraphique et sur la comparaison chamito-sémitique[2].

Aussitôt après que la thèse de Leslau eût été acceptée, Marcel Cohen en tirait parti. Dès le premier semestre de 1936, il ne manquait pas de consigner dans

---

2 École pratique des Hautes Études, Section des sciences historiques et philologiques, *Annuaire, 1932-1933*, Melun, Imprimerie administrative, 1932, p. 98-100.

son rapport annuel: «la thèse de M. W. Leslau sur le lexique soqotri a été l'objet d'un rapport favorable, et il s'est montré apte à donner un enseignement de sud-arabique ancien et moderne»[3]. Ces trois lignes devaient permettre d'autoriser Leslau à faire des conférences libres dans le cadre de l'École. C'est une des voies qui peuvent favoriser la candidature à une chaire de directeur d'études (titre traditionnel des professeurs à cette École).

Aussi, dès novembre 1936, Leslau, avec le titre d'élève diplômé, commençait-il à donner un cours libre qui s'inscrivait dans la dépendance de celui de M. Cohen et qui suivait (le vendredi après-midi) celui que donnait ce dernier sur la comparaison chamito-sémitique en supplément à ses cours du samedi après-midi sur l'éthiopien et le sudarabique. L'intitulé donné par Leslau était le suivant: "Sudarabique ancien et moderne. Explication d'inscriptions minéennes en comparaison avec les dialectes modernes. Grammaire et textes de soqotri".

J'avais fait la connaissance de Leslau en suivant, à partir de l'année académique 1933-1934, les cours de Marcel Cohen à l'École des langues orientales, en amharique, puis l'année suivante à l'École pratique des Hautes études pour l'éthiopien, le sudarabique et le comparatisme chamito-sémitique. Je suivis donc tout naturellement les leçons de Leslau et j'ai conservé les notes que j'y pris pendant les années académiques 1936-1937 et 1937-1938. J'ai ainsi eu l'honneur d'être un des tout premiers élèves de W. Leslau avec Gerhard Salinger, aujourd'hui aux États-Unis. Dans son rapport sur les cours de 1936-1937, Leslau note que j'ai «suivi la conférence avec zèle jusqu'au bout». Pour l'année 1937-1938, il indique que j'ai fait à ce séminaire un exposé sur l'article de D. H. Müller, *Die Form qátlal und qátlil in der Soqotri-Sprache* (dans le *Florilegium Melchior de Vogüé*, Paris, 1909) et aussi que je me suis «chargé de l'explication des textes [en sudarabique épigraphique] pendant toute l'année». Les mêmes leçons étaient suivies par le R. P. Henri Fleisch qui préparait alors sa thèse sur les verbes à allongement vocalique interne en sémitique.

---

3 Id., *Annuaire 1936-1937* (Melun, *ibid.*, 1936), p. 75. Dans le rapport sur les cours de 1932-1933, il est dit que «M. W. Leslau a dû rester éloigné, mais non oisif une partie de l'année pour raffermir sa santé; après son retour, il a pris la part la plus active aux exercices [d'éthiopien] et a présenté l'éthiopien comme langue principale au certificat [de licence] de langues sémitiques anciennes» (*Id., Annuaire, 1933-1934*, Melun, *ibid.*, 1933, p. 68, cf. p. 69). La «participation active» de W. Leslau est aussi notée pour les cours des années suivantes que Marcel Cohen donnait non seulement sur l'éthiopien classique (guèze) et le sudarabique, mais aussi sur le comparatisme chamito-sémitique. Pour les cours de 1934-1935, il est dit que W. Leslau «assiste» M. Cohen pour l'étude des textes éthiopiens de confession (*Annuaire 1935-1936*, Melun, *ibid.*, 1935, p. 80). On ne peut suivre d'aussi près la participation de Leslau aux cours d'amharique de Marcel Cohen à l'École nationale des langues orientales vivantes du fait que cette dernière institution ne publie pas d'Annuaire.

A ce petit séminaire, Leslau partageait en effet le temps entre une initiation au sudarabique épigraphique et l'étude des langues sudarabiques modernes. Après le soqoṭri étudié en 1936-1937 et en 1937-1938, il aborda en 1938-1939 ce qu'on appelait alors le šḥawri d'après les publications de M. Bittner. Pour des raisons que j'ai oubliées, je ne suivis pas les leçons de cette dernière année académique, que fréquenta en revanche Roger Schneider.

Ces cours libres n'étaient qu'une activité non rénumérée dont l'intérêt pour W. Leslau était avant tout qu'ils pouvaient lui préparer un avenir plus satisfaisant dans l'université française, sans doute même une carrière brillante. L'évolution des relations internationales devait en décider autrement.

Leslau a toujours été un travailleur acharné. Il publiait à l'époque, outre son *Lexique soqoṭri*, deux courts articles sur le sudarabique moderne, l'un en allemand et l'autre en français qui furent ses premières publications si je ne me trompe[4]. Il fut l'une des cinq ou six personnes qui furent à l'origine du petit groupe d'études dont Marcel Cohen prit la direction et qu'il anima longtemps, qui se réunissait chaque mois à la Sorbonne, dans les locaux de la IVe section de l'École pratique des Hautes Études et qui le fait encore aujourd'hui sous le direction maintenant de David Cohen. Il s'agit du Groupe linguistique d'études chamito-sémitiques, en abrégé G.L.E.C.S. On trouvera les abrégés de ces communications imprimés dans les tomes I, II et III des Comptes Rendus du G.L.E.C.S., précieuse collection que connaissent bien et qu'utilisent les chamito-sémitisants[5].

C'est vers cette époque qu'un glissement s'opéra dans les domaines d'étude auxquels Leslau accordait une attention prioritaire. Il délaissa de plus en plus le domaine sudarabique sans jamais l'abandonner tout à fait et s'adonna de plus en plus aux études éthiopiennes. On le comprend. Leslau était avant tout un linguiste. L'étude linguistique du sudarabique épigraphique demande à chaque pas des travaux préalables très complexes de type philologique, historique et archéologique. En ce qui concerne les dialectes sudarabiques modernes, le mehri avait été assez bien étudié et Leslau, après l'achèvement de son travail lexicographique sur le soqoṭri, ne voyait pas de possibilité

---

4 «Remarques sur quelques mots du sudarabique moderne» (*Mémoires de la Société de linguistique de Paris*, 23, fasc. 6, 1935, p. 407-409); «Der š-Laut in den modernen südarabischen Sprachen» (*W.Z.K.M.*, 44, 1937, p. 211-218).

5 «Explications et rapprochements à propos de quelques éléments du vocabulaire mehri» (séance du 20 décembre 1933), *C.R. du GLECS*, I, p. 35; «Sur le préfixe *n-* en soqoṭri» (séance du 26 février 1936), *ibid.*, II, p. 45 s.; «Le passif interne en soqoṭri» (séance du 26 mai 1937), *ibid.*, II, p. 91 s.; (en collaboration avec M. Cohen) «Mots amhariques présentant le traitement *k > č*» (séance du 26 janvier 1937), *ibid.*, III, p. 11 s.; «Observations sur quelques faits éthiopiens et sudarabiques» (séance du 23 mars 1938), *ibid.*, III, p. 19 s.; «Notes sur le tigrigna (éthiopien septentrional)», *ibid.*, III, p. 37-40.

d'étendre ses études linguistiques sur les autres dialectes. Il n'y avait guère de perspectives à l'époque d'enquêtes nouvelles réalisables possibles en Arabie du sud. Notre condisciple juif palestinien, Sigismund Reich (qui devait devenir plus tard citoyen britannique, professeur et prendre le nom de David Storm Rice) s'acharnait en vain à obtenir des autorités britanniques l'autorisation de se rendre au Ḥaḍramawt pour réaliser un ambitieux plan de recherches[6].

Par contraste, le domaine des langues sémitiques modernes d'Éthiopie ouvrait de vastes perspectives. On a vu que Leslau avait obtenu son diplôme d'amharique en 1934. Depuis l'année académique 1937-1938, il suppléait Marcel Cohen pour le cours d'amharique à l'École nationale des langues orientales vivantes. Mais, si l'amharique commençait à être assez bien connu, les autres langues sémitiques modernes d'Éthiopie étaient encore fort peu étudiées. On pouvait considérer comme réalisables et prometteuses des enquêtes sur le terrain et, même à Paris, on pouvait rencontrer des locuteurs. Aussi, dans son rapport sur ses cours de 1936-1937, M. Cohen note: «W. Leslau a travaillé spécialement sur le harari et le gouragué en élaborant des documents inédits»[7]. L'année suivante, il est dit que W. Leslau «a poursuivi des études sur les langues modernes d'Abyssinie; son travail sur le harari est sous presse au *Journal asiatique*, la rédaction de son travail sur le gouragué est avancée»[8]. L'année suivante encore, Marcel Cohen notait: «W. Leslau, après la parution au *Journal asiatique* de son travail sur le harari, a poursuivi l'élaboration d'un gros lexique du gouragué. Il a entrepris en outre des études sur le tigrigna avec des informateurs présents à Paris; deux articles sont terminés, un livre va l'être. En outre, il a publié dans la *Revue des études sémitiques* un article sur la forme fréquentative dans toutes les langues éthiopiennes»[9].

Tout cela parut rapidement malgré les circonstances comme il va être dit. Pour le «gros lexique du gouragué», il en fut autrement. Il a été rédigé entièrement et dactylographié à l'époque! Leslau m'en confia alors une copie

---

6 Une trace en est laissée par la revue critique des ouvrages sur cette région publiée par S. Reich dans le *Bulletin d'études orientales* de l'Institut français de Damas, t. 6 (1936), p. 108-118.

7 *Id.*, *Annuaire 1937-1938* (Melun, *ibid.*, 1937). Corriger le titre général des rapports sur les cours; il ne s'agit pas de ceux de 1935-36, mais bien de ceux de 1936-37.

8 *Id.*, *Annuaire 1938-1939* (Melun, *ibid.*, 1938), p. 87. Il s'agit de l'article «Contributions à l'étude du harari (Abyssinie méridionale)», *Journal Asiatique*, 229 (1937), p. 431-479, 529-606.

9 *Id.*, *Annuaire 1939-1940* (Melun, *ibid.*, 1939), p. 90s. Pour le tigrigna, il s'agit des articles «Essai de reconstitution des désinences verbales du tigrigna» (*Revue des études sémitiques*, 1938, p. 70-99) et «Observations sur quelques dialectes du tigrigna (dialectes d'Akkele Gouzay, d'Adoua et du Hamasen)» (*Journal Asiatique*, 231, 1939, p. 78-115). L'autre article mentionné est «Le thème verbal fréquentatif dans les langues éthiopiennes» (*Revue des études sémitiques*, 1939, p. 15-31).

relue par Marcel Cohen. Celui-ci y avait apposé au crayon quelques remarques et suggestions, surtout sur le plan des étymologies. Je possède toujours cette copie. Mais les circonstances n'en permirent pas l'impression et, plus tard, Leslau ne tarda pas à recueillir des matériaux nouveaux en grande quantité. Le dictionnaire en question ne pouvait se concevoir sans être fortement remanié. Leslau n'a pas cessé d'y travailler et cet ouvrage, qui a pris des dimensions considérables, n'a pu paraître que plus de quarante ans après les notations de Marcel Cohen [10].

La situation matérielle du couple Leslau s'améliorait nettement. Charlotte se voyait confier la direction d'un patronage d'enfants financé par la baronne de Rothschild à Belleville. Wolf y travaillait aussi. Il s'agissait de garder et d'occuper les enfants pendant les jours de la semaine où l'école s'interrompait, à l'époque le jeudi et le dimanche. Le travail acharné de Wolf était mis en valeur par Marcel Cohen qui essayait obstinément d'obtenir pour lui de meilleurs moyens d'existence et finissait par y réussir. A partir de 1937, Leslau bénéficia d'une bourse de la Caisse nationale de la recherche scientifique, qui devait devenir plus tard le Centre national de la recherche scientifique. M. Cohen ne négligeait pas d'explorer d'autres possibilités comme celle de centres français au Proche-Orient ou une bourse de la fondation Rockefeller.

Mais les nuages s'accumulaient. W. Leslau faisait toujours des démarches pour obtenir la nationalité française, «avec toutes les obligations qu'elle comporte, notamment le service armé» comme devait l'écrire Marcel Cohen en novembre 1939. Sa demande de naturalisation était encore ajournée en 1937. En septembre 1938, au moment de la menace de guerre qui devait être retardée par la conférence de Munich, il avait demandé à s'engager dans l'armée française. Confiant dans le résultat de ses démarches, ayant coupé tout lien avec la Pologne dont les événements ne faisaient que confirmer et accentuer les orientations antisémites et de plus en plus nettement fascistes, il négligeait de renouveler son passeport polonais. En attendant l'éventuelle naturalisation française, alors que Charlotte restait de nationalité autrichienne, il entrait donc dans la catégorie des apatrides (*heimatlos*) alors que celle-ci se gonflait dangereusement de nombreux Allemands ou citoyens des territoires annexés progressivement par l'Allemagne et que dénationalisait le régime nazi.

Cela n'était que le prodrome inquiétant de développements catastrophiques comme on le sait bien, mais aussi celui d'une très attristante évolution d'une grande partie de l'opinion française. Ce n'est pas le lieu d'analyser ici ses

---

10 W. Leslau, *Etymological Dictionary of Gurage* (*Ethiopic*), Wiesbaden, Harrassowitz, 1979, 3 vol.

causes ni l'ensemble de ses manifestations. Mais il est indispensable de les
évoquer brièvement. Autrement, les événements que je vais raconter risque-
raient d'être totalement incompréhensibles aux membres des générations qui
n'ont pas connu cette période tragique et des peuples qui ne sont pas passés par
cette expérience. Il ne leur resterait que la plus banale, la plus agréable à la
bonne conscience de chacun, mais aussi la moins explicative des explications,
le recours proprement raciste à une certaine perversité fondamentale de l'âme
française.

On peut d'ailleurs renvoyer à la brillante et vivante esquisse que donne,
avec son talent habituel, Arthur Koestler, compagnon d'internement de
W. Leslau pendant près de trois mois et victime des mêmes errements. Son
livre, écrit immédiatement après la même expérience [11], reste encore au total la
meilleure tentative d'analyse et d'explication de ces faits lamentables.

En résumé, il faut poser que la tendance à la xénophobie est malheureusement le sentiment le plus répandu chez tous les peuples, latent souvent et
même contrebalancé par d'autres tendances plus bénéfiques, mais toujours
prêt à resurgir. En France, dans les années 1930, plusieurs facteurs l'attisèrent
de façon croissante. La crise mondiale atteignait le pays, menaçait son genre
de vie relativement tranquille et prospère. A l'Est, les développements
politiques faisaient craindre de plus en plus la guerre alors que le souvenir
terrible de la grande saignée de 1914-1918 (plus d'un million et demi de morts
français) était toujours vivant. Dans cette période de récession économique,
on voyait arriver en France des centaines de milliers d'émigrés dont beaucoup
de réfugiés d'Europe centrale et orientale (de 1921 à 1931, la proportion des
étrangers en France était passée de 3, 95 à 6, 58 %). Chacun pouvait craindre
les conséqences de cet afflux pour son niveau de vie. Les classes dirigeantes et
possédantes, dont les privilèges avaient été ébranlés par la poussée du Front
populaire en 1936, encourageaient les tendances habituelles à chercher des
boucs émissaires, de préférence étrangers, aux maux du siècle. Gagnées par
la crainte à une idéologie fascinante, admiratrices de Hitler et de Mussolini
qui assuraient l'ordre, elles dénonçaient ces masses d'étrangers comme
responsables de la misère, inspirateurs de la révolte, prêts surtout à entrainer
les Français paisibles à une guerre inutile et sanglante contre des pouvoirs
bien disposés à leur égard.

Naturellement, aux diffuseurs sincères et convaincus de cette vision des
choses s'ajoutaient les agents conscients ou inconscients des États fascistes. A

---

11 *Scum of the earth*, London, V. Gollancz, 1941. Je cite la traduction française (par Jeanne
   Terracini) *La lie de la terre*, Paris Charlot, 1946, d'après la deuxième édition, revue et corrigée
   (1947), publiée en livre de poche, Paris, Calmann-Lévy, 1973.

mesure que la guerre approchait, l'espionnite fleurissait et tout réfugié était soupçonné à la fois d'exciter à la guerre antifasciste (sans l'intention d'y participer personnellement ajoutait-on) et/ou d'être un agent de l'ennemi fasciste soigneusement camouflé. Ajoutons (*last but not least*) la puissance universellement assurée de la crédulité, de la bêtise et de la cruauté.

La bureaucratie y ajoutait encore en appliquant mécaniquement des catégories juridiques tranchées à une guerre qui était au moins autant une guerre idéologique, une guerre civile internationale en somme, qu'une guerre nationale. De nombreux Allemands opposés au régime hitlérien (juifs ou non) qui avaient fui le nazisme et cherché refuge dans les démocraties occidentales furent internés au minimum un certain temps, comme sujets ennemis! Le résultat en fut très souvent des issues tragiques. En principe, un «criblage» devait séparer rapidement les «bons éléments» des «mauvais». Il ne se fit pas pas toujours. Quand il se fit réellement, ce fut tard et mal.

Quand la guerre fut déclarée, le 3 septembre 1939, il fallut tenir compte aussi des effets sur la France du pacte germano-soviétique que le Parti communiste français, après quelques jours d'hésitation, se décida à approuver. Le résultat en fut la mise hors-la-loi du Parti et la suspicion étendue à ses membres, tendant à déborder sur les millions de Français qui avaient voté pour lui ou s'étaient associés à l'une ou l'autre de ses initiatives. Ici, il faut rappeler que Marcel Cohen, le protecteur de W. Leslau, outre son activité scientifique universellement admirée et respectée, était, comme je l'ai dit ci-dessus, un militant communiste, familier d'un cercle d'amis de même tendance, certains très connus et réputés comme son ami intime, l'écrivain Jean-Richard Bloch. Il continuait naturellement à exercer dans leur plénitude ses fonctions universitaires. Mais il était dès lors soupçonnable ainsi que tous ceux qui gravitaient autour de lui. Les étrangers parmi eux pouvaient en être atteints, même ceux dont l'apolitisme était manifeste comme Leslau. En état de guerre, on n'y regarde pas de si près.

En septembre 1939, on n'avait aucune idée des aspects que pourrait prendre la guerre qui commençait. On craignait notamment beaucoup que des attaques allemandes utilisent les gaz contre les populations civiles, avant tout celles des grandes villes et de Paris même. Nous étions tous munis par les autorités de masques à gaz. La plupart des Parisiens qui le purent partirent en province. La Bibliothèque nationale, avec bien d'autres institutions, fermait ses portes dans le but d'utiliser toutes les ressources qui lui restaient, après le départ de beaucoup de ses employés pour l'armée, à mettre à l'abri ses collections. Je partis pour un village du Sud-Est en attendant ma mobilisation qui ne devait se produire qu'en décembre, car j'avais été exempté de service militaire pour faiblesse de constitution. La déclaration de guerre avait surpris Marcel Cohen

à Fressines, petit village du département des Deux-Sèvres où il passait toutes
ses vacances. Il pressa les Leslau de quitter, eux aussi, la région parisienne et
les confia à son ami intime Jean-Richard Bloch. Celui-ci disposait en effet
d'une vaste demeure de famille, une sorte de gentilhommière, la Mérigote, tout
près de Poitiers dont Fressines n'est éloigné que d'une cinquantaine de
kilomètres. Il trouva à loger les Leslau dans le voisinage. Charlotte Leslau
était dans un état de grossesse avancé. Wolf travaillait d'arrache-pied à son
livre sur le tigrigna. Il avait renouvelé sa demande d'engagement dans
l'armée française en juin 1939; elle n'avait pas abouti par suite de ses
déplacements lors des convocations à l'examen médical préalable. La guerre
déclarée, il se présenta aux autorités militaires de Poitiers et l'examen médical, le 13 septembre, fut positif. Mais la complication de son statut national
— Polonais devenu apatride — fit renvoyer à plus tard son incorporation.

Dès le début de septembre et même un peu avant, les autorités avaient
déclenché une vague d'arrestations d'étrangers. Les camps d'internement
d'étrangers «suspects» ou «indésirables» avaient déjà commencé à fonctionner
— sous le nom d'abord de bon augure, mais sinistrement inadéquat, de
«centres d'accueil» — pour concentrer et isoler les réfugiés espagnols et les
miliciens des Brigades internationales fuyant la victoire franquiste à partir du
printemps 1939. Ils furent équipés et multipliés pour «accueillir» un nombre
bien plus élevé d'internés[11bis]. Dès la nuit du 2 au 3 septembre, la police
parisienne vint arrêter un voisin de Koestler, médecin, réfugié allemand, qui
venait de quitter un sanatorium suisse pour s'engager dans l'armée française,
et Koestler lui-même, de nationalité hongroise (la Hongrie était neutre alors),
dont la rupture avec le communisme, un an et demi auparavant, avait été
commentée, qui était violemment attaqué par la presse communiste. Absent, il
échappa à l'arrestation cette fois-là. Il ne fut arrêté — après s'être présenté en
vain plusieurs fois à la police — que le 2 octobre. Pour Leslau, à Poitiers,
l'arrestation se fit le 24 octobre à la clinique même où sa femme venait
d'accoucher le 13 d'une petite fille, Eliane.

Dans la seconde quinzaine de septembre, le Ministère de l'Intérieur français
avait pris des décisions générales concernant l'internement des étrangers
résidant en France en commençant par les sujets allemands et autrichiens, mais

---

11 bis Quelques milliers d'Allemands et autres étrangers jouirent à partir de février 1940 du
statut relativement privilégié de «prestataires» dont W. Leslau demanda un moment à
relever. Réunis dans des camps spéciaux, ils devaient (en principe) «fournir des prestations
(c'est à dire exécuter des travaux) aux autorités militaires pour une durée égale à la durée
du service militaire imposé aux Français» (Schramm et Vormeier, [ouvrage cité ci-dessous
n. 12], p. 240, 256, 321-3, 370). Des savants, dont certains illustres et maintenant aux
États-Unis, passèrent par cette condition.

en débordant aussitôt cette limitation. Leslau fut immédiatement envoyé au «centre d'accueil» du Vernet dans le département de l'Ariège. Ce camp était réservé aux «éléments dangereux et indésirables». On le considérait comme un «camp répressif» où on envoyait aussi en punition ceux qui avaient mécontenté leurs surveillants dans des camps jugés plus «doux» [12].

En fait, l'internement et la répartition dans les divers camps avaient été en grande partie le fait du hasard ou de caprices bureaucratiques. On comptait plus ou moins sur l'avenir pour démêler les cas douteux, trier «bons» et «mauvais» éléments. Un document officiel du début de mai 1940, une lettre du ministère des Postes au directeur du camp, énonce: «Le département de la Défense nationale et de la guerre vient de faire connaître que les internés du camp du Vernet sont en effet des suspects de toutes nationalités qui ne sauraient être considérés comme internés civils admis au bénéfice des dispositions de la convention de Genève» [13]. On voit que l'administration du camp elle-même n'était pas très bien renseignée sur le statut des internés confiés à sa garde. Ceux-ci étaient naturellement encore plus dans l'obscurité. Leslau s'interrogeait en vain sur la cause de son arrestation et, dès qu'il le put, questionna là-dessus les autorités du camp. Le 18 novembre 1939, il écrivait à Marcel Cohen: «J'ai subi un interrogatoire. Mon dossier se trouve au Ministère de l'Intérieur, mais j'ai cru comprendre que le Ministère de l'Intérieur me soupçonne de la fréquentation de milieux allemands ou extrémistes [sic! M. R.] ... Il faudrait, en premier lieu, connaître l'accusation exacte et rassembler ensuite les documents pour réfuter les soupçons».

En fait, les critères avaient été des plus vagues et l'administration répondait un peu au hasard pour justifier a posteriori ses mesures. On rencontre de multiples exemples de cas des plus aberrants dans les documents et souvenirs

---

12 Sur ces camps en général, on trouvera beaucoup d'informations dans le livre de Hanna Schramm et Barbara Vormeier, *Menschen in Gurs, Erinnerungen an ein französisches Internierungslager, 1940-1941*, Worms, Georg Heintz, 1977, dont le contenu dépasse de beaucoup le titre. J'ai utilisé et cité ici la traduction française, *Vivre à Gurs, Un camp de concentration français, 1940-1941*, traduit de l'allemand par I. Petit, Paris, Maspero, 1977. Voir aussi le livre trilingue (allemand, français, anglais) de Barbara Vormeier, *Die Deportierungen deutscher und österreichischer Juden aus Frankreich*, (Paris), Éditions La Solidarité, 1980 et le livre d'Arthur Koestler cité ci-dessus. Je remercie Pierre Vidal-Naquet de m'avoir orienté à travers cette littérature. Voir Schramm et Vormeier, p. 180 sur les changements de dénomination des camps et l'extrait du règlement de Gurs reproduit pl. VIII qui menace le contrevenant récidiviste du «camp répressif du Vernet». Sur Le Vernet, cf. aussi le même livre p. 249-250, 251 n. 21, 254, 264, 267, 274, 278, 301ss. (rapport Bondy cité ci-dessous), 321, 335ss.

13 Cité par B. Vormeier dans H. Schramm et B. Vormeier, *op. cit.*, p. 251, n. 21, d'après un document d'archive.

publiés plus tard sur ces camps. On pourra en trouver dans le livre bien connu de Koestler, déjà cité, qui fut interné au Vernet d'octobre 1939 au 17 janvier 1940. François Bondy, journaliste et écrivain suisse, d'origine juive allemande, fut arrêté à Paris dans la vague d'arrestations encore plus massives et opérées encore plus au hasard qui suivit le déclenchement de l'offensive allemande de mai 1940. Il se retrouva au Vernet avec six autres Suisses dont un ingénieur envoyé en France par son usine suisse pour une démonstration d'appareil à la Société nationale des chemins de fer français. Libéré le 26 juillet, il écrit dans un rapport daté du 2 août: «On (y) trouve surtout des hommes internés sans motif, par suite d'une dénonciation anonyme non vérifiée ou à cause de leur lieu de naissance ou pour des raisons encore plus futiles» [14].

François Bondy — qui dirigea plus tard, de 1951 à 1969, la revue d'orientation spécialement anticommuniste *Preuves*, au surplus de haute tenue — note le cas Leslau comme typique: «Je tiens à citer le cas d'un apatride d'origine polonaise, M. L. qui, pendant plusieurs années, professa les langues sémitiques à l'École des hautes études et à l'École des langues sémitiques (lire: orientales M. R.) à Paris; il ne s'est jamais intéressé à la politique. Sa libération fut demandée à plusieurs reprises par des pétitions de professeurs de la Sorbonne et du Collège de France. On fit sur lui une enquête entièrement favorable. Ce jeune savant réputé est interné au Vernet sans avoir pu revoir sa femme et son enfant» [15].

En effet, dès son arrestation, en route vers le camp par chemin de fer, Wolf envoyait de la gare de Bordeaux deux cartes postales de détresse à son seul protecteur actif, Marcel Cohen, à Fressines. Celui-ci venait d'être mis au courant de la situation par Charlotte Leslau. Il ne perdit pas de temps pour tenter d'agir en faveur de Wolf, cherchant à faire intervenir des professeurs éminents et peu suspects du point de vue politique. Il commença par solliciter l'intervention du Directeur du Service central de la Recherche scientifique dont Leslau avait reçu des bourses les années précédentes et dont il avait compté en recevoir à nouveau pour la nouvelle année académique, Henri Laugier. Sur la demande de celui-ci, il «se porta garant des sentiments de loyalisme de Leslau envers la France». M. Cohen rédigea l'attestation exigée. Il prenait soin d'y dire: «Je l'ai toujours vu se consacrant exclusivement à sa vie de famille, avant tout à son travail scientifique très dense et absorbant, rigoureusement à l'écart de toute manifestation ou mouvement d'opinion politique». Cela devait permettre à Laugier de demander au Ministère de l'Intérieur la libération de

---

14 «Rapport sur le camp du Vernet (Ariège) et sur les conditions de l'arrestation et de l'internement de nombreux étrangers en France», in H. Schramm et B. Vormeier, *Vivre à Gurs*, p. 301-312. Le passage cité se trouve p. 306.
15 *Ibid.*, p. 306-7.

l'interné. On fit intervenir aussi des savants comme Mgr Sylvain Grébaut, ecclésiastique de rang élevé, professeur d'éthiopien à l'Institut catholique de Paris et Régis Blachère, alors professeur d'arabe à l'École nationale des langues orientales vivantes. Un vote unanime des professeurs de cette École s'associa à ces demandes.

Parmi ceux qui demandaient ainsi la libération de Leslau, il y avait un homme dont le témoignage aurait dû peser d'un poids tout particulier. Il s'agit de Jean Nougayrol, assyriologue réputé qui venait d'être chargé (en novembre 1938) du cours de religion assyro-babylonienne à la Vᵉ section (sciences religieuses) de l'École pratique des Hautes Études. Il allait être nommé directeur d'études dans le même enseignement en novembre 1941. En attendant, comme beaucoup, il était parti pour une résidence dans le sud du pays, et a dû faire des cours à l'Université de Toulouse. Mobilisé, il avait été affecté par les autorités militaires au camp du Vernet à titre d'«officier d'information» avec le grade de capitaine. Son excellente connaissance de l'allemand (il avait traduit des lettres de Rilke) avait dû jouer un rôle dans cette affectation. Il put aider un peu quelques intellectuels internés dont un écrivain allemand prénommé Albert et Koestler lui-même. Celui-ci parle avec sympathie du «capitaine N.», «homme charmant», «officier du 2ᵉ bureau qui était dans le civil lecteur de langues orientales à l'Université de Toulouse», que «les autorités militaires avaient affecté au camp», mais qui «n'avait aucune influence sur l'administration du camp» [16].

Jean Nougayrol avait encore plus de raisons de s'intéresser à un sémitisant comme W. Leslau. Du camp même, le 10 décembre 1939, il envoya une attestation: «Bien que je ne connaisse pas intimement M. Wolf Leslau, j'ai eu de fréquentes occasions de le rencontrer et de lui serrer la main au Collège de France et à la Sorbonne où nos recherches nous appelaient souvent l'un et l'autre avant la mobilisation. Je savais d'ailleurs que Monsieur Wolf Leslau était un jeune savant de grand avenir et *entièrement* adonné à ses études. Je serais heureux que son cas fût examiné avec un soin tout particulier et la

---

16 A. Koestler, *La lie de la terre*, p. 197s., 203. Dans les Annuaires de la section des sciences religieuses de l'E.P.H.E., on mentionne une mise à la disposition de l'Université de Toulouse de Nougayrol par arrêté ministériel de janvier 1941. Il s'agit sans doute d'une régularisation administrative a posteriori. Il fut plus tard démobilisé et put reprendre ses cours à Paris au début de 1942. Né à Toulouse en 1900, il fut mis à la retraite en 1970 et mourut d'un cancer en 1975. Voir l'article nécrologique de H. Cazelles (*Journal Asiatique*, 263, 1975, p. 3-5) qui contient quelques erreurs sur cette période. Cf. École pratique des Hautes Études, section des sciences religieuses. *Annuaire 1938-1939*, (Melun, Imp. administrative, 1938), p. 45, 99; *Annuaire 1939-1940*, (*ibid.*, 1939), p. 45, 60s.; *Annuaire 1940-1941 et 1941-1942 (ibid.*, 1941), p. 50, 113; *Annuaire 1942-1943 (ibid.*, 1942), p. 33, 49-50, 79.

bienveillance qu'il mérite»[17]. Il rédigea aussi en janvier et février 1940 deux rapports officiels qui devaient être transmis à Paris. Il écrivit à Marcel Cohen le 5 mars qu'il s'étonnait que l'ordre ne soit pas encore venu «d'ouvrir nos portes devant mon excellent collègue dont j'ai pu apprécier à plusieurs reprises le courage dans l'adversité et la charmante discrétion». Au début d'avril, il conseillait à Leslau de «ne pas remuer trop les choses» pendant qu'il intervenait lui-même en sa faveur. À la fin d'avril, il partit pour Paris avec le dossier de Leslau entre autres. Il revint au Vernet vers la mi-mai en pensant avoir obtenu de la Sûreté nationale que l'internement soit transformé en une assignation à résidence dans une localité donnée à moins que le Ministère de la Guerre n'accepte l'engagement de Leslau dans l'armée.

Pourtant, il y avait des libérations. Koestler avait été libéré en janvier avec une cinquantaine d'autres. «Mais nous étions des exceptions» écrit-il. De retour à Paris et désirant régulariser sa situation, il se heurta d'ailleurs sans succès au monstre administratif, renvoyé de bureau en bureau et toujours menacé d'être arrêté à nouveau. Les démarches pour la libération de Leslau se perdirent-elles dans le même labyrinthe de la routine et des règlements ou y eut-il une particulière mauvaise volonté de quelque fonctionnaire irrité par quelque détail de son dossier? On n'en saura sans doute jamais rien.

En attendant, Wolf demeurait au camp aux prises avec le supplice de l'espoir toujours déçu d'une libération prochaine, séparé de sa femme et de sa petite fille. Au moins, ses conditions d'existence s'y étaient un peu améliorées, entre autres grâce à Nougayrol. Il put y corriger les épreuves de son article «Observations sur quelques dialectes du tigrigna (dialectes d'Akkele Gouzay, d'Adoua et du Hamasen)» qui devait paraître au *Journal Asiatique* (voir ci-dessus n. 9). Surtout, ce qui lui importait tout particulièrement, il pouvait reprendre la correction de celles de son livre *Documents tigrigna*. Commencée à Mâcon par l'imprimerie Protat en septembre 1939, l'impression en fut terminée en 1941. Dans la préface, Leslau, très discrètement, indique: «La partie grammaire a été revue par mon maître Marcel Cohen. Le travail aurait gagné à être entièrement corrigé par lui; malheureusement, du fait de la guerre, les circonstances ne l'ont pas permis [...]. Je m'excuse auprès du lecteur des fautes qui ont échappé à mon attention [...], mais les pénibles conditions matérielles

---

17 Le mot «entièrement» est souligné (avec intention évidemment) par J. Nougayrol lui-même dans son attestation dont une copie se trouve dans le dossier conservé par Marcel Cohen. On y trouve aussi la copie d'une attestation parallèle de Mgr Sylvain Grébaut. Il dit qu'«il connait depuis plusieurs années M. Wolf Leslau qui a été son élève et peut se porter garant de la parfaite loyauté ainsi que des sentiments d'attachement et de fidélité à la France de cet orientaliste hautement méritant».

dans lesquelles j'ai dû corriger la première partie de l'ouvrage sont responsables des fautes d'impression qui ont subsisté dans cette partie» [18].

Ces conditions étaient en effet fort mauvaises et il faut admirer que Leslau
ait pu mener à bien ce travail. Marcel Cohen s'imaginait mal cette situation et
avait demandé à Leslau de rédiger un compte rendu de son livre, *Nouvelles
Etudes d'éthiopien méridional* paru en 1939, dans la «série de guerre» (comme
porte la couverture) de la «Bibliothèque de l'École des Hautes Etudes».
Leslau dut lui répondre (en mars 1940): «Il m'est très difficile de faire
actuellement le compte rendu [...]. Il est tout à fait impossible de faire ici un
travail suivi parce qu'il y a continuellement la chasse à l'homme pour exécuter,
très souvent, des travaux inutiles. Je n'ai même pas de table à ma disposition
sans parler du manque de la documentation nécessaire pour pouvoir réétudier
de près votre ouvrage».

Dans l'ensemble du pays, on vivait alors la curieuse période que l'on a
appelée «la drôle de guerre». Après quelques semaines d'hésitation, on s'était
aperçu avec étonnement que les Allemands n'attaquaient pas la frontière
française, on en attribuait au moins en partie la cause à l'efficacité de la ligne
Maginot. Cette situation semblait dès lors durable jusqu'à des évènements
imprévisibles préparés sur des théâtres d'opérations lointains: la Finlande, la
Norvège. En attendant, on s'installait dans la guerre. A Paris, l'Ecole pratique
des Hautes Etudes avait repris ses cours. Dès lors, Marcel Cohen et sa femme
étaient rentrés à leur domicile de Viroflay près de Paris, quittant Fressines où
étaient hébergées désormais Charlotte Leslau et la petite Eliane. Les cours
étaient d'ailleurs plutôt théoriques. Rédigeant à l'été 1940, après l'invasion de
la France, son rapport annuel, Marcel Cohen écrivait: «Il ne s'est présenté en
début d'année (i.e. en novembre 1939) aucun étudiant pour cette langue (le
guèze) non plus que pour le sud-arabique. M.W. Leslau n'a pu enseigner cette
année. Il a poursuivi la correction des épreuves de ses travaux sur le tigrigna:
un livre à paraître dans la collection de la Société de linguistique et un mémoire
à paraître dans le *Journal asiatique*; un article de lui a paru dans la *Revue des études
sémitiques*» [15].

Dans ce rapport officiel, dont Marcel Cohen avait assurément soigneusement pesé la formulation, il croit utile, en vue d'un avenir imprévisible,
d'insister sur les travaux en cours de Leslau. Mais il a recours délibérément
à des euphémismes. Il continuait en même temps à faire des démarches et
surtout à pousser d'autres personnes mieux placées à intervenir en faveur

18 *Documents tigrigna (éthiopien septentrional), grammaire et textes*, Paris, C. Klincksieck, 1941,
   p. VI.
19 École pratique des Hautes Études, Section des sciences historiques et philologiques.
   Annuaire 1940-1941 et 1941-1942 (Melun, *ibid.*, 1942), p. 135-6.

de Leslau. Mais tout semblait se perdre dans les méandres administratifs. Comme, des casernes successives où j'avais été affecté en tant que soldat, je m'inquiétais de son sort, notre amie commune Deborah Lifchitz, l'ethnographe et éthiopisante qu'un destin tragique attendait bientôt, m'écrivait le 10 avril 1940: «Leslau est toujours au même endroit; on ne peut rien faire pour lui. Il se porte à peu près bien et corrige assidûment ses épreuves de tigrigna. Il parait que cela sera remarquable»[20].

$$*\quad*\quad*$$

Cette relative quiétude commença à s'écrouler avec l'offensive allemande déclenchée le 10 mai 1940 contre la Belgique et la Hollande, et qui atteignit la France au bout de cinq jours. Une semaine plus tard, on se rendait enfin nettement compte que ce n'était pas la guerre de 1914 qui se répétait, que les Allemands ne pourraient être arrêtés quelque part au Nord de Paris. Comme l'avaient fait les Belges quelques jours auparavant, on procéda à de nouvelles arrestations, faites en grande partie au hasard, des sujets allemands et autrichiens, ainsi que des «étrangers suspects». On arrêta à nouveau certains qui avaient été libérés comme Arthur Koestler. Les exceptions faites dans un premier temps n'étaient plus de mise. La hantise des espions était plus forte que jamais, on criait à la trahison et tous les éléments hostiles à la démocratie, dont la xénophobie se colorait d'admiration pour Hitler et de haine pour

---

20 Répondant de New York à la première lettre que je lui écrivais de Beyrouth après la libération de la France et après avoir obtenu son adresse américaine, Leslau s'inquiétait: «Paul Rivet (le directeur du Musée de l'Homme où elle travaillait M.R.) m'a dit que Lifchitz a été transférée en Pologne, mais j'espère que ce n'est pas exact» (lettre du 17 janvier 1945). C'était malheureusement exact. Marcel Cohen apprenait vers cette date, au retour en France d'«une autre de nos amies captive à Auschwitz», qu'elle y était morte. Il me l'écrivait à Beyrouth en mars 1945 comme il en informait au même moment le couple Leslau avec qui il pouvait enfin, également en mars, reprendre la correspondance. Auschwitz avait été libéré par l'armée soviétique le 27 janvier 1945. Plus tard, il faisait publier, dans le *Journal Asiatique*, le dernier travail qu'elle avait rédigé, qui aurait dû paraître en 1940 dans le *Journal de la Société des Africanistes* et qu'elle lui avait remis. Il y ajoutait des indications supplémentaires obtenues en 1948 d'un lettré éthiopien («Le Livre d'Emmanuel, poème éthiopien», *Journal Asiatique*, t. 236, fasc. 1, 1948, p. 65-86). Il y insérait cette notation sobre: «Deborah Lifchitz, arrêtée en février 1942, a été déportée en septembre 1942 au camp d'Auschwitz où elle a été gazée dès l'arrivée» (p. 67). Cf. la notice nécrologique d'E. C[erulli], *Oriente Moderno*, 25, 1945, p. 63. Deborah Lifszyc (qui écrivit son nom en France Lifchitz) était attachée au Musée d'ethnographie du Trocadéro (plus tard Musée de l'homme) à Paris et chargée d'enseignement à l'École des langues orientales pour l'amharique. Elle était née le 5 juin 1907 à Kharkov en Ukraine.

les réfugiés allemands, prenaient le dessus dans l'administration. Le Vernet «accueillit» quelques centaines de nouveaux «hôtes» de toutes nationalités dont des Belges et des Italiens. Parmi eux se trouvaient les quelques Suisses dont il a été parlé ci-dessus [21]. En juillet-août 1940, une commission allemande devait y trouver 3728 internés «de nationalités diverses dont 283 ressortissants allemands du Reich, juifs pour la plupart» [22].

Le 21 juin 1940, l'armistice avec l'Allemagne était signé. Une grande partie de la France était occupée. Le Vernet se trouvait dans la zone dite libre c'est à dire non occupée. On a dû y suivre l'irrésistible avance allemande avec encore plus d'anxiété qu'ailleurs. Leslau, qui avait eu beaucoup d'espoir dans les résultats de la tournée de Nougayrol à Paris, comprit que, même si des décisions en sa faveur avaient été prises, il n'y avait plus à compter sur leur application dans cette atmosphère de désastre, de désordre et de capitulation. Nul ne savait ce que les Allemands décideraient.

La convention d'armistice franco-allemande du 26 juin 1940 obligeait le gouvernement français à livrer à l'Allemagne tous les Allemands se trouvant en France et dans les possessions françaises qu'elle réclamerait (art. 19). Alors que le désordre eût aisément permis de les laisser quitter leurs camps d'internement, la plupart des commandants de camps prirent plutôt des mesures de surveillance renforcée pour empêcher les évasions ... et les suicides. Il y eut pourtant de très remarquables exceptions, notamment à Gurs, où beaucoup furent libérés. Rien n'était prévu pour les non-Allemands. Il faut se garder de transposer anachroniquement à cette époque les conditions qui régnèrent à partir de 1942. Les Allemands ne réclamèrent nominativement, au début, que des sujets allemands compromis politiquement. Les autres les intéressaient peu. On expulsait d'Allemagne vers la France en octobre 1940 quelque 6500 juifs de Bade et du Palatinat. Ils furent internés dans les camps baptisés désormais «centres d'hébergement». Selon l'optique nazie d'alors, il s'agissait de se débarrasser d'éléments indésirables dont la France aurait la charge et dont elle pourrait faire ce qu'elle voudrait. On opposait des réponses dilatoires aux protestations et interrogations françaises. La France, de son côté, voulait se décharger et favorisait l'émigration. Des comités s'étaient formés dans le

---

21 Cf. F. Bondy in Schramm et Vormeier, *op. cit.*, pp. 303ss. J'avais personnellement vu passer le convoi de Belges transporté, dans des conditions assez horribles, de Belgique vers le Sud dont il est question p. 304. J'étais des soldats de l'Intendance chargés de ravitailler (un peu) ce convoi — pour la première fois apparemment depuis plus de 48 heures à partir de la Belgique — à St Pierre-des-Corps, nœud ferroviaire près de Tours où j'étais alors encaserné.

22 Rapport de la commission Kundt in Schramm et Vormeier, *op. cit.*, p. 321; cf. p. 265ss.

même but, notamment pour aider à l'émigration des juifs vers les États-Unis. Le principal obstacle était les quota américains restreignant l'immigration[23].

A l'été 1940, on ne pouvait guère prévoir que la continuation de la domination allemande sur la France avec ou sans troupes d'occupation, soit qu'une paix victorieuse soit imposée par l'Allemagne à l'Angleterre, soit que la guerre se poursuive longuement. Au Vernet, au moment de l'avance allemande et de sa dernière déception après le retour de Nougayrol de Paris, Leslau avait pris son parti. Le 12 juin, il écrivait à Marcel Cohen: «J'ai longuement réfléchi sur ma situation future. On ne peut évidemment rien prévoir actuellement, dans les circonstances que nous traversons, mais, à la réflexion, je suis arrivé à la conclusion que je ne pourrai plus vivre en France si je dois rester interné pour la durée de la guerre. J'ai beaucoup d'exemples à l'appui de cette supposition dans le milieu où je me trouve. La police ne pardonne pas. Et même si je dois pouvoir continuer à vivre en France, je ne veux pas rester interné pour des années peut-être, qui sait? J'ai eu de la patience pendant huit mois, mais je ne veux pas être usé complètement, car j'ai des responsabilités envers ma famille. Vous penserez peut-être à tous ceux qui font la guerre séparés de leur famille, mais faire la guerre actuellement est une nécessité alors que mon internement ne rend aucun service au pays, tout au contraire. Il y a encore d'autres réflexions qu'il m'est difficile d'exposer par lettre. J'ai donc décidé d'émigrer en Amérique pour recommencer mon existence pour la troisième fois. Je ne peux pas compter sur le quota ordinaire car ça prendra des années; il y a un moyen d'accélérer la chose, c'est d'obtenir une nomination comme professeur dans une Université [...]. Je vous prie de croire une fois de plus que j'ai longuement réfléchi avant d'avoir pris la décision de l'émigration [...]».

Leslau ajoutait des indications sur les universitaires américains intéressés par la linguistique sémitique auxquels il priait Marcel Cohen d'envoyer des lettres en sa faveur, ainsi que des indications pratiques. Marcel Cohen — qui avait regagné Fressines — se rangea immédiatement à ses raisons. Dès le 4 juillet, il envoyait à deux collègues américains une lettre recommandant Leslau. Mais les premières réponses furent pour expliquer qu'aucune perspective d'emploi dans une Université américaine pour un sémitisant n'était en vue.

Leslau s'y attendait et demandait, en attendant une réponse américaine favorable, qu'on le sorte du camp en l'assignant à résidence quelque part en

---

23 Pierre Vidal-Naquet me signale que Wolf Leslau est encore cité (comme «célèbre linguiste»), parmi d'autres, dans un livre de souvenirs encore inédit dont il a pu consulter le manuscrit. Le titre (provisoire) en est *Échec à l'article 19* et il a été rédigé précisément par M. Daniel Benedite, qui fut collaborateur d'un Comité américain de secours aux internés.

France. Il pensait, entre autres, à une intervention de l'École pratique des Hautes Études, le réclamant pour un emploi. Mais cela se heurtait encore à des obstacles administratifs. Il en était de même pour les démarches qu'aurait pu faire la Caisse de la recherche scientifique. Pendant ce temps, Leslau poursuivait toujours la correction de ses épreuves pour son livre sur le tigrigna.

La solution vint de ce côté. Leslau avait suggéré à Marcel Cohen d'écrire à l'imprimeur de son livre, Protat, à Mâcon pour lui demander d'établir un contrat de travail fictif l'engageant à son service. Ce serait une façon d'obtenir sa libération et son assignation à résidence forcée à Mâcon.

Emile Protat (associé à son frère Pierre) obtint de Vichy en 1941 que Leslau fût autorisé à quitter de temps à autre le camp pour venir à Mâcon surveiller l'impression de son ouvrage. A peu près à la même époque, il fut d'ailleurs transféré du Vernet au camp des Milles. Les Milles est un village au Sud-Ouest d'Aix-en-Provence, non loin de Marseille. On y groupait les internés étrangers qui étaient en voie d'obtenir pour les États-Unis un de ces précieux visas que délivrait le consulat américain à Marseille. Des Milles Wolf allait donc parfois à Mâcon. Toutes ces localités se trouvaient, comme le Vernet, en zone dite libre. Par contre, Fressines où se trouvait Charlotte était en zone occupée. Elle ne put rejoindre Mâcon avec sa petite fille qu'en risquant l'arrestation. Autrichienne exilée, il lui était pratiquement impossible d'obtenir un permis comme on en délivrait parcimonieusement aux Français présentant toute garantie. Dans le chemin de fer, elle réussit à échapper au contrôle d'une patrouille allemande en tançant sa fille en excellent allemand naturellement. Les militaires allemands, attendris par cette mère allemande, n'insistèrent pas pour lui demander ses papiers.

Il était temps. Les conditions s'aggravaient. Peu à peu, l'étau se resserrait. Le gouvernement de Vichy organisait de plus en plus la répression des opposants réels ou potentiels, prenait de plus en plus de mesures xénophobes et antisémites en attendant que les déportations allemandes ne soient décidées et ne s'organisent à partir de mars 1942. A Fressines, Marcel Cohen était averti qu'il allait être arrêté et prenait les devants en partant à bicyclette, le 6 octobre 1941, et en gagnant des refuges clandestins. Sa femme et sa fille cadette, à leur tour menacées, quittaient Fressines le 18 juillet 1942.

Wolf Leslau, après quelque temps passé à Mâcon, put gagner Marseille, non sans péripéties nouvelles. Il passa à nouveau par un camp de regroupement, mais il y disposait de fréquentes permissions de sortie et rejoignait sa femme qui demeurait à Mâcon. Il pouvait en recevoir des colis de nourriture qui étaient bien nécessaires. A Marseille commençait une suite de démarches pénibles du genre de celles qu'a décrites Koestler pour les exilés allemands :

«Finalement quelques uns réussirent à gagner Marseille et à obtenir des visas pour les U.S.A. ou d'autres pays de l'Amérique. C'était l'élite intellectuelle et les riches, des gens qui avaient des relations, des écrivains, des journalistes, des étudiants, peut-être 200 sur 10 000. Les visas pour les États-Unis leur étaient délivrés selon une liste «d'intellectuels de valeur» établie par les comités de New York. Même ces hommes de réputation mondiale devaient attendre des mois, écrire, faire la queue, s'humilier, jusqu'à ce que le cachet magique fût imprimé sur leurs passeports [...]. Puis, quand tout était en règle et que le miracle de leur évasion allait se réaliser, les autorités françaises leur refusaient le visa de sortie ...»[24].

Les Leslau faillirent s'embarquer à la fin de décembre 1941. Mais, au dernier moment, un nouvel obstacle avait surgi. A la suite de l'attaque japonaise sur Pearl Harbor le 7 décembre 1941, l'Allemagne et l'Italie avaient déclaré la guerre aux États-Unis le 11 décembre. Pour l'administration américaine, Charlotte, citoyenne de l'Autriche annexée par l'Allemagne, devenait un «sujet ennemi». Il fallut continuer les démarches sur une nouvelle base. Wolf, au moment de la reprise de nos relations, m'écrivait en janvier 1945 : «Comme vous le savez, j'ai été interné et cet internement a duré deux ans et demi. Réflexion faite, ça m'a probablement sauvé la vie [...]. Je ne sais pas si vous vous rendez compte de ce que c'est (que) d'entreprendre des démarches pour aller en Amérique : les attentes et les déceptions n'avaient pas de fin».

Enfin le visa était délivré à la fin de mai 1942. Le couple Leslau et la petite Eliane s'embarquaient à Marseille à bord du *Gueydon* le 31 mai. Il devait les mener par Oran à Casablanca d'où un vieux navire portugais, le *Serpa Pinto*, chargé au double de sa capacité d'êtres humains fuyant l'Europe en feu, les transportait à New York au début de juin. Encore une fois, il était temps. En novembre 1942, à la suite du débarquement des Américains en Afrique du Nord, les Allemands occupaient toute la zone «libre» de la France, y compris Marseille et Toulon. Tous ceux qui se trouvaient en France étaient bloqués et pris au piège. Du Vernet et des Milles entre autres, de sinistres convois allaient bientôt être dirigés vers l'Est, vers les camps de la mort.

*   *   *

La longue expérience française des Leslau s'était donc achevée de façon désastreuse, même si le pire avait été évité *in extremis*. Pourtant, les liens avec la France n'étaient pas rompus. Aux États-Unis, au départ, Wolf eut du mal à trouver un travail suffisamment rémunéré dans les institutions d'enseigne-

---

24 A. Koestler, *La lie de la terre*, p. 372s.

ment, alors que sa famille s'était agrandie avec la naissance de Sylvia, le 19 janvier 1943. Il dut cumuler les emplois. Bientôt, il put — entre autres emplois — enseigner dans deux institutions francophones en exil: d'abord l'Institut de philologie et d'histoire orientales et slaves (à base d'exilés belges), puis l'École libre des Hautes Études. Vers la fin de 1943, il était secrétaire-trésorier du Cercle linguistique de New York que l'on fondait pour continuer en exil, avec des linguistes français, américains et autres, l'activité de la Société de linguistique de Paris. Quand la paix se fit en Europe, Marcel Cohen pensa un moment le faire nommer à un Institut français qui devait être créé à Addis Abeba (mais le projet échoua), puis le faire désigner comme maître de recherches au Centre national de la recherche scientifique (qui avait remplacé la Caisse nationale de la recherche scientifique). Tous ces projets, dans l'esprit de Marcel Cohen, pouvaient le pousser à revenir en France et même à s'y installer définitivement. Il n'avait pas encore passé aux États-Unis les cinq années nécessaires pour acquérir la nationalité américaine.

Marcel Cohen aurait bien aimé que Wolf Leslau choisisse la France et devienne son successeur pour l'enseignement des langues éthiopiennes comme celui qui lui paraissait le plus qualifié pour cet emploi. Il s'employait de son mieux à lui préparer une place en France. Il avança formellement sa candidature. W. Leslau, qui tenait aussi à ne pas décevoir son vieux maître et son meilleur protecteur, n'oppose pas, dans ses lettres, un refus absolu qui aurait manqué d'égards et de politesse. Mais il accumule les objections et se déclare hésitant. Marcel Cohen, assez souvent, plaçait ainsi ses protégés devant le fait accompli de démarches tendant à leur obtenir une position, à son avis très désirable pour leur propre bien et pour celui de la science. A la même époque, après le refus de Leslau, il pensa à moi pour le même projet d'Institut français d'Addis Abeba. Pour de multiples raisons, je n'y tenais pas non plus, mais je n'osais contrarier mon bon vieux maître que quand il ne fut plus possible de tergiverser et il me reprocha de ne pas lui avoir exprimé plut tôt mon refus. De même, Wolf Leslau — qui d'ailleurs avait aussi exprimé dans sa correspondance avec Marcel Cohen son scepticisme devant ce dernier projet me concernant — avait d'excellentes raisons de s'en tenir fermement à son choix américain. Marcel Cohen, comprenant mal les réponses quelque peu embarrassées de Leslau, pensant aussi sans doute qu'il fallait un peu lui forcer la main pour qu'il accepte une situation très enviable, persista quelques années dans ses illusions et dans ses démarches unilatérales. D'ailleurs, celles-ci se heurtaient à de forts obstacles bureaucratiques en France même, vieux pays où l'insertion des étrangers ne peut se faire qu'avec des étapes longues et précautionneuses, alors que les États-Unis, nation composite formée de couches successives d'émigrants, est plus habituée à de telles intégrations. Les démarches de Marcel Cohen, de façon bien curieuse pour qui n'a pas de familiarité avec les contradictions de la conscience idéologique, trouvaient aussi leurs limites en lui-même. Dans cette période de guerre froide, en tant que militant communiste, ne devait-il pas s'opposer à la pénétration culturelle de «l'impérialisme américain»? La correspondance des deux hommes porte la marque de ces insistances parfois hésitantes de M. Cohen en face des réticences polies de W. Leslau. Le ton monta parfois un peu entre les deux hommes, mais l'amitié affectueuse qui les unissait apaisa vite ces remous avec l'aide de l'intervention conciliante de leurs épouses. Le débat se faisait d'ailleurs de plus en plus abstrait. Wolf devenait définitivement citoyen américain comme sa femme. Sa situation s'améliorait peu à peu aux États-Unis où il obtenait des subventions pour des voyages d'enquête linguistique en Éthiopie. Il réalisait enfin un de ses vœux les plus chers: aller enquêter sur place au lieu de se contenter de travailler sur les notations plus ou moins fiables de chercheurs et surtout de voyageurs antérieurs. Marcel Cohen se résigna à ne pas le voir devenir un professeur français.

Cependant les liens avec la France subsistaient. Toutes les fois que Leslau allait en Ethiopie ou en revenait, il faisait son possible pour passer par Paris et se concerter avec son maitre. Ainsi, dès l'automne 1946, il tint à passer son doctorat en France et en français. Cela se fit en juillet 1953. Selon les règles de l'époque, Leslau présenta deux ouvrages sous forme dactylographiée, l'un étant sa «thèse principale» et l'autre sa «thèse complémentaire». La première était son *Étude descriptive et comparative du Gafat*, la seconde ses *Coutumes et croyances des Falachas*. Outre Marcel Cohen dans les deux cas, le premier jury comprenait les linguistes Pierre Fouché et Michel Lejeune, le second l'arabisant Régis Blachère et le sociologue Georges Gurvitch. Les deux livres devaient paraitre dans des collections françaises[25]. Marcel Cohen avait consacré beaucoup d'efforts et de temps à discuter avec Leslau le choix des travaux à présenter et plusieurs points de ses exposés comme à s'occuper de former le jury et de fixer une date convenable pour tous, etc.

*   *
*

J'arrêterai ici ces notations biographiques entremêlées quelque peu de souvenirs personnels. Je me suis limité a peu près, comme on l'a vu, à la

---

25 W. Leslau, *Étude descriptive et comparative du Gafat (Éthiopien méridional)*, Paris, Klincksieck, 1956 (*Collection linguistique* publiée par la Société de linguistique de Paris, LVII); id., *Coutumes et croyances des Falachas (Juifs d'Abyssinie)*, Paris, Institut d'Ethnologie, 1957 (*Travaux et mémoires de l'Institut d'ethnologie*, LXI).

période française de la vie de Wolf Leslau et à ses relations douces-amères avec la France dont on pourrait narrer encore d'autres péripéties secondaires. Puisqu'aucune autre contribution biographique n'est prévue pour ce volume — le répertoire de l'œuvre scientifique considérable de Leslau figurant ci-dessus n'en tient pas lieu exactement —, je donnerai maintenant de très succinctes indications sur sa carrière professorale aux États-Unis.

J'ai indiqué ci-dessus les institutions francophones, installées à New York pendant la guerre, où il enseigna. Elles avaient pour fonction essentiellement de donner asile et de procurer un gagne-pain à des savants français et belges exilés tout en continuant en territoire libre l'œuvre d'Écoles prestigieuses, pour le moment sous contrôle allemand. Elles ne devaient pas survivre beaucoup à la fin des hostilités. Wolf Leslau devait, avec des titres encore limités, se frayer un chemin dans le monde des établissements d'enseignement américains où règne une concurrence acharnée. Dans les années 1947-1951, il enseigna ainsi à New York, à l'Asia Institute et à la New School for Social Research. En octobre 1951, il put accéder enfin à un poste plus en rapport avec ses orientations et lui laissant plus de temps pour la recherche, plus prestigieux également. Il commença à enseigner en effet l'hébreu, l'arabe et la linguistique sémitique en général à la Brandeis University, à Waltham, Massachusetts. Ses publications se multiplièrent. Sa réputation s'étendit. En 1955, on lui offrit le poste de professeur à l'Université de Californie à Los Angeles (UCLA). Il quitta donc la Brandeis University, institution dont la vocation spécifique-ment juive (conformément aux désirs de son fondateur) limitait l'ouverture linguistique.

À l'UCLA, Wolf Leslau put enfin trouver une position qui lui convenait parfaitement. En plus de ses dons scientifiques et pédagogiques, ses qualités d'organisateur se révélèrent. Il y forma de très nombreux élèves et y fonda le Département des langues du Proche-Orient dont il fut le président. Je n'insisterai pas ici sur les services qu'il rendit dans ce poste au progrès des études. La plupart des lecteurs en sont très avertis. Puisque j'ai choisi pour thème de parler des rapports de Wolf Leslau avec la France, je noterai seulement ici qu'il fit venir à Los Angeles, à titre de *visiting professors*, des savants français éminents, parmi lesquels je citerai à titre d'exemples les iranisants Jean Aubin et Gilbert Lazard et l'arabisante Nada Tomiche.

A Los Angeles enfin, jusqu'à sa retraite en 1976, Wolf Leslau put donner sa pleine mesure. Notons encore, pour terminer ce court aperçu général, que cette activité lui valut de recevoir en 1965 le prix fondé par l'empereur d'Éthiopie Hailé Sellassié. Le prix venait d'être fondé et le premier récipiendaire en avait été, en 1964, Marcel Cohen. Après consultation de nombreux éthiopisants, il parut que Wolf Leslau était la personnalité la plus désignée pour recevoir

cet honneur, immédiatement après son vieux maitre. L'empereur, quels que
fussent ses défauts par ailleurs, marquait beaucoup d'intérêt pour le progrès
des études sur l'Ethiopie, du point de vue archéologique ou linguistique
notamment. Les monarques, les meilleurs et les pires, affectionnent souvent
la tradition du mécénat.

*   *   *

J'avais eu l'intention, au départ, de limiter cette contribution à quelques
souvenirs personnels. Mais comme je l'ai dit, ils étaient insuffisants, en ce qui
concerne la période d'avant-guerre, pour donner un tableau un peu cohérent.
En écrivant cet article, j'ai pu vérifier une fois de plus combien la mémoire est
traitresse. Si je n'avais pas contrôlé mes souvenirs et mes impressions au
moyen des lettres de Leslau et d'autres documents, j'aurais avancé bien des
inexactitudes. Avant la guerre, nos relations avaient été cordiales, mais
n'avaient pas été poussées jusqu'à l'intimité. Aussi mes souvenirs précis se
réduisaient-ils à quelques scènes gravées dans l'inconscient pour des raisons
mystérieuses au détriment d'autres bien plus importantes. Ainsi Wolf m'in-
terrogeant au carrefour de l'Odéon sur la possibilité d'utiliser dans un article
scientifique français la formule allemande «resp.» pour «respektive», en
français «respectivement», équivalente de «bezw.» (beziehungsweise). Je
l'avertis que cela ne serait nullement compris et qu'il fallait écrire simplement
«ou bien». Cela illustre en tout cas les efforts qu'il faisait alors pour s'assimiler
au milieu scientifique français. En contraste, de façon bien plus frivole, je
l'interrogeai sur le sens précis du mot *einstellen* pour bien comprendre la
fameuse chanson de Marlene Dietrich dans *l'Ange bleu*: «Ich bin von Kopf bis
Fuss auf Liebe eingestellt»!

Ce genre de réminiscences n'a pas un grand intérêt. Mais l'accumulation des
rencontres, des conversations, des lectures, des lettres, de souvenirs laisse à la
longue un sédiment plus valable. C'est sur cette caractérisation de Wolf Leslau
que je terminerai.

Wolf Leslau a énormément écrit sur la linguistique sud-sémitique. Mais ce
n'est pas une mécanique à écrire des articles linguistiques. C'est un homme
sensible, cordial, amical, affectueux. Il a le plus grand amour pour sa famille,
il a montré qu'il était prêt à se dévouer pour ses amis et pour les siens.
Cependant il est vrai qu'il est possédé par une passion, la passion scientifique.
Cette passion s'est fixée très tôt sur un domaine spécial, celui de la linguistique
sémitique. A l'intérieur de ce domaine il a choisi les langues du sud,
spécialement les langues éthiopiennes comme étant la branche où il y avait le
plus de champ pour la découverte. Il s'y est tenu.

Il n'y a pas sacrifié les intérêts humains. Mais il était dès le début persuadé de la validité de la loi de la spécialisation. Dans la tradition de la science du XIXᵉ siècle, il évaluait la masse de travail nécessaire pour accumuler les connaissances sur ce terrain et il s'y est voué. Il accepte de se situer dans le courant d'un immense travail collectif, de continuer August Dillmann, Franz Praetorius et Marcel Cohen, de préparer la voie pour d'autres.

Si l'on choisit ce mode de vie, c'est qu'on a pour lui au moins un certain goût. Wolf s'occupe de sa famille et s'accorde un nombre raisonnable de distractions. Il aime les enfants et, parfois, s'est chargé de tâches pédagogiques auprès de groupes de bambins. D'autres fois, pour se délasser, il s'est fait bûcheron ou menuisier. Mais il ne s'agit que d'activités secondaires par rapport à sa tâche principale. En celle-ci il trouve son bonheur. «Je suis un homme heureux» lui arrive-t-il de dire.

J'ai parlé quelque part, d'un point de vue sociologique, d'une tendance humaine à l'autonomisation des tâches. Une société peut assigner aux individus des tâches particulières subordonnées à son mécanisme général. Mais beaucoup débordent de la fonction qu'il doivent ainsi remplir, prolongent la trajectoire qui leur est assignée. La tâche en question, ils la poursuivent jusqu'à ses dernières conséquences, même si la société accepte mal cette extrapolation. Wolf Leslau ne se sent lié par aucune limitation dans sa tâche. Il y passe toutes les heures que lui laissent ses capacités de travail et les devoirs ou les affections de la vie sociale. Il accepte les honneurs, mais ne les recherche pas. L'essentiel est de travailler et de publier les résultats de ses recherches. Toutes ses errances ont eu pour but essentiel de trouver la position qui lui permettrait de travailler avec le meilleur résultat. Il a fallu l'insistance de Marcel Cohen pour lui faire prendre du repos et des soins quand la tuberculose le guettait. Encore n'était-il nullement oisif au sanatorium. Dans des conditions exécrables, au camp du Vernet, déplorant de ne pas pouvoir faire plus, il corrigeait ses épreuves. Pérégrinant à travers l'Ethiopie à la recherche de nouveaux matériaux linguistiques (voire de langues supposées disparues comme le gafat, de dialectes à peu près inconnus comme beaucoup de ceux groupés sous le vocable de gouragué) ainsi que de compléments et d'éclaircissements aux domaines déjà connus, il multiple ses enquêtes pour profiter au maximum du laps de temps qui lui est imparti alors qu'il doit être presque toujours en route et aussi maintenir par des visites de bons rapports avec les autorités, donner des conférences, participer à des cérémonies. Il n'oublie pas de rendre compte à Marcel Cohen de ses activités et de ses découvertes. Voici un extrait de lettre qui donne une bonne idée de cette activité inlassable. Elle est envoyée à Marcel Cohen d'Addis Abeba le 14 mars 1950:

«... Je viens de rentrer d'Ankober. En auto jusqu'à Debra Berhan [à partir d'Addis Abeba soit 130 km], réception chez le gouverneur dans le bon style éthiopien. Loué des mulets à Debra Berhan pour Ankober; [j']avais avec moi un *baldäräba* [«introducteur officiel auprès d'un chef»] et un cuisinier [huit heures de marche selon la *Guida dell' Africa orientale italiana* «par des sentiers fatigants» «à travers des rochers et des précipices».]. Passé la nuit et la matinée suivante à Ankober; allé après-midi à Aliyu Amba, quatre heures [la *Guida* commente: deux heures 30 d'un sentier abrupt et malaisé avec 1000 mètres de dénivellation sur 7 km de distance à vol d'oiseau], au S. E. d'Ankober. Passé deux jours à Aliyu Amba, retour à Ankober, visite des églises et retour à Debra Berhan — Addis Abeba. Les Argobba se trouvent à Aliyu Amba, un village mi-chrétien mi-musulman. Les jeunes ne savent plus bien l'argobba. Les quelques Argobba se trouvent à Čanno dans le *q"allâ* [«vallée, plaine de climat chaud»] et je n'y suis pas descendu parce que très fatigué et, de plus, mes informateurs d'il y a trois ans sont de Čanno [et] actuellement à Addis Abeba et ça me paraissait inutile de me fatiguer trop. Mon objet principal était de contrôler mes documents anciens et j'avais la satisfaction de constater que c'était du bon argobba [...]. Je n'ai pas fini l'enquête complètement et je tâcherai de la finir à Addis Abeba. — De retour à Addis Abeba, j'ai rempli le temps avec des enquêtes sur les dialectes gouragué. J'ai presque fini l'aymallal, ai réexaminé le chaha et commencé le walane. Les dialectes gouragué sont une aubaine, car ils remplissent bien mon séjour à Addis Abeba entre les voyages. — Actuellement, je prépare le voyage pour le lac Zway. — Berland, [proviseur] du Lycée français m'a demandé une conférence. Je la donne vendredi. Le grand problème est de convaincre les Éthiopiens — petits et grands (et surtout grands) — de la nécessité et de l'importance d'étudier toutes les langues éthiopiennes et non seulement l'amharique. Je propage cette idée dans la mesure de mes forces ...»[26].

On voit par ces phrases écrites rapidement, à chaud, ce qu'était un voyage d'étude pour W. Leslau. On se doute que les journées passées dans les pays où il enseigne et met au point ses travaux ne sont pas moins laborieuses. Tout ce qu'entreprend Wolf, il s'y applique totalement et sans ménager sa peine.

Telle est cette vie, consacrée en majeure partie au travail, qui évoque, sur un autre plan, cette éthique protestante décrite par Max Weber. C'était aussi l'éthique savante du XIXᵉ siècle dont beaucoup perpétuent le modèle. Marcel Cohen, aussi, était de ce type. C'est cette religion du travail savant qui le

26 Camparer le récit de ce voyage et de toute cette mission éthiopienne de 1950 mis au point plus tard par Leslau, «Report on a second trip to Ethiopia» (*Word*, 8, 1952, p. 72-79). Il a publié d'intéressants rapports du même genre, «Preliminary Report on a trip to Ethiopia» (*Transactions of the New York Academy of Sciences*, series II, vol. 10, nᵒ 8, June 1948, p. 291-297); «A year of research in Ethiopia, (*Word*, 4, 1948, p. 212-225); W. Leslau et S. Chojnacki, «On Mule-Back through Guraghe in Ethiopia» (*Canadian Geographical Journal*, 58, nᵒ 3, March 1959, p. 90-99), etc.

rapprochait le plus de Wolf Leslau sans préjudice d'autres affinités dans les qualités humaines. Seulement Marcel Cohen était aussi l'adhérent d'une autre religion séculière, le communisme auquel il jugeait de son devoir de consacrer une partie déterminée de son temps et de ses efforts, de se sacrifier le cas échéant, puisqu'il pensait contribuer ainsi au bonheur et au progrès de l'humanité. Autour de lui, tout un milieu partageait les mêmes tendances, Wolf Leslau regardait avec scepticisme, avec un peu d'étonnement, peut-être avec une certaine admiration — car ils risquaient leur vie pour leurs rêves et certains, très proches de M. Cohen, l'ont réellement perdue — ces gens avec lesquels le hasard l'avait mis en contact et leurs illusions qui eurent tant de conséquences désastreuses. L'histoire a justifié ce scepticisme et cette sagesse, au moins en grande partie. Mais cela n'empêchait pas Wolf et Charlotte de comprendre les motivations généreuses qui poussaient Marcel Cohen, d'être sensibles à ses immenses qualités humaines, de lui pardonner les errements auxquels son engagement l'entrainait, bref de l'aimer. Entre eux, le problème politique était soigneusement passé sous silence et ainsi était sauvegardée leur grande amitié.

C'est avec regret que je quitte cette évocation d'une vie, d'une certaine façon exemplaire. Ce n'est pas que d'autres modèles de vie ne puissent être tout autant valables. Mais il n'est pas mauvais, en ces jours, de mettre en relief les mérites des hommes qui s'adonnèrent à ce type d'activité scientifique dans un environnement particulièrement difficile. Un écrivain israélien de grand talent, dans une gamme contestataire, a écrit: « Je crois que la génération qui a grandi et agi entre les deux guerres mondiales était l'une des plus héroïques, étonnantes et malheureuses de l'humanité »[27]. Même si Wolf Leslau a eu la chance d'échapper aux conséquences les plus tragiques de cette situation, il fallait en effet un certain héroïsme pour s'obstiner à mener jusqu'au bout un projet vital dont la réalisation au cours d'une époque tranquille et dans des conditions favorables exige déjà beaucoup de sacrifices. Je ne crois pas être obnubilé par la mentalité du *laudator temporis acti* en constatant et en déplorant que, dans certains secteurs de la recherche en sciences humaines au moins, la mode soit d'en prendre à la légère avec ces exigences en se couvrant de prétextes dont plusieurs ont d'ailleurs une part de validité. On est tombé trop facilement d'un excès dans un autre. Ni la nécessité de procédures synthétiques souvent méprisées dans un autre stade ni la myopie que peut développer chez certains une activité trop limitée à la quête érudite des matériaux n'excusent le laxisme à l'égard du travail lent et pénible,

27 Amos Kenan, *Holocauste II*, récit traduit de l'hébreu par l'auteur et par Christiane Rochefort, Paris, Flammarion, 1976, p. 37.

minutieux et attentif, toujours sur ses gardes vis à vis de lui-même, aux
conclusions prudentes et mesurées, qui doit toujours rester à la base et qui
exige beaucoup du savant. Il n'exclut nullement mais conditionne la validité
des efforts plus poussés vers la théorie. Travailleur minutieux et scrupuleux
à l'esprit ouvert, attentif aux suggestions des généralistes, n'hésitant pas
à conclure quand des chances raisonnables sont en vue d'aboutir à des
déductions assurées, Wolf Leslau, avec bien d'autres de même orientation
dans leur travail, pose ainsi des jalons sur la route d'un avenir idéal mais
problématique où les exigences contradictoires de la science seront également
et harmonieusement respectées.

INTELLECTUAL LABOURER

Sahle Sellassie Berhane Mariam*
Addis Ababa

'How do you say "to eat" in your language?'
'Webra.'
'Wobra?'
'No. Webra.'
'Say it again.'
'Webra.'

He would write it down on a rectangular card not bigger than a quarter of a page. He had piles of them, held together in a rubber band.

'Did you say "Wabra"?'
'No. Webra.'
'Say it again.'
'Webra.'
'Webra?'
'That's right.'

He would add the necessary dots, dashes, and other signs to indicate the accurate pronunciation of the word. A layman would not be able to read these signs: only linguists like him could. He would pronounce the word inwardly to himself again and again, and go to the next word.

'How do you say "to drink"?'
'Westte.'
'Wostte?'
'No. Westte.'
'Say it again.'
'Westte.'

He would use another card to jot down the word, and before proceeding to add the necessary linguistic signs for the accurate pronunciation he would ask me:

---

* Sahle Sellassie was Wolf Leslau's linguistic informant for the Chaha text of *Ethiopians Speak: Studies in Cultural Background*, vol. 2, and for most of the Chaha texts of *Ethiopians Speak*, vol. 5.

'Did you say, "wastte"?'
'No. Westte.'
'Say it again.'
'Westte.'
'Westte?'
'That's right.'

I met him the first time, as a child, in a district town known as Emdeber, about one hundred and eighty kilometres south-west of Addis Ababa. He came all the way from the United States of America to do research on Ethiopian Semitic languages, one of which happened to be my mother tongue. He lived under difficult conditions in Emdeber, coming from a society that enjoyed the highest standard of living on earth. But he was a scholar and had to go the roots to get what he wanted.

Years later I met him again in Addis Ababa, and later still in his adopted homeland, U.S.A. (originally he was from Poland), and he was still working on his dictionary of the Guraghe language.

I often wondered why he took so much pains to write a dictionary of a language spoken nowhere else but in a tiny section of Ethiopia. But then linguistics is a science, and a linguist is a scientist studying any language, written or unwritten, spoken by a few thousand people or by millions. And so he went to ask me the old types of questions, in his office this time, in the University of California, Los Angeles, fondly known as U.C.L.A.

'How do you say "twig" in your language?'.
'Bweretta.'
'Boretta?'
'No. Bweretta.'
'Say it again.'
'Bweretta.'

He was using the same kinds of rectangular cards he used years back. He still had piles of them on his desk. He jotted down the word and proceeded to the confirmation questions.

'Did you say "bwaratta"?'
'No. Bweretta.'
'Say it again.'
'Bweretta.'
'Bweretta?'
'That's right.'

Professor Wolf Leslau has written several dictionaries of the Ethiopian Semitic languages, one of which alone, "English-Amharic Context Dictionary", has over 1500 pages. Apart from dictionaries he wrote several other books on Ethiopian themes — textbooks, folklore, proverbs, grammars, etc.

Why don't you use texts to collect words for your dictionaries?' I remember having asked him one day.

'I do when I can,' he told me, 'I have no problem with my research on the Amharic language, for example. But the other Ethiopian Semitic languages do not have written literature, at least not in sufficient quantity, and I have to depend on informants for my study.'

In the early sixties he was a man of middle age, with a regular face, roundish in shape, always shaven cleanly. The most prominent feature in him, however, was the heavy curve around his shoulders. He looked almost bent double due to excessive work, I presume, a veritable intellectual labourer that he was, and that he still is.

LINGUISTICS AND PHILOLOGY

PRINCIPLES FOR THE CREATION OF NEW SCIENCE AND TECHNOLOGY TERMS IN AMHARIC

Amsalu Aklilu
Addis Ababa University

Many developing countries are now living in the twentieth century—an epoch of scientific and technological revolution. Until recent times the majority of these nations used to learn one of the major international languages such as English and French in order to gain an education in a certain field of learning. The colonial masters of bygone days were in favour of spreading their respective languages, while at the same time weakening the use of local languages. This tendency however had to discontinue. Many African and Asian languages are now trying to be modernized in order to serve the spread of science and technology.

Some of these countries have indeed succeeded in their venture. Tanzania in Africa and Indonesia in Asia could be very good examples of this.

Since the close of the 19th century, Ethiopia has witnessed an uncontrolled influx of scientific and technological terms which have found their way in the languages. To some, adequate renderings were given; others were left as they were only to be understood by those exposed to modern education. It was then very seriously felt among intellectuals and government circles that a centralized effort should find a solution to the problem. This has resulted in the establishment of an Academy and among the several responsibilities that it shoulders, the creation of Amharic terms for various disciplines was one. It was after the establishment of a Language Academy that an adequate and systematized solution has been found. Coining of Amharic terms has been centralized and therefore no other institution or individuals are allowed to undertake such an activity unless they are given the mandate by the Academy to do so.

The Academy, before starting to undertake actual coinage activity, has taken quite a long time to lay down principles and guidelines for the creation of new terms. Linguists and specialists in science and technology from Addis Ababa University and other institutions had to get together and discuss key papers, presented by specialists. Study tours to Israel and Egypt were also felt necessary, and therefore two linguists and two natural scientists had to visit pertinent institutions in these countries. Discussions with experts was

very fruitful and helped a lot in our task. Following this I shall try to
mention the major principles we have been following in creating new terms.

A) *Intrinsic Characteristic of the Concept*

— Shape, as in:
U-tube   ሀ ፡ ቱቦ *
corrugated sheet   ሽንሽን ፡ ቆርቆር
horseshoe magnet   ፈረስ ፡ ኮቴ ፡ መግነጢስ
nut   ቅርንፉድ
T-joint   ፐ ፡ ሙላ
grinding wheel   ሽክርክር፡ መሳል
grid   ፍርግርግ
cone shaped   ቅንብብ ፡ ቅርፅ
dome mountain   እንቁላል ፡ ተራራ
oxbow lake   ዶጋ ፡ ሐይቅ
annular   ቀለበታዊ   from   ቀለበት   ring
cylinder   በርሜሎ   from   በርሜል   barrel
cap rock   እፈያ ፡ አለት

— Volume, as in:
crater lake   ገሞራ ፡ ቆሬ ፡ ሐይቅ
2-litre flask   ሁለት ፡ ሊትር ፡ ፋሽኮ
cumulus   ቁልል ፡ ደመና
density of population   ሕዝብ ፡ ዝፈት
cube (of a number)   ሥልስ ፡ አርቢ
stock   ክምችት ፡ ሀብት
layer   ንብባሬ
layering   ንብብራት

— Strength, as in:
abutment   ግፈት ፡ አዘል ፡ ግንብ
active earth pressure   ግፈታፈር ፡ (ግፈት ፡ አፈር)
beating force   ሽክማካፋይ (ሽክም ፡ አካፋይ)
bearing surface   ሽክማዘል (ሽክም ፡ አዘል) ፡ ወለል
astable   ርጋቴለሽ (ርጋት ፡ የለሽ)

---

*   These terms should not be considered as final since they have not yet been approved by the
    Language Academy.

torque	ኃይላዙሪት (ኃይል ፡ አዙሪት)
point load	ትኩር ፡ ክብደት
charging	ጉስራ
gauge pressure	የወደር ፡ ግፊት

— Special characteristics, as in:

swivel chair	ተሽከርካሪ ፡ ወንበር
air drying	አየር ፡ ድርቆሽ
alignment	መሥመር ፡ ቅምጥ
anchor bolt	አሳሪ ፡ ችካል
archway	ቅሥት ፡ መሻለኪያ
barbed wire	ቆንጥር ፡ ሽቦ
adjustable wrench	ተስተካካይ ፡ መፍቻ
check valve	መቆጣጠሪያ ፡ ክፍክድ (ክፍት ፡ ክድን)
condenser	ተን ፡ መላሽ
explosive rivet	ባለፈንጂ ፡ ከምሱር
grinding wheel	ሽክርክር ፡ መሳል
internal combustion engine	ውስጠ ፡ ቃጠሎሽ ፡ ሞተር

— Material as in:

adobe	ፀሐይ ፡ ጡብ
alloy steel	ቅይጥ ፡ ከሰል ፡ ብረት
mallet	የዕንጨት ፡ መዶሻ
ferromagnetic	ብረትማ ፡ መግነጢስ
earth pillar	ሸክላ ፡ ዐምድ
rock flour	ድንጋይ ፡ ዱቄት
margarine	የዕንጨት ፡ ቅቤ
clay soil	ሸክላ ፡ አፈር
salt water	ጨው ፡ ውሃ

B) *Extrinsic characteristics of the concept*

— Application, as in:

absorbing well	ውሃወግድ ፡ ጉድጓድ
adjusting screw	ልካንኂ (ልክ ፡ አንኂ)
bit brace	የጅ ፡ መሠርሠሪያ
carport	መኪና ፡ መጠለያ
amplifier	አጉሊ (አጉዪ)
chassis	ረከቦት

choke   አፋኝ
circuit breaker   ዙር ፣ መቋረጫ
conduit   ችቧቃፈ (ችቦ ፣ አቃፈ)
control grid   ተቆጣጣሪ ፣ ወንፈት
coupling   ማቀናጃ

— Location, as in:
head room   ደረጃ ፣ ራስ
lawn   ዳጃፍ ፣ መስክ
base line   መነሻ ፣ መሥመር
center line   ማህል ፣ መሥመር
collar beam   ቋንጮ ፣ ወጋግራ
canopy   ዳጃፍ ፣ ጠለል
neutral   ወገን ፣ የለሽ
longitudinal valley   ግድሞሽ ፣ ሸለቆ
coastal plain   ጠረፋዊ ፣ ሰታቶ
frontal rain   ግንባር ፣ ዝናብ

C) *Characteristic of origin*

— Method of manufacture, as in:
hybrid circuit   ቅይጥ ፣ ኤሌክዙር
impregnated coil   የተሰረገ ፣ ጥንጥን
magnetic tape   መግነጢሳዊ ፣ ጥብጣብ
industrialized building   ፍብርክ ፣ ሕንፃ
animal product   የእንስሳት ፣ ውጤት

— Discover, as in:
Angstrøm unit   የአንግስትሮም ፣ አሀድ
Brownian movement   ብራውናዊ ፣ ቅስቅሳት
Cariolis force   የካርዮሊስ ፣ ኃይል
Doppler shift   የደፕለር ፣ ሽግሽግ
Love wave   የላሽ ፣ ሞገድ

— Describer, as in:
Poupart's ligament   የፑፓርት ፣ መለያልይ
Marxist philosophy   ማርክሳዊ ፣ ፍልስፍና

— Producer, as in:
Bunsen burner   የቤንሰን ፡ ኩራዝ
Mercedes Benz   ሜርሴዴስ ፡ ቤንዝ

— Country of origin, as in:
Scotch whisky   ስኮች ፡ ዊስኪ
Taunus   ታውኖስ ፡ መኪና

There are no fast and hard rules in creating new terms. One has to try various ways of coining and using the one that seems more appropriate in expounding the content of a concept. Sometimes it becomes difficult to find an appropriate or even an approximate equivalent to a term. This is due to the very nature of the language from which the translation is made i.e. terms in the language of origin from which the translation is made are sometimes ambiguous, and therefore a transparent rendering in the receptor language becomes difficult. In such a case, there is no better way than to leave the term untranslated or adopt it with some phonological modification if found necessary.

The following are general guidelines followed in the translation of concepts into Amharic.

a) The more special the term, it is better to leave untranslated, e.g.: atom, actinomycetes, amphibolite, ampere etc.

b) Translate all those terms that are used for general education as far as possible.

c) Even when a term is one that is internationally accepted and thus left untranslated it must be modified to fit into the phonological system of the receptor language, eg.:

physics   ፊዚካ
magnet   መግነጢስ
theory   ቲዮሪ
vitamin   ቪታሚን
turbine   ቱርቢና

d) do not translate terms which have more or less found their way into the language, e.g.:

X-ray   ኤክስ ፡ ሬይ
kilowatt   ኪሎዋት

antenna	አንቴና
camera	ካሜራ
compass	ኮምፓስ
telescope	ቴሌስኮፕ

e) When adopting a term grammatical affixes should be translated, e.g.:

Brownian	ብራውናዊ
atomic energy	አቶማዊ ፡ ጉልበት
diamagnetism	ዳይማግኔትነት
Doppler effect	የዶፕለር ፡ ውጤት

f) Using the same term for many branches of science should be avoided, e.g.:

solution	in chemistry	ብጥብጥ
solution	in mathematics	ፍቺ
base	in chemistry	ቤዝ
base	in mathematics	ተራቢ
axis	in geography	ዘንጎ
axis	in zoology	ዘንጎ ፡ አጥንት

g) Naming of terms should be based not only on the English term but also on other languages as well. Accordingly, the term should be selected from different languages in accordance with their adaptability into the receptor language, e.g.:

hollow masonry units	ብሎኬት
bearing	ኩሽኔታ
gypsum	ጀሶ

h) Avoid as far as possible, using very common and overcharged terms for scientific purposes, e.g.:

development	ግምባታ	instead of	እድገት
absorption	ምጠት	instead of	መምጠጥ
adhesion	ጥብቀት	instead of	መጣበቅ
auditory	ስማታዊ	instead of	የመስማት
axial	ዘንጓዊ	instead of	ዘንጋዊ
outbreak	ፍንዳታ	instead of	መፈንዳት

i) Terms which have subtle similarities or differences of meaning should be carefully delineated, e.g.:

force	ኃይል
power	አቅም
energy	ጉልበት
sketch	ቢጋር
drawing	ርስስ
design	ዲዛይን
diagram	ስምረ ፣ ንድፍ
outline	ንድፍ

j) As far as possible very common affixes should have fixed corresponding affixes in the receptor language, e.g.:

anti-freeze	ፀረ ፣ አብራጅ
anti-knock agent	ፀረ ፣ ኳኳቴ
PreCambrian	ቅድመ ፣ ካምብሪያዊ
prehistory	ቅድመ ፣ ታሪክ
postgraduate	ድኅረ ፣ ምረቃ
biology	ሥነ ፣ ሕይወት
seismology	ሥነ ፣ እንቅጥቃጤ ፣ መሬታ

k) Verbalize Amharic nouns, if this will help in translating the concept adequately, e.g.:

easting	ማመሥረቅ	from	ምሥራቅ	east
polarize	ማዋለት	from	ዋልታ	pole
calcine	መከልሰን			
afforest	ማድነን	from	ደን	forest

e) The new term must fit into the language so that the form of the term coined, if a noun it should be declined with ease, and if a verb it should be conjugated without difficulty, e.g.:

—amplify	ማግነን
amplifier	አግናኝ
amplification	ገነና
amplitude	ግነት
—elastic	ልስትክ
elasticity	ተለስታኪነት

—absorb	መምጠጥ
absorber	መጣጭ
absorptance	ምጦሽ
absorption	ምጠት
—accelerate	ማጥደፍ
acceleration	ጥድፈት
accelerator	አጥዳሪ

The above short remarks in our experience in creating new terms for science and technology concepts are not exhaustive by far. As I mentioned earlier since there are no hard and fast rules to be followed in translating terms, the principles and guidelines enumerated above could serve only as a spring board in starting such an endeavour. I feel also that setting up principles of terminology creation might differ from language to language. But it is of paramount importance to think in advance about such a problem before starting to undertake a project of this kind; otherwise the attempt could be unsystematic and perhaps also lacking in diversity.

ÉGYPTIEN, ARAMÉEN ET ÉTHIOPIEN

Parallélismes et symétries morphogénétiques
dans l'évolution des systèmes verbaux

DAVID COHEN
Sorbonne, Paris

Le système verbal de l'égyptien ne se laisse réduire, pour sa constitution, à aucun de ceux que connaissent les autres branches du chamito-sémitique. Historiquement, il représente l'aboutissement de développements indépendants fondant des renouvellements sur des bases distinctes. Mais derrière la forme matérielle, la comparaison morphogénétique laisse apparaître des parallélismes et des analogies dans l'évolution témoignant tous d'un même phénomène: la verbalisation de prédicats nominaux. L'objet de la présente étude est de réunir des exemples de ces parallélismes, dont il se trouve qu'ils sont nombreux en araméen et dans les langues éthiopiennes (sémitiques et couchitiques), pour éclairer la constitution et l'évolution du système égyptien.

De ce système, seul un paradigme hétérogène à l'ensemble, et sans doute vestigiel [1], le pseudo-participe, à valeur de statif, a fait l'objet d'hypothèses le reliant à des formes chamito-sémitiques.

A. Erman l'avait rattaché, comme manifestant la même construction originelle, à l'*accompli* du sémitique occidental [2]. G. Lefebvre, entre autres, a suggéré de se référer, au moins partiellement, au *permansif* akkadien, qui expliquerait mieux en particulier la forme de la première personne [3]. E. Zyhlarz de son côté, invoquait la conjugaison des verbes qualitatifs dans certaines langues berbères [4]. Mais toutes ces conjugaisons semblent bien se ramener à un prototype unique de «statif» constitué morphogénétiquement par une base verbo-nominale suivie d'une forme courte de pronom sujet [5].

---

[1] Le caractère archaïque du paradigme est généralement reconnu, voir par exemple, G. R. Driver, *Problems of the Hebrew Verbal System*, Edinbourg 1936, 9-31.

[2] *ZÄS*, 27 (1889), 65; *Aegyptische Grammatik*, 1-3. Voir aussi Th. Nöldeke, *Beiträge zur semitischen Sprachwissenschaft*, Strasbourg 1904, 89.

[3] *Grammaire de l'égyptien classique*, 2ème éd. Le Caire 1955, 167-8.

[4] *Ursprung und Sprachcharakter des Altägyptischen*, Berlin-Hambourg, 1933, 7-8, 18.

[5] Voir D. Cohen dans *Mélanges linguistiques offerts à Émile Benveniste*, Paris 1975, 88-98.

Est-ce le cas du *pseudo-participe*? Voici les données sur lesquelles se fonde l'hypothèse:

		Pseudo-participe (Égyptien)	Accompli (Arabe)	(guèze)	Permansif (Akkadien)	Prétérit qualitatif (Kabyle)
Sing.	1	-*kwἰ*	-*tu*	-*ku*	-*a-ku*	-*(ə)γ*
	2 m.	-*tἰ*	-*ta*	-*ka*	-*ā-ta*	-*(ə)d̲*
	f.	-*tἰ*	-*ti*	-*ki*	-*ā-ti*	-*(ə)d̲*
	3 m.	*(-ἰ)*, -*w*	-*a*	-*a*	-Ø	-Ø
	f.	-*tἰ*	-*at*	-*at*	-*at*	-*(ə)t*
Plur.	1	-*wyn*	-*nā*	-*na*	-*ā-nu*	
	2 m.	-*tἰwny*	-*tum*	-*kəmu*	-*ā-tūnu*	
	f.	-*tἰwny*	-*tunna*	-*kən*	-*ā-tīna*	-*it*
	3 m.	*(-ἰ)*, -*w*	-*ū*	-*ū*	-*ū*	
	f.	-*tἰ*	-*na*	-*ā*	-*ā*	

On aperçoit immédiatement la difficulté de l'hypothèse. L'élément *kw* est certes présent, en même temps qu'en égyptien, dans l'«accompli» éthiopien, dans le «permansif» akkadien et dans le «prétérit qualitatif» du berbère kabyle. Mais comment expliquer le second élément -*ἰ/y* qui se trouve dans l'ensemble du paradigme à l'exception des troisièmes personnes du masculin (pour lesquelles néanmoins des formes archaïques en -*ἰ* sont attestées)? Par ailleurs, au pluriel, ni la deuxième personne ni la troisième du féminin ne s'éclairent par le sémitique. C'est ce qui conduisit Marcel Cohen à proposer un parallèle morphogénétique à partir du couchitique[6].

Dans ce groupe de langues, le verbe est constitué en général par une base invariable augmentée de morphèmes suffixés marquant la personne en même temps que le genre, le nombre et l'aspect. Mais d'après une explication généralement admise, ces morphèmes sont issus de la conjugaison par préfixes, représentée en sémitique, en berbère et même dans une partie du couchitique, de verbes auxiliaires très courts signifiant «dire», «être». Ainsi voici comment s'analyserait par exemple, en bédja, le verbe *tam* «manger» à l'accompli:

---

6 «Sur la forme verbale égyptienne dite pseudo-participe», *Mémoires de la Société de linguistique*, 22 (1922), 242. L'hypothèse est sérieusement prise en considération par G. Lefebvre (*op. cit.* note 3, p. 167) et A. Klingenheben, *Mitteil. d. Inst. f. Orientforschung*, 4 (1956). A. Gardiner semble plus sceptique et ne considère comme assuré que le rapport avec le sémitique (*Egyptian Grammar*, 3ème éd., Oxford 1969, 235).

Sing. 1   tam - *n*a ($<$ *'an)   Plur. 1 tam - *n*a

  2 m. tam - *t*a   2 tam - *t*a*n*a

  f. tam - *t*a*i*

  3 m. tam - *y*a   3 tam - *y*a*n*

  f. tam - *t*a

La proposition de M. Cohen est de voir dans les désinences du «pseudo-participe», un verbe **i* «dire» (peut-être apparenté à *y* «dire» dans diverses langues couchitiques) et dont l'existence est constatée dans d'autres formes de conjugaison égyptiennes[7]. L'hypothèse rendrait bien compte, au singulier, des deuxième et troisième personnes, ainsi que de la deuxième du pluriel, mais laisserait inexpliquées les premières personnes.

Peut-être l'amorce d'une solution serait-elle dans la combinaison des deux hypothèses, selon une proposition faite par I. M. Diakonov[8]. Il faudrait alors poser comme base, non pas le simple prédicatif du nom verbal, mais un veritable statif conjugué, auquel l'auxiliaire également conjugué viendrait s'adjoindre. Les formes du singulier se justifieraient alors pleinement, à condition toutefois de maintenir la forme *i* ($=y$) proposée par M. Cohen et non pas de la remplacer par *iw* comme le fait I. M. Diakonov. Le tableau suivant met en regard des formes telles que les reconstruit I. M. Diakonov au moyen de *iw*, celles qu'on obtiendrait avec **i* comme auxiliaire:

1.   **sḏm-ku 'ʾ(a)-iw $>$ sḏm-kwi*   **sḏm-ku 'i $>$ sḏm-kwi*

2. m.   **sḏm-t(a)-ta-iw $>$ sḏm-tì*   **sḏm-t(a)-tì $>$ sḏm-tì*

  f. **sḏm-t(i) ta-iw-i $>$ sḏm-tì*   **sḏm-t(i) tì $>$ sḏm-tì*

3. m.   **sḏm-aw ya-iw $>$ sḏm-w/y*   **sḏm-yì $>$ sḏm-ì/w*

  f. *sḏm-at t/ya-iw $>$ sḏm-tì*   **sḏm-(a)t tì $>$ sḏm-tì*

Le tableau suffit à montrer que l'hypothèse de *iw* comme auxiliaire n'est propre qu'à introduire des complications supplémentaires dans la reconstruction. Son apparence de justification réside dans la forme de la 3ème personne du masculin en -*w*. Mais il semble bien que cette forme est secondaire, la plus ancienne étant -*ì*[9]. En outre la supposition d'une désinence -*aw* pour la 3ème personne du masculin ne s'impose pas, puisqu'il est vraisemblable que la

---

7 Sur cet élément *y* et les conjugaisons avec *y*, voir D. Cohen, *Les langues chamito-sémitiques*, dans M. Cohen et J. Perrot, *Les langues dans le Monde* t. II (sous presse).

8 *Semito-xamitskie jazyki*, Moscou 1965, 86.

9 Voir K. Sethe, *Das aegyptische Verbum im Altaegyptischen, Neuaegyptischen und Koptischen*, Leipzig, 1899-1902, II, 7; G. Lefebvre, *op. cit.* note 3, 170; A. Gardiner, *op. cit.* note 6, 235.

forme la plus conforme à la morphogénèse du paradigme est celle qu'atteste l'akkadien (avec désinence Ø)[10].

I. M. Diakonov n'envisage que les formes du singulier et ne s'exprime pas sur celles du pluriel. Dans l'hypothèse proposée, elles ne pourraient s'expliquer que par des processus extrêmement complexes. Mais si on admet pour le pluriel une base prédicative non conjuguée, les évolutions ne poseraient pas de graves problèmes : *sḏm-w nì > sḏmwyn; sḏm-wt tìwn > sḏmtìwn. La 3ème personne du masculin serait purement et simplement, comme en akkadien, la forme prédicative au pluriel. Il resterait cependant à expliquer les formes (analogiques l'une de l'autre?) en -ì pour le pluriel, en -w pour le singulier.

La difficulté est évidemment que le prédicatif de base est supposé conjugué au singulier et non conjugué au pluriel. Mais telle est exactement la situation pour le qualitatif berbère où la désinence en -it commune à toutes les personnes est, selon toute probabilité, une simple marque de pluriel[11] (voir ci-dessus p. 82 le paradigme que présente le kabyle).

Quoi qu'il en soit, l'origine nominale du pseudo-participe demeure hautement vraisemblable et sa constitution semble, dès les stades les plus archaïques, manifester l'une des constructions attestées fréquemment dans le reste du chamito-sémitique. En fait ce que montre l'analyse de l'ensemble du système verbal égyptien au cours de sa longue histoire, c'est que les processus de formation et de renouvellement qui y apparaissent ne s'écartent guère de ceux qui se manifestent dans les autres branches de la famille, fondés sur la «verbalisation» progressive de constructions à prédicat nominal.

Les formes qu'on relève dès le stade le plus ancien se caractérisent par un mode de conjugaison significatif. La forme est constituée par une base apparemment invariable et des marques personnelles identiques aux pronoms possessifs suffixés. La conjugaison la plus simple ne comporte pas d'autres éléments. Ainsi pour le verbe sḏm «entendre», les formes sont les suivantes : Sing. 1 sḏm-ì, 2 m. sḏm-k, f. sḏm-t, 3 m. sḏm-f, f. sḏm-s, plur. 1 sḏm-n, 2 sḏm-tn, 3 sḏm-sn.

La base sḏm est d'origine verbo-nominale, mais l'écriture égyptienne ne permet malheureusement pas de distinguer le ou les schèmes que recouvre la graphie sḏm. En particulier, rien, en principe, ne permet de décider, par la considération de la base elle-même, quelle(s) forme(s) verbo-nominale(s) elle

---

10 Pour une analyse détaillée, D. Cohen, *La phrase nominale et l'évolution du système verbal sémitique* (sous presse).

11 Voir A. Basset, *La langue berbère*, Londres 1969, 19-20, 25, 32.

peut représenter. L'accord n'est pas fait à ce sujet parmi les égyptologues. Pour les uns, la base représenterait une forme de participe actif, la construction équivalant à une phrase nominale à deux termes complète par elle-même: *sḏm-f* «il (est) entendant = il entend»[12]. Le procédé qui consiste à construire une forme verbo-nominale comme prédicat d'une phrase nominale à sujet pronominal est abondamment illustré dans l'histoire des langues chamito-sémitiques. Mais s'agit-il ici d'une telle construction? Dans *sḏm-f*, la base est accompagnée d'un pronom suffixe («possessif») et non d'un pronom indépendant («pronom sujet»). «Il (est) entendant» aurait été *sḏm sw*[13].

Mais en fait le problème que pose cette forme n'est pas celui du suffixe personnel, mais de la base elle-même. La construction ne parait difficile à analyser que parce que la base est supposée participiale. Mais les langues sémitiques présentent bien en réalité des formes verbales issues de la construction d'une base verbo-nominale avec un pronom suffixe. Ainsi en est-il en particulier du *gérondif* de certaines langues éthiopiennes. Mais il s'agit alors non d'un participe, mais d'une sorte d'infinitif, un nom d'action[14]. La difficulté qu'oppose le guèze, c'est que la forme gérondive *nagiro* est à analyser comme *nagira-(h)u* et équivaut littéralement à «à son-(action de) dire», soit: «tandis qu'il dit, en disant». Comme on le voit par cette traduction, une telle forme, du fait même de sa morphogénèse, est d'abord «converbiale», c'est-à-dire qu'elle n'est apte à remplir en principe qu'un emploi de «circonstanciel». Mais le cas du tigrigna, langue proche du guèze, témoigne d'une évolution de ce point de vue. En effet dans cette langue, le gérondif fonctionne comme une forme non subordonnée à valeur de «parfait-présent». Ainsi dans la phrase *ḥaḍe maṣḥaf hibunni* «il m'a donné un livre», la forme *hibunni* est morphologiquement un gérondif[15]. En réalité en tigrigna (comme en amharique d'ailleurs), le «parfait-présent» a dû être exprimé normalement, et l'est encore en partie, par la forme composée du gérondif, c'est-à-dire par le gérondif accompagné d'un auxiliaire «être» conjugué à un mode personnel, lequel permet d'autonomiser la construction. C'est encore le cas en amharique. En tigrigna, le processus par lequel une forme subordonnée d'origine nominale est devenue indépendante et s'est intégrée à l'organisation aspectuelle du système verbal, réside donc ici dans

---

12 A. Erman, *ZÄS*, 36 (1901), 123; K. Sethe, *ZÄS* (1918); F. Lexa, *Philologica* 2 (1923-4), 25-53. G. Lefebvre, *op. cit.* note 3, 126 et J. Polotsky, *Études de syntaxe copte*, Le Caire, 1944, 92 envisagent l'hypothèse sans défaveur, mais n'y adhèrent pas expressément.

13 Ou *ntf sḏm*, voir A. Gardiner, *op. cit.*, note 6, 288-9, 326.

14 Pour la comparaison avec gérondif guèze, H. Satzinger, avec références dans *Mitteil. d. Deutschen Archäol. Inst. Abhand.* Kairo, 23 (1968), 163-6.

15 Voir Wolf Leslau, *Documents tigrigna (Ethiopien septentrional)*, Paris, 1941, 85.

l'omission (possible et non nécessaire) de l'auxiliaire. Un tel développement serait-il inconcevable pour le *sḏm-f* égyptien?

Quoi qu'il en soit, il n'est pas douteux que l'égyptien connaît au moins une autre forme de construction «possessive», à savoir *sḏm-n-f*. Ici l'analyse ne semble pas poser de problèmes. La base verbo-nominale *sḏm* est augmentée, en guise de marques personnelles, de pronoms suffixes précédés de la préposition attributive *n*; si bien que *sḏm-n-f*, dans la mesure où *sḏm* est à comprendre comme une sorte de «participe passif», ne peut signifier étymologiquement que «entendu *(est)* *à-lui* = *il a* entendu»[16].

La construction de *sḏm-n-f* est reproduite, de la façon la plus rigoureusement parallèle, au cours de l'histoire de l'araméen. Attestée principalement dans les états récents, elle a pour base un participe passif avec un complément (pronominal ou nominal) introduit par la particule attributive *l-*: *šmiε l-ī* littéralement «entendu (est) à-moi = j'ai entendu». La construction, dans tous les cas où elle a été relevée, assure l'expression d'un parfait (du moins dans un premier stade; elle peut évoluer ensuite pour ne plus assurer que l'expression d'un accompli général ou d'un narratif). En fait on distingue clairement, dans l'histoire de cette forme, deux étapes. Dans la première, l'ensemble de la construction est attribué à un sujet extérieur avec lequel s'accorde le participe: «Le chant (est) entendu à moi» peut être traduit par «j'ai entendu le chant». Mais l'ordre des mots et l'accord indiquent bien que le véritable sujet est le terme qui correspondrait à l'objet dans la traduction. Cette construction apparait, à une époque ultérieure, sous une forme évoluée. *Šmiε l-ī* est désormais analysé comme une phrase nominale à deux termes complète et le terme qui se trouvait antérieurement en fonction de sujet se présente, par sa position comme par son inaptitude à imposer un accord à ce qui était originellement un participe, comme le complément d'objet de ce participe[17].

Dès les plus anciens textes, *sḏm-f* et *sḏm-n-f* qui constituaient le système fondamental, étaient flanqués de trois autres formes relevant comme eux d'une conjugaison suffixale: *sḏm-in-f*, *sḏm-ḫr-f*, *sḏm-kꜣ-f* dont les emplois sont ainsi définis par A. Gardiner: «They are used in main clauses only; and all three may be employed to express future consequences of one sort or another, whether enjoined or merely asserted. The *sḏm-in-f* and *sḏm-ḫr-f* forms

---

16 K. Sethe, *ZÄS*, 47 (1910), 140, Anm. 2.
17 D. Cohen, *op. cit.* note 10 (avec références).

may serve as rather impressive narrative tenses, and the *śdm-ḥr-f* tense has in addition a not very clear use in reference to the present» [18].

L'intérêt de ces formes, dans la perspective de cette étude, est dans leur constitution même. Les hypothèses à ce sujet sont diverses. La plus simple et la plus ancienne est qu'il s'agit de formes parallèles à celle de *śdm-n-f*, comportant, outre la base, une préposition suivie d'un pronom suffixe [19]. Mais s'il existe des prépositions *in* et *ḥr* dont la fonction est d'introduire le complément d'agent, *kś* ne correspond à rien de tel [20].

Une autre explication est cependant possible: *kś-f* pourrait n'être que la forme *śdm-f* du verbe *kśi* «penser, avoir dans l'idée, se proposer de», si bien que *śdm-kś-f* serait littéralement «entendre (*ou* entendu) se propose-t-il = il entendra». Mais si cette hypothèse est admise pour *kś-f*, elle pourrait l'être aussi pour *in-f* qui ne serait alors que la forme *śdm-n-f* du verbe *i* «dire»; d'où: *śdm-in-f* «entendu a-t-il dit = il a entendu» [21].

Il n'y a là certes qu'une hypothèse difficile à vérifier. Elle mérite néanmoins d'être signalée pour les parallélismes qu'elle suggère entre les faits égyptiens et ceux qui sont attestés principalement dans les langues couchitiques.

L'exemple du bédja est particulièrement significatif. Dans cette langue, il semble possible de dégager deux stades historiques dans la forme de la conjugaison, le premier se caractérisait par des désinences en *-i* à l'accompli, *-a* à l'inaccompli, comme dans une grande partie des langues couchitiques. Ces désinences sont constituées, comme il a été indiqué plus haut, par un verbe très court: «dire, être» conjugué. Dans le stade le plus récent, le système a été renouvelé par l'utilisation d'un autre verbe «dire» (*an/in*) comme marque de l'inaccompli, selon le schéma suivant:

	Modal	Accompli	Inaccompli
Stade I		**tami*	**tamia*
Stade II	*tami*	*tamia*	*tamini*

Si bien qu'aux deux stades, les formes I **tamia*, II *tamini* signifiant «il mange» sont morphogénétiquement: «manger il (a) dit» [22].

---

18 *Op. cit.* note 6, 347. À propos de *śdm.ḥr.f* qui semble marquer non pas un futur, mais un présent gnomique, Junge, *Journ. of Egypt. Archaeol.* 58, 133-9.

19 K. Sethe, *ZÄS*, 54 (1919), 98.

20 Pour J.B. Callender, *Middle Egyptian*, Malibu, 1975, 41, *in* représenterait un ancien démonstratif.

21 F. Lexa, *Philologica*, 2, 22-53, *Arch. Orient.*, 8, 210; R. E. Faulkner, *Journ. of Egypt. Archaeol.*, 21, 186; A. Gardiner, *Proceed. of the Brit. Acad.*, 23 (1937), 12; G. Lefebvre, *op. cit.* n. 3, 145. Ce dernier propose de voir dans *ḥr.f* le *śdm-f* d'un verbe *ḥrw* 'crier'.

22 Voir D. Cohen, *GLECS* 14 (1970) et, dans J. M. C. Thomas et L. Bernot (éd.), *Langues et techniques*, Paris 1971, I, 57-63 (avec références).

Mais en outre, dans l'usage actuel, s'est instaurée, au moyen d'un autre verbe «dire, se proposer de» l'expression d'une sorte de futur, d'un «intentionnel»: *tami indi* «il va manger, il a l'intention de manger», *tami nead* «nous avons l'intention de, nous allons manger». Comme on le voit, la base reste invariable (sauf à prendre parfois une marque de pluriel), et la signification littérale de telles formes est: «manger il s'est / nous nous sommes proposé de» [23].

Pour ce qui concerne les formes *sḏm-f* et *sḏm-n-f*, il importe de souligner que, dès le moyen empire, l'emploi de la première est soumis à des restrictions syntaxiques. Elle ne constitue plus que fort rarement une forme réellement indicative, mais «prospective» ou «emphatique». La seconde, *sḏm-n-f*, est également l'objet d'une «modalisation», mais qui n'est pas encore achevée [24]. En fait, le système est déjà soumis à un renouvellement selon un double processus. Le premier porte sur les anciennes formes elles-mêmes. Celles-ci sont, dans leur emploi primaire, augmentées d'un élément auxiliaire, les formes non augmentées étant réduites alors à des emplois syntaxiquement conditionnés [25]. L'augment est ici l'élément *iw*, dont la valeur est approximativement «c'est» ou «la situation est que». *iw sḏm-f* correspondrait littéralement à «c'est que / la situation est qu'il entend = il entend».

Le second processus est particulièrement important. C'est lui qui commandera l'évolution ultérieure au bout de laquelle seront pratiquement éliminées les formations précédemment décrites fondées sur *sḏm-f* et *sḏm-n-f*. Il consiste en la verbalisation d'une phrase nominale à prédicat prépositionnel dont le centre est un infinitif.

Ce type de formation est représenté essentiellement par trois constructions différant par la préposition: *iw-f ḥr sḏm* «sa situation (est) sur (le procès d')entendre = il entend maintenant, il est en train d'entendre». C'est la préposition *m* qui est utilisée lorsque l'infinitif prédicatif appartient à un verbe de mouvement: *iw-f m iit* «il est *dans* (le procès de) venir = il est en train de venir».

De telles constructions réfèrent donc à un procès que le contexte situe dans le temps. La préposition *r* «vers» confère par son sens même à la construc-

---

23 *Tu Bedawie* (E. M. Roper), Herford, Herts, s.d., 84.

24 Voir H. J. Polotsky, *Egyptian Tenses* (The Israel Academy of Sciences and Humanities, Vol. II, no 5, 1965), 2. Pour le détail des emplois, *ibid.* 15-17.

25 Pour des manifestations de ce processus, J. Kuryłowicz dans *Proceedings of the 9th International Congress of Linguists*, Cambridge (Mass.), 1964; M. Cohen dans *Scientia*, 94 (1959), 166-72; F. Rundgren, *Intensiv und Aspektkorrelation*, Uppsala, 1959, 14 et passim.

tion, une valeur de futur: *iw-f r śdm* «il est *vers* (le procès d') entendre = il entendra» ...

Ainsi donc si on met à part les formes verbales qui ne seraient représentées en moyen égyptien que comme des archaïsmes utilisés dans des contextes stylistiques particuliers, le système verbal présenterait, pour l'essentiel, l'organisation suivante:

	α: non progressif	β: progressif
A Inaccompli	*iw(f) śdm-f*	*iw-f ḥr/m śdm*
B Accompli	*(iw) śdm-n-f*	
C «Prospectif»	*śdm-f*	*iw-f r śdm*
D Statif	**(iw)-f śdm-w*	

Ce sur quoi il convient d'insister est la qualité de phrases nominales à prédicat prépositionnel des constructions «progressives» en β. Il suffit de comparer les deux séries de propositions suivantes pour en avoir la notion claire [26]:

nsw ḥr tšš «Le roi (est) sur la frontière)»: *nsw ḥr iit* «le roi vient»
bšk-k m *pr-k* «Ton serviteur est dans ta maison»: *iw-f* m *iit* «il vient»
iw-f r *bšk* «il sera un serviteur»: *iw-f r śdm* «il entendra».

Le fonctionnement de ces formes et leur fréquence sont tels que dans les étapes ultérieures, elles devaient constituer l'essentiel du système verbal. L'essentiel mais non la totalité. En fait une autre construction fait normalement partie du système, c'est celle qui a été désignée plus haut par le terme de «statif». Elle est constituée par le pseudo-participe introduit par l'élément *iw*. En moyen égyptien, le pseudo-participe est encore conjugué. Il aboutit dans une étape ultérieure à une forme invariable qui laisse à l'élément *iw* la charge de fournir l'indication de personne.

Rappelons au passage que les constructions du type β ne sont pas absentes du sémitique. Ce sont précisément de telles constructions qui ont renouvelé le système verbal néo-syriaque dans ses stades les plus récents, selon le schéma suivant:

	Aα	Aβ
Stade I	*gāriš*	*ki gāriš*
Stade II	*ki gāriš*	*ile b-grāša*

ile b-grāša «il tire» est littéralement «il est dans (le procès de) tirer» [27].

26 Voir G. Lefebvre, *op. cit.* note 3, 324.
27 Le type de construction d'une forme verbale au moyen d'une forme (verbo-)nominale précédée d'une particule locative n'est propre ni à l'égyptien ni au chamito-sémitique. Il est

L'évolution vers un renouvellement du verbe par intégration au système, de constructions à prédicat (verbo-)nominal s'accentue fortement en néo-égyptien[28]. Plusieurs traits doivent être dégagés.

1. L'ancienne conjugaison attestée dès les premiers stades connus, à savoir la conjugaison suffixale: *śḏm-f* et *śḏm-n-f*, ne constitue plus apparemment qu'un vestige. Les formes qu'on peut relever pour *śḏm-f* sont en majeure partie «modalisées»: elles fonctionnent comme subjonctif, comme coordinatif, comme optatif ou dans des subordonnées temporelles. Pour la forme *śḏm-n-f*, elle est d'une grande rareté et présente une forte connotation d'archaïsme. Des autres conjugaisons anciennes, *śḏm-ìn-f*, si fréquent en moyen égyptien, n'est plus guère utilisé que pour le verbe *ḏd* «dire» et le verbe auxiliaire *wnn* «être» dans une construction périphrastique: *wn-ìn-f (ḥr) śḏm* qui renouvelle dans une certaine mesure l'ancien *śḏm-f*. Les conjugaisons au moyen de *ḥr* et de *kś* ont disparu.

En fait les formes anciennes, bien que d'un usage réduit, se comportent comme des conjugaisons «fortes» du fait qu'elles caractérisent encore la conjugaison des auxiliaires qui entrent dans la constitution de la nouvelle conjugaison, en grande partie périphrastique.

2. L'ancienne conjugaison à suffixes ne recule pas seulement dans sa forme simple. Mais la forme *śḏm-f* composée avec *ìw* connaît des restrictions à son emploi. En fait elle subit, elle aussi, un phénomène de «modalisation». Désormais, on ne la relève guère que dans des phrases circonstancielles, exprimant un procès accessoire au procès principal[29].

3. La conjugaison nouvelle se développe quant à elle selon deux lignes principales. D'une part, au moyen des constructions à prédicat «préposi-tionnel». Le degré de «verbalisation» de ces constructions peut se mesurer en quelque sorte à un fait remarquable. Le point de départ est, comme on l'a vu, dans la structure: sujet + préposition + infinitif. La présence de la

---

à la base d'une théorie «localiste» de l'aspect, v. J. Anderson, *An essay concerning aspect*, La Haye 1973; J. Miller dans *Journal of Linguistics*, 8, pp. 217-36, B. Comrie, *Aspect*, Cambridge 1976, 129-30.

28 Voir à ce sujet G. Maspéro dans *Recueil de travaux relatifs à la philologie et à l'archéologie égyptiennes et assyriennes* 24 (1902), 152; W. Edgerton, dans *Bul. of the Amer. Sch. of Orient. Research*, n⁰ 122 (1951), 9-12; F. Hintze dans *Zeitschrift f. Phon. u. allgem. Sprachwiss.* I (1947), 89; G. Fecht, *Wortakzent und Silbenstruktur*, Glückstadt 1960, 423-5.

29 A. Gardiner, *op. cit.* n. 6, 94; voir aussi A. De Buck dans *Journ. of Egypt. Archaeol.* XXIII (1937), 152 et suiv.; F. Hintze, *Untersuchungen zu Stil und Sprache neuägyptischer Erzählungen* I, 57 et suiv., J. Černy dans *Studies in Egyptology and Linguistics in Honour of H.J. Polotsky*, Jerusalem, 1964, 81 et suiv.

préposition est absolument indispensable pour donner un sens à l'ensemble, une phrase: sujet + infinitif étant agrammaticale. Mais ceci précisément ne vaut que dans la mesure où la construction est interprétée comme une phrase. On conçoit que si elle se «paradigmatise» en quelque sorte, la préposition cesse d'être essentielle. Elle peut tendre à être éliminée, servant ainsi, par sa présence ou son absence, de discriminant entre une simple forme verbale à valeur déterminée et une véritable phrase à prédicat prépositionnel. C'est précisément ce dont témoignent les textes néo-égyptiens où la préposition dans ces constructions verbalisées apparait comme optionnelle et devient de moins en moins fréquente au cours de l'évolution. Ainsi les textes les plus anciens ont souvent, comme le moyen égyptien, une construction *iw.f ḥr sḏm* (litt. «il [est] dans entendre») qui, dans les textes les plus récents, est représentée par *iw.f sḏm* désormais sémantiquement inanalysable.

Le même phénomène est constaté en néo-syriaque où l'élément *b-*, représentant la préposition signifiant «dans», bien que toujours écrit, n'est plus réalisé dans certains usages. Chez les Juifs d'Ourmia, *b-* a disparu entièrement devant la forme d'origine infinitive *garoš*, lequel est désormais conjugué au moyen de suffixes, à l'instar de l'ancien participe.

4. L'autre ligne de développement de la conjugaison met en jeu également la construction à prédicat nominal, mais sans préposition cette fois. En adoptant pour le néo-égyptien une terminologie qui est traditionnelle en copte, on indiquera qu'il s'agit là de formes où la base (verbo-)nominale est constituée par un «qualitatif». Cette forme, on l'a vu, est elle-même, l'aboutissement d'un processus d'agglutination d'une construction à prédicat nominal. En ancien et moyen égyptien, elle est conjuguée. En néo-égyptien, cette conjugaison est réduite à sa plus simple expression. Quelques formes archaïques apparaissent encore, mais toutes les formes peuvent comporter, en guise de désinence, le seul élément *-t*[30]. C'est dire que le «pseudo-participe» peut fonctionner comme une sorte de prédicatif, et il apparait désormais en construction avec des composantes: pronoms ou auxiliaires conjugués indiquant le sujet. Ces constructions peuvent-elles être considérées comme des formes verbales dans l'ensemble du néo-égyptien?

La seule chose qu'il semble possible d'affirmer est que dans l'état ultérieur, en copte, une telle analyse ne pourrait soulever aucune objection. Quoi qu'il en soit, en néo-égyptien, les constructions où entre cette forme, ont une valeur de statif résultatif.

---

30 Ce *t* s'amuït vraisemblablement en fin de mot, J. Vergotte, *Phonétique historique de l'égyptien. Les consonnes*, Louvain, 1945, 114.

5. Une innovation du néo-égyptien est dans la réalisation d'un conjonctif dont l'origine est obscure et qui est constitué par le préfixe *mtw* + pronom suffixe représentant le sujet et une base (verbo-) nominale.

Il ne semble pas qu'il soit possible, dans l'état actuel, de donner un tableau morphologique où les formes laisseraient apercevoir avec précision le fonctionnement du système verbal. En fait si on laisse de côté les formes des conjugaisons anciennes, on se trouve devant de très nombreuses constructions à prédicat nominal qui souvent se doublent et dont un grand nombre est mal attesté. Dans certains cas, on l'a vu, des phénomènes comme le caractère optionnel de la préposition, témoignent en faveur d'une morphologisation. Dans d'autres, on peut à la rigueur tirer des indications du système copte. Mais quel statut donner par exemple aux soixante-cinq paradigmes différents que M. Korostovtsev relève et classe[31]? Ce qui importe ici, c'est de voir la dynamique de ce fonctionnement verbal à travers les modes de constitution des constructions. Or de ce point de vue les faits sont d'une grande simplicité. Ces constructions mettent en jeu quatre séries de morphèmes:

a. Formes en fonction d'auxiliaires. Ces formes portent, lorsque le sujet n'est pas exprimé autrement, les marques personnelles «possessives» représentant le sujet. Ces auxiliaires illustrent donc, comme on l'a dit, l'ancienne conjugaison.

b. Pronoms. Le sujet peut être représenté par un pronom autonome, ce qui rend non nécessaire la conjugaison de l'auxiliaire.

c. Prépositions. Celles-ci sont présentes dans la forme pleine des constructions à prédicat prépositionnel. Elles peuvent cependant être absentes dans les conditions qui ont été indiquées ci-dessus, p. 91, l. 14 sq.

d. Bases (verbo-) nominales. Elles sont au nombre de deux: l'infinitif et le qualitatif.

Sur la base de ces quatre séries de formes, tous les «modèles» relevés, à l'exception toutefois des anciennes conjugaisons, sont couverts par la forme canonique suivante:

$$(\text{Auxiliaire non conjugué}) \begin{bmatrix} \text{Auxiliaire conjugué} \\ \\ \text{Sujet pronominal} \end{bmatrix} (\text{Prépositions}) \begin{bmatrix} \text{Infinitif} \\ \\ \text{Qualitatif} \end{bmatrix}$$

31 *Grammaire du néo-égyptien*, Moscou 1972, 402-8. Voir maintenant J. Černy et A. Groll, *A Late Egyptian Grammar*, Rome 1978, P. J. Frandsen, *An Outline of the Late Egyptian Verbal System*, Copenhague, 1974, H. Satzinger, *Neuägyptische Studien*, Vienne 1976.

Les éléments entre parenthèses ne sont pas obligatoires. L'auxiliaire non conjugué caractérise certains paradigmes; les prépositions, qui ne s'emploient qu'avec la base infinitive, sont optionnelles. Les éléments entre crochets alternent à l'intérieur d'une même colonne. Autrement dit, les bases infinitives ou qualitatives peuvent se construire l'une et l'autre avec un auxiliaire conjugué et avec un sujet pronominal.

Voici, à titre d'illustrations, quelques unes des formes les plus fréquentes (à la 3ème personne du singulier masculin):

Conjonctif: préfixe + pronom suffixe + infinitif *mtw-f sḏm*; présent I: pronom ou nom (+ préposition) + infinitif *sw (ḥr) sḏm*; Ia: pronom ou nom + qualitatif *sw sḏm*; présent II: auxiliaire conjugué + préposition + infinitif *ìw-f ḥr sḏm*; présent IIa: auxiliaire conjugué + qualitatif *ìw-f sḏm-*; futur III: auxiliaire conjugué + préposition *r* + infinitif *ìw-f (r) sḏm*; futur relatif: *ìw* + futur III *ìw ìw-f sḏm*.

D'autres constructions mettent en jeu, à titre d'auxiliaires conjugués, *wn* «être» ou *ìrj* «faire». Mais celles-ci ne connaîtront de développement véritable que dans les états ultérieurs.

Le copte, dernier état attesté de l'égyptien, réalise au terme d'une évolution qui s'amorce dès le moyen empire et s'épanouit sous le nouvel empire, à partir de l'époque de la XVIIIᵒ dynastie, une véritable mutation. Le système verbal, dans sa structure, apparaît comme profondément différent de celui de l'ancienne langue. Pour ce qui concerne les verbes autonomes, la vieille conjugaison n'est plus représentée que par quelques fossiles, guère plus d'une douzaine, dont quatre verbes d'état et quatre impersonnels[32]. Mais à considérer les faits du point de vue de la genèse des formes, son rôle se révèle fondamental dans la nouvelle conjugaison.

Comment se présente le système sur le plan synchronique? Les points suivants sont à considérer:

1. Une forme verbale est constituée par une base, invariable dans le même paradigme, représentant la racine verbale précédée de morphèmes exprimant les différentes modalités: «temps», modes, personnes (avec des distinctions de genre et de nombre). La base est soit un infinitif soit un qualitatif.

2. Les constructions suivent deux modèles fondamentaux[33]:

---

32 Voir A. Mallon, *Grammaire copte*, 4ème éd. revue par M. Malinine, Beyrouth 1956; W.C. Till, *Koptische Dialekt Grammatik ...*, Munich 1928; H.P. Houghton, *The Coptic Verb: Bohairic Dialect*, 2ème éd. Leyde 1959; H. J. Polotsky dans *Orientalia* XXIX (1960), 392-422.

33 H. J. Polotsky, *Ibid.*, 393-4 distingue une conjugaison à structure tripartite et une conjugaison à structure bipartite.

    I Préfixe + marque personnelle (+ infixe) + base
    II Marque personnelle (+ infixe) + base

Ces conjugaisons sont fort complexes. Le tableau suivant en facilitera l'analyse. Il représente les éléments susceptibles d'entrer dans la constitution d'une forme verbale, l'ordre des colonnes (horizontalement) étant celui dans lequel ils se présentent dans cette forme:

	(A)			B	C	(D)			E
	α	β	γ			α	β	γ	
I a				e		na	e	šan	
b				ne-	marques				
c	nt	s	es	a-	1				infinitif (qualitatif)
d	ma	ta		-re-					
II					marques 2		na		infinitif qualitatif

Les éléments des colonnes désignées par une lettre entre parenthèses sont absents des formes verbales les plus simples. Celles-ci, dans le modèle I, comprennent un élément des colonnes B, C et E. Dans le modèle II, seules les colonnes C et E sont nécessaires.

Col. E. Elle contient les bases verbales. Celles-ci apparaissent sous la forme de l'infinitif exclusivement pour la plupart des formes dans le modèle I, de l'infinitif ou du qualitatif dans le modèle II.

Col. D. Les éléments peuvent se combiner avec ceux de la ligne (a). *na* et *e* sont des marques de futur; *šan* entre dans la forme verbale d'une protase dans une phrase conditionnelle. Les trois marques sont mutuellement exclusives.

Col. C. C'est celle des marques personnelles proprement dites. Deux séries: la première est caractéristique des formes verbales du modèle I: singulier: 1. *-y-*, 2m. *-k-*, f. *-re-*, 3m. *-f-*, f. *-s-*; pluriel: 1. *-reten-*, 2 *-w-*, 3. *-re-*.- La deuxième série est utilisée pour les formes de modèle II, mais aussi dans la phrase à prédicat nominal adverbial ou prépositionnel: singulier 1. *ti*, 2.m. *k*, f. *te*, 3.m.*f*, f. *s*; pluriel 1. *tn*, 2. *tetn*, 3. *se*.

Dans les deux modèles, les marques des troisièmes personnes alternent avec des noms en fonction de sujet.

Col. B. Ces éléments sont nécessaires dans les formes verbales du modèle I. Ils constituent donc des indices des divers «temps» et «modes» de la conjugaison. Dans la terminologie traditionnelle, *e* est le préfixe de la forme désignée comme «Présent II»; dans les formes de «futur», elle est accompagnée des éléments *e* ou *na* de la col. D; le «conditionnel» est marqué par *e-*

et *šan-*. Seuls ou avec des éléments de (A), *ne* caractérise les «imparfaits», *a* les «parfaits» et les «habituels»; -*re*- ne se trouve jamais isolément, il est joint aux autres éléments de B à certaines personnes et se combine aux éléments Ad pour la formation de l'«optatif» et du «final».

Col. (A). Combinés avec ceux de B, les éléments de (A) fournissent les deuxièmes formes de «parfait» et l'«habituel». Pour les éléments en (d), voir ci-dessus à propos de (B).

D'où les formes suivantes (à la troisième personne masculin singulier):

Présent I	*f-sōtm*	(II C E)
Futur I	*f-na-sōtm*	(II C D E)
Présent II	*e-f-sōtm*	(I B a C E)
Futur II	*e-f-na-sōtm*	(I B a C D α E)
Futur III	*e-f-e-sōtm*	(I B a C D β E)
Conditionnel	*e-f-san-sōtm*	(I B a C D γ E)
Imparfait	*ne-f-sōtm*	(I B b C E)
Imparfait futur	*ne-f-na-sōtm*	(I B b C D α E)
Parfait I	*a-f-sōtm*	(I B c C E)
Parfait II	*nt-a-f-sōtm*	(I A c α B c C E)
Habituel	*s-a-f-sōtm*	(I A c β B c C E)
Optatif	*ma-re-f-sōtm*	(I A d α B d C E)
Final	*ta-re-f-sōtm*	(I A d β B d C E)

On voit par ce tableau les raisons pour lesquelles le système de conjugaison du copte est habituellement caractérisé comme «préfixal» par opposition à la vieille conjugaison égyptienne qui apparait comme «suffixale», puisque les éléments variables précèdent la base dans un cas et la suivent dans l'autre. Mais ces caractérisations, valables sur le plan synchronique, ne doivent pas en déguiser la nature morphogénétique. En effet, au moins pour ce qui concerne les formes du modèle I, la conjugaison «préfixale» ne peut s'expliquer diachroniquement comme celle du sémitique, par la préfixation des marques de personnes au thème verbal. En réalité les marques ici sont à très peu près les formes d'une série de pronoms suffixables aux noms (avec valeur «possessive») et sont en tout cas distincts des pronoms en fonction de sujet. C'est que la conjugaison des formes I est historiquement fondée sur celle d'anciens verbes conjugués à l'ancienne mode, c'est-à-dire par l'adjonction des pronoms personnels suffixés à valeur «possessive». Dans le tableau donné ci-dessus, les colonnes B et C, toutes deux nécessaires pour le modèle I, constituent historiquement des verbes conjugués qui avaient été utilisés dans les constructions dites «pseudo-verbales» dans les états antérieurs:

> *ne* provient de *wnn* «être»; *a* de *i.ir.f*, forme «emphatique» de *irj* «faire»; *re* de *irj.f* «subjonctif» du même verbe *irj*. Quant à *e*, il est à rattacher à l'élément *iw*, sur lequel voir ci-dessus p. 88 l. 17 sq.

Les éléments de la col. (A) sont étymologiquement de nature diverse: *nt* est une particule relative en copte même; *s̆* est l'aboutissement de l'ancienne particule proclitique *ḫr*, sur laquelle voir ci-dessus p. 89; il peut être précédé de l'élément *e* qui n'est autre que celui de Ba; *ma-* qui se présente toujours en combinaison avec *-re-* de la col. B, est la forme conservée de l'impératif du verbe «donner» (*im.j*); elle permet de constituer un «optatif»; *ta-*, toujours en combinaison avec *-re-*, représente une ancienne première personne de forme *s̆dm.f* du verbe *di* «donner, causer, être cause»: «je serai cause que …».[34]

Les éléments de la col. (D) sont aussi d'étymologies variées:

> *na* provient de *nɛj* «aller» dont il pourrait constituer le qualitatif, à moins (plus vraisemblablement) qu'il ne continue une construction prépositionnelle: *m* «dans» + l'infinitif *nɛf*[35]; *e* représente l'ancienne préposition *r* «vers» dont il a été question ci-dessus p. 88. *na* et *e* fonctionnent comme des morphèmes de futur; *s̆an* entre dans une construction dont la formation étymologique est obscure.

A partir de ces éléments, les constructions dont sont sorties les formes verbales du copte sont attestées dans les états antérieurs de l'égyptien. Elles se réduisent à quatre types étymologiques: a. sujet + qualitatif; b. sujet + préposition + infinitif; c. auxiliaire «être» conjugué + préposition + infinitif; d. auxiliaire «faire» conjugué + infinitif.

Ainsi si on laisse de côté les quelques verbes qui ont conservé la conjugaison au moyen de morphèmes suffixés attestée dans les états antérieurs de l'égyptien, le système verbal du copte apparaît comme entièrement renouvelé. Les formes continuent certes en grande partie des constructions néo-égyptiennes ou même moyen-égyptiennes. Mais ce qui fait la caractéristique du copte, c'est que ces constructions ne sont plus analysables en synchronie; les éléments morphologiques qui peuvent être dégagés ne sont pas des formes autonomes, mais des marques spécifiques. Dans *a-f-sōtm*, c'est la recherche étymologique qui reconnaît un ancien auxiliaire conjugué *a-f*;

---

34 Voir H. J. Polotsky, *op. cit.* note 12, 14-5.
35 Voir W. C. Till, *op. cit.* note 32, 122.

une base *a-* n'a plus d'autre fonction que de marquer certains «temps» et «modes» du verbe et ne peut être considéré en copte comme un verbe «être». Il est donc légitime, comme cela a été indiqué plus haut, de considérer la nouvelle conjugaison comme préfixale, c'est-à-dire fléchie au moyen d'éléments antéposés à la base.

Ainsi apparait le sens général de l'évolution du système verbal de l'égyptien à travers une histoire de quelque quatre millénaires. Au point de départ, une conjugaison à base nominale avec des morphèmes flexionnels suffixés. Au terme de l'évolution, une conjugaison à base nominale avec des morphèmes préfixés. Dans cette inversion, deux processus distincts. L'un est entièrement innovant: c'est d'une part l'agglutination des pronoms sujets à un prédicat (verbo-)nominal, construit directement, aboutissant à un statif; d'autre part, c'est la réduction à une forme unique d'une construction où le prédicat (verbo-)nominal est introduit par une préposition (laquelle peut disparaitre au cours de l'opération).

Le processus, sous son premier aspect, est attesté dès les débuts de l'histoire en sémitique avec le statif et l'«accompli» occidental à suffixes; au cours de l'évolution de l'araméen, c'est l'ancienne conjugaison à préfixes qui a été renouvelée de la sorte. Aussi en néo-syriaque, certaines des formes de l'inaccompli sont constituées morphogénétiquement par un ancien participe actif comme base + des formes réduites des pronoms sujets selon le schéma suivant [36]:

Sing. 1 m. *pātiḫ+ana > pathin*   j'ouvre (mas.)
       f. *patḫa+ana > pathan*   j'ouvre (fém.)
     2 m. *pātiḫ+at > pathit*   tu ouvres (mas.)
       f. *patḫā+at > pathat*   tu ouvres (fém.)
     3 m. *pātiḫ*   il ouvre
       f. *pātḫa*   elle ouvre
Plur. 1 *pātḫī+aḫnan > pathaḫ*   nous ouvrons
     2 *pātḫī+attun > pathītun*   vous ouvrez
     3 *pathī*   ils ouvrent

En néo-araméen de Ma'lula, le même processus a conduit à la formation de conjugaisons préfixales [37].

---

36 Voir Th. Nöldeke, *Grammatik der neusyrischen Sprache*, Leipzig 1868, 216; K. G. Tsereteli, *Sovremennij assirijskij jazyk*, Moscou, 1964, 55.
37 D. Cohen, *Journ. of Sem. Stud.*, XXIV (1979), 219-24.

Sing. 1   ana+kōtēb > nkōtēb   j'écris
           hačč+kōtēb > čkōtēb   tu écris (mas.)
           kōtēb   il écrit
           kōtba   elle écrit

Le second processus consiste à constituer en morphème flexionnel portant toutes les déterminations d'une forme verbale, un auxiliaire conjugué à l'ancienne mode, c'est-à-dire par suffixes. Le phénomène ne semble pas attesté dans l'histoire connue du sémitique, mais il est à la base de ce qu'on peut déceler de l'évolution du système couchitique. L'évolution ici est parallèle et inverse. Comme on l'a vu, en effet, une forme conjuguée couchitique est constituée, dans le type dominant, par une base invariable qui sert souvent d'infinitif, et d'un morphème flexionnel suffixé mais formé lui-même par un auxiliaire conjugué par préfixes. L'inversion dans un cas comme dans l'autre s'explique comme le reflet, sur le plan morphologique, des règles syntaxiques de construction de la phrase :

	Égyptien	Couchitique (bédja)
1.	*śḏm.f*	*y*-x [= base -verbo-)nominale]
d'où	*ìrj.f* («faire»)	*yini* («être, dire»)
2.	*ìrf.śḏm*	*tam yini*
3.	*af-śōtm*	*tamīni*

L'évolution de la structure du système et des formes qui le constituent attestent ainsi des processus de renouvellement connus dans le reste du chamito-sémitique. La dynamique sémantique est aussi la même. L'évolution a abouti en égyptien, comme en araméen et en arabe, à organiser l'expression de la concomitance : d'une part adaptée au moment de l'énonciation : présent «actuel» ou progressif («Présent I»), parfait-présent («Parfait I»), futur «proche» (il est sur le point de faire, il va faire, he is going to do); d'autre part relative à un moment quelconque : imparfait ou futur «relatifs» formés au moyen respectivement des morphèmes *ne* et *na*. Dans le temps où s'opérait cette organisation, les formes anciennes étaient éliminées (formes à suffixes) ou «modalisées» réduites soit au rôle de formes de subordonnées soit à celui de «temps seconds» caractéristiques de la phrase coupée [38].

---

38 H. J. Polotsky, *op. cit.*, note 12, 20 et suiv.

A GEEZ PROLOGUE
CONCERNING THE WORK OF *MÄMHƏR* KƏFLÄ GIYORGIS
ON THE TEXT AND INTERPRETATION
OF THE BOOK OF EZEKIEL

ROGER COWLEY
Oak Hill College, Southgate, London

Biographical traditions and literary remains demonstrate that there have been many Ethiopian scholars, such as Bähaylä maryam [1], Bähaylä mika'el [2], Märqoryos [3], Giyorgis of Gasəčča [4] and Məhərka dəngəl [5], who learnt non-Ethiopian languages, pursued textual researches, and utilized and translated non-Ethiopian materials. Historical information about most of them is fragmentary, but the life history of a more recent scholar, *Mämhər* Kəflä giyorgis (1825-1908 A.D., henceforth KG), who appears to belong to this same category, and who is the subject of the Geez text translated below, is of interest as it gives some indications of the motivations, researches, and legacy of a person of this type.

The paper MS which contains the following text on fols. 1r-4v is labelled "Jerusalem Ethiopic 301 E", and "Däbrä gännät 116", and is kept in the bookstore of the Ethiopian Church in Ethiopia Street, Jerusalem. Fol. 5r contains some dates associated with Ezekiel's life, and fols. 6r-116r contain a Geez text (of Septuagintal type) of the book of Ezekiel, lightly annotated in the margins in Amharic. The volume is dated as written in Jerusalem in 1908 E.C. in the month *Yäkkatit*, and was given by *Abba* Gäbrä mädhən to *Abba* Sinoda (who, to judge from the other MSS which also bear his name, was a man of fine scholarly inclination).

---

1 Appendix to MEHI; *ACD* IV pp. 12-3; EMML 932 fol. 121r.

2 Guidi pp. 55-6; catalogue notes to EMML 2161.

3 Ullendorff pp. 42-3; in addition to B.N. Zotenberg 7, Bible Society (London) MS Ethiopic I also contains a note relating to his collation of Geez and Hebrew texts (see *Historical Catalogue of the Manuscripts of Bible House Library*, (ed.) A.F. Jesson, London, 1982, p. 71). Possibly he is to be identified as Zär'a Ya'qob's Minister of the Pen; see MS CCR 25.

4 Taddesse pp. 222-5; catalogue notes on EMML 1838; Getatchew Haile. "On the Writings of *Abba* Giyorgis Säglawi from Two Unedited Miracles of Mary", *Orientalia Christiana Periodica*, 48 (1982) 65-91.

5 *ACD* II pp. 227-8; catalogue notes on EMML 2101.

MS JE 301 E = DG 116

f.1a
በስመ ፡ እግዚእብሔር ፡ መሐሪ ፡ ወመስተሣህል ፡
ናቄፍዮ ፡ ወንዱኅፉ ፡ ምክንያት ፡ ተጻኖኑቱ ፡ ወተረክቦቱ ፡
ለትርጓሜ ፡ ሕዝቅኤል ፡ ነቢይ ፡ እምቃለ ፡ መምህር ፡ ዳሬ ፡
እሳዲሁ ፡ ለዝንቱ ፡ ትርጓሜ ፡ እምኢትዮጵያ ፡ ወሮሜ ፡ ዘእንበለ ፡
ቃንዓት ፡ ወሕመሜ ።

        እእኑው ፡ ንዜንዎስው ፡ በእንተ ፡ ውእቱ ፡ መዱሐሪ ፡
ሕዝቅኤል ፡ ነቢይ ፡ ዘሀሎ ፡ እምቅፍዮም ፡ ውእቱ ፡ ውስተ ፡ ናሉ ፡
ብሔረ ፡ ኢትዮጵያ ፡ እንዘ ፡ ይትነሰብ ፡ ወይተረጐም ፡ እመዋዕለ ፡
እበርሀ ፡ ወእጽብሐ ፡ እስከ ፡ ወእንግሥተ ፡ ትንቤር ፡ ፉዳሪስ ፡
እንዘ ፡ እበው ፡ የኃልፉ ፡ ወውሉፉ ፡ ይተርፉ ፡ ኮነ ፡ ይተረጐም ፡
በብሔረ ፡ ጐናዳረ ፡ ባሕቲቱ ፡ ወእምንጐዳርኒ ፡ እነ ፡ በናሉ ፡
ጐ ግኔ ፡ እኅ ፡ በሳዕሳይ ፡ ቤት ፡ እስመ ፡ ሮ ፡ እለ ፡ ይብልዎሙ ፡
ቤት ፡ ዘሳዕል ፡ ወቤት ፡ ዘታሕት ። ወዝንቱ ፡ ፋዕው ፡
1b
ፉፉ |ፉዋፀ(ዮሙ ፡ እሊቃውንት ፡ ቤት ፡ ሳዕሳይ ፡ እምኑኮሙ ፡
ሊቃውንተ ፡ ጐናዳረ ፡ ወበእንተዝ ፡ ጛፉረ ፡ ሳዕኬዎሙ ፡
መንፈስ ፡ ትንቢት ፡ ወትዝሃሮት ፡ ምስለ ፡ ሕመሜ ፡ ወቃንዓት ፡
ብቱዓ ፡ እስከ ፡ ፉፉዳ ፡ ለዝንቱ ፡ መንፈት ። ወእምባዝኝ ፡
ሕመሜ ፡ ወቃንዓት ፡ እናዙ ፡ ይተርጐምዎ ፡ በብዙኝ ፡ ተዓዖበ ፡
ወተጠናቀቅ ፡ በዊኦሙ ፡ ቤተ ፡ ወእጻዋዎሙ ፡ ኛፉት ፡ ከመ ፡
ኢይስማዕ ፡ መኑሃ ፡ ዘኢኮነ ፡ እምኝየዎሙ ። ይተርፉስ ፡
ዘኢኮነ ፡ እምኝየዎሙ ፡ የኝርይ ፡ ኮቱ ፡ እርፉዕት ፡
እምእርዳእይዎሙ ፡ ለሰዋይ ያ ፡ ወለእንባቦቱ ፡ ወለእመሮ ፡
እምእርፉኝት ፡ ዘእዱንኝ ፡ ትርጓሜሁ ፡ ወተጠየቅ ፡ ይምሰጤዎ ፡
ይኤዝዝዎ ፡ ከመ ፡ ኢዱንሯ ፡ በካልዕ ፡ መካን ፡ ወኢይርኢ ፡
ወዱሐዕ ፡ ዘኮቱ ፡ ትንምርት ፡ ወሪሰዱዋ ፡ ምስጤሪ ፡ ሩብሪ ፡
ታር ፡ እስከ ፡ እመ ፡ ይትከሰት ፡ በዓፉሜሁ ። ወበእንተዝ ፡
2a
ፉኑው ፡ እግዚእ |ብሔር ፡ ሳዕኬዎሙ ፡ መቃሰፉተ ፡ መኑቱ ፡
መቃሰፉተ ፡ ወመመንሱት ፡ ወሕማው ። ወእምኝኝ ፡ ጻሞት ፡
ለናፉሶሙ ፡ ወዓፀወ ፡ ውስተ ፡ ሞት ፡ እርዳእይዎሙ ፡
ወኢተርፉ ፡ ፬ እምውስቴቶሙ ፡ ለዜና ። ዝንቱ ፡ ውእቱ ፡
ምክንያት ፡ ተኛኖኑቱ ።

ክፍል ፡ በእንተ ፡ ተረጓቦቱ ፡፡ ይቤ ፡ መተርጉም ፡
ክፍለ ፡ ጊዮርጊስ ፡ ዘብሔር ፡ ሸዋ ፡ ወስመ ፡ ሀገሩ ፡
እንየበር ፡ ወሐር ፡ እማባ ፡ እንዩ ፡ በር ፡ ይእቲ ፡ ምፍር ፡
መላሏ ፡ ወሐር ፡ እማባ ፡ ርስተ ፡ ነዳዪ ፡ እምፍቋሬ ፡
ፈደያኩ ፡ ትምህርተ ፡ ብሉይ ፡ ወሐዲስ ፡ ወሊቃውንት ፡
ወመጻሕፍተ ፡ ወነነያሳት ፡ ኢወሀበከዎን ፡ ንዋየ ፡ ለእዕይንትዮ ፡
ወኢፍቋስ ፡ ለቋራንብትዮ ፡ ወኢዐራፍተ ፡ ለመላትሕዮ ፡
እስከ ፡ እሬክብ ፡ መፅሐዎ ፡ ለሕዝቅኤል ፡ ነቢይ ፡ ወያፍኩ ፡
ኍሎ ፡ እፍግራተ ፡ ወጋዳማተ ፡ ወፋሰያተ ፡ ወኢረከብኩ ፡

26 መጽሐፈ ፡ ርቶዕ ፡ ዘ|ሀሎ ፡ ውስተ ፡ እዴ ፡ መዓምህራን ፡
ቋፋምት ፡ ዘእንበለ ፡ በሐር ፺ ፡ ወሀለው ፡ ህያ ፡ ፪ቱ ፡
መጻሕፍት ፡ ፮ ይኄስ ፡ እምናብራሙ ፡ ወ፮ስ ፡ ዘበበን ፡
ሎቱ ፡ መለጹ ፡ እሉጺ ፡ ኢሐወዙኒ ፡፡ ወገዝቹ ፡ ረከብኩ ፡
ትእምርተ ፡ ትርጋሜ ፡ ወሥዕለ ፡ ኤስኬፋሬ ፡ ጽሉፈ ፡
ለገህቴ ፡ መዐጠነ ፡ ፮ ናራዝ ፡ ወተፈሣሕኩ ፡ ፃቃ ፡ ነገመ ፡
ዘሬክባ ፡ መፍፈነ ፡ ሳሉዓ ፡ ወእዐለውንያ ፡ በኮመ ፡ ሀሎ ፡፡
ወናሲእዮ ፡ ዘንተ ፡ ሐርኩ ፡ ብሔረ ፡ ክሬን ፡ ወይምጵዋዕ ፡
እስመ ፡ ሰማዕኩ ፡ ከመ ፡ ቦ ፡ ህያ ፡ መጻሕፍቲሁ ፡ ለመምህር ፡
ጓቢይ ፡ ዘበሙ ፡ ወልፉ ፡ እብ ፡ ሊቃ ፡ ሊቋውንት ፡፡ ወረከብኩ ፡
ውስተ ፡ ቤተ ፡ እፍርኜ ፡ ፪ መጻሕፍት ፡ ሠናያ ፡ ወርቶና ፡
ዘ፮ ቋሎውሙ ፡ ወ፮ ካብሮሙ ፡ ወኢቦአ ፡ እምውስቴቶሙ ፡
መለዋ ፡ እላ ፡ እምኝንትሙ ፡ ዘተፍእፈ ፡ በእፉ ፡ መዓምህራን ፡፡
ወእዐለውኩ ፡ እምኜሬዮሙ ፡ ዘንተ ፡ መጽሐፈ ፡ እንዘ ፡ እሠይም ፡.

3a ውስ|ቴቱ ፡ ምዕራፈተ ፡ በበካኑ ፡ ከመ ፡ ሠርዓተ ፡ እፍርንኜ ፡
ወኍሎሙ ፡ ፀናፍዉ ፡፡ ወእያዓዝ ፡ እኝዝነኩ ፡ እትመሀር ፡
ልሳነ ፡ መማይስኝ ፡ ወረተኚ ፡ ወበእንተዝ ፡ ፈቋድኩ ፡
እርእይ ፡ ለመሙኜ ፡ ወወራፉይ ፡ ብሔር ፡ ሮሜ ፡ ረከብኩ ፡
፮ዱ ፡ ብእሴ ፡ ማእያምሬ ፡ ጽርዕ ፡ ወእብራይስኝ ፡ ምስለ ፡
ሱርስት ፡ ወዓረብ ፡ ዘምሁር ፡ ፃቀ ፡ እምኍሎሙ ፡ ሊቋውንተ ፡
እፍርኜ ፡፡ ወደቤለኒ ፡ እሊቀ ፡ ኢትዮጵያዊ ፡ መሐሬኒ ፡ ልሳነ ፡
ግዕዝ ፡ ወእምሐራ ፡ ወእነሃ ፡ እምሀርከ ፡ ኍሎ ፡ ዘፈቋድከ ፡
ወተሰናዳውን ፡ በዝንቱ ፡ ምጵንር ፡ እስከ ፡ መሀሬኒ ፡
ወመሠርገ̣ዋ ፡ ወዉኜቱ ፡ ዘእጻብረ ፡ ሌተ ፡ ተስዐወቱ ፡

ኩሉ ፡ ንገብ ፡ ወትርጓሜ ፡ ዘመጽሐፈ ፡ ሕዝቅኤል ፡ ነቢይ ።
ወእምፍጻሬ ፡ ፲ወ፮ዓመት ፡ ናዴግዋ ፡ ለሮሜ ፡ ወዳረት ፡
ኢየሩሳሌም ፡ እስጓፈ ፡ ነበ ፡ ቆሎ ፡ እጊእኑ ፡ እንዘ ፡ እንዘ ፡

36 እብል ፡ ዘቲ ፡ ይእቲ ፡ | ምዕራፍይ ፡ ለዓለም ።። ወአእኩ ፡
ማዕካለ ፡ ሕዝብየ ፡ እስ ፡ ሀለዉ ፡ ውስቴታ ፡ ከመ ፡ እርኦደ ፡
እመየ ፡ ጠቢብ ፡ ዘየኅሥሥ ፡ ለዝንቱ ፡ ወጽሐፈ ።። እልቦ ፡
ወኢ፮ እምኔየሰዉ ።። ወተፈጸመ ፡ ኃዝን ፡ ለፈስሐየ ፡ ፱ት ፡
ዓመት ፡ እስክ ፡ እሬክብ ፡ ብሴ ፡ ምኅመነ ፡ ወጠቢበ ፡
ውስት ፡ ጽሒፍ ፡ ዘይርነብ ፡ አፈሁ ፡ ወእመልየ ፡ ሎቱ ።።
እስመ ፡ ይፈልዋ ፡ ለረቂእ ፡ ቀጠወ ፡ ይድሐፈ ፡ ቃሎ ፡
ወእምዝ ፡ ያገብብ ፡ ወይትመሀር ፡ ትርጓሜሁ ።።

ስዕለተ ፡ ረፉእ ፡ ለዝቱ ፡ ወተርጓሚ ፡ ዘነበሪ ፡
ምስኬሁ ፡ ፱ት ፡ ዓመት ።። እስእል ፡ ወእስተበቁዕ ፡ እምኃበ ፡
ዘይጽሕፈ ፡ ዘንተ ፡ መጽሐፈ ፡ ወእመዕን ፡ እማነ ዕናተ ፡
በስመ ፡ እግዚእብሔር ፡ አፍቅዶ ፡ ወበበቀር ፡ ሕዝቅኤል ፡
ነቢይ ።። ከመ ፡ ይሳሣ ፡ ለዘቲ ፡ ምኅንይት ፡ ውስተ ፡ ዓፅነ ፡
ዝንቱ ፡ ወጽሐፈ ፡ በከመ ፡ ሄምንኩ ፡ እነ ።። ወረሰይኩዋ ፡

4a መቅፉወ ፡ ከመ ፡ ይኅ | ፡ ፍር ፡ ካልዕ ፡ ትዉልፈ ፡ ዘነመ ፡
ተኃኅለ ፡ ቀዳሚ ፡ ወዘነበ ፡ እኍ ፡ ተረክብ ፡ ፈነሪ ፡ እዉ ፡
ወመኔ ፡ ፈፈወ ፡ ባሕሪ ፡ ወተታየጠ ፡ ወመኔ ፡ ዓርገ ፡
ወልዕለተ ፡ ፈመናት ፡ ወእጡረ ፡ እስመ ፡ ተረስነ ፡
እምኑሉ ፡ ሰብእ ፡ ወተኃብጋ ፡ እምኔሉ ፡ እዕዋረ ፡ ሰማይ ።።
ወእመ ፡ ዩም ፡ ፈፈወ ፡ ሎቱ ፡ ለዝንቱ ፡ እብ ፡ ክንፈስ ፡
ጊዮርጊስ ፡ ፲ወ፬ ፡ ዓመት ፡ እምእሰ ፡ ተወልዳ ፡ ዘዉኅተ ፡
ተፈደዓት ፡ ፲ወ፱፬ ፡ ዓመት ፡ ሠጋዊ ፡ እመ ፡ ፲ወ፬ ፡ ለገንቦት ፡
ይቤለኔ ፡ ሊተ ፡ ለረቂእ ፡ ዮም ፡ ይእቲ ፡ ዕለተ ፡ ልፈትየ ፡
ስምዓኔ ፡ ወልፈየ ፡ ወእንግርከ ።። በ፲ወ፮ ዓመት ፡ ወዓእኑ ፡
እምዓርየ ፡ ወተፈረኛኑ ፡ እምእዝዛጣፉየ ፡ ፮ወ፮ ዓመት ፡
ነበርኩ ፡ በምሀር ፡ ወበተምህሮ ፡ እንዘ ፡ እዓዉፈ ፡ ኑሎ ፡
እኃገሪ ፡ ኢትዮጵያ ።። ወኑኔ ፡ ውስተ ፡ ቤተ ፡ እፈርንጁ ፡
፲ወ፯ ዓመት ።። ይ.ሰስለኔ ፡ ዘቀርበ ፡ ፈልስትየ ፡

4b ወበጽ | ሐኔ ፡ ዕፉዐየ ፡ ለእዕርፎ ፡ ወኢተረፈኔ ፡ ዘእንበሰ ፡

ሳጓን ፡ መዋዕል ፡፡ ዱዮ ፡ ውስተ ፡ ልብክ ፡ ለዝንቱ ፡ ነገር ፡፡
እስክ ፡ እሞ ፡ ትክፍን ፡ እዕይንትዮ ፡ መታፈርን ፡ ሥጋየ ፡
ውስተ ፡ መሬት ፡ ይኀብሬ ፡ ኢትትሀነይ ፡ ተኈሶኈትዮ ፡
መዓልት ፡ መሌሊተ ፡ በኈንተ ፡ ዝንቱ ፡ መዷሐዴ ፡ መእብኁተ ፡
፮ፉ ፡ ዚቤ ፡ ለኅልእንከ ፡ ትሬጵበሙ ፡ እየመነልእን ፡ እስሞ ፡
እእየምር ፡ ከመ ፡ ፉሙነ ፡ ይኁቲ ፡ ስጣሎ ፡ ዘዮ ፡ እየምኑክ ፡፡
መእየፍጓሬ ፡ ፳ እውራነ ፡ መ፲ ዕለት ፡ እመ ፡ ፲ ለፉጐመዬ ፡
ዚቤ ፡ ፲ መ፭ ሰዓት ፡ ዘመዓልት ፡ ዘውኈት ፡ ፉና ፡ ሠርኀ ፡
ተሬልመት ፡ ነፉሉ ፡ እየምሠጋሉ ፡ ዘኅስለ ፡ ዓዐር ፡
መዷኈይም ፡፡ መተቀብሬ ፡ በፅርሐ ፡ ጽዮን ፡ ቀፍስት ፡ ኃስ ፡
ተቀብሬ ፡ እኈቱ ፡ ተኈስ ፡ ጽዮን ፡ በከመ ፡ ይቤ ፡ ቀዲጢ ፡
እንዘ ፡ ይመዷእ ፡ እየምሮዬ ፡ ዘቲ ፡ ይኁቲ ፡ ምዕሬፉዮ ፡
ለኈለዎም ፡   እዐዝን ፡፡

Translation

(1r) In the name of God, the forgiving and merciful, we will commence, and write the reason of the loss and of the finding of the interpretation of Ezekiel the prophet, from the word of the elect teacher, the compiler of this interpretation, from Ethiopia and Rome, without jealousy or spite.

O brethren, we will relate to you concerning that book of Ezekiel the prophet, which existed from former times[6] in all districts of Ethiopia, being read and interpreted, from the times of Abrəha and Aṣbəha until the kingdom of Gondar. But later, when the fathers passed on and the sons remained, it used to be interpreted in the city of Gondar alone, and even in Gondar not in every school[7], but (only) in the "upper house"; for there are those which they call "upper house" and "lower house"[8]. This is the only greatness (1v) of the scholars of the upper house[9] over all the scholars of Gondar; and because of this, a spirit of pride[10] and contention abode upon them, together with much spite and jealousy, so that they buried this talent[11]. And because of the degree of spite and jealousy, they started to interpret it (Ezekiel) with much secrecy

---

6 Allusion to the Geez text of 1 John 1.1.
7 *Guba'e*—the assembly for instruction.
8 On the "houses" see OTIAC p. 165.
9 "house" (*bet*) is the reading of a corrector of the text; the original erased reading was *gondär*.
10 Reading *mänfäsä tə'əbit* for *mänfäs tənbit*.
11 Allusion to the parable of the talents, Matt. 25 and parallels.

and caution, entering the house and closing the door, lest anyone hear who
was not one of themselves. Let alone the one who was not one of themselves,
they would select for him (the teacher of Ezekiel) a pupil from among their
pupils, for hearing (the interpretation) and reading (the text). And if there
should be one of the pupils who had studied the interpretation and ascertained
its meaning, they would order him not to speak (of it) in another place, and
not to show his book in which were the marks [12]. And they made it "the
mystery of Däbrä Tabor" [13] until it should be revealed in its own time. And
because of this, God (2r) sent upon them plagues of his wrath, plague, and
destruction, and sickness, and did not deliver their souls from death, and
enclosed their pupils in death. Not one of them remained as a witness. This
is the reason for its loss.

    Section–concerning its finding: the interpreter Kəflä giyorgis, of the
land of Shoa–the name of his home-country is Ankobärr and Harr amba,
Ankobärr being the place of his birth, and Harr amba the inheritance of
his family–said, "After I had completed the study of the old and new
(testaments), and the scholars (patristic writings) and the books of the monks,
I gave no sleep to my eyes, nor slumber to my eyelids, nor rest to my jaws [14],
until I should find the book of Ezekiel the prophet. And I toured all the
churches and monasteries and islands, but I did not find a correct book
that (2v) had been in the hands of the former teachers, except at Däräsge [15].
And there were 2 books there; 1 was better [16] than its companion, and 1 had
many erasures [17]. They, too, did not satisfy me. Nevertheless, I found the
mark of the interpretation, and the picture of the *eskedere* [18], written by itself,
in 1 binding [19]. And I rejoiced greatly like the one who found the hidden
treasure [20], and I copied it just as it was. And taking this, I went to the district
of Keren and Massawa, because I had heard that there were there the books

---

12 *Tə'əmərt* — probably marginal annotations, memoranda of the AC.

13 I.e. a secret like the secret of the Transfiguration, Matt. 17 and parallels.

14 Allusion to Ps. 132.4.

15 The name has been corrected; "Darge" appears to have been written originally. In his
    book *Märha ləbbuna*, A.A., 1943 E.C., p. 81, Aklilä bərhan Wäldä qirqos says that the "old"
    Tərgwame ḥəzqə'el was to be found at Gundagundi and at Dimma.

16 Reading *yəḥeyyəs*.

17 Reading *mälaṣi*, i.e. a razor.

18 *Eskedere* is the "chamber", Gk. *exedra*, Heb. *liška*, see *MḤ* on Ezek. 40.19, and *MSWG*
    p. 245. The "mark of the interpretation" was probably a collection of notes on obscure
    words and passages, such as is found in MSS B.L. Orient 506, fols. 149r-159r, Orient 5085
    fols. 186r-192r, B.N. d'Abbadie 190, d'Abbadie 211 III, and d'Abbadie 39, fols. 199r-201v.

19 *Traz*—small parchment volume or "gathering", or paper exercise book or ledger.

20 Allusion to Matt. 13.44.

of the great teacher, of the name of Wäldä ab[21], the greatest of scholars. And I found in the house of the foreigners two fine and correct books which had the same text and the same appearance, and had no erasures, but which were originally written by the hand of the teachers. And I copied from them this book, marking in (3r) it the chapters in each place[22], according to the system of the foreigners and all the white (people). And then I started to learn the Roman[23] language, and I was successful, and because of this I desired to see Rome. And, having descended to the city of Rome, I found a man[24] learned in Greek and Hebrew, together with Syriac and Arabic, who was very learned, more than all the foreign scholars. And he said to me, "O Ethiopian scholar, teach me the language of Geez and Amharic, and I will teach you all that you wish", and we arranged matters according to this counsel, so that he taught me and I taught him. And it was he who collated for me the arrangement of all the text and the interpretation of the book of Ezekiel the prophet. And after 11 years I left Rome, and went up to Jerusalem, that I might worship where our Lord stood, saying[25], "This is (3v) my resting place for ever". And I came among my people who were there (in Jerusalem), so that I should see if there was any wise person who would seek this book. There was no single one among them, no not one. And sorrow was added to my joy for 2 years, until I found a man[26] faithful and wise in literature, who would open his mouth and I would fill it for him—for it is fitting for a pupil that first he write his text, and then he read and learn its interpretation".

The request of the pupil of this[27] interpreter, who was with him for 9 years. I request and I beseech of the one who writes this book, and I make supplication[28] in the name of God, Adonay, and by the love of Ezekiel the prophet, that he place this explanation inside the covers[29] of this book, just as I myself have placed it and made it an introduction, so that (4r) the next generation may know how it was lost at first, and how it was found latterly, or

---

21 On Wäldä ab, see appendix to MEHI. Concerning the book(s), Keren MS 4 is a text of En., Job, Isa., Jer., Dan., Ezek., and Apoc. Ezra, bearing the name *Mäl'akä bərhanat* Wäldä ab, see C. Conti Rossini, I manoscritti etiopici della Missione Cattolica de Cheren, *RRAL* (5) 13, 1904, pp. 233-55, 261-86.

22 Reading *bäbbämäkanu*.

23 *Romayəst*, probably Italian rather than Latin, though possibly both are intended; certainly KG used Dillmann's *Lexicon Linguae Aethiopicae*, see *MSWG* p. 7.

24 This must be Ignazio Guidi.

25 Reading *ənzä* once only.

26 Reading *bə'əse*; the man is KWK.

27 Reading *läzəntu*.

28 Reading *amaḥaṣṣən*.

29 *Ḥəṣən*—probably meaning "on the end papers", or perhaps "in the interior".

who crossed the sea and bartered for it, and who ascended above the clouds and brought it down, for he was forgotten of all men, and was concealed from all the birds of Heaven [30]. And at the time when the 84th [31] year of this father, Kəflä giyorgis, was completed for him, from the time when he was born, that is, the completion of the 1900th year of the incarnation, on the 14th of *Gənbot*, he said to me, his pupil, "Today is my birthday. Hear me, my son, and let me speak to you. In my 25th year I went out from my home-country [32], and was separated from my relatives; I remained 26 years in teaching and learning, touring all parts of Ethiopia, and I spent 33 years in the house of the foreigners. It seems to me that my departure has drawn near, and (4v) my age for rest has overtaken me, and there only remains for me a short period. Place this matter in your heart until the time when you close my eyes and cover over my body in the earth. Now do not neglect my request, day or night, concerning this book; and interpret it once for all. As for other (books), you will obtain them from other (people) [33]; for I know that this flight of mine from you will be speedy".

And after 3 months and 20 days, on the 3rd of *Pagume*, at the 11th hour of the day, that is, towards evening [34], his soul was separated from his flesh without pain or suffering. And he was buried on holy Mount Zion, where his brother Täklä ṣəyon was buried [35], just as he said at the first, when he came from Rome, "This is my resting place for ever". Amen.

This text translated above was almost certainly composed by Kidanä wäld Kəfle; the story of the Ezekiel commentary is continued in a prefatory note in Amharic (by Dästa Täklä wäld) to the Geez grammar and dictionary *MSWG* by KG and KWK [36]:

---

30 Allusion to Baruch 3.29-30 (23-4 in Amharic).
31 Apparently meaning "when he was 83 years old".
32 Reading *əmhagärəyä*.
33 The translation of *wä'abṣəho ... əmkal'an* is not clear to me, but the intention appears to be that KWK shall develop KG's work after his death, cf. *MSWG* p. 8.
34 I.e. at 5 p.m.
35 There are 2 defaced Ethiopian gravestones in the Latin cemetery on Mt. Zion, to the right of the path leading directly forward from the entrance, but I have been unable to verify that they are KG's and Täklä ṣəyon's. Also, books of KG's are reported to be in the library of the Latin Patriarchate in Jerusalem (S. Zanutto, *Bibliografia etiopica*, Rome 1929-32, p. 137), but enquiries have failed to locate them.
36 It is often overlooked that the title page of this work names its 2 authors as Kəflä giyorgis and Kidanä wäld Kəfle Wäldä abba täkle. "Wäldä abba täkle" or "Betä täklä haymanot" forms part of KWK's name because of his link with the monastery of Däbrä Libanos.

"The great scholar *Aläqa* Kidanä wäld Kǝfle Beta Täklä haymanot lived in Jerusalem, having left Ethiopia in 1882 E.C., 20 years after he was born, and then returned to his country in 1912 E.C. The reason he came back was that the Crown Prince of the kingdom of Ethiopia (*Aṣe* Haylä sǝllase the first) wrote a letter to him, saying, "If you can, come and interpret Ezekiel for me".

After he had published and delivered the text of Ezekiel together with its complete commentary, he began again in Dire Dawa to prepare this illuminating book which he had begun in the Holy Land. If, having spent the day working, a thought occurred to him when he went out to take the air in the evening, he would return to the house from outside, to write a memorandum. If an interpretation entered his thoughts at lunch or supper, he would leap up, leaving his food. If a meaning came to him while he was sleeping at night, he would rise from his bed, light a lamp, and write.

At that time, it was the honorable *Wäyzäro* Bälaynäš Gwäbäna, the wife of the honourable *Blatta* Aššǝne Kidanä maryam[37], who used to assist him with daily needs, while she prepared the provisions and allowance which His Majesty Emperor Haylä sǝllase the first ordered for him.

After all this perseverance and toil–even though he became blind because the Fascists imprisoned him in darkness, because he spoke, in 1929 E.C., without trace of shame or fear, of the Emperor's return and of the freedom of the whole of Africa, beginning from Ethiopia–he was still considering assembling in order place names and personal names, and interpreting them, as he explained on page 868[38], when he died on *Säne* 24 1936, E.C., and was buried at Däbrä Libanos".

Some further information is found in EMML MS 1555, fols. 27v-30r[39], which contains 15 numbered Geez poems, composed mostly of rhyming couplets, and written in *qǝne* style. They cover KG's erudition (1), birth (2), death (3), travels and studies in Ethiopia (4-6), sojourn in Rome (7), sojourn in Jerusalem (8-9), death (10), and the death and scholarly legacy of Täklä ṣǝyon[40] (11-15). This further information is incorporated into the following chronological table:

---

37 His photograph appears in *AMQ* p. 1232; he is probably the *Ato* Aššǝne of EMML 1522.
38 *MSWG* p. 868 — which defines the concept of proper names, rather than explaining KWK's intentions.
39 EMML 1523, 1557, 1558, 1560, 1561 are also relevant, see EMML catalogue vol. V; and EMML 2334 and 2335, in vol. VI.
40 For references on Täklä ṣǝyon, see appendix to MEHI.

A.D.   1825   Saturday, May 21 (= Gənbot 14, 1817 E.C.)[41], birth of KG;
              he was baptised on Säne 23.

       1849   (1841 E.C.) onwards, KG leaves Ankobärr and travels around
              in Gojjam, Amhara, Lasta, Begemder, Gondar, Simen, Tigre
              and Hamasen[42], for study.

c.   1850? death of Wäldä ab[43]; subsequent removal of his MSS from
              Gondar to Keren.

       1869   Friday, February 5 (= Ṭərr 29, 1861 E.C.), death of *Aratt ayna*
              Gwäsu[44].

c.   1872   (1864 E.C.), birth of KWK (said to be 20 in 1882 E.C.[45], but
              72 in 1936 E.C.[46]).

c.   1875   KG goes to the "house of the foreigners" at Massawa and
              Keren; during this time he makes a brief visit to Jerusalem,
              and translates the *Imitatio Christi* from the "language of Rome"
              into Amharic[47].

       1878   Tuesday, May 28 (= Gənbot 21, 1870 E.C.), council of Boru
              meda; Täklä ṣəyon leaves Ethiopia and goes to Jerusalem[48].

       1883   KG at Keren writes a treatise on Christology[49].

c.   1886   KG goes from Ethiopia to Rome; during his stay he works
              with I. Guidi on the *Vocabolario*[50], the *Fətḥa nägäst*[51], and the
              text of Ezekiel.

       1888   Friday, December 7 (= Ḫədar 29, 1881 E.C.) death of Täklä
              ṣəyon, burial on Mt. Zion[52].

       1890   (1882 E.C.), KWK goes from Ethiopia to Jerusalem.

c.   1897   KG goes from Rome to Jerusalem[53].

---

41 EMML 1555 f. 27v.
42 EMML 1555 f. 28r.
43 Appendix to MEHI.
44 ZL p. 374.
45 Foreword to *MSWG*, translated above.
46 *MSWG* p. 4; p. 3 has photographs of KG and KWK.
47 EMML 1555 f. 28v.
48 ZL pp. 189-190.
49 Yaqob, pp. 9-13, 18-19, and "Documento B" (pp. 49-211).
50 I. Guidi, *Vocabolario Amarico-Italiano*, Rome, 1901; see p. viii, and *AMQ* p. 5.
51 EMML 1555 f. 28v, 1523 f. 69r; published as I. Guidi, *Il Fetha Nagast o "Legislazione dei Re"*,
   Rome, 1897-9.
52 ZL pp. 189-190; EMML 1555 f. 29v.
53 EMML 1555 f. 29r. In general, see also K. Pedersen, *The History of the Ethiopian Community
   in the Holy Land from the time of Emperor Tewodros II till 1974*, Hebrew University, Jerusalem,
   M. A. Thesis, 1981.

1897-9 publication in Rome of the *Fǝtḥa nägäst*.

c. 1899 KG meets KWK in Jerusalem.

1901 publication in Rome of Guidi's *Vocabolario*.

1905/6 KG writes Amharic treatise EMML 2333 (23).

1908 Tuesday, September 8 (= *Pagume* 3, 1900 E.C.), death of KG in Jerusalem at age of 83, burial on Mt. Zion[54].

1916 February, writing of MS JE 301 E.

1920 (1912 E.C.), KWK returns to Ethiopia, and stays at Dire Dawa, working on the Ezekiel commentary.

1924 (1916 E.C.), publication in Dire Dawa of *MH*.

1929 (*Yäkkatit* 27, 1921 E.C.), KWK is asked by Crown Prince Täfäri to assist with work on an Amharic dictionary[55].

1935 publication in Dire Dawa of (?KG's) translation of the *Imitatio Christi*[56].

1937 (1929 E.C.), imprisonment of KWK.

1944 Saturday, July 1 (= *Säne* 24, 1936 E.C.), death of KWK, burial at Däbrä Libanos[57].

1956 publication in Addis Ababa of KG's and KWK's *MSWG*.

1970 publication in Addis Ababa of Dästa Täklä wäld's dictionary *AMQ*, the work for which occupied the years 1929-1958.

The fruit of the labours of KG and KWK on Ezekiel is the printed commentary, *MH*, made up as follows[58]:

Title page — (recto) "The Book of Ezekiel with its interpretation: its text in Geez, its interpretation in Amharic. Written by Kidanä wäld Kǝfle. Printed in 1916".
— (verso) photograph of Crown Prince Täfäri Mäkwännǝn.

4 unnumbered pages, headed "Announcement of the reason why I ... Täfäri Mäkwännǝn published this book", and containing the preface also contained in several other printed volumes of AC material[59].

---

54 EMML 1555 f. 28r, *MSWG* p. 8, Yaqob pp. 18-9.

55 *AMQ* p. 4.

56 Wright, p. 103.

57 The monks of Däbrä Libanos tried to prevent this, because of KWK's alleged heretical connections.

58 For bibliographical details see Wright pp. 99-100.

59 For references see *TIA* ch. 3.

Pp 1-6:   Preface (*Mäqdəm*) "of Ezekiel the prophet", containing
                   much traditional Ethiopian material also to be found e.g. in
                   the AC introductions to Isaiah and the corpus of the minor
                   prophets, but probably given its present form by KWK, as
                   it also contains material from Jewish sources concerning
                   Hananiah (*TB Ḥagigah* 13a) and a reference to Josephus'
                   Antiquities (not to the "Book of Josippon").

Pp. 7-504:   The text of Ezekiel in Geez, and commentary in Amharic,
                   with some illustrations. The Geez text is a careful translation
                   from the Hebrew of Ezekiel[60], and includes (p. 502) a
                   translation of the Massoretic note at the end of the book
                   giving the number of verses and chapters, and the mid-point.
                   The division into chapters (*mə'əraf*) follows the customary
                   modern arrangement, except that ch. 3 v. 1 falls at Hebrew
                   ch. 3 v. 4. The division into verses follows that in modern
                   printed Hebrew Bibles (and is not that of the Vulgate). Some
                   chapters are further divided into sections (*kəfl*), of which the
                   majority correspond with *parašot ptuḥot*, fewer correspond
                   with *parašot stumot*, and a few not with any formal text
                   division I can discover–possibly they are taken from an
                   Ethiopic MS.

                   The illustrations (and some of the notes of dimensions
                   relating to plans of the Temple) are reproduced from the
                   commentary on Ezekiel in L-Cl. Fillion, *La Sainte Bible*[61],
                   with the exception of the map on p. 503, which was probably
                   specially drawn. KWK was evidently aware of other illustra-
                   tions, as on p. 504 he mentions a "Hebrew picture" of the
                   plan of Ezekiel's temple.

                   The Amharic commentary itself contains material from
                   traditional Ethiopian[62], and from other, especially Jewish,

---

60 Cf. A.A. National Library MS 10 (*Catalogue*, 1962 E.C. pp. 6-7). On the questions raised by
   another Biblical text apparently translated from Hebrew into Geez, see H. A. W. Pilkington,
   A critical edition of the Book of Proverbs in Ethiopic, Oxford D. Phil. thesis, 1978, and
   E. Ullendorff, "Hebrew, Aramaic and Greek; the versions underlying Ethiopic translations
   of Bible and intertestamental literature", in G. Rendsburg et al (edd.), *The Bible World.
   Essays in Honor of Cyrus H. Gordon*, New York, 1980, pp. 249-257.

61 Paris, 1888-1904, vol. 6. For the original of the drawing on *MḤ* pp. 49 and 435 see
   M. Peeters Wilbaux in *Bulletins de la Société historique et littéraire de Tournai*, Tournay, tome I,
   1849, facing p. 266.

62 On the sources of the AC, see *TIA* ch. 6. Some of the traditional material in *MḤ* is also

sources; it is neither a mere edition of the Ethiopian AC, nor a mere adaptation of a non-Ethiopian work. The sources include the following:

a) KG himself, named in comment on 42.4 as favouring a symbolic understanding of details of Ezekiel's temple vision.

b) Sources typical of the remainder of the AC corpus, such as *Aksimaros*, *Zena əskəndər*, John of Nikiou, and most importantly the Biblical and patristic texts commented on in the AC, together with the Amharic commentaries themselves.

c) Readings of the *säba liqanat* (LXX translators), correctly cited on 1.4, 4.5, 8.2, 42.19 etc.

d) Readings or parallels in Arabic, on 1.4, 1.7, 1.11.

e) KWK appears to have used a Bible dictionary or encyclopedia, e.g. in comment on Tammuz in 8.14.

f) Jewish sources:

   (i) References to "Hebrew" (words or grammar) on 1.4, 2.4, 4.2, 6.14 etc.

   (ii) *Targum Yerushalmi*, cited by name on 1.3, doubtless from Radak.

   (iii) *Targum "Jonathan"* to Ezekiel, cited by name on 1.6 (and on pp. 505-6).

   (iv) "Midrash" is named as a source on 24.8, on "worship of Joash" (*Exodus Rabba* VIII.2 and parallels) and on "Zechariah's blood" (*TB Sanhedrin* 96b[63]).

     In addition, references to *mätärgwəman* or *liqawntä ayhud* are mostly to the targumim and midrashim; e.g. the *mätärgwəm* of 23.5 is *Targum "Jonathan" in loc.*, and the "Jewish scholars" of 17.1 refers to *Ecclesiastes Rabba* I.12.

---

found in the AC to other books–e.g. some of the material on Melchizedek in comment on Ezek. 16.3 is also found in AC *Filkəsyus* p. 39.

63 The tradition recorded in the comment on Ezek. 24.8 that 94,000 people were killed agrees with *TB Sanhedrin* 96b rather than with other versions of the story (see J.-D. Dubois, *Études sur l'Apocryphe de Zacharie et sur les traditions concernant la mort de Zacharie*, Oxford D. Phil. Thesis, 1978): the tradition recorded alongside it, that 1500 were killed, does not appear in Jewish sources, and may be Ethiopian (though AC Matt. 23.35 gives the number as 7, and *Sənkəssar, Mäskäräm* 8 does not record a number).

(v) KWK also seems to have drawn on the Talmud directly, and not via other Jewish or non-Jewish commentators—e.g. on 16.49 he cites the story of Sodom from *TB Sanhedrin* 109b, and on 43.3 he takes Hananiah's defence of the integrity of the book of Ezekiel from *TB Ḥagigah* 13a, though without naming these sources.

(vi) Later Rabbinic commentators. Surprisingly, the only one named is Shadal, once on 3.9[64]; but it is clear that Radak and Rashi have been used most extensively throughout the commentary, and doubtless KWK used the *miqra'ot gdolot*. E.g. the interpretation of the "third sword" of 21.19 as that of the Ammonites is that of Rashi; the ingenious comment on the "40 years" of 29.11 is that of Radak. The two interpretations of the "mountain" of 40.2 are those of Rashi and Radak respectively. In the Geez text of 46.22, KWK transliterates the Hebrew *qṭurot*, and then mentions in the comment the "reading" *ǝḥuẓat*, representing Radak's understanding *qšurot*. Examples occur on most pages of the commentary, and are too many to be accidental correspondences. The Jewish interpretations may lie alongside specifically Christian ones (e.g. in 44.2 on the "closed gate"), but the disparate materials are blended into a remarkably harmonious unity.

Pp. 505-6:   Report (*zena*) "from the Hebrew", in Geez. It gives some particulars about Ezekiel's life and death, including the claim that Pythagoras was his disciple[65]. It is probably translated from a Hebrew encyclopedia; its major source is the section on Ezekiel's grave in the *Travels* of Rabbi Petaḥiah of Regensburg[66].

---

64 3.12 in Hebrew; see *Peruše šadal ... 'al yirmya yeḥizq'el mišle ve'iyyob*, by Shmuel David Luzzatto, Lemberg, 1876.

65 See L. Ginzberg, *The legends of the Jews*, Philadelphia, 1947, vol. VI, p. 422.

66 A. Benisch, *Travels of Rabbi Petachiah of Ratisbon*, London, 1856, pp. 19-33; the material does not appear in the corresponding section of the *Itinerary* of Benjamin of Tudela (or in the Ethiopic version of lives of the prophets, see M. A. Knibb in *BSOAS*, XLIII (1980) pt. 2, 197-206).

Pp. 506-7:   Geez text of the section on Ezekiel in *Sənkəssar* for *Miyazya* 5 [67].

Pp. 507-10:   A *mälkə'* of Ezekiel, in Geez, probably KWK's original composition.

Pp. 511-3:   Appendix in Amharic on "The number of the books", discussing the Hebrew and LXX canons and text.

Pp. 514-5:   Errata, and note that work on the book was commenced on *Säne* 4 and completed on *Yäkkatit* 30.

We cannot quantify KG's contribution to this printed Ezekiel commentary. However, the evidence above suggests that KG gave KWK his interest in Ezekiel, his concern for establishing its correct text, extensive factual information concerning the traditional Ethiopian interpretation of Ezekiel, and a desire to extend his studies beyond traditional Ethiopian circles; and alongside this, he must have shared, as an outstanding teacher to an outstanding pupil, his vision of scholarly enquiry.

Acknowledgements

I am indebted to Prof. J. Tubiana and the Laboratoire Peiresc for using their Ethioconcord computer programme to supply Gregorian equivalents of Ethiopian dates; and to the staff of the Hill Monastic Manuscript Library for making available printouts from EMML MS 1555.

I am grateful to *Abunä* Matyas, *Abba* La'əkä maryam, Msgr. Batthish, Sister Kirsten Pedersen, Drs. Getatchew Haile, Yaqob Beyene, H. Rosenau, and S. Brock, and Mr E. Silver, for extensive and varied assistance (especially to Dr. Getatchew for corrections to my translation).

I am grateful to Prof. W. Leslau, both for the general contribution his studies have made, and for stimulating my work on this subject by writing to me about a closely related matter.

---

67 English translation in E. A. W. Budge, *The Book of the Saints of the Ethiopian Church*, Cambridge, 1928, pp. 783-4.

Abbreviations

AA	Addis Ababa.
AC	*Andəmta* commentary/corpus.
ACD	*Amharic Church Dictionary*, (ed) Sergew Hable Sellassie, draft ed., A.A., 1977 onwards.
AMQ	*Addis yamarəñña mäzgäbä qalat*, Dästa Täklä wäld, A.A., 1970.
BL	British Library, London.
BN	Bibliothèque Nationale, Paris.
CCR	Carlo Conti Rossini (see S. Strelcyn, *Catalogue des MSS éthiopiens de l'Accademia Nazionale dei Lincei*, Rome, 1976).
E.C.	Ethiopian Calendar.
EMML	Ethiopian Manuscript Microfilm Library (see Catalogues by W. F. Macomber and Getatchew Haile).
Guidi	I. Guidi, *Storia della letteratura etiopica*, Rome, 1932.
KG	Kəflä giyorgis.
KWK	Kidanä wäld Kəfle.
MEHI	R. Cowley, *Mämhər* Esdros and his interpretations, *Proceedings of the Sixth International Congress of Ethiopian Studies* (forthcoming).
MH	*Mäṣḥafä Ḥəzqə'el*, KWK, Dire Dawa, 1916 E.C.
MSWG	*Mäṣḥafä säwasəw wägəss wämäzgäbä qalat ḥaddis*, KG and KWK, A.A., 1948 E.C.
OTIAC	R. Cowley, Old Testament Introduction in the Andemta Commentary Tradition, *Journal of Ethiopian Studies*, vol. XII, no. 1, pp. 133-175.
RRAL	*Rendiconti, Regia Accademia dei Lincei* (classe de Scienze, Morali, Storiche e Filologiche).
Taddesse	Taddesse Tamrat, *Church and State in Ethiopia 1270-1527*, Oxford, 1972.
TB	*Talmud Babli*.
TIA	R. Cowley, *The Traditional Interpretation of the Apocalypse of St. John in the Ethiopian Orthodox Church*, University of Cambridge Oriental Publications, 33.
Ullendorff	E. Ullendorff, *Ethiopia and the Bible*, London, 1968.
Wright	S. Wright, *Ethiopian Incunabula*, A.A., 1967.
Yaqob	Yaqob Beyene, *L'Unzione di Cristo nella Teologia Etiopica*, Orientalia Christiana Analecta 215, Rome, 1981.
ZL	*Mäṣḥafä qəne, zəkrä liqawnt, Mäl'akä bərhan* Admasu Jämbäre, A.A., 1963 E.C.

THE AMHARIC FIRST ORDER VOWEL*

MONICA S. DEVENS
Pomona College

Amharic possesses seven vowel phonemes, known in traditional grammar as the seven vowel "orders". There is general agreement among scholars of Ethiopic concerning the phonetics of six of these seven vowels, orders two through seven. They are [u], [i], [a], [e], [ə], and [o], respectively. There is, however, no consensus about the phonetic description of the first order vowel. The purpose of this article is to resolve the controversy surrounding the first order vowel by specifying it acoustically.

There are three schools of thought concerning the nature of the first order vowel. One group of scholars claims that it is a front vowel, a second group hears a central vowel, while a third group places it somewhere between front and central positions. All agree that it lies in the mid-to-low range.

Among the proponents of the front vowel theory are Guidi, Mittwoch and Baeteman. Guidi (1889:6) employs the symbol ä for the first order vowel, which he specifies as the vowel in English "bad" (=IPA[æ]?). Mittwoch (1907:193-194) transcribes the most common occurrence of the first order vowel as a̭ and describes it as "ein ausserordentlich enges a", resembling the "broad e" in German "Mensch", but being somewhat closer to a (again = [æ]?). Baeteman (1929:xii-xiv), after reviewing the usages of others and finding them all unacceptable, settles on an analysis of the first order vowel as an "è ouvert" (= IPA[ɛ]?).

Cohen, Obolensky and Hudson all report that the first order vowel is a central vowel. Cohen (1936: 42-48) uses the symbol ä, which he defines as a central vowel, higher than a and lower than ə. But Cohen's ə is actually in the position of IPA [ɨ] on his chart, i.e. high central, thus making ä a

* I would like to thank the Ethiopians whose co-operation made this research possible and, in particular, the indulgence of the management of Walia Restaurant, Los Angeles. The spectrographic analysis was made possible through the generosity of Dr. Ronald K.S. Macaulay of Pitzer College. Most of all, I am grateful to Dr. Wolf Leslau who is totally responsible for my involvement in, and knowledge of, Ethiopic.

A preliminary version of this paper was read at the North American Conference on Afroasiatic Linguistics in Boston, March 13-15, 1981. I am grateful to all the participants at that meeting for their insightful comments.

mid central vowel (=IPA [ə]?). (It is actually mid-low as Cohen places a noticeably lower than e and o). Obolensky (1964), in agreement with Cohen, uses [ə] for the first order vowel, transcribing the sixth order vowel as the higher [ɨ]. Hudson, too, hears a mid central vowel (1978:198).

The third opinion is expressed in the work of Sumner, Ullendorff, Leslau and the group of Cowley, Bender and Ferguson. Sumner (1951:67), in an experimental phonetic study, analyzes the first order vowel as [ɛ] in open syllables but finds it somewhat centralized ([ë]) in closed syllables. Ullendorff (1955:161) reports a pronunciation which is "... a half-open fronted a-sound spoken with fairly well spread lips". He later goes on to call it "centralized". Leslau (1968:6) places the first order vowel in the position of [ɛ] on his chart, but describes it as being "... like the sound one makes while hesitating in speaking and which is represented in writing by 'uh'", i.e. English [ʌ]. Both Ullendorff and Leslau transcribe the first order vowel by ä. Finally, Cowley, Bender and Ferguson (1976:79) call it a central vowel, but further state that it actually is "... roughly between the vowels of English 'bed' and 'bud', generally nearer the former", i.e. between [ɛ] and [ʌ].

In addition, there has been some discussion of allophonic variation. Guidi, for example, claims that after [w] the first order vowel frequently has a sound which is "almost o". Cohen and Ullendorff, as Guidi, find a variant after [w] which they transcribe as å, a vowel intermediate between a and o. Cohen also hears a variant in the environment of palatals, transcribed ä, and equated with the vowel in English "man" (= IPA[æ]?). Both Guidi and Sumner note that totally unaccented first order vowels are short and indistinct. For Guidi, they are "almost ě", while for Sumner, they are [ə].

In order to determine the position of the first order vowel, a spectrographic analysis of the Amharic vowel system was undertaken. The data were taken from tape recordings made in 1974 of four native speakers from Addis Ababa, male students in their twenties and thirties. Both isolated word data and contextual data (though from reading, not casual speech) were utilized. As the recordings had been made for another purpose, it was impossible to get the same number of examples for each vowel or for each speaker. In the case of speaker #1, only one example of the vowel [o] was found and no examples of [e] or [u]. In general, however, at least four or five examples of each vowel per speaker were obtained, and between nine and twenty-four examples per speaker of the first order vowel. Spectrograms were made on a Kaye sonograph 6061-B. They were then analyzed and plotted separately for each speaker. After variants which had clearly been affected by particular phonetic environments were removed from the calculations (see

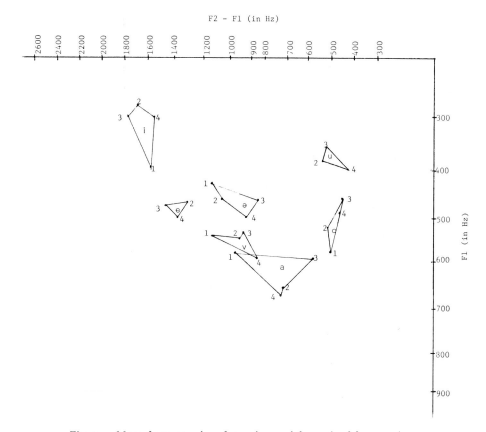

Figure 1. Mean formant values for each vowel for each of four speakers.
v stands for the first order vowel.

below), a master plot was made showing the mean formant values for each vowel for each speaker. A similar master plot was constructed using the median values. Finally, two new recordings (1980) were made of isolated words in almost a six-way contrast: /fvlləgi/ "want! (f.s.)", /fvlləga/ "she having wanted", /fvlləgo/ "he having wanted", /fvlləgu/ "want! (pl.)", /fvlləgge/ "I having wanted", and /fvlləgvh/ "you (m.s.) having wanted", /v/ representing the first order vowel here. The speakers were one of the original group of four (speaker #2) and an additional young man (identified as speaker #5 on the chart). These tapes were then analyzed spectrographically and plotted.

Figures 1 and 2 show the mean and median values, respectively, for each of the four speakers and each of the seven vowels as contained in the original

MONICA S. DEVENS

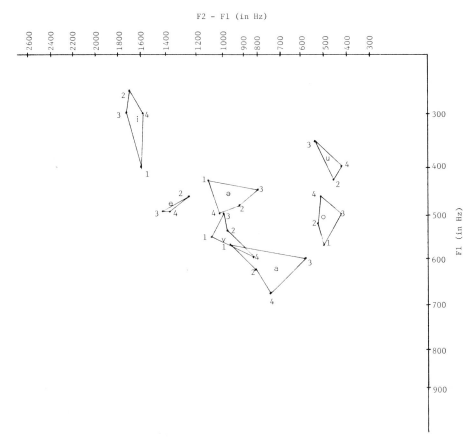

Figure 2. Median formant values for each vowel for each of four speakers.
v stands for the first order vowel.

recordings. The overall view of the vowel system is the same in both figures. Figure 3 shows the values obtained from the later recordings of the two speakers when the vowels were in near minimal pair position. Here every occurrence of every vowel is plotted. This figure, of course, shows a much greater spread in the vowel positions. Figure 4 shows a composite of all the graphs, with each vowel denoted by a single point. These were computed by taking the mean formant values of all the examples of each vowel, ranging from 12 examples of [e] to 74 examples of the first order vowel. The first order vowel shows up as a central vowel mid-way between [ə] and [a], i.e. IPA [ɐ]. Figure 5 is a spectrogram of the word /fʋlləga/ as recorded by speaker #2. One can clearly see that the first formant (F1) of /v/ is higher

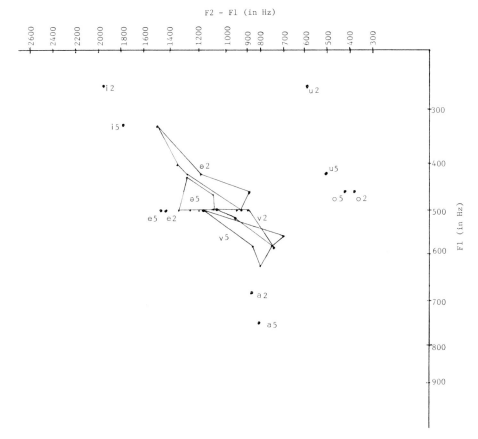

Figure 3. Plot of vowels occurring in six words recorded by two speakers.
Larger dots indicate vowels in near minimal contrast.
v stands for the first order vowel.

than that of [ə] and that the distance between F1 and F2 (the second
formant) is smaller for /v/ than for [ə]. Thus, again, /v/ is a vowel lower
and farther back than [ə].

Some phonetic environments clearly caused consistent shifts in the vowels.
In most cases, these occurred in the environment of semi-vowels. In four out
of the five examples of /wv/ in the data (again /v/ standing for the first order
vowel), the first order vowel was realized as a sound between its normal
position and [o] (mean formants 530, 1195), thus confirming the reports of
Guidi and Cohen. A pure [o] was recorded in the one case of /vw/ in the data
(/svw/ "man"). /ə/ in the environments /yə/ and /əy/ was invariably rendered
[i]. The data was insufficient to examine any other environment.

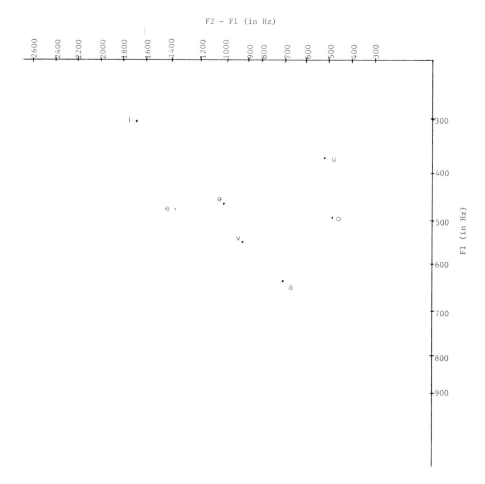

Figure 4. Composite plot showing the mean value of all examples for each vowel.
v indicates the first order vowel.

It is interesting to note that descriptions of the first order vowel in other Ethiopian Semitic languages have often been in accord with these findings. In his studies on Argobba (1959:252) and Soddo (1968:6), Leslau defines the first order vowel as "higher-low, central" and just below [ə] (= IPA [ɐ]). Palmer (1962:6) gives [ɐ] as the phonetic equivalent of the first order vowel in Tigre.

While the phonetic specification of the first order vowel is of primary interest here, the question of its transcription must, of necessity, also arise.

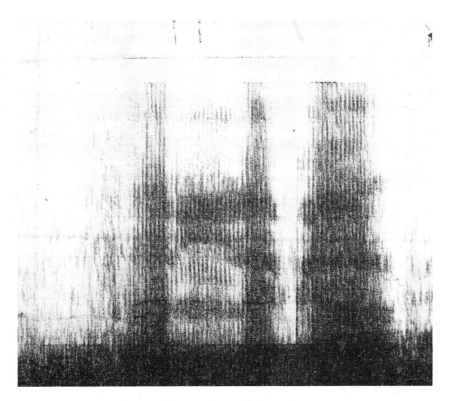

Figure 5. Spectrogram of the word /fvlləga/ as spoken by speaker #2.
/v/ stands for the first order vowel.

Ideally, it should be transcribed using the proper IPA symbol, [ɐ]. As the
International Phonetics Association states in its *Principles* (1949:7), "if a
language contains two unrounded central vowels, it is recommended that ə
be used to denote the closer one and ɐ for the opener one". Unfortunately,
however, economic reality makes that an unlikely prospect as the symbol [ɐ]
is not available to many printers. Five symbols used in the literature have
already been mentioned: ɛ, ə (using ɨ for the sixth order vowel), a, ạ and ä.
ɛ and the ə/ɨ set should be rejected, since they are IPA symbols with very
specific phonetic values which do not accurately represent the phonetics of
the Amharic first and sixth order vowels. a, ạ and ä have the advantage of
not leading the reader to an incorrect interpretation quite so immediately. Of
these, both a and ä use accepted diacritics which denote centrality but ä, it
seems fair to say (along with Hudson 1978:198), has been the most common

symbol in much of the recent literature, carrying with it the weight of "tradition".

This is not an ideal solution. As the International Phonetics Association notes (1949:1), "when two sounds occurring in a given language are employed for distinguishing one word from another, they should whenever possible be represented by two distinct letters without diacritical marks" and further (1949:16) in commenting on the diacritical mark ¨, "the use of ¨ is to be recommended when the vowels are special members of back or front vowel phonemes". But of all the available options, ä seems best when [ɐ] is unavailable.

The Amharic first order vowel is a mid-low central vowel, halfway between [ə] and [a]. It is the vowel expressed by the IPA symbol [ɐ]. While ä will probably continue to be the symbol used to transcribe it, it should be understood to express this phonetic fact: /ä/ = [ɐ].

References

Baeteman, J., *Dictionnaire amarigna-français* (Imprimerie Saint Lazare, Dire Daoua 1929).

Cohen, M., *Traité de langue amharique* (Institut d'ethnologie, Paris 1936).

Cowley, R., Bender, M. L., and Ferguson, C. A., "The Amharic Language: Description" in *Language in Ethiopia*, M. L. Bender, J. D. Bowen, R. L. Cooper and C. A. Ferguson (eds.) (Oxford University Press, London 1976).

Guidi, I., *Grammatica elementare della lingua amarica* (Rome 1889).

Hudson, G., Review of Bender et al., *Language in Ethiopia*. Language 54: 196-201 (1978).

International Phonetics Association, *Principles* (International Phonetic Association, London 1949).

Leslau, W., *Amharic Textbook* (Otto Harrassowitz, Wiesbaden 1968).

Leslau, W., *Ethiopians Speak III. Soddo* (University of California Publications, Near Eastern Studies II. University of California Press, Berkeley and Los Angeles 1968).

Leslau, W., "A Preliminary Description of Argobba", Annales d'Éthiopie 3: 251-273 (1959).

Mittwoch, E., "Proben aus amharischen Volksmunde", Mitteilungen des Seminars für orientalische Sprachen zu Berlin, West-asiatische Abteilung 10: 185-241 (1907).

Obolensky, S., *Amharic basic course* (Foreign Service Institute, Washington, D.C. 1964).

Palmer, F. R., *The morphology of the Tigre noun* (Oxford University Press, Oxford 1962).

Sumner, C., *Étude expérimentale de l'amharique moderne* (d'après la prononciation d'Abraha François) (Montreal 1951).

Ullendorff, E., *The Semitic languages of Ethiopia: a comparative phonology* (Taylor's Press, London 1955).

SEMITIC AND EAST CUSHITIC:
SOUND CORRESPONDENCES AND COGNATE SETS

ARON B. DOLGOPOLSKY
University of Haifa

o.   The purpose of this paper is to compare East Cushitic (as reconstructed on the Proto-East-Cushitic level by H.-J. Sasse, 1979, and on the Proto-Lowland-East-Cushitic level by Paul Black, 1974) to Semitic. I have tried to choose the most reliable cognate sets in order to establish regular consonant correspondences. This paper considers all classes of consonants except the laryngeals and the sonants.

I have used Sasse's and Black's reconstructions, as well as Bernd Heine's Proto-Sam (Somali-Boni-Rendille) reconstructions and my own East Cushitic reconstructions based on available material. Wherever possible, the Egyptian correspondences are taken into account as well.

1. Sem. *b, Eg. b = ECush. *b

(1.1)   Sem. *ba'raḵ- 'lightning' > Hebrew ba:'ra:ḵ, Aram. bar'ḵa:, Arab. barq-un, Tigre bärḵ, Akkad. birḵ-um 'lightning'; Sem. *√brḵ 'to lighten' > Akkad., Hebrew, Eth. √brḵ, Arab. √brq 'to lighten' = ECush. *barḵ-/ birḵ- > Elmolo ibirga, Dasenech biddi (< *birḵ-ti), Sidamo (Cerulli) biraḵo 'lightning'. Cp. also Eg. b'ḵ 'to be bright', Coptic ebrêce, ebrêč 'lightning'. See Sasse 1979.49, cp. Dolgopolsky 1972c.227-8.

(1.2)   Sem. *√'bd (basic stem *-'bad-) 'to get lost' > Hebrew √'bd (impf. yo:'baḏ < *ya-'bad-u) 'to get lost', Ugar., Phoen., Aram. √'bd id., Arab. √'bd 'to become wild' (cattle) = ECush. *bad- 'to get lost, to be extinguished' > Saho, Afar ba(:)d- 'to perish, to be extinguished', Dasenech bad-, Elmolo pɛd-, Galla bad- 'to be lost', Konso pat- 'to be ruined', Gidole pat- 'to disappear, to be lost, to die', Burji bas-s- (< caus. *bad-s-) 'to extinguish', Gawwada, Harso pat- 'to disappear', Gollango pat- 'to get lost'. See Black 1974.176, Sasse 1979.14.

(1.3)   Sem. *baẟan/m- 'venomous snake' > Akk. baŝm-um 'a mythic venomous snake', Ugar. bɵn 'snake', Arab. baẟan-un 'venomous snake' = ECush. *bos- 'snake' > Galla bofᵃ 'snake' and perh. Somali abe:so 'type of snake', Saho, Afar (')abe:so 'snake'. See Sasse 1976.127.

(1.4) Sem. *√bḥl or *√bxl > Aram. (Pehl.) bḥl 'fierce animal' = ECush. *baḥal- 'wild animal' > Somali baḥal 'wild animal', Rendille baḥaši (< *baḥal-ti) 'lion'. See Sasse 1979.41.

(1.5) Sem. *√bḳ' 'to split' > Hebrew, Aram. √bḳ' (impf. -bḳa') 'to split', cp. *√bḳw > Eth. (caus.) 'a-bḳawa 'distendere, aperire (os), hiare', bəḳw 'hians, hiscens' = ECush. *baḳ- 'to crush' > Afar bak- 'to crush', Somali baq- 'to curdle', Galla baḳ- 'to melt', baḳaḳ- 'to crack', Konso (caus.) paḳ-š- 'to chop', Gidole paḳ-ḳ-iyy- (sg. caus.) 'to chop', Gawwada paq-q-as- (sg. caus.) 'to chop'. See Black 1974.197, 253, Sasse 1979.48, 49.

(1.6) Eg. b'' 'snake's hole' (if it is not cognate with Sem. *√b'r 'hole') = ECush. *boḥl 'hole' > Saho bo:l (< boḥol), Somali boḥol, Galla bo:l-a (< *boḥol-a) 'hole in the ground', Gidole poḥol-a 'wall', Hadiyya bo:r-a 'salt-hole'. See Black 1974.120, Sasse 1979.16, 41.

(1.7) Sem. *bV ṣṣ- > Hebrew biṣ'ṣa: 'swamp', Christian Pal. Aram. bṣy 'swamp' (and perh. Sem. *ba:ṣ- 'sand' > Akk. ba:ṣ-um 'sand', Ar. ba:ṣ-un 'sand', cp. Hebrew boṣ 'silt') = ECush. *baẓ- 'lake, sea' > Saho, Som. bad 'sea', Rendille bey 'lake', Dasenech baẓ 'lake Rudolf', Elmolo paw 'lake Rudolf', Gollango, Dobase pas-o 'lake'. See Sasse 1976.137, Sasse 1979.20, Dolgopolsky 1966.54.

(1.8) Sem. *'a'b- (i.e. nom. *'a'b-u, gen. *'a'b-i, acc. *'a'b-a) 'father' > Akkad. ab-um, Hebrew 'a:b, Arab. 'ab-un (see Dolgopolsky 1978.1, 3-9) = ECush. *'a:b-/*'abb- 'father' > Saho, Afar abb-a, Somali a:bb-e 'father' and abb-a:n 'protector', Rendille ab-a, Bayso abb-o 'father', Galla abb-a: 'father' (general), a:bb-o: 'own father', Konso a:p-a, Gidole app-a 'father', Hadiyya a:bb-a 'father', Burji a:bb-o 'father'. See Sasse 1979.15.

(1.9) Sem. *√'bb > Arab. √'bb (pf. 'abba, impf. -'ubb-) 'to gulp, to swallow water in one draught', Eg. b'b' 'to drink' = LECush. *-a-'ab- 'to drink' > Afar -a'ab- (juss.), -a'ub- (pf.) 'to drink', Saho -o:'ob- (pf.) 'to drink', Somali 'ab-b- 'to drink'. See Black 1974.150, Dolgopolsky 1973.139, 225-6.

(1.10) Sem. *√dbr 'back, behind' = ECush. *dib-/*dub- 'tail, behind', *dab- 'tail' (see 3.2).

(1.11) Eg. dbḥ 'to need, to ask for (esp. food, water)' = POromo *ḍe:b-oḍ- 'to become thirsty' (see 5.6).

(1.12) Sem. *√gb' 'hill', *√gbl 'mountain' = ECush. *gub- 'mountain' (see 6.6).

(1.13) Sem. *√lb' 'lion' > OAkkad. lab'um id., Hebrew la:'bi:(') 'lioness' = PSam *liba:ḥ 'lion' > Somali libaḥ, Boni ği'wa, ğiwah 'lion'. See Heine 1978.67.

(1.14) Sem. *√gbb > Akkad. *gubbubu* 'to roast' = ECush. *gub- 'to burn' (see 6.7).

(1.15) Sem. *ganb- 'side' = SLECush. *ga₂b- 'bank, ditch' (see 6.12).

(1.16) Eg. gb' 'arm' = ECush. *gVb- > Saho, Afar *gaba* 'hand' (see 6.14).

(1.17) Eg. ḳ'b 'knee' = ECush. *gilb-/*gulb- 'knee' > Afar, Saho *gulub*, Somali, Rendille *ǧilib*, Boni *šilub*, Bayso *gilib*, Galla *ǧilba*, Konso *kilpa*, Gidole *kilp*, Gawwada *kilp-ayho*, Tsamay *gilib-ko*, Hadiyya *gurubbo*, Burji *gilba* 'knee'. See Black 1974.148, 163, 182, Sasse 1979. 5, 6, 18, Heine 1978.61, Dolgopolsky 1973.75.

(1.18) Eg. ḳb(b) 'cold' = ECush. *kab- 'cold' (see 8.5).

(1.19) Sem. *δa'nab- 'tail' = ECush. *ẕanb-/*ẕinb- 'tail' (see 11.1).

(1.20) Sem. *'δi'(V)b- 'wolf' = ECush. *ẕo:b 'lion' (see 11.2).

(1.21) Sem. *√sby 'to moisten, to dye' = ECush. *ṣub- 'to dip in' (see 12.1).

(1.22) Sem. *'libab- 'heart' > Hebrew *leb*, etc. (see Dolgopolsky 1978.2, 10-11) = ECush. *lubb- 'heart' > Elmolo *rup-ai'* 'heart', Galla *lubb-a'* 'life', Konso *lupp-o:ta* 'heart, soul' (see Black 1974.259) = Eg. ìb 'heart'.

Apparent deviations from the above sound correspondence are sometimes found in the intervocalic position and in one case in a consonant cluster, where ECush *f (rather than *b) happens to correspond to the Sem. *b:

(1.23) Sem. *'ar'ba'- 'four' > Hebrew *'ar'ba'*, Arab. *'arba'-*, Akkad. *erbe*, *erbû-m*, etc. = LESuch. *'af(a)r- (~ *'arf-) 'four' > Saho and Afar (Reinisch) *afar* 'four', Somali *áfar*, Rendille *afar*, Bayso *afar(-i)*, Arbore *afára*, Dasenech (Heine) *'affur* 'four' and the ordinal numeral ('fourth'): Somali *afr-a:d*, Galla *afr-afa* ~ *arf-afa*, Konso *arf-atta*, Gidole *arf-iyya*. The fact that the consonant in question is unvoiced in other Semito-Hamitic languages (Bedawye *faḍig* 'four', Eg. *ifd* 'Vierzahl', Chadic probably *fwVḍV ~ *VfwVḍV 'four' > Hausa *huḍu* ~ *fuḍu*, Bolewa *poḍḍo*, Angas *fi:r*, Margi *fwàḍà*, Wandala *úfáḍé*, Mubi *fáḍà*) suggests that the underlying Proto-Semito-Hamitic phoneme was unvoiced and therefore the irregular correspondence of Sem. *b to ECush. *f has to be explained by voicing in Semitic rather than by unvoicing in Cushitic. See Black 1974.153, 104, 167, Dolgopolsky 1973.231-2.

(1.24) Sem. *√rbṣ 'to lie' > Aram. √rb' 'to lie', Hebrew √rbṣ 'to lie, couch' (animals), Arab. √rbḍ 'to lay down, to cower', Akkad, √rbṣ 'sich lagern' = ECush. *raf- 'to sleep, spend the night' > Dasenech, Harso, Gollango *raf-* 'to spend the night', Elmolo *rap-* 'to sleep', Galla, Gawwada *raf-* 'to sleep', Hadiyya *lap-* 'to sleep'. See Sasse 1979.22.

2. Sem. *p (and Eg. f, p?) = ECush. *f

(2.1) Sem. *√pry 'to bear fruit, be fruitful' > Hebrew pa:'ra:, Aram., Syr.
pǝ'ra:, Eth. farya; Sem. *'pir(i)y- 'fruit' > Hebrew pǝ'ri:, 'pɛri:,
Phoen., Ugar. pr, Aram., Syr. pe:'ra: 'fruit' = ECush. *fir- > Saho
(Reinisch) fire 'flowers, fruit', faray- 'to blossom, bear fruit', Galla
(Thiene) firi 'frutto'; cp. Agaw: Bilin fir 'fruit', fri- 'to bear fruit' =
Eg. pr.t 'fruit'. See Dolgopolsky 1966.64.

(2.2) Sem. *put- 'vulva' > Hebrew poṯ = ECush. *fut- 'slot' > Somali
Isaaq fúto 'anus', Galla fuči 'vulva'; cp. Chadic: Angas fut 'deep hole'.
See Dolgopolsky 1973.247.

(2.3) Sem. *√p'l 'to do, to make' > Hebrew, Phoen., Aram. √p'l 'to do,
to make', Arab. √f'l 'to do, to act', Tigre √f'l 'to weave' = ECush.:
Proto-Sam *fal- > Somali fal- 'to do, make', Boni fal- 'to make'; cp.
Omotic: Kaffa hal- 'to do, to create', Mocha φalli- 'to create', Gofa
pol- 'to be fulfilled'. See Heine 1978.58, Dolgopolsky 1966.61.

(2.4) Sem. *pars-at- 'hoof' > Hebrew par'sa: 'hoof', Syr. parsǝ'ta: 'hoof' =
ECush. *fer- 'finger' > Afar fe:ra, Somali far, Boni per, Rendille fár,
Elmolo 'far-ro' 'finger', (Heine) parro 'Klaue', Kambatta (Fleming) far
'finger'; cp. Omotic (Koyra parta: 'finger') and Chadic (e.g., Hausa
farče 'finger-nail'). See Heine 1978.59, Black 1974.117, Dolgopolsky
1966.60-61, 1973.41-2.

(2.5) Sem. *√prh > Eth. √frh 'to fear' = ECush.: Proto-Konso *fu:r-
'to fear' > Konso fu:r, Gidole hu:r 'to fear'. See Black 1974.167.

(2.6) Sem. *√pγr 'to open wide (mouth)' > Hebrew, Syr. √p'r, Arab.
√fγr; perh. also Sem. *√prg > Arab. √frǧ 'to open (a door, the
mouth), to part (the legs)' = ECush. *fur- 'to open, to free, to untie'
> Somali fur-, Rendille, Boni fur-, Dasenech, Galla, Konso fur-,
Gidole (Black) fur-iyy-, (Sasse) hur-, Burji fur-; cp. Berber *√frk
(Ahaggar sǝffǝrǝkǝt 'ouvrir, découvrir'). See Sasse 1979.19.

(2.7) Sem. *√pls or *√plϑ > Eth. ta-fa:laṣa 'minutatim diffringi vel
diffindi' = ECush. *falč- (i.e. *fald'₁- in Sasse's symbolization) 'log',
'to split (wood)' > Galla (Thiene) falaṭa 'pezzo di legno spaccato,
travicello', Yāku pilč 'small sticks of firewood'. See Sasse 1979.31, cp.
Dolgopolsky 1973.42.

(2.8) Sem. *'p- (i.e. nom. *'p-u, gen. *'p-i, acc. *'p-a) 'mouth' > Hebrew
'pɛ:, st.c. 'pi:, Arab. fam-, st.c. fu:, fi:, fa:, Akkad. pûm, etc. (see
Dolgopolsky 1978.1, 3-9) = ECush. *'af- 'mouth' > Saho, Afar af,
Rendille, Boni af, Somali af, Dasenech 'af-u, Galla af-a:ni (pl.), Konso
af-a: (pl.), Sidamo, Darasa, Alaba af-o, Burji af-a. See Sasse 1979.19,

51, Dolgopolsky 1973.230-231 (with cognates in other branches of Cushitic).

(2.9) Sem. *√wpʿ > Akkad. *(w)apû* 'sichtbar sein', Hebrew *ho:'p̄i:aʿ* 'to appear, to shine', *yip̄'a:* 'beauty, splendour' = ECush. *ʾif-* 'light (Licht)' > Saho *if-o*, *if-tíin* 'light', Afar Saho *if-is-* (caus.) 'to illuminate', Galla Borana *ib-se* 'light', *ib-s-* (caus.) 'to illuminate', Somali Isāq *i:f* 'daylight, light'. See Black 1974.104, Dolgopolsky 1973.232-3.

(2.10) Sem. *√npx 'to blow' > Akk. √npx 'to blow up (the fire)', Hebrew, Aram. √npḥ, Eth., Arab. √nfx 'to blow', Ugar. mpxm (√npx) 'Blasebalg' = Eg. nf 'breath, wind' = ECush. *nef* > Saho *nef* 'face', Somali *náf* 'soul, self', Galla Borana *nafa* 'body', *nab-se* 'soul'. See Black 1974.166, cp. Dolgopolsky 1973.177.

(2.11) Sem. *√tpl 'to spit' = ECush. *tuf-* 'to spit' (see 4.5).

(2.12) Sem. *√ḳlp 'bark of tree' = ECush. *ḳolf-* 'bark of tree' (see 8.2).

(2.13) Sem. *√zḥp 'to creep' = ECush. *za:f-* 'to creep' (see 11.3).

(2.14) Sem. *√ṣpr 'to plait' = ECush. *ċifr-* 'braid, smth. plaited' (see 12.9).

(2.15) Sem. *√npš 'to breathe' = ECush. *nafs-/*nefs-* 'to breathe, to rest' (see 10.12).

However in the intervocalic position the ECush. correspondence of Sem. *p is sometimes *b:

(2.16) Sem. *√ṣpp 'to press (?)' = ECush. *ċi:p-* 'to squeeze, press' (see 12.10).

(2.17) Sem. *√ṭpʾ 'to close' = ECush. *dib-* 'to cover, to bury' (see 5.4).

(2.18) Sem. *√rʾp 'to drip, trickle' > Arab. *ruʾu:f-* 'fine rains', √rʾf 'to flow (blood)', Hebrew √rʾp 'to drip, trickle' = ECush. *ro:b-* 'rain' > Saho, Afar *rob*, Somali, Boni *ro:b*, Galla *ro:ba*, Konso *ro:pa*, Gidole *ro:p* 'rain', Galla *ro:b-*, Konso, Gidole *ro:p-* 'to rain'. See Black 112, 164, Heine 1978.72, Sasse 1979.22, Dolgopolsky 1973.173.

3. Sem. *d (and Eg. d) = ECush. *d

(3.1) Sem. *dakk-/*dikk- 'thin, fine, minute' > Hebrew *dak(k-)* 'thin, fine', Ug. dḳ 'zart, schwach', Arab. *diqq-* 'fine, minute', *daqqa* 'was fine, minute' = ECush. *dikk-/ dukk-* > Somali *di:q-* 'to become faint, tenuous', Galla *dikk-a* 'small', Hadiyya *ṭukk-a* 'narrow', Harso *ti:kk-assa* 'small'. See Sasse 1979.50.

(3.2) Sem. *√dbr 'hinder, back' > Arab. *dub(u)r-* 'back', *dabu:r* 'western wind', Hebrew *dǝ'ḇi:r* 'the hinder (or western) part of the temple',

Eth. *ta-dabara* 'to fall backwards' (see Leslau 1958.16) = ECush. **dib-/*dub-* 'tail, behind' > Somali *dib* 'short tail', Rendille *dub* 'tail', Boni *tib* 'tail', Elmolo *dup* 'tassel of animal's tail', Dasenech *dum* id., Galla *du(:)b-a* 'behind', Konso *tup-a* 'behind', *tup-p-a:* 'upper back', Alaba *dubb-o* 'tail', Hadiyya *dubb-o* 'behind', Gawwada, Harso, Gollango *tup-* 'behind, after'; ECush. **dab-* 'tail' > Somali *dab-o*, Bayso *deb-e* 'tail'. See Black 1974.177, Sasse 1979.16.

(3.3) Sem. **dall-* 'weak, meager, without strength' > Ugar. dl 'schwach, dürftig', Hebrew *dal(l-)* 'weak, meager, poor', Punic dl 'imparfait, défectueux', Akkad. *dall-u* 'small, inferiour' = ECush.: Somali Isāq *da:l-* 'to be/become tired', *dà:l* 'fatigue'; cp. Omotic: Kaffa *dalli-* 'diventar magro', Mocha *dallo* 'hunger'. See Dolgopolsky 1966.74, 1973.74.

(3.4) Sem. **'daϑ(V)'-* 'grass' > Akk. *dīšu, diš'u, daš'u* 'spring grass', Hebrew *'dɛšɛ* 'grass', OSArabian dϑ', Arab. *daϑa'iyy-* 'spring rain' = SLECush. **de:ẓ-* (or **de:d-*) 'grass' (prob. < **de:s-* > **de:s'-*) > Galla *ḍe:d-*, Konso *ḍe:t-* 'grass', Elmolo *ḍé:t-a*, Arbore *ḍe'd-anta* 'grass'. See Black 1974.260, 266.

(3.5) Sem. **√drr* 'to flow' > Hebrew *dǝ'ro:r* 'flowing' (*mɔr-dǝ'ro:r* 'flowing myrrh'), Arab. *√drr* 'to flow abundantly' (milk) = ECush.: Galla (Thiene) *dorani* 'puddle after the rain'.

(3.6) Eg. dg' 'gehen' = ECush. **dak̲-* 'to come, to go' > Sidamo *da'-*, Hadiyya *ṭa'-* 'to go', Galla *ḍak̲-* 'andare' (in Hadiyya and Galla **ḍak̲-* < **dak̲-* by assimilation?). See Sasse 1979.49.

(3.7) Sem. **ḥadd-* 'sharp' > Hebrew *ḥad(d-)* 'sharp', Arab. *ḥadd-* 'pungent', 'hot' (sun), 'hot tempered', Akkad. *eddu* 'spitzig' = ECush. **ḥadd-* 'bitter' (< **ḥadd-* under the influence of the laryngeal **ḥ*, cp. **ḥek-/ *ḥok-* 'to scratch' < **ḥVk-*, cognate of Sem. **√ḥkk*) > Galla *ḥadd-aa* 'bitter', Konso, Gidole *ḥadd-aw* 'to become bitter', Konso *ḥadd-a:* 'snake venom', Rendille *ḥa'ḍâḍ* 'bad tasting', Boni *ḥa'ré:r* 'bitter'. See Black 1974.196, Sasse 1979.54, Heine 1978.63, Dolgopolsky 1973.249.

(3.8) Sem. **√'bd* 'to get lost' = ECush. **bad-* 'to get lost' (see 1.2).

(3.9) Sem. **√ḳdḥ* 'to bore, to perforate' = ECush. **ḳadḥ-/*ḳudḥ-* 'thorn' (see 8.3).

(3.10) Sem. **√rdy* 'to step, to run' > Syriac *√rdy/w* 'to walk, to run', Arabic *√rdy* 'to beat the ground in running', Hebrew *√rdy/w* 'to tread', Akkad. *redû* 'gehen, (mit sich) führen, begleiten' = ECush. **-rd-* 'to run' > Afar *-erd-*, Somali *ord-* 'to run', Boni, Rendille *-irid-* 'rennen', Somali *rà:d* 'footprint' = Eg. rd 'foot'. See Black 1974.152, Sasse 1979.23, 1980.163-72, Dolgopolsky 1973.241.

(3.11) Sem. *√wrd 'to descend' > Akkad. √wrd 'hinab-, herabsteigen, hinuntergehen', Hebrew √y/wrd (pf. ya :'rad, caus. pf. ho :'ri :d) 'to descend' = Saho, Afar (Reinisch) ra :d- 'to fall'.

(3.12) Sem. *√w'd 'to bury' > Arab. √w'd 'to bury (alive)', ta-wa :'ada 'to conceal somebody (the land)' = ECush. *wV't- 'to sow', 'seed' > Bayso (Bender) wuta 'a seed', Sidamo (Moreno) wite id., Hadiyya (Plazikowsky-Brauner) wi :to id., Kambatta (Cerulli) wiṭ- 'to seed'. For this method of reconstructing ECush. *' see Black 1974.210, Sasse 1979.54. See Dolgopolsky 1973.189. The irregular correspondence of Sem. *d to ECush. *t is perhaps due to assimilation in a consonant cluster.

(3.13) Eg. wdd 'to boil' (itr., tr.) = ECush. *wa :d- 'to roast' > Galla wa :d-, Konso, Gawwada wa :t- 'to roast'. See Black 1974.101.

4. Sem. *t (and Eg. t) = ECush. *t

(4.1) Sem. *t-, prefix of 2nd pers. forms of the verb (prefix-conjugation) = ECush. *t-, prefix of 2nd pers. > Saho, Afar, Somali, Rendille, Boni, Dasenech t-, 2nd pers. marker in prefix-conjugation, as well as ECush. *-t-, initial element of the 2nd pers. suffixes in suffix-conjugation (going back to the 2nd pers. prefix of an auxiliary verb in ancient periphrastic conjugations, see Dolgopolsky 1972b.103-5, Zaborski 1975a).

(4.2) Sem. *t-, prefix of 3 sg. f. of the verb (prefix-conjugation) = ECush. *t-, prefix of 3 sg. f. (prefix-conjugation) > t-, 3 sg. f. prefix in Saho, Afar, Somali, Rendille, Boni, Dasenech, as well as 3 sg. f. prefix *-t- of an auxiliary verb in periphrastic conjugations, underlying the tenses of suffix-conjugation in ECush. languages: Galla 3 sg. f. impf. -ti, pf. -te, Somali 3 sg. f. impf. -ta :, pf. -tay', Sidamo 3 sg. f. dependent imperfect -ta, 3 sg.f. dependent perfect -te, etc. See Dolgopolsky 1972b.103-5, Zaborski 1975a.

(4.3) Sem. *till-/*tall- 'hill, heap (of stones)' > Hebrew tel, till-, JAram. til'l-a :, Syr. tɛll-a :, Arab. tall-un = SLECush. *tu :l- 'to pile up' > Somali, Galla, Konso tu :l- 'to pile up'. See Black 1974.185.

(4.4) Sem. *√tk' 'to strike' > Hebrew √tk' 'to drive, to thrust', Aram. √tk' 'to strike, to blow', Eth. √tk' 'to blow (trumpet)' = ECush. *-tak-/*-tuk- 'to touch, to push, to strike' > Afar -o :tok- 'to strike', Galla tuk- 'to touch', Rendile (Heine) tax- 'to push', Dasenech ta'- 'to push'. See Sasse 1979.48, Dolgopolsky 1973.276.

(4.5)　Sem. *√tpl > Arab. √tfl 'to spit' = Eg. tf 'to spit' = ECush. *tuf- 'to spit' > Afar, Somali, Galla, Arbore, Konso, Sidamo tuf-, Gidole šuh-, Dullay tuf- ~ čuf- 'to spit'. See Black 1974.166, 184, Sasse 1979.10.

(4.6)　Sem. *'anta 'thou' (m.), *'anti 'thou' (f.) = ECush. *'ati 'thou' > Saho, Afar at-u, Somali adi(-ga), Boni adi, Bayso, Rendille, Galla, Sidamo ati, Konso at-ti, Gidole at-te, Dullay ato ~ ačo, cp. Agaw *'ənt(i) 'thou' and Eg. intk 'thou' (m.), intč 'thou' (f.). See Sasse 1981.144, 1979.10, Black 1974.131-2, 184, Diakonoff 1965.71, Dolgopolsky 1973.133-4.

(4.7)　Sem. *√'ty 'to come' = ECush. *-'tʾiʾ 'to come' (> Boni, Elmolo). See Sasse 1980.

(4.8)　Sem. *'antim 'you' (pl. m.) = ECush. *'atin/*'itin 'you' (pl.) > Saho átin, Afar ísin, Somali idín-ka, Dasenech itini, Konso išina; cp. Agaw *'əntən 'you' (pl.). See Sasse 1981.144, 1979,11, Black 1974.131, Dolgopolsky 1973.134-5.

(4.9)　Sem. *√ḥtt > Arab. √ḥtt 'to rub off (mud)' = SLECush. *ḥa:ḍ- 'to sweep, rub off' (*t > *ḍ under the laryngealizing influence of *ḥ, cp. 3.7 and 7.10) > Somali ḥa:ḍ- 'sweep', Rendille (Heine) hár, Galla ḥa:ḍ- 'grattare, raschiare, raspare', Dasenech e:t (imp.) 'sweep'. See Black 1974.260, Dolgopolsky 1973.249.

(4.10)　Eg. ḥwtf 'to steal, to rob' = SLECush. ḥat- 'to steal' > Somali ḥad-, Galla, Konso ḥat-, Gidole ḥaš- 'to steal'. See Black 1974.185, 200.

(4.11)　Sem. *put- 'vulva' = ECush. *fut- 'slot, vulva' (see 2.2).

(4.12)　Sem.: Syr. kəta:ya:, kəta:ta: 'pit' = ECush. *kot- 'to dig' (see 8.8).

(4.13)　Sem. *-mu:t 'to die' > Hebrew, Aram. (impf.) -mu:t, Arab. (impf.) -mu:t-, Eth. (subj.), Akkad. (pret.) -mu:t 'to die' = Eg. mt 'to die', 'death' = ECush. *-mu:t 'to die' > Rendille (Schlee) amut 'ich sterbe', Gidole mu:t 'totkrank'. See Heine 1978.35, 52, Schlee 1978.17-9, Sasse 1980.165-7.

5. Sem. *ṭ (and Eg. d?) = ECush. *ḍ

(5.1)　Sem. *ṭa'lay- 'young (of an animal), young person' > Hebrew ṭa:'lɛ: 'lamb', JAram. ṭalya: 'Jüngling, Lamm', Syr. ṭalya: 'a youth', Arab. ṭala-n 'young (of a sheep, goat, antelope)', Eth. ṭali: 'goat' = ECush. *ḍal- 'to beget, to give birth' > Saho, Afar, Somali ḍal-, Rendille ḍel-, Boni ḍel-, Dasenech, Galla ḍal-, Konso ḍal-/ḍel-, Gidole ḍal-, Dullay ḍal-, Yāku del-. See Black 1974.163, 195, Sasse 1979.21, 30, cp. Dolgopolsky 1973.58.

(5.2) Sem. *√*ṭʿm* 'to taste, have taste' > Hebrew, Aram., Eth. √*ṭʿm* id.,
Arab. √*ṭʿm* 'to taste', Akkad. *ṭeːmu* 'Verstand' = SLECush. *ḍaʿm-
'to taste' > Saho (Welmers) *ḍaʿam-* 'to taste', Somali (Reinisch) *ḍaʿan*,
pl. *ḍaʿmo* 'taste, juice, sauce', Galla (Thiene) *ḍama* 'sugo, succo, stero'.
See Dolgopolsky 1973.317-8.

(5.3) Sem.: Arab. *ṭawwaḥa* 'to strike with a stick' = ECush. *ḍaw-* 'to hit,
strike' > Galla *ḍa-e* (pf.) 'he hit', Konso, Gidole (pf.) *ḍáw-é* 'he hit',
Elmolo *ḍa-* 'to hit, strike', Arbore (pf.) *da-y-iy*, Dasenech *ḍo-*. See Black
1974.212, Sasse 1979.43.

(5.4) Sem. *√*ṭpʾ/w* > Aram., Syr. *ṭᵊpaː* 'to close, be closed', Arab., Eth.
√*ṭfʾ* 'to go out' (fire) = ECush. *ḍib-* 'to cover, to bury' (see Sasse
1979.54), cp. Agaw *√*dbb* 'to cover, to bury' (Agaw *d* corresponds
to ECush. *ḍ* and Sem. *ṭ*).

(5.5) Sem. *-xiːṭ/*-xuːṭ 'to sew' > Arab. *xaːṭa* (impf. *-xiːṭ-*), Aram. *ḥaːṭ*
(impf. *-ḥuːṭ*) = ECush. *ḥiḍ-* 'to tie' > Afar *ḥiḍ-* 'to attach camels in
Indian file', Somali, Rendille *ḥiḍ-* 'to tie', Galla, Konso, Gidole *ḥiḍ-*,
Dasenech *ḥiẕ/t-* 'to tie'. See Black 1974.195, Sasse 1979.36, Heine
1978.64, Dolgopolsky 1973.159, 222.

(5.6) Eg. dbḥ 'to need, ask for (esp. food, drink)' = ECush. *ḍeːb-* 'thirst,
to be thirsty' > Galla *ḍeːb-oḍ-*, Konso, Gidole *ḍeːp-oḍ-* 'to become
thirsty', Galla *ḍeːbu*, Hadiyya *ṭeːba* 'thirst'. See Black 1974.110,
Dolgopolsky 1973.230.

6. Sem. *g (and Eg. g, ǧ) = ECush. *g

(6.1) Sem. *gir(r)-* > Akkad. *gir-um*, *girr-um* 'fire, god of fire' = Eg.
ǧr 'fire' = ECush. *gir-* 'fire', 'to burn' > Saho, Afar *gira* 'fire',
Sidamo, Hadiyya *gir(a)* 'fire', *gir-* 'to burn', Kambatta (Leslau) *giräta*,
Tembaro *girato* 'fire', Burji (Moreno) *ǧira* 'fire'. See Dolgopolsky
1973.202-3.

(6.2) Sem. *√*grʿ* 'to cut (hair)' > Hebrew, Aram., Syr., Mehri (Šxauri
dial., Bittner) √*grʿ*, Soḳoṭri (Leslau) √*grḥ* = ECush. *-grVʿ-* 'to cut'
> Saho (Welmers) *-egreʿ-*; ECush. *gawraʿ-* 'to cut throat' > Somali
gowraʿ- id., Boni *kuːraʿ-* 'to butcher' (see Heine 1978.60, Sasse 1979.45,
Dolgopolsky 1973.316).

(6.3) Sem. *-giːʾ* > Arab. *ǧaːʾa* (basic form *-ǧiːʾ-*) 'to come, to arrive' =
ECush. *gay-* 'to arrive' > Afar *gay-*, Somali (caus.) *geː-y-* (< *gay-y-*),
Galla *ga(y)-*, Konso *kay-*, Dullay *o-kay-*. See Sasse 1979.43.

(6.4) Sem. *√*gnḥ* 'wing, arm' > Arab. *ǧinaːḥ-* 'arm, wing', Mehri (Šxauri
dial., Bittner) *giʾnaḥ* 'wing' = Eg. ǧnḥ 'wing', gnḫ 'wing' = ECush.

*gan'- 'palm of hand, hand' > Saho gina', Afar gena'-ta, Somali ga'an, Boni ka'an, Bayso gene, Galla gana-a, Konso kan-a:ta, Gidole kana'-at, Dullay kana'-'-e (pl.), Yāku kinnɛ'-. See Black 1974.141, 161, Sasse 1979.17, 26, 54, Dolgopolsky 1973.316.

(6.5)   Sem. *√glḫ > Arab. ġaliḫa (impf. -ġlaḫ-) 'to be bald-headed', Hebrew gillaḫ 'to cut one's hair' = ECush. *√glḫ > Somali (Reinisch) galaḫ-i 'baldness of the head', galḫo, galḫadi 'seitwärtige Glatze von den Schläfen aufwärts'; cp. in other Cushitic languages: Bilin (Reinisch) gʷalḫay- 'to be bald-headed', Bedauye (Reinisch) gʷal'a 'baldness of the head'. See Dolgopolsky 1973.71.

(6.6)   Sem. *'gab(V)'- 'hill' > Ugar. gb', Hebrew 'gɛba', gib''a: 'hill', Akkad. gab'a:ni (pl.) 'heights'; Sem. *gabal- > Arab. ġabal- 'mountain' = ECush. *gub- 'mountain' > Galla (Thiene) gubba, -n 'cima, sommite', Dasenech gum 'mountain'. See Sasse 1979.15.

(6.7)   Sem. *√gbb > Akkad. gubbubu 'to roast' = ECush. *gub- 'to burn' (tr.) > Somali, Rendille, Galla gub-, Konso kup-, Boni kub- 'to burn', Yāku kup 'rot'. See Black 1974.182, Heine 1978.61, Sasse 1979.17.

(6.8)   Syr. gls 'monkey' (< Sem. *√gls or *√glš?) = ECush. *gelẓ- 'baboon' > Galla ġald-e:sa, Konso, Gidole kelt-ayta, Sidamo galad-o, Harso kals-akko. See Sasse 1979.18, 20.

(6.9)   Sem. *√g'y 'to call, to cry' > Hebrew ga:''a: (impf. -ḡ'ɛ: < *-g'ay) 'to cry', Syr. √g'y/w 'to call', JAram. √g'y/w 'brüllen' = ECush. *mag'- 'name' (a derived noun with the prefix *ma- fr. a verb *√g' meaning 'to call'?) > Saho, Afar miga', Somali maga', Rendille magaḫ, Bayso me:ge, Konso maxxa, Gidole maḫḫ(a), Arbore meke'e, Boni ma'ag, Galla maka:, Gawwada makḫ-akko, Harso makaḫ-ko. See Sasse 1979.17.

(6.10) Sem.: Akkad. gaṣṣ-at-u 'firewood' = ECush. *ge:ẓ- 'tree' > Somali geid, (Jabarti) ge:d, Rendille gey, Boni ke:, pl. ke:tĕ. See Heine 1978.60, Sasse 1976.137, Dolgopolsky 1973.62.

(6.11) Sem. *√grn 'to be old (?)' > Arab. √ġrn 'to be worn out' (clothes), 'to be trained' (beast) = ECush. *ger'- 'to grow old' > Galla ġa:r-, Konso ker-, Mashile, Bussa ker'-, Gidole ker'- ∼ kerḍ- 'to grow old', Arbore gair 'old', Dasenech ge:re, Elmolo gere, Sidamo (Moreno) ge:r-čo 'old'. See Black 1974.207, Sasse 1979.37, Dolgopolsky 1972a.208.

(6.12) Sem. *ganb- 'side' > Syr. gabba: 'side (latus)', Arab. ġanb- 'side' = ECush. *gVb- 'river bank, ditch' > Somali géb-i 'river bank', Konso káp-a, Gidole káp 'irrigation ditch', Gawwada kap-te id.; cp. Bilin gaf 'side, half', Hamir gǝba id., Bedauye gäb ∼ geb 'side'. See Black 1974.136, Dolgopolsky 1972a.199.

(6.13) Sem. *-gu:r 'to dwell (temporarily)' > Bibl. Hebrew ga:r (impf. -gu:r) 'to dwell as a guest (foreigner)', Middle Hebrew ga:r, -gu:r 'to dwell', Arab. ǧa:wara 'to live close by', ta-ǧa:wara 'to live near together' = ECush. *gir- 'to be, exist' > Somali, Rendille, Galla ǧir-, Boni šir-, Bayso gir- 'to be, exist', Konso kir-a 'life'. See Black 1974.182, Sasse 1979.18.

(6.14) Eg. gb' 'arm' = Saho gabaá, Afar gaba 'hand'. See Black 1974.297, Dolgopolsky 1972a.206 (comparaison with Chadic cognate words).

(6.15) Sem. *√ϑgg 'to flow' = ECush. *si:g- 'to move, come, go' (see 9.4).

(6.16) Eg. nǧm 'health' = ECush. *nagay- 'well-being' > Saho (Reinisch) naga: 'peace, well-being, health', Galla naga(y)a, Konso nakay-ta 'well-being', Dullay nakay-ho 'peace, health'. See Black 1974.160, Sasse 1979.43.

(6.17) Eg. dg' 'gehen' = ECush. *dak- 'to come, go'; *ḳ < *g' (see 3.6).

7. Sem. *k (and Eg.) = ECush. *k

(7.1) Sem. *ka 'thee, thy' (m.) > Akkad., Arab., Eth. -ka, Hebrew -ka: 'thee, thy' (m.), Akkad. (Babyl.) kâta 'thee' m., kûm 'thy' m., Old Assyr. kuāti 'thee' m., ku'ā'um 'thy' m. (vowels on analogy with šuāti 'him', šu'ā'um 'his') = Eg. -k 'thy' m. = ECush. *ku ~ *ke 'thee' > Saho, Somali, Boni ku, Dasenech kô, Konso ke, Hadiyya ke:-s, Sidamo -he:, Burji še 'thee'; ECush. *kV 'thy' > Saho ku, Galla (-káŋ, -táŋ)-kê, Rendille (ka-, ta-)ha, Sidamo -ki, Hadiyya ki, ki:(k). See Sasse 1973.13, Tucker-Bryan 1966.521-3. For cognates in other Cushitic, Berber and Chad languages see Diakonoff 1965.71-7, Dolgopolsky 1973.77-8.

(7.2) Sem. *'kulay-at- (~ *'kalay-at-?) 'kidney' > Bibl. Hebrew kəla:'yo:t pl., Middle Hebrew (Babyl. vocalization) kul'ya: sg., Arab. kulyat-un, Ugar. *klyt, Eth. kʷəli:t, Akkad. kali:t-u = ECush. *kal- 'kidney' > Somali kal-lí, Konso xal-l-a:, Galla kal-ê. See Black 1974.136, 192, Sasse 1979.12, Dolgopolsky 1973.77.

(7.3) Sem. *karkar- 'a circle' > Hebrew kik'ka:r 'round loaf of bread, disk, circle', Akkad. kakkar-u 'round bread, disk', Old South Arabian krkr 'load' or 'measure' = ECush. *kar-/*kir- /(?)*kor- 'round, a circular formation' > Konso kur-eta 'circular dance', Galla kor-a, Somali šir 'assembly'. See Sasse 1979.9.

(7.4) Eg. kp 'Fußsohle', čb.t, čb.w 'Sandale' = ECush. *kob 'shoe, sandal' > Afar kab-el, Somali kab, Boni kôb, Rendille kob, Dasenech ko-ti,

Arbore *kób-o*, Elmolo *kop(-o')*, Galla (Borana) *kob-e'*, (Wollega) *kop-e'*,
Konso *xop-ta*, Gidole *hop-a:*, Gawwada *xopé*. See Black 1974.151, 175,
Sasse 1979.12, Heine 1978.66.

(7.5) Sem. **k-*, **ka:* 'in this (?)' > Aram., Syr. *ka:* 'here', Hebrew *ko:* 'so',
Akkad. *ka:*, *ki:a(m)* 'thus' = ECush. **ka*, nom. **ku*, masc. demonstr.
pronoun > Somali *-ka/-ga/-ha* (nom. *-ku/-gu/-hu*) 'the', Bayso *hikina*
'this' m. (cp. *atina* f.), Galla *-k-*, masc. marker in forms with pronominal suffixes (e.g. *-k-o*, *-k-iya* 'my' m., *-k-e:* 'thy' m., *-k-e:na* 'our'
m.), Sidamo *-ha* (nom. *-hu*), substantivizing article m., *ko*, *ku*, *konne*
'this' m. (cp. *te*, *tenne* f.), Hadiyya *ka*, *kak*, nom. *ku*, *ka(h)* 'this' m.
(cf. fem.: *ta*, *tat*, nom. *tu*, *ta*, *tah*), Darasa *kuni* 'this' m., Kambatta
konni 'this'. See Sasse 1979.62, Dolgopolsky 1973.258-9.

(7.6) Sem. **kawr-* 'stove, furnace' > Syr. *kawra:*, Eth. *kawr*, Akkad. *ku:r-*
(> Hebrew *ku:r* 'furnace') = SLECush. **kar-* 'to boil' (itr.) >
Somali *kari* 'to cook, boil' (tr.), Boni *'kárĕ* id., Rendille *'kári* id.,
Konso *xar-*, Gidole *har-* 'to boil' itr. Elmolo *kar-is-* 'to cook'. See
Black 1974.190, Heine 1978.66.

(7.7) Sem. **kV* 'to' > Minaean *k* 'to', Mehri, Śxeri, Ḥarsusi, Soḳoṭri
k(ə)- 'with', prob. also Ugar. *k-* 'als', 'zu' (final) = ECush. **kV* 'to'
> Saho *-(a)k* 'to' (*faras-ak* 'to the horse'), Somali (Benadir, Darod)
ku 'to (him)' (*Liba:ḥi: waḥow wara:bihi: ku yiri* 'The lion said to the
hyaena', lit. '... the hyaena to said'), Dasenech *ká* 'to', 'her-' (preverb),
Sidamo *-ho* 'to' (*he:'to:-ho* 'to the girl'), Burji *-ha/-ga* 'to' (dative
marker). See Dolgopolsky 1973.259.

(7.8) Sem. **√nkϑ* 'to bite' > JAram., Syr. *√nkt* 'to bite', Eth. *√nks* 'to
bite' = ECush. **kis-* (or **kiš-*) > Sidamo (Cerulli) *kis-* 'to bite'; cp.
Berber: Tahaggart *əkš* 'to bite, eat'.

(7.9) Sem. **√'lk* > Arab. *√'lk* 'to champ (the bit)' (horse), and Sem.
-lu:k- > Arab. *la:ka* (impf. *-lu:k-*) 'to chew' = ECush. **'ilk-* 'tooth'
> Saho *ik-o*, Somali *ilig-*, pl. *ilk-o*, Rendille *ilaḫ*, pl. *ilk-o*, Boni pl. *ilk-*
ĕ, Bayso *ilk-o*, Arbore *ilk-wa*, Elmolo *ilk-o'*, Galla *ilk-a:ni*, Konso
ilk-itta, Gidole *ilh-*, Gawwada *ilg-e*, Harso *ilg-akko*, Burji *ilka ~ irka*,
(?) Sidamo *(h)inko*; cp. Agaw **ərkʷ-* (> Bilin, Awngi *ərkʷi*, etc.)
'tooth'. See Sasse 1979.12, Dolgopolsky 1973.269-70.

(7.10) Sem. **√ḥkk* 'to scratch' > Arab. *√ḥkk*, Akkad. *eke:ku* = ECush.
*ḥek-/*ḥoḳ- 'to scratch' (**k* > **ḳ* under the influence of **ḥ* ? — cp.
3.7 and 4.8) > Saho *hokuk-*, Somali *ḥoq-*, *ḥaqḥaq-*, Rendille *ox-*, Boni
ho'-, Arbore *hek-*, Galla *ho:ḳ-*, Gidole *hek-*, Burji *hoḳo:ḳ-*. See Sasse
1979.48, 50.

8. Sem. *ḳ (and Eg. ḳ) = ECush. *ḳ

(8.1) Sem. *ḳall- 'small, light (levis)' > Akkad. ḳall-u 'light, small, small in
       number', Hebrew ḳal(l-) 'light', ḳal(lo:-) pf. 'was light', Arab. ḳall-a
       'was small in number, rare' = ECush. *ḳall- (or *ḳal'-) 'thin,
       insignificant' > Saho all-o 'vanity, nothingness', Galla ḳall-a: 'subtle,
       thin, meager', Konso qalla'- 'thin', Gidole ḳalla'- 'narrow', Burji ḳall-
       ane: 'thin'. See Sasse 1979.22, 78, Dolgopolsky 1973.190.

(8.2) Sem. *√ḳlp 'to strip off bark' > Akkad., Aram., Syr., Middle
       Hebrew √ḳlp, Arab. √qlf; Sem. *'ḳil(V)p- 'bark, skin' (> Akkad.,
       Arab., Middle Hebrew), *ḳula:p-(at-) 'bark' (> Akkad., Syr., Arab.)
       = ECush. *ḳolf- 'bark of a tree' > Saho ḳolof-o, Somali qolóf, Konso
       qólf-a: 'bark', Galla ḳolof-a 'foreskin'. See Black 1974.144, Sasse
       1979.22, 48.

(8.3) Sem. *√ḳdḥ 'to bore, perforate, grind fire' > Arab. √qdḥ 'to make
       a hole, perforate, strike fire', Aram., Middle Hebrew √ḳdḥ 'to bore,
       perforate, kindle' = ECush. *ḳadḥ-/*ḳudḥ- 'thorn' > Somali qodáḥ,
       Galla ḳor-atti', Gidole ḳudd-eét, Konso qeét-ta, Elmolo eḍ, Sidamo uta,
       Hadiyya utta 'thorn', Rendille xadaḥ 'leaf'. See Black 1974.180, Sasse
       1979.49, Dolgopolsky 1973.81.

(8.4) Sem. *√ḳṣṣ 'to cut' > Ugar., Hebrew, Aram., Syr. √ḳṣṣ, Arab. √qṣṣ
       'to cut (off)' = ECush. *ḳaṣ 'to cut' > Saho (Reinisch) aḍ- 'to cut
       hair', Dullay qaṭṭ- 'to cut, hoe up, fold', Yāku qaṭ- 'to cut'. See Sasse
       1979.31, 48.

(8.5) Eg. ḳb(b) 'cold' = ECush. *ḳab- 'cold' > Somali qabow, Rendille
       'xóbo 'cold', Galla ḳab-ban-a, Konso qap-pan-na:w-, Gidole ḳap-pan-
       naw- 'to become cool', Arbore ḳab-ata, Elmolo -ap-an- 'cold'. See
       Black 1974.198, Heine 1978.71, Sasse 1979.49.

(8.6) Sem. *ḳa(:)r- 'beam, stick' > Hebrew ḳo:'ra:, Aram., Syr. ḳa:ri:ṭa:
       'beam', Arab. qari:yat- 'stick', Akkad. ḳari:t-u 'Kornboden, Speicher'
       = ECush. *ḳor- 'wood, tree' > Saho or- 'to hew', Somali qori, Boni
       'orĕ, Rendille 'xóro 'wood, firewood', Somali qor- 'to trim timber',
       Galla 'ḳor-a:ni, Konso 'qor-a:, Gidole 'ḳor-a:, Dasenech gôr, Elmolo
       'or-o', Arbore 'ḳoro 'wood'. See Black 1974.111-2, 97, Heine 1978.71,
       Sasse 1979.48, 49, Dolgopolsky 1973.24.

(8.7) Sem. *√ḳr' 'to tear' > Hebrew, Aram. √ḳr', Arab. (Maghreb) √qr'
       'to tear' (and prob. Sem. *√ḳrṣ 'to cut' > Arab. √qrḍ, Middle
       Hebrew √ḳrṣ, Sem. *√ḳrṣ 'to curtail' > Akkad. √ḳrṣ, Arab. √qrṣ)
       = ECush. *ḳer-/*ḳu:r- 'to cut' > Galla (Thiene) ḳŏr-u 'incidere,
       cesellare, lavorare il legno', Gidole ḳu:r-, Elmolo ur-, Arbore ḳur-
       'to cut', Konso qu:r- 'to cut up'. See Black 1974.260, Sasse 1979.5.

(8.8) Sem.: Syr. *ḳəta:ya:*, *ḳəta:ṭa:* 'pit' = ECush. **ḳot-* 'to dig' > Somali *qod-*, Boni *od-*, Rendille *xut-* 'to dig, cultivate', Galla *ḳot-*, Gidole *ḳoš-* 'to dig', Arbore *ḳot-* 'to plow', Dasenech *got/ẓ-* 'to dig, bury', Gawwada *qot-* (or *ġot-*) 'to dig'. See Black 1974.112, Heine 1978.71, Sasse 1979.10.

(8.9) Sem. **ḳarr-* 'cold' (adj.) > Hebrew *ḳar*, Arab. *qarr-* 'cold'; Sem. **ḳurr-* 'cold' (n.) > Hebrew *ḳor*, Arab. *qurr-*, Eth. *ḳ"ər(r)* = ECush. **ḳorr-* 'cold' > Galla (Thiene) *ḳorra* 'intense cold', Sidamo (Cerulli) *ḳorr-e:* 'cold'.

(8.10) Eg. nḳw.t 'Feuchtigkeit' = ECush. **ḳoyy-* 'wet' > Somali, Konso *qoyy-*, Arbore *ḳuy-iy'oa* 'wet'. See Black 1974.198, Sasse 1979.49.

9. Sem. *ϑ (and Eg. s) = ECush. *s

(9.1) Sem. **-ϑi:n-* 'to urinate' > Akkad. *šia:num* (pret. *-ši:n*), Syr. *ta:n*, Eth. *še:na* 'to urinate', Arab. *maϑa:nat-* 'bladder'; Sem. **'ϑay(V)n-* 'urine' > Akkad. *ši:na:t-um*, Hebrew *'šayin*, Syr. *ti:na:*, Eth. *šənt* = ECush. **sinç-* 'urine' > Galla *finç-a:ni*, Konso, Gidole *sind-a:*, Arbore *iy-sind-aye*, Dasenech *sinn-a* 'urine'. See Black 1974.216, Sasse 1979.24.

(9.2) Sem. *$\sqrt{}$$\vartheta$km* 'shoulders, back' > Hebrew *šə'ḳεm* 'shoulders, upper part of the back', Ugar. ϑkm, Eth. (denom. verb) $\sqrt{}$*skm* 'to carry on the shoulders' = ECush. **sug-/*'s'unk-/?*'s'akm-* 'shoulders, back' > Dasenech *sugu* 'back', Galla (Foot) *fugiso* 'upside down', Saho *sunku* 'shoulder joint' (cp. Bedauye Ammar'ar *'u sink"a* 'shoulder'), Somali (Reinisch) *sagan*, pl. *sagmo* 'Nacken, Genick'. See Sasse 1976.127-8, Dolgopolsky 1973.91. More accurate reconstruction of the ECush. root will be possible only when the development of consonant clusters is better explored.

(9.3) Sem. *$\sqrt{}$$\vartheta$'w* 'sheep' > Ugar. ϑà-t 'ewe', Arab. ϑ*a:'aw-at-* 'old sheep' (Aistleitner 1967.329-30) = Berber: Tahaggart *i-sa:-n* 'meat, flesh' = ECush. **so'-* 'meat' > Galla *fo:-ni*, Konso *sów-a:*, Gidole *sóh-a:*, Gato *só'-a*, Bayso *so:*, Dasenech *sú*, Elmolo *sow'*, Arbore *só-ra*, Somali *so'*. See Black 1974.205, Sasse 1979.50, 52.

(9.4) Sem. *$\sqrt{}$$\vartheta$gg* > Arab. *$\sqrt{}$$\vartheta$ġġ* 'to flow' = ECush. **si:g-* 'to move, to come and go' > Saho (Reinisch) *si:g-* 'to advance', Galla *fi:g-* 'to run', Konso *si:ḳ-* 'to come and go (like bees)'. See Black 1974.104, 168.

(9.5) Sem. *$\sqrt{}$lϑlϑ* > Arab. *$\sqrt{}$lϑlϑ* 'to be weak, feeble' = ECush. **lVs-* > Saho *lislis* 'soft', Galla *la:fa* 'soft'; cp. Agaw **ləs-* 'soft' > Hamir (Reinisch) *lis-* 'to be soft'.

(9.6) Sem. *baϑan/m- 'venomous snake' = ECush. *bos- 'snake' (see 1.3).

(9.7) Eg. sn 'riechen' = ECush. *san-/*sin-/*son-/*sun- 'nose' > Afar san, Somali san, Boni sa, Rendille sám, Galla fún-na :ni, Gidole sín-a :, Gato són-a, Dasenech sò :n-ò, Arbore són-o, Sidamo, Darasa, Alaba sano, Kambatta sänuta, Hadiyya sane :, Burji suna. See Black 1974.151, Sasse 1979.5, 24, Dolgopolsky 1973.109-110.

In one root Sem. *ϑ corresponds to ECush. *s:

(9.8) Sem. *√γ/ϑ 'to be thick, bulky' > Arab. √γ/z̧ id. = ECush. *'ils-/*'uls- 'heavy' > Afar 'ils-i, Somali 'ulús, Galla úlf-āta', Konso uls-, Dasenech iliš, Elmolo ils-ída, Arbore ilč-íɣda 'heavy', Rendille ḥulês 'heaviness'. See Black 1974.139, 168.

In the root for 'three' (Sem. *√slϑ = ECush. *sazih/*šVz̧h-, see 10.8) we find ECush. voiced *z̧ corresponding to Sem. unvoiced *ϑ, which is prob. to be explained by combinatory factors (*ls > *z̧?).

10. Sem. *š, *ś (= Eg. s and perh. š) = ECush. *š

(10.1) Sem. *š-, causative prefix > Akkad., Ugar., Minaean š-, Modern South Arabian š- (causative-reflexive), Sabaean, Hebrew, OAram. h-, JAram., Syr., Arab., Eth. '- = Eg. s-, causative prefix = ECush. *-š-, causative verbal prefix or suffix, with the allomorph *s before consonants, according to the ECush. morphophonemic rule *š → *s / —C. See Sasse 1979.32, Diakonoff 1965.98-101, Dolgopolsky 1973.287.

(10.2) Sem. *ya'šar- 'straight' > Akkad. išar-, Hebrew ya :'ša :r, Aram. yaš'ra :'straight', Arab. yasar-'easy, gentle, tractable' = ECush.*šVr- 'straight' > Galla (Thiene) sir(-ri) 'straight', Sidamo (Moreno) se :ra 'straight'.

(10.3) Sem. *-šu :p > Arab. sa :fa (impf. -su :fu) 'to smell a th.', Aram. šay'yeβ 'anblasen (Wind), anfachen (Feuer)' = ECush.: Galla (Thiene) suf-'to smell a th.' (Galla s < ECush. *š).

(10.4) Sem. *-šu :p 'to rub (off)' > Hebrew, Aram., Syr. ša :β (impf. -šu :β) = ECush. ≈*šo :f- 'to file' > Galla (Thiene) so :f- 'to file, to saw', Somali só :f-e 'lime'. See Reinisch 1900-3 :2.336, Zaborski 1975b.324.

(10.5) Sem. *√špy (or *√ϑpy) 'to sew, to tie up' > Eth. √sfy 'to sew', Akkad. šapû 'einbinden, einnesteln' = ECush.: Galla (Thiene) supp- (< *šub'- ?) 'to darn'.

(10.6) Sem. *šibb-, *√šbb 'vein, rope' > Syr. šɛbbe : 'veins', Arab. sibb- 'turban, piece of thin stuff', sabab- 'rope' = ECush. *še :b- 'leather strap' > Galla *se:p-ani*, Dasenech *se:b* 'leather strap', Harso *še:p-akko* 'leather belt'. See Sasse 1979.33.

(10.7) Sem. *√*šḳ'* (or *√*sḳ'*) > Arab. √*sq'* 'to knock' = ECush. *šoḳ- 'to beat, hit' > Galla *soḳ* 'to weed, cut off', Hadiyya *sukk-* 'to beat, hit', Dullay *šoq-* 'to hit'. See Sasse 1979.33. Perhaps Sem. and Eg. verbs with root-"élargissements" (such as Sem. *√*škp* > Syr. √*škp* 'verberavit, contudit' and Eg. skr 'to beat') also belong here.

(10.8) Sem. *√*ślϑ* 'three' > Akkad. √*šlš*, Sabaean, Minaean, Mehri, Śxeri √*šlϑ*, Eth. √*šls*, CSem. *√*ϑlϑ* (assimilation fr. *√*šlϑ*) > Ugar., Arab. √*ϑlϑ*, Hebrew √*šlš*, Aram. √*tlt* = ECush. *šaziḥ/*šVzḥH- 'three' > Afar *sidoḥu*, Somali (Isāq) *saddeḥ*, (Jiddu) *seye*, Rendille *séyyaḥ*, Boni *siddè'*, Bayso *sɛdi'*, Galla *sadi'*, Konso *sessa*, Arbore *sezi-ra*, Dasenech *seddi*, Sidamo *sasse*, Kambatta, Alaba, Hadiyya *sasso*, Burji *fadia*, Gawwada *ẓe:*, Gobze *sezɛh*. See Sasse 1976.138-9, 135, Heine 1978.73, Dolgopolsky 1973.92-4.

(10.9) Sem. *√*ś('*)r* 'food grain': Eth. *śərna:y* 'wheat', CSem. *śV'a:r-* 'barley' > Hebrew *śə'o:'ra:*, Ugar. š'r, Aram., Syr. *sə'a:rəta:'*, Arab. (derivative) *ša'i:r-* 'barley' = Eg. šr.t 'barley' = LECush. *šo:r- 'food' > Somali *só:r*, Boni *só:r*, Galla *só:r-a* 'food', Gidole *so:r-* 'preserved melted fat'. See Black 1974.169. The consonant *' in CSem. (which is absent in the Eth., Eg. and ECush. forms) is perh. due to popular etymology, the word for 'barley' having been associated in CSem. with *√*ś'r* 'hair' ('barley' as 'haired').

(10.10) Sem. *''iś(V)b- 'herb, herbage' > Hebrew *''eśɛb*, Ugar. 'šbt, JAram. '*isba:*, Syr. '*ɛsba:*, Arab. '*ušb-*, cp. Akkad. *išḫabtu* 'grass' = ECush. *'awš-/*'ayš- (perh. < *'awiš- ?) 'grass' > Saho, Afar '*ays-o* 'grass, straw, vegetation', Somali '*aws* 'dry grass', Boni *a:šĕ* pl., Rendille *ḫos*, Bayso *e:s*, Dasenech '*i:š* 'grass', Galla *e:s* 'a kind of corn', Dullay '*awš-* 'to become ripe', '*aš-ko* 'grass', Sidamo *ays-o* 'grass'. See Sasse 1979.44, 45, 47, Heine 1974.77, cp. Dolgopolsky 1973.149.

(10.11) Eg. šnč (a kind of snake) = ECush.: Galla (Thiene) *soti* 'aspid' (perh. < *šonti*; for Cush. *-nt- > ECush. *-t- > Galla -t- cp. *'anti > *'ati > Galla *ati* 'thou').

In one root we find Sem. *š corresponding to ECush. post-consonantal *s (special development in a consonant cluster?):

(10.12) Sem. *√*npš* 'to breathe', *'nap(V)š- 'breath, soul' = ECush. *nafs- ∼ *nefs- 'to breathe, to rest' > Saho -*mfes-/-mfis-*, verbal noun *nafs-e* ∼ *nefs-e*, Rendille *nefsó | nef'saḍa*, Boni *ne:fso* 'to breathe', Somali *nas-o*, Rendille *nâs* 'to rest', Elmolo *nas-i* 'to breathe, rest', Galla *naf-i:* 'fermezza, sicurezza, energia, potere' (?), Konso *ness-a* 'soul, breath', Gidole *nass* 'voice, character', Dullay *nass-aḍ-* 'to breathe', *nass-o* 'soul, breath', Yāku *nes-i* 'breath' (see Sasse 1979.59, 23, Heine 1978.69-70). Cp. also Berber *√nfs* > Tahaggart *su-nfᵊs* 'to breathe', *unfas* 'breath'.

11. Sem. *δ, *ẓ (and Eg. z) = ECush. *ẓ

(11.1) Sem. *δa'nab- 'tail' > Hebrew *za:'na:b*, Arab. *δanab-*, Akkad. *zibb-at-*, etc. = ECush. *zinb-/*zaban- 'tail' > Saho *daban*, dial. *zaban ∼ δaban* 'back', Galla *daban* in compound and derived words (*daban-killie* 'partridge', < *daballe *daban-le:* 'plait of hair'), Harso *sinp-o:* 'uncircumcised penis'. See Sasse 1976. 140, cp. Leslau 1980.126.

(11.2) Sem. *'δi'(i)b- 'wolf' > Hebrew *zᵊ'eb*, Arab. *δi'b-*, Aram. *de:b-a:* 'wolf', Akkad. *zi:bu* 'jackal' = Eg. z'b 'jackal' = ECush. *zo:bb- 'lion' > Sidamo *do:bb-iččo*, pl. *do:bb-a*, Alaba *zobe-ččo*, Kambatta *zo:bbe-čču*, Ṭembaro *zobbé-čču*, Ḳabenna *zo:bbo:* 'lion', Gogot (< Highland ECush.) *dobbiččo* 'kind of wild animal', cp. Iraqw *du'uma* 'leopard'. See Sasse 1976.141, Leslau 1979.3:195, 1980.120, Dolgopolsky 1973.106.

(11.3) Sem. *-zhap 'to crawl' > Arab. √zhf (impf. -zhafu) 'to drag oneself, creep' = ECush. *za:f- 'to crawl, drag oneself (as a baby)' > Konso *ta:f-*, Dasenech *za:f-*. See Sasse 1976.139-40.

(11.4) Sem. *'zah(V)r- 'flower' > Arab. *zahr-*, *zahrat-* 'flower', Syr. *zahr-a:* 'flower' = HECush. *zara:r- 'flower' > Sidamo *dara:ro*, Darasa *dara:ro*, Kambatta, Ḳabenna, Alaba *zara:ruta*, Ṭembaro *zära:ruta*. See Leslau 1980.120.

(11.5) Sem. *√zrḳ 'to throw, strew, push' > Akkad., Bibl. Hebrew √zrḳ 'to strew, sprinkle', Aram., Middle Hebrew √zrḳ 'to throw'. Ḥaḍramaut Arab. √zrq 'to throw', Arab. √zrq 'to shift (its load: camel)', 'jeter un javelin' = ECush. *-zrig-/*-zrug- 'to move (tr.), push' > Saho *-izrig-*, *-idrig-* 'to stir', Somali *durk-/durug* 'to shift one's position', Elmolo *yuruk-*, Arbore *zarug-* 'to push'. See Sasse 1979.20.

(11.6) Sem. *ḥiza:m- 'strap, girdle' > Syr. *ḥᵊza:m-a* 'girdle', Arab. *ḥiza:m-at-* 'strap, girth of a saddle' = ECush. *ḥizz- 'root, vein' > Somali *ḥídid*, Rendille *ḥiy*, Galla *hidd-a*, Konso *hitt-ina*, Gidole *hittin* 'root, vein', Boni *'hí:dĕ* 'root', *'híddĕ* 'vein', Bayso *hidid-i*, Dasenech *hiz*, pl. *hizzo*, Elmolo *hiwɛ'*, Arbore *hiyds-o* (= *hizzo* pl.?), Gawwada *ḥiss-e*, Harso *ḥi:s-e* 'root' (see Black 1974.177, 200, Sasse 1979.20, Heine 1979.20). The underlying semantic change is 'root, vein' → 'rope' → 'strap'.

(11.7) Sem. *√*r'ẓ* > Arab. *mi-r'iẓẓ-*, *ma-r'aẓ-* 'fine goat's hair' = ECush. *ri(:)ẓ-*, *√*'rẓ* 'hair, beard' > Saho *ri:d*, Galla *are:dă* 'beard', Bayso *adar* id. (?), Burji, Sidamo, Darasa *orda*, Kambatta, Alaba, Ḳabenna *or'ẓa-ta*, Ṭembaro *orẓäta*, Hadiyya *odda* 'hair of body', Yāku *ris-in-i*, pl. *risín* 'hair'. See Sasse 1976.138, Leslau 1980.120.

(11.8) Eg. *zm'.w* 'branches' = ECush. *ẓa:m-* 'branch' > Galla (Thiene) *dam-e*, Konso *ta:ma*, Harso *san-če:*. See Sasse 1976.140.

(11.9) Eg. *z* 'man, person' = ECush. *ẓat-* 'person, people' > Somali *dad*, Jiddu *yed*, Boni *dad*, Dasenech *-zat* 'person' and perh. Sago *da:t* ∼ *ẓa:t* 'Versammlung'. See Sasse 1976.140, Heine 1978.56.

(11.10) Eg. *z'b* 'to pass through' ('/ein Ort/ durchziehen') = ECush. *ẓarb-* 'to pass' ('vorbeigehen') > Galla *darb-/dabr-*, Konso *tarb-*, Gidole *tarp-*, Harso *sarp-*, Yāku *-seur-* (< *-sebr-* ?). See Sasse 1976.140. Erman and Grapow's interpretation of Eg. *z'b* as derived fr. *z'b* 'jackal' (Erman-Grapow 1926-31.3:420) is not convincing.

(11.11) Eg. *čzj*, wčz 'to raise, carry' = ECush. *siẓ-* 'to carry' > Somali *sid-*, Rendille *síd-*, Dasenech *siẓ-* 'to carry', Galla *fid-* 'to bring, give'. See Black 1974.168, 177, Heine 1978.73.

12. Sem. *ṣ*, *ṣ́* = ECush. *ç* (= Sasse's *d'₁*, Black's *D₁*)

(12.1) Sem. *√*ṣbγ* 'to moisten, to dye' > Arab. √*ṣbγ* 'to soak, to dye', OAram. ṣb' 'gefärbt', Bibl. Aram. *məṣabbə''i:n* 'those who moisten' =ECush. *çub-* 'to dip in' > Galla *çup-* ∼ *çub-* 'to dip in', Dullay *ṭup-* 'to swim' and prob. Yāku *ṭo:b-* 'to sift'. Cp. in Omotic: Kaffa *ṭipp-* 'immergere, tuffare'. See Sasse 1979.30.

(12.2) Sem. *√*ṣ'r* 'to be reproached' > Syr. *ṣə'ar* 'opprobio affectus est', Aram. *ṣa''er* 'beschimpfen', Arab. *ṣa''ara* 'to turn away the face in disdain' = ECush. *çe:r-* 'to be ashamed' > Konso *ǧe:r-*, Gidole *çe:r-* 'to be ashamed'. See Sasse 1979.27.

(12.3) Sem. *√*ṣll* 'to make pure', 'to clarify (a liquid)' > Aram., Middle Hebrew, Arab. √*ṣll* id., Syriac *ṣəla:la:* 'puritas', *ṣəli:la:* 'purus' = ECush. *çall-* 'only' > Galla, Darasa *çalla*, Moreno, Burji (Moreno) *čalla* (i.e. *çalla?*), Hadiyya *ṭala'em* 'allein'. Cp. Dolgopolsky 1973.104. The comparaison is valid unless Sem. *√*ṣll* is fr. *√*ṣll* 'to sink'.

(12.4) Sem.: Arab. *ma:ṣa* (impf. *-mu:ṣu*) 'to wash' = ECush. *mVyç-* 'to

wash' > Somali   Galla *mi:č-*, Kambatta *mečče'*, Ḳabenna *mečči-*.
See Dolgopolsky 1973.308, Sasse 1979.26.

(12.5)   Sem. *√plṣ 'to split' = ECush. *falč- 'log', 'to split' (see 2.7).

(12.6)   Sem. *√kṣṣ 'to cut' = ECush. *ḳač- 'to cut' (see 8.4).

(12.7)   Sem. *√w/yṣk or *√w/yṣḳ 'to pour' > Ugar., Hebrew √yṣk 'to
         pour, cast', Phoen. *yṣk* 'statue fondue' = ECush. *čak-/*čik- 'to
         wash' > Somali *ḍaqo*, Boni *'dá'o*, Rendille *'ḍíxo* 'to bathe, have a
         bath', Dasenech *ǧik-* (?), Yāku *ṭɔq-*, Konso *ǧaq-*, Gidole *čik-* 'to
         wash'. See Sasse 1979.27, 29, 30, Heine 1978.57.

(12.8)   Sem. *√ṣpy 'to wrap over' > Ugar. √ṣpy (G-stem), Hebrew *ṣip'pa:*,
         Syr. *'appa:* 'to wrap over, pull over' = ECush. *čuf- 'to close, to
         shut' > Somali *ǧuf-*, Galla *čuf-*, Konso *ḍuf-*, Gidole *ḍuh-*, Dullay *čup-*.
         See Black 1974.167, 215-6, Sasse 1979.29, 31.

(12.9)   Sem. *√ṣpr 'to plait' > Arab. √ḍfr, Eth. √ṣfr 'to plait, twist',
         Middle Hebrew *ṣə'pa:r* 'Geflecht' = ECush. *čifr- 'braid, smth.
         plaited' > Gidole *čirf-*, Konso *ǧirf-* 'braid', Galla *čifr-a:* 'women's
         hairdo'. See Sasse 1979.27, 29.

(12.10) Sem. *√ṣpp 'to press (?)' > Middle Hebrew *ṣa:'pu:p* 'gedrängt,
         beengt', Arab. *ḍaff-at-* 'crowd of people', *ta-ḍa:ffa* 'to throng in a
         point (crowd)' = ECush. *či:b- 'to squeeze, press' > Dullay *ṭi:p-* 'to
         press', Somali (intens.) *ḍi:bḍi:b-* 'to bring thighs together to close
         crutch'. See Sasse 1979.29, 30.

      There are cases in which a Sem. geminated emphatic sibilant
corresponds to ECush. *ẓ: Sem. *bVṣṣ 'swamp' = ECush. *baẓ-
'lake' (see 1.7) and Akkad. *gaṣṣat-u* 'firewood' = ECush. *ge:ẓ- 'tree'
(see 6.10).

Signs and symbols

In Proto-Semitic and in Sem. languages: x stands for traditional *ḫ*, and *ṣ́ for *ḍ.
In Ethiopian (Geez): ś symbolizes Śawt, and ṣ is used for Ṣappa.
In Old South Arabian: Beeston's s¹, s², s³ are rendered by š, ś, s.
In Egyptian: z stands for traditional (Erman-Grapow's) *s*, s for *ś*, x for *ḫ*, ' for *ȝ*, č for *ṯ*, and
    ǧ for *ḍ*.
In Cushitic: glottalized consonants are dotted (ḳ, ṭ, p, ḍ, g, ǧ, č), retroflex d is symbolised by ḍ,
    *ḍ stands for Sasse's *d', and *č for Sasse's *d'₁.
In all languages: hushing sibilants are denoted by ⁀: ǧ stands for the sound of Engl. j and
    č (rather than c) for ch, š for sh; ǧ symbolizes the palatal voiced injective stop (Sasse's *ɟ*).
Roman type is used for transliterating consonantic script, while italics symbolizes
transcription. Half brackets ⁀ ⁀ denote dubious phonemes in reconstructions: e.g., *⁀s'unk- (in
9.2) means "*sunk- or *šunk-". Consonantic roots are symbolized by √.

Abbreviations

Sem. = Proto-Semitic; ECush. = Proto-East-Cushitic; LECush. = Proto-Lowland-East-Cushitic (see Black 1974); PSLECush = Proto-South-Lowland-East-Cushitic (see Black 1974); PSam = Proto-Sam (i.e. Somali-Boni-Rendille, see Heine 1978); CSem. = Central Semitic (Canaanite-Aramaic-Arabic).

References

Aisleitner, J. 1967. *Wörterbuch der ugaritischen Sprache.* Berlin.

Black, P. D. 1974. *Lowland East Cushitic: Subgrouping and Reconstruction.* Doctoral Dissertation. Yale University.

Diakonoff, I. M. 1965. *Semito-Hamitic Languages. An Essay in Classification.* Moscow.

Dolgopolsky (Dolgopol'skij), A. B. 1966. "Materialy po sravnitel'no-istoričeskoj fonetike kušitskix jazykov: gubnye i dental'nye smyčnye v načal'nom položenii". In B. A. Uspenskij, ed., *Jazyki Afriki.* Moskva. 35-88.

Dolgopolsky (Dolgopol'skij), A. B. 1972a. "Materialy po sravnitel'no-istoričeskoj fonetike kušitskix jazykov: veljarnyj zvonkij v anlaute". In N. V. Oxotina, B. A. Uspenskij, eds., *Problemy afrikanskogo jazykoznanija.* Moskva. 197-216.

Dolgopolsky (Dolgopol'skij), A. B. 1972b. "O proisxoždenii ličnyx okončanij glagolov v vostočnosidamskix i irakvskix jazykax". *Africana. Afrikanskij ètnografičeskij sbornik,* 9 (= *Trudy Instituta Ètnografii im. N. N. Mikluxo-Maklaja,* N.S. 100). Leningrad. 103-112.

Dolgopolsky (Dolgopolski), A.B. 1972c. "La permutation des *m et *b initiaux dans les racines couchitiques". *Congrès International des Africanistes. Deuxième session, Dakar, 11-20 décembre 1967.* Paris. 225-234.

Dolgopolsky (Dolgopol'skij), A. B. 1973. *Sravnitel'no-istoričeskaja fonetika kušitskix jazykov.* Moskva.

Dolgopolsky, A. 1978. "On Phonemic Stress in Proto-Semitic". *Israel Oriental Studies* 8:1-12.

Erman, A. und Grapow, H. 1926-31. *Wörterbuch der ägyptischen Sprache.* I-VI. Berlin.

Heine, B. 1978. "The Sam Languages". *Afroasiatic Linguistics* 6/2:1-93.

Leslau, W. 1958. *Ethiopic and South Arabic Contributions to the Hebrew Lexicon* (University of California Publications in Semitic Philology, vol. 20).

Leslau, W. 1979. *Etymological Dictionary of Gurage (Ethiopic).* I-III. Wiesbaden.

Leslau, W. 1980. "Proto-*Sidamo *z". *Afrika und Übersee* 63.119-129.

Reinisch, L. 1900-3. *Die Somali-Sprache.* I-III. Wien.

Sasse, H.-J. 1975. "Galla /š/, /s/ und /f/". *Afrika und Übersee* 58:244-63.

Sasse, H.-J. 1976. "Weiteres zu den ostkuschitischen Sibilanten". *Afrika und Übersee* 59:125-43.

Sasse, H.-J. 1979. "The Consonant Phonemes in Proto-East-Cushitic", *Afroasiatic Linguistics* 7/1:1-66.

Sasse, H.-J. 1980. "Ostkuschitische und semitische Verbalklassen". In W. Diem, S. Wild, ed., *Studien aus Arabistik & Semitistik. A. Spitaler zum 70. Geburtstag ... überreicht.* Wiesbaden. 153-73.

Sasse, H.-J. 1981. "Afroasiatisch". In B. Heine a.o., ed., *Die Sprachen Afrikas.* Hamburg. 129-48.

Schlee, G. 1978. *Sprachliche Studien zum Rendille.* Hamburg.

Tucker, A. & Bryan, M. 1966. *Linguistic Analyses. The Non-Bantu Languages of North-Eastern Africa.* London.

Zaborski, A. 1975a. *The Verb in Cushitic.* Warszawa-Kraków.

Zaborski, A. 1975b. "Material for a Comparative Dictionary of Cushitic Languages: Somali-Galla Comparaisons". In J. and Th. Bynon, ed., *Hamito-Semitica.* London 321-31.

UNA SCARAMUCCIA POETICA TRA 'AFAWARQ GABRA 'IYASUS ED IL BLĀTTĀ GABRA 'EGZI'ABEHĒR

Luigi Fusella
Istituto Universitario Orientale-Napoli

Elena Sengal, in *Annali Istituto Universitario Orientale di Napoli*, 1943 (pag. 292), nelle sue «Note sulla letteratura moderna amarica» scrisse che 'Afawarq Gabra 'Iyasus, sotto lo pseudonimo di «cittadini di Asmara», aveva stampato, nel 1912, una poesia in risposta ad una poesia diffamatoria scritta contro l'Italia da un certo Blāttā Gabra 'Egzi'abehēr in occasione della guerra italo-turca e che sapeva per certo che, sotto il detto pseudonimo, si nascondeva lo 'Afawarq. La notizia è stata ripresa dal Gerald A.S. nelle sue *Four African literatures* (University of California Press, pagg. 280, 411 e 431) e la si può considerare certa dato che la Sengal riferiva, sicuramente, notizie avute dal Prof. Gallina che fu il suo tutore.

Fra le carte del mio venerato Maestro ho trovato, stampata su un foglietto volante, la poesia dello 'Afawarq e ne do qui il testo e la traduzione insieme con la traduzione di due delle quattro poesie del Blāttā Gabra 'Egzi'abehēr pubblicate da Y.I. Eadie nel suo *Amharic Reader* (Cambridge, University Press, 1924, pag. 195/202) la seconda delle quali, più che la prima, sembra essere, dalla frase «osservate Asmara» [verso 16], quella che 'Afawarq considerò diffamatoria par l'Italia. Ed affermo ciò pur se la poesia era conservata insieme con altro foglietto volante su cui era stampata la prima delle due poesie del Gabra 'Egzi'abehēr.

Sulla vita del nostro Blāttā nulla conosco in più di quanto è stato pubblicato dal Merab in *Impressions d'Éthiopie* (Paris, 1929, pag. 259) ove si legge che il Gabra 'Egzi'abehēr fu imprigionato da Ras Makonnen nel 1902 per aver sostenuto la teoria Copernicana e che, buon conoscitore dell'italiano, era vissuto a lungo nella colonia eritrea ed aveva giocato un gran ruolo a favore dello Scioa durante gli anni che precedettero la guerra italo-abissina del 1896 e dal Pankhurst R. in *Ethiopia Observer* (Vol. VI, pag. 260) ove si legge che egli fu il primo giornalista editore di un giornaletto manoscritto, che nacque a Tsada Kistan nello Hamāsēn, che fu imprigionato dagli italiani a Nocra e che, dopo la battaglia di Adua, raggiunse la corte di Menilek ove divenne una specie di satirico di corte (a kind of court satirist).

Questa poesia di 'Afawarq, scritta nel 1912, precede quella da lui scritta in occasione della ascesa al trono della Regina Zaweditu e da me pubblicata negli atti del V⁰ Congresso Internazionale di Studi etiopici (*Modern Ethiopia*, A.A. Balkema, Rotterdam, 1980, pag. 1) ed è un bell'esempio dello stile poetico dell'Autore e, specialmente nelle due prime strofe, della violenza della sua satira.

Sarebbe assai interessante, anche a completamento della scarsa sua produzione poetica a noi nota, poter accertare se il sospetto di A. Triulzi in *Atti del IV Congresso Internazionale di Studi Etiopici* (Roma, Accademia dei Lincei, 1974, vol. I, pag. 710, nota n. 41) sia fondato e se questa poesia sia contenuta nella raccolta indicata dal Triulzi, il che conferemerebbe che essa appartiene al nostro Autore.

Dei sentimenti filo-italiani dell'˒Afawarq ho già detto in *Dictionary of African Biography* (Reference Publications, Inc. New York, pag. 45) e questa poesia dimostra che, a prescindere dai legami che lo legavano all'Italia sia per aver sposato un'italiana, sia per l'attività prestata a fianco del Prof. Gallina, la sua attività di giornalista filo-italiano nel periodo dell'occupazione fascista dell'Etiopia non affondava le proprie radici, come potrebbe sospettarsi, in un desiderio di conformismo ai nuovi tempi o di tornaconto personale, ma in un più inveterato, disinteressato sentimento.

La mia traduzione, anche se a scapito della forma italiana, è strettamente letterale. Le parole tra parentesi non figurano nel testo. Messo in buon italiano, per es, l'ultimo verso si sarebbe dovuto tradurre: «Egli non sa neanche scrivere l'amarico e pretende fare il poeta!». Ometto, per motivi di spazio, qualsiasi osservazione stilistica o grammaticale.

Le poesie di Blāttā Gabra ˒Egzi˒abehēr

I

Ascoltami, ti prego, Šawā, Harar, Kāffā, Kontā,
Goǧǧām, Bagēmeder, Tegrē fino all'Endartā,
Wallo, Yaǧǧu, Wāg, Awessā fino al Lāstā,
Abissinia tutta, ovunque tu sia.
Mentre ti parlo, interpreta il (mio) dire con investigazioni[1].
Il Turco, gente forte, che da Gerusalemme, da padrone,
ha sciolto[2] il mondo a colpi (lett. scudiscio) di spada

---

[1] Leggi, cioè, e medita attentamente!

[2] *Ha sciolto* = ha fatto alto e basso, ha fatto quel che voleva. Cfr. Il mio «Il Dagmāwi Menilek ecc» in *Rassegna degli Studi Etiopici*, vol. XVII, 1961, pag. 12.

era arrivato anche da noi: un brigante, Grāñ [3],
non si trovò un prode che lo frenasse!
Quest'anno, invece, lo han colpito i guai
poichè viveva ammalato (lett. nella malattia) di superbia,
senza apprendere un'arte, senza approntar colline (su cui difendersi)
e nell'invidia, in segreti conciliaboli,
uccidendo e battendo, con la scusa della religione,
di notte con le donne, di giorno coi giochi,
sempre saziandosi delle gioie mondane,
senza mai pensare, da mattina a sera, al suo governo.
Essendogli stato consigliato di esser paziente, di viver tranquillo
ed avendo egli risposto: «non ascolto», si consigliarono contro di lui,
— affinchè la sua voce, il flauto musulmano, si spegnesse, —
al fine di spodestar(lo dal)la sua carica, (dal)la sua posizione onorevole.
Un istruito, che non conosce facezie
governo libero [4] gli venne immediatamente contro
per mare, per terra, dalle altezze del cielo,
battendo, da lontano, il (tasto del) telegrafo senza fili [5].
Lo sgozzò, lo fece a pezzi, lo ridusse vagabondo (= lo scacciò).
Esso [6] aveva navi, poche e scadenti,
e, non potendo (esse) difendersi da quelle dei prodi,
se ne fuggirono e si ammassarono nel porto dei Dardanelli.
Se (pur) presentava [7] reclami a tutti gli Stati,
se (pur) piangeva e gridava, donde poteva arrivagli un aiuto
dato che era crudele, ozioso e corrotto?
In qual modo esso fu, a proposito del Golgota [8], ingiusto a nostro danno
da quel che, man mano abbiamo sentito, impariamolo ormai!
E, poi, stiamo attenti, prima che giunga il (nostro) turno!
Impariamo dagli Europei, diventiamo quant'è più possibile forti
e sian molti, affinchè il nostro cuore non sia dubbioso, i consiglieri
sì che, nel giorno dello scontro, il nemico non vinca!
Studiamo la storia, leggiamo i giornali,

---

3 Il noto Mohamed, soprannominato «il Mancino» che invase l'Etiopia nel 16º secolo.
4 *Governo libero* = il Governo Italiano.
5 Cfr. *postea*, nota nº 18.
6 *Esso* = il Governo Turco.
7 Soggetto è il Governo Turco.
8 L'Etiopa possiede, fin dal XIIº secolo, in Gerusalemme alcune località e chiese tra le quali quella del Golgota. Si accenna, forse, ad una qualche discussione fra i due Governi, essendo allora Gerusalemme sotto dominazione turca, a proposito di questa chiesa.

impariamo le lingue, guardiamo le carte geografiche!
E' esso (= lo studio) che ha aperto gli occhi ai popoli.
Le tenebre sono sparite, son diventate alba;
dormire di giorno, è una vergogna il letto!
Affinchè nostra madre, l'Etiopia, non si separi dal marito
diamole oggi consigli sì che non diventi prostituta
e noi, suoi figli, non siamo sbattuti qua e là.
Un patrigno è crudele, (vive) ad adirarsi ed a percuotere
e non imbandisce, poi, la mensa della gloria!
Se io do sempre consigli, ogni domenica,
non ho trovato alcuno, nè un signore che mi disapprovi
nè uno che dica: «Altro che, ha ragione!»
Dal momento che le cose stanno così, è meglio il silenzio!
Dato che non ho guadagno, perchè insistere?
Che importa a me? Ad un tal vagabondo?
Guai a chi è abituato (a dir)[9]: «Son qui, son qui, Signor mio!»

Ha parlato il Blāttā Gabra 'Egzi'abehēr.

II

Ascoltatemi tutti, musulmani e Amara (= Cristiani),
metropoliti, monaci, sacerdoti di turno e dabtarā,
(ascoltate) quel che è accaduto quest'anno: la congiura di guerra,
la infelicità[10] che ha colpito i Turchi.
(Venendo) dal gran mare, fin (dal) mare eritreo[11],
navigando su navi, in ordine di guerra,
han cominciato a bruciarli, con inferno di cannonate,
per prendersi il paese, per piantarvi la (loro) bandiera.
Che cosa mostruosa quest'onta! E', mentre è temibile, terribile!

---

9 Interpretazione incerta, diversamente tradotto da Eadie. Credo che voglia dire: Guai ai popoli che non sono indipendenti, che sono abituati a rispondere «Eccomi, eccomi, padrone!».

10 *Hasār* è vocabolo ge'ez = disgrazia, angustia, ristrettezza. È in stato costrutto.

11 Così traduco, essendo notorio che alla guerra italo-turca il Governo italiano fece partecipare molti reparti di ascari eritrei i quali, poi, rientrati in patria, presero il nomignolo di «Trembulē» (= Tripolini). Cfr. *Fusella*, «Una poesia amarica di Aqā Gabru sui fatti di Sagalē», in *Atti del 6° Congresso Internazionale di Studi Etiopici* (in corso di stampa). Ma si può anche tradurre: «l'infelicità che ha colpito i turchi, dal Mediterraneo al Mar Rosso».

Adesso, prima che giunga l'avvoltoio, occorre esser cauti,
(l'avvoltoio) che depreda, con la violenza, il pane onorato;
(che) non ha pietà per i vecchi nè bontà verso i fanciulli.
E' fratello di Erode, soldato di Pilato.
Quando arriva, amaro come il fiele,
dicono che non dà mai neanche un posto per una tomba [12].
Se non mi credete, osservate 'Asmarā!
Se oggi andiamo d'accordo, senza che alcuno di noi si insuperbisca,
così come ci disse Davide con la cetra del canto:
«il consiglio, per colui che lo pone in opera, è bello
e colui che lo accetta non teme alcuno»
diventerà [13] come il Giappone, forte in tutto.

Ha parlato il Blāttā Gabra 'Egzi'abehēr.

La Poesia di 'Afawarq Gabra 'Iyasus segue alla pagina 148

---

12 A questa accusa l'Afawarq risponde col verso 4, strofa 10, della sua poesia.
13 *Diventerà*: soggetto è l'Etiopia.

Testo della poesia di 'Afawarq Gabra 'Iyasus

አስተርጓሚ ፥ ሁኖ ፥ ሰሐን ፥ ሲፈገፍግ ፥
እሁን ፥ ማን ፥ አገባው ፥ ከጨወታ ፥ ተወግ ፥
ታዛባ ፥ ሳይለይ ፥ ወድቆ ፥ ሲአድር ፥ ተፍግ ።

አክብረውህ ፥ ነበር ፥ ብለውህ ፥ በላታ ፥
በግር ፥ ብረት ፥ ገባህ ፥ ስለሆንህ ፥ ወስላታ ፥
ዐር ፥ ስትጠርግ ፥ የነበር ፥ ስትደፉ ፥ ባሬታ ፥
ትሰድብ ፥ ጀመረ ፥ የብርሃኑን ፥ ጌታ ።

ሁለቱ ፥ መንግሥቶች ፥ ፍቅራቸውን ፥ ወደው ፥
ስልክ ፥ ሸቦ ፥ ዘረጉ ፥ መድፋቸውን ፥ ትተው ፥
ፍቅር ፥ እንደ ፥ ሸማ ፥ ሊኖሩ ፥ ተላብሰው ።
እንኳን ፥ ለንግዴው ፥ በሬት ፥ ተጠጥተው ፥
መሐላ ፥ ባልጠሉም ፥ እንዳይፈርስ ፥ እርቃቸው ።

በዚህ ፥ መሀል ፥ ገብቶ ፥ ምን ፥ ያስቀባጥራል ፥
ለሱ ፥ ሳያውቅበት ፥ ለሌላው ፥ ይመክራል ፥
ለሱ ፥ ባያልፍለት ፥ ለኛስ ፥ ደስ ፥ ብሎናል ፥
ጨለማ ፥ ተሽሮ ፥ ብርሃን ፥ ገብቶልናል ።

ከንፈሩ ፡ አክንባሎ ፡ ው.ቃቢ ፡ የሴለው ፡
ፍቅር ፡ እንዲፈርስ ፡ ነው ፡ እሱ ፡ የሚጥረው ።

ብልህት ፡ ተኖረው.ስ ፡ ታወቀ ፡ ፈረነጇ ፡
ለጠብ ፡ ምን ፡ ባስጣረው ፡ ለማፉቀር ፡ እንዲ ።

ተንግዬህ ፡ አይመጣም ፡ ያዱአው ፡ ጦርነት ፡
ተዛንተህ ፡ ተቀመጥ ፡ ያበሻ ፡ ፍጥረት ፡
የቀጣፊ ፡ ወሬ ፡ ይቅርብህ ፡ መስማት ።

ተንግዬህ ፡ ቢመጣ ፡ የጦርነት ፡ ስራ ፡
ሰማይ ፡ ሰማዩን ፡ እይ ፡ ሲ.በር ፡ እንዳሞራ ፡
በላይህ ፡ ይዘንባል ፡ እሳተ ፡ ገሞራ ፡
እንኳን ፡ ያየር ፡ መንገድ ፡ መርፊ ፡ የማትሰራ ፡
እንዲህ ፡ ባለው ፡ ጠላት ፡ አበሻም ፡ አትኩራ ፡
ተፉቅራ ፡ ትቀመጥ ፡ ተኢጣሊአ ፡ ጋራ ፡
ይኼን ፡ ብታረግ ፡ ነው ፡ የምትኖር ፡ ጠንክራ ።

ለእያሱ ፡ ሲ.ጥር ፡ የኢ.ጣሊአ ፡ መንግሥት ፡
ምን ፡ ያጠራጥራል ፡ በቀጣፊ ፡ ሐሜት ፡
ብርሃን ፡ ተጠይፎ ፡ ጨለማ ፡ ለመግባት ።

ያሥመራ ፡ ከተማ ፡ እንዴቱን ፡ ትደነቅ ፡
ውሽት ፡ ገጠመባት ፡ እውነቱን ፡ ሳይጠይቅ ፡
የጥንት ፡ ወሬ ፡ ይዞ ፡ የዛሬውን ፡ ሳያውቅ ፡
ገዢው ፡ ለኛ ፡ ሁኖ ፡ ርስትን ፡ ሲጠብቅ ።

ነገሩ ፡ ይድነቅህ ፡ እረ ፡ ስማ ፡ ስማ ፡
አርነት ፡ የወጣህ ፡ ያሥመራ ፡ ከተማ ፡
ኢጣሊአ ፡ ተገባች ፡ ተሾሮአል ፡ ጨለማ ።

እንኳን ፡ ተግዛቱአ ፡ ታሰብ ፡ እስተ ፡ ቍርደት ፡
ለጋላ ፡ ተርፈታል ፡ የኢጣሊአ ፡ ብልሀት ።

ሸዋ ፡ ደስ ፡ ይበልህ ፡
ጐጃም ፡ ደስ ፡ ይበልሁ ፡
ትግሬም ፡ ደስ ፡ ይበልሁ ፡
ወሎም ፡ ደስ ፡ ይበልሁ ፡
ሁሉም ፡ ደስ ፡ ይበልሁ ፡
በኢ.ጣሊ.አ ፡ ኃይል ፡ ነው ፡ የከፈተው ፡ ዓይንህ ።

ኢ.ጣሊአ ፡ በጠብዋ ፡ እንዲህ ፡ ከጠቀመች ፡
ተንግዴህ ፡ በፍቅርዋ ፡ ዓለም ፡ ታሳያለች ።

ላገር ፡ ማን ፡ አይረዳዎ ፡ ክፉት ፡ ተኖረማ ፡
እያየው ፡ ነው ፡ እንጂ ፡ አገሩ ፡ ሲለማ ።

የወዛበት ፡ ለሱ ፡ ገንዘቡን ፡ ማን ፡ ደፍሮት ፡
ቤቱ ፡ ክፍቱን ፡ ቢአድር ፡ አሳብ ፡ የለ ፡ ፍራት ፡
ጉብ ፡ መቅቡጥ ፡ የለ ፡ ለዳኛ ፡ ለመስጠት ፡
እንዲእው ፡ ዓለም ፡ ቱኖአል ፡ ያሥመራማ ፡ መንግሥት ።

የቀድሞ ፡ ግዛቱአን ፡ ተቀምታ ፡ ኑራ ፡
ሮማ ፡ ተነሳች ፡ ለመውሰድ ፡ ጠንክራ ፡
ቱርክን ፡ ምን ፡ አገባት ፡ ባልተገባት ፡ ስፍራ ።
እንኳን ፡ ትሪፖሊ ፡ ይቀራል ፡ ኤርትራ ፡
ገና ፡ አልተጀመረም ፡ ታያለች ፡ መከራ ፡
እስጥምቡል ፡ ክፉ ፡ ኑት ፡ ያረመኒ ፡ ኖራ ፡
ነገ ፡ ትፈርሳለች ፡ በክርስቲያን ፡ ሴራ ።

ገጣሚ ፡ ደፋር ፡ ነው ፡ ነገሩን ፡ እያውቀው ፡
ኢቶጵያን ፡ ከቱርክ ፡ ምን ፡ አመሳሰለው ።

የቱርክ ፡ ስም ፡ ተሰብሮአል ፡ ተገምሶአል ፡ ጨረቃው ፡
ያበሻ ፡ ስም ፡ ቅዱስ ፡ ከዚያ ፡ ከላይኛው ፡
አላማው ፡ አንበሳ ፡ የሚአስፈራ ፡ ግርማው ።

ገብረእግዚአብሔር ፡ ገጥሞ ፡ ክፉ ፡ የሚያወራ ፡
ኢጣሊአ ፡ ቢዋጋ ፡ ከቱርክ ፡ እስላም ፡ ጋራ ፡
አበሻ ፡ ምን ፡ ልትሆን ፡ በፍቅር ፡ ጠንክራ ።

የሞትወጣው ፡ ንጉሥ ፡ እያሱ ፡ ምኔልክ ፡
ፍቅርህን ፡ አጥብቀው ፡ ልብህ ፡ አይታወክ ፡
ሰካር ፡ በሚገጥመው ፡ የማይጠጣ ፡ በልክ ።

ተንግዴህ ፡ ኢጣሊአ ፡ አትመጣም ፡ በክፋት ፡
እጅግ ፡ ትመኛለች ፡ ያበሻን ፡ አንድነት ፡
እንዳይነካት ፡ ብላ ፡ ያልታሰበ ፡ ጠላት ፡
አሳቡእም ፡ ላንተ ፡ ነው ፡ እንዲገባ ፡ ብልሐት ።
የሮማ ፡ ልማድዋ ፡ የነበራት ፡ ተጥንት ፡
ባለሙ ፡ መዝራት ፡ ነው ፡ ብልሐትና ፡ እውቀት ።

ምላስህ ፡ መርዛም ፡ ነው ፡ ከንፈርህ ፡ መግሏሊት ፡
ሰባት ፡ ጊዜ ፡ ክደህ ፡ የለህም ፡ ሃይማኖት ።
ለሞኝ ፡ ይመስለዋል ፡ ገብረግዚሐር ፡ ሲሉት ።

ድርውን ፡ ሳያርዱ ፡ ይገኛልን ፡ መረቅ ፡
ግጥም ፡ ገጠምሁ ፡ ይላል ፡ አማረኛ ፡ ሳያውቅ ።

ያስመራ ፡ ልጀች ።
ለብላታ ፡ ገብረ ፡ እግዚአብሔር ፡ የጅ ፡ መንሻ ።

እሥመራ ፡ ፲፱፻፳፪ ፡ ዓመተ ፡ ምሕረት ፡

Traduzione

Mentre, come interpetre, strofinava [14] i piatti
chi, ora, lo ha introdotto dalle cose futili in quelle serie [15],
mentre, senza distaccarsi dallo sterco, passa la notte nel letame?

Ti avevano onorato, facendoti Blāttā [16],
entrasti in catene [17] (= in prigione) perchè fosti imbroglione;
tu che, mentre spazzavi via lo sterco, mentre versavi il pitale,
cominiciasti ad ingiuriare il padrone della luce (= l'Italia).

I due Governi, desiderosi di pace (lett. amore),
abbandonati i cannoni, stesero il filo telegrafico [18]

14 *Strofinava i piatti* = era sguattero. È riferito al Blāttā Gabra 'Egziabehēr cui è dedicata la
   poesia.
15 *Wag* = consuetudine, tradizione, usanza, diritto. Qui traduco: cosa seria.
16 Sembra che a nominarlo «blāttā» sia stato il Governo Italiano. Sul significato e valore di
   detta carxica, oltre a quanto detto da Bairu Tafla in *Atti del 4° Congresso internazionale di
   Studi Etiopici* (Acc. Lincei, Roma, 1974, pag. 611) ed ai riferimenti da lui indicati in nota,
   traduco quanto dice Takla Ṣādeq Makuriyā nella sua *Storia d'Etiopia. Da Aṭē Lebna Dengel
   a Tēwodros* (Artistic māttamiyā bēt, 2° ed. 1945 (1952/53) pag. 72): *Blāttā* o *Blāttēnā*
   significano «ragazzo». Anticamente così eran chiamati i trenta ragazzi che prestavano
   servizio nello *elfeň* e nello *elfeň addarāš*. Costoro, quando uscivano dallo *elfeň*, non potevano
   uscire da soli, ma in corteo e come addetti alla sicurezza del re (*baṭabbāqinnā bāğğābi kālhona
   baqar bīččāččawen ayewaṭum*). In seguito il loro numero aumentò fino a 150 divisi in tre
   reparti di 50 ragazzi ciascuno: un reparto addetto al *faras bēt*, uno al *zafan*(?) *bēt*, alla
   camera in cui il negus riceveva gli ospiti, un altro addetto al servizio del negus nella camera
   privata del re chiamata *anbassā bēt*. Costoro, al tempo d'oggi, sono chiamati *rāsgē bētoč*,
   anṭāfiwoč, *yalfeň zabaňňoč* ed *ačkaroč* ed alcuni anche *ženžā ačkaroč*.
       Ai tempi dell'Imperatore Sarza Dengel, divisi in due parti, i primi si chiamavano «piccoli
   blāttēnoč» ed i secondi «grandi *blāttēnoč*» ed i loro capi, quelli dei piccoli, si chiamavano, in
   amarico «*Teqāqen blāttēn gētā*» (in ge'ez: *liqa ne'usān blāttēnoč*) (sic!) e, quelli dei grandi, in
   amarico «*tāllāq blāttēn gētā*» (in ge'ez: *liqa 'abiyyān blāttēnoč*) (sic!). Il loro compito, mentre
   quello dei «piccoli» era di addetti allo *elfeň* ed ai servizi interni della casa reale, quello dei
   «grandi» era di addetti ai servizi esterni e corrispondeva, all'incirca, all'attuale compito del
   ligābā. Si dice che, in sovrappiù, talvolta, sia a loro, sia ai loro comandanti, si aggiungeva il
   compito di custodia del sigillo e di capo della polizia.
       Cfr. anche R. Greenfield *Ethiopia, A new political history*, Pall Mall, London, 1965
   (pag. 463) e Māḥtama Sellāsē Walda Masqal, *Zekra nagar*, 2° ed. pag. 20 e *passim*.,
   e Dassetā Takla Wald *Yāmāriňňa mazgaba qālāt*, 1970, pag. 1151. Forse, invece di *zafan bēt*
   (= casa dei canti) si deve leggere *zufān bēt* (= stanza del trono).
17 Qui sembra accennarsi alla prigionia in Nocra, disposta dal Governo Italiano e non a
   quella disposta da Ras Makonnen o, forse, ad ambedue.
18 Le prime linee telegrafiche e telefoniche furono stese da Menilek nel 1892 (= 1899/1900).
   Cfr. Māḥtama Sellāsē Walda Masqal, op. cit. (pag. 490).

per vivere ammantati di amore come da uno šammā.
Meno male che per l'avvenire, precedentemente pentitisi[19],
essi non rifiuterebbero di giurare a che la loro pace non crolli.

Entrato in mezzo a quest'affare, che cosa (lo) fa cianciare?
Senza saper (lo fare) per sé, dá consigli agli altri!
Se a lui (le difficoltà) non passano, quanto a noi, siamo contenti[20]:
la tenebra è stata fugata, è entrata, a nostro favore, la luce.

Il suo labbro (è come) un akenbāllo[21], disgustoso[22];
quel per cui egli si sforza è perchè l'amore crolli.

Se avesse intelligenza, se conoscesse gli europei,
che cosa mai lo farebbe affaticare, invece che per l'amicizia, per l'odio?

In avvenire non avverrà più la battaglia di Adua;
o popolo (lett. creatura) abissino, stattene a tuo agio,
cessi, per te, l'udire le notizie dell'imbroglione.

Se, in avvenire, venissero operazioni di guerra,
guardalo[23], in cielo, volare come un avvoltoio;
pioverà, su di te, un fuoco infernale.
L'Abissinia che non sa costruire, non diciamo vie aeree, ma neanche un ago,
non si insuperbisca per (aver vinto ad Adua) un tale nemico!
Se ne stia in amicizia con l'Italia;
è, se farà così, che vivrà forte.

Mentre il Governo italiano si sforza in favore di 'Iyāsu,
che cosa rende dubbiosi? Per ripiombare, per le calunnie di un imbroglione,
nelle tenebre tenendosi a schifo la luce?

Quanto, la città di 'Asmarā, rimarrà stupefatta:
(Gabra 'Egzi'abehēr), senza informarsi sulla verità, ha composto contro di
essa versi di falsità,

19 Passo di interpretazione incerta. Forse vuol dire: pentitisi per quel che in precedenza era
   accaduto.
20 Cioè: se lui è nei guai, noi, sotto il governo italiano, ce la passiamo bene.
21 *Akenbāllo* «grosso coperchio del *meṭād*, ovvero, del forno per cuocere lo *enḡarā*».
22 Rectius: *yalēllaw. Weqābi yalēllaw*, letteralmente «che non ha bellezza».
23 *Guardalo*: si riferisce agli italiani ed alla loro aviazione.

prendendo (a base) vecchie notizie e senza conoscere le attuali
mentre il governatore, essendo dalla nostra parte, difende (la nostra) terra
avita [24].

La cosa ti stupisca! Oh, ascolta, ascolta,
o città di Asmara uscita a libertà:
la tenebra, da che è arrivata l'Italia, è stata fugata.

Non solo nei suoi dominii, da Asab fino a Querdat [25].
(anche) per i Galla la civiltà italiana è stata sovrabbondante.

Šawā, rallegrati,
Goǧǧām, rallegrati,
Tegrē, rallegrati
Wallo, rallegrati
tutti quanti siate felici,
è per la potenza dell'Italia che (Iddio) ha aperto i vostri occhi!

L'italia, se con la sua inimicizia, ha giovato tanto,
con la sua amicizia, in avvenire, farà apparire la felicità.

Se vi fosse del male, chi non aiuterebbe il (proprio) paese?
Ma è vedendolo prosperare (che l'etiopico non corre in aiuto del proprio
paese).

Chi mai gli [26] ha strappato il denaro per cui egli ha sudato?
Se la sua casa resta aperta di notte, non vi è preoccupazione o timore,
non vi è donativo di corruzione o gubbo [27] da dare al giudice;
il governo di 'Asmarā è diventato una felicità!

Essendo stata depredata dei suoi antichi dominii,
Roma, divenuta forte, è sorta a (ri)prenderseli.
Che cosa ha fatto entrare la Turchia in località che non le spettavano?
Verranno a mancarle non solo Tripoli, anche (i possedimenti sul mar) eritreo.
Le cose non sono ancora iniziate, essa ha ancora da vedere (i suoi) guai!

---

24 *La nostra terra avita*: evidente risposta all'affermazione del Gabra 'Egzi'abehēr nella 2a
   poesia, verso 15, ove egli accusa il Governo italiano di non lasciare agli etiopici neanche
   un po' di terra per seppellirvi i morti.
25 *Querdāt* «Agordat».
26 *Gli* = all'etiopico.
27 *Gubbo* «donativo di corruzione dato ai giudici per guadagnarne i favori».

Istambul è cattiva, (è) una costruzione[28] di infedeli,
crollerà domani per la congiura dei cristiani.

Il poeta è audace! Le cose non le conosce!
Che cosa gli ha fatto paragonare l'Ethiopia alla Turchia?

Il nome della Turchia si è rotto, la sua luna si è spezzata,
quello dell'Etiopia è santo. Là, sulla sua parte superiore[29]
(del) suo vessillo (c'è) il leone la cui maestosità è temibile.

(E') Gabra 'Egzi'abehēr che, componendo poesie, sparge cattive notizie.
Se l'Italia combatte con i Turchi musulmani
che mai diverrà l'Etiopia forte nell'amore (= pace)?

O sorgente[30] re, 'Eyāsu Menilek[31],
rinsalda il tuo amore. Che il tuo cuore
non si agiti per quel che va poetando un ubriacone che beve senza misura!

D'ora in poi l'Italia non verrà più in cattiveria[32].
Essa desidera assai l'unità dell'Etiopia
allo scopo che non la attacchi un nemico cui non si è pensato (= improvviso).
Il suo pensiero è per te, affinché entri (in Etiopia) la civiltà.
L'abitudine di Roma, l'abitudine che essa ha fin dall'antichità,
è di seminare nel mondo civiltà e sapere.

La tua[33] lingua è velenosa, il tuo labbro (è come) un coperchio[34],
poiché hai tradito sette volte, non hai fede!
Quando lo chiamano «Gabra 'Egzi'abehēr», allo sciocco sembra vero[35]!

---

28 *Norā*, letteralmente «calce» = è una rocca di infedeli.
29 Oppure: «Il nome dell'Abissinia è santo, lì, nel cielo, (opp. è benedetto dal cielo?).
30 Nel testo: *yammetewaṭā*. Liǧ 'Eyāsu, infatti, all'epoca della guerra italo-turca era ancora sotto la tutela di Rās Tasammā. Egli, d'altro lato, non assunse mai il titolo di negus.
31 *'Eyāsu Menilek*: La dizione non è esatta poiché Menilek era il *nonno* ex filia e non il *padre* di Liǧ 'Eyāsu.
32 *In cattiveria* cioè «da nemica, con intenzioni ostili e aggressive».
33 *La tua lingua*: qui il poeta si rivolge al Gabra 'Egzi'abehēr.
34 Nel testo: *maglālit* «coperchio di marmitta». Vedi nota n. 21.
35 Cioè: solo gli sciocchi, sentendoti chiamare col nome di Gabra 'Egzi'abehēr, possono credere che tu sia veramente «servo di Dio» che, cioè, il significato del tuo nome corrisponda al tuo modo di agire.

Senza che si sgòzzi la gallina se ne può ricavare il brodo?
Egli, senza conoscere l'amarico, dice: «Ho composto poesie».

> I ragazzi di 'Asmarā
> Omaggio a Blāttā Gabra ῾Egzi'abehēr.
> 'Asmarā, 1905 anno di grazia (= 1912/13).

Post scriptum: durante la correzione delle bozze di stampa di quest'articolo ho potuto esaminare, grazie alla cortesia del Prof. Triulzi, gli scritti di 'Abbā Tasfā Sellāsē, oggetto del suo studio cui ho fatto cenno innanzi.

Alle pagg. 41/43 delle carte del Tasfā Sellāsē non vi è, come il Triulzi indica, «una lunga serie di poesie dello 'Afawarq» ma un'unica poesia, la nostra, trascritta con lievissime varianti e preceduta dal seguente titolo: «La risposta che diede (opp.: che *gli* diede) il Sig. 'Afawarq Gabra Yasus del paese di Zagē, Goǧǧām» e le varie strofe sono state scambiate, ad un'affrettata lettura, per singole poesie. A pag. 40 vi sono sei *geṭem* ed a pag. 39 vi è la poesia del Gabra 'Egzi'abehēr da me innanzi indicata col n° 2. Ciò conferma che, malgrado la intercalazione, nelle carte Tasfā Sellāsē, del foglio n. 40 e la riunione, nella carte Gallina, della nostra poesia con quella del Gabra 'Egzia'abehēr da me qui indicata col n° 1, quella alla quale lo 'Afawarq risponde è la seconda. La intitolazione data dal Tasfā Sellāsē, poi, ammesso che ve ne fossero, fuga ogni incertezza sull'identità del nostro Autore.

OLD AMHARIC FEATURES
IN A MANUSCRIPT FROM WOLLO (EMML 7007)

GETATCHEW HAILE

St. John's University, Collegeville, Minnesota

EMML[1] 7007 (19 × 17cm., 112 fols.[2], 2 cols., 19 lines to a column) is not particularly old. The genealogy of Ethiopian rulers on fols. 15v-16r ends with Iyyasu II, suggesting that it was copied between 1730 and 1755. But it contains features which thus far have been considered old by scholars of Amharic. If two centuries are not enough to make a language old, we may have to revise our knowledge about the dialects of Amharic; we may have been considering regional variations as phenomena of archaism. EMML 7007 is the microfilm of a manuscript from Wollo (Awas/Ḥawas Śəllase in Allamaṭa). But the old features which its texts preserve are found in manuscripts coming from other parts of the country as well. We should also bear in mind that EMML 7007 could have been copied from an older manuscript originating in the Gojjam-Gondar region. This may, in fact, explain why it has both the old and the new forms of some words such as *ḫand* and *and* for "one" (e.g., fol. 31v: *ḫandənnätun and qän tänaggäräw* "He [God/Christ] spoke [about] his oneness on one [and the] same day," or *gʷeta* and *geta* "master" (e.g., fols. 32r and 61v respectively), and why a few archaic conjugational elements (e.g., the object suffix *-waččäw* or *-waččo*, for *-aččäw* "them"[3] are wanting in it. In other words, the copyist of this manuscript may have altered some words and copied others as they appear in the old manuscript from which he was copying. The chronology of the rulers of Ethiopia that ends with *Aṣe* Susənəyos (1607-1632) and the paragraph on the "seven deadly sins" (fol. 20v), a Western thought not common in Ethiopia, may indicate that the exemplar of this manuscript was written during the Jesuit enterprise in Ethiopia in the seventeenth century.

With the exception of the first twenty-nine leaves[4], the original contents

---

1 For abbreviations and full reference see Bibliography.

2 Numbered 1 to 121, with the numbers 91 to 99 omitted from the series.

3 See, for example, *wälag siläwaččäw* "because he calls them begetter(s)" Wright (1877) no. 277, 1, p. 286 (col. 2). See also Praetorius (1879), p. 113; Cowley (1974), p. 604; and Guidi (1889), p. 59.

4 Fols. 3r-15r: the Apocalypse of Baruch, Br. Lib. MS Or. 503, fol. 63r, Wright (1877), pp. 20-1; fols. 15r-16r: chronology of the rulers of Ethiopia; fols. 16r-25v: two

of EMML 7007 are in Amharic. They include commentary on *Bä-səmä Ab* or the Gəʻəz Opening Prayer[5] (fols. 30r-31v, 33rv and 32v); commentary on the Our Father[6] (fols. 32v, 32r, 49rv and 34rv); commentary (with the usual lengthy introduction) on the Nicene Creed[7] (fols. 34ᵛ-74ᵛ); admonition in a composition that *rhymes* in very short lines (fols. 74v-80r); and the symbolic meanings of the letters of the Gəʻəz alphabet, in Gəʻəz and Amharic[8] (fols. 80r-110v). The rest (fols. 111r-121r) contains different hymns and litanies in Gəʻəz in a later hand[9]. Since poems are not always good sources for the study of grammar and since editing it is in progress, the present study excludes the unique poem in fols. 74v-80r.

1.0. *Orthography*

The beautiful eighteenth century hand of the relatively careful copyist of EMML 7007 makes it easy for one to see clearly the different forms of the letters of this manuscript.

1.1.   The letter for *ž̌* is ጀ, not ዠ[10]. Its first order form *ž̌ä*, is not distinguishable from its third order form, *ž̌i*; both are ጀ:

    ጀመራቸው ፡ (fol. 39v, for MA: ዠመራቸው ፡)

    ረጀም ፡ (fol. 41v for MA: ረዠም ፡)

1.2.   The sixth order form of *č̌* is not different from its third order form; both *č̌i* and *č̌(ə)* are rendered with ጪ. The form ጭ is very rare in this manuscript[11].

---

unidentified admonitions, with the second (fols. 18r-25v) having a paragraph on the seven deadly sins, 7 *ḫaṭawə' əmuran əllä yəqättəlu näfsä* (f. 20v); fols. 25v-26r: a shorter version of the genealogy of Shoan monks, *cf.* EMML 1760, fols. 110v-130r, Getatchew Haile-Macomber (1981), p. 207; fols. 26r-27r: ages of biblical and other historical personalities; fols. 27r-29v: commentary on the creation, *Sənä fəṭrät*, and genealogy of rulers from Adam to *Aṣe* Susənəyos (1607-1632), concluded with some historical notes.

5 Br. Lib. MS Or. 792, fol. 2r, Wright (1877), p. 286.

6 *Ibid.*, fol. 3r.

7 *Cf.* d'Abbadie 101, fol. 2r, Conti Rossini (1912), no. 102, I, p. 483.

8 Probably d'Abbadie 212, fol. 1r, Conti Rossini (1913), no. 151, p. 27.

9 Fols. 111r-112r: *Bä'əntä Śəllasekä*, Hammerschmidt (1960), pp. 16-18; fols. 112r-115r: *Bəzə't anti wä-nəgəstä ṣədq*, Chaine (1913), no. 292, p. 345; fols. 115r-117v: *Nä'a Giyorgis* [MS: *Giworgis*], Br. Lib. MS Or. 568, fol. 112r, Wright (1877), no. 181, b. p. 117 (col. 2); fols 117v-119v: *O-zä-wärädkä*, Hammerschmidt (1960), pp. 20-24; and fols. 119v-121v: *Täfäśśəhi Maryam lä-Addam fasikahu*, Chaine (1913), no. 302, p. 345.

10 *Cf.* Strelcyn (1968), p. 31; Praetorius (1879), p. 3.

11 *Cf.* Strelcyn (1981), p. 73.

Furthermore, its first order form, ቸ (čä), and its fifth order form, ቼ (čе), interchange freely [12].

1. ነበረቼ ፣ (fol. 34v, MA: ነበረች ፣).
   ነቼ (fol. 35r, MA: ነች ፣).
2. እርሳቸውም ፣ and እርሷቸውም ፣ (fol. 35v).
   አላቸው ፣ (fol. 38v) and አላች ፣ (fol. 35v).

1.3. The free interchange can be seen also between the first order form of š, ሻ (šä), and its fifth order form, ሼ (šе) [13].

1. አሽክመው ፣ (fol. 31r).
   ተሼልም ፣ (fol. 68r).

1.4. The labials *l*ʷä and *m*ʷä are consistently written as ኻ and ኟ respectively.

1. የሚኻት ፣ (fol. 41v, MA: የሚሏት ፣).
   ይኻል ፣ (fol. 35r [four times]).
2. ከደኟ ፣ (fol. 63r, MA: ከደኟ ፣ and ከደሟ ፣).

2.0. *Morphology*

2.1. As in the old Amharic text studied by R. Cowley [14], the (Gə'əz) verb ጠበወ ፣ is changed to ጠበ ፣, not to ጠባ ፣ as in MA.

1. በደረትዋ ፣ ተቀምጦ ፣ ሲጠብ ፣ ተገኘ ፣ (fol. 34v).
   He was found sitting on her chest and suckling.

The last radical of the verb from which አወራ ፣, አስወራ ፣, etc., are derived could have been የ (* ወረየ ፣ cf., Arabic روى). This manuscript preserves the form አስወረ ፣ "to disseminate, to spread news"

2. አብላ ፣ ወለድሁ ፣ ብላ ፣ አስወረቼ ፣ (fol. 84v)
   Lying, she made the news spread, saying, "I have borne (a child)".

2.2 We know that (Gə'əz) verbs ending in ወ/የ change sometimes like those ending in ሀ, ሐ, ኅ/አ, ዐ in MA; e.g., ጠበወ ፣ becomes ጠባ ፣ just as ሰምዐ ፣ becomes ሰማ ፣. The influence of the analogical construction seems to work in

---

12 On the use of the forms of *č*, see Griaule (1932), pp. 4-7; and Strelcyn (1981), p. 73.
13 *Cf.* Strelcyn (1981), p. 73.
14 Cowley (1974), pp. 597-607; Getatchew Haile (1980), p. 579.

the reverse as well. That is, verbs ending in **ሀ**, **ሐ**, **ጎ/አ**, **ዐ** change sometimes like those ending in **ወ/የ** in MA; e.g., **ፈርሁ ፡** > **ፈረሁ ፡** > **ፈረ ፡** "to fear" [15].

1. **ጸላቱም ፡ ይፈረዋል ፡**   (fol. 31r).
   His enemy, too, would fear him.
2. **አየና ፡ ነገሩን ፡ ፈረ ፡**   (fol. 67r).
   He saw the matter and was afraid.
3. **እርሱም ፡ ቢፈር ፡ ደፈረና ፡ ማለ ፡**   (fol. 37v).
   And he, since he was afraid, dared and swore.

2.3. There are several derived verbs in this manuscript which are not common in MA, e.g., **አሄደ ፡** "to cause to go, to make one go" (MA: **አስኬደ ፡**).

1. **ግራ ፡ መንገድ ፡ የሚያሄዱ ፡ አጋንንት ፡**   (fol. 30v).
   Demons which cause one to go the wrong [lit. "left"] way.

In MA, **አሄደ ፡** means "to thresh, to tread grain, to let animals walk on cereal plants for the purpose of threshing". Interestingly, the object in this present day meaning is not "animals" but the cereal plant:

2. **ገበሬው ፡ ገብሱን ፡ አሄደ ።**
   The farmer threshed the barley.

The above example taken from fol. 30v (sentence 2. 3, 1) would mean that a sentence such as

3. **አጋንንት ፡ ምእመኑን ፡ ግራ ፡ መንገድ ፡ አሄዱት ።**
   Demons caused the faithful to go the wrong way

was possible.

አኛ "to cause or to assist one to lie down". This verb, which is obviously the causative of ***ኛ**, is very common in older Amharic [16].

4. **እንደሰው ፡ አኙኝ ፡ አንሱኝ ፡ እገሙኝ ፡ ተኩሱኝ ፡ አላለም ፡**   (fol. 64v).
   [Christ] never said like others, help me lie down, raise me up, treat me with *wagämt* (or) treat me with medical fire.

In MA (of Shoa), the verb **አገመ ፡** is type B (O$_2$), not type A (O$_1$) as in this example [17].

15 Strelcyn (1981), p. 74 (parag. 2.2.8).
16 *Cf.* Strelcyn (1968), p. 68; Getatchew Haile (1970), p. 71.
17 For similar examples in the Amharic dialect of Wollo, see Getatchew Haile-Seifu Metaferia (1973), p. 118.

አሰለበ ፡ "to take off one's clothing" (from Gəʿəz ሰለበ ፡ "to take away, usually by force").

5. እንግዲያስ ፡ ልብስሽን ፡ ሁሉ ፡ አስልቢ ፡ አንድ ፡ ልብስ ፡ ልበሺ ፡   (fol. 43v).
   If so, take off all your clothes; put on (only) one dress.

6. ሁሉን ፡ አሰለበቺ ፡ ዓይነ ፡ ርግብም ፡ የራስ ፡ መሸፈኛ ፡ አልቀራትም ፡ ሁሉን ፡ አሰለበቺ ፡
   (fol. 43v).
   She took off every(thing). She did not spare even (her) veil (which is) the head cover; she took off every(thing).

አሻሻለ ፡ "to compare, to choose, to see which of the many choices is the better one" (MA: "to improve").

7. የማነን ፡ ን (fol. 44v) ጉሥ ፡ ልጅ ፡ ላግባ ፡ ብሎ ፡ ሲል ፡ ሲያሻሻል ፡ ነበረ ፡
   (fol. 44rv).
   He was comparing (girls) and choosing (a wife) saying, "Whose king's daughter should I marry?".

8. መጽሐፍ ፡ ላሻሽል ፡ ከአፈ ፡ መምህር ፡ ልጠይቅ ፡ ሳይል ፡   (fol. 51v).
   Without saying, "Let me choose/compare book(s); let me inquire from the mouth of a teacher".

ተባባለ ፡ "to disagree, to contradict each other" (from አለ ፡ "to say"; MA: "to say to each other")

9. መጽሐፍት ፡ ተባባሉን ፡   (fol. 55v).
   "Did the (holy) books contradict each other"?

10. አልተባባሉም ፡ ጉባኤያቸው ፡ አንድ ፡ ቀን ፡ አይዶለውም ፡   (fol. 55v).
    They did not disagree; the council(s about which each of the so-called differing books reported) did not take place in one (and) same day.
    They did not disagree; they are not reporting about the same council.

2.4. ጸ/ፀ are very well preserved. The texts in this manuscript are very much influenced by the Amharic of Gondar. My examples are limited to words that are not common.

ልጸ ፡ "bark" (MA: ልጥ ፡)

1. የቤቱ ፡ ልጹ ፡ እንዳይበጠስ ፡   (fol. 110r).
   In order that the bark of the house (with which the walls were tied together) might not be cut.

(See also fol. 107v).

ቀጸ ፡ (< ቀጽዐ) "to cut, to tailor, to rule, to decide, to straighten".

2. ስንክሳር ፡ እግዚእነ ፡ ኢየሱስ ፡ ክርሰቶስ ፡ በአንድ ፡ ሐብር ፡ ሲሰራ ፡ ሲቀጸ ፡ ይውል ፡ ነበረ ፡ ይላል ፡   (fol. 55v).
The Synaxary says, "Our Lord Jesus Christ used to spend the day together with (them) laying down rules and deciding on (matters concerning the Church)".

ጸይም ፡ "brown" (for human skin complexion, ጸሊም ፡ > ጸይም ፡ > ጠይም ፡?)

3. አይቀላም ፡ አይጠቁርም ፡ ጸይም ፡ ነው ፡   (fol. 100r).
It shall neither be red (i.e. "light") nor black: it (shall) be brown.

ጸፈጠ ፡ "to be tasty" (MA: ጣፈጠ ፡)[18]

4. በትምህርት ፡ ጨው ፡ ጸፍጣቹሁ ፡ እንድትጸድቁ ፡   (fol. 108r).
That you may be justified spiced with the salt of learning.

2.5.   The plural marker

The MA plural marker -*oč̆č̆* which is suffixed to a singular (e.g., *bet* "house", *betoč̆č̆* "houses") may have its origin in *at*, one of the plural markers in Gə'əz (e.g., *gäṣṣ* "face", *gäṣṣat* "faces,"). In this manuscript, the plural for ልጅ ፡ "child" is in most cases ልጃቹ *ləğač̆(č̆)*[19],.

1. አዳምን ፡ ከነልጃቹ ፡ አወጸው ፡   (fol. 55v).
[Our Lord] brought out (of Sheol) Adam with (all) his children,
(See also fols. 35r, 36v, 102r and 102v).
The plural for ሰው ፡ "person", "man", "human", is always ሰዋቹ *säwač̆(č̆)*.

2. ሰዋቹ ፡ ከጽርዕ ፡ ሀገር ፡ መጽተው ፡   (fol. 36v).
His people coming from Greece [inquired about him].

(See also fols. 37r [twice], 38r, 53r and 84r).

2.6.   The MA ምንድር ፡ "what", is always ምንዱር ፡

1. ምንዱር ፡ ነው ፡ ግንድ ፡ ነው ።   (fol. 44v).
What is it, a log?

(See also fol. 51r).

---

18 Getatchew Haile (1970), p. 80.
19 *Cf.* Cowley (1974), f. 4v (Plate III). For a similar form in Gafat, see Leslau (1956), p. 42.

2.7. As mentioned in the introduction, both forms ጔታ ፥ and ጌታ ፥ "master, lord" are common, although the earlier is more frequent than the latter.

1. የበጎውም ፥ የክፉውም ፥ ጔታ ፥ እሱ ፥ ነው ፥   (fol. 106r).
   He is the Lord of the good as well as the bad (things).
2. እግዚአ ፥ ማለት ፥ ጔታ ፥ ማለት ፥ ነው ፥   (fol. 67v).
   Ǝgzi'o (in Gəʿəz) means gʷeta ("master, lord", in Amharic).

(See also fol. 101v [three times]). ጔታ ፥ is very common in older Amharic[20].

3. እግዚእነ ፥ ማለት ፥ ጔታ ፥ ማለት ፥ ነው ፥   (fol. 61v).
   Ǝgzi'ənä (in Gə'əz) means gʷeta [sic] ("master, lord" in Amharic).

2.8. The MA ያለ or አለ "without" is invariably እንበለ as in Gəʿəz[21].

1. እንበለዚሁ ፥   (fol. 87v, twice).
   Without this.
2. እንበለ ፥ መጠን ፥   (fol. 102r).
   Without limit.
3. እንበለ ፥ እርሱ ፥   (fol. 110v).
   Without him.
4. እንበለ ፥ ባዲ ፥   (fol. 41r).
   Other than her husband.
5. እንበለ ፥ ልብሴ ፥   (fol. 41v).
   Without my clothes.

2.9. The auxiliary verb allä retains its final vowel in the 3rd person plural in the compound verb.

1. ካህናት ፥ በጸጋ ፥ አምላክ ፥ ተብለዋሉ ፥   (fol. 59v)
   Priests are called god(s) by grace.
2. ምእመናንም ፥ የጸጋ ፥ ልጅ ፥ ተብለዋሉ ፥   (fol. 61v).
   The faithful, too, are called children (of God) by grace.
3. እስራኤልም ፥ ወልድየ ፥ ዘበኩርየ ፥ ተብለዋሉ ፥   (fol. 61v).
   The Israelites, too, have been called "My first-born child".

2.10. It is a well known fact that the mm (of the relative clause, የም) drops

---

20 Praetorius (1879), p. 202; Getatchew Haile (I forthcoming).
21 Griaule (1933), p. 6 (line 5); Getatchew Haile (1970), p. 74. The form is still used in Səmen.

out in the negative [22]. There are apparently conditions in which it drops out
in the affimative as well.

1. ይነግራት ፥ [MA : የሚነግራት ፥] የለም ፥ ብየ ፥ እነግርሽ ፥ ብየ ፥ መጻሁ ፥ (fol. 41v)
   I came to tell you saying to myself (that) there is no one who would
   tell you [lit. "her"].

2. አይሰማ ፥ [MA : የማይሰማ ፥] ታቦት ፥ አለና ፥ ቤተ ፥ ክርስቲያኑን ፥ አቃ[ጸለው ፨]
   (fol. 38r).
   He burnt the church saying, "(What use is) a *tabot* that does not
   listen (to prayers)"?

3. መናፍቅ ፥ ኪመለስ ፥ [MA : ከሚመለስ ፥] የሰይፍ ፥ ሞት ፥ ይቀበል ፥ ይወዳል ፥
   (fol. 58v).
   A heretic would love to accept death by [lit. "of"] sword rather than
   returning (to the true faith).

4. ምነው ፥ የሰማይ ፥ አባቴ ፥ በሉኝ ፥ ኪል ፥ [MA : ከሚል ፥] ወይ ፥ መምህሬ ፥ ወይ ፥ ጌታየ ፥
   በሉኝ ፥ ባለ ፥ (fol. 32r).
   Why should he have said, "call me either 'my teacher' or 'my
   master'" instead of saying, "call me 'my heavenly father'"?

2.11. It is extremely interesting to note that the etymology of MA
እባክህ ፤ እባክሽ ፤ etc., "please", could be ባረከ ፥ "to bless".

1. ይባርካችሁ ፥ [MA : እባካችሁ ፥] ወንድሞቼ ፥ ሳጽን ፥ አለኝ ፥ ... በመርከብ ፥ ላይ ፥
   ጫኑልኝ ፥ (fol. 43v).
   May [God] bless you [MA "Please"], my brothers, I have a box ...
   load (it) on (the) ship.

3.0. *Grammar*

3.1. The object marker ን can be used with an object that lacks a definite
article.

1. መቃብርን ፥ ቢከፍቱ ፥ ከሆድዋ ፥ ልጅ ፥ ወጥቶ ፥ በደረትዋ ፥ ተቀምጦ ፥ ሲጠብ ፥ ተገኘ ፥
   (fol. 34v).
   When they opened (the) tomb, a child was found (who), having
   come out of her womb, was suckling sitting on her chest.

---

22 For the same use of the form, see Griaule (1933), p. 26, no. 5; Getatchew Haile-
   Seifu Metaferia (1973), p. 115.

2. ከዚያ ፡ ኋላ ፡ ሬሳን ፡ ቀብረው ፡ ያነን ፡ ልጅ ፡ አንስተው ፡ ሄዱ ፡   (fol. 34v).
   Then they buried (the) corpse, took up that child and left.
3. የሚታዮነም ፡ የማይታዮነም ፡ ለፈጠረ ፡ አምላክ ፡ እናምናለን ፡   (fol. 61r).
   We believe in God who created (the) visible and (the) invisible.
4. ያነግዜ ፡ ሰይጣን ፡ ዝሙ-ትን ፡ አሳደረባት ፡   (fol. 35r).
   At that time Satan made sexual lust dwell in her.

What is striking in the first three cases is not the presence of the object marker but the absence of the definite article (መቃብርን ፡ for መቃብሩን ፡, ሬሳን ፡ for ሬሳውን ፡ and የሚታዮነም ፤ የማይታዮነም ፡ for የሚታዮትንም ፡ የማይታዮትንም ፡ respectively). According to MA (of Shoa), the object marker in 3.1.2 is redundant or unnecessary, if not ungrammatical. However, the use of the Amharic definite article has not been thoroughly investigated yet.

3.2. The double introduction of quotations (with ሲል ፡ አለ ፡ , ብሎ ፡ አለ ፡, etc.) is now so well known in older Amharic that commenting on it might be unnecessary. It may be fair, however, to say that this phenomenon is disappearing just in this century. Such quotations are introduced commonly by mentioning two forms of the verb አለ ፡ "to say".

1. አርዮስ ፡ ሲል ፡ እርሱን ፡ ቀድሞ ፡ ፈጠረ ፡ በርሱ ፡ እኛን ፡ ፈጠረ ፡ ይላል ፡   (fol. 62v).
   Arius says, "He first created him and through him he created us".
2. ዘእንየ ፡ ኪያየ ፡ ርእዮ ፡ ለአቡየ ፡ ብሎ ፡ ሲል ፡ ተናገረ ፡   (fol. 31v).
   He spoke saying, "He that hath seen me hath seen my father".

3.3. At least in one case, a finite or a compound verb, ይደብላል ፡ (i.e., a verb with an auxiliary verb), is used in a subordinate sentence.

1. በገና ፡ በመታ ፡ ጊዜ ፡ ፈረሱ ፡ ከጋጽ ፡ ሆኖ ፡ ይደብላል ፡ ሆነ ፡   (fol. 35r).
   It so used to happen that when he played the harp, the horse in the stable danced (?).

3.4. On the other hand, the gerund, the verb form which in MA is considered non-finite (in Shoa), is used in the main sentence[22].

1. የናቱ ፡ ሰዋቺ ፡ ዘመዶቹ ፡ በቅንዓት ፡ ሰኞ ፡ መከሩ ፡ ተፈታባቸው ፡ ማክሰኞ ፡ መከሩ ፡ ተፈታባቸው ፡ ረቡዕ ፡ መከሩ ፡ ጸንቶ ፡ (fol. 84r).
   His [Christ's] mother's people, his relatives, conspired in jealousy on Monday; (their conspiracy) was foiled. They conspired on Tuesday;

it was (again) foiled. They conspired on Wednesday; (this time) it held.

See also 3.6.2 below.

3.5.   The verb **ነገሠ ፥** "to be a king", which is intransitive in MA, takes an object, "to rule (?)".

    1.   **ያባቱን ፥ መን** (fol. 36v) **ግሥት ፥ ነገሠ ፥**   (fol. 36rv).
       He ruled his father's kingdom.

3.6.   The particle **ና**, suffixed to a verb in the subjunctive, joins a subordinate sentence, with the meaning "so that, in order that".

    1.   **እስኪ ፥ ያነን ፥ ሕፃን ፥ ስደድልኝ ፥ ለምዶም ፥ እንደሆነ ፥ አየውና የተማረውንም ፥ እጠይ
       ቀውና ፥ ሲል ፥ ላከበት ፥** (fol. 37r).
       He sent him (a missive) saying, "Please let that child come to me so that I may see (on) him if he is accustomed (to being here) and that I may inquire from him what he has learnt".
    2.   **እኔም ፥ አምንበታለሁና ፥ ስትመለሱ ፥ ትነግሩኝና ፥ ድረሱብኝ ፥ አላቸው ፥ አርደው ፥ ብሎ ፥**
       (fol. 83r).
       Since I, too, believe in him, come to me when you return so that you may tell me (about what you saw). He meant, "so that I may slay him".

3.7.   The **ና**, when suffixed to an imperfect, seems to have the meaning of "if":

    1.   **ይህንስ ፥ አልክኝና ፥ እስክታሳየኝ ፥ ድረስ ፥ ቀድሜ ፥ በወንጌልና ፥ በመስቀል ፥ አምልሃ
       ለሁ ፥** (fol. 37v).
       If you say this to me, I shall make you first swear by the Gospel and the Cross until you show me (the corpse).
    2.   **በን ፥ ይህንንስ ፥ አልክኝና ፥ ለማን ፥ እሰግዳለሁ ፥ ትላለህ ፥**   (fol. 57r).
       Well, if you say this to me, who do you say you [lit. "I"] worship?

3.8.   The verb **አመነ ፥** "to believe" takes the preposition **ለ** (MA: **በ**).

    1.   **ሰማዮን ፥ ካልነበረ ፥ እንደነበረ ፥ አድርጎ ፥ ለፈጠረ ፥ ለ**(fol. 61r) **ምላክ ፥ እናምናለን ፥**
       (fols. 60v-61r).
       We believe in God who created the heaven/sky from non-existent to existent.

2. ለባሕርይ ፡ ለጠባይ ፡ ልጁ ፡ እናምናለን ፡   (fol. 61v).
   We believe in his natural Son.

3. በሕንድነት ፡ በሶስትነት ፡ ለሚኖር ፡ አምላክ ፡ እናምናለን ፡   (fol. 61v).
   We believe in God who exists in unity and trinity.

3.9.   The particle ት.

The grammatical role of the suffix ት found in old Amharic texts is not
very clear. Goldenberg has valid reasons to consider it as a marker of an
equative sentence, a variant of ነው ፡ "to be"[23]. I had an opportunity to
furnish materials in questioning the position of Goldenberg[24]. The materials
presented here make my position, that the particle may not be a simple
variant of ነው, stronger.

1. እለ ፡ እስክንድሮስም ፡ ጠየቀው ፡ ም፡ነው ፡ ወልድን ፡ ፍጡር ፡ ያልኸው ፡ ቢለው ፡ እኔት ፡
   አልሁት ፡ መጽሐፍ ፡ ይላል ፡ እንጂ ፡ አለው ፡   (fol. 56v).
   Alexander asked him (a question). When he said to him, "Why is it
   that you call the Son creature?" Arius said, "Did I call him (so)?
   (No); but the scripture did."

It may be tempting to suggest a translation such as, ... Arius said, "*Is* it I
(who) called him (so) ...". But such a translation could be accepted only if
the structure was, ... እኔት ፡ ያልሁት ፡ ...

2. መቅዶንዮስም ፡ መለሰና ፡ እኔት ፡ አልሁት ፡ መጽሐፍ ፡ ይለዋል ፡ እንጂ ፡ አለው ፡   (fol.
   69v).
   And Macedonius replied saying, "Did I call him (so) or the scripture?".

3. እለ ፡ እስክንድሮስም ፡ ምሳሌህ ፡ ይህት ፡ ነው ፡ ሌላ (fol. 57r) ን ፡ አለህ ፡ ቢለው ፡ አ
   ርዮስ ፡ የለኝም ፡ አለ ፡   (fols. 56r-57r).
   When Alexander said to him, "Is this your only proof-text [lit.
   "example"]? Do you have any other one?". Arius said, "I do not
   have (any other; yes, this is all)".

This is a unique example where both ት and ነው ፡ appear in one (grammatical) place, making the equation of ት with ነው ፡ impossible. More examples
of this type, which are lacking in our manuscript, are essential to show that
ት is not a variant of ነው ፡. It may be argued that in this unique example the

---

23 Goldenberg (1974), p. 247; Goldenberg (1976), 131-7; Cowley (1977), pp. 139-43;
   Getatchew Haile (1979), pp. 119-121. Gafat has a copula in the form of a geminated *t*,
   Leslau (1956), p. 78.
24 Getatchew Haile (II forthcoming).

word **ነው ፡** could have been added by the copyist of this manuscript who may have not understood the role of **ት** in the old manuscript from which he was copying.

> 4. **አባቶቻቸን ፡ ለሃይማኖት ፡ አልተመቸከም ፡ ሲሉ ፡ አስወጽተው ፡ ሰደዱት ፡ እኔት ፡ አገባ ዋለሁ ፡ አይቻለኝም ፡ አለ ፡** (fol. 67r).
>
> "Our fathers expelled him and excommunicated him saying, 'You are not fit for the faith'. Would I let him back? I cannot", he said.

I see no way of understanding the **ት** in **እኔት ፡** in this example as any form of the verb *to be*.

The usual examples such as

> 5. **ለመንፈስ ፡ ቅዱስና ፡** (fol. 104r) **ለወልድ ፡ አካል ፡ አብ ፡ ምናቸውት ፡** (ff. 103v-104r).
>
> What is the Father for the person(s) of the Holy Spirit and the Son?

are also found in this manuscript.

After spending so much time in defining the role of this particle, I am inclined to believe that it is a certain type of a definite article, the same article that appears with a relative verb in the plural, e.g., **የሄዱት ፡** "the ones who left". There should be nothing new in the Amharic pronouns (e.g., **እኔው ፡**) taking the definite article:

> 6. **እኔው ፡ አገባዋለሁ ፡**
>
> The I (of all people) shall let him in/back.
>
> 7. **እኔት ፡ አገባዋለሁ ፡**
>
> The I (of all people) shall let him in.

Abbreviations and Bibliography

BSOAS = *Bulletin of the School of Oriental and African Studies*.

Chaine (1913) = M. Chaine, "Répertoire des Salam et Malke'e contenus dans les manuscrits éthiopiens de la bibliothèques d'Europe", *Revue de l'Orient Chrétien*, 2ᵉ série 8/18 (1913), pp. 183-203 and 337-357.

Conti Rossini (1912; and 1913) = C. Conti Rossini, "Notice sur les manuscrits éthiopiens de la collection d'Abbadie", *JA*, (Mai-Juin 1912 - Novembre-Décembre 1915).

Cowley (1974) = Roger Cowley, "A Text in Old Amharic", *BSOAS*, vol. 37/3 (1974), pp. 597-607.

Cowley (1977) = Roger Cowley, "Additional Sources for a copula *tt* in Old Amharic", *IOS*, vol. 7 (1977), pp. 139-143.

EMML = Ethiopian Manuscript Microfilm Library, Addis Ababa/Collegeville; see Getatchew Haile-Macomber.

Fol(s). = Folio(s).

Getatchew Haile (1970) = Getatchew Haile, "Archaic Amharic Forms", *Proceedings of the Third International Conference of Ethiopian Studies II, Addis Ababa 1966*, Addis Ababa (1970), pp. 61-80.

Getatchew Haile (1979) = Getatchew Haile, "Some Archaic Features of Amharic", *Proceedings of the Fifth International Conference of Ethiopian Studies, Session B, Chicago 1978*, Chicago 1979, pp. 111-124.

Getatchew Haile (1980) = Getatchew Haile, "Some Notes on 'A Text in Old Amharic' of Roger Cowley", *BSOAS*, vol. 43/3 (1980), pp. 578-80.

Getatchew Haile (I Forthcoming) = Getatchew Haile, "Panegyrics in Old Amharic", *IOS*.

Getatchew Haile (II forthcoming) = Getatchew Haile, "Materials on the theology of the *Qəb'at*, or Unction", *Proceedings of the Sixth International Conference of Ethiopian Studies*, Tel-Aviv 1980.

Getatchew Haile-Macomber (1981) = Getatchew Haile and William F. Macomber, *A Catalogue of Ethiopian Manuscripts Microfilmed for the Ethiopian Manuscript Microfilm Library, Addis Ababa and for the Hill Monastic Manuscript Library, Collegeville, Vol. V: Project Numbers 1501-2000*, Collegeville, 1981.

Getatchew Haile-Seifu Metaferia (1973) = Getatchew Haile and Seifu Metaferia, "The Dialect of Gojjam", Habte Maryam Marcos (ed.), "Regional Variations in Amharic", *Journal of Ethiopian Studies*, vol. 11/2 (1973), pp. 113-129.

Goldenberg (1974) = Gideon Goldenberg, "L'étude du Gouragué et la comparaison chamito-sémitique", *IV Congresso Internazionale di Studi Etiopici, II Roma 1972*, Roma 1974, pp. 235-249.

Goldenberg (1976) = Gideon Goldenberg, "A Copula ✝ in Old Amharic", *IOS*, vol. 6 (1976), pp. 131-137.

Griaule (1932) = Marcel Griaule, "Règles de l'Église (documents éthiopiens)", *JA* (Juillet-Septembre 1932), pp. 1-42.

Guidi (1889) = I. Guidi, "Le canzoni geez-amariña in onore di Re Abissini", *Rendiconti della Reale Accademia dei Lincei. Classe di scienze morali, storiche e filologiche*, vol. V, ser. 4 (1889), pp. 53-66.

Hammerschmidt (1960) = Ernst Hammerschmidt, *Äthiopische liturgische Texte der Bodleian Library in Oxford*, Berlin 1960.

IOS = *Israel Oriental Studies*.

JA = *Journal Asiatique*.

Leslau (1956) = W. Leslau, *Étude descriptive et comparative du Gafat*, Paris 1956.

MA = Modern Amharic.

MS = Manuscript.

Praetorius (1879) = F. Praetorius, *Die amharische Sprache*, Halle 1879, reprint Leipzig 1972.

Strelcyn (1968) = S. Strelcyn, *Médecine et plantes d'Éthiopie*, Warsaw 1968.

Strelcyn (1981) = S. Strelcyn, "Les mystères de Psaumes, traité éthiopien sur l'emploi des Psaumes (Amharique ancien)", *BSOAS*, vol. 44/1 (1981), pp. 55-84.

Wright (1877) = William Wright, *Catalogue of Ethiopic Manuscripts in the British Museum Acquired since the Year 1847*, London 1877.

NOMINALIZATION IN AMHARIC AND HARARI:
ADJECTIVIZATION

GIDEON GOLDENBERG
Tel-Aviv University

1.   Early in the history of Amharic studies it was well recognized that as the exponents of "genitive" and "relative" (including "conjunctional" substantivization) were identical it would be unadvisable and improper to treat those forms separately in the grammatical description. In fact, this observation, which Praetorius compressed into an incidental foot-note (AS 318 n. 2), is one of the most pregnant statements on Amharic syntax that were made in *Die amharische Sprache* (see also ibid. 3-4 and 458 §343a). Not only are all nominalizations effected by the same "translatif", but the syntactically-nominalized transforms pass beyond the bounds of syntax in their becoming noun-like. Such syntactical constructions, especially in Amharic and in Harari, will be found capable of assuming post-nominal suffixes and even susceptible of entering, as bases, into further morphological noun-derivation.

Nominalization is the process by which any expression may be formed into a noun or into a construction assuming the function of a noun. The idea that linguistic expressions are often made to pass, whether by morphological or by syntactical means, from one grammatical category to another has long been conceived, referred to under various names such as "Überführung", "conversion", "Verwandlung", "transposition", (Fr.) "translation" (or Eng. "transference"), "rank-shifting" (in some sense), or the vogue term "transformation" in some of its uses [1].

---

[1] F. Praetorius (AS 319:10-11) referred incidentally to an adjective-derivational suffix as "der Ansatz zu formaler Überführung ins Adjektiv". H. Schuchardt's "Ueberführung in eine andere Wortklasse" has been mentioned by H.J. Polotsky (1976, p. 2 fn. 1); "Überführung" is now common, without being a technical term, as a German rendering of the French "translation". "Conversion" was H. Sweet's term for what Ch. Bally later called "transposition implicite" (Sweet 1891 I § 105). [Revived by A.F.L. Beeston, "conversion" (or rather "clause conversion") was differently employed for the substitution of a morphological transform for its syntactically equivalent clause; see Beeston 1970 ch. 12 etc.]. For "Verwandlung ganzer Sätze etc. in substantivische Satztheile" or "in adjectivische adnominale Attribute" v. G. von der Gabelentz ²1901, pp. 104, 463-470. A short historical survey of Ch. Bally's "transposition" and L. Tesnière's "translation" will be found in Tesnière 1959 ch. 163 (pp. 381-384). R.P. Stockwell 1977 pp. 51 & 142 will suffice as one possible reference for the rest.

The equivalence itself of a word to its syntactical parallels was brilliantly recognized in

Noun being understood as a generic term embracing substantive and adjective, nominalization consequently comprises substantivization and adjectivization as two special classes to be described in the sequel.

2. *Adjective and Adjectivization*

The adjective will be characterized as reflecting, in reduced form, some of the properties of the predicative nexus typical of the verb (or verb-like) complex from which it is considered to be derived. Like finite verbs it contains within itself its pronominal subject, which here represents the qualified entity. According to this conception, the deverbal adjective would take, in the first place, the form of a participle, other adjectival forms being regarded as quasi-participial[2]. Teaching this doctrine, the Arab grammarians would explain the difference between a noun which is not an adjective (*ism ġayr ṣifa*) and a noun which is an adjective (*ism huwa ṣifa*) defining the former as *ǧins ġayr ma'xūḏ min fiʻl* "a common noun not drawn from a verb" (like 'man', 'horse' etc.) and the latter as *ma'xūḏ min al-fiʻl* "drawn from the verb"[3]. The adjective is simply *ṣifa* when it has the form of a participle (*ism fāʻil* or *ism al-mafʻūl*), otherwise it will be regarded as *ṣifa mušabbaha bi(-smi) l-fāʻil* etc., or, in short, *ṣifa mušabbaha*. Considering an Arabic sentence like *marartu bi-raǧulin ḥasanin* "I passed by a nice man" it has been said that *yakūnu fī ʻḥasan' ḍamīr yaʻūdu 'ilā l-mawṣūf wa-huwa fī mawḍiʻ marfūʻ bi-ʻḥasan'* "there is in 'ḥasan' ("nice") a personal pronoun referring to the qualified (substantive) [and in apposition to it], which (pronoun) is in the position of a nominative with relation to 'ḥasan'"[4]. It is also said that the adjective which is in predicative position *yataḍammanu l-ḍamīra* "contains a pers. pron." referring to the subject[5]. The implicit presence of the pronominal agent is typical of all

medieval Arabic grammar, where *al-ism | fiʻl al-ṣarīḥ* ("the plain noun | verb") and *mā fī taʼwīlihī* (or *al-muʼawwal bihī*) are presented as belonging to the same syntactical category. In the Becker-Herling system of sentence analysis clauses would be regarded as 'developments' of the simple words for which they stood (Becker [2]1841 p. 510, Pfister 1972; 32; my attention was drawn to these writings by H. J. Polotsky).

2 For such characterization of adjectival forms cf. Polotsky 1976, esp. § 2.1 (pp. 4-7).

3 Ibn Yaʻīš, *Šarḥ al-Mufaṣṣal* I 26:16-17 (ad § 3); cf. Zamaxšarī, *Muf.* 5:3, 85:1.

4 Ibn Yaʻīš, *Šarḥ al-Mufaṣṣal* VI 82:14-15 (ad § 348).

5 The examples are *zaydun qāʼimun* "Zayd is standing" and *'amrun ḥasanun* "'Amr is nice"; see Ibn al-Anbārī, *Inṣāf* 30. The Arab grammarians are said to be in full agreement on this point; the "Kūfans" even went further in claiming that any nominal predicate, not only an adjective, should be regarded as containing a pronoun referring to the subject (see ibid.).

nominal forms of the verb[6]; in the deverbal adjective this hidden pronoun forms the head. If a finite verb-form can be characterized by the presence of (1) the pronominal subject and (2) the verbal lexeme with (3) nexal (predicative) relation between them, an adjective could be defined by the presence of (1) its implied pronominal subject and (2) the description or qualification, with (3) attributive relation between them. With the pronoun as head it is markedly nominal. Needless to say, free adjectives are not necessarily less adjectival than those modifying some substantive; they should not be described indiscriminately as substantivized.

Adjectivization is the transformation of any expression, whether nominal or pronominal or adverbial or a verb (i.e. a nexus-complex), into an adjective. Adjectivizations, the same as adjectival forms, imply a pronominal head. Besides the pronominal agent contained in the verb, any form capable of being extraposed in a nexal construction can equally be made the pronominal(ized) head of an adjectival clause[7].

In the tradition of the Ethiopic *säwasäw* the equivalence of (a) adjectival forms to (b) adjectival phrases and clauses is made conspicuous through the terminology employed, the former being called *wəsṭä-zä qəṣṣəl* (adjectives with implicit *zä-*) and the latter *gəlṣä-zä qəṣṣəl* (adjectives with explicit *zä-*)[8]. By describing plain adjectives as containing within themselves the inherent translatif, the simple forms are shown as "converted". The particle *zä-* which is here mentioned has become in Gəʿəz "ein allgemeines Bezüglichkeits-zeichen" (Dillmann 1857, 264:9.11-12, §147a). Where no longer susceptible of the distinctions of gender and number, the *zä-* can hardly be considered in itself pronominal; it has rather become a nominalizing function-word. As such it resembles its southern parallels.

As already mentioned above (fn. 8), an adjective can always occur as a *bäqi qəṣṣəl*, i.e. without an explicit modified substantive, and will then behave like substantives and assume any nominal marker. If in the following

---

6 "Die Partizipialien, unter denen wir die Partizipien, Infinitive, Gerundien und Supine begreifen ... drücken zwar nicht mehr, wie das Verb, die Aussage aus, werden aber immer noch mit einem Subjekte gedacht" (Becker 514-515). The subject will be explicitly added to such "participials" where necessary (v. ibid.).

7 Indirect attributive expressions, the same as indirect predication couched in extrapositional construction, quite similarly involve a referential pronoun; just another manifestation of the structural affinity between attributive and predicative relations.

8 See MSäw. 311:6-19, 324:5, 332:34, 333:7; cf. ib. 213 (no. 31); MSG 73-74, 89-91; AMQ 469b:12-14; ASäw. 57. An adjective can also be *bäqi* (self-sufficient) when it is predicative or with qualified substantive understood. In such forms as well the implicit *zä-* is said to be present.

discussion adjectives are mostly quoted in attributive position connected with a substantive, this is done because it is precisely in such context that the special syntax of adjectival expressions is discernible.

ADJECTIVIZATION IN AMHARIC

3.   The morphological formation of adjectives (as of other forms) by root × thematic pattern is available in Amharic as in its cognates. Adjectives so formed are mostly (a) participial; some other adjectives, limited in number, are (b) special primary words. Non-verbal forms will be adjectivized morphologically through (c) base + affix derivation. The syntactical value of the adjective will be the same in any case, in (a) *fäsaš wəha* "running water", (b) *dägg säw* "a good man", the same as in (c) *dərrito-am ləbs* "patchy clothes", *särdo-amma märet* "weedy land" (lit. "full of couch-grass"), *andənnät-awi yänuro ədgät* "united development", *hayl-änña agär* "strong country", *sənt-änña šəraššər* "which walk" (lit. "of which time"), *yəhəčč-ənña-wa ləgagäräd* "this girl", or *yät-ənña-w təmhərt* "which study?".

The inclusion of syntactical constructions with *yä-* (or any of its allo-morphs)[9] in the chapter describing the formation of adjectives, as found in Hartmann's *Amharische Grammatik*, pp. 238-250, is completely justified, and could have been regarded, had it been done with consistency, as reflecting a profound conception of Amharic structure. In fact, however, Hartmann follows the Ethiopian tradition in recognizing the *gəlsä-yä qəssəl* as adjectival (ASäw. 57); more closely he treads in the steps of P. Agostino da Hebo, whose *Grammatica amarica* 49-56 seems to have been one of Hartmann's immediate models. But the bringing here of such expressions as *yä-käbbärä* "ehrenwert" and *yä-zare* "heutig" etc. together with *awaqi* "weise" or *kuratänña* "stolz" in a chapter describing the morphology (!) of adjectives seems mostly to reflect the author's awareness of just the lexical equivalence of those "Verbaladjektivische Relativformen" (§ 5.2.1.1) and "Adjektivierte Nomina" (§ 5.2.3.18) to morphologically-derived adjectives in Amharic (like *käff yalä* "high" — *käffətänña*, *däss yämmiyassäñ* "glad(dening)" — *asdässač*, *yäzälaläm* "eternal" — *zälalämawi*)[10], or — more plausibly — his feeling that they are translatable as adjectives into German and other languages[11].

---

9 These are *yä-*, pronounced or *wəstä tawaqi* (ASäw. § 247), *yämm- | mm- | m-*, or, for the Imperfect in absolute usage and in some survivals, zero.

10 Compare the following instance where a *wəstä-yä qəssəl* and a *gəlsä-yä qəssəl* are found parallel in the same context: ƎD 47:4 *əǧǧəg təlləq wäyəmm yannäsa waga* "a very big or small reward".

11 See, e.g., the heading of Hartmann's § 5.2.3.20 (p. 248): "Adjektivische Gliedsätze, die

Structurally there is no real difference between such adjectival expressions and any other "genitive" or "relative" like *yä-nəgus ləǧ* "(the) king's son", *yä-nnantä bet* "your house", *yä-šwa set* " Shoan woman", *yä-aksum nəgus* "king of Aksum", *yagär säw* "countryman", *yä-rswo mämṭat* "your coming"; *yämm-iṭoh wəšša* "a barking dog", *bəzu yä-täläwawwäṭä assab* "many different ideas", *bäzziyačč agär yallu säwočč* "people who are in that country", *yä-bäddälhuh bädäl* "the injustice which I did to you", *baločʼaččäw yä-motubbaččäw hulätt setočč* "two women whose husbands died upon them". In all such instances the forms or constructions marked with /yä-/ are equally "adjectival" in their syntactic value. And in Amharic, as already mentioned above, the syntactically-adjectivized and the morphologically-adjectivized "transférés" are much like the plain adjective in their syntactical and even in their morphological behaviour.

4. Adjectivizations having the form *yä——awi* or *yä——(ä)ňňa* are markedly hypercharacterized. These are mainly common in "adjectival expressions of position" (v. FA 85, n. 3) like *yäfitäňňa* "first", *yähʷaläňňa* "last", *yälayəňňa* "upper", *yätačəňňa* "lower", *yäwädihəňňa* "nearer", *yäwädiyaňňa* "farther", and, formerly, in gentilic adjectives like Gen. xxiii 10 (C. 1886) *Efron yähetawi-w* "Ephron the Hittite", I Kings xxi 4 (C. 1886) *yäyəzreʼelawi-w nabot* "Nabot the Jezreelite", John xix 25 (C. 1886) *maryam yämägdälawitu* "Mary Magdalene", Traité 80 *yäfransawi säw* "Frenchman"; but also in *yamarəňňa qʷanqʷa* "the Amharic language", Zeph. ii 15 (C. 1886) *yädässtäňňa-yitu agär* "the rejoicing city", MČ̣8:10 *yäwädiyaňňa-yitu aläm* "the next world" (ibid. 15:11-12 *yäwädiya-w aläm*), AZ 25 Hədar 1962 5d-e *yädəngätäňňa ṭäqlalla səbsäba* "an extraordinary general meeting", QQ 7:3-4 *yätarikawi qərs* "historical heritage", QQ 7:23-24 *yämängəstawi aqʷam* "official position". See AS 317-320 (§ 249); (Guidi, *Gr.* § 61); Traité 80, 113; (NÉ 128); Agostino da Hebo, *Gr.* 56; FA 85 n. 3, 88 n.l.

It will hardly be possible to determine whether, e.g., *yäfitäňňa, yähetawi* are to be analysed as *(yä-fit)-äňňa, (yä-het)-awi* (AS 319) or as *yä-(fit-äňňa), yä-(het-awi)* (Traité 80), and whether there is at all one single way of analysis good for all such forms. Besides *yäfitäňňa* there are also attested *yäfit* and *fitäňňa*; besides *yähʷaläňňa* — *yähʷala* and *hʷaläňňa*; so there are *yälay* — *yälayəňňa* — *layəňňa, yätač* — *yätačəňňa* — *tačəňňa*. The tendency in the historical development of the language is apparently to replace the older *yä——(ä)ňňa* forms by the simpler ——*(ä)ňňa* and the *yä——awi* forms by

im Deutschen durch einfache Adjektive· wiedergegeben werden". "Der Attributsatz" is discussed in another part of Hartmann's grammar, among the other dependent clauses, pp. 448-452.

——*awi*; yet the simple *yä*—— is also found as an alternative form for gentilic names as well[12]. The formation of adjectival expressions through *yä*——*(ä)ñña* or *yä*——*awi* is not actually alive any more. The extant derivational means may well be employed for achieving differentiation; cf. *yägǝll* "private" — *gǝlläñña* "isolationist" — *gǝllawi* "secluded, individual-istic" etc. [13]

5. *Syntax of Attribute + Substantive: Marking of Plural*

Two ways of marking the plural of indefinite A + S are possible: (I) A + S^{pl} and (II) A^{pl} + S^{pl}. These will equally apply, in principle, to any adjectival expression. The examples which follow are arranged under three heads: (a) A = morphologically-formed adjective [in Tesnière's notation: A, > A], (b) A = *yä-* + noun/pronoun/adverb ("genitive") [Tesnière's (syntacti-cal) "translations" O > A, E > A], and (c) A = *yä-* + verb ("relative") [I ≫ A]. [Construction (b) as here defined refers to the "plain genitive" only (*yähǝsan(u) lǝbs* "(the) baby's dress"), and does not include the construction *yähǝsan lǝbsu*; see Hailu 1964].

I A + S^{pl}

(a)   IT I 273:9 *awwaki säwočč* "unruly people"; LTA 13:12-13 *bǝrtu mǝsässowočč* "strong pillars"; ƎD 45:20 *bǝzu nägäročč* "many things"; MI I:22 *bǝzu säwočč* "many people"; LZG 13:2 *kǝfu säwočč* "bad people"; ibid. *mälkam säwočč* "good people"; HSN 17:22 *tallaq šumamǝnt* "high officials"; ČS 12:3-4 *läǝrogit akǝstočču, lätǝllǝq ǝhǝtočču* "to his old aunts (and) to his elder sisters"; LTA 13:12-13 *bǝherawi tǝmhǝrt-betočč* "national (traditional) schools"; ƎD 47:9 *mänfäsawi sǝrawočč* "pious deeds"; Fables 130:2 *hulätt set-mänäk^{w}sewočč* "two nuns".

(b)   II Sam. xiii 33 *yänǝgus lǝǧočč* "(the) king's sons"; Neh. vii 6 *yagär lǝǧočč* "the children of the province"; IT I 211:29 *yäaksum nägästat* "kings of

---

12 The substitution of the simpler forms for the pleonastic ones can probably be learnt from comparing Bible translations such as Pl. 1829 and C. 1886 with A.A. 1947-53. For the gentilic *yä-* see, e.g., the rendering of "Egyptian" as *yä-mǝsr säw* or *yä-gǝbṣ säw* in the Amharic Bibles.

13 *gälältäñña* approaches in meaning some uses of the last two forms; it is also normal now for "neutral". An attempt to introduce *gǝlläñña* for "neural" (SA 5 Oct. 1960 1d:62) seems to have been unsuccessful.

Aksum, Aksumite kings"; MTəzz. 21:31 *yäňňa wägänočč* "those of our side, our folks"; WL 50:18, IMS 15:1 *yäqädmo säwočč* "the ancients"; MTəzz. 127:3 *yäṣägga ləgočč* [13a].

(c)   Amharic syntax requires that the modified entity, expressed or not, should be represented pronominally in the adjectival ("relative") clause, wherever that is possible [14]. See AS 453-457, Traité 116-119, NÉ 119-120, Polotsky 1936 119-120 [= 456-457], Polotsky 1960 120 [= 6], FA 108-111, Goldenberg 1965 12, id. 1978 141-143. If the modified noun is in the plural, its pronominal representative too will be plural. But pronominal representation and the agreement it carries do not belong to the relative clause in its capacity as an adjectival expression. What concerns us here is the special marking of the relative as plural to make it agree, qua adjective, with its *man'ūt*, and it will be seen in § 6c that such marked agreement is also possible in relative clauses, parallel to the $A^{pl} + S^{pl}$ construction in the other attributive expressions. In this section suffice it to quote, for comparison, a few instances of $A + S^{pl}$ where the adjectival clause taken as a whole is not marked plural.

LM 92apu *abrän yämmənnəsära säwočč* "we people who work together"; LTA 11:25 *čəlot lay yämmiqqämmäṭu-t daňňočč* "the judges sitting in court"; IMS 20:6-7 *yäbarənnät qänbär yäwäddäqäbbaččäw säwočč* "people upon whom the yoke of slavery came". Textual evidence for the construction with *na't sababiyy* like *tarikaččäw yämmiṣṣaf(-äw) wäṭṭaṭočč* "youngsters whose story is being written" is adduced below § 8c (I have got no such example with the modified subst. indefinite, but that is due to mere chance).

6. II $A^{pl} + S^{pl}$

(a)   FK I 85:27 *täkättayočč wättaddäročč* "escort soldiers"; SWärq II 55:14 *bəzuwočč a'waf* "many birds"; ƏD 27:9 *bəzuwočč čačutočč* "many chicks";

13a *yäṣägga ləgočč* is the appellation given to the followers of the Däbrä Libanos doctrine of the Hypostatic Union.

14 In cases where such representation should have involved the verbal complex itself, it is impossible when the position of the required cataphoric pron. suff. is occupied by another pronoun representing some "indirect" complement, as, e.g., in *əgziabəher yäsäṭṭäňň ləgočč* "the children whom the Lord has given me"; the pron. suff. representing the recipient person, or a mediate suffix in any function, will be given preference over the object suffix, and as the "slot" available for post-verbal suff. cannot accomodate more than one suffix, the pronominal representation of the *ism man'ūt* will often have to be left out; cf. Polotsky 1960 120 [= 1971, 6], Hetzron 1966, 95-97.

IT III 145b:11-12 *qʷärraṭočč mäləktäňňočč* "determined messengers"; ƎD 49:8 *räžžəmočč täraročč* "high mountains"; ƎD 14:17 *leločč säwočč* "other people"; ĠT 141:1 *talallaq säwočč*, MTəzz. 74:25 *təlälləq säwočč*, AWDjA 11:26-27 *təlälləqočč säwočč* "great men, gentlemen"; ĠT 143:9 *dägagg säwočč*, ibid. 28apu *dägaggočč säwočč* "kind people"; Hirut 205:6 *zämänawiwočč wäṭṭatočč* "modern youngsters"; IT III 2:22 *mänfäsawyan ṣähafiwočč* "spiritual writers"; HSN 15:20 *wanna wanna ṭəqmočč* "main interests", AWDjA 1apu *wanna wannawočč färänǧočč* "most important Europeans"; LTA 13:22-23 *wändočč-ənna setočč ləǧočč* "boys and girls".

(b)   NÉ 102 *yähagäročč säwočč* "les gens du pays" [plural of *yähagär säw*]; IT I 211:33 *yäaksumočč nägästat* "Aksumite kings, kings of Aksum"; Traité 136 *yänewočč* "my ones, mine"; KBT 7:26 *yäqädmowočč abbatoččaččən* "our forefathers"; MSäw. 51:22 *yäruqočč setočč* "distant females, 3rd pers. fem. pl.". The "genitival" adjectives are marked as plural like any adjectival form in the A^{pl} + S^{pl} construction, the plural marker referring to the adjectival complex as a whole: *(yä-aksum)-očč*, *(yä-əne)-očč*.

(c)   The agreement in number (also in gender) of the relative clause, as complex, with the modified S is readily seen when the adjectivized verb is in a compound tense with *näbbärä*. It has already been observed that the plural marked in the form of the auxiliary refers to the adjectival complex as such and not to the verbal compound as it is in the sentence underlying the relative:

transférende	*ləǧočč hedäw näbbär* (or, less commonly, *näbbärä/näbbäru*)
	"the children had gone"
tranféré	*(hedäw yänäbbär)-u ləǧočč*
	"children who had gone"
transférende	*näfsaččäw täṭämta näbbär* (or *näbbäräčč*)
	"their soul(s) had been thirsty"
transféré	*(näfsaččäw täṭämta yänäbbär)-u säwočč*
	"people whose soul(s) had been thirsty"

The marking of the plural in the form of the auxiliary *yänäbbär-u* in the first example is obligatory only because of the adjectivization [in the substantival "abstract relative" the aux. need not be plural]; in the second example its status as A^{pl} is even clearer since it agrees with the S^{pl} but not with the subject of the relative clause. See Goldenberg 1965 12, Hailu 1972 499-500, and mainly Goldenberg 1978 141-143. The same rules apply to the agreement in gender.

The plural in *yänäbbär-u*, then, does not belong to the verb *näbbär* but to the adjectival complex *yänäbbär-*, and only because in the sequence of morphemes it is immediately attached to a verb-form, this plural is marked by a verbal plural morpheme, a typical example of morphology crossing syntactic structure. The nominal status of the relative, analogous to any other adjectival form or complex, finds full expression in the dialectal construction of relative complex + *-očč* pl. Such plural relatives, found in the Amharic of Goǧǧam (and Wollo?), are mostly quoted as free adjectives (i.e. as primaries) or else furnished with a definite article. See IA I 71 n., Traité 117 (§IV,11), Goldenberg 1966 65 n. 3 & 74 n. 3, Getatchew & Seifu 1973 116, Goldenberg 1978 141-143. Relative complex + nominal plural marker is common in Harari; see below § 15c.

IA I 71 n. *yähedočč naččäw, yämmihedočč naččäw* ("they are those who came/ those who come"); Traité 117 *yämäṭṭočč* "(ceux) qui sont venus"; Getatchew & Seifu 1973 116 *qəddəm yämäṭṭočč wändəmmoččä naččäw* "those who came a moment ago are my brothers"; *yäballočč tännətäw* "those who ate have slept"; *yäqomočč dannočč naččäw* "those who are standing are judges"; *mihedočč* "those who go"; *mibäločč* "those who eat"; *misämočč* "those who hear". A few examples of relative complex + *-očč* in a printed text have been discovered by Roger Cowley: KH 190:34-35 *kä-Pawlos qal yäwäṭṭahäw antä bäənna balwäṭṭanočč lay ləttəṭäqsäw yəggäbbal-ənə ayəggäbbamm* "is it proper that you, who have departed from the word of Paul, should impute it to us, who have not departed? certainly not!"; ibid. 202u *kähawaryat həgg baltänawwäṣnočš lay* "to us, who have not moved away from the ordinances of the Apostles"; ibid. 223:18-19 *ənna bääṣädä səga yallänočč bääṣädä näfs lallut žämädoččaččən ənnəsälləyallän* "we, who are in the "realm of the flesh" [= the "land of the living", earthly life], pray to our relatives who are in the "realm of the soul" [= the world to come, (above of) after-life]". See also below, § 9c.

7. *Syntax of Attribute + Substantive: Definite in Sg. and Pl.*

Both the position of the definite article, attached to the attribute, and, in many cases, the forms of the article as well, show the structural equivalence of (a), (b) and (c) [15]. The syntax of the definite A + S in the singular and in the plural:

15 As elsewhere in the present paper, we have no intention of presenting a full description of the facts. The examples adduced here are meant to illustrate the diveristy of expressions which may enter the constructions discussed. A + S formular compounds are here

III A^{art} + S

(a) SWärq II 81:24 *čär-u amlak* "the gracious God"; SṬ 189:2 *təlləq-u säw* "the great man"; AWDjA 2:30 *dägg-itu nəgəst* "the kind queen"; HSN 15:20 *addis-itu iṭalya* "the new Italy"; MTəzz. 24:2 *galla-ytu balabbat* "the Galla lady"; ÇS 8:17 *yəhəččəňňa-wa ləğagäräd* "this girl"; IT II 105:20 *əňňəh-u mänäkʷse* "this monk"; AA 17:21 [² 17:4] *assər-u bərr* "the ten dollars".

(b) IT I 70:1 *yänəgus-u mäls* "the king's reply"; AWG 274:29 *däne-w korəčča* "with my saddle"; SWärq II 73:24 *yäne-yitu-mma* "as to my one ..."; WL 68u *yäṭorənnät-u mässariya* "the weapons of war"; IT IV 116b:23 *wädä täsfa-yitu agär* "to the promised land"; MSäw. 51:21 *yäruq-u wänd* "3rd pers. m. sg." ("the distant male"); ZI (title) *yäzare-yitu ityopya* "Today's Ethiopia"; AA 48:16 [² 40:24] *yäzare-wa miste* "my present wife"; ID 28 Mäsk. 1957 1a-b: -4 *yäsera liyone-wa wäyzäro* "the beauty queen of Sierra Leone" ("Miss. Sierra Leone").

(c) MSG 26:30 *kämäṣaḥəft yätägäňňä-w-ənna yämmiggäň-äw əwnätäňňa-w tarik* "the true story which has been found and will be found in the books"; Zad. 57:6 *dəro yadärg-äw yänäbbärä-w asdässač wäg* "the delightful talks which he used to have [with her] previously"[16]; LA 22:5-7 *ṣəyon mogäsa lämmattəbbal-äw, bäsetočč gädam lämmattəmmar-äw ləğagäräd* "to the girl called Ṣ.-M. who learns in the convent"; IT II 40:11-12 *yodit yämmattəbbal-äwa yäfälaša set* "the Falasha woman called Judith"; IT III 84b:25 *yodit yätäbaläčč-əw* "the one called Judith"; ZI 14 Gənb. 1957 1d:34-35 *madam eyliš elis yätäbaläčč-itu* "the one called Mme. E. E."; SWärq II 36:3 *käbet yalläčč-itu əhətəš* "your sister who is at home"; SA 27 Mäsk. 1957 4a:1-2 *wəb bähonäčč-əw bäaddis abäba* "in the beautiful Addis Ababa"; ID 29 Mäsk. 1957 1e:16-17 *aššännafi yähonäčč-wa wäyzärit məsraq alämayyähu* "Miss M. A. who was the winner"; AWT 12:24 *lägäzzaňň-u arämäni* "to the pagan who bought me"; GMB 69apu *yämmifälləgäňň-u* "he who seeks me"; AWT 13:18-19 *wädänäbbäräbbät-u mäsk* "to the meadow in which he was"; FA 109 n. 3 *yänäggärat-u ləğ* "the boy who told her".

ignored. These have $(A + S)^{art}$ structure, like *ṭäqlay-ministər-u* "the prime minister", *yäfäqad-wäräqät-u* "the licence". Neither do we discuss here A + S where possessive suffixes do also interfere. For some important details of the "genitive" constructions one should refer to Hailu Fullas' thoughtful study (Hailu 1964), where due attention is paid to constructions like *yäḥəṣan(u) ləbsu* (which is intermediate between the simple "genitive" *yäḥəṣan(u) ləbs* and the extrapositional constr. *ḥəṣan(u) ləbsu* ...).

16 The *-äw* in *yadärg-äw* is the cataphoric pronoun; the *-w* in *yänäbbärä-w* is the definite article referring to the "noun phrase" whose head is *wäg*.

8. IV   A^{art} + S^{pl}

(a)   Plural substantives, when definite, require as a rule that their attributive adjective (which carries the article) should agree in number, i.e. be marked as plural: A^{pl-art} + S^{pl}. C. H. Dawkins seems to have been the first to formulate this rule (FA 87 § 173), later repeated by Klingenheben (1966, p. 19) and Hartmann (292 § 5.5.2.2, 303-304 § 5.8.2.1, R 76). An accurate formulation of the rule should not refer to the plural marker *-očč* (Dawkins, Hartmann) but to the agreement in number as such; numerals other than "one", which are plural in any case, do not assume the plural suffix: AWG 275:27-28 *hulätt-u wättaddäročč* "the two soldiers"; ƎD 19:23 *sost-u-mm säwočč* "all three men". The Goǧǧame *arattočč, ammǝstočč, hulločč* have only been observed "when there is no noun to be head of a noun phrase" (Getatchew & Seifu 1973, p. 116).

(b)   Definite "genitive" + S^{pl} with the A unmarked as plural is never allowed in cases of "*žärf astäne*", but tolerated with real "*žärf*" (possessive): AWG 300:15 *yäm"ač-u žämädočč* "the relatives of the deceased". Cf., however, below, § 9b.

(c)   If the attribute is a relative clause, agreement in number with a plural S will be marked wherever possible; v. supra § 6c, also §5c. Definite relatives will further be marked by the definite article attached to the A. The normal structure of definite A + S in the plural will then be A^{pl-art} + S^{pl}. The construction A^{art} + S^{pl} can only be said to exist where the explicit marking of A (qua adjectival complex) as plural is impossible, as in cases of *na't sababiyy* like LTA 11:7 *ǝnnih tarikaččäw yämmiṣṣaf-äw wäṭṭatočč* "those youngsters whose story is being written". The definiteness of the A + S is marked in any case by the article attached to the relative as to any other A.

9.   V   A^{pl-art} + S^{pl}

As mentioned above (§8a), this is the structure required as a rule in definite plural A + S.

(a)   ST 7:12 *addisočč-u särratäññočč* "the new workers"; MTǝzz. 143apu *lätǝlǝllǝqočč-u säwočč* "to the noblemen"; ib. 195:29; GAW 830:18 *bǝžuwočč-u yägrañ yätor aläqočč* "the many military commanders of Grañ"; SWärq I 240:10-11 *ǝndä leločč-u awraǧǧawočč* "like the other districts"; AL 437:3 *käddatäññočč-u ṣǝftočč* "the treacherous rebels"; AFS 31:6 *mǝnočč-u mogädäññočč-u säwočč gäṭṭämu* "what defiant people have joined (here)"; FK I 85pu-u *arbäññočč-u wättaddäročačačən* "our valiant soldiers".

(b) IT I 211:25 *yäaksumočč-u nägästat* "the Aksumite kings, the kings of Aksum"; GAW 286:32 *yäññawočč-u wättaddäročč* "our soldiers"; YG (title) *yänewočč-u gärädočč* "my maids"; BG 39:25 *bäqädmowočč-u nägästat* "in the former kings ..."; HSN 49:8 *yäzarewočč-u qänočč* "the present days"; IT I 368:26 *yäzarewočč-u grikočč* "the peresent-day Greeks"; IMS 14:1 *yämäǧämmäryawočč-u säwočč* "les hommes à l'origine".

(c) As stated above (§ 6c), the agreement in number of a relative A to its S is readily seen when the adjectivized verb is in a compound tense with *näbbärä*. The same is true when the construction is marked definite by the article attached to the A: in HSN 29:24 (*ṭäbbəqänačʼčäw yänäbbär)-u-t wädagačʼčən* "our friend whom we have been expecting", the 3rd pers. pl. afformative, though verbal in form, belongs clearly to the adjectivization and not to the underlying "transférende" (whose subject is 1st pers. pl.). In other cases, like Const. 1931 art. 18 *yämmiyasfälləgu-t akkʷaḥʷanočč* "the requisite conditions", AWG 266:20 *yäqärru-tu aškäročč* "the remaining boys", the subject of the relative verb and the modified S are referentially identical, and this identity might be said to be reflected in the agreement of the verbal 3rd plural with both. The definite article in all relatives marks the adjectival complexes as nominal, also where the exponents of the article are object suffixes.

Relative complexes assuming the nominal plural marker *-očč*, thus manifesting their nominal structure even morphologically, have been mentioned in § 6c. Such relatives when definite are attested as (1) (*yä-* + verb)ᵃʳᵗ⁻ᵒᶜᶜ or (2) (asynd. rel. Imperf.)ᵒᶜᶜ⁻ᵃʳᵗ.: (1) AWGu. 132:18-20 *əndäñña mädhanit mənəmm əndämmannawq-äw-očč abäšočč hullu* "comme nous autres Abyssins qui ne comprenons rien aux remèdes"; (2) IT I 81:24 *kämäsafəntočču yəbälṭ-očč-u* "most of the dukes"; cf. IT IV 107b:9 (= *yämmibälṭut*, v. AS 460).

Syntax of Attribute + Substantive: Marking of the Accusative

10. The syntactical equivalence of the various adjectival expressions can also be shown by examining the syntax of the accusative *-n* marker. The conditions of when this marker is to be used and in what syntactic position are rather difficult to describe, because when the accusative complement is indefinite the *-n* is normally avoided, and when it is definite (whether explicitly marked as such or with a "zero article") the *-n* hankers after the form that carries, or could have carried, the definite determiner. A detailed

study of the use of the accusative *-n* is O. Kapeliuk's (1972), where the various constructions of direct object with and without *-n* are properly classified and profusely illustrated. O. Kapeliuk well mentions the fact that "avec un complément non déterminé formellement" some writers would use *-n* more than others, and that in KBT and ASäw. the use of the *-n* for the accusative is almost generalized. Seemingly limited to the writings of language teachers, the stylistic status of this almost generalized use of *-n* with indefinite accusative looks rather questionable, and O. Kapeliuk therefore chooses (ib. § 6) to examine the use of the *-n* with indefinite accusative "chez les auteurs qui ne l'emploient pas toujours". It is, however, interesting to examine the syntax of the really-indefinite accusative with *-n*, because only with the indefinite the *-n* will be found in the basic position which it should occupy in the first place. In addition to KBT and ASäw., the indef. accus. with *-n* will also be found in AFS, a lively story written by Täklä-Maryam Fantaye, another language teacher, but also here and there in ƎD, MTəzz. and elsewhere. It appears to have some roots "bäkahnat-ənna bähagärä säb qʷwanqʷa".

With object expressions that are really indefinite, where the *-n* is normaly avoided by most Amharic speakers and writers, those who have the *-n* at all will place it suffixed to the modified substantive: VI A + S^accus. With object expressions that are definite in one sense or another, whether that definiteness is formally marked or not, the construction will be VII A^(def)-accus + S [17]. To show this, suffice it to quote some pairs of phrases, definite and indefinite, all drawn from the same source, and some even taken from the same context:

VI	VII
(a) AFS 24:23 *sost aynät məgbočč-ən* "three kinds of food"	AFS 24u *sost-u-n-əmm aynät məgbočč* "the three kinds of food"
(b) AFS 23:13-14 *yäduqet-bəṭbəṭ wəha-n* "water of flour-dilu-tion"	AFS 23:22-23 *yäduqet bəṭbəṭ-u-n wəha* "the water of the flour-dilution"
(c) AFS 3u-4:1 *läamarəňňa mäm-mariya yähonu mäṣaḥəft-ən* "Amharic text-books"	AFS 115:13 *yassäbaččəhu-t-ən gänzäb* "the money (of) which you have thought"

17 To say that "l'adjectif ou son équivalent s'attirent normalement le *-n* et l'article" (Kapeliuk 1972, 198 § 11a) is inaccurate. What could in fact be said is that the adjective attracts the article and the article attracts the *-n*. That is true for Kapeliuk's examples as well: both *bəzu čəggər-ən* "much trouble" (quoted ibid. 198) and *andand dərsätočč-ən* "some essays" (194) are of constr. VI. In the absence of a formal definite determiner, the use itself of constr. VII might serve to show the definiteness of the whole expression. For *and-ən säw* ("l'un …", "l'autre") (Kapeliuk ib. 191) see below, footnote 18.

Some further examples:

VI (a)   AFS 3:15 *ṭäqami əwqät-ən* "valuable knowledge"; ibid. 10:8-9 *asč̣äggariwoč̈č̈ nägäroč̈č̈-ən* "things causing difficulty"; ibid. 22:19-20 *andit fəyyäl-ən* "one goat"[18]; MTəzz. 36:26 *hulätt mäto-n* "two hundreds"; KBT 166b:22-23 *dəngəlt ləǧ agäräd set-ən* "a virgin young woman".

VI (b)   AFS 7:12 *ləyyu ləyyu yäaggälaläs bahrəyoč̈č̈-ən* "various qualities of expression"; ƏD 57:9 *quṭər yälelläw yätänk"äl yäkəfatəmm sərawoč̈č̈-ən* "innumerable deeds of deceit and wickedness".

VI (c)   ƏD 21:6 *räž̌ž̌əm yähonu təmhərtoč̈č̈-ən* "extensive studies"; ƏD 76:1-2 *läsämay betač̈č̈ən yämmismamma məghar-ən* "work that is appropriate for our celestial home".

VII (a)   AWT 13:19-20 *yan dägg adragi-w-n säw* "that beneficent man"; MSG 22:16-17 *anditu-n qän ənk"a sayəfäṣṣəm motä* "he died without even filling one day" (cf. fn. 18); Zad. 28:17 *yəhač̈č̈-ən set* "this woman"; ČS 16:10 *ya-nn-ən-u qän* "that day"; WL introd. (1):4-5 *mälkam-u-n nuro* "the good life".

VII (b)   Hirut 221:14 *yabbat-u-n səm* "the name of the father [my father]"; AFS 22:20 *yägəlgäloč̈č̈-u-n af* "the mouth(s) of the kids"; MSäw. 51-21 *yäruq-itu-n set* "the 3rd fem. sing." (lit "the distant female"); ƏD 48:14 *yäñña-yitu-n aläm* "our own (small) world"; IT I 67:29 *yäzare-w-n ityop̌ya* "present-day Ethiopia"; SṬ 189:24 *yäbälay-u-n baläsəltan* "the high official".

VII (c)   ChrMən. 286:19 *yäwässädäw-n əqa* "the things which he had taken"; AWT 30:4 *yalläbbät-u-n-u geta* "the master who is in it"; AL 310:21 *yänäffägäč̈č̈əññ-ən səm* "the name which she denied me".

11. *Adjectivization in Amharic: Synopsis*

		(a)	(b)	(c)
	A + S	dägg säw	yäaksum nəgus	yämmič̈oh wəšša
		səntäñña šərəššər	yärswo mämṭaṭ	yäbäddälhuh bädäl
I	A + S^{pl}	awwaki säwoč̈č̈	yagär ləǧoč̈č̈	yäsäṭṭäññ ləǧoč̈č̈
		bəzu nägäroč̈č̈	yäñña wägänoč̈č̈	abrän yämmənnəsära säwoč̈č̈
			yaksum nägästat	

---

18 If the same author writes elsewhere *and-ən nägär* (AFS 12:7), it is because that was intended to mean "something, anything", and in Amharic the expression for "(any)one", "one another", "l'un ... l'autre ..." mostly require "one" marked definite (*andu, andu landu, andu ... lelaw ...* etc.) of which *and*, when employed, is the zero-marked equivalent.

II	$A^{pl} + S^{pl}$	täkättayočč ⎱ wättaddäročč ⎰ bəzuwočč aʼwaf	yagäročč säwočč yänewočč yaksumočč nägästat	näfsaččäw tätämta ⎱ yänäbbäru säwočč ⎰ yämäṭṭočč
III	$A^{art} + S$	čäru amlak däggitu nəgəst assəru bərr	yäzarewa miste yäneyitu yäsera liyonewa wäyzäro	lägäzzaňňu arämäni käbet yalläččitu əhətəš yänäggäratu ləǧ
IV	$A^{art} + S^{pl}$	hulättu ⎱ wättaddäročč ⎰	yämʷaču zämädočč	tarikaččäw yämmiṣṣafäw ⎱ wäṭṭatočč ⎰
V	$A^{pl-art} + S^{pl}$	däggočču säwočč bəzuwočču aläqočč	yänewočču gärädočč yäzarewočču qänočč yaksumočču nägästat	ṭäbbəqänaččäw yänäbbärut ⎱ wädaġaččən ⎰ yämmannawqäwočč abäšočč yebälṭočču
VI	$A + S^{accus}$	ṭäqami əwqätən hulätt mäton	yätänkʷäl ⎱ sərawoččən ⎰ yaggälaläṣ ⎱ bahrəyoččən ⎰	lä- ... yämmismamma ⎱ məgbarən ⎰ mämmariya yämmihonu ⎱ maṣahəftən ⎰
VII	$A^{(def)-acc} + S$	mälkamun nuro yəhəččən set	yabbatun səm yäňňayitun aläm yäbälayun baläsəlṭan	yäwässädäwn əqa yalläbbätunu geta yänäffägäččəňňən səm

ADJECTIVIZATION IN HARARI

12. The adjectivized verb in Harari discloses immediately its nominal character by being, as complex, susceptible of consistently assuming the suffixed pronouns (3rd pers., also as exponents of the definite article) in their "possessive", i.e. post-nominal forms [19]: [245:6 *wīǧ-ẓo* "the child(ren)"]; ibid. *gidīr-ẓo* "the big one(s), the adult(s)" — 1:2 & 10:4 *zigädärä-ẓo* "the biggest"; [54:10 *bäǧīḥ usu'* "many people" — 54:9 *abẓaḥ usu'* "most people" —] 62:3, 66u *abẓaḥ-ẓo* — 9u *yibäẓḥi-ẓo* "the (its) majority"[20]; 43:6 *yansi-ẓo* "lesser (of it)", 201:3 *yansi-ẓiyu* "a few of them"; cf. Leslau 1965b 157b *yägädräẓal-ẓo*, *yəkätbäẓax-ẓo*. In the marking of the plural, too, nominalization in Harari goes further than in Amharic as it uses freely the nominal plural marker with the relative as with any other noun.

The turning of non-verbal forms into an attribute is only marked by position: any such form may function as modifier of a substantive by just

---

19 References to Harari texts, when not otherwise specified, are to Leslau 1965a.

20 This example and the two following ones are bare Imperfects having the value of relative forms. Of such forms there will be found survivals in Amharic as in Harari; they were in general use in Old Amharic as they still are in some other South Ethiopian languages; see Goldenberg 1977 487-489 (with references to earlier literature on the subject), Leslau 1958 21 §14d, id. 1965b 157b.

being placed immediately before it. The adjectivizing "translatif" *ẓ*-, still attested in Old Harari as employed in a way parallel to that of the Amharic *yä*-, has completely disappeared in the modern language before non-verbal forms: what in the older language was, e.g., *ẓa-ḥay ẓär* "river of milk" (Cerulli 294-5 = 312:33, v. ib. 379 § 147) became *ḥay-ẓär* in Modern Harari (also used as a name for a kind of a drum). While in Amharic such a process is mostly limited to the development of formular compounds[21], Harari is no more capable of marking as adjectivized any non-verbal form, and consequently no "free genitive" is there available. Substantives that are thus functioning as attributes just in virtue of their pre-substantival position cannot fulfil this function without their head word. In the absence of a modified substantive (as when it has already been mentioned and its repetition is undesirable) a prop-word is indispensable. In Harari, *ẓāṭ* "property" is called for in such cases[22]. May it here be repeated that genuine adjectives as well as adjectivizations, which, as characterized above, contain within themselves the pronominal representation of the modified entity, are in principle self-supported and independently adjectival. In modern Harari little is left of this adjectival independence (see below, § 15b).

The syntax of A + S in Harari is much simpler than in Amharic because of the greater consistency in the implications of the "turanisirende Wortstellung"[23]: the accusative marker and the definite article (as well as the "adpositions") find their proper place at the end of the whole construction (after the S) and thus cannot directly contribute to the formal characterization of A as nominal. But the nominal plural suffix attached to A marks the syntactically-transformed A as morphologically noun-like.

13. The A + S construction may have in Harari, as in Amharic, but with significant alterations, three types of A: (a) A = adjective, (b) A = substantive etc., (c) A = *ẓ*- + verb ("relative").

(a) The construction of (a) adjective + substantive is fairly common: 9:1, 57:13, 58:11 *gidīr gār* "big building"; 11:9 *qäčīn ūga* "narrow street"; 2:7 *rŭḥuq zämān* "far time, a long time ago"; 158:2 *gudōr timfāš* "long breath";

---

21 See Leslau 1964, p. 19.

22 Examples for *ẓāṭ* as prop-word: 28:5 *indōč irāz-wā abōč-ẓāṭ yäsīmalu* "they sell women's clothes and men's ones"; 99:12-13 *rägāč bärṭa-ẓiyu därmāč-ẓāṭ-be fiẓ-be yitlāyumēl* "the bärṭa (*ṭat*-ceremony) of the old men does not differ much from that of the young men"; 230-1 *mēgäl-ẓāṭ-āč-u naḥdägeyu* "let me leave (them) the first ones (lit. those of the beginning)".

23 See Praetorius 1871 p. 2 n. 1; cf. Polotsky 1960 117 [= 1971 p. 3].

8:1 *ḫurdi gār* "yellow building"; 55:7 *näṣ̌īḥ afär* "white earth"; 8:3-4 *yī gār* "this building".

(b)   Besides the basic construction of (b1) substantive[a] + substantive[b], where the former constituent modifies the latter, there may also be considered in Harari in the same connexion the construction (b2) subst[a] + (subst[b] + suff[a]). This we do not because (b2) does structurally deserve to be presented on a par with (b1), but because its examination here may be found expedient for the accurate description [24].

Construction (b1) is commonly employed wherever a substantival form is to function as a modifier, whatever might be the underlying relation between the modifier and the modified: 9:3 *dūk gār* "Duke's house"; 9:13, 10:1 *aräqe gār* "liquor house"; 9:14 *däwwa dukkān* "medicine shop, pharmacy"; 156:4 *toya usu'* "people of the neighbourhood, neighbours"; 1:4 *gē sinān* "the language of Harar"; 247:13 *ašūra yäm* "the day of Ašura"; 209:1 *qur'ān kitāb* "a Koran book"; Cerulli 224, no. 92 *yi zaman esuât̂* "the people of today"; 60:2 *gār näzāfa* "cleaning of the house"; 60:8 *gār mäṭräg* "sweeping of the house".

Construction (b2) is in its structure extrapositional, and often employed accordingly. Except for its outward appearance it has nothing analogous to the Turkish izafet, though it may be suspected that if not the seeming resemblance to the Turkish it would have had lesser chance to find its way into the chapters on genitive and possessive relation in Harari grammar (v. Cerulli 147-148, 380) as a type of noun + noun construction. Examples of (b2) are: 99:12 *rāgāč bärḍa-ziyu därmāč-zāṭ-be fiz-be yitlāyumēl* "the older people their *bärḍa* (*čāt*-ceremony) does not much differ from that of the young men"; 124:3-4 *liǧi wäldi qaḥat āwā āy-ze-wā qurra aḥlāč gār ūgaw yilīṭumēl* "the boy will not pass by the house of the girl's parents and close relatives" (lit. "the girl — her parents and close relatives"); Cerulli 213:29 = XI:12 *ilawá amîr čilôtziyu-bê adīǧó* "they brought him to the emir's tribunal" ("unto the emir in his law court"), cf. Cerulli 147-148.

However, the sequence subst[a] + subst[b] + suff can also stand for (b1) + suff, i.e. (subst[a] + subst[b]) + suff [25]. When the suffix does not agree with

---

24 Compared to Amharic, (b1) corresponds more or less to the type *yähəsan ləbs*; in (b2) there is an extraposition corresponding in fact to the Amharic *həsan(u) ləbsu*, but perhaps to the intermediate *yähəsan(u) ləbsu* as well; v. supra, fn. 15. For the indication of definiteness in these constructions see below.

25 Suffixes whose referents are outside the (A + S) have nothing to do with the construction as such and should not be allowed to interfere in the description. For instance 191:13 *wīǧnät umri-ziyu* "their (age of) childhood", suff. referring to "boys and girls" which

subst[a] the construction can only be (b1) + suff, but when it does, any possible expression of formal opposition between (b1) + suff and (b2) is neutralized, and the interpretation is left to intuition (for possible help that may come from the accusative marker -*u*, see below). When the suffix is -*ẓo*, it can also stand for the definite article referring to (b1); see Cerulli 148 § 82. As 30:2 *ḥarši bisāya* means "agricultural products" ("product of the farm"), 50:8 *ḥarāši bisāya-ẓo* appears most likely to mean "the agricultural products" ("the products of the farmer"): *(ḥarāši bisāya)-ẓo*[26]. So also 116:5 *gōyta qudra-ẓō-be* "by the power of the Lord", but for 110:4-5 *liǧi wäldi ṭaba-ẓo ḥafīš mäxna yīglal* the translation which might better suit the context (*liǧi wäldi* "the boy" being in contextual contrast with *qaḥat wäldi* "the girl") will probably be "the boy — his voice begins to become thick", that is with *liǧi wäldi ṭaba-ẓo* as construction (b2).

(c)   The nominal character of the adjectivized verb as evidenced in Harari is shown in § 12. Many examples of relative clauses in Harari have been adduced by Cerulli (pp. 162-171, 387-391) and Leslau (1958) (p. 16, §§ 8c & 9c, and p. 22, § 17). Some further instances are 47:3 *qāṭi-be ẓidīǧa usu'* "a man who has come from outside"; 47:7 *alāy yisūčal ayna* "another kind that has fragrance"; 1:9 *gē tiṭṭärahbāẓat sum* "the names by which Harar is called".

Syntax of A + S in Harari: Marking of the Plural

14.   I A + S^pl

(a)   207:13, 243:7 *gidīr usu'āč* "elderly people"; 11:2 *qäṭīn ūgäč* "narrow streets"; 232:7.8 *alāy wäḥačäč* "other girls"; 201:8 *abōč āwäčäč* "male saints"; 66:5 *indōč dälläläč* "female brokers"; 171:9 *islām wäldäč* "muslim children" (cf. 196:5 *islāmäč*); 10:3 *yī dukkänäč* "these shops".

(b)   Cerulli 224, no. 92 *yi ẓaman esuäč* "the people of today"; 173:4 *tōya wīǧäč* "the children of the neighbourhood".

(c)   With a modified noun in the plural, the relative verb will most usually carry the agreement in number through its subject morpheme or otherwise[27].

---

follows; 199:7 *mäsgid-ẓo wäqfi* "the waqf of his mosque", suff. referring to the *lāzim* mentioned before.

26 50:7-8 *gē-usú' ḥarāši ẓināra-bew ẓämān-be yitxätätẓal ḥarāši bisāya-ẓo yārdu-bō nār* "in the time when the Harari people were farmers, one used to place in it (viz. in the main upper-storey room) the agricultural products that can be stored up".

27 I have got no evidence for A being an indirect attribute (cf. § 8c).

As explained in § 5c, such agreement does not belong specifically to the relation of a relative modifier, qua adjectival expression, to its *ism man'ūt*. The following instances can be regarded as carrying no marked agreement between A and S specifically belonging to the relative in its capacity as adjective; they represent A + S^{pl}. For A^{pl} rel. in A^{pl} + S^{pl} Harari has the nominal -*āč* plural marker freely employed; see § 15c. Examples: 57:12 *ziqäru gārāč* "the remaining houses"; 75:13 *yiṭrāmätleyuzal usu'āč* "people for whom it is provided"; 201:2 *bäqla-be yitḥēläqzalu āwāč* "holy shrines (lit. "fathers") that are counted in hundred(s)". In the following instance a plural subst. (inanimate) shows no agreement with the relative A nor with its predicate: 62:10-12 *aräb sinān, aḥmara sinān, tigrē sinān-baḥ yitmisāsalzal isaḥad kilmāč gē sinām-bēm yiträxäbal* "some words^{pl} that resemble^{sg} Arabic, Amharic or Tigre are found^{sg} in Harari".

15. II   A^{pl} + S^{pl}

(a)   162:5-6 *rāgāč indōčāč* "old women"; Cerulli 145, 157 *azziyāč mistāč* "those wives"; ibid. 157 *hiyač indočāč* "these women".

(b)   It is remarkable that in spite of the fact that in construction (b) no sign except position is usually left to show the attributive relation, there will be found besides forms like 211:7 *tōya wīǧ*, pl. 173:4 *tōya wīǧāč* "the children of the neighbourhood" also 215:7 *tōyāč ūgāč* "the streets of the neighbourhood"; cf. supra § 6b. Of special interest is 241:4 *indōčāč azzo tōyāč zitayāč* "women, those who are^{pl} of this^{sg} neighbourhood^{pl}", i.e. (those who are)$^{nominal\ pl}$ (*azzo toy*)^{āč} (of this neighbourhood)^{pl}. The nominal plural marker is the only formal sign which still marks in such cases what is left of the adjectival character of A. We may thus feel relieved to find in this sign some justification for including the Harari constr. (b) among the forms of adjectivization.

(c)   Relative marked as adjectivized by the nominal plural suffix, which in Amharic is limited to some form of local dialect (v. § 6c in fine), is very common in Harari: 34:14 *čat yäsīmzal-āč gē indōčāč* "Harari women who sell čat"; 214:7 *zissiqāqäl-āč qälädāč* "strips of leather that are hanging"; 215:5 *zisäma'-āč usu'āč* "people who have heard"; Cerulli IV:11-12 (p. 206) *Mákka zihār-âč gey suâč* "Hararis who went to Mecca"; 162:4-6, 213:3, 215:4, 218:11, 219:1, 220:9; Cerulli 169 (§ 102), cf. Leslau 1958 15 (§ 7c).

16. III   A + S^accus

As A + S^accus is a common and regular construction, involving no intricacies, it would have been practically unnecessary for it to be profusely illustrated, were it not for the comparison to Amharic. A few examples, however, will be helpful, especially as Cerulli's § 84 (p. 151) is somewhat confusing.

(a)   *gidīr mägāla-w* "the Main Market"; 175:2 *ši'ištäň dāg-u* "the third stage"; 83:1 *yī dilāga-w* "this work"; 74:2 *isbälbälāt qäbīla-w* "the different tribes"; 170:5 *wīǧ wäldi-w* "the baby".

(b)   11:1 *dukkānāč ūga-w* "the street of the shops"; 215:7 *tōyāč ūgāč-u* "the streets of the neighbourhood"; 118:12 *därma mugād-u* "the young men's association"; 228:4 *sāsa sōmänzo-w* "the thirty-day fast"; 208:4 *qur'ān kitāb-u* "the Koran"; 58:9-10 *gār hawāz hangūr-u* "the food of the family"; 124:3-4 *qurra ahlāč-ze gār ūga-w* "the street of the house of her close relatives"; 73:13-14 *ahmara wäldi yilīqbāzal adāb ūga-w* "the *adab* way (good manners) in which the Amhara child is brought up".

Extraposition will involve repetition of the accusative marker: 152:10-11 *wäldi-w qāmzo-w yahatbo* "one washes the body of the child"(lit. "the child, his body", a typical case of the σχῆμα καθ' ὅλον καὶ μέρος, Arab. *badal al-ba'd min al-kull*); Cerulli 217:13 = XIII:24 *qahassina-w simzie-w* "the name of our daughter" (lit. "our girl, her name").

(c)   Cerulli 225, no. 16 *zitrōǧa riyāl-ú* "the stolen money"; 74:2-3 *yätfälsāzal sifätāč-u* "qualities that make them be praised"; 71:2 *yätxīšzal xurūǧiyazo-w* "its (or: the) necessary expenses"; 48:11-12 *mäqōrahti tähay-le zāl wäntäf lūh-u* "the threshold board which is below the locker"; 241:10 *yisägdizalāč usu'āč-u* "the people who pray"; 50:5, 122:10-11, 81:4-5, 63:8-9.

17.   *A + S in Harari: Synopsis*

		(a)	(b)	(c)
	A + S	qäčīn ūga yī gār	gē sinān gār mäträg	zidīǧa usu' yisūčzal ayna
I	A + S^pl	qäčīn ūgāč yī usu'āč	yī zamān usu'āč tōya wīgāč	ziqāru gārāč yitmisāsalzal kilmāč
II	A^pl + S^pl	rāgāč indōčāč azziyāč mistāč	tōyāč ūgāč	zihārāč usu'āč yäsīmzalāč indōčāč
III	A + S^accus	gidīr mägāla-w yī dilāga-w	därma mugād-u tōyāč ūgāč-u	zitrōǧa riyāl-u yätxīšzal xurūǧiyazo-w

References

AA   [Həruy Wäldä-Səllase], *Addis aläm. Yäqənočč-ənna yädägg adragiwočč mänoriya.*
            Yagärun yä-Ityopyan betä-krəstiyan mättadäs kämmiwädd kand säw yätäṣafä.
            Addis Ababa 1925 E.C.
            Second edition in: Zämänfäs Qəddus Abrəha, *Ityopyawyan filosofiwočč.* Asmara
            1948.

A.A.1947-53 *Mäṣhaf qəddus: yäbəluy-ənna yähaddis kidan mäṣahəft,* bägərmawi Qädamawi
            Haylä-Səllase nəgusä nägäst zä-Ityopya mälkam fäqad-ənna təəzaz tarrəmo
            täzägaġto tattämä. Addis Ababa 1947 E.C. (NT), 1953 E.C. (OT).

AFS   Täklä-Maryam Fantaye, *Ǝnnä-Asfaw-ənna fəyyälä säsočču.* Andäñña mäṣhaf. Ləbbä
            wälläd. Addis Ababa 1958 E.C.

Agostino da Hebo (1955), *Grammatica amarica.* Asmara.

AL   Abe Gubäñña, *And lännatu. Tarikawi ləbb wälläd.* Addis Ababa 1961 E.C.

AMQ   Dässta Täklä-Wäld, *Addis yamarəñña mäzgäbä qalat bäkahnat-ənna bähagärä säb
            qᵘanqᵘa.* Addis Ababa 1962 E.C. (1970).

Anbārī v. Ibn al-Anbārī.

AS   Praetorius, Franz, *Die amharische Sprache.* Halle 1878-1879.

ASäw.   Märsəe-Hazän Wäldä-Qirqos (Blatta), *Bäaddis sər'at yätäsänadda yamarəñña
            säwasəw.* (Addis Ababa 1935 E.C.) Fourth edition, Addis Ababa 1948 E.C.

AWDjA   Afevork G. J., *Yä-Ityopya mängəst alga wäraš lə'ul Ras Täfäri Mäkᵘännən wädä
            Ġəbuti-nna wädä Adän sihedu-nna simmälläsu yämängädaččäw akkᵘahᵘan.* Dire Dawa
            1915 E.C.

AWG   Afevork G. J., *Grammatica della lingua amarica.* Roma 1905.

AWGu.   Afevork G. J., *Guide du voyageur en Abyssinie.* Rome & Paris 1908.

AWT   Afevork G. J., *Ləbb wälläd tarik.* Roma 1900 E.C. (1908).

AZ   *Addis Zämän* (newspaper). Addis Ababa.

Becker, Karl Ferdinand (1841), *Organism der Sprache.* 2. neubearbeitete Ausgabe. Frankfurt am
            Main.

Beeston, A. F. L. (1970), *The Arabic Language Today.* London.

BG   Wäldä-Giyorgis Wäldä-Yohannəs, *Bəlsəgənna bägəbrənna.* Addis Ababa 1942 E.C.

C. 1886   *Mäṣhaf qəddus, ərsumm yäbəluy-ənna yaddis kidan mäṣahəft. The Holy Bible containing the
            Old and New Testaments.* At the Mission Press of St. Chrischona, Basle, 1886.

Cerulli, Enrico (1936), *La lingua e la storia di Harar* (= Studi Etiopici I). Roma.

ChrMən.   Gäbrä-Səlasse (Ṣähafe təəzaz), *Tarikä zämän zä-Dagmawi Mənilək nəgusä nägäst zä-
            Ityopya.* Addis Ababa 1959 E.C.

Const. 1931 *Yä-Ityopya həggä-mängəst. The Constitution of Ethiopia.* Addis Ababa 1923 E.C.
            (1931).

ČS   Bərhanu Zäryəhun, *Čäräqa səttəwäṭa.* Addis Ababa. n.d.

Dillmann, August (1857), *Grammatik der äthiopischen Sprache.* Leipzig.

ƎD   Mahtämä-Səllase Wäldä-Mäsqäl (Balambaras), *Ǝṣub dənq.* Addis Ababa 1943
            E.C.

FA   Dawkins, C. H., *The Fundamentals of Amharic.* Addis Ababa 1960.

Fables   *Cent fables amhariques,* mises en écrit par le dabtara Kenfé, traduites et annotées
            par M. M. Moreno (Cahiers de la Société Asiatique XI). Paris 1947.

FK   *Fəre känafər zä-Qädamawi Haylä Səllase nəgusä nägäst zä-Ityopya.* vols. I & II. Addis
            Ababa 1944-1955.

Gabelentz, Georg von der (1901), *Die Sprachwissenschaft, ihre Aufgaben, Methoden und bisherigen Ergebnisse*. 2. Aufl. v. Albrecht Graf von der Schulenburg. Leipzig.

GAW   Täklä-Ṣadəq Mäkʷriya, *Yägrañ ahmäd wärära*. Addis Ababa 1966 E.C.

Getatchew Haile & Seifu Metaferia (1973), "The Dialect of Gojjam", in: Habte Mariam Marcos (ed.), "Regional Variations in Amharic", *Journal of Ethiopian Studies* XI,2 (July 1973) 115-120.

GMB   Alämayyähu Mogäs, *Gäbrä-Mäsqäl hariyaw: tarikawi ləbb wälläd*. Addis Ababa 1955 E.C.

Goldenberg, G. (1965), "Studies in Amharic Syntax", *Journal of Ethiopian Studies* III,1 6-22.

Goldenberg, G. (1966), *The Amharic Tense-System* (in Hebrew). (Hebrew University doctoral thesis) Jerusalem.

Goldenberg, G. (1977), "The Semitic Languages of Ethiopia and Their Classification", *Bulletin of the School of Oriental and African Studies, University of London* XL,3 461-507.

Goldenberg, G. (1978), "Congruence and Comitative and a Problem of Linguistic Typology", *Atti del Secondo Congresso Internazionale di Linguistica Camito-Semitica (Firenze 1974)* (= Quaderni di Semitistica 5). Firenze, 133-147.

ǦṬ   Mäkʷännən Əndalkaččäw (Ras Bitwäddäd), *Ǧoro ṭäbi*. Addis Ababa 1951 E.C.

Guidi, Ignazio (1924), *Grammatica elementare della lingua amarica*. Terza ed. Napoli.

Hailu Fullas (1964), "The Particle *yä-* in Amharic", *Rassegna di Studi Ethiopici* XX 103-119.

Hailu Fulass (1972), "On Amharic Relative Clauses", *Bulletin of the School of Oriental and African Studies, University of London* XXXV, 3 497-513.

Hartmann, Josef (1980), *Amharische Grammatik* (Äthiopistische Forschungen hrsg. v. E. Hammerschmidt, 3). Wiesbaden.

Hebo v. Agostino da Hebo.

Hetzron, Robert (1966), "Pronominalization in Amharic", *Journal of Semitic Studies* XI 83-97.

Hirut   Ilala Ibsa, *Hirut abbatʷa mannäw?* Addis Ababa 1956 E.C.

HSN   *Gərmawi nəgusä nägäst Qädamawi Haylä-Səllase bäyyägizew yadärräguwaččäw nəgəggəročč 1944-1949 E.C.* vol. II. Addis Ababa 1953 E.C.

IA I   Armbruster, C.H., *Initia Amharica: An Introduction to Spoken Amharic*, I *Grammar*. Cambridge 1908.

Ibn al-Anbārī, Abu'l-Barakāt, *Kitāb al-Inṣāf fī masā'il al-xilāf bayn al-naḥwiyyīn al-Baṣriyyīn wa-l-Kūfiyyīn — Die grammatischen Streitfragen der Basrer und Kufer*, ed. Gotthold Weil. Leiden 1913.

Ibn Yaʿīš, Muwaffaq al-Dīn, *Šarḥ al-Mufaṣṣal* I-X. Cairo, al-Munīriyya, n.d.

ID   *Yä-Ityopya Dəmṣ* (newspaper). Addis Ababa.

IMS   Käbbädä Mikael, *Ityopya-nna məərabawi sələṭṭane*. Addis Ababa 1941 E.C.

IT   Täklä-Ṣadəq Mäkʷriya, *Yä-Ityopya tarik*. I 1951 E.C., II 1951 E.C., III 2nd ed. 1945 E.C., IV 4th ed. 1946 E.C. Addis Ababa.

Kapeliuk, Olga (1972), "L'emploi de la marque de l'accusatif *-n* avec le complément d'objet direct en amharique", *Israel Oriental Studies* II.

KBT   Täsämma Habtä-Mikael Gəṣṣəw, *Käsate Bərhan Täsämma, yä-Amarəñña mäzgäbä qalat*. Addis Ababa 1951 E.C.

KH   Mäl'akä-Bərhan Admasu Ǧänbäre, *Kʷäkʷəha haymanot. Wäṭṭat tämälkät əndattəssasat*. Addis Ababa 1949 E.C.

Klingenheben, August (1966), *Deutsch-amharischer Sprachführer nebst einer grammatischen Einführung ins Amharische*. Wiesbaden.

LA   Həruy Wäldä-Səllase, *Yäləbb assab: yä-Bərhane-nna yä-Ṣəyon Mogäsa gabəčča*. Addis Ababa 1923 E.C.

Leslau, Wolf (1958), *The Verb in Harari (South Ethiopic)*. Berkeley and Los Angeles.

Leslau, Wolf (1964), "Towards a History of the Amharic Vocabulary", *Journal of Ethiopian Studies* II,2 12-20.

Leslau, Wolf (1965a), *Ethiopians Speak: Studies in Cultural Background, I. Harari*, Berkeley and Los Angeles.

Leslau, Wolf (1965b), "Gleanings in Harari Grammar I", *Journal of the American Oriental Society* LXXXV 153-159.

LM   Taddäsä Libän, *Lelaw mängäd*. Addis Ababa 1952 E.C.

LTA   Bäəmnät Gäbrä Amlak, *Ləǧənnät tämälləso aymäṭamm*. Addis Ababa 1949 E.C.

LZG   Həruy Wäldä-Səllase, *Yäləqso zema gəṭəm. məsṭiru kämäṣahəft gara yätäsmamma*. Addis Ababa 1910 E.C.

MČ   Zännäb, *Mäṣhafä ṭäwata səgawi wämänfäsawi*. 2nd ed. Addis Ababa 1951 E.C.

MI   Alämayyähu Mogäs, *Mälkə'a Ityopya (yä-Ityopya mälk)* I. Asmara 1952 E.C.

MSäw.   [Tayyä Gäbrä-Maryam (Aläqa)] *Mäṣhafä säwasəw. yä-Gəəz qʷanqʷa mämmariya yämäṣhaf mägläča yämmihon*. Monkullo 1889. [1st ed. repr. Asmara 1958 E.C.; 2nd ed. Addis Ababa 1918 E.C.]

MSG   (Kəflä-Giyorgis &) Kidanä-Wäld Kəfle, *Mäṣhafä säwasəw wägəs wämäzgäbä qalat haddis*. Addis Ababa 1948 E.C.

MTəzz.   Lämma Haylu Wäldä-Tarik (Aläqa), *Mäṣhafä təzzəta*. Mängəstu Lämma əndäṣafäw. Addis Ababa 1959 E.C.

NÉ   Cohen, Marcel, *Nouvelles études d'éthiopien méridional* (Bibliothèque de l'École des Hautes Études 275). Paris 1939.

Pfister, Raimund (1972), "Zur Geschichte der lateinischen Grammatik Teil II: Satzgliedsystem Becker-Herling; 20. Jahrhundert", *Linguistik für Latinisten* (Dokumentation einer Einführungstagung), Akademie für Lehrerfortbildung Dillingen, Akademiebericht Nr. 9, pp. 28-37.

Pl. 1829   *Novum Testamentum ... in linguam Amharicam vertit Abu-Rumi Habessinus*, ed. Thomas Pell Platt. London 1829.

Polotsky, H. J. (1936), review of M. Cohen, Traité de langue amharique in: *Institut français de Damas, Bulletin d'études orientales* VI 118-123 [= Polotsky 1971 455-460].

Polotsky, H. J. (1960), "Syntaxe amharique et syntaxe turque", *Atti del Convegno Internazionale di Studi Etiopici, Roma 1959* (Accademia Nazionale dei Lincei, Problemi attuali di scienza e di cultura. Quaderno N. 48). Roma [= Polotsky 1971 3-7].

Polotsky, H. J. (1971), *Collected Papers*. Jerusalem.

Polotsky, H. J. (1976), "Les transpositions du verbe en égyptien classique", *Israel Oriental Studies* VI 1-50.

Praetorius, Franz (1871), *Grammatik der Tigriñasprache in Abessinien*. Halle.

QQ   Täklä-Ṣadəq Mäkʷriya, "Yäqʷanqʷa qərs", in: *Yäqʷanqʷa qərs-ənna yäwaṡṡa abyatä krəstiyanat*, Addis Ababa 1963 E.C., 7-17.

SA   *Sändäq Alamaččən* (newspaper). Addis Ababa.

SṬ   Täklä-Ṣadəq Mäkʷriya, *Yäsäw ṭabay-ənna abro yämänor zäde*. Addis Ababa 1943 E.C.

Stockwell, Robert P. (1977), *Foundations of Syntactic Theory*. Englewood Cliffs, New Jersey.

SWärq   Alämayyähu Mogäs, *Säm-ənna wärq — amarəñña əski ənnəwäq* I-II. Asmara 1953-1955 E.C.

Sweet, Henry (1891), *A New English Grammar, Logical and Historical*, Part I. Oxford.

Tesnière, Lucien (1959), *Éléments de syntaxe structurale*. Paris.

Traité   Cohen, Marcel, *Traité de langue amharique (Abyssinie)* (Travaux & mémoires de l'Institut d'Ethnologie, XXIV). Paris 1936.

WL   Həruy Wäldä-Səllase, *Wädağe ləbbe. yäsäwn ṭäbay-ənna nuro bäməssale yämmigälṣ.* Addis Ababa 1915.

YG   Pawlos Ñoñño, *Yänewoččǔ gärädočč.* Addis Ababa 1965.

Zad.   Voltaire, *Zadig wäyəmm əddəl.* tärgʷamiw: Šambäl Afä-wärq Yohannəs. Addis Ababa 1956 E.C.

al-Zamaxšarī, *K. al-Mufaṣṣal fī l-naḥw,* ed. J. P. Broch. Christiania ²1879.

ZI   *Yäzareyitu Ityopya* (newspaper). Addis Ababa.

REPRESENTATION OF LANGUAGE SIMILARITY
IN A SAMPLE OF SEMITIC

GENE GRAGG
University of Chicago

This frankly exploratory paper is a report on a preliminary application in a linguistic context of some techniques for bringing out groupings and patterns of similarity and difference in complex data arrays. The long-term perspective of the present limited undertaking is a project for assembling extensive comparative files in Afroasiatic, and the eventual goal is to see what can be done with a realistic range of data—type-systemic and token-textual, lexical, phonological, morphological, and syntactic, over a wide spectrum of languages, living and dead, well-attested and poorly-attested. Techniques of the kind examined here may or may not result in improved explanatory models of synchronic relations of similarity and diachronic relations of phylogenetic succession. But a sufficient reason for their continued exploration is, in my opinion, the prospect of being able to use currently available large-scale data processing techniques in order to periodically "take the temperature" of growing historical-comparative language data files, and to derive preliminary hypotheses about relations existing in the data and suggest directions for further data collection.

As an initial step a feasible approach to the longer-term goal seemed to be a study of lexical and grammatical similarities in a short, accessible text in a sample of better-understood Semitic languages. An obvious accessible text is the Bible, and, in order to keep the Hebrew data comparable to that of the other languages, I chose the New Testament. Hence the trial data is Luke 7,1-19—A text-token sample of about two hundred words of a simple narrative, translated into seven different languages: Geez, Tigrinya, Amharic, Arabic, Hebrew, Syriac, and Neo-Aramaic ("Assyrian")[1]. The textual histories of these translations, and their relations to one another, to the Greek original, and to translations not considered here are complicated in

---

[1] As a Cushitic (Oromo) lexicographer (whence the impulse to make a representative Afroasiatic language-data file), I can claim some professional competence in Ethio-Semitic. I have a "gentlemen's knowledge" of Arabic and Hebrew; but the reader should be forwarned that I am a rank outsider in Aramaic, and that, in this exploratory exercise, my conclusions about Aramaic should be taken hypothetically and by way of example.

the extreme. Hence I wish to make no exaggerated claims about these seven passages as adequate samples of the seven languages in question. For the present purposes it is sufficient that they permit us to consider with a degree of realism certain aspects of data processing with language data of this type. This having been said, it would of course be surprising if nothing at all could be learned from them about the languages they represent; and apart from the technical aspect of the problem, which is our primary focus here, I think some interesting working hypotheses about developments and relations of "West Semitic" languages are suggested by our analyses.

Because the sample texts are seven different renderings of a single narrative, it was possible to make a text comparison of lexical cognacy. Only major lexical categories (noun, verb, adjective, adverb) were counted. Passages where, because of translational idiosyncrasies in one or more of the versions, comparison was problematic were left aside. Likewise, an identical set of words was not counted more than once (e.g. "say" Eth. *bhl* = Arb. *qwl* = Heb., Syr., Nam. *7mr* occurred eight times; "hear" *sm9* in all languages occurred three times—each of these counted as a single correspondence set, one for "say" and one for "hear"). This left seventy-one septuplets on which cognates were counted. The raw similarity data are as follows:

	GEZ	TGA	AMH	ARB	HEB	SYR	NAM
GEZ							
TGA	29						
AMH	19	37					
ARB	9	9	7				
HEB	12	10	8	18			
SYR	13	12	11	16	24		
NAM	9	11	9	19	30	36	

Table 1: Lexical Cognates in Semitic Sample

From this one can see that Tigrinya and Amharic, for example, share 37 cognates, Syriac and Geez 13, Neoaramaic and Hebrew 30, etc.

Because of the shortness of the sample, only grosser typological features in morphology and syntax could be accounted for (mean number of morphemes per word, relative predominance of prefixing, suffixing, simple word order features—as opposed to tense/aspect distinctions, use of case, types of subordinate constructions, etc.). For the technique of counting these features I follow here the general technique of Greenberg (1960), who himself is trying to present in quantified form the typological approach of Sapir. Thus the features in Table 2 are scored in terms of Greenberg-like ratios. Previous

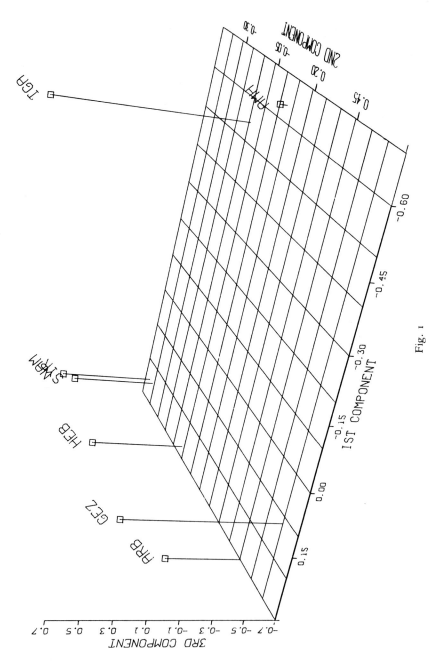

Fig. 1

	GEZ	TGA	AMH	ARB	HAB	SYR	NAM
1. morpheme / word	3.11	2.39	3.22	2.97	2.87	2.50	2.78
2. derivational-morpheme / word	.22	.11	.11	.35	.22	.34	.26
3. inflectional-morpheme / word	2.90	2.28	3.11	2.62	2.64	2.17	2.25
4. proclitic / word	.37	.05	.07	.32	.61	.38	.48
5. prefix / word	.26	.26	.43	.13	.21	.05	.00
6. derivational-prefix / word	.06	.01	.02	.07	.00	.04	.03
7. ablaut / word	.44	.31	.47	.31	.34	.32	.33
8. derivational-ablaut / word	.13	.09	.06	.23	.18	.12	.07
9. gemination / word	.08	.06	.21	.03	.01	.00	.00
10. suffix / word	.72	.52	.72	.84	.41	.33	.65
11. derivational-suffix / word	.02	.01	.02	.05	.04	.17	.17
12. enclitic / word	.02	.05	.18	.00	.01	.08	.07
13. infix / word	.00	.00	.00	.02	.00	.00	.00
14. genitive-pronoun / word	.21	.11	.13	.14	.21	.18	.15
15. concord-word / word	.07	.03	.03	.05	.06	.07	.06
16. article / word	.01	.03	.04	.09	.11	.00	.00
17. case (# of indications) / word	.26	.11	.23	.52	.33	.24	.30
18. genitive-particle / case	.02	.00	.08	.00	.00	.15	.21
19. preposition / case	.66	1.00	.46	.39	.84	.85	.79
20. postposition / case	.00	.00	.13	.00	.00	.00	.00
21. case-inflection / case	.32	.00	.33	.61	.16	.00	.00
22. "gerund" / verb (inflected verb)	.10	.18	.16	.00	.00	.00	.00
23. "participial-verb" / verb	.00	.00	.00	.00	.00	.30	.81
24. infinitive / verb	.01	.01	.00	.00	.10	.02	.01
25. subordinate-form / verb	.08	.15	.28	.09	.00	.00	.00
26. finite-verb (main) / verb	.77	.59	.55	.83	.76	.58	.05
27. copula-construction / verb	.04	.06	.01	.08	.14	.10	.11
28. subject-marker / verb	0.92	1.00	1.11	1.00	.89	.74	.78
29. object-marker / verb	.27	.22	.24	.06	.01	.03	.03
30. relative-marker / verb	.08	.11	.11	.02	.03	.11	.13
31. auxiliary / verb	.00	.07	.11	.00	.00	.19	.03
32. oblique-object-marker / verb	.00	.02	.03	.00	.00	.00	.00
33. internal-plural / plural	.86	.70	.14	.50	.00	.00	.00
34. suffix-plural / plural	.14	.30	.86	.50	1.00	1.00	1.00
35. V - S / V, S	.79	.00	.00	1.00	.73	.60	.64
36. S - V / V, S	.21	1.00	1.00	.00	.27	.40	.36
37. V - O / V, O	.96	.00	.00	1.00	.94	.86	.78
38. O - V / V, O	.04	1.00	1.00	.00	.06	.14	.22
39. Adj - N / Adj, N	.50	1.00	1.00	.00	.00	.00	.00
40. N - Adj / Adj, N	.50	.00	.00	1.00	1.00	1.00	1.00
41. Gen - N / Gen, N	.00	.17	.86	.00	.00	.00	.00
42. N - Gen / Gen, N	1.00	.83	.14	1.00	1.00	1.00	1.00
43. Rel - N / Rel, N	.00	1.00	1.00	.00	.00	.00	.00
44. N - Rel / Rel, N	1.00	.00	.00	1.00	1.00	1.00	1.00
45. Mod - N / Mod, N	1.00	1.00	.50	.50	1.00	.43	1.00
46. N - Mod / Mod, N	.00	.00	.50	.50	.00	.57	.00

Table 2: Grammatical Indices for Semitic Sample
(Cf. Table 4 for denominator counts, from which actual ratios can be calculated)

SYNTACTIC DISTANCES FOR SEMITIC SAMPLE

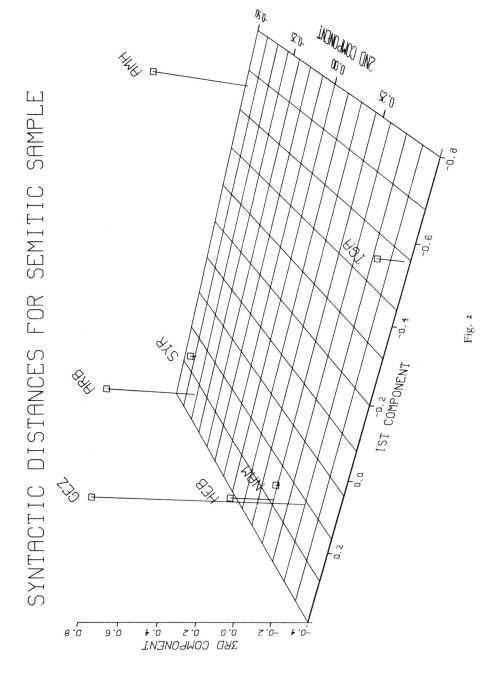

Fig. 2

experience with the specific indices of Greenberg (1960) convinced me that they are not well-suited for conveying important distinctions in Semitic, and the indices used here are those which seem best to differentiate the data at hand[2].

A more definitive set of indices would demand and merit a detailed justification, but for our purposes the following remarks will, I hope, suffice. Indices 1-34 are morphological in character. Index 1, the ratio of morphemes (i.e., concrete formatives) to words, is Greenberg's "index of synthesis". In 2 and 3 "derivational" morphemes are those which signal a part of speech (the Aramaic -ā formative with nouns was classified here, perhaps problematically), or which change one part of speech into another (e.g., formatives involved in verbal nouns and adjectives). Formatives involved in the Semitic so-called "derived verb stems" (causative, passive, frequentative, etc.) are in practice difficult, if not impossible to extricate from the inflectional formatives, and are here classified as "inflectional". Note that 2 and 3, with allowance for rounding, sum to Index 1. Indices 4-13 have to do with Sapir's "morphological technique"; while 14-16 and 33-34 cover some prominent nominal features (by "concord word" in 15 is meant a member of the pronominal or demonstrative system showing inflection for gender, number, or person). Index 17 gives the relative frequency of morphological indications of case, while 18-21 gives their relative distribution (and hence sum to unity). Indices 22-27 give the different types of verbal word (including a few cases of zero copula), and sum to unity also. "Gerund" is the Ethiopian converb; "participial verb" is the new suffix conjugation developed in Aramaic (Syriac and Neoaramaic). 25 covers morphologically marked subordinate clause forms (e.g., subjunctive in Arabic, relative verb in Amharic). In 26, «finite verb» is a residual category which in effect means a descendent of the West Semitic so-called perfective or imperfective, and hence may be a covert historical category. Indices 28-32 deal with morphological sattelites of the verbal word; 32 refers to the -b-/-l- suffixed object markers in modern Ethiopic Semitic (Amharic, Tigrinya here). The syntactic indices 35-46 are pair-wise dichotomous, and represent the most basic word-order features. Thus 35-36 account for all of the clauses in each of the languages which have a verb, and a morphologically independent noun as subject; they give the proportion of cases where the subject follows the verb (35) and proportion

---

[2]   This raises important issues in the philosophy or general approach one adopts to questions of taxonomy, particularly the choice, weighting, and number of distinguishing characteristics. For a discussion of this in the context of biological numerical taxonomy cf. Sneath and Sokal (1973: Ch. 3).

of cases where the subject precedes the verb (36)—similarly for the other pairs
of indices. In 45-46 "Mod" stands for modifiers not covered by 39-44.

The next step in deriving an overview of the relative similarity of these
languages consists in deciding on a measure of similarity/dissimilarity between
the individual pairs of languages. A large variety of such measures are
available and discussed in the literature[3]. For this investigation, for the
morphological and syntactic indices, I chose to use the widely employed
Euclidean distance measure, according to which the distance between individuals a and b in a space of n variables is:

$$D_{ab} = \sqrt{\sum_{i=1}^{n} (a_i - b_i)^2}$$

where, in our case, a and b are languages and a_i, b_i is the "score" of a, b on
the i-th index. Note that this reduces to the familiar Pythagorean Theorem for
the length of the hypoteneuse of a right triangle:

$$ab = \sqrt{(a_1 - b_1)^2 - (a_2 - b_2)^2}$$

in the special case where n = 2, and a_1, a_2 and b_1, b_2 are the coordinates of
points a, b in a two-dimensional Cartesian coordinate system. In the case of
the Euclidean distance measure, o is the limiting case of identity between two
individuals, while the upper limit is simply the square root of the largest sum
of differences; inbetween, the smaller the number D, the more closely related
are the items being measured. For the numerical ratios, therefore, the distance
between two languages as measured by the ratios in Table 2 is simply the
square root of the sum of the squared differences between the corresponding
entries in the columns representing the two languages in Table 2. This
number, for different combinations of indices, is given in Table 3A 2-5.

For the purposes of the present investigation, lexical distance was calculated
simply as the square root of raw lexical difference:

$$\sqrt{71 - N}$$

3 Sneath and Sokal (1973: Ch. 4). There are several reasons for chosing straight Euclidean
distance on non-standardized data in the present explanatory context. Among them are the
intuitive accessibility of this measure, and the fact that it has a history of use in linguistic
contexts (Altmann and Lehfeldt, 1973). Recent work on the ordination technique used here
(Mather, 1976) however suggests that better results may sometimes be obtained with some
less intuitively obvious similarity measures, and with standardized data matrices. The point
obviously merits further investigation.

where N is the number of cognates between two languages, and 71 is the total number of correspondence sets. Note that under one possible interpretation, this measure of lexical distance differs from a strict Euclidean distance only by a factor of $\times 2$. That is, a Euclidean distance can be obtained by multiplying the distances of Table 3A 1 by $\times 2$. This effect will follow if each etymologically distinct word is considered a separate dichotomus feature, and languages are scored 1 or 0 according as they possess or do not possess this feature[4]. Note that for any two languages, the four possible cases of "distance" are 1-0, 0-1, 1-1, 0-0. The latter two possibilities are equal to 0, and hence do not contribute to the distance. Since, as the reader can verify, there are exactly 71—N "1-0" terms, and 71—N "0-1" terms, the Euclidean distance formula reduces to:

$$\sqrt{2(71-N)} = \sqrt{2} \cdot \sqrt{71-N}$$

Given the provisional nature of the original data, I will not dwell here on the results of this first step — although I believe that they are interesting in their own right, and worthy of consideration. They show very well, and in fact more accurately than the graphs, the distance between pairs of languages (or language samples) in the domains measured. However, as is often the case with similarity matrices of this sort, and as the reader can verify, many aspects of the global picture are not at all clear. What one can also verify for oneself very concretely (say, by cutting wires to scale and attempting to model concretely the distances among the set of languages as a whole) is that the distances represented in the matrices of Table 3A 1-5 are not two or even three dimensional (the wires will not connect properly without a lot of bending and stretching). In fact the raw dimensionality of the last matrix might be considered to be on the order of 200.

Hence the need for the next, mathematically and computational most complex step. There is a large and higly technical literature involved, which I have neither the competence nor in any case the space to summarize[5].

4 On this interpretation the lexical material would represent in effect a large number of binary variables (186, in fact). The ease of deriving a distance matrix for a large collection of lexical material should be obvious. This ease, and the fact that with this similarity measure one can use a computationally convenient ordination technique makes the development of a similarity measure of this sort an interesting goal, which merits a good deal of intensive consideration. For the moment note that ordination either by $\sqrt{71 - N}$ or by $\sqrt{2} (71 - n)$ yields perceptibly the same result.

5 Here, as elsewhere, Sneath and Sokal (1973) provided a valuable initiation. Cooley and Lohnes (1971) was a general computational guide, with useful computer programs; while Mather (1976) gave specific detail on Principal Coordinates. In particular my Principal

A. Distance Matrices   B. Components

1. (Lexical)

	Gez	Tga	Amh	Arb	Heb	Syr	Nam	Comp 1	Comp 2	Comp 3
Gez								.335	.109	.585
Tga	6.48							.488	—.065	—.105
Amh	7.21	5.83						.471	—.134	—.385
Arb	7.87	7.89	8.00					—.268	.752	—.407
Heb	7.68	7.81	7.94	7.28				—.293	.189	.528
Syr	7.26	7.68	7.75	7.42	6.86			—.350	—.455	.016
Nam	7.87	7.75	7.87	7.21	7.14	5.92		—.387	—.396	—.232

R = .759/.787

2. (Morphological: Indices 1-34)

	Gez	Tga	Amh	Arb	Heb	Syr	Nam	Comp 1	Comp 2	Comp 3
Gez								.518	.126	.139
Tga	1.20							.090	.741	.235
Amh	1.22	1.62						.258	—.563	.329
Arb	0.86	1.36	1.15					.326	—.104	—.394
Heb	1.40	1.41	1.20	1.14				—.173	—.186	—.565
Syr	1.75	1.27	1.63	1.48	0.87			—.488	.184	—.266
Nam	1.81	1.65	1.58	1.62	1.20	0.95		—.531	—.198	.522

R = .407/549

3. (Syntactic: Indices 35-46)

	Gez	Tga	Amh	Arb	Heb	Syr	Nam	Comp 1	Comp 2	Comp 3
Gez								.169	.359	.743
Tga	2.38							—.547	.477	—.264
Amh	2.75	1.21						—.638	—.482	.212
Arb	1.05	2.93	3.08					.322	—.372	.196
Heb	0.71	2.63	2.97	0.81				.263	.215	—.147
Syr	1.11	2.63	2.77	0.61	0.84			.219	—.421	—.360
Nam	0.78	2.47	2.83	0.93	0.26	0.82		.212	.225	—.379

R = .606/.807

4. (Morpho-Syntactic: Indices 1-46)

	Gez	Tga	Amh	Arb	Heb	Syr	Nam	Comp 1	Comp 2	Comp 3
Gez								.118	.610	.302
Tga	2.66							—.546	—.143	.662
Amh	3.01	2.01						—.636	.063	—.651
Arb	1.36	3.23	3.29					.298	.447	—.196
Heb	1.57	2.98	3.20	1.40				.273	—.087	—.032
Syr	2.08	2.92	3.22	1.60	1.20			.246	—.430	—.080
Nam	1.98	2.97	3.24	1.87	1.23	1.25		.247	—.460	—.005

R = .731/.635

5. (Total: Lexical plus Indices 1-46)

	Gez	Tga	Amh	Arb	Heb	Syr	Nam	Comp 1	Comp 2	Comp 3
Gez								.222	.446	.660
Tga	7.01							.514	—.092	—.008
Amh	7.81	6.17						.530	—.256	—.383
Arb	7.99	8.51	8.65					—.275	.591	—.601
Heb	7.84	8.36	8.56	7.41				—.299	.152	.177
Syr	7.89	8.22	8.39	7.59	6.96			—.334	—.415	.160
Nam	8.12	8.30	8.52	7.45	7.25	6.05		—.359	—.427	—.004

R = .702/.800

Table 3: Distance and Component Matrices for Semitic Sample

Let me simply state for the present that there exist mathematical transformations whose function is to produce the most satisfactory low-dimensional approximation to high-dimensional numerical data arrays—for graphing and visualization purposes, two- and three-dimensional approximations are obviously what are frequently envisaged. Criteria for "most satisfactory" can obviously differ from researcher to researcher and from project to project. Hence there is an embarras de choix of techniques. The technique used here, Gower's Principal Coordinates, is a Principal Component analysis of a transformed similarity matrix[6]. It works directly from the distance matrix, without going back to the original data matrix, or going through the intermediate step of a variable × variable correlation matrix[7].

In table 3 B I give the first three principal coordinates (i.e., a "best" three-dimensional approximation) for the seven languages as measured by the corresponding distance matrices in Table 3 A. As a check, I offer under each distance-matrix/coordinate-matrix pair two values for "R", the so-called

Components program is based on the PRINCO program listed in Cooley and Lohnes (1971), Ch. 4. Good programs for these purposes are readily available in all academic installations. However, in the interests of testing the feasibility of this type of data processing, and seeing how far a relatively untutored linguist could maintain some control over the computational steps involved, I adapted their programs into BASIC and ran them on a microcomputer (TRS 80 Model III). The resulting program was monumentally slow and undoubtedly inefficient—but accurate to about three decimal places, as tested with selected data sets against the Principal Component routines of SAS.

6 Ordination is a term used for any one of a number of methods involving "display in graphical form of inter-object similarities in a low dimensional space" (Mather, 1976: p. 307). In Principal Component Analysis a p x n (in our case, for example, a 7 (language) x 46 (variable)) matrix, in which each of the p objects (the languages) is represented by n coordinates (the score for each of the indices), is replaced by a p x r matrix (7 × 3 in our case) in which each object is represented by a smaller number of coordinates (the components) "which in some sense retain approximately the same information as the original coordinates" (Kruskal, 1978). Principal Coordinate Analysis, stemming from Gower (1966), is treated in Mather (1976). In addition cf. the recent evaluations and comparisons of Principal Coordinates in Thorpe (1980) and Pimentel (1981). Besides Principal Component Analysis and Principal Coordinate Analysis, a third frequently used technique is Multidimensional Scaling—for an application in linguistics cf. Black (1978). My own initial trials with Greenberg and Greenberg-like indices seem to indicate that these three techniques result in what for our purposes are quite comparable ordinations.

7 This would have involved, for this initial trial, the processing of an n x n matrix where n is larger than 200 (and would be much larger than that in more realistic lexical probes), approaching the normal limits of the matrix processing routines of some of the standard statistical packages. With the approach used here I was able to derive the component matrices on a microcomputer, and could have done so with an indefinitely large number of variables (but not of languages).

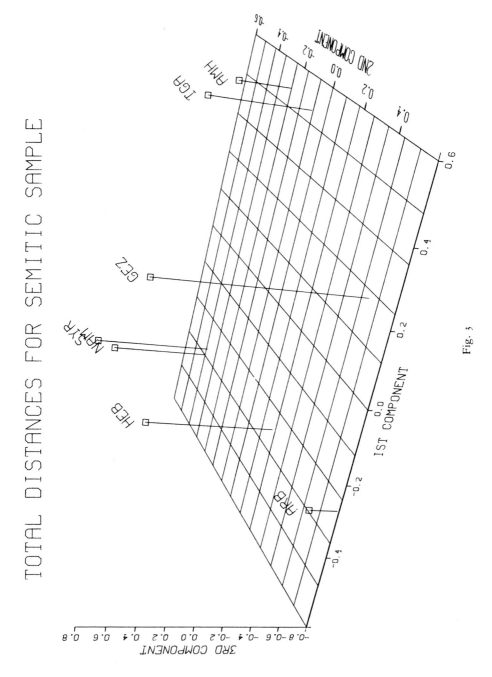

TOTAL DISTANCES FOR SEMITIC SAMPLE

Fig. 3

"cophenetic" correlation coefficient. This is simply the product-moment correlation coefficient between the original distance matrix and a new Euclidean distance matrix (not given here, but calculable from the figures in Table 3 B) derived from the coordinates in the reduced variable space. The first value is for three principal coordinates, and the second for two. An "R" of between .6 and .95 is apparently considered normal in biological numerical taxonomy, and on these grounds all of our ordinations seem to fall within acceptable limits, with the exception of the morphological ordination, where the data are obviously not satisfactorily described in two or three dimensions (see below)[8].

The results of this reduced dimensionality are plotted in Figures 1 to 5[9]. For these graphs I availed myself of a wide range of graphic software and hardware options avalable to the general user at the University of Chicago installation in order to produce a visually effective set of graphs. I should emphasize however, since practicality is a consideration in the context of this investigation, that the essential points made by the graphs could be made also, if less vividly, by a series of two-dimensional (e.g., Comp 1 by Comp 2, Comp 1 by Comp 3) scattergrams of the kind that can be produced by the humblest of microcomputers. These graphs are in no sense a definitive statement. But they certainly suggest some interesting questions for further investigations along these lines. Among the observations that might be made are the following:

The first graph gives a fairly close approximation to the clustering one might expect from the traditional Stammbaum of the Semitic language family. The cleavage between Ethiopian Semitic and Non-Ethiopian Semitic, however, is much deeper than one might have predicted; and Arabic, although neatly segregated in a corner by itself, is definitely on the same side of the fence with Northwest Semitic, as opposed to Ethio-Semitic, with which it

---

8 On the cophenetic coefficient see Sneath and Sokal (1971: pp. 278-80) and references cited there. Note that in Principal Component Analysis, as many principal components can be extracted as there are variables, with the first principal component accounting for the largest proportion of variance in the data, the second component for the second largest proportion, and so on. In the types of social science and biological data considered so far in multivariate analysis, it has been found to be usually the case that a large amount of the variance in a data array can be accounted for by a smaller number (e.g., two to four) of components. We have of course no specific precedents on which to base expectations for language data. In any case, the exploratory and ordination-oriented reduction of dimensionality undertaken here must be strictly distinguished from a more sophisticated type of analysis in which we would try to determine optimal or inherent dimensionality, and attempt substantive interpretations of these dimensions.

9 The data points were converted into graph vectors by means of the graphics language, DISSPLA, and plotted on a Calcomp drum plotter.

LEXICAL DISTANCES FOR SEMITIC SAMPLE

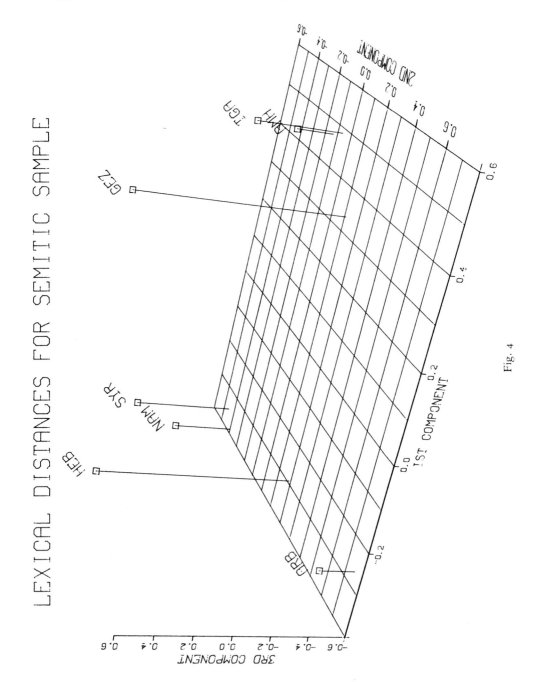

Fig. 4

	Gez	Tga	Amh	Arb	Heb	Syr	Nam
word	184	285	225	234	205	226	223
case	47	30	52	121	68	55	66
verb	77	88	93	64	72	80	80
plural	7	10	5	10	19	8	8
V, S	14	19	15	13	22	15	14
V, O	18	16	19	12	17	7	9
Adj, N	4	3	4	9	7	3	3
Gen, N	6	6	8	6	12	8	8
Rel, N	2	7	11	2	1	9	7
Mod, N	6	14	6	2	4	7	9

Table 4: Raw Counts of Ratio Denominators in Table 2

is often linked in a subfamily called South Semitic. It is interesting that Neoaramaic behaves like a proper Northwest Semitic language in this and other graphs, and not like the maverick it is sometimes made out to be. (In these graphs, Amharic and Tigrinya are the real mavericks). It is fascinating to speculate what the addition of Akkadian would do to the alignment depicted here. (In the absence of an Akkadian version of Luke, it was obviously out of the question to include Akkadian in this initial limited investigation). Another notable aspect of the first graph is its striking isomorphism with a somewhat distorted map of the geographical distribution of the Semitic languages—as viewed, say, from somewhere above Malta (Arabic is foreshortened into the North, and Ethiopia looms disproportionately large). This is perhaps the kind of map to be expected of lexical differences among languages which diffused gradually from a single core over a contiguous area. If this is the case, a graph for, say, Romance, might well share these features, while other language families (Indoeuropean as a whole, perhaps) might show some interesting differences. Finally, note that this method of measuring cognacy, although limited in its applicability (e.g. the Akkadian case), achieves some of the results looked for in lexicostatistics without involving assumptions about basic vocabulary or family tree structure. It might be worthwhile investigating whether the method might be extended to texts which are not literal translations of a single original text.

Graph two is much less clear—note also its low "R" (cf. above). The highly inflecting Arabic, Amharic, and Geez cluster together, and Hebrew occupies a medial position between them and Aramaic, whose solidarity and isolation is interesting. The extreme isolation of Tigrinya is noteworthy and hard to explain. As noted above, no clear low-dimensional picture seems to emerge from these counts, and more collection seems in order.

The syntax graph, not surprisingly, neatly separates SOV languages from

MORPHOLOGICAL DISTANCES FOR SEMITIC SAMPLE

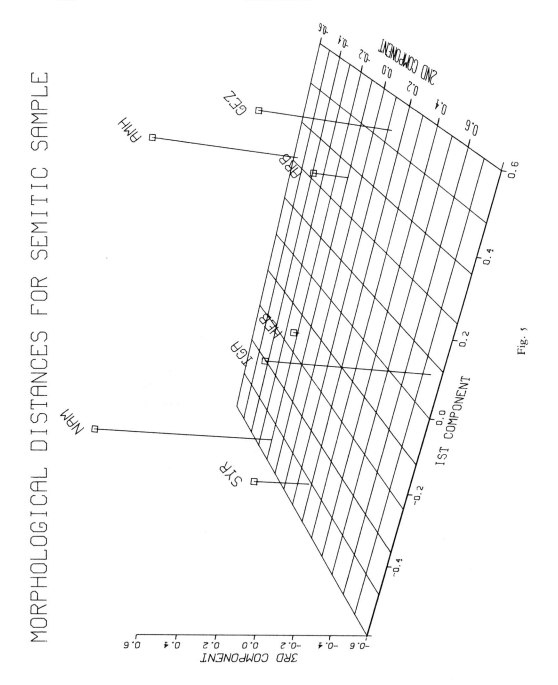

Fig. 5

the rest, and the more "classically" Semitic Arabic and Syriac from languages that have made more concessions to SOV-type syntax. Note here the usefulness of scoring word-order features in ratio terms, rather than forcing an all-or-none classification of word-order features—i.e., of recognizing that some languages are more or less VSO, SVO, etc. than others.

Given the differences between the two preceding graphs, what is surprising about Graph 4, which is based on the features underlying 2 and 3 combined, is that it provides as close an approximation to Graph 1 as it does. The single major exception is that Geez has frankly joined the rest of Semitic, leaving Tigrinya and Amharic at the edge of the Semitic universe. This suggests that lexical change may have worked relatively faster for Geez than morphological and syntactic change in combination, although obviously much more data are required. It will be interesting to see in larger collections of data to what extent grammatical and lexical features each give roughly the same configuration for language similarity, with allowance made for "swing languages" such as Geez.

The last graph is, not surprisingly, something of a compromise between Graphs 1 and 4, and perhaps gives the most balanced picture of the relations of similarity and distance which exist among these languages. As a single picture, graphs of this kind will obviously be preferred; but it will obviously be important to be able to "decompose" them into their underlying partial similarity configurations.

In conclusion I would like to observe, first of all, that there is no lack of problematic aspects in the approach to language difference projected here. We need to know more about the appropriateness and limitations of ratio-based indices. They seem to work well enough for text-count measures, but systemic measures will surely have to work more with ordinal, nominal, and dichotomous scales. Moreover some serious questions of homology have been glossed over in the above: In language difference measures, exactly what categories are to be taken as equivalent to what other categories? Thus gerundive verbs in Ethiopic and "participial" verbs in Aramaic were taken as distinct innovations in the finite verb system, and not equated with anything else. But should the gerundive verbs have been counted as just one more class of subordinate forms, and the "participial" as mainclause finite[10]?

Granted the existence of these problems, whose discussion and investigation can only advance our knowledge of language typology and language change, a use of techniques like those presented here as a heuristic adjunct to a

---

10 This is a classic problem in all kinds of numerical taxonomy. Cf. footnote 1, and the linguistics-oriented discussion in Altmann (1976).

comparative language data file seems feasible. Given properly encoded files, it seems possible, and potentially useful, to derive a similarity matrix and ordination based either on the file as a whole, or on some subselection of languages and/or properties. In particular, using some technique such as Principal Coordinates, lexical cognates, which in any case form the core of any traditional comparative language data file, can be interpreted as above to yield an easily derived measure of lexical distance.

Of course the number of practical details that remain to be solved (file structure, encoding, updating, revision, missing data) should not be underestimated; and the fact should be kept in mind that there are surely as many workable "solutions" as there are different perspectives which can be brought to bear on the task. I will mention in closing only one long-term perspective. On the one hand, by substituting a time-axis for the third component and providing a hierarchically arranged succession of ancestor nodes, graphs of the kind given here can easily be transformed into three-dimensional trees. Given suitable means for choosing the coordinates of intermediate nodes, this could result in an interesting graphic display of the extent and rate of change in lexical, morphological, and syntactic domains [11]. On the other hand, the limitations of the family tree diagram as well as the artificial or unverifiable nature of some of its assumptions have been a topic of discussion among historical linguists since the last century. Ordination of languages in various two- or three-dimensional variable spaces, with or without a complete system of subtending ancestor nodes, may well function as a valuable complement to traditional representations of language relationship, and better display aspects of language relationship obscured by them.

---

[11] A good illustration of this in the context of paleontology is Rowell (1970); cf. further Sneath and Sokal (1973: pp. 356-61).

Bibliography

Addis kidan (New Testament in Amharic) (1965), (Yämäṣhaf Qəddus Mahbär, Addis Ababa).

al-9ahd al-jadııd (New Testament in Arabic) (1971), (Society for Distributing the Holy Scriptures, Middlesex).

Altmann, Gabriel (1976), "Homologiekriterien in der Linguistik und der Biologie", *Aufsätze und Reden der Senkenbergischen Naturforschenden Gesellschaft* 28, 184-91.

Altmann, Gabriel and Werner Lehfeldt (1973), *Allgemeine Sprachtypologie: Prinzipien und Messverfahren* (Fink, München).

Black, Paul (1976), "Multidimensional Scaling Applied to Linguistic Relationships", *Cahiers de l'Institut Linguistique (Louvain)* 3, 43-92.

Cooley, William, and Paul Lohnes (1971), *Multivariate Data Analysis* (Wiley, New York).

Gower, J.C. (1966), "Some Distance Properties of Latent Root and Vector Methods Used in Multivariate Analysis", *Biometrika* 53, 325-38.

Dobson, Annette, and Paul Black (1979), "Multidimensional Scaling of some Lexicostatistical Data", *The Mathematical Scientist* 4, 55-62.

Greenberg, Joseph (1960), "A Quantitative Approach to the Morphological Typology of Languages", IJAL 26, 178-94.

Habbərīt habʰdāšā (New Testament in Hebrew) (1971), trans. Franz Delitsch (Society for Distributing the Holy Scriptures, Middlesex).

Ḥaddəš kidan (New Testament in Tigrinya) (1974), (Maḥbär Mäṣhaf Qəddus, Addis Ababa).

Kruskal, Joseph (1978), "Factor Analysis and Principal Components: Bilinear Methods", in W. Kruskal and J. Tanur (eds.), *International Encyclopedia of Statistics* (Free Press, New York), vol. 1, pp. 307-330.

Kruzuta dLuqa (Luke in Neoaramaic) (1965), (The Bible Societies in the Near East, Beirut).

Mather, P.M. (1976), *Computational Methods of Multivariate Analysis in Physical Geography* (Wiley, New York).

Pimentel, Richard (1981), "A Comparative Study of Data and Ordination Techniques Based on a Hybrid Strain of Sand Verbenas", *Systematic Zoology* 30, 260-67.

Rowell, A.J. (1970), "The Contribution of Numerical Taxonomy to the Genus Concept", in E.L. Yochelson (ed.), *Proceedings of the North American Paleontological Convention, Chicago 1969* (Allen Press, Lawrence), vol. 1, part C, pp. 264-93.

Sankoff, David, and H. Cedergren, (1976), "The Dimensionality of Grammatical Variation", *Language* 52, 163-178.

Sneath, Peter, and Robert Sokal (1973), *Numerical Taxonomy* (Freeman, San Francisco).

The New Testament in Syriac (1920), (British and Foreign Bible Society, London).

Thorpe, R.S. (1980), "A Comparative Study of Ordination Techniques in Numerical Taxonomy in Relation to Racial Variation in the Ringed Snake Natrix Natrix (L.)" *Biol. J. Linn. Soc.* 13, 7-40.

Wängel qəddus wämäṣaḥəftihomu lähäwaryat qəddusan (New Testament in Geez) (1899) (British and Foreign Bible Society, Leipzig).

A NOTE ON GE'EZ RELATIVE CLAUSES

Hailu Fulass
Howard University, Washington

Introduction

To my knowledge, the most detailed discussion on Ge'ez relative clauses is found in Dillmann (1907; see especially pp. 332-333, 380, 527-537). Dillmann's discussion of the Ge'ez relative clause is so detailed and complete that it would be most difficult, if not impossible, to cite a relative clause construction that is not mentioned therein.

The purpose of the present study is, therefore, not to give examples of relative clause constructions which are not found in Dillmann but to clarify aspects of the grammar of one type of relative clause construction in Ge'ez and to show that, as regards this particular type of construction, typologically Ge'ez forms a different set as against the present day Ethio-semitic languages.

The relative clause in Ge'ez is characterized by the particle $z\ddot{a}$ and its morphologically and syntactically conditioned variants (see Dillmann, p. 332; 527ff.). Dillmann and others call this morpheme a relative pronoun. However, it has been convincingly argued by Palmer (1961; 1962) and Hailu (1972) that the relative marker $z\ddot{a}$ (and its equivalents in the other Ethio-semitic languages) is not at all a pronoun, but a particle which indicates that the clause to which it is attached functions as a relative clause. What Palmer (1961:26) pointed out in connection with relative clauses in Tigre is equally true in Ge'ez that the so-called relative pronoun "... does not mark the kind of distinction that is shown by the relative pronouns 'who', 'whom', 'whose', etc. ... These (distinctions) are marked ... by the concord between the noun and certain elements within the relative clause".

That this observation of Palmer's is true for Ge'ez is illustrated by the following examples.

> (1) männu wɨʔɨtu säbɨʔ zäyɨkɨl   D:335
>   "who is the man that is able to?"
> (2) ʔabäw zätägabɨʔu bänɨk'ɨya   D:333
>   "the fathers who assembled in Nicaea"

In example (1) zäyɨkɨl and in example (2) zätägabɨʔu function as adjectives qualifying säbɨʔ and ʔabäw respectively. The particle *zä* in all such cases marks the clause as adjectival and the elements that serve as relative pronouns are the third person masculine singular (= msg) subject marker in sentence (1) and the 3mpl subject marker /-u/ in (2). More generally, in Ge'ez and other Ethio-semitic languages if the head of the relative clause is (coreferential with the underlying) subject of the relative verb, that is, the verb with which the relative marker is associated or to which it is attached, then there is always agreement, expressed by subject markers affixed to the relative verb, between the head noun-phrase and the relative verb.

Since the relative clause is adjectival, it occupies the position of modifier; that is, it follows (in the overwhelming number of cases) the noun phrase which it modifies.

(3) bɨʔisi zäyähawwɨr   D:531
    "The man who goes"
(4) wäldɨyä zäʔafäk'k'ɨr   Mk 9:8
    "my beloved son (more literally 'my son whom I love')"

There are, however, cases in which the relative clause precedes the noun phrase it modifies.

(5) ʔitɨrʔayu zäwädäk'ä ɨklu   D. 530
    "gather not up the corn which has fallen aside".
(6) kullu zätɨgäbbɨru k'alä   D. 530
    "all the things that you do".

Observations such as the above concerning the position of the relative clause are common knowledge and, therefore, do not need any elaborated or detailed discussion. It would be, nonetheless, interesting to study in detail the conditions which determine the position of the relative clause in relation to its head. Dillmann (p. 530) hints at one or two specific conditions governing the position of the relative clause; in a projected comprehensive study of the relative clause in Ge'ez, the present author will attempt to investigate these conditions in a more systematic and detailed manner.

I

To come back to the subject of this note. Although Dillmann (p. 332) declares that *zä* (and its variants) "serve as *Relative Pronoun* in Ethiopic, without any further combination", and although he asserts (p. 527) that

"Ethiopic has no other personal Relative", he, nevertheless, expresses a reservation—or, if you like, he makes his strong assertion *conditional*—by saying (p. 351), "The ordinary way of indicating ... (case) relations ... is by treating the Relative Pron. ... merely as a general mark of relations which needs to be supplemented by Personal Pronouns". As was argued by Palmer and Hailu in the above mentioned works, there is a fundamental distinction between a relative marker and a relative pronoun, and, consequently, in Ethio-semitic languages (in fact, in Semitic languages in general) the recalling of the antecedent and case relations in relative clauses are indicated by what Dillmann calls "Personal Pronouns". It is, in fact, these "Personal Pronouns", or pronominal affixes, that function as relative pronouns in the relative clause, even though they may be realized as o under given conditions.

In the other Ethio-semitic languages, there are well specified conditions which prohibit the recalling of the head noun of a relative clause by a relative pronoun. Thus, if the relative verb has an indirect object which is non-coreferential with the head noun then the head noun may or may not be recalled. In Ge'ez this alternative does not exist. The head noun in this type of construction cannot be recalled. Thus the Amharic sentences below,

> (7:a) läwändɨmme yäs'afkut däbdabbe
>   (b) läwändɨmme yäs'afkullät däbdabbe
>   (c) *läwändɨmme yäs'afku däbdabbe

mean (except (7c) which is ungrammatical) "the letter which I wrote to my brother". In (7a) the morpheme *-t* is the 3msg. direct object marker and agrees with däbdabbe. This is so because the direct object of the relative verb yäs'afku which was coreferential with the head of the whole relative clause, namely, däbdabbe, has been deleted. In such cases Amharic requires a pronominal copy of the deleted noun phrase unless this is blocked by the recalling of the indirect object, if any, in underlying structure. In (7b) the "prepositional" suffix *-llät* refers to wandimme and blocks the appearance of the direct object marker which would have recalled the deleted noun in the relative clause coreferent with däbdabbe. Similarly, in the Tigriñña sentences below:

> (8:a) nɨhawwäy zɨs'ɨhafkuwwo däbdabbe
>   (b) nɨhawwäy zɨs'ɨhafkullo däbdabbe
>   (c) *nɨhawwäy zɨs'ɨhafku däbdabbe

a situation exactly parallel to the Amharic obtains. In Kɨstanɨñña, a Guraghe language, one finds exactly the identical structure, e.g.,

(9:a)   näzämmiddi yäs'afkunni däbdabbe
   (b)   näzämmiddi yäs'afkuläyi däbdabbe
   (c) *näzämmiddi yäs'afku däbdabbe

The Tigriňňa and Kistaniňňa clauses mean the same as the Amharic clauses
in (7). The clauses in the three languages have identical structures which can
be represented by:

(10)

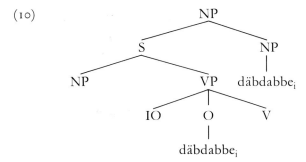

The subscripts /i/ indicate that the two nouns are coreferential.

If in the S cycle the IO is also recalled by a suffix attached to V, that is, if
the underlying sentence is, nihawwäy däbdabbe s'ähafkullo, then on the
matrix NP cycle O is deleted without leaving a pronominal copy. That is,
one derives the (b) sentences in (7), (8) and (9) above. If, on the other hand,
the IO is not recalled by V on the S cycle, i.e., if you have näzämmiddi
däbdabbe s'afki in which the indirect object zämmidi "my brother" is not
recalled by the corresponding suffix pronoun, then on the matrix NP cycle O
will be deleted but it will be recalled by a pronominal copy attached to V.
Thus are derived the (a) sentences in (7) and (9). These two are the only
alternatives in the derivation of correct relative clauses having the underlying
structure indicated in (10). Hence, the ungrammaticality of the (c) sentences
in (7), (8) and (9) are automatically accounted for. This analysis holds in the
case of all the Ethio-semitic languages spoken today.

Geez, however, diverges from this pattern. The Geez equivalents of the
sentences cited in the other three languages are:

(11:a)   mäli?ikt zäs'ähafku lä?ihuyä
   (b)   mäli?ikt zäs'ähafku lottu lä?ihuyä
   (c) *mäli?ikt zäs'ähafkuwwo ?ihuyä

In Geez if the head noun is coreferential with the direct object of the
relative verb, the direct object is deleted and no pronominal copy of it is
attached to the relative verb. Thus whereas

(12) zɨntu wɨʔɨtu wäldɨyä zäʔafäk'k'ɨr　　　　　Mk 9:78
"This is my beloved son"

(13) wäzäʔasärkä bämɨdr yɨkäwwɨn ʔɨsurä bäsämayat　　　Mk 16:19
"and whatever you bind on earth shall be bound in heaven"

are sentence patterns which are grammatical, sentences such as:

(14) zɨntu wɨʔɨtu wäldɨyä zäʔafäk'k'ɨro

(15) wäzäʔasärko bämɨdr yɨkäwwɨn ʔɨsurä bäsämayat

are ungrammatical. This is exactly the reverse of what is found in present-day spoken Ethio-semitic languages. For instance, the translation of (12) and (13) in Amharic are (16) and (17) respectively.

(16) yämmɨwäddäw lɨje yɨh näw

(17) bämɨdr yassärkäw bäsämayɨm yätassärä yɨhonall

In terms of the overt presence of a recalling pronominal suffix, note that -w attached to yämmɨwädd in (16) and yassärk in (17) are pronominal copies of the deleted lɨje and säw which are O's of wäddädku and ʔassärk, respectively, in underlying structure. As such (16) and (17) translate in a morphologically equivalent manner (14) and (15) rather than (12) and (13). Translations of (12) and (13) into other Ethio-semitic languages would show a similar form as (16) and (17) above.

For the sake of simplicity, consider the case in which the only object of the main verb of the relative clause is a direct object which is coreferential with the head of the relative clause. Leaving details aside, Geez relative clause formation is roughly as follows:

(18) NP_i (X V NP_i Y) $\longrightarrow$
　　　NP_i (X V Ø Y)

In present-day Ethio-semitic languages, however, the rule is roughly as follows:

(19) (X NP_i V Y) NP_i $\longrightarrow$
　　　(X Ø V_{npi} Y) NP_i

where both in (18) and (19) the outer NP_i represents the head, and the inner NP_i represents the direct object, and $_{npi}$ in (19) represents a pronominal copy of the inner NP_i.

Here are some more examples in Geʕez, illustrating (18).

(20:a) wärɨʔyä kullo zägäbrä Gen. 1:31
　　　"and God saw everything that He had made"

(b) *wärɨʔyä kullo zägäbäro
(21:a) ʔɨsmä zäyɨmehhɨru ʔiyɨgabbɨru Mt. 23:3-4
    "for they preach, but do not practice".
(b) *ʔɨsma zäyɨmehhɨrɨwwo ʔɨyɨgäbbɨru
(22:a) ʔalbomu zäyɨbälliʕu Mk 8:1
    "and they had nothing to eat".
(b) *ʔalbomu zäyɨbälliʕɨwwo

Compare sentence (20) - (22) with their respective Amharic equivalents
which illustrate the operation of rule (19).

(23:a) yäsärrawɨn hullu ʔayyä
(b) *yäsärran hullu ʔayyä
(24:a) yämmiyastämɨrutɨn aysärummɨnna
(b) *yämmiyastämɨru(n) aysärummɨnna
(25:a) yämmibälut ʔalnäbbäraččäwɨmm
(b) *yämmibalu alnäbbäraččäwɨmm

Notice that in the structures above wherever the Geez sentence is grammatical the corresponding Amharic sentence is not and vice versa. A parallel situation is found if the Geez constructions in (20) - (22) are translated into another Ethio-Semitic language.

II

In this section we shall show a construction which again marks Ge'ez as typologically distinct from the rest of Ethio-semitic.

As is well known, in Ge'ez one of the ways the direct object is indicated is by the suffix -a attached to it. The suffix -a becomes Ø after nouns ending in vowels other than -i and -u. In the latter case a phonetic rule reduces -i + a to -e and u + a to -o.

One way of indicating the fact that a proper noun is a direct object is by attaching the suffix morpheme ha to the noun. Another way is to attach the prefix morpheme lä to the proper noun, or to any noun serving as direct object. (For more details see Dillmann p. 317ff.) Now, in Ge'ez when the direct object is marked by the prefix lä then in the overwhelming majority of cases the direct object is also recalled by a suffix pronoun attached to the verb which governs the direct object. In the two pairs of sentence below

(26:a) nɨgbär säbʔa bäʔarɨyanä   Gen. 1:26
    "Let us make man in our image".

(b) wägäbäro ʔɨgziʔabɨher läsäb?   Gen. 2:7
     "and God created man".

(27:a) wäfaressɨnni wälädä ʔesromha   Mt. 1:3
        "and Perez begat Hezron"

(b) wayɨshak'ɨnni wälädo läyaʔɨk'ob   Mt. 1:2
     "and Isaac begat Jacob"

we note that when the direct object is indicated by the morpheme *ha* it
is not recalled by a suffix pronoun, and when it is indicated by *lä* it is recalled
by the corresponding object suffix pronoun. This is a general grammatical
fact in Geʿez grammar. It is, therefore, easy to see that in

(28) wäzässä yafäk'k'ɨra länäfsu yɨgäddɨfa   Jn. 12:25
      "He who loves his life loses it"

(29) wäzässä ʔafk'äro läʕaläm ʔihallo fɨk'rä
      ʔɨgziʔabɨher habehu   I Jn. 2:15
      "If anyone loves the world, love for the Father is not in him".

The presence of the object markers *-a* and *-o* attached to the relative verbs
yafäk'k'ɨr and/afk'ärä respectively is due to *lä* which is affixed to näfsu and
ʕaläm respectively. In constructions where the object of the relative verb is
not indicated by *lä*, the object, in the overwhelming number of cases, is not
recalled by the corresponding object suffix as the following examples
illustrate.

(30) kullu zäyɨhaddɨg bɨʔisito   Mt. 5:32
      "every one who divorces his wife"

(31) wäkullu zäs'äwwɨʔa sɨma ʔɨgziʔabɨher yɨdɨhɨn   Acts 2:21
      "whoever calls on the name of the Lord shall be saved".

In Amharic and the other Ethio-semitic languages the corresponding
relative clause structure is parallel to the examples cited in (30) and (31)
rather than those in (28) and (29). That is, the relative verbs do not take
direct object suffixes. For instance, in Chaha, a west Guraghe language, the
equivalents of (28) and (29) are,

(32) ʔarɨwäta yɨrämɨd yɨbähurɨn

(33) ʔaram yɨrämd säb yɨgzär nɨmajä bähwat ʔeräbärä

And in Amharic the equivalents of (28) and (29) are

(34) näfsun yämmiwädd yat'äfatall

(35) ʔalämɨn yämmiwädd yäʔɨgziʔabɨher fɨk'ɨr bärsu zänd yälläm

It should be noted that (28) and (29) (and, of course, their equivalents in the other Ethio-semitic languages) express universal statements. This observation is important because in present-day Ethio-semitic languages if a sentence of the form of, e.g. (34) nafsun yämmiwädd yat'äfatall, expresses a particular state of affairs, then the relative verb takes a direct object suffix or the whole noun phrase is made definite, with the definite marker attached to the modifier, i.e., the verb of the relative clause. Thus, if the relative clause mentions implicitly a particular person as loving his soul then the relative verb may take the object suffix referring to soul as in (36a) or the definite marker -u (-w after vowels as in (36b). Hence sentences

  (36a) näfsun yämmiwäddät (säwiyye) yat'äfatall
    (b) näfsun yämmiwäddäw (säwiyye) yat'äfatall

can only mean "the man (Mr. so and so) who loves his soul (is bound to or) will lose it"; the sentences in (36) can never mean the universal statement "he who loves his soul will lose it". The same constraint applies in the modern Ethiop-semitic languages.

Conclusion

This short note has demonstrated that in terms of some grammatical conditions that have to be satisfied in order to derive grammatical relative clauses, Ge'ez shows well specified divergences from modern Ethio-semitic languages. From this fact one may draw the tentative conclusion that any work in Ge'ez that systematically "fails" to show these divergences is a relatively recent work influenced by Tigriñña and/or Amharic.

A deeper and more detailed comparative syntactic analysis may exhibit other divergences between Ge'ez and its "sister" Ethio-semitic languages. Whether such divergences are of mere typological interest or whether they imply evolutionary divergence and genetic grouping should be investigated, since it could throw light on the origin of Ethio-semitic in general.

* The following are abbreviations and conventions used in this paper: D = Dillmann (all citations and quotations from Dillmann refer to Dillmann 1907); IO = indirect object; O = Direct object. (*) placed initially before a phrase or sentence indicates that the phrase or sentence is ungrammatical or at least unacceptable.

Bibliography

Chaine, C.: 1938. *Grammaire éthiopienne* (Nouvelle Édition). Imprimerie Catholique, Beyrouth.

Dillmann, August and Carl Bezold: 1907. *Ethiopic Grammar* (tr. A. Chrichton). Williams and Norgate, London.

Getatchew Haile: 1971. "The Suffix Pronouns in Amharic" in *Papers in African Linguistics* (eds. Chin-Wu Kim and H. Stahlke). Linguistic Research. Inc., Edmonton Champaign, pp. 101-110.

Hailu Fulass: 1972. "On Amharic Relative Clauses", *Bulletin of the School of Oriental and African Studies*, Vol. XXXV, Part 3, pp. 497-513.

Palmer, F. R.: 1961. "Relative Clauses in Tigre", *Word*, Vol. 17, No. 1, pp. 23-33.

Palmer, F. R.: 1962. "Relative Clauses in Tigrinya", *Journal of Semitic Studies*, VII, 1, 36-43.

Hetzron, R. and Marvin L. Bender: 1976. "The Ethio-Semitic Languages" in *Language in Ethiopia* (eds. M. L. Bender, J. D. Bowen, R. L. Cooper and C. A. Ferguson). Oxford University Press, London.

SOME ASPECTS OF THE PHONOLOGY OF ULTIMATE VOWELS IN SAHO-ƐAFAR

R. J. HAYWARD
University of London

This paper broaches three problems. The first concerns itself with an explanation of the substantive difference in the inventories of final unaccented vowels in Saho and Ɛafar; the second considers whether there is an underlying distinction of length in the final vowels of Ɛafar; the third tackles the irregularity of length alternations in the vowels preceding final consonants in Ɛafar. Resolution of the last problem requires the introduction of a new hypothesis about long vowels and accent for the languages of this group. Athough my title does delimit the topic accurately enough, there is a need to distinguish two types of ultimate vowel. This distinction separates elements which, in addition to being the last vowels in words, are also the final segments of those words from elements which, although being the ultimate vowels in words, are followed by consonants. The first type of vowel will be referred to as 'terminal' (T vowel), and the second type as 'non-terminal' (NT vowel). The analyses advanced here have as their primary data my own field-notes on Southern Ɛafar and Irob Saho. As will appear other works on the languages have been taken extensively into account. As far as Ɛafar is concerned the privilege of access to the first draft of the forthcoming Ɛafar—English Dictionary has been of enormous value [1].

I

Examination of surface contrasts between T vowels shows the number of possible oppositions as less when the vowel is unaccented. Though this is true both for Saho and Ɛafar, the systems are different. viz:

[1] This is an acknowledgement of indebtedness to Dr. E. M. Parker, upon whose unflagging labours the compilation has depended. Gratitude is also expressed to the British Academy for the financial grant which is enabling us to bring this project to completion.

accented T vowels		unaccented T vowels			
both		Saho		Ɛafar	
i *u*		*i*		*i*	*u*
e *o*		*e* *o*			
a		*a*		*a*	

Comparison of cognates having unaccented T vowels reveals regular correspondence between low vowels. In the case of front vowels, however, it appears that Saho has retained a distinction which was lost in Ɛafar. But it must be added that Saho words which contain an unaccented terminal *i* are rare, and most of these that occur are obviously loanwords, e.g.: *ẓéyti* 'oil', *ḳáyši* 'priest', *ḳobábi* 'metal cup', *ḳórsi* 'breakfast', *sánti* 'knife', *šúkki* 'suspicion'. However, in addition to a few words which are not obvious loans, but for which I have not been able to find sure Ɛafar cognates[2], there is a set of nouns which originated as compounds with the affirmative and negative forms of the verb *li-* 'have'. Such nouns are clearly indigenous and occur widely. The important point here is that both in Saho and Ɛafar the masculine forms have unaccented terminal *i*. Apart from these, however, the situation is that where Ɛafar has unaccented terminal *i* Saho has *e*. e.g.: S. & Ɛ. *naɛabtóoli* m. 'enemy (male)'; S. & Ɛ *dirábli* m. 'liar (male)'; S. & Ɛ. *afmáli* m. 'dumb man'; but S. *ɛáre*: Ɛ. *ɛári* m. 'house'; S. *gíle*: Ɛ *gíli* m. 'thumb'; S. *dúrre* m. 'disease': Ɛ. *dúrri* m. 'trouble'. As there are no instances of unaccented terminal *e* in Ɛafar it is concluded that a sound shift must have occurred during the development of the language, raising Proto-Saho-Ɛafar (PSƐ) **e*, and merging it with **i*[3].

In the case of unaccented rounded T vowels there is simply no evidence that a high: mid distinction ever existed in PSƐ. Now we find only a straight correspondence of Saho *o* to Ɛafar *u*. e.g.: S. *agábo*: Ɛ. *agábu* m. 'women'; S. *ífo*: Ɛ. *ífu* m. 'light'; S. *írro*: Ɛ. *úrru* m. 'children'; S. *fúgo*: Ɛ. *fígu* m. 'God'; S. *sído*: Ɛ. *sídu* m. 'pelt'. It seems almost certain that in the proto-language the back rounded vowel was a mid one. There are at least two pieces of evidence for this. All Saho and Ɛafar varieties exhibit interesting processes of

---

2   E.g.: *ḥági* 'faeces', *ɛáḍḍi* 'friend', *ɛawáani* 'locusts'. The last word here is probably to be connected with Ɛafar *ɛánay* 'locusts', but the two forms cannot be related in terms of regular correspondences. Concerning the transcription used here *ḍ* and *ḷ* represent retroflex stop and lateral phonemes respectively, *ḳ* represents an ejective velar stop, and *ḥ* represents a voiceless pharyngeal spirant.

3   Bliese also concludes that final unaccented *i* and *u* in Ɛafar result from a raising process, though for him the process is seen as a synchronic rule of the phonology; see Bliese 1981: 230.

dissimilation in nouns[4]. Of course here is the fact that in the singulative suffix -*yta* (-*ta* with C-final stems) the low vowel must be replaced by *o* when the final root vowel is low. e.g.:

	class noun	singulative	
Saho:	*ɛiidó* f.	*ɛiidoytá* f.	sheep
	dummú f.	*dummuytá* f.	cat
	diḷaaḷé f.	*diḷaaḷeytá* f.	bee
	ɛimboobá f.	*ɛimboobaytó* f.	flower
Ɛafar:	*ɛawʿí* f.	*ɛawiytá* f.	kite
	ḍuuné f.	*ḍuuneytá* f.	ants
	darsá f.	*darsaytó* f.	pupil, disciple (female)

It is important to note that all the immediately preceding singulative forms are feminines, and, as such have ultimate accent. In masculine nouns, however, the accent (in vowel-final words) is never ultimate. Thus, when the final root vowel is low the vowel of the suffix will be an unaccented back rounded vowel; and here the qualitative difference emerges, e.g.:

	class noun	singulative	
Saho:	*bakḷí* f.	*bakḷíyta* m.	mule
	síyye m.	*siyyéyta* m.	palm-tree
	ɛaḷḷó f.	*ɛaḷḷóyta* m.	inner bark
	sáɛa m.	*saɛáyto* m.	livestock
Ɛafar:	*kullúm* m.	*kullúnta* m.	fish
	boḥó f.	*boḥóyta* m.	word, stick
	ɛánay m.	*ɛanáytu* m.	locust
	islám m. Islam	*islántu* m.	Muslim

Since there is no obvious morphological explanation for why it is that in Ɛafar only masculine singulatives should appear with -*(y)tu*, we conclude that the explanation is an historical one, namely that unaccented terminal **o* in PSƐ became *u* in Ɛafar. This first argument is nicely buttressed by a second, which takes account of certain lexicalized singulatives in Ɛafar, in which the earlier stem-final mid vowel has been "fossilized" word-internally. In the cognate class nouns the stem-final vowel is now high. e.g.: Ɛafar: *daboytá* f. 'transportable house used by Ɛafar nomads', cf. *dábu* m. 'house made of unhewn stone'; *andóyta* m. 'foreskin', cf. *ándu* m. 'pieces of (camel)

---

4 Attention was first drawn to these fascinating processes in Bliese 1967, and subsequently developed in Bliese 1975.

skin undergoing curing'; *ifóyta* m. 'lamp', cf. *ífu* m. 'light'. This shift of articulation can perhaps be seen to be coupled with that which brought about the merger of unaccented **e* with **i* in Ɛafar. The asymmetry of the proto-language has undergone repair.

II

In view of the existence of two independently made proposals for the hypothesis that final single vowels of Proto-East-Cushitic had undergone elision by the time PSƐ emerged, I do not intend to embark upon another; I shall assume it here [5]. All Saho and Ɛafar varieties exhibit systematic contrasts based upon vowel length, though not in all contexts. One case where vowel length is non-contrastive is in T vowels. The explanation for this, of course, is provided by the hypothesis just cited, from which it may further be inferred that T vowels in Saho and Ɛafar are the reflexes of earlier long vowels. The phonetic observation is that except in monosyllables (see below) the T vowels of words uttered in isolation are durationally more or less the same as short vowels elsewhere. The matter comes to be of interest on account of the claim that synchronically in Ɛafar a particular set of T vowels has to be regarded as underlyingly long; see Bliese 1981:209. The vowels in question are the accented T vowels of feminine nouns. Indeed the very fact of their attracting accent is on account of their underlying length, for Bliese's "root stress rule" operates wholly with phonological factors. "The root stress rule has word-final long vowels stressed, roots with final short vowels taking penultimate stress, and consonant-final roots taking stress in the last syllable" (op. cit. 209). Other linguists engaged in Ɛafar studies have regarded noun accent as lexically governed (cf. Morin 1977:356), so that a rule which could predict accent placement solely in terms of phonological determinants would be highly desirable. "This rule avoids marking stress on nouns in the lexicon by listing the stressed final vowel as long in the feminine class. Under this analysis, final long forms (feminine) and consonant-final (masculine) nouns have the last syllable stressed, while masculine nouns with short final vowels have penultimate stress" (op. cit. 209). Since diachronically all the T vowels of Ɛafar reflect earlier long vowels, and phonetically all T vowels are durationally pretty similar, marking some vowels (i.e. those in feminine nouns) as long in the lexicon requires justification, if it is not to be regarded merely as a diacritic

---

5 The reader is referred to Black 1974: 117, 133 ff. and Sasse forthcoming.

device. The support which Bliese offers takes account of the length alternations which appear in a type of reduplicative plural formation commonly found with feminine nouns. e.g.: 1. *amó* f.: *amoomá* f. 'head(s)', 2. *gilé* f.: *gileelá* f. 'knife/knives', 3. *angú* f.: *anguugá* f. 'breast(s)', 4. *abeesá* f.: *abeesaasí* f. 'viper(s)', 5. *boodá* f.: *boodaadí* f. 'meadow(s)', 6. *dalá* f.: *daloolí* f. 'gourd(s)', 7. *lafá* f.: *lafoofí* f. 'bone(s)' (Selection of *-i*, rather than *-a* (egs. 4-7), as the final sufix is governed by the dissimilatory principle that the suffix occurs when the terminal vowel of the singular is low. The occurrence of *oo* (egs. 6 & 7) is governed by another dissimilatory principle that this must occur when the preceding vowel of the stem is low). Bliese accounts for the shortness of the vowel in the singulars by an extension of a rule which shortens long vowels in closed syllables—the "closed syllable vowel shortening rule" (op. cit. 225) (hereafter referred to as the CSVS rule).

Although this evidence looks quite convincing there are, in fact, many snags. Firstly, not all feminine nouns form plurals in this way, and many have no plural at all; which means that we could assign underlying long vowels to these words only in virtue of the fact that they were feminines, or that they were accented on the T vowel, which would, of course, entail a certain circularity in the argument. But even granting them underlying long vowels *by analogy* with the feminines that do show alternation, there are still problems. There is no guarantee that length in this type of plural form has not been morphologized, i.e. become a part of the plural formation process—like the reduplication of the stem-final consonant. There is some indication that this might be the case. In considering the somewhat similar case of the plurals of C-final masculine nouns it is claimed that "*-a* alone is the normal plural when the last stem vowel is underlying long. The underlying long vowel surfaces when the *-a* suffix puts it in an open syllable. If the last two stem vowels are *a*, the last one will dissimilate to *oo*" (op. cit. 178). E.g.: *hutúk* m.: *hutuuká* f. 'star(s)'; *lifíɛ* m.: *lifiɛá* f. 'claw(s)'; *alíb* m.: *aliibá* f. 'tendon(s)'; *magáɛ* m.: *magooɛá* f. 'grave(s)'; *daɛár* m.: *daɛoorá* f. 'wadi(s)'. There are, however, other completely regular processus in Ɛafar, and these do not bear out the claim that C-final nouns of this type invariably have underlying long last stem vowels. One such regular process operates in nominal predicates (NPd) in affirmative present tense equative sentences. Here the copula *kinn-* does not usually appear unless it is in contrastive focus, so that the NPd comes sentence-final. If the final (= head) element of the predicate is a C-final noun a vowel of predictable quality is added. Since this suffixation creates an open syllable for the last stem vowel, the CSVS rule does not apply, with the result that an underlying long vowel will surface. E.g.: *ah lifíiɛi* 'this is a claw', cf. *lifíɛ* m. 'claw'; *woh daɛáara* 'that is a wadi', cf. *daɛár* m. 'wadi'. It is emphasized that this is an absolutely regular process, and so furnishes a better test for revealing underlying length contrasts than the plural process, which probably belongs more in the realm of derivational morphology[6]. The significance of this here is that comparison of the two processes shows frequent disagreement. E.g.:

absolutive singular	nominal predicate	plural	
alíb	*alíbi*	*aliibá*	tendon(s)
magáɛ	*magáɛa*	*magooɛá*	grave(s)
ramád	*ramáda*	*ramoodá*	vein(s)
ɛafúr	*ɛafúra*	*ɛafuurá*	gecko(s)
aráḥ	*aráḥa*	*arooḥá*	place(s)

Since the unfailing appearance of long vowels is confined to these plurals perhaps the feature should simply be regarded as part of the plural formation process. Furthermore, if plural forms cannot be fully relied upon to reveal underlying length here, perhaps they should also be viewed with suspicion in the case of feminine nouns. For these, however, the nominal predicate "test" is not available. There is another process, however, which might be applied. Before the coordinating conjunction *kee* T vowels lengthen. It is plausible to suggest that the marked rising pitch on *kee* is a prosodic marker of non-finality[7], rather than of word accent as such; so that it may be possible to account for this lenthening as being due to the fact that *kee* is enclitic in Ɛafar—as it certainly is in Irob Saho. Lengthening of T vowels is observed, however, not only in feminine, but also in masculine nouns. E.g.: *gabáa-keě* 'a hand and ...', cf. *gabá* f. 'hand'; *baaḍóo-keě* 'land and ...', cf. *baaḍó* f. 'land'; *gítaa-keě* 'a road and ...', cf. *gíta* m. 'road'; *ḍáaguu-keě* 'news and ...', cf. *ḍáagu* m. 'news'. If this lengthening *is* indicative of underlying long vowels, so well and good, but surely it also seems to indicate that phonetic duration is predictable and therefore redundant in the T vowels of nouns; ergo it cannot be utilized in the prediction of accent placement[8].

6 For further discussion of the category of number in East cushitic and the problem of treating it as part of the inflectional morphology see Hayward 1981.

7 A convincing demonstration that rising pitch at the end of non-final phrases in Ɛafar is not necessarily associated with accent (stress) is provided by the suffix *-y*. Topicalized (non-verb) phrases are fronted in Ɛafar and commonly take the clitic *-y* phrase-finally as a topic marker. Rising pitch occurs on the syllable closed by the *-y*, even when the word is accented on another syllable. E.g.: *awkǎay tet máaḍiga* '(as for the) girl, I don't know her', cf. *awká* 'girl'; *áwkǎay kaa máaḍiga* '(as for the) boy, I don't know him', cf. *áwka* 'boy'. The point is, even if *kee* is not enclitic in Ɛafar, *-y* certainly is. It should be noted, moreover, that the T vowels of both *awká* and *áwka* are equally long.

8 A similar conclusion would have to be reached for (at least) Irob Saho. In Irob when

III

In all Saho and Ɛafar varieties we find innumerable instances of morphological alternations involving long vowels in open syllables and short vowels in closed syllables. We have already had occasion to note such alternations between the absolute (citation) forms and NPd forms of Ɛafar words such as *lifíɛ* ~ *lifíiɛi*, *daɛár* ~ *daɛára*, etc.[9]. The absolutive form cannot tell us whether or not a long vowel will appear in the NPd form, so that lexical entries will need to be marked in some way. Morin (1977) indicates this by means of a parenthesized vowel following the absolutive form. Thus, 'wadi' would be represented as *daɛar(a)*, while the non-alternating word for 'vein' would be simply *ramad*[10]. Since within his grammar stress will be assigned to long NT vowels, Bliese's underlying forms for the preceding would be *daɛaar* and *ramad* respectively. Now how do we account for the short NT vowel alternant? Bliese's CSVS rule purports to do this. Leaving out the (angle bracket) expansion dealing with T vowels in polysyllabic words[11] the rule is

$$V \rightarrow [\text{-long}] \, / \, - C \left\{ \begin{matrix} \# \\ C \end{matrix} \right\}$$

The problem is that the rule is too powerful. Out of 427 C-final nouns with long NT vowels 162, i.e. 38%, do not contract in closed syllables. Morphophonemically then C-final nouns fall into three groups. viz.:

	absolutive	NPd form	
1. short	*bád* m.	*báda*	sea
	wadár m.	*wadára*	goats
2. long — noncontracting	*ráat* m.	*ráata*	track
	sagáal m.	*sagáala*	nine

the postposition *-ko* 'from' is suffixed to a vowel-final noun that vowel undergoes lengthening, whether it carries accent (i.e. is a feminine) or not. E.g.: *gádab gimóoko* 'from very early morning', cf. *gimó* f. 'morning'; *gúbaako* 'from below', cf. *gúba* m. 'inferior location'.

9 Although this alternation is by no means restricted to NT vowels, attention is restricted to these.

10 Parker 1980 follows Morin in this.

11 It is not clear to me that contraction of T vowels is really the same process as the contraction of NT vowels. It seems that the latter would furnish a real argument for the recognition of the syllable in Ɛafar phonology (cp. Hayward 1976:57)—an argument that is vitiated by the attempt to couple with it a process which has nothing to do with closed syllables.

| 3. long — contracting | *yáb* m. | *yáaba* | speech |
| | *migáɛ* m. | *migáaɛa* | name |

There are two good reasons why the fact that a large number of the exceptions to the CSVS rule are loanwords[12] should not encourage us to give up the attempt to account for them, or to mark them in the lexicon as "[+ foreign]". Firstly, there are plenty of equally obvious loanwords that do obey the rule[13]. Secondly, there are many exceptions that bear no signs of a borrowed origin, and for some of these cognates are found in other East Cushitic languages[14].

I believe that the problem resides in the incompleteness of the analysis of long vowels in Ɛafar. When confronted with contrastive length in vowels a linguist usually tries to decide whether the length is an inherent feature or represents a sequence of identical vowels; that is, one decides between a one-segment analysis (long vowel = [+ syllabic, + long]) or a two-segment analysis (long vowel = [+ syllabic] [+ syllabic]). In the case of Ɛafar there is every reason to adopt the former—I have myself argued for this (Hayward 1974:401). With this analysis long vowels constitute single syllabic nuclei, just as short vowels do. The mistake has been to assume that in carrying the analysis this far we have all the prerequisite apparatus for accentual considerations. I shall suggest here that for the latter there is need to refer to another entity, one which enables us to divide long vowels at one level of analysis, while maintaining their segmental and syllabic integrity at another. The traditional "mora" is invoked to meet these desiderata. Long vowels are analysed as bimoraic, short vowels as monomoraic. A second suggestion is that placement of accent has to refer to morae, rather than to syllables or vowels. The immediate advantage of this is that it enables us to specify what the essential distinction is that blocks the CSVS rule. In contracting words the accent is on the first mora, in noncontracting words it is on the second, i.e. *yáab* 'speech', but *raát* 'track'. The CSVS rule requires revision in order to refer to such distinctions. Viz.:

---

12 For example: *seéf* 'sword'; *tuút* 'cotton'; *daás* 'booth'; *buúk* 'book'; *miidaán* 'balance'; *muraár* 'bitter substance'; *saraáb* 'juice, sock'; *safíir* 'ambassador', etc.

13 For example: *ḥál* (NPd *ḥaála*) 'behaviour'; *sandúg* (NPd *sanduúgu*) 'box'; *sirág* (NPd *siraága*) 'lantern'; *taswír* (NPd *taswiíri*) 'picture'; *baabúr* (NPd *baabuúru*) 'bus'; *barmíl* (NPd *barmiíli*) 'barrel', etc.

14 For example: *duúl* 'hippopotamus', cf. Bayso *dúulo* 'id.'; *faál* 'omen', cf. Somali *fáàl* 'id.'; *máar* 'skin of calf used to induce milk in the mother cow', cf. Arbore *maár* 'calves'; *raát* 'track', cf. Somali *ráàd* 'id', etc.

$$\text{CSVS - mark II} \quad \begin{matrix} \text{mora} \\ \text{[-accent]} \end{matrix} \rightarrow \emptyset / \text{X mora} - \text{CS}$$

I.e. A second mora drops in a closed syllable unless it bears the accent. The rule will apply equally in the case of C-final nouns with accent in the ultimate or penultimate syllables, i.e. in *saábuun* 'soap' (absolutive *saábun* ∼ NPd *saabuúna*) as well as in *migáaɛ* 'name' (absolutive *migáɛ* ∼ NPd *migaáɛa*)[15].

There is further justification for this analysis. This is based on the predictions which this analysis would make about the possible surface absolutive forms of polysyllabic C-final nouns; in particular it would predict the nonoccurrence of nouns having a long NT vowel but bearing accent in some pre-ultimate syllable. Empirically this proves to be the case; nouns of the form (C)V́CVC and (C)V́VCVC occur, as do (C)VCV́C, (C)VVCV́C, (C)VCV́VC and (C)VVCV́VC, but I have yet to find either (C)V́CVVC or (C)V́VCVVC. Secondly, there is some phonetic evidence from long monosyllabic nouns of the form CVVC. Since according to this analysis accent would oocur on the second mora, one might expect the syllable to be pronounced with rising pitch, and this is sometimes the case, it being notably so in nouns with final sonorants, e.g.: *duúl* m. 'hippopotamus', *saár* m. 'waterskin', *boón* m. 'ironsmith', etc.[16]. Thirdly, there is an argument based on the advantage of this approach in explaining the strikingly different proportions of monosyllabic to polysyllabic words that are not subject to the CSVS rule. With monosyllables it is 62%, while with polysyllables it is only 35%. Referring simply to the monosyllable/polysyllable dichotomy offers no reason for this discrepancy. However, in terms of a mora-based accentuation words such as *subáḥ* m. 'butter' and *dírab* m. 'lie' are respectively comparable to words such as *guút* m. 'grudge' and *néef* m. 'face'. What we ought to be calculating in all cases is the proportion of words which have accent on the final mora[17]. Once seen in these terms the proportion compared cannot be CVV́C:CV́VC::XCVV́C:XCV́VC (where X is a variable representing any permitted sequence of segments), since with respect to the last two morae

---

15 It also accounts for contractions in verb forms such as *rubté* 'she sent': *ruubé* 'he sent', etc., where the accent occurs *to the right* of the eliding mora.

16 A concomitant of this analysis for ᴇafar (though not for Irob; see later) would be a rule regressively spreading the high pitch feature (the exponent of accent) when accent is located on the final mora—except perhaps when there is a word-final sonorant. Jointly the CSVS rule and this one render the more abstract distinction between CV́VC and CVV́C obscure in surface forms.

17 Although it is not the case that accent in nouns is restricted to the ultimate or penultimate mora, the number of cases where accent occurs farther to the left is so small as to be negligible here.

polysyllabic words, by definition, have more possibilities than monosyllables. Thus, the proportion compared should be $CV\acute{V}C : C\acute{V}VC :: XCV\acute{V}C + XVC\acute{V}C : XC\acute{V}VC + X\acute{V}CVC$. Once this is adjusted the discrepancy disappears. Thus, the percentage of polysyllabic words accented on the final mora turns out to be 61.6%, and compares exactly with the percentage of monosyllabic words not subject to the CSVS rule *on account of being accented on the final mora.*

The concern for a mora-based account of accent did not originate in an attempt to provide an explanation for the exceptions to the CSVS rule in Ɛafar, but in order to explain accentual alternations in long-vowelled monosyllables in Irob. There are certain nouns in which accentual shift occurs from the left to the right of a syllable when the noun functions as subject. This is observed as a change from falling to rising pitch. Such a phenomenon is a clear candidate for an analysis based on morae. E.g.: *bóoḷ yublé* 'he saw a hundred', cf. *booḷ yemeeté* 'a hundred came'; *ḷaá dággegid yané* 'the cattle are in the kraals', cf. *ḷáa* 'cattle'. It is of note that *bóoḷ* is durationally shorter than *booḷ*[18]. Another phenomenon in Irob posing somewhat similar problems for a syllable-based analysis are singular/plural pairs such as *faás : fáos* 'axe(s)', *saár : sáor* 'waterskin(s)', for which a statement according them structural similarity to *farás : fáros* 'horse(s)', *maláb : málob* 'beer(s)', *waɛág : wáɛog* 'monkey(s)', etc. is required. But even if here we were tempted to say that *faás* and *saár* were bisyllabic on account of their plurals, there could be no such argument in the case of *ḍaáḷ : ḍaaḷá* 'house(s)', *buún* 'coffee', *maáḷ* 'money', *koón* 'five', etc. It should be emphasized, moreover, that in the case of Irob in all nouns that resist the CSVS rule one hears an unmistakably clear rising pitch[19]. Returning to the CSVS rule there is one piece of evidence in Irob that shows conclusively that this rule is sensitive to accent. Plural possesive pronouns are formed by suffixing *-im* to the possessive definitive. Since the definitive always takes the accent in these words our hypothesis predicts that the extra mora of vowel length provided by the suffix would be lost unless the definitive were C-final. In the case of V-final definitives such as *yi* and *ni*, this is exactly what happens; thus *sínim* 'yours (pl.)', *ténim* 'theirs', but *yím* 'mine' and *ním* 'ours'.

---

18 Perhaps the reason why this word does not contract fully is because of the extremely low frequency of occurrence of *bóol* as compared with *booḷ*, which is the form used in counting and as a noun modifier. The same behaviour is found in the case of *súb* 'thousand'.

19 In marked contrast to Irob the Saho variety described by Welmers (1952) would appear to have dropped considerations of accent in the CSVS rule, for even the cognates of Ɛafar and Irob *faás* and *saár* contract (op. cit. 159).

While the approach to length and accent advocated here is novel as regards the Saho-Ɛafar group, it is not altogether novel for Cushitic, for it is implicit in Black's statements concerning Somali (Black 1974: 125)[20], and Hudson has argued for something similar in Beja[21]. It is hoped that the proposals advanced here somewhat sketchily may be proved in a more profound treatment of accent in the Saho-Ɛafar group.

20 For the significance of the mora in Somali scansion, see Johnson (1979).
21 While the inclusion or exclusion of Beja from Cushitic proper is a genetic question under debate, there can be no doubt at all about the strong typological similarities of this language to languages such as Saho and Ɛafar.

References

Black, P. D.
1974 *Lowland East Cushitic: Subgrouping and Reconstruction*, unpublished PhD dissertation, Yale University, New Haven, (available from University Microfilms).
Bliese, L. F.
1967 *Selected Problems in Noun Morphology in the Aussa Dialect of 'Afar*, unpublished MA dissertation, University of Texas, Austin.
1975 "Afar Vowel Dissimilation: A Problem in Rule Ordering", *Anthropological Linguistics* 17.3: 102-6.
1981 *A Generative Grammar of Afar* (SIL Publications in Linguistics 65) Dallas: SIL and University of Texas at Arlington.
Hayward, R. J.
1974 "The Segmental Phonemes of 'Afar", *BSOAS* 37.2: 385-406.
1976 *Categories of the Predicator in 'Afar, with Especial Reference to the Grammar of Radical Extensions*, unpublished PhD dissertation, University of London.
1981 "Nominal Suffixes in Dirayta (Gidole)", *BSOAS* 44.1: 126-44.
Hudson, R. A.
1973 "Syllables, Moras, and Accents in Beja", *Journal of Linguistics* 9:53-63.
Johnson, J. W.
1979 "Somali Prosodic Systems", *Horn of Africa* 2,3: 46-54.
Morin, D.
1977 "Le nom en Afar du sud", *BSOAS* 40.2: 354-70.
Parker, E. M.
1979 *Prerequisites for an Adequate Lexicography of Afar*, unpublished PhD dissertation, University of London.
Welmers, W. E.
1952 "Notes on the Structure of Saho", Part 1, *Word* 8.1:145-62, Part 2, *Word* 8.3:236-51.
Sasse, H. J.
Forthcoming — "Case in Cushitic, Semitic and Berber", to appear in the proceedings of the Third International Congress on Hamito-Semitic Linguistics, London 1978.

ZUR FUNKTION VON INFINITIV UND DEMONSTRATIVEN IM ALTSÜDARABISCHEN

Maria Höfner
Universität Graz

1. Infinitiv

Eine in den altsüdarabischen Inschriften sehr häufige und bekannte Erscheinung ist die Aneinanderreihung von zwei oder mehreren durch *w* verbundenen Zeitwörtern, wobei an der Spitze ein Verbum finitum steht (3. Pers. Perf. oder Impf.), während die folgenden Infinitive sind. Im Sing. sind die 3. Pers. masc. Sing. des Perfekts in der vokallosen altsüdarabischen Schrift von den Infinitiven nicht zu unterscheiden, doch wird der Unterschied augenfällig, wenn das erste Zeitwort ein Plural oder ein Imperfekt ist; die folgenden Verba haben dann weder Endungen, noch Präfixe, es sei denn fallweise eine Endung *-n* im Sabäischen. Dazu zwei Beispiele zur Verdeutlichung.

> CIH 40, Z. 2: *br'w/w-ḥwṭr/w-ḥqwḥ/w-ḥšqrn*
> CIH 581, Z. 16: *fl/yšrḥn/w-šwf/w-mt'n*

Das eben Gesagte gilt sowohl für alle Dialekte, als auch für alle Verbalstämme. Der II. Stamm jedoch (im Altsüdarabischen sehr häufig von kausativer Bedeutung). nimmt insofern eine Sonderstellung ein, als hier zwei Infinitiv-Formen nebeneinander stehen, eine mit *t*-Präfix, eine ohne Präfix: *tqtl* und *qtl*, letztere wohl mit verdoppeltem zweiten Konsonanten (was aber in der Schrift nicht zum Ausdruck kommt). Und zwar findet man in den erwähnten Verbalketten die Formen *ohne* Präfix, außerhalb solcher Verbindungen die Form *tqtl*, d.h. die *qtl*-Formen haben verbalen Charakter, die anderen nominalen. Besonders deutlich wird dieser Unterschied in jenen Fällen, wo beide Formen in einer Phrase nebeneinander stehen, wie etwa in den folgenden Beispielen.

> Nami 15, Z. 5 f: *bn/ǧlt/w-tnkr/fqd/w-ǧll/w-nkrn/'lmqh/b'ly/'bdhw*
> ebda., Z. 18 ff: *bḏt/ḥmr/sdqhmw/......./bkl/sry/w-tbšr/w-šft/w-tḥwd/sry/w-šft/*
> *w-ḥwdn/w-tbšrn/'lmqh*

Im zweiten Beispiel ist *tḥwd-ḥwdn* II. Form, *tbšr-tbšrn* dagegen V.

Aber auch in anderen Fällen ergibt sich aus der Bedeutung, daß eine II.
Form (kausativ) vorliegt.

> RES 4766, Z. 2: *bnyw/w-mlʾ/qbrhmw*; hier kann *mlʾ* nur heißen »voll =
> fertig machen, vollenden".
> RES 4107, Z. 2: *brʾ/w-ṯwbn*
>   *ṯwb* I. »zurückkehren«, II. wörtlich »zurückkehren lassen«, d.h.
>   (einen Bau) »wiederherstellen«

Angesichts der zwei verschiedenen Infinitivformen des II. Stammes erhebt
sich die Frage, ob in den übrigen Stämmen der »nominale« und der »verbale«
Infinitiv ebenfalls unterschieden wurden. Der Unterschied könnte hier nur in
der Vokalisation liegen, eventuell noch in einer vokalischen Endung; das
konsonantische Schriftbild ist ja, wie schon bemerkt, in beiden Fällen gleich.

Was die Funktion des »verbalen« Infinitivs betrifft, so bieten sich zum
Vergleich vor allem die äthiopischen Sprachen Geʿez, Tigriña und Amharisch
an, die ja auch eine infinitivische Form in ähnlicher Verwendung kennen, das
sogenannte Gerundium[1], das ja nichts anderes ist als ein Infinitiv der Form
qatil, verbunden mit den Pronominal-Suffixen. Die Suffixe fehlen zwar bei den
in Frage stehenden Infinitiven des Altsüdarabischen, aber auch sie versehen,
wie im Geʿez, »nicht die Stelle eines Nomens, sondern die eines Verbums und
sind eigentlich nichts anderes als das der Zeitsphäre beraubte Verbum«[2], und
kommen ebenso wie dort nur in Verbindung mit einem Verbum finitum vor,
das Tempus und Numerus bestimmt. Man kann also diese Infinitive des
Altsüdarabischen sehr wohl zu dem Gerundium der äthiopischen Sprachen in
Parallele setzen. Ob man daraus schließen darf, daß der »verbale« Infinitiv
auch im Altsüdarabischen *qatil* (und entsprechend in den abgeleiteten
Stämmen) lautete, ist zwar nicht zu beweisen, doch läge eine solche Annahme
nicht allzu fern[3].

---

[1] A. Dillmann, *Grammatik der äthiopischen Sprache* (2. Aufl., 1899), S. 235 unterscheidet
im Geʿez den »nennwörtlichen« und den »tatwörtlichen« Infinitiv und nennt letzteren
Gerundium. — Im Tigriñña heißt die entsprechende Form bei L. de Vito, *Grammatica
elementare della lingua Tigrigna* (Roma 1892) »zusammengesetztes Perfekt«, bei M. da Leonessa,
Grammatica analitica della lingua Tigray (Roma 1928) »Permansiv«, bei W. Leslau, *Documents
Tigrigna* (Paris 1941) »Gérondif«. — Das Tigrē kennt zwar eine ganze Anzahl von Infinitiv-
Formen, vor allem auch *qatil*, aber nicht die Bildung des Gerundiums.

[2] So beschreibt Dillmann, *a.a.O.* (s. Anm. 1) die Funktion des Gerundiums.

[3] Ebenso ist es eine offene Frage, wie der »nominale« Infinitiv tatsächlich gelautet hat;
die Formen *qatāl* etc. in Höfner, *Altsüdarabische Grammatik*, S. 60f, sind eine mögliche
Annahme, aber nicht mehr.

2. Demonstrativa

Das Altsüdarabische kennt zwei Gruppen von Demonstrativen, eine gebildet von einem Stamm *h*- im Sabäischen, *s*- im Qatabanischen, und eine von einem Stamm *ḏ*- in allen Dialekten, zu dem ein Plural *'l* gehört. Während Beeston [4] die beiden Gruppen nebeneinander anführt, ohne einen Bedeutungsunterschied zu vermerken, werden in meiner Grammatik [5] die Bildungen mit *ḏ*, bzw. die Formen *h'*, *hw'* etc. als Demonstrativa für das Nähere angenommen und dementsprechend mit »dieser« übersetzt, während *hwt* etc. »jener«, das Entferntere bezeichnen sollte. Ferner entsteht aus der dortigen Darstellung der Eindruck, als wären die *h*- Demonstrativa seltenere (und ältere) Formen im Vergleich mit *ḏ*-.

Hier sind einige Richtigstellungen von nöten. Die *h*-Formen sind weder seltener, noch älter als die anderen, wie die Untersuchung einer großen Anzahl von Texten klar erwiesen hat. Vielmehr ergibt sich daraus ein anderer Unterschied. *ḏ*-Demonstrativa bezeichnen das Nähere, das, was vor Augen steht, worauf man sozusagen den Finger legen und damit hindeuten kann, während *alle* Formen vom *h*-Stamm dann gebraucht werden, wenn von etwas die Rede ist, das zeitlich oder räumlich fernliegt; kurz, der Unterschied von *ḏ*- und *h*-Demonstrativen ist der von Gegenwart und Nicht-Gegenwart, von sichtbar und unsichtbar. Wie gesagt, gilt dies für alle Ableitungen vom *h*-Stamm, sowohl für *h(w)'*, als auch für *hwt*. Der Unterschied zwischen *diesen* Formen ist vielmehr ein anderer: wie J. Ryckmans erkannt hat [6], werden die Formen mit *t*-Endungen im casus obliquus gebraucht, die anderen im Nominativ. Diese Tatsache ist besonders bei der Übersetzung eines Textes im Auge zu behalten. So kann z.B. in Ja 577, Z. 15 *st'wln/hw'* nicht heißen »in bringing back *him*«, sondern »daß *er* (jener) zurückkehrte« (was sich übrigens schon daraus versteht, daß *'wl* X. nicht Kausativ ist). Ebenso kann in Ja 644, Z. 10 *hw'/'ysn* nicht Objekt der Verba sein, sondern ist deren Subjekt [7].

Zur Veranschaulichung des Unterschiedes zwischen *ḏ*- und *h*-Demonstrativen mögen noch einige Beispiele dienen.

Zunächst zum *ḏ*-Stamm [8]. Am Beginn der zahllosen Votivinschriften wird die Widmungsformel niemals lauten *hqny/hwt/slmn*, sondern immer

---

4 A. F. L. Beeston, *A Descriptive Grammar of Epigraphic South Arabian* (London 1962), S. 47f.

5 M. Höfner, *Altsüdarabische Grammatik* (Leipzig 1943), S. 36ff.

6 *Bibliotheca Orientalis* 34 (1977), S. 301.

7 So richtig bei A. F. L. Beeston, *Qahtan* 3, S. 56.

8 Zu den einzelnen Formen (masc., fem., Dual., Plural) der *ḏ*- und *h*-Demonstrativa s. *a.a.O.* (Anm. 4 und 5).

ḥqny/ḏn/ṣlmn. Die Statue (*ṣlmn*) steht ja vor den Augen des Empfängers (des Gottes), ist gegenwärtig und sichtbar. Oder CIH 601, Z. 17: *w-kwnt/ḏt/mṯbtn* »und es fand statt diese Anordnung«, womit eben die Inschrift gemeint ist, die da, jedermann sichtbar, auf einem Pfeiler vor dem großen Tempel in Ṣirwāḥ steht.

Demonstrativa vom *h*-Stamm dagegen bezeichnen Ferneres, wie folgende Beispiele zeigen.

Ja 649, Z. 13: *w-'tw/hʾ/w-šʿbhw* »und es kehrte zurück *jener* und sein Stamm«. *hʾ* ist Nominativ und bezeichnet den Stifter der Inschrift, der am Anfang bereits genannt wurde und dessen Rückkehr aus einem Kampf in der Vergangenheit liegt. Ganz Analoges gilt für Ja 631, Z. 14: *hwʾ/w-kl/šwʿhmw* »jener und alle, die sie begleitet hatten«, auf einem Kreigszug nämlich, der vorher geschildert und bereits vergangen ist. Oder Ja 635, Z. 38: *bn/hwt/brtn* »von jenem Feldzug«, der im Text vorher beschrieben wurde und zeitlich zurückliegt; ein Beispiel für den casus obliquus.

Ein besonders instruktives Beispiel für den Gebrauch des *ḏ*-, bzw. *h*-Demonstrativs bietet Ja 633, eine Widmung, dargebracht für die Errettung aus einer Krankheit, die in Z. 5 erwähnt wird. Z. 8f und 14f kommen darauf zurück und hier steht beidemale *hwt/ḥlẓn*; Z. 10f und 15 dagegen erwähnen »diese Weihgabe« mit den Worten *ḏt/ḥqnytn*, das ist *ṣlmn/d-ḏhbn*, die Statue, die zusammen mit der Inschrift dargebracht wurde, die zwar schon einmal erwähnt wurde (Z. 3), die jedoch sichtbar und gegenwärtig ist, während die Krankheit nun vorbei und vergangen ist.

Es ließen sich noch zahlreiche Beispiele beibringen, doch dürften die angeführten genügen, um den unterschiedlichen Gebrauch der *ḏ*- und *h*-Demonstrativa aufzuzeigen.

Die beiden Stämme *ḏ* und *h* sind in den meisten semitischen Sprachen zur Bildung von Demonstrativen verbreitet, doch wird der Unterschied von Nähe und Ferne im allgemeinen nicht durch sie, sondern in anderer, in den einzelnen Sprachen verschiedener Weise ausgedrückt. Bildungen mit *h* für die Bezeichnung von Entferntem sind im Tigrē anzutreffen: *lahay, lohay*. Für die Nähe wird hier zwar nicht der Stamm *ḏ* gebraucht, sondern *ʾl*, jener Stamm, der im Altsüdarabischen als Plural zu den *ḏ*-Demonstrativen fungiert.

EVIDENCE OF THE NOMINAL ORIGIN OF THE PERFECT IN AMHARIC

GROVER HUDSON
Michigan State University

This paper discusses some of the noun-like characteristics of the perfect verb in Amharic, which are evidence of the nominal origin of this conjugation. The opinion appears to remain somewhat controversial within Semitic linguistics that the West and South Semitic perfect conjugation has nominal origins as seen, in general, in the Akkadian stative. The theory that Akkadian shows an archaic state of the Semitic verbal system in this regard was first proposed by Paul Haupt (1878), and has received qualified support since then. A recent synopsis of the Semitic verbal system (Janssens 1975: 80-1), however, rejects it, and accepts the common alternative hypothesis, that the ancient West Semitic already verbal perfect is a better model for Proto-Semitic, Akkadian being divergent. Thus the hypothesis seems still worthy of argumentation.

The claim that modern Amharic illustrates a Proto-Semitic feature seen more clearly in the ancient language Akkadian reinforces the claim of Haupt (1889, p. cclv, regarding Ge'ez) of the relative archaicness of Ethiopian Semitic, and the repeated urgings of Wolf Leslau for greater consideration of Ethiopian Semitic languages in the reconstruction of Proto-Semitic.

Recently Carleton Hodge (1975) presented evidence for a general universal in the evolution of languages: that new verb conjugations have derived from nominal sentences. This paper offers a further proof of this tendency. Finally, the explanation of several peculiarities of the Amharic verb system as owed to the origin of perfect as a nominal conjugation may contribute to the realization of the importance of the evolution of languages in understanding issues in synchronic descriptive and theoretical linguistics (cf. Givón 1979, Ch. 7; Sampson 1980, Ch. 6).

Before the evidence is presented one other point is necessary regarding the place of the hypothesis in Semitic linguistics. Amharic has another verb form, the so-called gerundive, which is transparently nominal in origin. Some, for example Moscati et al (1965: 133), would offer the Amharic gerundive as a parallel to the Akkadian stative, a quite inappropriate comparison for the purposes of reconstruction. The Amharic gerundive is first of all very recent in origin, as shown by its non-reconstructability for Ethiopian or even South Ethiopian Semitic, and its transparent nominal basis and origin (it conjugates with the present-day Amharic possessive pronoun suffixes). Furthermore, its non-stative character is quite unlike the Akkadian stative. The "defectiveness" of the Akkadian stative—its limitation to certain verbal roots (Goetze 1942)— seems to me to be often ignored in the comparative Semitic literature; the Amharic gerundive by contrast is formed freely from every verb, not just the statives.

The following facts about Amharic will be discussed here as evidence of the nominal origins of the perfect: (1) the element -*l*- of the negative of the perfect; (2) the use of the prefix *yä*- to express both the genitive of nouns and the relative of the perfect; (3) the element *mm*- of the relative imperfect; (4) the use of some clause subordinators only with the imperfect; (5) the use of some clause subordinators only with the perfect; (6) the variable use of *mm*- and the imperfect with certain clause subordinators; and (7) the form of the 2nd plural suffix of the perfect.

1. *The form of the negative perfect*

Negation of the Amharic perfect, as commonly in southern Ethiopian Semitic, is by a prefixed *a-l-*; -*m(m)* is suffixed: *al-säbbärä-m* "he did not break" vs. *a-y-säbr-əm* "he does not break". In Amharic the negative of the infinitive is by *al-ä*: *alämäsbär* "not to break", and a prefix *yalä-*, presumably *yä-al-ä*; it is used to express the negative of nouns in the expression "without": *yalä-bet* "without a house". Various speculations are possible on the etymology of this negative -*l*-. My point is just that it constitutes a connection between the noun and the perfect which does not exist between the noun and the imperfect.

2. *The genitive and relative functions of yä*

The use of a single or cognate morphemes to express the genitive of nouns and to subordinate a relative clause is not uncommon in the world's languages, it seems, but perhaps these cases are always the result of developments such as argued here: nominal origin of a verb. In Amharic this is illustrated by examples like *yä-mätta-w säw* "the man who came". The dual use of this morpheme would naturally result from the stage of Amharic in which the verb was nominal. The pre-perfect, like many other nouns, would have functioned as an attribute of nouns when genitive. The phrase above would at that stage have the gloss "the man of (his) coming", "the coming man", hence today's "the man who came", upon the nominal's reanalysis as verbal-aspectual.

It can be immediately objected that this interpretation as an argument for the nominal origin of the perfect fails since *yä-* is seen as well with the verb in the imperfect: *yä-mm-i-mäta-w säw* "the man who is coming". The interesting thing here is that the additional element *mm-* is necessary with the relative imperfect.

3. The element mm- of the relative imperfect

The use with the relativizer-genitive of this element with the imperfect and not with the perfect requires an explanation, and one consistent with the present argument immediately suggests itself: *mm-* was a nominalizing prefix, cognate with the *m*-prefix nominalizers common in Semitic, including for example the infinitive formative of Amharic: *mämṭat* "to come", *mäsbär* "to break". As nominal the pre-perfect would have accepted genitive *yä-* directly, but as a verb the imperfect would have required nominalizing affix. Alternatively, *mm-* of the relative imperfect could be descended from a relative indefinite pronoun cognate with the Semitic interrogative pronouns, for example Amharic *man* "who?", *mən* "what?". The pre-Amharic relative clause would then have been of the type seen in English and other European languages, formed by use of relative pronouns, *who, which,* etc. In the former possibility the pre-Amharic relative clause in the perfect would have been more of the approximate type seen in the current Amharic quasi-noun clause of *mähed-u-n al-sämma-hu-m* "I didn't hear of his going"; *mähed* is an infinitive, but provided with the possessive pronoun suffix this can function as a clause, "I didn't hear that he went". In either case the predecessor of *yä-* would not have been at first employed with the imperfect, but was extended to use there with the rise of the perfect as a model for verbs.

There is some evidence that the suggestion that *mm-* derives from a relative indefinite pronoun may be right: older Amharic texts have relative clauses in the imperfect in which *yä-* is absent and the imperfect verb is prefixed by *mm-* alone. This seems rare at most nowadays, and its frequency in the past suggests that *yä-* has been extended to relative imperfects with *mm-*, by analogy with the perfect.

Further evidence that the relative verb of Amharic was nominal, and hence, since the simpler relative verb is that of the perfect, that the perfect has nominal origins, is the reported use in Gojjam and Wällo dialects of the usual plural suffix of nouns with the relative verb (Armbruster 71; Cohen 117): *yä-hed-očč* "those who went", *yä-mm-i-hed-očč* "those who go".

It seems likely, owing to evidence presented by Hetzron (1973), that the prefix *mm-* of the relative is cognate with the *-mm* suffix of the Amharic negative main verb (*a-y-säbr-əmm* "he doesn't break"), itself cognate with the *-mm* "topicalizer" (*əne-mm al-hed-ku(-mm)* "I didn't go either"). However, these connections are completely compatible with the possibility that *-mm* of the relative imperfect goes back to an indefinite pronoun, itself a reasonable source—if rather removed in time—for all three functions (for reconstruction and possible cognates see Gelb 138 ff and Blejer).

4. *Clause subordinators used with only the imperfect*

Three clause subordinators are used only with the imperfect: *s(ə)-* "when", *s-i-mäta ayyä-hu-t* "when he came, I saw him"; *b(ə)-* "if", *b-i-mäta lə-ngär-äw?* "if he comes, shall I tell him?"; *l(ə)-* "in order that/to", *l-i-hed kot läbbäsä* "he put on a coat in order to go". These three prefixes cannot be attached to verbs in the perfect; all other clause subordinators combine with both. As seen in the first example, with *s(ə)-*, the imperfect with these subordinators expresses the past if the main verb so requires, and perhaps more could be made of this fact in the argument for the nominal origins of the perfect.

That these three morphemes are archaic is suggested by the facts that their origins as prepositions (vs. *bä-* "at, when", *kä-* "from, since") or their use as separate words (vs. *səlä* "because", *əndä* "that, like") is not attested nor apparent. These morphemes must predate the perfect conjugation, which when it appeared was not extended to use with these pre-eminently verb-combining morphemes. An explanation of this would be the origin of the perfect outside the verb system.

5. *Clause subordinators used with only the perfect*

Unlike the subordinators used only with the imperfect, which are of obscure and presumably archaic origin, those used only with the perfect are largely of prepositional origin, and transparently so (see Dawkins 102-5 for the associations of subordinators and verb forms). They are homophonous with prepositions, and often construct as clause subordinators with the help of noun complements. A couple of examples are *bä-...gize* (*bä* "at, in", *gize* "time"): *bä-mäṭṭa gize* "when he came"; and *kä-...ğämməro* (*kä-* "from", *ğämməro* 3 m. sg. gerund of *ğmr* "begin"): *kä-mäṭṭa (ğämməro)* "since he came". Such clauses are traditionally understood to be constructed with historical or hypothetical "underlying" synchronic relative clauses, i.e., *bä-yä-mäṭṭa gize* "at the time (at) which he came", *kä-yä-mäṭṭa* "from which he came"(?); *yä-* after prepositions is assumed to be elided as a phonological process (Praetorius 452).

The details of use and interpretation of such constructions as these are innumerable. My emphasis is on just the fact of their occurrence with the perfect and not the imperfect. That these subordinators are prepositional and the verbs perfect cannot be accidental, and again the hypothesis of the nominal origins of the perfect is explanatory: we suppose the clauses to have come from prepositional phrases constructed with participial heads: respectively: "at the time of his coming", and "from his coming". Notice that "from his coming" is a better paraphrase of *kä-mätta* "since he came" than is "from which he came".

6. *Variable use of mm- with certain subordinators*

The quasi-verbal stage of the perfect would have encouraged some variation in the use of a nominalizer *mm-* with imperfects, since prefixes whose use as subordinators is earlier with nominal verbs would tend to lose the necessity for nominal verbs as the perfect became fully verbal and, being more frequent (and earlier learned), encouraged a tendency for uses of the perfect to be extended to the bare imperfect. In such a case there would result some use of the imperfect with and without *mm-* with certain, perhaps quasi-prepositional, subordinators such as *ənd(ə)-* and *əsk(ə)-*, and this is exactly what we find. These two may or may not employ *mm-* when constructed with the imperfect.

Interestingly, however, *əsk(ə)-* may not construct with the negative imperfect without *mm-*. That is, we find *əsk-i-mäta* "until he comes" alongside *əskä-mm-i-mäta*, but only negative *əskä-mm-a-y-ččal-äññ* "until I could not" (Dawkins 104). The persistence of archaic forms of negative rather than affirmative verbs is well known.

Modern Amharic appears to be in the process of bifurcating the variable use of *ənd(ə)-* with and without *mm-* with the imperfect (Goldenberg 1965: 11, Dawkins 104-5). The former, *ənd(ə)* + *mm-* comes to be used in contexts were contrasts of tense/aspect are useful; for example, *əndə-mm-i-l* "as he says" replaces earlier *ənd-i-l* (Goldberg 11), where a contrast with *əndä alä* "as he said" is useful. Without *mm-*, *ənd(ə)-* persists in use in the "purposive" meaning: *ənd-i-mäta azzäzu* "they ordered him to come" ("... that he come"). That is, the *mm*-prefixed imperfects are more and more seen as in contrast with perfects, which is what we would expect if both these forms were formerly not seen as verbal, but now are—that is, if the perfect had non-verbal origins. (For a somewhat different interpretation of these facts, see Hetzron, p. 6.).

7. The 2nd plural suffix

Finally, perhaps the most interesting evidence, concerning as it does a striking departure from common Semitic morphology, is the form of the Amharic 2nd plural (common) suffix of the perfect. Here Amharic differs in two ways from the more typical Semitic languages. Amharic lacks the distinction of masculine and feminine in the 2nd plural generally, and in the perfect the suffix found is -*aččəhu*: *säbbär-aččəhu* "you pl. broke". The suffix must certainly be analyzed into -*ačč*- and -*hu*, the latter part being cognate with the common Semitic 2nd pl. masc. suffixes, in southern Ethiopian Semitic with *hu* < **kəmu* (Leslau 1956: 98). But what of -*ačč*-? This must be seen as a relic of the noun plural, **-ati* > -*ačč*, and on this hypothesis, of course, the stem of the perfect must have been a noun.

Several other particulars of Amharic grammar might be raised as part of the argument, but not without much abstract and probably unhelpful discussion. One such fact is the archaic use of *yä*- with relative imperfect verbs, but only negative forms (and all of these 3 m. sg. forms: Praetorius 1879: 126; Goldenberg 1977: 487-8; Getatchew 1978: 121). This fact as well as all those discussed above plus some others were discussed at length in Hudson 1973. The Amharic perfect shares with the other Semitic languages those fundamental characteristics that suggests the origins of this verb as a sort of participle conjugated with pronoun suffixes, presumably earlier a nominal sentence, for example the use of suffixes vs. the prefixes of the older verbs, and the similarities of these suffixes with the endings of the independent pronouns. The seven pieces of evidence discussed here are new support for an old hypothesis, which perhaps ought not be particularly controversial.

References

Armbruster, C. H. 1908. *Initia Amharica*. Cambridge: University Press.
Blejer, Hatte. 1978. *Two Semitic Discourse Particles*. MS, Linguistics Dept., University of Texas, Austin.
Cohen, Marcel. 1936. *Traité de langue amharique*. Paris: Institut d'Ethnologie.
Dawkins, C. H. 1969. *The Fundamentals of Amharic*. Rev. ed. Addis Ababa: Sudan Interior Mission.

Gelb, Ignace J. 1969. *Sequential Reconstruction of Proto-Akkadian* (Assyriological Studies no. 18). Chicago: University of Chicago Press.

Getatchew Haile. 1970. "Archaic Amharic forms". *Proceedings of the Third International Conference of Ethiopian Studies*, II, 61-80. Addis Ababa: Institute of Ethiopian Studies.

Getatchew Haile. 1979. "Some archaic features of Amharic". *Proceedings of the Fifth International Conference on Ethiopian Studies*, Robert L. Hess, ed. 111-124. Chicago: University of Illinois at Chicago Circle.

Givón, Talmy. 1979. *Understanding Grammar*. New York: Academic Press.

Goetze, Albrecht. 1942. "The so-called intensive of the Semitic languages". *JAOS* 62: 1-8.

Goldenberg, G. 1965. "Studies in Amharic syntax". *Journal of Ethiopian Studies* III: 6-22.

Goldenberg, G. 1977. "The Semitic languages of Ethiopia and their classification". *BSOAS* XL: 461-507.

Haupt, Paul. 1878. "The oldest Semitic verb-form". *Journal of the Royal Asiatic Society of Great Britain and Ireland* 10: 244-52.

Haupt, Paul. 1889. "Prolegomena to a comparative Assyrian grammar". *JAOS* 13: ccxlix-cclxvii.

Hertzron, Robert. 1973. "The element *-mm* in the Amharic verbal system". *Annali dell'Istituto Orientale de Napoli* 33: 1-10.

Hodge, Carlton T. 1975. "The nominal sentence in Semitic". *Afroasiatic Linguistics* 2/4: 1-7.

Hudson, Grover. 1973. "The relative clause in Amharic". Paper for the Conference on Word Order and Word Order Change. Santa Barbara, January 1974.

Janssens, G. 1975. "The Semitic verbal tense system". *Afroasiatic Linguistics* 2/4:9-14.

Leslau, Wolf. 1956. *Étude descriptive et comparative du Gafat* (Collection linguistique, Société de Linguistique de Paris LVII). Paris: Librairie Klincksieck.

Moscati, Sabatino et al. 1965. *An Introduction to the Comparative Grammar of the Semitic Languages*. Wiesbaden: Harrassowitz.

Praetorius, Franz. 1878. *Die Amharische Sprache*. Halle: Verlag der Buchhandlung des Waisenhauses. [Reprinted 1970. New York: Georg Olms Verlag].

Sampson, Geoffrey. 1980. *Making Sense*. Oxford: OUP.

AN UNPUBLISHED GEEZ-AMHARIC MAGIC MANUSCRIPT

Thomas L. Kane
Washington

The manuscript which is the subject of this paper was purchased by the writer in Addis Ababa in 1977. It is written on ledger paper which has been stapled together to form a booklet 11 × 18 cm. containing 94 leaves. Unlike most mss. of this kind, it is carefully written in black ink probably with a traditional reed pen. There are 22 lines to a page. Not all pages have text: ff. 36B, 37B, 38-45 and 46A are blank as are ff. 71, 76-93 and 94A. Folio 72 contains a computus entitled 'Hassabä fənot' and ff. 74-75 contain a computus entitled 'Hassabä Noh' which are written in purple pencil in a hand different from the rest of the text. These two entries appear to be later entries which were entered by another person on the blank pages of the manuscript.

The uniformity of the handwriting and the color of ink suggest that this ms. is a careful copy of an older text. In his 'Le livre des recettes d'un dabtara abyssin, Marcel Griaule states that such mss. as this represent an accretion of 'recipes' collected over the years by däbtäras[1]. The condition of other such mss. in the writer's possession indicates this is indeed the case: the variations in the ductus, the kind of writing instrument, the color of the ink and even the kinds and sizes of paper in a given ms. indicate clearly that they are anything but unified compositions. The age of this ms. is difficult to determine. The discoloration of the paper shows that it is not recent. A 'recipe' for changing paper into paper money (f. 17A) indicates that this ms. could not have been written before paper currency became accepted as a medium of exchange. Although Haile Selassie introduced paper currency in the 1930's, it was neither widely known nor accepted until the Italian occupation of 1936-1941. This ms. could have been written anytime between 1938 and 1960.

The 'recipes' in this (or in any other such ms.) are not arranged in any kind of order. The user of such a ms. undoubtedly relies on his memory to locate a given 'recipe' and in this ms. has apparently used symbols, usually an eight-pointed linear star written in red pencil, to indicate the most reliable ones. The writer has therefore grouped the 'recipes' into five categories:

---

[1] Griaule, Marcel, Le livre des recettes d'un dabtara abyssin, Paris, 1930, p. 4.

physical ailments, mental ailments, personal (for 'recipes' designed to protect the practicant from harm or to enhance certain of his skills or characteristics), interpersonal ('recipes' designed to influence the actions of others or to vitiate 'recipes' used by enemies to harm the practicant), those concerned with property and a miscellaneous category for a few which do not fit into the foregoing.

The effective power of these 'recipes' derives from the following:

1) natural substances, mainly plants and seeds but frequently animal substances such as skin, hair, blood, feces, vomit, butter, eggs and occasionally animal limbs or whole animals (if small). Noxious substances are rarely ingested but are encapsulated in a piece of sewn leather and worn next to the body.

2) magic names. Such names betray origins of the most diverse sort: Greek, Hebrew and Arabic being the most common. Others are clearly mumbo-jumbo, names formed by the combination of speech sounds which are outside the normal phonetic patterns of Amharic. In this ms., transcriptions into Ethiopic characters of several suras of the Quran, e.g. the Fatiḥa and suras 113 and 114, have taken the place of these magic names[2]. Each invocation of magic names must be followed by a *gäbir* or effectuation in order to produce the desired effect. These *gäbirs* direct that the names or the charm be written in a special ink on a special substance such as parchment made from the skin of a rock hyrax or be recited while standing on a special substance, often a large rock protruding from the earth. By changing the *gäbir*, the charm may be made to serve an entirely different purpose[3]. Without a *gäbir*, the invocation lacks force. Older magic mss. the writer has seen are without *gäbirs*, probably because the possessor wished to protect his stock of 'recipes' against theft.

3) designs. These are of two kinds: *sänṭäräž* and *ṭälsäm*. The first kind comprises rectangles which are divided into cells by parallel lines intersecting at right angles and are so named for their resemblance to a chessboard (*sänṭäräž*). Usually the cells contain symbols, usually words or syllables,

---

2 Lists of these magic names are given in Strelcyn, S., *Prières magiques éthiopiennes pour délier les charmes*, Warsaw, 1955, Index I (p. 327ff.) and Index V, (p. 411ff.); Griaule, M. op. cit., p. 166ff., and Lifchitz, D., *Textes éthiopiens magico-religieux*, Paris, 1940, p. 250ff.

3 The *məsḥabä nəway* (charm for attracting money) on f. 29B can be used for selling *ṭäǧǧ*-mead by omitting the *gäbir* which calls for the slaughter of a white chicken and a white goat, the burning of white incense and the scattering of fragment substances around the dwelling and instead writing the charm around a *ṭälsäm*-design (which design is not specified) and placing the drawing underneath a crock of mead.

generally the latter. The well-known palindrome square SATOR AREPO is probably the archetype of this kind of design[4]. This type of design is very common in Arabic magic and several of the designs in this manuscript are clearly derived from this source.

The *ṭälsäm* (from Greek *telesma* via Arabic *ṭilsim*) designs follow no definite pattern. Some are letter-like symbols with lunettes, others are geometrical figures inscribed with magic names or drawings such as the star-eye so common to magic scrolls[5]. Designs are considered to have such magic powers that they are usually without *gäbirs*.

Despite the fact that the *sänṭäräẑ* is probably meant to provide magic words or names by being read in various directions in keeping with its presumed derivation from the SATOR AREPO palindrome, there is no indication given in the recipes as to how they are to be read. The *sänṭäräẑ* on f. 4A, a *ma'särä säräqt* or 'binder of thieves' which consists of a simple pair of doubled parallel lines intersecting another such pair at right angles (reminiscent of the square used in thicktacktoe), has directions which state that the design is to be drawn on a piece of paper after which the name of the stolen item, the names of the owner and the owner's mother are to be written around the design while reciting Sura 2, verses 7 and 19.

The second *sänṭäräẑ* (f. 9A), a rectangle of 12 columns divided into 9 rows, contains symbols, mostly one to a cell, which when read as a normal text give the magic names *haruruel* and *həfrəriwael* some meaningless syllables (but possibly magic words) and the magic words *Adonay*, *Ḥbnodi*, *Ṣäba'ot* and the magic phrase *ahya šärahya alsaday*. *Adonay* is the well-known Hebrew term for Jehovah, *Ḥbnodi* has been identified by Strelcyn as the Coptic *fnout* 'God', *Ṣäba'ot* is Geez for 'Lord of Hosts' and the phrase is a reasonably accurate transcription of Exodus 3:14 in Hebrew[6]. The purpose of the design appears to be for countering refractory oxen and sorcerers.

The third such design (f. 24A) contains Arabic words in transcription, each word in a separate cell, written from left to right across the top and vertically down the sides, the remaining cells being filled by repeating the words in such a way that the repeated words form diagonal lines across the design. The words are from Sura 9, verses 128-129. This should be enough to indicate that most such designs cannot be read like their prototype or as in Arabic magic probably because neither Geez nor Amharic lend themselves to such a procedure.

---

4 For an interesting note on the origin of this palindrome, see Strelcyn, op. cit., p. 80.

5 Strelcyn, op. cit., p. XXXII. A number of these designs are reproduced in: Strelcyn, S., *Médecine et plantes d'Éthiopie* (I), Warsaw, 1968.

6 See the entry *əmnodi*, Strelcyn, *Prières*, p. 448.

The Recipes

Recipes dealing with physical manifestations

'afterbirth' *yäängədih ləǧ* (for afterbirth) 57B, *läängədeh* 59A, *səng läqärräbbat* (for a woman whose *səng*[7] has failed to come out) 59A, *läsəng* 49A.

'allopecia' *lašät lälasäw* (for one whom a *lašät* 'lizard'[8] licked) 4B, *lälašit ǧoro* (for an ear [licked by] a *lašit* 'lizard') 10A, *lärasä šällata* (for a bare scalp) 55B.

'appetite' *yäwäsfat* (for the intestinal worm) 59A.

'back' *ǧärbawn lätammämä* (for one whose back aches) 55B, *yäǧärba* (for the back) 57B, *ǧärbawn lämmiqäṭäqqəṭäw* (for one whose back is afflicted by a chronic illness) 56B.

'bleeding' *läset* (for menstrual bleeding) 4A, *argəza sallä̌čč däm lämmimätat* (for a woman who is afflicted by [an effusion of] blood even though she is pregnant) 5A, *ṭälsäm*-design for menstrual bleeding or nosebleed 54A, *yädäm* (for blood) 57A, *əyyämälalläsä əndä məraq bäafu däm lämmitäfa* (for one who repeatedly spits blood from his mouth like sputum) 56A.

'broken-windedness' (an equine disease) *länəddəft* 60B, *yämändäf* (for becoming broken-winded) 46B.

'chapping' *yäägər nəqaqat* (for cracks in the skin of the feet) 2B, *yääǧǧ färqəq labbätä nägär hullu* (for cracks in the hands and for all swellings) 57B.

'colic' *mägañña* 4B, *ganen bädäm əndayṭaläh* [for *əndayənṭalläh?*] (so that a demon may not cause your blood to pour?) 48B.

'cough' *läsal* 47B, *yäsal mädhanit* (medicine for a cough) 60A.

'crying child' *läzäybäkki həṣan* (for a child who cries) 8B.

'deafness' *ǧoro lädänäqqʷäräw* (for one whose ear has become deaf) 7B, 59A.

'diarrhea' *täqmaṭ* 4B, 10B.

'ear' *käǧoro qənqan lägäbbabbät* (for one who has a chicken louse in his ear) 56B

'ear inflammation' *ǧoro yämmimägəl* (one whose ear suppurates) 55B.

'eye ailment' *lä'ayn həmäm* (for eye illness) 7A, 7B; *yäfera*[9] 7A.

'epilepsy', see 'mental ailments'.

'eye rheum' *yä'ayn mädd* 12A.

'fetus' *lä'aynä ṭəla läsəns lämmizzawwär däm lämmihon* (for Shadow Eye[10], for a newly-conceived fetus which moves about and becomes blood) 51A.

---

7 Armbruster, C.H., *Initia Amharica*, Part III, p. 683. The entry reads: 'part of the placenta adhering to the uterus (if this fails to come away, it causes death)'.

8 Armbruster, C.H., ibid., p. 37.

9 So identified by my informant but Strelcyn, *Prières*, p. 336 has 'a serious contagious illness'.

10 See Griaule, P., op. cit., p. 142 and Strelcyn, *Prières*, p. 45.

'fever' *länədad, lämänšo* [11] 56A.

'fright' *ṣälotä dəngaṣe* (prayer for fright) [12] 49A.

'genitalia' *qʷəlaw labbäṭä* (for one whose genitals are swollen) 4B, 51A.

'gonorrhea' *čäbṭ* 4B, 27A, 47B.

'headache' *yäfəlṣät* 4B, 56B; *läras fəlṭät* (for splitting of the head) 7A, 59B; *läras həmäm* (for sickness of the head) 6A.

'heart trouble' *ləbbən lätammämä* (for one whose heart is sick) 56A, 56B, 57A.

'hydrophobia' *wəšša länäkkäsäw* (for one whom a [mad] dog bit) 5A, 5B; *yäəbd wušša* (for a mad dog) 57A, *əbd wušša länäkkäsäw* (for one whom a mad dog bit) 59A.

'hymen' *həgg mägsäs laššännäfäw* (for one who is unable to deflower his virgin bride) 26B, *yähəgg mäftəhe* (breaking of the hymen) 54B.

'illness' *lähəmam* 47B, *läbäššəta* 18B, 48A, 54A; *läsəray* 4B, 6A, 7B; *läləkkəft* 47B [13]

'illness—congenital' *lätəddaqi* 8B, 17B, *läsəga ṣəddaqi* 56B [14].

'illness—diagnosis' *həmam lämäläyyät* (for identifying a disease) 53A [15].

'illness—prevention of' *yäbäššəta yämmayasnäkka* (which does not allow a disease to affect one) 6B.

'impotence' *bəllətu lämotäbbät* (for one whose genitalia have died to his detriment) 4B, 5B; *qʷəlaw lämotäbbät* (for one whose genitalia have died to his detriment) 6B, *läzämotä 'əskit* (for a dead penis) 54B, 60B; *mäftəhe 'əskit* (breaking of [a spell on] the penis) 55B, *akalatum lämotä säw* (for a man whose male member is dead) 56B, *läzänomä 'əskit* (for a penis which is asleep) 60A.

'inebriation' *läsəkar* 9B.

'insanity' *bämädhanit labbädä säw* (for a person made insane by poison) 50B [16].

'itch' *läəkäk* 4B, 17B.

---

11 *Nədad* is malarial fever, *mänšo* an intermittent fever.

12 Presumably the purpose of this recipe is to overcome the effects of fright.

13 *Həmam* is the Geez term for illness, the same as the Amharic *bäššəta*. *Səray* means 'charm, evil spell' while *ləkkəft* is indicated by the two native dictionaries (AYMQ and KBT) as being the initial symptom of disease. The KBT adds that it is also an 'infection by a subtle spirit, lethargy of body and mind'.

14 Identified as an unspecified congenital illness by the informant. This disease is cited in Griaule, M, op. cit., p. 90 but is not translated nor explained.

15 This charm also reveals *ẕar*-demons.

16 Despite the many references to the use of poison in Ethiopian literature and in books written by Westerners on Ethiopia, there are no recipes for the preparation of poison known to the writer.

'jaundice' *lä'of* (for the bird [disease]) 5A, *ṣälotä bä'əntä həmamä 'aynä wärq* (prayer for the gold-eye disease) 11B [17].

'labor pains' *yämət* 7A, 25B.

'leprosy' *śəga däwe* 4B, 6A; *lädäwe śəga* 5A.

'malaria' *yäwäba mädhanit* (medicine for malaria) 60A.

'miscarriage' *läwərǧa* 54B.

'pain' *läwəgat* 56B.

'puerpural fever' *läśotälay* 5A, 12A; *'anqäṣ ẓäśotälay* (chapter on puerpural fever) 27A; *lähəmam dähar läm"aṭäṭa* (for the illness of an abraded back?) 47B [18].

'relapse' *lägərśa* 4B.

'rheumatism' *läq"ərtəmat* 17B, 54A.

'scrofula' *läməśśəro* 3B, 6A, *bäməśśəro ǧoro lämmimägəl* (for one whose ear suppurates on account of scrofula) 6A, *yäməśśəro* 57A, *länäqärsa* 6A, *mäqqämäčaw yäməśśəro laq"ässäläw* (for one whose posterior has been wounded by scrofula) 5A.

'snakebite' *läəbab* 56A, *yäəbab mädhanit* (medicine for snake [bite]) 60B.

'sterility' *yämäkan set yämmiyaswälləd* (for causing a barren woman to give birth) 9A, untitled charm included with a *mäftəhe səray*, 30B, *lämäkan* 54A, 60B, 61B.

'stomach ailment' *lähod näqärsa* (for scrofula of the stomach) 6A, *lähod* 47B, *hodun lätammämä* (for one whose stomach is ill) 56A, 57A, 59B.

'stomach pains' *yäq"ərṣät* 50B, 56B.

'swelling' *(ə)bäṭ* 4B, *läəbäṭ hullu yämmiyamägəl mädhanit* (a medicine which makes all swellings suppurate) 58A; *yägussay mädhanit* (medicine for *gussay*) 61B.

'syphilis' *wurde* (a mild form) 4B, 6A, 7B, *läqiṭṭiñ* 5B, *qəččəñ lawäṭṭat ləǧwa əndaywäṭa* (so that a woman who has syphilis may not transmit it to her child) 17B, *yäqiṭṭəñ mädhanit* (medicine for syphilis) 58A, untitled remedy for preventing transmission of a disease by touch, sweat or sleeping [together] 26B.

'tapeworm' *koso lämälalläsäbbät bíggäñ* (if one is found to have tapeworm repeatedly) 58A.

'typhus' *tässəbo* or *wärrärśəñ* 18B.

---

17 *Yäwäf bäśśəta* is Amharic for 'the bird sickness'. This is jaundice or viral hepatitis. *'Aynä wärq* more commonly denotes a psychic affliction similar to *'aynä ṭəla* or Shadow Eye, but *AYMQ*, p. 925, confirms that *'aynä wärq* is also used for jaundice.

18 Identified by my informant as *śotälay*. For information on this illness, see Griaule, M., op. cit., pp. 144-145.

'urinary ailment' *lämmətəšän* (for a woman who urinates) 10B, 19A, 49B; *yäšənt maṭ* (painful urination due to inflammation of the urethra caused by gonorrhea and other ailments) 57B.

'uterus, prolapse of' *maḥəšänwa läwäṭṭabbat* (for one whose uterus has gone up) 5A.

'uterine ailment' *zäyarättə' 'aṣmä bə'əsit zämaḥəsan* ([charm] which straightens the bone in the uterus of a woman)[19] 7B; *aṭənt lähonäbbat hodwan länäffat set* (for a woman who has a bone in her uterus and whose abdomen is swollen) 25B.

'uvula' *lääntəl* 18B, 57A.

'vomiting' *lätəfat* 4B, 5B, 11A, 19A, 32A, *ṣälot bä'əntä həmamä təfat wäfähaq wätäqmaṭ* (prayer concerning the illness of vomiting, hiccoughs and diarrhea) 60B, *yänəzzaži* (food expelled through the nose or mouth due to ilness) 56B [a prayer on 11A entitled *ṣälotä nägär zäasfäraqəw* has the notation *yätəfat* 'for vomiting' pencilled over it but this notation is apparently erroneous. See the entry 'enemy' under 'interpersonal relations' below].

'warts' *läähəyya kəntarot* 49B.

'yaws' *läqʷəsəl* 47B, 56A, *yäqʷəslä səga* 57A, 59B; *lägʷärmiṭ biggäññ* (when the *gʷärmiṭ* sore is found) 58B.

An unclassifiable recipe is: *bäsäwnätu ṭälsäm zäwäg'at 'adi bäwäräqät* (one who has tattooed a *ṭälsäm*-design on his body or on paper) 60A.

Recipes dealing with property

'batter utensils' *läbuho əqa* 26A.

'beverage' *ṭägg lämäšäṭ* (for selling *ṭägg*-mead) 30A, *ṭägg ṭälla əndayəbbälašš* (so that *ṭägg*-mead and *ṭälla*-beer do not spoil) 30B.

'bloodstains' *däm länäkkaw šämma* (for a *šämma*-garment which has come in contact with blood) 56A.

'hail' *zäbäräd* (to protect crops against hail) 4B.

'household' *yäbetəhən zuriya* (for the area [around] your house) 11B.

'livestock' *awre yämmiyalämd* (one who domesticates animals—the text indicates that it is used for wild birds such as the francolin and the partridge) 5A, *läbota käbärät käbt lämmiyawärd* (for one taking cattle down from the pen?) 6B[20], *lam ləgʷan sətətäla* (when a cow rejects its calf) 12B, *lägärgari*

---

19 Strelcyn, S., *Médecine et plantes d'Éthiopie*, p. 525.

20 The informant identifies this as a 'recipe' for inducing cattle to abort. In fact, a pencilled 's' has been written above the word *'yämmiyawärd'* 'who brings down' which would provide

färäsənna bäqlo labäyya bäre (for bolting horses and mules and for refractory oxen) 11A.

'locusts' *mäṣhafä 'anbäṭa* (charm for locusts) 3A, *ṣälot bä'əntä 'anbäṭa zäṣälläyä 'elyas bäwəstä bä'at* (prayer for locusts which Elijah prayed while in the cave) 14B.

'milk vessels' *yäwätät əqa əṭan* (fumigating milk vessels) 10B.

'money' *kəfəl gänzäb əndigäba ṭəru wärq* (so that fractional currency will turn to pure gold) 26A, *wäräqätun bərr yämmiyadärg* (which turns paper into paper currency) 17A, *məṣhabä nəway* (for attracting money) 32A, *ṣälot bä'əntä məṣhabä nəway, məṣhabä 'elyas wäməṣhabä särägälla 'elyas* (prayer for attracting money, Elijah's [money] attracter and the [money] attracter of Elijah's chariot) 28A, *läwəhiba nəway* (for being given money) 3A, *läzäṭäf'a nəway* (for lost money) 8B.

'property' *käsate habt* (revealer of property) 33B, *lähabt* 12B, 51B, *lämäftəhe habt* (for breaking a spell [cast on] property) 50A [21], *ṣälot bä'əntä mäftəhe habt zätä'asrä bä'aynä ṭəla wä'əg̱g̱ä säb'* [22] *wäbä'aynä nas* (prayer for breaking a spell cast on property by Shadow Eye, Əg̱g̱ä Säb' and Eye of Copper) 31A, *ṣälot bä'əntä mäkəstä habt wämäftəhe śəray zäsäb' wäzäaganənt* (prayer for revealing property and breaking spells of man or demon) 22B, *lämändəg* (charm which enables its owner to get anything he wants from others) 47B, 53A, 61B, *yätäqäbbärä yämmiyawäṭa* (which unearths anything buried) 8B.

'rutting' *lämmətəśaffəd bäqlo* (for a rutting mule) 11A.

'selling' *ṣälot bä'əntä śeṭ wätäśayäṭ* (prayer for selling and trading) 28A, *ṣälot bä'əntä məśyaṭ* (prayer for selling) 33B.

'theft' *yäleba* (for a thief) 5B, 18B; *yäleba yätäfättänä* (for a thief. Tested) [23] 9B, *läsällabi* (for one who takes property by stealth) 2B, 10B, 26A, 34B; *läsällabi läawdəmma* (for one who takes by stealth, for a threshing floor) 10A, *läbetäsäb* (lit. for the family—the text indicates that it is to keep servants from stealing) 58B, *ma'särä säräqt* (binder of thieves) 4A.

Recipes which are designed to protect the practicant from harm or to improve himself in some way

'burns' *ṣälot zäṣälläyä Räwqə'el mälakä bəheru läkoreb* (prayer which Rawqiel, the angel of the land of Horeb, prayed—protects against burns) 8A.

'*yämmiyaswärrəd*' 'which causes abortions' but this may have been done because the text is not entirely intelligible.

21 This charm consists of Suras 113 and 114 in transliteration.

22 Əg̱g̱ä säb' is defined by Strelcyn as an *être maléfique*. He suggests the term may be derived from Geez *ədä səb* 'magic hand'. See Strelcyn, *Prières*, note 6, p. 41.

23 Tested to the efficacy of the recipe. Ordinarily this is expressed by the Geez *fətun* 'tested'.

'combat' untitled prayer for protection from bullets, sword blows, stoning, beatings and wars 24B, *'aqqabi ẓäṭəyyət* (protector from bullets) 24B.

'handwriting' *yäṣəfät* (for improving handwriting) 9A.

'imprisonment' *ṣälotä moqəḥ* (prayer for fetters) 18B.

'insect bites' *lätək"an* (for bedbugs) 4A.

'intelligence' *mäkəstä ẓä'iyo'el* (discloser of the secrets of Joel—for improving the intelligence) 19A, *läləbb bəlhat* (for acuity of the mind) 56B.

'invisibility' *lämäsäwwär* 48A, *läsəwware* (for being invisible) 50B.

'life' *lä'əmä konä lämot aḥəsəro wälä'əmä konä läḥəywät arzəmo* (if it is [a matter of] death, make it short and if [a matter of] life, lengthen it—an untitled charm for easing the agony of death or for prolonging life) 35B.

'memory' *nəgruni ẓäḥaläyä ləbbunäyä* (tell me what my mind has thought) 52B, *ẓä'iyagäddəf* (which does not let one omit [something]) 9B, 19A.

'mien' *lägərma mogäs* (for dignity and esteem) 31B, 47A, 53A; an untitled *gərma mogäs* 14A, *ṣälot bä'əntä gərma mogäs* (prayer for dignity and esteem) 13A.

'panther' *yänäbər* 60B.

'protection' *'aqqabe rə'əs* (guardian of the head i.e. the self) 10B, 26A, 32B, 48A, *ṣälotä näbabi* (prayer of the speaker—a prayer for protection against insults and blows) 51B.

'wild animals' *läawṭ läawre hullu* (for the orycteropus [24] and for all wild animals).

Interpersonal relations

The recipes in this category fall into two groups: those designed to harm one's enemies and those designed to win the favor or affection of other persons. It will be observed that the former has the greater variety.

'court case' *lämuggət* 55A.

'enemy' *läṣärr* 5A, 13B, 46B, 47B; *mädfənä ṣärr* (closing up of the enemy) 24A, 34A, 61B; *yämästäḥaməm* (charm for making someone ill) 5B, 24A, 53A (the same prayer with a *mändəg* charm) 60B, untitled prayer for making people fight each other 51B, *mästäṣabi'* (charm for creating enmity between two persons) 52A, *lädänqara* (charm for casting a spell on someone) 50A, *ṭälat agär ṭəlo əndihed* (so that an enemy will leave the district and go away) 51B, *yəthatäm mäsob wäqäst yäəgäle* (may the table and bow of so-and-so be sealed—

---

24 An animal which is believed to dig up and eat human corpses. It is also called *resa awṭ* 'unearther of corpses'. A photograph of this animal published in the Ethiopian newspaper *Addis Zämän* in the early 1960's shows a powerfully built animal with shaggy fur and large, sharp digging claws.

a charm to deprive an enemy's household and property of any blessing) 37A, untitled recipe for casting fear into those who look at the practicant 34B, *ṣälotä mägräre ṣärr mäkaməẕ mädängəẕ* [25] (prayer for controlling the enemy, poisoning? [him] and stupefying [him]) 34A, *ṣälotä bä'əntä mäläṣär [mädfən läṣärr?]* (prayer for closing up an enemy) 32B, an untitled *mädfənä ṣärr* 10B, *ṣälotä nägär ẕä'asfärraččäw* (prayer for a thing which frightened them—this prayer bears a pencilled notation 'for vomiting' but as the prayer refers to the Biblical incidents in which Moses dealt with Pharaoh, Hezekiah with Sennacherib and David with Nabal, this is clearly erroneous) 10A, *läbalängara* (for an opponent) 11A, *läḥasän* (Arabic?—identified as a *mästäḥaməm* by the informant) 13B, *yäḥayyu* (Geez 'who gives life' but identified as a *mädfənä ṣärr* by the informant) 13B,34B, untitled charm for hurting an enemy by causing his genitalia to be twisted by magic 55A, *'aläm ẕäšärak* (the phrase is distorted Arabic, the charm has been identified as a *mädfənä ṣärr* by the informant) 7B [26].

　　'friend' *läfəqər* (for love) 26B, 60B, 61B, an untitled *mästäfaqər* (love-philtre) 2A, 34A, 60B, *mästäfaqər* 46B, *läset mästäfaqər* (philtre for a woman's love) 53A, *lämästäfaqər läbetä mängəst* (for gaining someone's affections, for [becoming popular] at court) 53A, *mästäwadəd* (for gaining someone's affection) 27B, *lämäyaẕ set* (for capturing [the favor of] a woman) 50B, *ṣälot bä'əntä məsḥabä säb' wänəway* (prayer for attracting people and money) 28B.

　　'illness' *yämmayasnäkka* (which does not let [illness] touch [one]—a charm which counters the *mästäḥaməm* charm by turning the sickness against the person using that charm) 5B.

　　'sorcerer' *läabayam läqumäññam* (a *säntäräẕ*-design to counter refractory oxen and sorcerers) 9A.

　　'wife' *'aqqabe ḥəgg* (protector of sexual virtue) 60A, *ḥəggä ṭäbbəq* (protect sexual virtue) 49B, *bə'əsa wäbə'əsit 'iyətfälṭu* (may husband and wife not separate) 37A, *wäyagəbə'a ḥabä ẕätəkat mänbära* (and cause her to come back to her place of residence of old) 13B.

Mental ailments

A considerable number of recipes deal with malign spirits or beings and the physical or mental manifestations induced by them. It seems appropriate to

---

25　This word is not attested in the dictionaries. The informant identified it as a 'name of God' i.e. a word having magical powers. Most charms of this kind have the word *mäfẕəẕ* 'stunner' at this point. See Strelcyn, S., *Prières*, p. 57.

26　The Arabic is Sura 94.

place them under the same heading, including *bariya* (epilepsy) given the association this disease has with demons which is apparent from the fact that it is generally linked with the demon Legewon—the Legion of Mark 5:9 and Luke 8:30—in the recipes.

'dream' *lähəlm* (occurs with a *mändəg* and *mästahaməm* recipe. It can be used to induce dreams merely by changing the *gäbir*) 53A, *həlm lämäläyyät* (for identifying dreams—this recipe also reveals the names of *zar*-demons) 53A.

'epilepsy' *zäbarya* 4B, 7A, 56B; *barya lämmitəlaw säw* (for a person who has had an epileptic fit) 51A, *mädhanit zäbarya wäzäbuda* (medicine for epilepsy and the *buda*-spirit) 10A; *ṣälot bä'əntä barya wälegewon* (prayer for epilepsy and the *Legewon*-demon) 48A.

'evil eye' *yaynät* (shares a recipe with *'aynä ṭəla*) 11B, *'aynu lätäṭaläbbät* (for one on whom the evil eye has been cast—shares an incantation with a small-pox remedy) 7A.

'evil spirit' *landärrəbi* 2B [27], *läbuda* (incantation shared with *səray, wərde, ṭəla wägi* and *mäftəhe wəllaǧ*) 7A, *läbuda* 7B, *läbuda* (incantation shared with one for *qumäñña*) 18B, *mädhanit zäbarya wäzäbuda* (medicine for epilepsy and for the *buda*-spirit) 10A, *yäbuda yäganen* (for the *buda*-spirit, for demons) 54B, *läganen* (for demons) 11A, 47A, 51B, *läganen mäṭäbbäqiya* (for protection against demons) 48A, *yälegewon yäganen* (for the *Legewon*-demon, for demons) 54B, *yälegewon mädhanit* (medecine for the *Legewon*-demon) 56B, *legewon əndä barya lämmitəlaw* (for one who had an epileptic-like fit caused by the *Legewon*-demon) 58B, *mägzə'a 'aganənt* (binder of demons) 31B, *mäftəhe wəllaǧ* (breaker of [spells cast by] lesser *zar*-spirits—shares a recipe against *səray, wərde, buda* and *ṭəla wägi*) 7B, *yätäyazä yämmiyasläfälləf* (which makes a possessed person talk) 48B [28], 49B, *ṣälot bä'əntä mäsgärtä mäsäriyan buda wäqummäñña wäzar wəllaǧ 'əm tayazi wä'əmṭämzazi fəls* (prayer for [rescuing someone] from the snares of sorcerers, *buda*-spirits, sorcerers, lesser *zar*-spirits, from chronic illness and crippling illness) 1A.

'insanity' *labbädä säw* (for a crazy person) 5A, *läzar bäššəta* (for the *zar*-disease) 5A.

'spells' *lämäftəhe* (for breaking spells—shares incantation with *qumäñña* and *ṭəla wägi*) 6B, 8A, 9B, 12A, 13A, 48A, 49A; *lämäftəhe səray* (for breaking spells) 4B, 30A, 50B, 54B; *səray* (spells—shares incantation with one for

---

27 The KBT explains *andärrəbi* as a malificent action brought against a person by *ṭänqʷay*-sorcerers or wicked *däbtära*-cantors who cause rain, hail or stones to fall on a person, sand to be sprinkled on the bread he is eating or for his house to catch fire. The AYMQ explains it as stones hurled during darkness by an unseen being or the dumping of excrement (human or animal) on the table.

28 See footnote 10.

wərde, buda, ṭəla wägi, mäftəhe wəllaǧ) 7B; *ṣälot bä'əntä mäftəhe səray* (prayer for the breaking of spells) 25A, 50A; *ṣälot bä'əntä mäkəstä habt wämäftəhe səray zäsäb' wäzä'aganənt* (prayer for revealing [lost] property and for breaking spells of man and demons) 22B, *ṣälot bä'əntä mäftəhe səray wämäftəhe habt wä'aynä ṭəla wä'aynä wärq* (prayer for breaking spells, breaking [spells] on property, Shadow Eye and Gold Eye) 25A, *lätädäggämäbbät* (for one who has had a spell cast on him) 5A, *lä'əǧǧä säb'* (for necromancy) 26A; *yäṭəla* (for Shadow Eye) 18B; *ṭəla wägi* (shadow piercer—shares an incantation with *səray, wərde, buda* and *mäftəhe wəllaǧ*) 7B; *läṣəla wägi* (for the shadow piercer) 60B; *ṣəla wägi lämästähaməm lädəggəmt* (shadow piercer, incantation for causing illness, spell-casting) 2A; *'aynä ṭəla* (Shadow Eye—shares an incantation with *yaynät*) 9A; *'aynä ṭəla läfärräkä 'əǧǧä säb'* (Shadow Eye, for one on whom necromancy has become strong) 6A; *ṣälot bä'əntä 'aynä ṭəla* (prayer for Shadow Eye) 27B; *lä'aynä ṭəla läsəns lämmizzawwär däm lämmihon* (for Shadow Eye, for a newly-conceived fetus which moves about and becomes blood) 51A; *ṣälot bä'əntä 'aynä ṭəla abro addäg wämäftəhe habt* (prayer for Shadow Eye, companion from childhood and for breaking spells on property) 30B.

Miscellaneous

A few 'recipes' cannot easily be fitted into the foregoing categories. They are: *b(ə)rät yämmibäla* (for eating [through] iron) 50B which might apply either to etching iron e.g. the name of the owner or a motto to be inscribed on a sword blade, or to eating through iron fetters in order to achieve escape from imprisonment; an untitled incantation appearing on 51A for keeping demons away from someone's grace; *mäl'ak lämmisəb* (for attracting angels) 53B; and the Fatiha (initial Sura of the Quran) as a charm for preventing rain while on a journey, 14A.

This ms. contains several incantations for ascertaining the future. Since dreams are considered to presage the future (for which the prototype is the Biblical account of Joseph's dream [29] as is proved by the title of one of these incantations 'The dream which You made Joseph dream in the land of Egypt'), several 'recipes' are for inducing dreams. They bear the following titles: *mäkəstä məṣṭirä zämän* (revealer of the secrets of the age) 2A; *yärä'əy* (for a vision—apparently to induce visions or trance-like states in which the future is presaged) 10B, 22A, 48A; an untitled prayer to St. Mary to reveal the future 18B; an untitled prayer for finding out the future 22A; *lähəlmä yosef*

---

29 Genesis 41, v. 11-32.

(for Joseph's dream) 53B; *ḥəlm zä'aḥlämkä läyosef bäbəḥerä gəbṣ* (the dream which You made Joseph dream in the land of Egypt) 22B.

In this ms. there are also several passages having the word '*ḥassab*' (computus) in the title. These computuses appear to provide means for the practicant to surmount many of the uncertainties of daily life. They appear to be derived from the zodiac and from the system of assigning values to the letters of the alphabet which are then computed on a base of varying value. For instance, the name Haylu is computed as follows: H has the value of 20, Y the value of 90 and L the value of 2. Computed on a base of 12, H has a remainder of 8 and Y a remainder of 6. These are added to make 14 which is again reduced by a factor of 12. This value is added to the value of L which gives a total value of 4 to the name Haylu[30].

There are eight computuses in this text: *ḥassabä mänazəl* (computus of the zodiac) 18A; *ḥassabä räwadi* (computus of the victor) 35A; *ḥassabä ḥabt* (computus of wealth) 35B; *ḥassabä käwakəbt* (computus of the stars) 62A; *ḥassabä bä'əntä nägärä wärḥ* (computus on telling the months) 69B; *ḥassabä fənot* (computus for a journey) 72A; *ḥassabä noḥ zätäfännäwät rəgb* (computus of Noah which was sent [with] the dove) 74A; and *ḥassab bäzäyətammär məwuq wäqorir* (computus by which heat and cold may be known) 94B. Only the *ḥassabä mänazəl*, the *ḥassabä käwakəbt* and the *ḥassabä räwadi* appear to be complete.

Comparison with the computuses of like nature appearing in a printed version of the 'Awdä nägäst[31] shows that there are a great many of these computuses (53 in this work alone) and taken together provide against almost any conceivable contingency. These computuses require further study but apart from a brief article by Conti Rossini, there is no information[32].

There are practically no peculiarities in the grammar or the lexicon of this text. *Tənnəsʷa* for *tənnəsʷa* ('small' + fem. def. art.) occurs several times, *ṭuhat* 'morning' instead of *ṭʷat* and *qəṭṭiñ* 'syphilis' for *qeṭṭiñ* are to be noted. They are nothing unusual and may be due to the fact that the 'recipe' in which they appear originated outside the area of the Shoan dialect in which most of these recipes appear to be written.

---

30 An illustration of how these work is provided by the *ḥassabä beta nəgus* 'computus of the palace' given here in its entirety: Compute [the practicant's] name and [his] mother's name on a factor of 3 plus [the numbers of] the day and the month. [A remainder of] one is good. It will turn out well for you, you will enter joyfully. [If it is] 2, you will lose money. [If] 3, straits and hunger await you' (p. 209, *Ḥatäta mänafəst wä'awdä nägäst*).

31 'Awdä-nägäst *wäfəkkare käwakəbt* and Ḥatäta mänafəst wä'awdä nägäst.

32 Conti Rossini, C. "Lo 'auda nagast'", *RSE*, 1941.

I wish to thank my informant, däbtära Gäbrä-maryam Dästa of Addis Ababa, for his help in elucidating some of the recipes and Dr. Muhammad Umar Memon for identifying the Suras of the Quran.

Bibliography

Anonymous, *'Awdä nägäst wäfəkkare käwakəbt*, Addis Ababa, 1953 A.M.

Armbruster, C.H., *Initia Amharica*, Part III, Amharic-English vocabulary with phrases, Cambridge, 1920.

Dästä Täklä-wäld, *'Addis yamarəñña mäzgäbä qalat*, Addis Ababa, 1962 (*AYMQ*).

Griaule, M., *Le livre des recettes d'un dabtara abyssin*, Paris, 1930.

Lifchitz, D., *Textes éthiopiens magico-religieux*, Paris, 1940.

Strelcyn, S., *Médecine et plantes d'Éthiopie* (I), Warsaw, 1968.

Strelcyn, S., *Prières magiques éthiopiennes pour délier les charmes* (*maftəhe šəray*), Warsaw, 1955.

Täsämma Habtä-mika'el Gəṣəw, *Käsate bərhan täsämma: yamarəñña mäzgäbä qalat*, Addis Ababa, 1951 A.M. (KBT).

Zämänfäs-qəddus Abrəha, *Ḥatäta mänafəst wä'awdä nägäst məslä fəkkare 'iyäsus wäsabela*, Asmara, 1953 A.M.

LES VERBES «REDONDANTS» EN AMHARIQUE

Olga Kapeliuk

L'Université Hébraïque, Jérusalem

Introduction

Il y a en amharique, de même que dans les autres langues néo-éthiopiennes de la famille sémitique, un petit groupe de verbes, dont la présence dans certaines constructions semble inexplicable. L'exemple suivant, tiré d'un texte de Käbbädä Mikael, dont le style est justement caractérisé par ce genre de constructions, est représentatif de cette tendance:

1. *yäHəndən mängəst čärrəsaččəhu yalagäňňaččəhu honaččəhu bəttəqäru təwäddal-*
   laččəhunə wäyəss dägmo yannantä yähonäˀn Šäkspirən fäṣṣəmo yalagäňňaččəhu
   bəttəhonu təwäddallaččəhu? täblän bənnəṭṭäyyäq noro mən ənnəmälləs noroall?
   bäwnätu yeh ṭəyyaqe käbbad hono bätägäňňä näbbär. yämängəst säwočč
   yähonut ofisiyal bähonä nəgəggər yämmimälləsu mähonaččäw ayəṭṭäräṭṭä-
   rəmm. (KMRJ 14/1-9) [1]

   «Si on nous avait demandé (étant dit) 'Auriez vous préféré rester (étant) ceux qui n'ont jamais possédé l'empire de l'Inde ou bien auriez vous préféré d'être ceux qui n'ont jamais eu votre Shakespeare' qu'aurions nous répondu? Vraiment cette question aurait été considérée (étant) difficile. Il n'y a pas de doute que ceux qui sont les hommes du gouvernement auraient répondu par un discours (qui est) officiel».

On peut distinguer dans cet extrait trois constructions différentes comportant la copule: *yalagäňňaččəhu bəttəhonu* et *yämmimälləsu mähonaččäw* où un verbe relatif précède directement la copule qui a la forme exigée par la structure de la proposition, se comportant en quelque sorte comme un auxiliaire; *yalagäňňaččəhu honaččəhu bəttəqäru, käbbad hono bätägäňňä* et *täblän bənnəṭṭäyyäq*, où le gérondif de la copule et de la forme passive du verbe «dire» sont placés entre un verbe et son complément et *yannantä yähonäˀn*

---

[1] Voir la liste des abréviations à la fin de cet article. Dans la traduction des exemples j'écris entre parenthèses les mots qui sont dans le texte amharique mais doivent être omis dans le texte français et entre crochets les mots qui ne se trouvent pas en amharique et sont ajoutés dans la traduction.

Šäkspirən, ofisiyal bähonä nəgəggər et *yämängəst säwočč yähonut*, où une forme relative de la copule intervient entre un qualifiant et son qualifié (sous-entendu dans le dernier exemple). J'ai décrit ailleurs la première construction[2]. La forme relative de la copule sera examinée ultérieurement, et c'est le gérondif de la copule et de quelques autres verbes qui fera l'objet de cet article.

Les constructions dont il sera question comportent le gérondif de la copule et des verbes *mässälä* «sembler, paraître», *adärrägä* «faire», *alä* «dire» et son passif *täbalä* et, occasionnellement, le parfait précédé de la conjonction *əyyä* ou, dans le cas de *alä*, l'imparfait précédé de la conjonction *sə*, donc toutes des formes indiquant la concomitance. Dans certains cas ces verbes ne possèdent pas leur sens plein et paraissent «redondants». C'est d'ailleurs le terme qu'emploie M. Cohen à propos du gérondif de *adärrägä* et de *honä* dans certaines constructions[3], tandis que L. Fusella s'élève contre l'emploi excessif des formes subordonnées de la copule dans l'amharique contemporain: «Che necessità c'è... in periodi già appesantiti e complicati da una serie di proposizioni subordinate ed incise, de dire *bämängäd sälam bämmiyafärəs akkʷakʷan huno yämmiggäññ* per tradurre quello che, con minor numero di parole, potrebbe tradursi *bämängäd sälam siyafärəs yämmiggäññ* ... Che necessità di dire ... *ṭəfatäñña huno täṭäyyaqi näw* (sarà ritenuto responsabile) invece di *əndätəfatäñña yəqqʷäṭṭärall*?»[4].

En fait les verbes cités constituent une catégorie spéciale en amharique même en dehors des constructions dans lesquelles ils paraissent de trop. Ils sont beaucoup plus «grammaticaux» que les autres verbes dans la langue et ont tendance à perdre leur contenu lexical au profit de leur fonction purement grammaticale. La copule *näw/honä* est vide de sens et ne sert qu'à fournir un auxiliaire ou à créer le lien de prédication entre le sujet et son attribut, *mässälä*, de par son comportement syntaxique et son contenu lexical, représente souvent un équivalent incertain de la copule[5], comme le montre l'exemple suivant:

---

2 Voir mon article «L'évolution de la phrase amharique: la nominalisation du verbe», *Comptes Rendus du Cinquième Congrès International des Études Éthiopiennes, Nice, 19-22 décembre 1977*, Rotterdam, 1980, p. 97-105.

3 Voir M. Cohen, *Traité de langue amharique*, Paris, 1936 p. 329 et id. *Nouvelles études d'éthiopien méridional*, Paris, 1939, p. 173; voir aussi G. Goldenberg, *Ma'areket hazmanim ha'amharit*, Jérusalem, 1966, § 109-110.

4 Voir L. Fusella, «Osservazioni linguistiche sull'amarico moderno», *Atti del Convegno Internazionale di Studi Etiopici, Roma 2-4 aprile 1959*, Rome, 1960, p. 85.

5 Voir mon article «Il semble que ou il semble qui — un problème de syntaxe amharique», *Studies Presented to H. J. Polotsky*, éd. D. W. Young, Gloucester MA, 1981, p. 53.

2. *baləssasat käzzih bäfit yagäbbahaččäw hullu fättočč yəmäsluññall?* —*naččäw.*
   (HIFK 112/1-2).
   «Si je ne me trompe pas toutes celles que tu as épousées auparavant
   me semblent des divorcées?» — «Elles [le] sont».

Les verbes *alä* et *adärrägä* perdent souvent complètement leur contenu lexical
pour servir comme un outil grammatical pur dans la création et la dérivation
de verbes à partir d'éléments non-verbaux. Les deux verbes se trouvent alors
normalement en distribution complémentaire *alä* permettant de former des
verbes intransitifs et *adärrägä* des verbes transitifs ou causatifs, par exemple
ṣätt alä «se taire», *ṣätt adärrägä* «pacifier», *wätta alä* «sortir un peu (intr)» et
wätta adärrägä «sortir un peu (tr.)». Parfois *honä* remplace *alä* dans la création
de verbes intransitifs et se trouve en distribution complémentaire avec
adäräggä, par exemple: *dəl honä* «subir une défaite» et *dəl adärrägä* «vaincre,
infliger une défaite»[6].

Cette capacité des quatre verbes mentionnés à se débarrasser de leur
contenu lexical au profit de l'expression de relations grammaticales pures
facilitera l'explication des constructions à verbes «redondants» en position
adverbale.

2. *Verbes « redondants » en position adverbale*

Seront considérés comme étant en position adverbale les verbes *honä, mässälä,*
adärrägä et *alä (täbalä)* au gérondif ou à une forme équivalente devant un
autre verbe régissant. Il faut, bien sûr, distinguer entre les verbes appartenant
à ce groupe qui ont leur sens plein et ceux qui sont employés de façon
superfétatoire. Dans l'exemple suivant le premier gérondif de la copule a un
sens plein et le deuxième est «redondant»:

3. *sədbunna mäddäfäru ləbsu hono lähulgize mässädäbiyawənna mäddäfäriyaw*
   hono yənorall (HAFM 103/15-17)
   «L'injure et l'offense étant devenus son vêtement, il vit tout le temps
   (étant) [comme] l'objet d'injures et d'offenses».

Lorsqu'ils n'exercent pas leur fonction pleine, ces verbes en position
adverbale lient au verbe régissant certains compléments prouvant ainsi que

---

6 Outre sa fonction de composante dans des verbes composés *adärrägä* tend en amharique
parlé d'aujourd'hui à devenir un véritable *empty verb* comme *do* en anglais, par exemple:
mähedaččəhu näw qurs sattəbälu? — *argänall* (Mängəstu Lämma, *Yalačča gabəčča*, Addis Abäba,
1957 c.é. p. 108/19-20) «Vous devez partir sans avoir déjeuné?» — «Nous avons fait (=
déjeuner)».

l'amharique conçoit en termes de subordination prédicative la relation entre un verbe et certains de ses compléments. Cette conception est illustrée le plus clairement dans l'emploi de la copule, qui est d'ailleurs le plus fréquent.

3. *honä*

En position adverbale on trouve occasionnellement à la place du gérondif de la copule, dans un entourage distributif, le «gerundio presente»[7] *əyyähonä*, par exemple:

4. *lämängəstumm səra yätor ministraččən fitawrari Habtä Giyorgis wanna honäw, ministročču hullu läyyäkəflaččäw səra alafi əyyähonu əndisäru* (HSHI 63/4-7).
    «Pour qu'ils travaillent, notre ministre de guerre le *fitawrari* H.G. (étant) [en tant que] principal [responsable] pour le travail du gouvernement, et tous les ministres (étant) [en tant que] responsables du travail de leurs départements respectifs».

Les deux formes verbales permettent de lier à un verbe un complément d'état ou de qualité (le *ḥal* des grammairiens arabes), ou un complément prédicatif (= attribut). Le complément d'état et de qualité se distingue du complément prédicatif par le fait que sa présence n'est pas indispensable sur le plan syntaxique et il ne fait qu'ajouter un supplément à un verbe plein. Sans le complément prédicatif, par contre, un verbe qui le demande reste incomplet; dans l'exemple suivant le premier gérondif accompagne un complément de qualité et le deuxième un complément prédicatif:

5. *məšt yagäbba, bet nəbrät yabäǧǧämm, qes däbtära hono yagäläggəlall. ançi gən yämməttəyəw dəngəl hono yəqər näw* (HAFM 35/18-20).
    «Celui qui épouse une femme et fonde une maison et une famille sert Dieu (étant) [comme] un prêtre ou un *däbtära*. Mais ce que tu dis c'est 'qu'il reste (étant) vierge'».

a. Dans le cas d'un complément désignant l'état ou la qualité le gérondif de *honä* permet de joindre à n'importe quel verbe un substantif ou un adjectif (y compris le verbe relatif et le participe) qui sans cela seraient incapables de s'attacher au verbe, sauf au moyen d'une préposition. Or, l'amharique préfère d'indiquer la relation entre un verbe et son complément d'état ou de qualité à l'aide d'un moyen verbal, le gérondif de *honä* en l'occurrence, au lieu

---

7 Pour ce terme voir AWGr p. 110.

de recourir à la subordination du nom à l'aide d'une préposition, par exemple :

6. *Bäzzabbəh Tori yäbərät hawəlt hono yəṭäbbəqatall* (MLṬB 13/20).
   «B.T. l'attend (étant) [comme] une statue de fer».

7. *əhtəhənənna wändəmməhən abbat honäh astaməraččäw* (AMYB 76/9-10).
   «Enseigne ta sœur et ton frère (étant) [comme] un père».

8. *mälku qʷərṭ ayatun[8] hono wäṭətoall* (BZBF 34/8).
   «Son visage est sorti (étant) exactement [comme] son grand père».

9. *mərkoňňočč ərräňňočč əyyähonu yagäläggəlu ğämmär* (Prog. Dic. 27/8).
   «Les prisonniers de guerre ont commencé à servir (étant) [comme] des bergers».

10. *əndä raswa ləsləs huno yätäwällädä ləğwa* (AGRA 22/7-8).
    «Son enfant qui est né (étant) délicat comme elle-même».

11. *säw ... käənsəsat yələq yätägʷädda hono yəwwällädall* (KMIM 14/12).
    «L'homme est né (étant) plus désavantagé que les animaux».

12. *läSäblä albašənna täkättay hona täsäṭṭäčč* (HAFM 204/20-21).
    «Elle a été donnée à S. (étant) [comme] habilleuse et suivante».

13. *əzzih Addis Abäba däğğ ṭäniwočč honaččəhu täqämmäṭu* (HSHI 12/4-5).
    «Établissez-vous ici, à Addis Abäba, (étant) [comme] des solliciteurs».

b. Dans les exemples 4-13 le gérondif de la copule fournit la seule expression sur la surface de la relation d'état ou de qualité entre un verbe et un de ses compléments. Il arrive toutefois que cette relation est déjà exprimée par une préposition et pourtant le gérondif de la copule fait son apparition, ici apparemment de façon tout-à-fait «redondante», par exemple :

14. *qäňňazmač Akalu səläne hono yənnägagär ... qäňňazmač Akalu səläne yəhun*
    (HAFM 104/22-24).
    «Que le *qäňňazmač* A. parle (étant) de ma part ... que le *qäňňazmač* A. soit de ma part».

15. *gərmawi nəgus Fuad bazägağğullən ləyyu babur honän wädä Iyärusalem*
    tägʷazn (HSHI 63/32-33).
    «Nous sommes partis à Jérusalem (étant) dans un train spécial que le roi Fuad nous a préparé».

16. *bäňňa səm honäw əndifärrəmu* (HSHI 56/9).
    «Pour qu'il signe (étant) en mon nom».

---

8 Sur l'accusatif avec le complément de la copule voir mon article «Quelques remarques sur l'emploi de l'accusatif en sémitique éthiopien et en arabe classique», *Studia Orientalia Memoriae D.H. Baneth Dedicata*, Jérusalem, 1979, p. 234-235.

17. *tallaqwa Britanyamm qal kidan kätägabbaččaččäw mängəstočč gara hona ... yämməttəttaggäl mähonwan tärädətaččəhut* (HSFK 185/19-21).
«Et vous avez constaté que la Grande Bretagne combat (étant) ensemble avec les pays avec lesquels elle a conclu une alliance».

18. *lafərsataw yätäsäbässäbäw həzb bägʷadd bägʷadd əyyähonä kand təlləq zaf sər täkämačto səlänäbbär* (HIFK 146/12-14).
«Puisque les gens qui s'étaient réunis pour l'*afərsata* étaient rassemblés (étant) par groupes sous un grand arbre».

c. Il est encore plus extraordinaire que des adverbes, aussi bien ceux qui comportent une préposition (surtout *əndä*) que d'autres, s'attachent parfois, eux aussi, à un verbe au moyen du gérondif de *honä*, malgré que leur place naturelle soit directement auprès du verbe. Dans ces constructions le gérondif reste parfois invariable et le verbe est intransitif ou passif, par exemple:

19. *mən aynät fätäna bigäʈməh näw əndäzzih honäh mäqno yaʈʈahäw* (MGLG 34/6-7).
«Quelle épreuve as tu subie que tu as (étant) tellement changé?».

20. *əndäzziya hoňňe bänorkubbat kätäma əndäzzih hoňňe alənorəmm* (PŇM 11/10).
«Je ne vivrai pas (étant) comme ça dans une ville où j'ai vécu (étant) ainsi».

21. *əndaggaʈami hono andande wädä wəčč səttəwäč* (MGLG 9/4-5).
«Si par hasard (littéralement 'comme le concours des circonstances étant') tu sors parfois dehors».

22. *əndä ədəl hono bäməsa säat tägänaňňu* (DAŠS 109/12-13).
«Par hasard (litt. 'comme la chance étant') ils se sont rencontrés à l'heure du déjeuner».

23. *bäzziya yätäsäbässäbäw hullu band qal hono ... tänaggärä* (HSHI 32/5-6).
«Tous ceux qui étaient rassemblés là-bas ont parlé (étant) d'une seule voix».

24. *käzare gämmero käbetä krəstiyan wəčči hoňňe əʈäbbəqallähu* (AMYB 11/1-2).
«À partir d'aujourd'hui j'attendrai (étant) à l'extérieur de l'église».

25. *täzzih huno yaw yettayyall* (AWGui 90/8).
traduit par l'auteur «Voilà on l'aperçoit d'ici» (litt. «étant d'ici»).

26. *yand gʷadd fəllagot əndiyaräka bəčča hono tämärräʈä* (DAŠS 49/4-5).
«Il a été élu (étant) uniquement pour satisfaire la volonté d'un camarade».

Le gérondif de *honä* permet aussi de créer des adverbes à partir d'un adjectif et d'un pronom interrogatif auprès de verbes intransitifs et passifs, par exemple:

27. *gəlṣ huno yaltänäggäräw yännatunna yabbatu yämäğämmäriya huneta* (AGRA 18/15-16).
    «L'état d'origine de ses parents qui n'a pas été indiqué (étant) d'une façon claire».

28. *mən hunäš tətäkkəžalläš əte?*
    «(Etant) [pour]quoi tu te soucies ma sœur?».

d. Lorsque les verbes intransitifs *norä* «vivre, rester», *qärrä* «rester», *qʷäyyä* «attendre, rester», les verbes transitifs *ayyä* «voir» et *agäññä* «trouver» et les verbes passifs *tägäñña* «être trouvé», *täsärra* «être fait», *täqʷäṭṭärä* «être considéré», *tayyä* «être vu, paraître», *täsämma* «être ressenti», demandent un complément prédicatif, celui-ci doit être introduit normalement par un gérondif d'un verbe «grammatical», surtout de la copule, qui crée un lien entre ce verbe et un substantif, un adjectif (y compris le participe et la forme relative)[9] ou une construction prépositionnelle qui lui sert de complément. Ce n'est que très rarement et avec le seul verbe *täqʷäṭṭärä*, que l'on trouve une préposition seule, l'amharique préférant normalement la subordination à caractère verbal, par exemple:

29. *yägetənnät wäg mähonu qärto känäwr täqʷäṭṭärä* (HAFM 113/18-19).
    «Ayant cessé d'être une coutume de seigneurs ceci a été considéré comme une disgrâce».

30. *yäne dämäwäz magñät kämagñät yəqqʷäṭṭärall!* (HIFK 76/19-20).
    «Comme si gagner mon salaire était considéré comme gagner?».

Les autres exemples comportent un gérondif de la copule:

31. *yəh həggənna sərat yämmayəlläwwäṭ zäläalämawi hono əndinor azəžžeallähu* (HAFM 26/2-3).
    «J'ai ordonné que cette loi et règle demeure (étant) inchangeable et éternelle».

---

9 Il faut pourtant signaler qu'à l'encontre du complément d'état et de qualité, le complément prédicatif peut être rendu par un verbe relatif sans l'intermédiaire d'un gérondif «redondant», par exemple *landafta ənkʷan yamänätta altägäññämm* (BGQK 19/19-20). «Il ne s'est trouvé hésiter un seul instant»; d'autre part l'emploi des verbes demandant un complément prédicatif avec un verbe subordonnée est normal: *räžmo tayyaččäw* (HAFM 50/8-9). «Il lui a paru long».

32. *əndä mäkʷanənt hono mänorən yämməttəmärṭ mäsloññ* (HSHI 13/1).
«Comme il m'a semblé que tu choisirais de vivre (étant) comme les princes».

33. *bəčča yäwällad mäkanočč honän əndannəqär* (HAFM 37/31-32).
«Seulement que nous ne restions pas (étant) stériles».

34. *kinä ṭəbabaččən dəha hono yäqʷäyyäw* (BGQK 82/28).
«Ce que notre art est resté (étant) pauvre».

Avec les verbes transitifs *hono* est employé lorsque le complément prédicatif indique une caractéristique inhérente à l'objet et non pas le résultat de l'action du verbe régissant, dans quel cas on utilise le gérondif *adrəgo* (voir §5b ci-dessous), par exemple:

36. *kähullumm yätäšalä hono yagäññähut käsäwəyyew gʷadd mähonən näw* (PŇD 69/12-13).
«C'est d'être le compagnon de l'homme que j'ai trouvé (étant) le mieux de tout».

37. *səlantä mənənnät lämawäq gən kämmiffällägäw bälay hono agñəččallähu* (DAŠS 186/23-24).
«Je l'ai trouvé (étant) au-delà du nécessaire pour connaître ta valeur».

38. *biyayäw mäkʷännən hono ayyäw* (PŇM 12/2).
«S'il le voyait il le voyait (étant) [comme] un prince».

Avec les verbes passifs c'est le gérondif de la copule qui est le plus fréquemment employé, par exemple:

39. *ṭəfatäññawa täqaẓwa əne bəčča hoññe tägäññähu* (HAFM 49/25-26).
«Moi seule j'ai été trouvée (étant) fautive et digne de punition».

40. *käleločču därasyan yätäläyyä səṭotanna muya yalläw hono yəggäññall* (KMRJ 17/6-7).
«Il se trouve être celui qui a un don et une qualification différente des autres auteurs».

41. *əndä wanna moya hono yämmiqqʷäṭṭärəllät ṭäbay* (KMRJ 15/15-16).
«La caractéristique qui est considérée [comme] étant sa qualification principale».

42. *däräga bädäräga hono yätäsärra yamarəñña mäṣhaf* (Tub. 74/10-11).
«Le livre d'amharique qui a été fait (étant) par degrés».

43. *mäsärrätawi ṭəyyaqe hono sälä täsämmaññ* (BGQK 33/7-8).
«Parce que [cela] a été ressenti par moi [comme] étant une question fondamentale».

44. *asfällagi hono tayyaččäw* (HIFK 143/28).

«Il lui parut (étant) nécessaire».

45. *hulätt əyyähonä yəttayyaččäw ğämmär* (HAFM 496/4).

«Il a commencé à lui paraître (étant) double».

Avec les deux derniers verbes *honä* peut être remplacé par *mässälä*.

4. *mässälä*

Le gérondif du verbe *mässälä* «sembler, paraître» est employé à la place du gérondif de la copule pour lier le verbe *tayyä* et occasionnellement les verbes *täsämma-w* et *qärrä* à leur complément prédicatif (qui a souvent la forme relative du verbe) [10], par exemple:

46. *asfällagi mäslo tayyaččäw* (HIFK 105/17-18).

«Il Lui parut (semblant) nécessaire».

47. *fəṣṣum and mäslo yettayyall. mänäṣəren awṭəčče bəmmäläkkät gən ṭəqit ṭəqit sost mäslo yəttayyall … and gize sost and gize and əyyähonä tayyäññ* (HWSW 8/22-9/3).

«Il paraît (semblant) tout-à-fait un, mais lorsque je regarde ayant sorti mes lunettes petit à petit il paraît (semblant) trois … Il m'a paru (étant) une fois trois et une fois un».

48. *kämäčemm gize yələq wädäne yäqärräbäčč mäslo täsämmaññ* (BZBF 12/17-18).

«J'ai ressenti qu'elle était (semblant) plus proche de moi que jamais».

Dans cet exemple le verbe est impersonnel et c'est la raison pour laquelle le gérondif reste invariable.

49. *hazän lay yätäqämmäṭä säw mäslo näbbär yäqärräw* (BGQK 79/4).

«C'est (semblant) [comme] un homme en deuil qu'il est resté».

5. *adärrägä*

Le gérondif du verbe *adärrägä* est employé systématiquement comme l'équivalent transitif du gérondif de *honä* dans les constructions comportant un complément d'état ou de qualité et un complément prédicatif. Il est en outre fréquemment employé auprès des adverbes de manière.

---

10 Voir mon article «Il semble que».

a. Les exemples d'un complément d'état et de qualité attaché au verbe au moyen de *adrəgo* ne sont pas fréquents, par exemple:

50. *addis ṭəyyaqe adrəgäw mamṭatwo* (HAFM 115/24-25).
«Le fait que vous avez posé ceci (faisant) [comme] une nouvelle question».

51. *mahbärun barya adrəgo əndigäzaw* (HAFM 122/16-17).
«Pour gouverner la société (faisant) [comme] des esclaves».

La présence d'une préposition n'exclut pas l'emploi du gérondif «grammatical», par exemple:

52. *säwən ... käleločč̣əmm fəṭrätočč̣ bälay adrəgäh səttəšomäw* (HSHI (II)/14-15).
«Lorsque tu nommes l'homme (faisant) au dessus des autres créatures».

b. Par contre la présence du gérondif de *adärrägä* auprès d'un verbe transitif, demandant un complément prédicatif, est de rigueur, par exemple:

53. *däha adrəgo yäfäṭṭäräññən amlak amäsäggənallähu* (HAFM 88/17-18).
«Je remercie le Seigneur qui m'a créé (faisant) pauvre».

54. *säwənnätwan yäwändočč̣ massäqaya mässariya adrəga näbbär yämməttəmmä- läkkätäw* (BGQK 54/27-28).
«C'est (faisant) [comme] un outil de torture pour les hommes qu'elle considérait son corps».

55. *yämot mot adrəgäw q"äṭräwət* (HAFM 100/9-10).
«Le considérant (faisant) pire que la mort».

56. *ənglizən lämaṭfat ačč̣ər nägär adrəgo yəgämmətäw näbbär* (KMIM 124/2).
«Il considérait la victoire sur les Anglais (faisant) [comme] une affaire courte».

Avec le verbe *ayyä* que nous avons déjà rencontré avec le gérondif de la copule (*cf.* §3d ci-dessus), le gérondif *adrəgo* est employé lorsque le complément prédicatif indique un état résultant de l'action du verbe régissant, par exemple:

57. *käato Täzärra əkkul adrəgäw ayayuwačč̣äwmm näbbär* (AGRA 27/6-7).
«Elle ne les voyait pas (faisant) [comme] des égaux de *ato* T.».

Quant au verbe *agäññä* que nous avons examiné sous *hono*, il semble que c'est son causatif qui s'attire le gérondif de *adärrägä*, par exemple:

58. *wägänun bädday adrəgo yämmiyasgäññäw yəhonall* (HSFK 176/25).
«Il peut le rendre (faisant) l'offenseur de ses proches».

c. Mais le gérondif *adrəgo* peut apparaitre même si le complément est déjà lié au verbe par une préposition, surtout la préposition *əndä* «comme», dont la caractère adverbal semble particulièrement faible, par exemple:

59. *ənnäzzihənəmm tämariwočč əndä setäñña adariwočč adrəgo yəgämmətaččäw nähbär* (MGLG 25/1-2).
«Et il considérait ces élèves (faisant) comme des prostituées».

60. *əndäwändəmmwa adrəga təwäddäw nähbär* (*Traité* 329).
«Elle l'aimait (faisant) comme son frère».

Il semble que *əndä* tend à s'attirer le gérondif *adrəgo* même lorsqu'elle fonctionne comme une conjonction devant le verbe d'une proposition de contenu, dont le caractère adverbal est, pourtant, incontestable, par exemple:

61. *yan mäsänakəl liyalfut əndämmayčəlu adrəgäw asayyuwaččäw* (HAFM 139/21-22).
«Ils Lui ont montré (faisant) qu'il ne pourra pas traverser cet obstacle».

d. *əndä* attire le gérondif *adrəgo* aussi lorsqu'elle sert à créer des adverbes auprès de verbes transitifs. Mais des adverbes de manière même sans *əndä* s'accompagnent souvent de *adrəgo*, par exemple:

62. *abbate yasaddägäñ əndih adrəgo näbbär* (BZBF 40/10).
«C'est (faisant) ainsi que mon père m'avait élevé».

63. *läbəčča adrəgo band bätäläyyä mäṣhaf wəṣt masattäm asfällagi honä* (KMQA 5/8-9).
«Il est devenu nécessaire d'imprimer (faisant) séparément dans un livre spécial».

64. *əǧǧəg adrəgo yəwäddattall* (AWR 55/23-24).
«Il l'aime (faisant) beaucoup».

65. *bäṭam adrəgo asazzənot yänäbbäräw* (HFIK 163/11-12).
«Ce qui l'avait (faisant) beaucoup attristé».

66. *dähna adrəgäh səmañ* (AMYB 75/21).
«Écoute-moi (faisant) bien».

adrəgo sert aussi à créer des adverbes à partir d'adjectifs dans le voisinage de verbes transitifs (pour l'équivalent avec *hono* et un verbe passif voir exemple no. 27), par exemple:

67. *gələṣṣ adrəgäh nəgäraččäw* (HAFM 137/23).
«Dis leur (faisant) clairement».

5. *alä*

L'emploi, dans les langues sémitiques éthiopiennes et dans certaines langues couchitiques, du verbe «dire» comme un moyen pour la création et la dérivation de verbes, de préférence intransitifs, à partir d'un élément non-verbal, a été traité de manière exhaustive dans plusieurs travaux [11]. Dans des constructions de ce genre le verbe «dire» perd presque toujours son contenu lexical pour devenir un outil dans la création et la dérivation de verbes. En amharique cette capacité du verbe *alä* à se débarrasser de son sens premier se manifeste également dans certaines constructions syntaxiques dans lesquelles il participe. Il est superflu de tenter d'expliquer le chemin parcouru par le verbe «dire» pour arriver à sa fonction d'outil abstrait, comme l'explique G. Guillaume: «Il faut se garder de vouloir à tout force ... retrouver dans un mot outil, quel qu'il soit, son sens initial de sémantème. Les filiations qu'on croit pouvoir établir de la sorte ne sont à l'ordinaire qu'une image sans vérité de la filiation plus subtile qui a eu lieu réellement das la pensée» [12].

Pour ce qui est du verbe *alä* l'on peut dire que dans certaines constructions il ne se distingue pas des autres verbes «grammaticaux» que nous venons d'examiner. Ainsi dans la proposition suivante le verbe *qäna alä* est transformé en *qäna mässälä* pour se conformer à la construction habituelle avec *tayyä*:

> 68. *ənen qäna mäslo kätayyäññ* (HIFK 107/12).
>
> «Puisque cela m'a paru (semblant) juste».

tandis que dans l'exemple suivant le gérondif de *alä* occupe la place réservée normalement au gérondif de *mässälä*:

> 69. *angätu əndä sibago sil bəla təttayyalläčč* (BGQK 81/16-17).

---

11 Voir pour l'amharique notamment M. Cohen, *Traité* p. 262-275 et *Nouvelles études* p. 286-300, J. Hartmann, *Amharische Grammatik*, Wiesbaden, 1980, p. 141-143, Afevork Ghevre Jesus, *Il verbo amarico*, Rome, 1911, p. 96-103; pour les autres langues sémitiques de l'Éthiopie voir W. Leslau, *Documents tigrigna*, Paris, 1941, p. 124, F. R. Palmer, «Some remarks on the grammar and phonology of the 'compound verbs' in Cushitic and Ethiopian Semitic», *Quattro Congresso Internazionale di Studi Etiopici*, *Roma aprile 10-15*, Rome, 1974, tome II, p. 71-77; W. Leslau, *The Verb in Harari*, Berkeley and Los Angeles, 1958 p. 70-73; W. Leslau, *Étude descriptive et comparative du Gafat*, Paris, 1956, p. 70; pour une bibliographie sur ce phénomène dans les langues couchitiques voir A. Waley et C. H. Armbruster, «The verb 'to say' as an auxiliary in Africa and China», *BSOAS* tome VII no 3 (1934), p. 573-576.

12 Dans «Theorie des auxiliaires et examen de faits annexes», *BSL*, tome XXXIX (1938), p. 10.

«Son cou paraît tendu (distant) comme une ficelle» (voir §5c ci-dessous).

En fait une forme subordonné de *alä*, que ce soit le gérondif, le «gerundio presente» ou l'imparfait précédé de la conjonction *sə*, peut servir à exprimer des relations syntaxiques pures, de la même manière qu'une forme subordonnée de *honä*, *mässälä* ou *adärrägä*. La principale différence entre les constructions avec ces trois derniers verbes et celles comportant *alä* réside dans le caractère du complément qu'ils introduisent. *honä*, *mässälä* et *adärrägä* joignent au verbe régissant des compléments (à l'exception des adverbes de manière introduits par *adrəgo*), dont le caractère prédicatif nous est encore clair, même si dans les langues qui nous sont familières il n'est pas exprimé sur la surface[13]. *alä*, par contre, introduit des compléments dans lesquels il est plus difficile de discerner le caractère prédicatif, comme le complément de but, d'instrument, d'objet direct et quelques adverbes.

a. Dans l'indication du but et de l'intention la construction comporte la préposition *lä* et soit le gérondif soit l'imparfait précédé de *sə* de *alä*, par exemple:

70. *yəhənnən fätäna bärase lay yamäṭṭahut lähagäre səl bəčča aydällämm. lärase läsäb'awinnäte səl näw* (BZBF 55/18-20).
«Ce n'est pas seulement (lorsque je dis) pour mon pays que j'ai fait venir cette épreuve sur moi-même. C'est (lorsque je dis) pour moi-même et pour ma personne humaine».

Cette construction est également courante avec un infinitif ou avec un verbe à l'imparfait, dans quel cas *alä* fonctionne comme un auxiliaire[14], par exemple:

71. *əndiyaw wändənnät yəzoňň mässariya lalämmäläyät bəyye näw əngi lälela aydällämm* (BGQK 129/4-5).
«Si je me suis conduit comme un fanfaron c'est (disant) pour ne pas me séparer des armes et non pas pour autre chose».

---

13 Mais comparer en français: «La politique de X s'est révélée être dangereuse» ou «La politique de X est considérée comme étant dangereuse».

14 Un autre cas où *alä* fonctionne comme un auxiliaire est celui de l'infinitif précédé de la préposition *əndä* et suivi du verbe «dire». La construction exprime une action qui se fait un peu, par exemple: *yädäkkämäččäw dəkam tənnəš əndämaläf kalälaččäw bähʷala* (HAFM 47/20-21) «Après que Sa fatigue a passé un peu». L'équivalent transitif de cette construction est obtenu à l'aide de *adärrägä*: *mäkinawn əndä mäqom adärrägä* (AGRA 16/19-20) «Il a arrêté un peu sa voiture».

72. *yačči ləǧ ləttəwädq näw alu baša Zəmam ləttəwädq səttəl tämälkətäw* (DASS 70/27-29).

«Cette enfant va tomber» a dit *baša Z.* en constatant qu'elle [allait] (lorsqu'elle dit) tomber».

b. Le complément d'instrument ou de moyen introduit par la préposition *bä* peut s'accompagner du gérondif *bəlo.* Etant donné que ce complément indique souvent l'instrument d'un acte violent certains amharisants attribuent au verbe *alä* le sens de «frapper». C'est ainsi, que Dässəta Täklä Wäld donne à *alä* et *balä* (?) aussi le sens de *mätta, bäbättər ṭäẓẓälä* et *däbäddäbä* et cite l'exemple *bädulla bälat* [15], tandis que M. Cohen écrit: «*alä* a aussi le sens de 'y aller' — *bäläw* 'vas-y (contre lui)', 'tape-le' ... *bäbättər aläw* 'il lui a donné du bâton'» [16]. Certains exemples semblent confirmer cette interprétation:

73. *bärəgaččanna bäṭəffi bəlo käbetu aswäṭṭaw* (ŠMMY 58/8-9).
«Il l'a fait sortir de sa maison (disant [ou le] frappant) par des coups de pied et des gifles».

74. *balagär bäsärraw dulla anatəhən bəlo bigälhəss?* (HAFM 303/17).
«Et si les paysans te tuent (disant [ou] frappant) [sur] ta tête avec un gourdin?».

Mais d'autres exemples prouvent que *bəlo* ne fait qu'accompagner, en tant que moyen abstrait exprimant la subordination, un complément de verbe, par exemple:

75. *babbatəh bäläh attəčäkkənəbbən* (ŠMMY 46/10).
«(Disant) par ton père, ne sois pas cruel avec nous».

76. *əňňa bafär bäqəṭälu əyyaln yäəsatun hayl ənnabärd gämmärn* (PŇM 56/10-11).
«Nous avons commencé à refroidir le feu (disant) avec de la poussière et des feuilles».

c. Avec un adverbe *bəlo* semble très proche de *hono,* par exemple:

77. *wädetəss bəyye əfälləgatallähu* (ŠMMY 76/19).
«Et (disant) où la chercherai-je?».

78. *həzbu and and əyyalä käbetä-krəstiyan əyyäwäṭṭa* (DASS 62/13-14).
«Lorsque les gens sortaient (disant) l'un après l'autre de l'église».

---

15 Dässəta Täklä Wäld, *Addis yamarəňňa mäzgäbä qalat,* Addis Abäba, 1970, p. 102, 173.
16 *Traité,* p. 263.

La ressemblance avec *hono* se manifeste aussi dans les constructions avec *əndä* «comme» (voir exemple no 69).

d. Le seul exemple d'un complément d'objet direct introduit par *bəlo* que j'ai trouvé peut également avoir la signification «frapper»:

> 79. *abbate attäk"akos səlasṭännañ gənbarun bəyye əṭəläwallähu* (LMND 14/4-5).
> «Puisque mon père m'a appris le tir je tirerai (disant [ou] frappant) dans son front».

Toutefois certains grammairiens considèrent aussi le discours direct accompagnant le verbe *alä* comme le complément d'objet direct[17]. Il est également bien connu que les verbes exprimant la parole, la pensée et le sentiment peuvent s'adjoindre le contenu de la parole, de la pensée etc. sous la forme du discours direct (correspondant à une proposition de contenu dans le discours indirect).Dans ces constructions le gérondif ou l'imparfait accompagné de la conjonction *sə* du verbe *alä* (ou *täbalä*) sert de lien entre le discours direct et le verbe régissant, par exemple:

> 80. *yäbärbärre čənät mähon alläbbät bəlo yänäbbäräwn hassab läwwəṭo ... lela nägär mähon alläbbät sil assäbä* (AGRA 14/7-11).
> «Ayant changé l'idée (disant) [que] cela devait être une charge de *bärbärre* ... il a pensé (lorsqu'il dit) 'cela devait être autre chose'».
> 81. *ṣähay yäfəṭrät aläm əmbərt näčč täblo yəttammänall* (KMIM 117/16).
> «On croit (étant dit) [que] le soleil est le centre de l'univers».

Il n'y a pas de doute que dans ces constructions l'amharique, en tant que langue à structure très stricte de la proposition, se sert du gérondif du verbe *alä* (ou *täbalä*) pour ne pas laisser une partie de la proposition — le discours direct — dans le vide, sans indiquer sur la surface la relation qui existe entre lui et le verbe. Malgré que son sens soit vivant, *bəlo* est ici très proche des autres verbes «grammaticaux» et sa présence est dictée seulement par la nature du complément. Dans l'exemple suivant sans le discours direct on aurait *adrəgo* à la place de *bəlo* (comparer exemple no 56):

> 82. *šärmuṭa näčč bəlo yəgämmətäññ yəhonall* (BGQK 91/30-31).
> «Peut-être me considère-t-il (disant elle est) [comme] une putain».

Le gérondif *bəlo* fournit donc à la partie constituée par le discours direct un moyen formel, à caractère adverbial, pour se joindre à un verbe en tant que

---

17 F. Praetorius, *Die amharische Sprache*, Halle, 1878, p. 434 et J. Hartmann *op. cit.*, p. 454.

complément de la même manière que *hono*, *mäslo* et *adrəgo* permettent à d'autres compléments de s'attacher à un verbe.

6. *Systemzwang*

La question qui se pose est de savoir pourquoi l'amharique (et les autres langues néo-éthiopiennes) exprime par des moyens verbaux la relation entre un verbe et certains de ses compléments, relation qui dans les autres langues sémitiques ou dans les langues indo-européennes reste soit inexprimée sur la surface, soit rendue par les moyens ordinaires de rection verbale à savoir les cas ou les prépositions. Même le guèze emploie régulièrement ces deux derniers moyens tandis que l'amharique les remplace par la subordination verbale, par exemple:

83. guèze: *na'ammər kämä əmhabä əgzi'abher mäṣa'əkä mämhərä* (Jean 3/2) [18].
«Nous savons que tu es venu de chez le Seigneur en tant que professeur».
amharique: *ənnawqallän kä'əgziabher zänd əndä mäṭṭah mämhər hunäh* [19]
84. guèze: *räkäbomu läsäb'a yə'əti hagär kämä 'ənsəsa* (*Gädlä Täklä Haymanot* 29/4) [20].
«Il a trouvé les gens de ce pays comme des animaux».
amharique: *əndä ənsəsa honäw agäññaččäw*.

En fait l'amharique ne se contente pas de remplacer l'accusatif et la préposition du guèze par un verbe «grammatical» subordonné. Il s'en sert de façon tout-à-fait «redondante» lorsque les éléments de rection verbale sont déjà présents et même auprès de certains adverbes. Cette tendance générale à concevoir en termes de subordination verbale, donc prédicatifs, la relation entre un verbe et ces compléments peut s'expliquer de deux façons:

a. Si l'on accepte la définition de Hermann Paul que «Das Verhältnis von Subjekt mit Prädikat ... ist das Verhältnis, aus dem die übrigen syntaktischen Verhältnisse entspringen mit einer einzigen Ausnahme, nämlich der kopulativen Verbindung mehrerer Elemente zu einem Satzgliede» [21], on dira que l'amharique exprime sur la surface une relation prédicative fondamentale, qui dans les autres langues reste enfouie dans la structure profonde.

18 *Ethiopic New Testament*, The Bible Society, London, 1899.
19 *New Testament in Amharic*, The British and Foreign Bible Society, Addis Abäba, 1951.
20 Edition en guèze, Addis Abäba, 1946 c.é.
21 H. Paul, *Prinzipien der Sprachgeschichte*, Halle, 1937, p. 138.

b. L'autre explication tient compte de la structure générale de la proposition amharique. La tendance bien connue des langues néo-éthiopiennes à l'hypotaxe, qui se manifeste surtout par la multiplication de propositions subordonnées comportant un gérondif (ou une forme équivalente), donc adverbales, représente l'une des caractèristiques les plus frappantes de la phrase amharique, au point que ces constructions y constituent l'un des modèles syntaxiques les plus courants. Mais le gérondif n'est pas seulement utilisé pour transformer une proposition en proposition adverbale. Il sert souvent lui-même d'adverbe au verbe qui le suit et le modèle structural d'un verbe précédé d'un gérondif le déterminant ou complétant est très habituel dans la langue. Vu cette forme verbale de nombreuses déterminations jointes à un verbe, il n'est pas surprenant que sous l'effet du *Systemzwang* d'autres déterminations, dépourvues au départ d'un verbe, s'en attirent un, vide de son sens et tout-à-fait «grammatical», rien que pour se conformer au système.

Il est très significatif qu'une autre langue exhibant un penchant extrême pour l'hypotaxe — le turc — emploie des constructions avec des formes adverbales des verbes «être» et «dire» qui sont presque identiques à celles de l'amharique, par exemple [22] :

Muallim olarak geldiğim şehir.
«La ville où je suis venu (étant) [en qualité de] professeur».

Ben de bu Şakir Beyi pek edepsiz biri olarak tanıyordum.
«Moi aussi je connaîs ce Ş. *Bey* (étant) [comme] quelqu'un de très mal élevé».

Ömründe ilk defa olarak üzere bir araba düşündü.
«(Etant) pour la première fois dans sa vie il a pensé à une voiture».

Bugün de dahil olduğu halde önümüzdeki üç gün zarfında.
«Au au cours des trois prochains jours, y compris (étant) aujourd'hui».

Yadigâr diye sütannem satmıyor.
«Ma nourrice ne laisse pas vendre (disant) [parce que] c'est un souvenir».

Mesut bir aile babası diye düşündüm.
«J'ai pensé (disant) 'un père de famille heureux'».

Bir sınıflamaya temel diye alınabilir.
«Il peut être pris (disant) [comme] une base de classification».

---

22 Les exemples sont tirés de A.N. Kononov, *Grammatika sovremennogo tureckogo literaturnogo yazika*, Moscou, 1956, §594, 595, 858, 1083, 1087.

Karagayı bülbül diye sater.
«Il vend le corbeau (disant) [comme] un rossignol».

Il semble que nous pouvons définir les constructions qui ont été trai-
tées dans cet article comme une expression de la tendance générale de
l'amharique, en tant que langue à structure hypotactique, à rendre par la
subordination verbale des relations existant entre un verbe et ses déter-
minants.

Abréviations

AGRA	Abe Gubäñña, *Yäräggäfu abäbočč*, Addis Abäba, 1964 calendrier éthiopien.
AMYB	Amarä Mammo, *Yäəwnät bəlləčta*, Addis Abäba, 1967 c.é.
AWGr	Afevork Ghevre Jesus, *Grammatica della lingua amarica*, Rome, 1905.
AWGui	Afevork Ghevre Jesus, *Guide du voyageur en Abyssinie*, Rome, 1908.
AWR	Afä Wärq Gäbrä Iyäsus, *Ləbb wälläd tarik*, Rome, 1908.
BGQK	Bäalu Gərma, *Yäqäyy kokäb ṭərri*, Addis Abäba, 1980.
BZBF	Bərhanu Zäryəhun, *Yäbädäl fəṣṣame*, Addis Abäba, 1956 c.é.
DAŠŠ	Dännäqäw Asaye, *Šəffənu säwənnät*, 1969 c.é.
HAFM	Haddis Alämayyähu, *Fəqər əskä mäqabər²*, Addis Abäba, 1962 c.é.
HIFK	Haylä Iyäsus Fəqadu, *Käəngədih wädih adära əndayəddäggäm*, Addis Abäba, 1953 c.é.
HSFK	Haylä Səllase, *Fəre känafər*, t. II, Addis Abäba, 1944 c.é.
HSHI	Haylä Səllase, *Həywätənna yäItyopya ərməǧǧa*, Addis Abäba, 1965 c.é.
HWSW	Həruy Wäldä Səllase, *Wädaǧe ləbbeᴬ*, Addis Abäba, 1949 c.é.
KMIM	Käbbädä Mikael, *Ityopyanna məərabawi sələṭṭane*, Addis Abäba, 1941 c.é.
KMQA	Käbbädä Mikael, *Yäqəne azmära*, Addis Abäba, 1956 c.é.
KMRJ	Käbbädä Mikael, *Romewonna Juliet*, Addis Abäba, 1956 c.é.
LMND	Lämma Mängäša, *Yänäṣannät däwäl*, Addis Abäba, 1968 c.é.
MGLG	Mängəstu Gädamu, *Ləǧagäräditwa*, Addis Abäba, 1960 c.é.
MLṬB	Mängəstu Lämma, *Tälfo bäkise*, Addis Abäba, 1961 c.é.
PŇD	Pawlos Noňňo, *Dəbləqləq*, Addis Abäba, 1957 c.é.
PŇM	Pawlos Noňňo, *Məsqələql*, Addis Abäba.
Prog. Dic.	*Täramaǧ mäzgäbä qalat*, Addis Abäba, 1969 c.é.
ŠMMY	Šəfäraw Məhräte, *Məkər yalmälläsäw mäkära därräsäw*, Addis Abäba, 1960 c.é.
Traité	Voir note 3.
Tub.	J. Tubiana, *Recueil de versions amhariques*, Paris, 1966.

ÄTHIOPISCHE MARGINALGLOSSEN
ZUM SABÄISCHEN WÖRTERBUCH

WALTER W. MÜLLER
Universität Marburg

Wolf Leslau hat in seinen bahnbrechenden lexikographischen Arbeiten, die mit dem *Lexique soqoṭri* (Paris 1938) begannen und als deren vorläufig letzte Frucht er das dreibändige *Etymological Dictionary of Gurage* (Wiesbaden 1979) vorgelegt hat, über die jeweilige semitische Einzelsprache hinaus nie den gesamtsemitischen Hintergrund aus dem Auge verloren. Davon legen die sprachvergleichenden Partien in den beiden genannten Werken sowie etwa in der *Étude descriptive et comparative du gafat* (Paris 1956) und im *Etymological Dictionary of Harari* (Berkeley and Los Angeles 1963) beredtes Zeugnis ab. Einige seiner Veröffentlichungen, wie z.B. *Ethiopic and South Arabic Contributions to the Hebrew Lexicon* (Berkeley and Los Angeles 1958) und *Hebrew Cognates in Amharic* (Wiesbaden 1969), sind ausschließlich etymologischen Fragen gewidmet. Da von Wolf Leslau als nächstes größeres Unternehmen ein vergleichendes Wörterbuch des Altäthiopischen zu erwarten ist, mag es vielleicht angebracht sein, einige Randglossen zum Wortschatz der Geʿez-Sprache anzubringen.

Bei den etymologischen Glossen soll vom Altsüdarabischen lediglich das Sabäische (abgekürzt: Sab.) in Betracht gezogen werden; das Qatabānische, Mināische und Ḥaḍramitische (abgekürzt: Qat., Min., Ḥaḍr.) werden nur gelegentlich erwähnt, wenn ein Wort auch in den Inschriften jener Dialekte belegt ist. Ebenfalls ausgeklammert bleiben die altsüdarabischen epigraphischen Dokumente, welche auf äthiopischem Boden gefunden wurden. Der Verfasser erkennt dankbar an, daß er neben seinen eigenen Sammlungen zum Altsüdarabischen auch das in Gemeinschaftsarbeit mit A. F. L. Beeston, M. A. al-Ghul und J. Ryckmans entstandene Manuskript eines *Sabaic Dictionary* benutzen konnte, das nunmehr zum Druck gegeben wurde. Dieses Wörterbuch berücksichtigt jedoch keine Etymologien, sondern vermerkt nur diejenigen Fälle, in welchen eindeutig Entlehnungen aus anderen Sprachen im Sabäischen vorliegen. Zu äthiopischen Wörtern, die sich in altsüdarabischen Inschriften finden, vergleiche man W. W. Müller, Abessinier und ihre Namen und Titel in vorislamischen südarabischen Texten, in *Proceedings of the Fifth International Conference on Ethiopian Studies, Session B, April 13-16, 1978, Chicago, USA*, Chicago 1979, S. 309-314. Auf etymologische Vergleiche des Sabäischen mit anderen semitischen Sprachen Äthiopiens, etwa mit dem Tigre und

Tigrinya, wurde verzichtet, für einige bislang unbeachtet gebliebene altsüdarabische Parallelen zu den südäthiopischen Sprachen sei verwiesen auf
die Rezension von W. W. Müller von Wolf Leslaus *Etymological Dictionary of
Gurage*, in *ZDMG* 131 (1981), S. 396-404.

Eine Auflistung aller sabäischen Wörter bzw. Wurzeln, für welche sich
auch im Altäthiopischen Parallelen nachweisen lassen, würde einige hundert
Nummern erbringen. In der anschließend gegebenen Liste wurden daher,
von vereinzelten Ausnahmen abgesehen, nur solche sabäische Wörter berücksichtigt, die entweder überhaupt keine Entsprechungen im Arabischen besitzen oder bei welchen die arabischen Wurzel nur in einer völlig anderen
Bedeutung belegt ist. Gelegentlich wurde jedoch auch eine auffallende Über-
einstimmung in der Nominal- bzw. Verbalform als genügend erachtet, um ein
solches Wort aufzunehmen. Neben längst bekannten Entsprechungen stehen
zahlreiche Beispiele, die noch nirgends registriert wurden oder die wieder in
Vergessenheit geraten sind. Fragwürdige Gleichungen auf Grund veralteter
oder unzulänglicher Interpretationen sabäischer Inschriften wurden nicht
wiederholt. Am Schluß der einzelnen Abschnitte wurde öfters auf Werke
verwiesen, in denen auch die etymologischen Entsprechungen in anderen
semitischen und in weiteren äthiopischen Sprachen zu finden sind, besonders
auf W. Leslau, *Etymological Dictionary of Gurage* (abgekürzt: *EDG*) und auf
L. Koehler und W. Baumgartner, *Hebräisches und aramäisches Lexikon zum Alten
Testament*. Dritte Auflage. Leiden 1967 ff. (abgekürzt: *KBL³*).

Es erübrigt sich wohl, Inschriftensiglen wie CIH, RES und manche andere,
die zeit Jahrzehnten eingebürgert sind, aufzuschlüsseln und mit den dazu
gehörigen Literaturangaben zu versehen. Für neuere Inschriftenpublikationen
und darin verwendete Sigeln sei verwiesen auf Alessandra Avanzini, *Glossaire
des inscriptions de l'Arabie du Sud* 1950-1973, Vol. I, Firenze 1977 (*Quaderni di
Semitistica* 3), S. 1-18: A. Bibliographie, S. 19-185: B. Les inscriptions. Um
den Ort der Veröffentlichung von Inschriften der Sammlung Eduard Glaser
aufzufinden, konsultiere man Maria Höfner, *Sabäische Inschriften* (*Letzte Folge*)
Wien 1981 (*Sammlung Eduard Glaser XIV*. Österreichische Akademie der
Wissenschaften. Phil.-hist. Klasse, Sitzungsberichte, 378. Band), S. 49-59:
Verzeichnis der seit 1944 publizierten Gl-Inschriften. Außerdem wird das
obenerwähnte *Sabaic Dictionary* eine Bibliographie und ein Siglenverzeichnis
zur Literatur über die sabäischen Inschriften enthalten. [*Korrekturzusatz*: Das
Werk ist Ende 1982 bei den Editions Peeters in Louvain-la-Neuve erschienen;
S. XX-XXV: Sigla of the Inscriptions Cited, S. XXXIV-XLI: Bibliography.]

Sab. *'bn* »Stein«, und zwar der zum Bau verwendete Bruchstein (CIH 448
+ Hakir 1,2; CIH 540,30), pl. *'bn* (CIH 540,74); auch im Qat., Min. und Ḥaḍr.

belegt. — Geʿez ʾəbən »Stein«, pl. ʾaʾbān; s. für weitere Entsprechungen W. Leslau, *EDG*, III, S. 49b unter əmən.

Sab. ʾfy-m »eine Sorte Lebensmittel«, vielleicht »Gebackenes« (CIH 562,7). — Geʿez ʾəfüy »gebacken«; zu dem bei Dillmann, *Lexicon linguae aethiopicae*, Sp. 810, angeführten einzigen Beleg ist ein weiterer aus der Kirchenordnung des Hippolyt nachzutragen, s. E. Hammerschmidt, *Stellung und Bedeutung des Sabbats in Äthiopien*, Stuttgart 1963, S. 43; s. auch *KBL*³, S. 75b.

Sab. ʾkl »Getreide« (Gl 1537,7), »Nahrung, Speise« (Gl 1773b, 4; CIH 563 + 956,2). — Geʿez ʾəkəl »Getreide, Speise«; s. auch W. Leslau, *EDG*, III, S. 33b.

Sab. ʾmt »Elle« (CIH 570,2), pl. ʾmm (CIH 540,75; u.ö.); auch im Min. belegt. — Geʿez ʾəmmat »Elle«; s. auch *KBL*³, S. 59b.

Sab. coll. ʾnm »Weber« (RES 3945, 11.13); s. N. Rhodokanakis, *Altsabäische Texte I*, Wien 1927 (Akademie der Wissenschaften in Wien. Phil.-hist. Klasse, Sitzungsberichte, 206. Band, 2. Abh.), S. 74; jedenfalls Bezeichnung einer niederen sozialen Klasse. — Äth. ʾanāmī »Weber«.

Sab. ʾrft in ʾrfthw (RES 4922,4) »seine Mauer« oder »seine Grenze«, kaum jedoch »seine Oberfläche«, wie G. Ryckmans im *RES* übersetzt hat, s. G. Garbini in *Annali dell'Istituto Orientale di Napoli* 33 (1973), S. 436. — Geʿez ʾaraft »Wand, Mauer«, falls nicht arab. ʾurfa »Grenze« zur Erklärung herangezogen wird.

Sab. ʿbṭ (Ja 567,27; u.ö.), ʿbṭt (Ja 635,45), bezeichnet etwas Böses, wovor die Gottheit behüten möge, vielleicht »Frondienst« oder »Verleumdung«. — Geʿez ʿabaṭa »nötigen, zwingen«, oder aber arab. ʿabaṭa »verleumden«.

Sab. ʿḍ »Holz« (Ja 557) als Baumaterial, dann übertragen auf Bauelemente aus Stein, welche die Funktion des Holzes übernahmen; auch im Qat., Min. und Ḥaḍr. belegt. — Geʿez ʿəd »Holz«; s. für weitere Entsprechungen W. Leslau, *EDG*, III, S. 12b unter äçä, wo jedoch altsüdarab. ʿḍ (statt ʿṣ) zu lesen ist.

Sab. coll. mʿqbt »Wachen, Wächter« (RES 5085,10), und vielleicht auch mʿqb (CIH 45 + 44,4), beide Belege spätsabäisch. — Geʿez māʾqäb, pl. maʾāqəbt »Wachen, Wächter«.

Sab. ʿsy »opfern« (RES 2740,8; haramisch), daneben häufig in der Bedeutung »machen, erwerben, kaufen«, auch im Qat. und Min. belegt. — Geʿez ʿasaya »vergelten, Dank abstatten«; s. auch F. Rundgren, Zur arabischen Wortkunde. 1. Die Wurzel ʿśw und ihre Verwandten, in *Studia Orientalia in memoriam Caroli Brockelmann*, Halle 1968, S. 161f.

Sab. ʿśq »Anlage« (z. B. von Weingärten, RES 4194,3); hʿśq »bauen, anlegen« (z. B. einen Brunnen, YM 544,1, oder einen Paßweg, YMN 8,4); auch im Qat. und Min. belegt. — Geʿez ʿaśq (neben ʿasq, s. Dillmann, *Lexicon*, Sp. 972) »Wirkware, kunstvolles Gewebe«.

Sab. *'ṣd* »Dörfer« (Ja 574,5; Ja 575,3.4); s. Y. Shitomi, Une note sur *'ṣd*, in *Raydān* 4 (1981), S. 127-129. — Geʿez *'aṣad* »Dorf«.

Sab. *'tb* »weihen, bestimmen (zur Vernichtung)« (RES 3945,5.6; CIH 516,8-9; u.ö.; sämtliche Belege altsabäisch). — Geʿez *'ataba* »bezeichnen, kennzeichnen, besiegeln«.

Sab. coll. *b'r* »Rinder, Vieh« (RES 3945,18; CIH 535,10; u.ö.). — Geʿez *bəʾrāwī* »Rind, Ochs«; s. für weitere Entsprechungen W. Leslau, *EDG*, III, S. 150b unter *bora*.

Sab. *brr* »durchbrechen, ausbrechen (Vulkan)« (CIH 323,2; s. W.W. Müller und H. v. Wissmann, Über die von einem Lavastrom bedrohten Tempel der Stadt Damhān ..., in *Anzeiger der phil.-hist. Klasse der Österreichischen Akademie der Wissenschaften*, 113. Jg. 1976, S. 117); »einen Ausbruch (zum Kampf) machen, sich (zum Kampf) stellen« (Ry 614,6; Ja 631,28.31); qat. *brr* »(einen Bergweg) durchstechen, durchbrechen« (RES 3550,3; RES 4328,5). — Geʿez *barara* »durchdringen«.

Sab. *d'* (CIH 540,66; CIH 541,12.50; Ry 507,7; sämtlich spätsabäisch), Bedeutung entweder »schon« oder »nicht«. — Zur Bedeutung »schon« wurde Geʿez *wadʾa* »vollenden« verglichen, vor einem Perfekt »schon«; zur Bedeutung »nicht« vergleiche man jetzt die Belege in der altäthiopischen, im altsüdarabischen Alphabet abgefaßten Inschrift des *Wʿzb*, etwa *lddʾ/ymt* »dem, der unsterblich ist«, s. R. Schneider, Quelques remarques linguistiques sur l'inscription de Wʿzb, fils de Kaleb, in *Comptes rendus du Groupe Linguistique d'études chamito-sémitiques* 18/23 (1973-1979), S. 93-95, wo nicht nur sämtliche Beispiele aus jener Inschrift gebracht werden, sondern auch die Literatur über die Erörterung der Bedeutung von sab. *d'* vollständig angeführt ist.

Sab. *dglmt-m* »Schmuckringe, Armspangen (aus Gold und Silber, als Beutestücke von den Äthiopiern)« (in Z. 13 einer der großen, noch unveröffentlichten Felsinschriften von Miʿsāl). — Geʿez *dəgʷəlmā, dəlgʷəmā* »Schmuckring, Armspange«, das nach Th. Nöldeke, Lehnwörter in und aus dem Äthiopischen, in *Neue Beiträge zur semitischen Sprachwissenschaft*, Straßburg 1910, S. 53, im Anschluß an S. Fraenkel der Prototyp von arab. *dumluǧ* »Armreif« sein soll.

Sab. *mdlt* »Gewicht, Wert, Preis« (RES 4191,6; Ja 609,5; u.ö.), ḥaḍr. *mdlw-t* »dessen Gewicht« (RES 2693,2-3). — Geʿez *madlōt*, pl. *madāləw* »Gewicht, Wert«.

Sab. *ḏmr* »eine Entscheidung treffen« (Gl 1574,7; Ja 669,20-21; u.ö.). — Geʿez *tazam(m)ara* »sich als Autorität berufen auf, als Zeugnis anführen« (*Qērellos*, ed. B.M. Weischer, 1973ff., III, S. 44,15; IV 2, S. 28,19-30,1).

Sab. *ḏnm* »regnen« (Ja 651,17; Ja 735,12), *ḏnm* »Regen« (CIH 28,7; Ja 651,17; u.ö.). — Geʿez *zanma, zanama* »regnen«, *zənām* »Regen«; s. für weitere Entsprechungen W. Leslau, *EDG*, III, S. 710a unter *zänäbä*.

Sab. *ḍbʾ* »einen Kriegszug unternehmen, Krieg führen« (CIH 516,6; RES 3884,9; u.ö.), *ḍbʾt* »Kriegszug« (YM 349,9; u.ö.), auch pl. (Ja 636,6-7). — Geʿez *ḍabʾa* »Krieg führen« (Dillmann, *Lexicon*, Sp. 1281 unter *ṣabʾa*), *ḍabʾ*, pl. *ḍabʾāt* »Krieg«; s. W. Leslau, *EDG, III*, S. 610a unter *ṭäbäññä*.

Sab. *ḍbḥ* »Abgabe leisten« (Gl A 744,4; s. Maria Höfner, *Sabäische Inschriften (Letzte Folge)*, S. 30f.). — Geʿez *ḍabbəḥa* »Tribut entrichten, Abgabe leisten« (Dillmann, *Lexicon*, Sp. 1278 unter *ṣabbəḥa*).

Sab. *ḍr* »Feind« (CIH 314,22; CIH 573,5; u.ö.); im Sab. und Min. *ḍr* auch »Krieg«. — Geʿez *ḍar(r)* »Feind«; s. W. Leslau, *EDG, III*, S. 629b unter *ṭärä*.

Sab. *fdfdt-m* »reichlich tragend, fruchtbar (von Palmgärten)« (RES 4781,2). — Geʿez *fədfād* »reichlich, zahlreich«.

Sab. *flś* »in die Flucht schlagen, verjagen« (CIH 334,11; Nāmī NAG 13 + 14,3). — Geʿez *ʾaflasa* »vertreiben«.

Sab. *flṭ* »(Land) zuweisen, übereignen« (Gl 1444,1), auch im Qat. belegt. — Geʿez *falaṭa* »absondern, trennen«.

Sab. *fnwt* »Wasserweg, (Haupt)kanal« (CIH 611,3; CIH 657,3; u.ö.), pl. *fnw* (CIH 329,2.4; CIH 380,4). — Geʿez *fənōt*, pl. *fənāw* »Weg«.

Sab. *hfśḥ* »mit Freude erfüllen« (Šarafaddīn, *Tārīḫ* III, Nr. 31,12; s. W. W. Müller, Eine sabäische Gesandtschaft in Ktesiphon und Seleukeia, in *Neue Ephemeris für Semitische Epigraphik* 2, 1974, S. 163). — Geʿez *astafaśśəḥa* »erfreuen, mit Freude erfüllen«.

Sab. *tgʿr* »(zusammen)gerufen werden, einberufen werden« (Ja 577,13; Ja 665,14; Iryānī 32,18; s. W. W. Müller, Das Ende des antiken Königreichs Ḥaḍramaut. Die sabäische Inschrift Schreyer-Geukens = Iryānī 32, in *Al-Hudhud. Festschrift Maria Höfner zum 80. Geburtstag*. Hrsg. von Roswitha G. Stiegner, Graz 1981, S. 237). — Geʿez *gəʿara, gaʿara* »rufen«; s. für weitere Entsprechungen W. Leslau, *EDG, III*, S. 288b unter *(a)gʷarra*.

Sab. *gbʾ* »zurückkehren« (CIH 541,50.80; CIH 621,8), »zurückbringen« (Ja 670,28); *hgbʾ* »zurückgeben« (RES 3910,4; Gl 1574,10.12), »übergeben« (Ja 576,2), »wiederherstellen« (CIH 365,9; RES 4775,2). — Geʿez *gabʾa* »zurückkehren«, *agbəʾa* »zurückgeben, zurückbringen«; s. für andere äthiopische Sprachen W. Leslau, *EDG, III*, S. 255 unter *gäba*.

Sab. *hgr* »Stadt«, d.h. eine von Mauern umgebene Siedlung; bis zum heutigen Tag wird Haǧar in manchen Gegenden Südarabiens für die Ruinen antiker Städte gebraucht; pl. *ʾhgr* (CIH 363,1; RES 3945,5; u.ö.). — Geʿez *hagar*, pl. *ʾahgur* »Stadt«; bei Dillmann, *Lexicon*, Sp. 20, bereits mit dem Hinweis auf arabisch *haǧar*, das als ḥimyarisches Wort überliefert ist; s. für andere äthiopische Sprachen W. Leslau, *EDG, III*, S. 26b unter *agär*.

Sab. *mhrk-m* »Beute« (Fa 119,8 = YM 358,8), falls nicht doch statt dessen *mhrgm* »Tötungen« zu lesen sein sollte (s. A. F. L. Beeston in *Corpus des inscriptions et antiquités sud-arabes*, Tome I, Section 1, S. 50). — Geʿez *məhrəkā* »Beute«; s. für andere äthiopische Sprachen W. Leslau, *EDG*, III, S. 421a unter *maräkä*.

Sab. *ḫdg* »lassen, verlassen« (Ja 643,29; Ja 644,9), »zurücklassen« (Gl 1369,2), »ablassen« (CIH 99,9; CIH 380,5), »unterlassen« (Ja 2834,4), wobei in den drei zuletzt angeführten Belegen *ḫdg* statt *ḫdl* gelesen wurde. — Geʿez *ḫadaga* »lassen, verlassen, zurücklassen, hinterlassen, ablassen, weglassen, unterlassen«; s. für andere äthiopische Sprachen W. Leslau, *EDG*, III, S. 15 f. unter *adägä*.

Sab. *mḫdr* »Wohnplatz, Residenz« (Ja 547,3-4; spätsabäisch). — Geʿez *māḫdar* »Wohnung, Niederlassung«; s. zur Wurzel *ḫdr* Leslau, *EDG*, III, S. 17b unter *addärä*.

Sab. *ḫrf* (häufig belegt) »Spätsommer, Herbst« (neben *dṯ'* »Frühjahr«), »Jahr«. — Geʿez *ḫarīf* »(laufendes) Jahr«.

Sab. *ḫry* »erretten, bewahren« (CIH 343,9; RES 3992,12; u.ö.). — Geʿez *ḫaraya, ḫarya* »(aus)wählen, vorziehen«.

Sab. *ḫḫ* in der Dualform *ḫḫnhn* »die beiden Durchgänge« (Ja 552,3). — Geʿez *ḫōḫt* »Tür, Tor, Eingang«; s. für weitere Entsprechungen *KBL³*, S. 284b.

Sab. *ḫyl* »Macht, Kraft« (CIH 541,1; Gl 1177,6; u.ö.). — Geʿez *ḫayl* »Macht, Kraft«; s. *KBL³*, S. 298b.

Sab. *mḫfd* »Turm, Bastion, Vorbau (einer Mauer)« (CIH 448 + Hakir 1,1; RES 4943,4; u.ö.), pl. *mḫfdt*; auch im Qat., Min. und Ḥaḍr. belegt. — Geʿez *māḫfad* (im Hinblick auf das Altsüdarab. besser so statt *māḥfad* wie bei Dillmann, *Lexicon*, Sp. 628) »Turm«, pl. *māḫfadāt*.

Sab. *ḫg* »Gesetz, Recht« (RES 3945,2; Gl 1143,3; u.ö.); auch im Min. belegt. — Geʿez *ḫəgg* »Gesetz, Recht«.

Sab. *ḫqw* in den Dualformen *ḫqwnhn* »die Hüften, Lenden« (Ja 711,5), *ḫqwyhw* »seine Hüften, Lenden« (Ja 700,13). — Geʿez *ḫaqʷē* »Hüften, Lenden« als erstarrter Dual; s. für andere äthiopische Sprachen W. Leslau, *EDG*, III, S. 72 unter *anqä*.

Sab. *ḫrḍ* »Mehlkuchen(?)« (CIH 562,6). — Geʿez *ḫarīḍ* »Mehl, Teig«; s. für andere äthiopische Sprachen W. Leslau, *EDG*, III, S. 93a unter *arṭ*, wo nach K. Conti Rossini, *Chrestomathia arabica meridionalis epigraphica*, Roma 1931, S. 158, altsüdarab. *ḫrṣ* »Mehl« angegeben wird, das aber höchstwahrscheinlich »Schätzung« bedeutet.

Sab. *mḫrm* »Heiligtum, Tempel« (CIH 140,8; CIH 398,12; u.ö.), pl. *mḫrmt* (CIH 323,5; Ja 629,28). — Geʿez *məḫrām*, pl. *məḫrāmāt* »Heiligtum, Tempel«.

Sab. *ḫyqn/qn'* »der Strand von Qanaʾ, der Anlegeplatz von Qanaʾ« (Iryānī 13§13); auch mehri *ḫayq* »Strand«. — Geʿez *ḫayq* »Küste, Strand«.

Sab. *ḫyw* »leben, am Leben bleiben« (RES 4938,7-8, Ry 375,4; u.ö.); *ḫywt*

»Leben« (Ja 764,3). — Ge'ez *ḥaywa* »leben«; *ḥaywat* »Leben«; s. für weitere Entsprechungen *KBL³*, S. 296b.

Sab. *khl* »imstande sein« (Ja 651,36); auch mehri *kəhēl* »vermögen, imstande sein«. — Ge'ez *kəhəla* »vermögen, imstande sein«; aramäisch *kəhal*; s. für andere äthiopische Sprachen W. Leslau, *EDG*, III, S. 173 unter *čalä*.

Sab. *kl'y* »beide« (Ja 557) neben *kly* (Ja 644,24; u.ö.), *kl'ty* (Ja 672,1). — Ge'ez *kəl'ē*, *kəl'ētū* »zwei«; s. auch W. Leslau, *EDG*, III, S. 356 unter *kʷett*.

Sab. *mkrb* »Tempel, Synagoge« (Gl 1194,4; Ry 520,4; u.ö.; sämtlich spätsabäisch). — Ge'ez *məkʷrāb* »Tempel, Synagoge«.

Sab. *l'l* »oberhalb, aufwärts« (Maṣna'at Māriya, 5), auch im Min. belegt; *l-l'l* »darüber hinaus« (CIH 80,11). — Ge'ez *lā'əla* »auf, über«; s. für andere äthiopische Sprachen W. Leslau, *EDG*, III, S. 378a unter *lalä*.

Sab. *mdr* »Boden (eines Grabes)« (RES 4231,5), pl. *'mdr* »Gebiete« (RES 3951,4). — Ge'ez *mədər*, pl. *'amdār* »Erde, Boden, Gebiet«; s. auch W. Leslau, *EDG*, III, S. 392a.

Sab. *mḥly-m* »Eid, Schwur« (Gl 1533,6; s. Maria Höfner, *Inschriften aus Ṣirwāḥ, Ḥaulān (I. Teil)*. Wien 1973 (*Sammlung Eduard Glaser VIII. Öster-reichische Akademie der Wissenschaften. Phil.-hist. Klasse, Sitzungsberichte, 291. Band, 1. Abh., S. 31). — Ge'ez *maḥalā* »Eid, Schwur«; s. für andere äthiopische Sprachen W. Leslau, *EDG*, III, S. 401b unter *malä*.

Sab. *mrt-n* »Kalkstein« (Fa 90,2), auch im Qat. und Min. belegt. — Ge'ez *marēt* »Lehm, Kalk«.

Sab. *myṭ* »Wein?« (Robin/Kāniṭ 6,2). — Ge'ez *mēs* »Honigwein«, bereits inschriftlich belegt, s. A. J. Drewes, *Inscriptions de l'Éthiopie antique*, Leiden 1962, S. 36.

Sab. *mzr-m/ḏtmr-m* »Dattelwein« (CIH 540,50-51; spätsabäisch). — Ge'ez *məzər* »Bier«; zu arab. *miẓr* s. Th. Nöldeke, Lehnwörter in und aus dem Äthiopischen, in *Neue Beiträge zur semitischen Sprachwissenschaft*, Straßburg 1910, S. 57.

Sab. *mẓ'* »(an)kommen, gelangen, erreichen« (CIH 364,1; CIH 581,7; u.ö.); *hmz'* »überlassen, überweisen« (Gl 1533,1; Gl 1572,1; u.ö.), »zukommen lassen, durchführen, ausführen« (Garbini AION 33, 1973, 37,6). — Ge'ez *maṣ'a* »kommen«; s. für weitere Entsprechungen *KBL³*, S. 585b, und W. Leslau, *EDG*, III, S. 437a unter *mäṭa*.

Sab. *nfq-n* »Sarkophag« (s. J. Ryckmans, Rezension von Sammlung Eduard Glaser VI, in *Bibliotheca Orientalis* 29, 1972, S. 92) (Gl 1656/1 = AM 221/2), auch im Min. in der Sarkophaginschrift RES 3427/1 bezeugt. - Ge'ez *nafq*, *nəfq* »Kasten, Sarg«.

Sab. *nfṣ* »aufbrechen, ausziehen, marschieren« (Iryānī 13§10; Iryānī 32,12; u.ö.; s. W. W. Müller in *Al-Hudhud. Festschrift Maria Höfner*, S. 238). — Ge'ez *nafṣa* »fliehen, weggehen«.

Sab. *ngš* »unter Kontrolle bringen« oder »Tribut auferlegen« (Iryānī 32,37; s. W. W. Müller in *Al-Hudhud. Festschrift Maria Höfner*, S. 244); auch im Min. belegt. — Äth. *nagśa* »die Herrschaft erlangen, herrschen«; s. für weitere Entsprechungen W. Leslau, *EDG*, III, S. 454b unter *nägäsä*.

Sab. *tnhy* »(Sünden) bekennen, (öffentlich) beichten« (CIH 523,1; CIH 533,1; u.ö.). — Ge῾ez *tanāḥaya* (so wohl besser statt *tanāḥaya*, Dillmann, *Lexicon*, Sp. 632; s. bereits Fr. Praetorius in *ZDMG* 66, 1912, S. 786f.) »(Sünden) bekennen«.

Sab. *ḥnśg* »zusammenfügen«, d.h. die einzeln gegossenen Teile einer Bronze-statue zusammenfügen und durch Querstücke miteinander befestigen; s. W. W. Müller, The Inscriptions on the Hellenistic Bronze Statues from Nakhlat al-Ḥamrā', Yemen, in *Proceedings of the Seminar for Arabian Studies* 9 (1979), S. 79. — Ge῾ez *nasaga* (Dillmann, *Lexicon*, Sp. 639, neben *naśaga*) »mit einem Bolzen befestigen, mit einem Riegel verschließen«; vgl. *mansag/manśag* »Riegel, Querstück (um etwas zu befestigen)«.

Sab. *mqdḥ* »Gefäß, (Opfer)schale« (CIH 972; RES 2740,7). — Ge῾ez *maqdəḥt* »Krug, Gefäß«.

Sab. *qšmt* »Gemüsegarten, Pflanzung« (CIH 308,9); vgl. auch jemenitisch-arab. *qušm* »Gemüse« (s. E. Glaser, *Altjemenische Studien*, hrsg. von O. Weber, Leipzig 1923, S. 83, Anm.). — Ge῾ez *qaśama* »ernten, sammeln, lesen«.

Sab. *qṭn-m* »klein« oder »niedrig« (CIH 609,7; Gl 1547,8; u.ö.; meist zusammen mit *bḥt-m* »groß« oder »hoch«); vgl. auch mehri *qeṭáyn* »dünn, fein«. — Ge῾ez *qaṭīn* »zart, klein«; s. für weitere Entsprechungen Gesenius-Buhl, *Hebräisches und aramäisches Handwörterbuch über das Alte Testament*, 17. Aufl., S. 710a, und W. Leslau, *EDG*, III, S. 508b.

Sab. pl. *rdyt* »Zinsen« (Gl 1547,2; s. Brigitte Schaffer, *Sabäische Inschriften aus verschiedenen Fundorten*. Wien 1972 (*Sammlung Eduard Glaser VII. Öster-reichische Akademie der Wissenschaften. Phil.-hist. Klasse, Sitzungsberichte, 282. Band, 1 Abh.*, S. 41). — Ge῾ez *rədē* »Zinsen«.

Sab. *rḥq* »fern sein« (CIH 343,9-10; CIH 609,7; u.ö.), *rḥq-m* »fern« (Fa 3,8; RES 3929,13; u.ö.); auch mehri *rəḥāq* »fern sein«. — Ge῾ez *rəḥqa* »fern sein«, *rəḥūq* »fern«; s. auch W. Leslau, *EDG*, III, S. 526b unter *raqä*.

Sab. *rḥś* »ein Libationsopfer darbringen(?)« (CIH 428,2). — Ge῾ez *rəḥsa* »feucht sein oder werden«, *'arḥasa* »feucht machen, eintauchen«; s. für andere äthiopische Sprachen W. Leslau, *EDG*, III, S. 527b unter *rasä*.

Sab. *sfrt* »Ausdehnung« (CIH 570,5). — Ge῾ez *səfrat* »Maß, Ausmaß«; zur Wurzel *sfr* s. W. Leslau, *EDG*, III, S. 538a.

Sab. *sm῾* »Zeuge sein, bezeugen« (CIH 570,9); *sm῾* »Zeuge(n)« (RES 4123,1), »Zeugnis, Urkunde, Dokument« (Gl 1572,4; u.ö.). — Ge῾ez *sam'a* »Zeuge sein, bezeugen«, *səm῾* »Zeuge, Zeugnis«.

Sab. *sslt* aus **snslt* »Kette« (Ry 508,8; Ja 1028,4.8), *sślt* (Ry 507,10), sämtliche Belege spätsabäisch; vgl. auch harsusi *senselēt* und südarab. *sinsila* neben *silsila* (C. de Landberg, *Glossaire Datînois*, S. 1964). — Ge'ez *sansal* »Kette«; s. für andere äthiopische Sprachen W. Leslau, *EDG*, III, S. 554a unter *sänsälät*.

Sab. *msty* »Trank, Getränk« (CIH 563 + 956,2). — Ge'ez *mastē* »Trinken, Trank«; zur Wurzel *sty* s. W. Leslau, *EDG*, III, S. 534b unter *säče*.

Sab. *hstw* »gewähren« (Gl 1574,14 = RES 4964,12; s. J. Ryckmans, Le sens de *d'l* en sud-arabe, in *Le Muséon* 67, 1954, S. 348). — Ge'ez *'asaṭṭawa, tasaṭwa* »annehmen, gewähren, erhören«.

Sab. *'yṭ* »(Wasser)güsse, (Wasser)zuflüsse (Ja 735,14). — Ge'ez *sōṭa* »gießen, ausgießen, vergießen«.

Sab. *śrh* »schützen, bewahren«, auch »erfolgreich durchführen« (Ja 564,13), *śrh* »Erfolg, Gelingen« (BR-M. Bayḥān 3,15). — Ge'ez *śarrəha* »erfolgreich sein«.

Sab. *śry* »heil bewahren, (er)retten« (Gl 1366,4), *hśry* (CIH 313,3). — Ge'ez *śar(r)aya* »heilen«.

Sab. *śym* »errichten« (Ja 651,32), »aufstellen« (Ja 576,13), »einsetzen« (CIH 496,5), »festsetzen« (CIH 349,6), etc. — Ge'ez *śēma* »einsetzen«; s. für weitere Entsprechungen W. W. Müller, *Die Wurzeln mediae und tertiae y/w im Altsüdarabischen*, Tübingen 1962, S. 71.

Sab. *mśwr* »Bewässerungskanal« (RES 4781,1). — Ge'ez pl. *masāwər* »Gießgefäß, Spund, Schnabel (zum Eingießen)« (eher unter *swr*, Dillmann, *Lexicon*, Sp. 385, statt unter *śwr*, ebd., Sp. 255).

Sab. *ṣhf* »schreiben, ein Dokument abfassen« (CIH 314 + 954,9), *ṣhft* »Schriftstück, Dokument« (CIH 314 + 954,8.11; YM 546,2); *ṣhft* auch im Qat. und Min. belegt. — Ge'ez *ṣahafa* »schreiben«, *ṣəhfat* »Schrift, Inschrift, Aufschrift«; s. für andere äthiopische Sprachen W. Leslau, *EDG*, III, S. 569b unter *ṣafä*.

Sab. *ṣlt* »Steinbau« oder »Steinpflasterung« (DJE 12,2.4; CIH 325,2), *ṣll* »Steinpflasterung« (CIH 40,3), auch im Qat. belegt; vgl. jemenitisch-arab. *ṣalla*, pl. *ṣalāl* »flache Pflastersteine«. — Ge'ez *ṣallē, ṣallā*, pl. *ṣallāt* »(steinerne) Tafel«; s. W. W. Müller in *Neue Ephemeris für Semitische Epigraphik* 1 (1972), S. 90.

Sab. *ṣn'* »befestigen« (Ry 508,8; Ja 1028,8, u.ö.); *tṣn'* »sich verschanzen« (CIH 353,6; CIH 541,77; u.ö.), *stṣn'* (CIH 621,8). — Ge'ez *ṣan'a* »stark, fest sein«, *taṣann'a* »sich stärken, Kräfte sammeln«, *astaṣānə'a* »befestigen«; s. für andere äthiopische Sprachen W. Leslau, *EDG*, III, S. 622b unter *(a)ṭänna*.

Sab. *ṣyh* »anlegen (z. B. eine Pflanzung)« (CIH 158,2; RES 4920,2; u.ö.). — Ge'ez *ṣēha* »ebnen«.

Sab. _t̠qr_ »(eine Zisterne) aushauen« (Grjaznevič 1,1). — Geʿez _saqʷara_
»durchbohren, durchstechen, durchgraben«.

Sab. _stwdd_ »übereinkommen« (Rathjens 14,5; Robin/al-Mašāmain 1,1;
Umm Laylā 1,4). — Geʿez _astawādada_ »gut ineinanderfügen, passen, überein-
stimmen«.

Sab. _wdq_ »stürzen« (Ja 619,7), »einstürzen« (Ja 651,20), »befallen, fallen
über« (YM 440,8); _dqt_ »Sturz« (Ja 619,7), _wdqt_ »Einsturz« (CIH 396,9; Ja
651,12). — Geʿez _wadaqa_ »fallen, einstürzen«, _dəqat, wədqat_ »Fall, Sturz,
Einsturz«; s. für andere äthiopische Sprachen W. Leslau, _EDG_, III, S. 644a.

Sab. _wḍ'_ »hinausgehen« (CIH 532,5), »ausfließen« (RES 3945,2), »heraus-
kommen, sich ergeben« (CIH 570,6); auch im Qat. belegt; _hwḍ'_ »hinausführen,
hinausleiten« (CIH 615,5), »hinaustreiben« (RES 4176,6). — Geʿez _waḍ'a_
»hinausgehen«, _'awḍə'a_ »hinausführen«; s. für weitere Entsprechungen _KBL³_,
S. 406a, und W. Leslau, _EDG_, III, S. 672a unter _wäṭa_, wo jedoch altsüdarab.
_wḍ'_ (statt _wṣ'_) zu lesen ist.

Sab. _mwfr_ »bebautes und bewirtschaftetes Land (das zu einer Stadt gehört)«
(CIH 506,3), _mfr_ (CIH 546,2; Gl 1142,5); auch im Min. belegt. — Geʿez _mūfār_
»(die zu einer Stadt gehörenden) Gehöfte, Grundstücke und Fluren«.

Sab. _wft̠_ »(nieder)brennen, verbrennen« (RES 3943,3; RES 3945,3; u.ö.;
sämtlich altsabäisch). — Geʿez _wafaṭa_ »verbrennen«.

Sab. _wgr_ »steinigen« (Robin/al-Mašāmain 1,10; s. W. W. Müller, Altsüdarabische Miszellen, in _Raydān_ 3, 1980, S. 68f.). — Geʿez _wagara_ »steinigen«.

Sab. _wkḫy-m_ »Streit, Auseinandersetzung?« (ST 1,15; A. F. L. Beeston in
Corpus des inscriptions et antiquités sud-arabes, Tome I, Section 1, S. 42:
»ignominiously«). — Geʿez _wakəḫ, wakḫat_ (_Qērellos_, ed. B. M. Weischer,
1973ff., IV 3, S. 106,3) »Streit, Lärm«; s. _KBL³_, S. 391bf., und W. Leslau,
EDG, III, S. 649b unter _wäkka_ III.

Sab. _wqr_ »Stein, in welchen etwas eingemeißelt ist« (CIH 438,1; CIH 601,14;
CIH 947,4); auch im Min. belegt. — Geʿez _wəqrō_ »behaune Steine«; s. für
andere äthiopische Sprachen W. Leslau, _EDG_, III, S. 659a.

Sab. _wrḫ_, pl. _'wrḫ_ »Monat« (zahlreiche Belege); vgl. auch mehri _wārāḫ, warḫ_.
— Geʿez _warḫ_, pl. _'awrāḫ_ »Monat«; s. _KBL³_, S. 418a, und W. Leslau, _EDG_,
III, S. 660a unter _wär_ I.

Sab. _wrq_ »Gold« (_bl̠tm/wrq_, »Goldmünzen«, Garbini AION 30, 1970,
540,2-3; _t̠lt̠y/wrqm_, »dreißig Gold(münzen)«, Grjaznevič 14,1); auch im Qat.
belegt. — Geʿez _wrq_ »Gold, Goldmünze«; s. für andere äthiopische Sprachen
W. Leslau, _EDG_, III, S. 664a.

Sab. _wrw_ »angreifen, Feindseligkeiten begehen« (RES 3945,13; altsabäisch).
— Geʿez _warawa_ »werfen«; s. W. Leslau, _EDG_, III, S. 666 unter _wəräwärä_.

Sab. _ḥwš'_ »erhören, (eine Bitte) gewähren, Gunst erweisen, (im Orakel) einen Respons verleihen« (CIH 314,6; Gl 1655,4; u.ö.; s. Maria Höfner, *Inschriften aus Ṣirwāḥ, Ḥaulān (I. Teil)*, S. 59). — Geʿez *awśəʾa* (wohl besser so statt mit Dillmann, *Lexicon*, Sp. 895 unter *wśʾ*) »Antwort geben, erhören«.

Sab. *wṣḥ* »ankommen, erreichen« (CIH 540,7; CIH 541,24; u.ö.; sämtlich spätsabäisch). — Geʿez *baṣḥa* »ankommen, erreichen«.

Sab. *wṭn* »Grenzsteine setzen, Grenze ziehen« (CIH 949,4; RES 3945,17), *twṭn* (CIH 610,2-3; Ry 366,2); *wṭn* »Grenzstein, Grenze« (CIH 389,4-5; Gl 1520,2; u.ö.). — Geʿez *wassana, tawassana* »begrenzen«, *wasan* »Grenze«; s. für andere äthiopische Sprachen W. Leslau, *EDG*, III, S. 668a.

Sab. *wyn* »Weingarten« (CIH 522,2; RES 4196,2; u.ö.), pl. *ʾwyn* (Nami NAG 13 + 14,3). — Geʿez *wayn*, pl. *ʾawyān* »Weinstock, Weingarten«; s. *KBL³*, S. 391.

Sab. *ẓlm* »schwarz?« (neben *ḥmrt* »rot?«; RES 3945,15; altsabäisch); auch in den sabäischen Inschriften aus Äthiopien belegt in der Form *ṣlm* (neben *ʾdm* »rot«), s. A. J. Drewes, The Lexicon of Ethiopian Sabaean, in *Raydān* 3 (1980), S. 39f. — Geʿez *ṣalīm* »schwarz«; s. W. Leslau, *EDG*, III, S. 180 unter *ṣällämä*.

LA COPULE NÄW EN AMHARIQUE
DANS UNE PERSPECTIVE CHAMITOSÉMITIQUE ET AFRICAINE

Karel Petráček
L'Université Charles, Prague

La copule *näw* en amharique a été plusieurs fois étudiée dans les grammaires respectives [1] dans son aspect formel, fonctionnel et temporel. Nous connaissons encore quelques études spéciales destinées à ce thème [2]. Dans ces travaux

---

1 M. Cohen, *Traité de langue amharique*, Paris 1936, 1970[2], 148ss.; Fr. Praetorius, *Die amharische Sprache*, Halle 1879, 257-8, 414-19; C. H. Armbruster, *Initia Amharica. An Introduction to Spoken Amharic*, P. I, Grammar, Cambridge 1908, 69-70; I. Guidi, *Grammatica elementare della lingua amarica*, Napoli 1924, 12; A. Klingenhaben, *Deutsch-amharischer Sprachführer*, Wiesbaden 1966, 42; C. H. Dawkins, *Fundamentals of Amharic*, Addis Ababa, 1960; W. Leslau, *Amharic Textbook*, Wiesbaden 1967,37; J. Hartmann, *Amharische Grammatik*, 1979; E. B. Gankin, and Kasa Gebre-Hiywot, *Amharsko-russkiy slovar*, Moskva 1969, 942-3.

2 Le problème de la copule en général:
J. Lyons, *Introduction to Theoretical Linguistics*, Cambridge 1968, 322; H. Gipper, *Bausteine zur Sprachinhaltsforschung*, Düsseldorf 1963, 135-214 (Arabisch 184); voir aussi la série par J. W. M. Verhaar, ed., *The Verb «Be» and its Synonyms*. Philosophical and Grammatical Studies, Dordrecht, 4 (1969), 5 (1972) et toute la série (depuis 1, 1967).
La fonction présentative:
R. Hetzron, «Presentative Function and Presentative Movement», *Studies in African Linguistics*, Suppl. 2, October 1971, 79-105.
Dans les langues sémitiques:
C. Brockelmann, *Grundriss der vergleichenden Grammatik der semitischen Sprachen*, II, Berlin 1913, 102ss.; M. Cohen, *Le système verbal en sémitique et l'expression du temps*, Paris 1924, 104-6; G. Ryckmans, «L'idée d'existence en sémitique», *Tijdschrift voor philosophie* 23, no. 2, 1961, 318-322; Fadlou Shehadi, «Arabic and 'to Be'», in: J. W. M. Verhaar, ed., *The Verb «be» and its Synonyms*, IV, 1969, Dordrecht, 112-125; Wolfram von Soden, *Sprache, Denken und Begriffbildung im Alten Orient*, Wiesbaden 1973, 21, 34 etc.; J. Barr, «The Expression of Being in the Semitic and the Related Languages», conférence pour Second Int. Congress of Hamito-Semitic Languages, Firenze 1974 (seulement dans le préprint!).
Dans les langues sémitiques éthiopiennes:
R. Hetzron, *Ethiopian Semitic. Studies in Classification*, Manchester 1972, 79-85; W. Leslau, «Supplement. Characteristics of the Ethiopic Language Group of Semitic Languages», in: A. N. Tucker, M. A. Bryan, *Linguistic Analyses. The Non-Bantu Languages of North-Eastern Africa*, London, 1966, 603; W. Leslau, *Etymological Dictionary of Gurage (Ethiopic)*, III, Wiesbaden 1979, 444 s.v. /ə/n; W. Leslau, *Étude descriptive et comparative du gafat (éthiopien méridional)*, Paris 1956, 79-80; G. Goldenberg, «The Semitic Languages of Ethiopia and their Classification», *BSOAS* XL, 1977, 461-506 (Copulas 478ss.; ici sur les copules à n, t, u, š; voir aussi G. Goldenberg, «A Copula ✝ in Old Amharic», *Israel Oriental Studies* VI,

nous constatons la forme spécifique de la copule *näw* consistant dans la base *na-* munie des suffixes pronominaux objectifs qui ont été en partie supprimés au cours de l'évolution et prouvent ainsi la transition de cette base vers la sphère verbale/parfait [3]; on met en relief l'assymétrie de sa forme du parfait et de son temps présent [4]. Parfois, on montre les formes analogues dans les autres langues sémitiques d'Éthiopie [5] et dans le cadre du sémitique en général [6].

L'étymologie de la base à -*N*- (*nä*) s'appuie sur les données des langues éthiopiennes et sémitiques et suppose son origine dans une particule présentative ou deïctique, alors dans la sphère non-verbale [7].

1976, 131-137; R. Hetzron, *The Gunnän-Gurage Languages*, Napoli 1977, 106; M. L. Bender, *Amharic Verb Morphology: A Generative Approach*, New Haven 1968, 140.

Pour le sudarabique moderne:

W. Leslau, *Lexique soqoṭri* (sudarabique moderne), Paris 1938, 66, s.v. *'ino*; E. Wagner, *Syntax der Mehri-Sprache*, Berlin 1953, 30ss.; T. M. Johnstone, *Ḥarsūsi Lexicon*, Oxford 1977, s.v. *'n(n)*.

En amharique:

Getatchew Haile, «The Copula **ነው** (näw) in Amharic», IV. *Congresso int. di studi etiopici*, Roma 1972, 1974, T. II., 139-154; G. Goldenberg, *The Amharic Tense System*, thèse de doctorat, Jerusalem 1966, §98-100, 101-123, 132; Ch. A. Ferguson, «Verbs of 'Being' in Bengali, with a Note on Amharic», in: J. W. M. Verhaar, ed., *The Verb «Be» and its Synonyms*. Philosophical and Grammatical Studies, Part 5, Dordrecht 1972, 74-114 (surtout 106ss.); Abraham Demoz, Hailu Fulas, «The Adjective and the *näw* Clauses in Amharic», *Proceedings of the Third Int. Conf. on Ethiopian Studies*, Addis Ababa 1966, I, 1977, 81-87.

À propos de la copule à *t* voir G. Goldenberg, «A Copula **ት** in Old Amharic», *Israel Oriental Studies* VI, 1976, 131-137 et son travail cité en ann. 2 (1977); L. Bender, Hailu Fulass, *A Morphology of Amharic*, Michigan (Occasional Paper 6, Linguistics and Languages, 1), inaccessible.

3 Cf. surtout R. Hetzron 1972, cité en ann. 2, 79-85; G. Goldenberg 1977, ibid. 478ss.

4 L'explication structurelle de ce fait, constaté passim dans les travaux descriptifs, est donnée pour le bilin et le tigriñña par F. R. Palmer, «Bilin 'to Be' and 'to Have'», *African Language Studies* 6, 1965, 101-111: it happened (past) = it is (present). M. Cohen, *Traité de langue amharique*, 148 constate une certaine diffusion temporelle de la copule *näw* en amharique.

5 Surtout dans les travaux sur les langues sémitiques d'Éthiopie, cf. ann. 2: R. Hetzron 1972, 1977; W. Leslau 1956, 1966, 1979; G. Goldenberg 1977.

6 Cf. ann. 2: M. Cohen 1924, C. Brockelmann 1913, W. Leslau 1938, E. Wagner 1953, T. M. Johnstone 1977; sur la base *'/hnn* cf. D. Cohen, *Dictionnaire des racines sémitiques ou attestées dans les langues sémitiques ...* fs. 1, 1970, 26, s.v.; J. Barth, *Die Pronominalbildung in den semitischen Sprachen*, Leipzig 1913, 97ss.

7 Pour l'origine non-verbale (particule présentative, deïctique, démonstrative etc.) cf. surtout M. Cohen, o.c. en ann. 2 (1924), 104-6; *Traité* 1936, 148, particule présentative, cf. présentatif *ǝnnäho* ch. IV, §7 ibid.; C. H. Armbruster, o.c. en ann. 1 (1908), 69 (particule démonstrative: look! see!); F. Praetorius, o.c. en ann. 1 (1879), 257 (allgemein hindeutend da!, siehe da!); A. Klingenheben, o.c. en ann. 1 (1966), 41 (particle); I. Guidi, o.c. en ann. 1 (1924), 12 (particella col senso originale di ecco ... *nän* — io sono — eccomi);

D'autre part, on estime [8] que la base de la copule *näw* soit d'origine verbale.
M. Cohen qui a étudié la copule *näw* dans la section des copules non-verbales
déjà dans son *Système verbal en sémitique*[9], a changé son opinion dans son
ouvrage postérieur sur le chamitosémitique [10] et trouvait que l'origine
démonstrative de la copule n'était pas prouvée.

Pour une origine non-verbale semblent témoigner les particules présentatives en sémitique (arabe *'inna*, *'anna*, hébreux *hinne*, ancien araméen *hn* etc.) et
dans les langues éthiopiennes du nord (guèze *na-hu*, tigriňňa *ənniho*) et du sud
(amhar. *ənnäho*, harari, gurage, gafat) [11], à côté de quelques formes parallèles
en sud-arabique moderne (soqoṭri, ḥarsūsi) [12]. Elles sont liées à l'accusatif
du pronom objectif qui met le sujet en relief. En tigriňňa, la forme *ənyehu*
(*ənniho*) pour la 1e personne du sg. montre déjà le suffixe personnel subjectif
(d'après M. Cohen analogue à celui-ci du parfait *-ku* et dans la forme du
pronom personnel *anā-ku* en accadien) [13].

Une fois, cette particule (*'inna* en arabe) a été interprétée comme la copule [14].

L'origine verbale de la particule présentative (et par là de la copule *näw*) est
démontrée par le fait connu que son sujet (et le sujet de la copule) sont

---

R. Hetzron, o.c. en ann. 2 (1972), 79ss. (élément deïctique d'origine non-verbale);
W. Leslau, o.c. en ann. 2 (1979), 444 (comparaison avec le guèze *na-* behold); O. Rössler,
cité chez Getatchew Haile, o.c. en ann. 2 (1972); pour l'opinion du dernier cf. dans le
suivant. Les opinions changées de M. Cohen cf. dans le suivant.

    D'après E. Cerulli, *Studi etiopici*, *IV*, *La lingua caffina*, 1951, 477, il s'agit d'un emprunt des
langues couchitiques d'origine démonstrative, cf. ann. 15.

8 L'origine verbale est supposée par Getatchew Hailu, o.c. en ann. 2 (1972), 147 (*nä* — le verbe
«to make one something»), «to be»; le morphème *-w* etc. représente l'objet pronominal; il
s'agit d'un verbe transitif (149) complété dans le passé et dans les clauses subordonnées
par *honä*. W. Leslau, o.c. en ann. 2 (1956), 79-80 parle de deux possibilités: d'un élément
présentatif ou d'un verbe (**hlw*); G. Goldenberg, o.c. en ann. 2 (1977), 480, contre
R. Hetzron, souligne l'origine verbale de la copule négative; ici aussi sur la verbalisation
de la copule négative ancienne (suffixes objectifs » → suffixes verbaux).

    Les comparaisons avec les autres langues chamitosémitiques mettent en évidence l'origine
verbale; le fait est bien documenté par le changement de l'opinion de M. Cohen qui passait
du terrain sémitique, dans son *Système verbal*, au terrain chamitosémitique, dans son *Essai
comparatif*. Les comparaisons seront encore citées dans le suivant (pour le tchadique, le
couchitique, l'égyptien et le berbère).

9 O.c. en ann. 2 (1924).

10 *Essai comparatif sur le vocabulaire et la phonétique du chamitosémitique*, Paris 1947, 185-6.

11 Les formes sont ramassées dans les travaux cités en ann. 2: M. Cohen 1924; R. Hetzron
1972; W. Leslau 1956, 1966, 1979; G. Goldenberg 1977.

12 Cf. les travaux de W. Leslau 1938, E. Wagner 1953, T. M. Johnstone 1977, cités en ann. 2
(le sudarabique moderne).

13 O.c. 1924, 104.

14 Fadlou Shehadi, o.c. en ann. 2 (1969).

marqués par un pronom objectif. E. Cerulli[15] réclame pour la copule *näw* l'origine couchitique.

Dans cette situation, nous pouvons élargir le champ de comparaison et observer les autres langues de la famille chamitosémitique ainsi que d'autres langues de différentes familles en Afrique, surtout dans son nord-est, pour en tirer une interprétation nouvelle des faits dans une perspective comparative, non seulement génétique mais aussi aréale et typologique. Par là, nous espérons aboutir à certains nouveaux résultats.

On se limitera à suivre dans quelques langues l'élément -*N*- que nous trouvons ici dans une fonction multiplexe: du verbe, d'une particule (ou copule) de génitif et d'un pronom (suffixé ou possiblement aussi indépendant). Quelques fois, la sémantique de ce verbe d'existence (ou de cette copule) est liée au verbe «dire», mais la distribution de ce fait semble avoir un caractère universel[16]. En tchadique, nous connaissons la racine reconstruite **na*- avec le sens «voir»[17].

La distribution de l'élément -*N*- dans ses fonctions différentes apparaît comme il suit:

Langue	verbe	génitif (copule génitive)	pronom	particule
le chamito-sémitique:				
égyptien	*wnn* (être)	-*n*-	*in*..	*in*
berbère	*ini* (dire)	-*n*- (préposition)		
couchitique	*an/na* (être)			
	n (dire)			

---

15 *Studi etiopici IV, La lingua caffina*, Roma 1951, 477 s.v. *ne*- (in funzione di copula) qui est entré en amharique *nä-w*. On peut admettre que l'origine de cette copule couchitique est démonstrative.

16 A. Waley, C. H. Armbruster, «The Verb 'to Say' as an Auxiliary in Africa and China», *BSOAS* VII, 1933-5, 573-76. Pour le chamitosémitique cf. la grammaticalisation du verbe «dire» en bédja (*an, in*), en berbère (*ini*) chez D. Cohen, «L'inaccompli en -*n*- du Bedja et le système verbal chamitosémitique», *GLECS* XIV, 1969-70, 69-75; N. A. Tucker, M. A. Bryan, o.c. en ann. 2 (1966), 501; sur la racine **j/A/* «dire, être» (<**[h]Aj* —) A. B. Dolgopolskiy, *Sravnitel'no-istoričeskaya fonetika kušitskich yazykov*, Moskva 1973, 184-5; sur la racine'*An/n/* «être» ibid. 208-210. Sur le verbe *nəŋ* en Agaw cf. R. Hetzron, *The Verbal System of Southern Agaw*, Berkeley 1969, 59, 83, 72 sur la fluctuation des verbes «dire, être». Pour le tchadique cf. Cl. Gouffé, «Sur les emplois grammaticalisés du verbe 'dire' en haousa», *GLECS* 15, 1970-71, 77-90; pour les langues sahariennes cf. dans le suivant, ann. 24.

17 P. Newman, «Chadic Classification and Reconstructions», *AAL* 1977, no. III **na* (Kk. *naa*, W. *nahau*, T. *na*, Bc. *na*).

Langue	verbe	génitif (copule génitive)	pronom	particule
sémitique	*kāna* (ar. etc.) (être)	*li-?* (préposition)	*'an-a*, *'an-ta*	*'inna*, *'anna*
	näw (copule)			*nä-w* (copule non-verbale)
tchadique	*nàà* (être?)	*-n-* (copule)	*su-nàa*, *su-n*	
	*na (voir)			
le nilo-saharien :				
saharien	*n* (penser, dire) (attribuer →)			*n-ər*, *n-əm* (etc. pron. dépendant possessif)
noubien		*-n-*		
fur		*-/i/ŋ*		
daju		*- aŋ*		
maba		*- n*		
voir aussi :				
souahili		*ni* (copule)		
yorouba		*ni* (copule) [18]		

Les langues citées appartenants à la famille chamitosémitique et à la famille nilo-saharienne de J. H. Greenberg (qui reste néanmoins assez problématique) [19], forment une zone assez cohérente et ouvrent la possibilité d'une interprétation aréale, supposée déjà par A. Zaborski [20] qui visait l'existence de -N- dans les langues couchitiques (omotiques) et tchadiques et dans le souahili. La distribution des faits analogues transversants les limites des familles des langues actuelles est bien connue en Afrique du nord-est, voir les

---

18 La littérature respective pour les langues chamitosémitiques sera encore discutée dans le suivant. La documentation pour les autres langues est accessible aisément chez A. N. Tucker, M. A. Bryan, o.c. en ann. 2 (1966), chez W. E. Welmers, *African Language Structure*, Berkeley 1973, et chez J. H. Greenberg, *Languages of Africa*, The Hague 1966.

19 M. L. Bender, «Nilo-Saharan Overview», in: M. L. Bender, ed., *The Non-Semitic Languages of Ethiopia*, East Lansing 1971, Part 4: *Nilo-Saharan* (439-483) et ses travaux en préparation; E. A. Gregersen, «Kongo-Saharan», JAL 11, 1972, 68-89; M. L. Bender, T. C. Schadeberg, ed., *Nilo-Saharan Proceedings. A Collection of Papers Presented at the First Nilo-Saharan Linguistics Colloquium*, Leiden Sept. 8-10, 1980, 1981.

20 *The Verb in Cushitic*, Warszawa-Kraków 1975, passim, sur la reconstruction du verbe «être» **Vn/n/* avec la littérature respective, p. ex. 17-18 (bédja), 39 ('afar-saho), 89 (konso-reconstruction par Dolgopol'skiy **Vn/n/* et Hetzron *wnn*); 118-19 le problème des copules en couchitique, en tchadique et en souahili: «It is possible that all this parallelism is due to relationship with some secondary interference ... Nevertheless one has to be cautious since there is also *ni* as copula even in Swahili»!

travaux de M. M. Bryan[21]. Dans ce dernier cas, on peut penser à l'influence
d'un substrat inconnu. Même pour notre problème, la solution aréale et
l'influence d'un substrat ou adstrat n'est pas exclue. La situation en Ethiopie
parle pour une telle solution[22].

Mais restons dans le cadre du chamitosémitique qui admet en même temps
la solution génétique ainsi qu'aréale grâce au fait que les subfamilles et les
langues chamitosémitiques isolées, à côté de leur origine commune supposée,
attestant des contacts dans leur développement postérieur, p. ex. les contacts
entre le tchadique et le berbère, entre l'égyptien et le libyco-berbère et entre
le sémitique et le couchitique, en se taisant des contacts hypothétiques entre le
couchitique et l'égyptien et les autres langues chamito-sémitiques de l'Afrique
du nord (le libyco-berbère) ou de l'Afrique centrale (le tchadique).

Déjà l'interprétation génétique des faits chamitosémitiques nous aidera à
éclaircir notre problème. Mais il faut voir les systèmes respectifs dans leur
développement et non seulement chercher la forme commune reconstruite. Le
flottement des fonctions de l'élément -*N*- est assez clair dans le tchadique où
les analyses successives de C. T. Hodge, Cl. Gouffé et P. Zima[23] faisaient
possible de ramasser le -*N*- hypothétique dans toutes ses fonctions postérieures
(c.-à-d. un prédecesseur de la copule génitive, un stabilisateur, — c.-à-d. la
copule —, la copule génitive actuelle et quelques éléments dans les pronoms
du sujet des formes -*su-nàa, su-n*). La racine *na-* «voir» n'a pas été étudiée
dans ce contexte.

L'analogie saharienne est extrêmement importante pour comprendre les
relations entre la copule (le verbe *nàà*) et les formes pronominales en tchadique,
bien qu'il s'agissait des langues appartenants à la famille nilo-saharienne: le
verbe *n* «penser, donner, ou dire» sert dans les langues sahariennes comme le
verbe auxiliaire pour la troisième classe verbale et en même temps il apparaît

---

21 «The *N/*K Languages of Africa», *JAL* 7, 1968, 169-217; «A Closer Examination of
some *N/*K Languages», in: *Second Int. Conf. «Language and Literature in the Sudan»*, 1970,
accessible en preprint.

22 Cf. la riche littérature sur les contacts des langues sémitiques et couchitiques, p. ex.
W. Leslau, M. M. Moreno, Ch. A. Ferguson, F. R. Palmer etc. Pour notre thème cf. la
thèse de E. Cerulli, o.c. en ann. 15; les travaux de F. R. Palmer (cf. ann. 4); R. Hetzron,
o.c. en ann. 2 (1972) pour le sémitique éthiopien (guraghé de l'est, *gunnän*-guraghé dans leur
position limitrophe 85). Les contacts aréaux ne sont pas rares en Afrique, au contraire.

23 C. T. Hodge, «Morpheme Alternants and the Noun Phrase in Hausa», *Language* 21, 1954,
87-91; «Hausa *nàa* "to Be" or "not to Be"», *African Language Review* 8, 156-62; Cl. Gouffé,
«Le problème de l'aspect en haoussa II», *GLECS* 11, 1966-7, 29-67; «Une corrélation
typologique dans quatre langues de l'Afrique occidentale: les fonctions de N», *AuÜ* 54,
1971, 286-302; P. Zima, *Problems of Categories and Word Classes in Hausa (The Paradigm of
Case)*, Prague 1972, surtout 80 ss.

comme la base des pronoms possessifs (*n-ər*, *n-əm* etc.)[24] et nous offre la possibilité de chercher aussi dans ce dernier cas le verbe «dire qch. pour, donner qch. pour, attribuer». D'ici s'ouvre, devant nous, la possibilité de joindre encore à cette notion la particule -*n*- pour le génitif (en égyptien) ou la copule génitive dans le tchadique.

L'interprétation des faits dans les langues tchadiques ramassant le verbe, la copule, le génitif et le pronom peut aussi nous guider à l'étude de l'égyptien (voir le verbe *wnn*, la particule de présentation d'origine démonstrative *in* et le pronom de la 1e personne du pl. en moyen égyptien)[25] et la particule -*n*- de génitif qui joue un rôle important dans le système verbal égyptien (*sḏm.n.f*)[26]. L'introduction de la notion verbale dans l'élément -*N*- dans les formes verbales égyptiennes nous aide à transformer ces formes dans les structures avec un verbe auxiliaire, comme l'a déjà supposé I. M. Diakonoff[27], et fonder ainsi la comparaison entre les formes égyptiennes analytiques et entre celles

24 La description comparative de ces langues cf. A. N. Tucker, M. A. Bryan, o.c. en ann. 2 (1966); sur l'analogie de la structure verbale et pronominale cf. M. A. Bryan, «The Verb Classes in the East Saharan Languages», in: *Afrikanische Sprachen und Kulturen — Ein Querschnitt*, Hamburg 1971, 224-235, surtout 225; N. Cyffer, «The Person Elements in Saharan Languages. A Step towards the Creation of Proto-Saharan», *Proceedings of the First Nilo-Saharan Colloquium*, Leiden 1981, 185-200; quelques détails aussi chez J. Lukas, «Die unabhängigen Personalpronomina in der westzentralsaharischen Sprachgruppe», *AuÜ* LXI, 1978, 279-294. Les deux auteurs n'ont pas observé l'identité de l'élément pronominal -*n*- et du verbe *n* (d'attribution). Notons encore ia fluctuation sémantique entre «être», «dire» et «donner» en teda-daza, Ch. et M. Le Cœur, *Grammaire et textes Teda-daza*, Dakar 1956, 97; le problème est discuté chez K. Petráček, «Zur inneren Rekonstruktion des zentralsaharanischen Verbalsystems», *Asian and African Linguistic Studies*, Prague 1979, *Studia Orientalia Pragensia* IX, 93-127, surtout 101ss. La base pour «être» et «dire» est ici *KI*, la racine avec -*N*- est liée plutôt à «penser», «dire», elle fonctionne aussi comme base des suffixes pronominaux possessifs (Ch. et M. Le Cœur, o.c. 73; cf. *nər* «j'ai pensé, j'ai dit, j'ai donné»; la forme verbale composée *la-nər* «j'ai vu»; possessifs *nər* etc.). Le sens sousjacent serait peut-être «penser qch. pour qn., dire que qch. appartient à qn., attribuer qch. à qn., appartenir à».

25 A. H. Gardiner, *Egyptian Grammar*, Cambridge 1927, 64; A. Erman, *Aegyptische Grammatik*, Berlin 1911, 84; G. Lefebvre, *Grammaire de l'égyptien classique*, Le Caire 1940, 57-8; E. Edel, *Altägyptische Grammatik*, Roma 1955, 173; J. Černý, «INN in Late Egyptian», *JEA* 27, 1941, 106-12; dans une perspective chamitosémitique I. M. Diakonoff, *Semitico-Hamitic Languages*, Moscow 1965, 70; K. Petráček, «Vers une conception dynamique du paradigme dans les études chamito-sémitiques», *MUSJ* XLVIII, 1973-4, 157-163.

26 Cf. seulement W. T. Thacker, *The Relationship of the Semitic and Egyptian Verbal Systems*, Oxford 1954, 272; A. Roccati, «Origine di forme verbali egizie», *AION* 30, 1970, 383-87; «La signification di *sḏm.n.f*», 2e *Congr. int. des égyptologues*, 1978, Grenoble, sous presse. La littérature respective cf. dans mon article «Zur Stellung des altägyptischen Verbalsystems im Rahmen des Hamitosemitischen», *Bulletin de la Soc. d'égyptologie*, Genève, 1982, t. 6, 83-101.

27 I. M. Diakonoff, o.c. en ann. 25, 84 avec l'analogie dans le haoussa et en couchitique: le verbe «être».

des autres langues chamitosémitiques (p. ex. couchitiques ou tchadiques) et utiliser aussi l'analogie des langues sahariennes, où la troisième classe formée par le verbe *n* représente la dernière étape de l'évolution du système verbal.

Notre manière de voir les faits se montre alors fructueuse aussi pour l'interprétation du système énigmatique de l'égyptien.

Pour le sémitique asiatique (et éthiopien), cette hypothèse d'unité de l'élément -N- ouvre de nouveau le problème de l'étymologie de l'élément *AN*[1] dans les pronoms sujet où on a voulu, déjà auparavant, trouver cet élément [28], parallèlement avec la base verbale en couchitique. Notons en marge que le pronom de la l. p. sg. *an-ā-ku* apparaît comme la forme régulière du statif accadien (*šar-ā-ku*) [29]. L'analogie structurelle en saharien (verbe→pronom) et en tchadique (verbe-copule génitive-stabilisateur [copule]-pronom sujet) parlent de nouveau en faveur de cette ancienne hypothèse.

L'interprétation verbale de l'élément -N- nous autorise aussi à repenser à l'origine de la forme verbale réflexive et passive à préfixe *n*-, c.-à-d. la VIIe forme verbale (en arabe, niph'al sémitique). L'analyse de la forme *j-a-N-qatil* formée sur la base intransitive *qatil* et munie d'un préfixe subjectif non-actif -*a*-semble être acceptable. Le problème exige une étude spéciale que je prépare. Dans les langues couchitiques ('afar), le verbe à -N- forme entre outre la forme du statif [30] que nous pouvons chercher dans la forme analytique *j-a-N-qatil* — «celui-ci comme sujet inactif EST *qatil* (part. passif)».

Le couchitique offre — à côté du flottement sémantique entre les verbes «être» et «dire» de la base -N- [31] — une analogie précieuse pour le système

---

28 L. Reinisch, *Das persönliche Fürwort und die Verbalflexion in den chamito-semitischen Sprachen*, Wien 1909; pour le pronom cf. aussi la dernière étude par E. Affuso, «I pronomi di I e II persona in semitico, egiziano e berbero», *AION* 37, 1977, 248-81 avec une pleine documentation.

29 Pour ces problèmes cf. l'étude de E. Affuso, o.c. en ann. 28.

30 Tout le système des thèmes dérivés en sémitique exige, d'après nous, une profonde réinterprétation, car il s'agit avant tout d'un système produisant la transitivation du verbe. Dans ce contexte cf. surtout l'étude de Abraham Demoz, *The Meanings of Some Derived Stems in Amharic*, Diss. California Univ. at Los Angeles, 1964, discutée positivement chez M. L. Bender, *Amharic Verb Morphology: A Generative Approach*, Ann Arbor 1968, 90 ss. Pour l'arabe cf. mes idées indépendantes sur ce problème dans «Le système de l'arabe dans une perspective diachronique», *Arabica*, 28, 1981, 162-177.

Pour les langues couchitiques cf. l'étude par R. J. Hayward sur le statif, «The Stative Conjugation in 'Afar», *AION* 38, 1978, 1-39, passim sur la copule (*kinni* — to be), le morphe *Vn* dans le verbe statif et la copule **in* (to be). Cf. aussi la formation en somali, C. R. V. Bell, *The Somali Language*, Oxford, 1969, 114, § 136; il mentionne aussi l'analogie en souahili (ann. 1) et en galla.

31 Les analogies couchitiques ont été déjà mentionnées, cf. les travaux de M. Cohen, o.c. en ann. 10 (1947), 185-6; A. Zaborski, o.c. en ann. 20 (1975), 118-19; F. R. Palmer, o.c. en

verbal égyptien avec ses formes analytiques et, comme nous avons déjà noté, pour le système tchadique (avec les formes à -N- su-naà, su-n). Nous avons trouvé la possibilité d'interpréter la VIIe forme verbale sémitique (arabe etc. sauf araméen, et avec d'autres fonctions en éthiopien) avec l'aide de la notion verbale de l'élément -N-. Ici, en couchitique, la copule avec -N- est largement répandue[32] et tirée probablement d'une racine verbale. L'analyse du statif en 'afar[33] montre l'importance de cet élément.

La préposition berbère -n- est, d'après F. A. Pennacchietti[34], liée à la préposition -n- en égyptien et li- en sémitique. Notre analyse de l'égyptien et du tchadique montre la possibilité d'accepter aussi, dans ce cas, la notion verbale ou copulative avec le sens d'appartenance, mais le problème reste à être d'abord étudié de proche.

Revenons finalement au sémitique éthiopien. La distribution ainsi que la fréquence de la copule avec -N- sont largement attestées dans les langues du sud[35], mais ce morphème n'est pas fondé dans les systèmes du nord bien qu'ici aussi existent les particules présentatives qui peuvent être interprétées comme le point de départ de l'évolution des copules postérieures dans les langues du sud. R. Hetzron a bien montré qu'il s'agissait d'un processus évolutif dans ces langues et il a découvert les deux étapes successives de cette évolution: n- avec le suffixe objectif et puis avec le suffixe subjectif verbal[36]. La transition du suffixe objectif au suffixe subjectif dans la forme verbale reflète, d'après notre avis, un trait typologique ancien lié au développement de l'opposition sujet-objet dans l'évolution typologique des langues, au moins dans la conception de la «typologie de contenu»[37].

---

ann. 4 (1965); E. Cerulli, o.c. en ann. 7 (1951), 477; A. N. Tucker, M. A. Bryan, o.c. en ann. 2 (1966), ann. 16; D. Cohen, o.c. en ann. 16 (1969); R. Hetzron ibid.; A. B. Dolgopol'skiy, o.c. en ann. 16 (1973); A. B. Dolgopol'skiy, *Nostratičeskiye etimologii i proizchoždeniye glagol'nych formantov*, Etimologiya 1968, 239-40; R. J. Hayward, o.c. en ann. 30 (1978); C. T. Hodge, o.c. en ann. 23 (1969).

32 Cf. les travaux de E. Cerulli et de A. Zaborski, en ann. 31.

33 R. J. Hayward, o.c. en ann. 30 (1978).

34 «Considerazioni sulla preposizione berbera N», *Atti del Secondo congr. int. di. linguistica camito-semitica*, Firenze 1974, 1978, 307-14 avec parallèles en égyptien et en sémitique.

35 Les sources citées en ann. 5 et 2 (R. Hetzron, W. Leslau, G. Goldenberg).

36 O.c. en ann. 2 (1972); accepté aussi par G. Goldenberg, o.c. en ann. 2 (1977).

37 Surtout G. A. Klimov, *Očerk obščey teorii ergativnosti*, Moskva 1973; *Tipologiya yazykov aktivnogo stroya*, Moskva 1977; «K vzaimootnošeniyu genealogičeskoy, tipologičeskoy i areal'noy klassifikacii yazykov», in: *Teoretičeskie osnovy klassifikacii yazykov mira*, Moskva 1980, 6-23; la théorie a été déjà appliquée dans les études des langues chamitosémitiques par I. M. Diakonoff, M. Korostovcev, M. Je. Mat'ye, M. L. Palmaitis. Le problème est connu sous le terme de la théorie ergative, élaborée aussi par d'autres savants et appliquée dans les langues chamitosémitiques, cf. Z. Frajzigier, «On the Proto-Chadic Syntactic

La dynamique du processus de transition de l'ancienne copule (avec les suffixes objectifs) à la copule nouvelle (avec les suffixes subjectifs verbaux) et la situation dans le nord éthiopien nous indiquent que la copule se développait surtout dans le terrain du sud. Ici, nous trouvons les langues couchitiques avec le verbe et avec la copule à l'élément -N- et nous pouvons alors supposer que les éléments présentatifs anciens ont été développés sous l'influence du couchitique, sinon repris par le sémitique de ces langues comme un élément déjà élaboré, utilisé et intégré dans le système comme tel. La théorie de E. Cerulli est basée sur cette hypothèse [38].

Bien qu'il reste toujours la possibilité que l'élément en question -N- représente une ancienne forme verbale, comme dans les langues chamito-sémitiques en Afrique, il n'est pas absolument exclu qu'il y a la possibilité d'y voir un élément présentatif sémitique renouvelé sous la pression des substrats ou adstrats couchitiques.

Mais finalement, rien ne nous empêche de voir dans les particules présentatives documentées en sémitique asiatique et en éthiopien, les éléments d'origine verbale, et de lier ainsi la situation en sémitique à la situation structurelle que nous connaissons dans le chamitosémitique en Afrique et dans quelques langue africaines.

Cette double interprétation prouve la complexité de la copule à -N- en chamitosémitique. À côté des arguments pour le caractère verbal de la copule «être», nous avons trouvé aussi la possibilité d'y voir la particule présentative. Mais dans ce dernier cas, il faut noter que cette particule pouvait être d'origine verbale, p. ex. tirée de la racine pour le verbe «voir» que nous avons trouvé en tchadique (*na*). Une interprétation analogue (voir → voici!) a été déjà supposée auparavant dans le cas de la particule *'inna* etc. en arabe.

L'orientation étymologique vers la sphère verbale semble être soulignée, mais à la place d'un unique verbe ancien «être», nous trouvons encore le verbe «voir» comme base possible de la copule à -N-. Le troisième verbe qui entrait dans nos arguments était le verbe «dire» dont la transformation en «être» est bien attesté dans les langues africaines [39]. Voilà un problème d'évolution morphologique et sémantique complexe dont les fondéments historiques semblent être plus larges que le résultat de l'évolution que nous observons en outre en amharique.

Pattern», *Third Int. Hamito-Semitic Congress*, London, 29-31 March 1978 (preprint-résumé); G. Böhm, «Two Types of 'Ergative' Predication in Chadic Languages», *Int. Kolloquium über die tschadische Sprachfamilie*, Hamburg 15.-18. Sept. 1981 (preprint). La littérature est ramassée dans mon étude citée en ann. 26 (1982 ann. 11); cf. aussi «Le système de l'arabe dans une perspective diachronique», *Arabica*, v. 28, 1981, 162-177.
38 Cf. ann. 15.
39 Cf. ann. 16, ann. 24.

AMHARIC MINUTIAE

H. J. Polotsky
The Hebrew University, Jerusalem

I

(A) N madräg-u vs. (B) yä-N madräg

1. During the last century a significant shift has taken place in what grammarians of Amharic have to say about the way, or ways, in which the nominal subject of an infinitive can be expressed.

2. From the scanty material at his disposal Praetorius concluded (§ 292 c) that the regular construction was the genitive (B). Though he was quite prepared, on the analogy of a number of languages [1], to find the nominative (A) too, the examples actually known to him were very few and not all of them certain.

3. The co-existence of the two constructions is positively stated by Afevork at the end of his chapter on the genitive (§ 117 p. 224): the genitival *yä-* "può omettersi" "nella proposizione completiva diretta o indiretta", i.e. before the substantival subject of an infinitive functioning as complement of a *verbum dicendi/sentiendi*:

[B] *ərgənna yä-motaččənän mäqqaräb yasassəbännall,* or
[A] *ərgənna motaččən mäqqaräbwan yasgänäzzəbännall*

"La vecchiaia ci avverte che la morte si avvicina"

Cf. § 6 end.

4. This couple of Afevorkian sentences is taken up, together with a few others, in Marcel Cohen's *Traité* p. 195 (ch. VI § 30), where we find for the first time an indication concerning the relative frequency of the two constructions: "Dans une phrase à proposition infinitive, l'anticipation du sujet logique (Chap. III, § 29 [p. 93]) est si fréquente qu'elle apparaît comme la

---

1 "Scholastic" grammarians had to acknowledge the nominative as subject of the gerund (Lat. *gerundium*, Fr. *gérondif*) in Psalm 125:1 In convertendo Dominus captivitatem Sion ...: Ch. Thurot *Extraits* 268-9.

construction la plus normale", i.e. the exact opposite of what Praetorius had thought. I for my part can only endorse Cohen's indication: in my experience construction A is markedly more common than construction B. Cf. § 8.

5. Though "la proposition infinitive" is one of the peculiarities of French (and Italian)[2] grammatical nomenclature, Cohen's use of the term—he refers himself to his ch. X §§ 7 and 27a (pp. 343-4 and 359 respectively)—will cause no more difficulty than Afevork's (§ 3) "proposizione completiva". I am less happy about his "anticipation". The possessive suffix attached to the infinitive (N madräg-u) need not be understood as anaphoric (epanaleptic), but can be understood literally as transformation or metamorphosis of the person-marker of the underlying verb-form. The difference is, however, not as great as it may appear at first sight. In a language where the nominal subject stands in front and the verb-form necessarily carries person-markers agreeing with the nominal subject in gender and number (and if the subject is an absolute personal pronoun, also in person), the difference between normal word-order and "anticipation" (extraposition, segmentation), between concord and anaphora, is reduced to a matter of subjective and impressionistic preference for the one or the other.

6. What both constructions have in common is that an underlying sentence (N adärrägä) is made to function as a substantive by converting the finite verb into the infinitive. They differ fundamentally in the range of the conversion (transposition). In construction A the conversion is limited to the verb, the possessive suffix reflecting the person-marker: N madräg-u; the rest of the sentence, i.e. the subject and the nexus, remains unaffected. In construction B the conversion extends over the whole sentence, the actor of the underlying finite verb being turned into the genitival adjunct of the infinitive: yä-N madräg. The initial unmarked N of construction A, to repeat it, is not an original genitive with "omitted" yä-, but the nominative which had been the actor of the underlying finite verb.

Just as N adärrägä is substantivized by converting the finite verb into the infinitive, so it is adverbialized by converting the finite verb into the gerund, and just as the 3rd person markers of the finite verb are transformed into the corresponding possessive suffixes with the infinitive, so they are transformed into the special personal endings of the gerund:

---

2 So far as *Infinitivsatz* was used at all in German [e.g. Ed. Mätzner *Französische Grammatik* (²Berlin 1877) p. 513 § 218 I 1,a] it was given a sense which will sound familiar to the student of Arabic: synonymous with *Substantivsatz* (cf. below fn. 5), because the infinitive is the "Partizipiale" corresponding to the substantive.

	m. sg.	f. sg.		pl.
Perfect	adärräg-ä	/	-äčč	/ -u
Infinitive	madräg-u	/	-wa	/ -aččäw
Gerund	adrəg-o	/	-a	/ -äw

The closest parallel to N (nominative) *madräg-u* is provided by the Gəʿəz ancestor of the gerund construction: *mäsəyo bəher* (Mark 6:47), *rəʾəyomu ʾardaʾihu* (Matthew 21:20), *ḫalifon ʾəmantu* (Matthew 28:11), etc.

Dillmann *Gr.* § 181 α [¹(1857) p. 354 = ²(1899) p. 399], in describing the construction, hints that he would have expected the accusative rather than the nominative: "[ein eigenes Subject] wird dann, nachdem das Suff. am [thatwörtlichen] Infinitiv [= the gerund] auf es hingewiesen, diesem Suff. frei in seiner nächsten Form (nicht im Acc.) beigeordnet".

Praetorius *Äth. Gr.* (1886) § 78 would have expected the genitive. He stresses that a nominal subject is added "unvermittelt" and that it "nicht etwa durch *lä* eingeführt wird, wie man nach § 133 [*məhrät-u lä-ʾəgzi'abəher*] erwarten könnte".

Thomas O. Lambdin *Introduction to Classical Ethiopic (Geʿez)* (1978) pp. 140-1 states that "a noun subject is added appositionally to the appropriate 3rd person form". The case is not explicitly commented upon, but the following sentence is added: "In English we tend to view an expressed noun as the subject of the following main verb; in Ethiopic, however, the noun subject clearly belongs to the subordinate phrase". Would it not have been both clearer and more economical to have stated that the expressed noun remains in the syntactic relation in which it had stood in the underlying main sentence (*näbiro ʾIyäsus* ← *näbärä ʾIyäsus*)?

7. The syntactic otherness of the two constructions stands out most clearly when the infinitive is governed by a preposition. Cf. two chapter-headings in Bl. Hɘruy's *Yä-ləbb asab*:

(A) *Ato Kəbrät-ənna Gännähoy Nəgatwa Ṣəyyon-Mogäsa-n sälä mäwläd-aččäw*
(*Dərsätočč* 133:2, chap. I)
(B) *Sälä Ṣəyyon-Mogäsa ləgg mäwläd* (ibid. 170:21, chap. VII)

In A the preposition *sälä* precedes the infinitive just as in the corresponding subordinate clause it would precede the substantivized *yä-wällädu*, extruding the subordinator *yä-*: *sälä wällädu*. In B, where the underlying sentence (*Ṣ.-M. ləgg wällädäčč*) is fully nominalized, the preposition precedes the whole group *yä-Ṣ.-M. ləgg mäwläd*, again extruding the subordinator *yä-*. Cf. the corresponding position of *-n* in §§ 11,12 and § 10 respectively.

We note that at the beginning of each of these two chapters the reader is in a different position with regard to what he is going to read. At the start he naturally knows neither the *dramatis personae* nor the subject-matter of the narrative which awaits him. By the time he reaches chap. VII he is already well acquainted with the heroine and, having read in the preceding chapter about her happy marriage, he expects, as a matter of course, just what the chapter-heading announces. It remains to be seen whether this difference corresponds to the syntactic difference.

8. Neither the fact that Afevork (§ 3) lets one single translation do duty for both constructions nor Cohen's expression "la construction la plus normale" (§ 4) implies that they are synonymous and differ merely in frequency. The lesser frequency of construction B suggests that it is subject to a condition of which A is independent and that the presence or absence of this condition finds syntactic expression in Amharic, but not in European languages. Although the syntactic difference between the two constructions (§ 6) may suffice to suggest certain deductions concerning their actual usage, we prefer to rely on the positive evidence of texts.

9. An instructive example occurs in *Araya* near the beginning of chap. XII. After his return from France Araya goes to Däbrä Bərhan in order to enquire after his mother with whom he has been out of touch since he left her, somewhat abruptly, fifteen years before. The matter weighs on his conscience and causes him "thoughts of fear and doubt (misgivings)".

> ["When he enquired after the relatives and friends whom he had formerly known, he heard that most of them had died or gone to another village"] *nägär gən sälä ənnatu andit əmmät Askalä yämmibbalutən yännatun gwaddäñña agñəto biṭäyyəqaččäw ənnatu bähəywät* <u>*mänor-ačäw-n-ənna*</u> *mänkwəsäw əzziyaw agäračäw əndämmiqqämmäṭu astawwäqut.*
>
> <u>*yä-nnatu-n mänor*</u> *barrägaggäṭä gize Araya yätäsämmaw dässta yəh näw lämalät yasčäg-gərall* "but concerning his mother, when he found and asked a friend of his mother called Mrs. Askalä, she (pl.) informed him that his mother was alive and that she (pl.) lived as nun in her same village. It is difficult to describe exactly the joy which Araya felt when he had ascertained that his mother was alive" (Gərmaččäw Täklä Hawaryat *Araya* [[1] 105:8-12 =][3] 131:3-7)

Our two constructions correspond here to a dramatic transition from anxiety to relief. In the sentence-like (§ 6) A the information conveyed by the infinitive has its full topicality; in the substantivized B the topicality is spent and the information is merely referential or anaphoric.

10. Construction B seems to be preferred when the infinitive refers back to a narrative (or declarative) passage:

yäkrəstiyanu nəgusəmm yä-ṭoru-n maläq, yä-sostu-n-əmm däǧǧazmačočč mämot, yandäññaw-n-əmm däǧǧazmač mättasär, yagäru-n-əmm mäzzäräf-ənna mäṭfat bäsämma gize wädiaw bähazän-ənna bädəngaṭe tammo käṭəqit qän wädia alä-qänu täqässäfä motä "when the Christian king heard that his army had been wiped out, that three³ [out of four] generals had died, that the one (remaining) general had been taken prisoner, that the country had been pillaged and devastated, he at once fell ill from grief and shock and died before his time a few days later" (Afevork *Ləbb wälläd tarik* 2:18-21, anaphoric to lines 7-15).

nəgusu gən yä-balämwaločawo-n-ənna yä-zäbäññočawo-n mäṭṭänäq, malqäs, tämäret mäwdäq aytäw ənba yanqäwo ǧämmärä "but when the king [Aṭe Fasil] saw how his courtiers and his guards were distressed, how they wept, how they fell to the ground, tears began to choke him" (Afevork *Gramm.* 276:9-10, anaphoric to lines 2-5)

ya yätäräbä mäläktäñña yä-nəgəstitu-n mäčoh-ənna märgäbgäb bayyä gize [......] *alä* "when that famished messenger saw how the queen was screaming and shaking with emotion he said: '[......]'" (Afevork *Gramm.* 314:9-(10)18, anaphoric to lines 5-8)

Ankobärəmm səttədärs wädä səlk bet hedäh yä-abbataččən-ən mättamäm läəhtočče bäsəlk nəgär "and when you arrive at Ankobär, go to the telephone office and tell my sisters by telephone that our father has fallen ill" (Bl. Həruy *Addis aläm* 8:u-9:2, anaphoric to 7:pu-8:29)

[In the church of Port-Said mass was to be celebrated in honour of the Empress. Therefore] *kämärkäb ndä wärrädn bäqäṭṭəta wädä beta krəstiyan hedn. yä-gərmawit ətegemm wädä beta krəstiyan mähed asqäddəmo səlä tawwäqä bäPort Sa'id yämminorut yäGəbṣ ortodoks krəstiyanočč* [...] *bätallaq dässta täqäbbälwaččäw* "as soon as we disembarked from the ship, we went straight to the church. Because it had become known beforehand that the Empress was (would be) going to the church, the Egyptian Christians living in Port-Said [.....] received her with great joy" (Bl. Həruy *Bäədme mäsänbät* 4:10-15)

"*säläzzih ərsaččäwn šərän yäAṣe Məniləkən ləǧǧ Wäyzäro Zäwditun angəsänall. yä-ləul Ras Mäkwännənən ləǧǧ Däǧǧazmač Täfärin Ras bəlän alga wäraš-ənna yämängəstu ndärase adrəgänall*". [.........]

Ləǧǧ Iyyasumm bäHarär kätäma sallu yä-rsaččäw-n mäššar, yä-nəgəst Zäwditu-n mängäs, yä-ne-n alga wäraš-ənna balämulu səlṭan ndärase mähon bäsämmu gize Sumalewoččun-ənna

---

3 Lit. "the three", cf. Praetorius §244e, first alinea. Cf. Brockelmann *Grundriss* II 69; Wackernagel *Vorlesungen über Syntax* II 136-7, 318 [the reference on p. 137 line 16 is to K. W. Krüger's *Griech. Sprachlehre* (⁵Berlin 1873) §50,2, A. 8 (II p. 95)]. A Chaucerian example: and borwed of him large botels three / And in the two his poyson poured he / The thridde he kepte clene for his drinke (*The Pardoner's Tale* 871-3).

Adaločč̣un säbsəbäw bäkätämaw šəbbər əndinnässa adärrägu "Therefore we have deposed him (pl.) and crowned Lady Zäwditu, the daughter of Aṣe Menelik. We have given the title of Ras to General Täfäri, the son of Ras Makonnen, and made him Heir Apparent and Representative of the Government'" [impeachment and condemnation of Lidj Iyasu, 17 Mäskäräm 1919 a.m. = 27 Sept. 1926 [...] "When Lidj Iyasu, being in the city of Harar, heard that he (pl.) had been deposed, that Queen Zäwditu had been crowned, that I had become Heir Apparent etc., he collected the Somalis and Adals and stirred up a disturbance in the city" (Emp. Haylä Səllase's Autobiography 32:1-3, 19-22).

11. Construction A is not excluded from similar passages. Whether it is allowed because of its neutral, unmarked, character, or whether it is intended to let the information retain its topicality, is more than the foreign student can presume to decide.

ləǧǧətumm yätäšännäsäč̣č̣əw bämuqät wärat bäMiyazya sälä honä [.....] *akalwa təlləq hono täwälda näbbär.*

Ato Kəbrätəmm ləǧǧətu təlləq hona mäwwäläd-wa-n bayyä gize "gäna səttəwwälläd əndäzz̧ih təlləq yähonäčč̣ kätəqit amät bähwala-mma mən tahəl yəhon? [.....] *käwädet əyyamäṭṭahu laläbsat näw?" əyyalä yagwrämärrəm ǧämmär* "because it was in the warm season, in (the month of) Miyazya [April-May] that the girl had been conceived [...] she had been born her body being big. When Mr K. saw that the girl was born being big, he started grumbling: 'If she is so big already when being born, what size will she be after a few years? [....] How (lit., bringing from where) am I going to clothe her?'" (Bl. Həruy *Dərsätočč̣* 133:11-19)
[Heinrich Schliemann, in search of a wife, had offered to marry the Athenian school girl who could best recite the Odyssey] *yəhən yämässälä[4] asab Šliman kätäbaläw liq mäqräb-un mämhəritu lätämariwočč̣u bägällätäč̣č̣əllač̣č̣əw gize bäzz̧iya təmhərt bet bänäbbärut ləǧǧagärädočč̣ mäkakkäl təlləq wədəddər honä* "when the schoolmistress disclosed to the students that such a suggestion had been offered by the scholar called Schliemann, there arose a great competition among the girls who were at that school" (Käbbädä Mikael *Talallaq säwočč̣* 40:30-41:1).

12. Where the information conveyed by the infinitive stands by itself, independently of the context, construction A seems to be the norm.

bäNoh gize qura wəhaw mägwdäl-u-n lämayät billak sayəmmälläs qärrä "when in Noah's time the raven was sent to see whether the water was diminishing (or, had diminished), he failed to return" (Afevork *Gramm.* 128, isolated sentence)
Z̧osefin gabəč̣č̣ač̣č̣äw bäbetä krəstiyan yätäbarräkä-nna yätäqäddäsä alä-mähon-u-n näggäräč̣č̣əw "Joséphine told him [the pope] that their [hers with Napoleon]

---

4 The *yä-* subordinates *mässälä* to *asab* only, not the whole group to the infinitive.

marriage had not been blessed and sanctified in church" (Bl. Hǝruy *Goha ṣǝbaḥ* 166)

"[...]" *yämmil därasi sǝttǝsämu* <u>*yǝḥ*</u> *säw wäyǝmm ḥassätäñña* <u>*mähon-u-n*</u> *wäyǝmm dägmo waga yälelläw dǝrsät* <u>*mäṣaf-u-n*</u> *lǝttǝrräddut tǝčǝlallaččǝhu* "when you hear an author who claims "[...]", you can be sure that this man either is a liar or else has written a worthless piece of writing" (Käbbädä Mikael *Sǝlǝṭṭane malät mǝndǝnnäčč?* 179:13-15)

čäräqa wädä märet ǝyyätäṭäggačč <u>*mähǝd-wa*</u> *yätärägaggäṭa sǝlähonä and qän bämäret lay wädqa lǝttaṭäfat tǝčǝlalläčč* "because it is certain that the moon more and more approaches the earth, it can one day fall upon the earth and destroy it" (Käbbädä Mikael *Sǝlǝṭṭane malät mǝndǝnnäčč?* 163:1-2)

wädagu Kat ǝndiggäddäl <u>*mäffäräd-u-n-ǝnna*</u> *bämmiggäddälǝbbätǝmm bota ǝssu rasu Frederik qärbo ammwamwatun ǝndimmäläkkät* <u>*mättazäz-u-n*</u> *näggärut* "they told him that his friend Katte had been condemned to be put to death and that he himself, Frederick, had been (or, was being) ordered to be present at the place where he was put to death and to watch the execution" (Käbbädä Mikael *Talallaq säwočč* 97:12-14)

II

The cleft sentence

1. An Amharic Cleft Sentence is a copula (c) sentence whose predicate (Z, the element which precedes *näw/näbbärä/aydällämm* etc.) is either a (pro)noun or an adverb (prepositional phrase, adverb clause, gerund) and whose subject (A) is a finite verb-form converted by the converter *yä-* into a noun, either a substantive ("abstract"[5], with adverbial predicate) or an adjective ("concrete", with nominal predicate); the arrangement is either A - Z - c or Z - c - A.

(a) "SIMPLE" AND CLEFT (A - Z - c) IN SUCCESSION

2. That Cleft Sentences are "derived" from underlying "simple", non-cleft, sentences is, of course, implied in the term "Cleft" ["Zerfällung eines Satzes in zwei Glieder" Ed. Mätzner *Frz. Gramm.* (² Berlin 1877) p. 509 lines apu - pu]; cf. Goldenberg 'Studies in Amharic Syntax', *Journal of Ethiopian Studies* 3 (1965) 18-19. In order to convince the student that this "derivation" is not a

---

5 If the terms "substantival/adjectival conversion", "substantive/adjective clause" are used, then "abstract" and "concrete" become superfluous. "Content clause" [= "Inhaltssatz"] is far from being an improvement ("vaut infiniment mieux" Sandfeld *Syntaxe* II XIII) on "substantive clause"; Jespersen's arguments against the latter (*MEG* III 2.1) are futile.

mere artifice invented to support a theory, it is sound didactic procedure to make use of a case where the shift from a "simple" to a cleft sentence takes place before our eyes. This occurs with the substantive variety in the arrangement A - Z - c:

Of two successive sentences the first culminates in an ordinary finite verb-form. The second culminates in a copula with adverbial predicate (Z - c), to which the verb of the first sentence, converted into a substantive, provides the subject (A).

Such sentences occur no doubt in all Neo-Ethiopian languages, but the only source from which a few examples have so far been collected seems to be Leslau's Čäxa volume of 1950: *Notes on Gurage Grammar* (Jerusalem 1951) 26-8.

In the translations of the following examples I have taken the liberty of violating English usage by placing the *that*-clause in front.

INTRANSITIVE

3. *bämäčärräša Troy bäzzihu wəggiya ṭäffačč yätäffaččəwəmm əsraelawyan käGəbṣ agär bäwäṭṭu bä-308 amätat yäwäha ṭəfat bähonä bä-1164 amätat näw* "in the end Troy was destroyed in this war, and that it was destroyed was 308 years after the Israelites left Egypt and 1164 years after the flood" (Käbbädä Mikael *L'Éthiopie* 27:16-19) *əwnätəmm abbatu əndaläw Frederik almotämm. nägär gən yalmotäw labbatu yəmäsläw əndä näbbäräw "mäṭfo sar" sälä honä aydällämm* "and really, as his father had said, Frederick did not die; but that he did not die was not, as his father thought, because he was a 'bad herb'"[6] (Käbbädä Mikael *Talallaq säwočč* 98:12-13)

TRANSITIVE

4. *Pilaṭos əǧǧun sayəttaṭṭäb bäfit Iyäsusən asgärräfä; yasgärräfäw gən əwnät haṭiat agňatobbät aydällämm gən əhew gərrəfat tämässäqälu yatärfäw mäslot näbbär yəlallu* "Before washing his hands Pilate caused Jesus to be scourged; but that he caused him to be scourged was not because he had really found a crime ("sin") in him, but because he thought that this scourging would save him from being crucified, so they say" (Afevork *Gramm.* 180). The corresponding *Domanda* (same page) has the infinitive: *masgärräfu haṭiat agňatobbätənə näw?* *tämariwoččumm yəwäddut näbbär yämmiwäddutəmm bäṭəbäbu wəsṭ təhtənna sälänäbbäräw näw* "his [Socrates'] disciples loved him, and that they loved him was because within his wisdom he had humility" (Käbbädä Mikael *L'Éthiopie* 34:25-26)

(b) ELLIPTIC: Z - c [- A]

5. In the following examples the sentence consists of two segments. The second segment clearly represents Z - c with adverbial predicate (*əyyä*[7], *lä-*).

---

6 "Unkraut vergeht nicht".

7 Rendered "while", though in our examples the meaning of the "concomitant circumstance" is modal rather than temporal.

But the first segment is not a normal constituent of the Cleft Sentence at all:
it is a substantive in extraposition, qualified by an adjectivized verb-form: in
the first example the substantive is the subject, in the other two examples the
complement, of the verb-form.

6. For the purpose of translation, the lexical elements of the two segments
can be somehow combined so as to yield a plausible sense; to construe them so
as to satisfy grammar seems less easy. The apparent difficulty arises from the
fact that the A part of the Cleft Sentence is omitted and has to be understood;
that this is really so is shown by the last example, where there is no verb to
govern the extraposed accusative. The reason for this ellipsis is that the
omitted substantivized verb-form fully or nearly falls together with the
adjectivized verb-form contained in the extraposition:

yämmihedu,	adj.	"(those) who go"
yämmihedut,	subst.	"that they go"
yämmissättaččäw {	adj.	"(those) to whom it is given"
	subst.	"that it is given them"
yämmiṣəfaččäw {	adj.	"(those) which he writes"
	subst.	"that he writes them"

7. *läqəddase ənkwa wädä setočč gädam yämmihedu qäsawəst bätam yäšämäggälu
mänäkosat käwändočč gädam əyyätämärräṭu näw* "even priests who go to the women's
convent for [= in order to celebrate] mass—it is while very aged monks are
chosen from the men's convent [viz. that they go, *yämmihedut*] (Bl. Həruy *Dərsätočč*
150:6-8)

*ẓeni yätäbaläw täqäbə'o səm yämmissättaččäw säwočč əndet yallä muya wäyəmm səṭota
yallaččäw honäw lämmiggäññut näw?* "the people who are given the honorific title
'genius'—to those who possess (lit., are found possessing) what kind of talent or
gift is it [viz. that it is given, *yämmissättaččäw*]?" (Käbbädä Mikael *Yäsəlaṭṭane
ayyär* 79:8-9)

yämmiṣəfaččäw-n mäṣahəft hullu käleločč därasyan əyyäqädda näw "all the books
[accusative] which he [Alexandre Dumas] writes it is by (lit., while) copying
from other authors [viz. that he writes them, *yämmiṣəfaččäw*]" (Käbbädä Mikael
Talallaq säwočč 23:8-9)

8. Bally *Linguistique générale et linguistique française* (²Berne 1944) §§ 89, 90
shows how a single substantive in extraposition (segmentation) is equivalent
to an adverb clause, especially of time and of condition, and stands to a
following sentence in the relation of A to Z. Bally's analysis applies, of course,
to a cleft sentence no less than to a "simple" one. Our examples thus are of
the same kind as the fairly frequent case where an adverb clause, most often

one introduced by s- "while, when", is followed by an elliptic Cleft Sentence: some examples are quoted by Goldenberg art. cit. 19; cf. also my contribution to the forthcoming *Mélanges Rodinson*, § 7. In all these cases the elliptic Cleft Sentence (Z - c [- A]) as a whole is Z in relation to the extraposed A:

$$A^1 \left| \begin{array}{c} Z^1 \\ \hline Z^2 - c\,[-\,A^2] \end{array} \right.$$

(c) ACCUSATIVE AS Z

9. The accusative marker *-n* differs from the prepositions *bä-, lä-, kä-, sälä, wädä, əndä, əskä* in two ways: it is suffixed to its noun and consequently does not extrude a genitival *yä-*: *yä-Troy-n kätäma* as against *bä-Troy kätäma* etc. [8]. This difference notwithstanding they belong to the same category. In the Cleft Sentence the accusative will therefore as a matter of course be treated exactly like a prepositional phrase, i.e. as an adverb, requiring a substantival A.

10. The rendering of this construction into English is sometimes awkward. With the arrangement A - Z - c it is often convenient to use a rendering which demands a nominative rather than an accusative, e.g.

ənna yämmənnawqäw bamarəñña yätäṭafäw-n näw əñǧi, yäfäräng qwanqwa annawqəmm "what we know (recognize) is the Amharic text (lit., that which is written in Amharic), Frankish we don't know" (Afevork *Mənilək* 78:3-5, Ṭaytu's retort to Count Antonelli)

In some cases we shall express the accusative in the relative, "whom". In Amharic the direct object suffix of the nominalized verb is invariably in the 3rd m. sg., also when the Z is a feminine or a plural: by this non-concord the verb is shown to be substantivized, the suffix functioning as article.

11. A - Z - c

lännantä gən yätänazzäzullaččəhu yann-ən yäMänzu-n qoda märet näw "but what he has bequeathed to you is that barren piece of land in Mänz" (Bl. Hɘruy *Addis aläm* 16:22-23)

antä yämmättənnaggäräw yämälkwa-n mamar bəčča näw "but it is only the beauty of her appearance that you are talking about" (Bl. Hɘruy *Dərsätočč* 140:14)

läzzihəmm səra bämäǧämmäriya märi yadärrägut Däǧǧazmač Balča-n näw "it was General Balča whom they [certain obstructive elements] at first made leader for this activity [? I wonder whether *səra* is not an error for *sera* 'plot']" (Emp.

---

8 Cf. in the genitival construction B discussed *supra* under I *yä-nnatu-n mänor* (§ 9 and examples in § 10) as against *sälä Ṣ.-M. ləǧǧ mäwläd* (§ 7).

Haylä-Səllase's Autobiography 124:18; my attention was drawn to this example by Professor Ullendorff, cf. his annotated translation *ad loc.*)

yakkärayyähuh ahəyyaye-n näw ənǧi, ṭəlawa-n č̣əmmər aydällämm "it is my she-donkey that I have leased to you, not her shade as well" (Käbbädä Mikael *Talallaq säwočč* 49:31)

dəbbəštu yämmiyasčäggəräw käbtočč-ən bəččamm aydällä "ce ne sont pas seulement les animaux que le sable gêne" (Afevork *Guide* 148:apu-u)

kämot yələq yämmifärut sayəqqäbbäru mäqrät-ən näbbär "what they feared more than death was to remain unburied" (Käbbädä Mikael *L'Éthiopie* 48:25-26)

12. **Z - c - A**

yäEwropa gazeta gən taṭe Mənilək yələq aṭe Yohannəs-ən näw lältyopya mängəst yätägäbbu adrəgo yanäsa yänäbbärä "but it rather of Aṭe Yohannəs than of Aṭe Menelik that the European press used to speak as deserving the kingship of Ethiopia" (Afevork *Guide* 228:4-6)

bäsäw ṭäbay wəsṭ fäṣṣəmo tämäsgañ-ənna č̣ärrəso tänäqqafi yällämm. yämmiyasmäsäggənəmm ṭäbay yalläw säw binor käyaẑəw yələq säč̣əw-n fäṭari-n näw yämmiyasmäsäggənäw "in the human character there is no (such thing as) completely praiseworthy and entirely blameworthy; and if there is a man who has a character which causes praise, it is the giver, the Creator, rather than the taker that it causes to be praised" (Täklä Ṣadəq Mäkwriya *Yäsäw ṭäbay* 17:apu-u)

ahzab yäqəddus Giyorgisən säwənnät əndä əhəl däqqusäw läbäre ahlətäwt əndägäna həyaw bono bäbärew šañña lay tämälləso əndäwäṭṭa yämmiyasayyäw-n səəl näbbär yämmilut? "Did you mean the painting which shows St George's body, after the heathen had crushed it like fodder and fed to an ox, re-emerging again alive on the hump of the ox?" (Haylä I. Fəqadu *Käəngədih wädih adära əndayəddäggäm* 82:7-10)

nəgəstä Saba Iyärusalem därsa bämämmäläswa Mənilək-ən bəčča alnäbbärämm yatärräfäččəw, nägär gən yältyopyan tarik yäṣafä and yäFäränsay därasi əndätänaggäräw "bämahṣänwa Məniləkən, bäləbbwa yäəwnätäññawn haymanot zena yəza tämälläsäčč" ənǧi "On her return after having arrived in Jerusalem it was not only Menelik whom the Queen of Sheba had gained, but, as a French writer who has written the history of Ethiopia has said, 'she returned with Menelik in her womb and with the tidings of true religion in her heart'" (Käbbädä Mikael *L'Éthiopie* 24:8-125)

läkka əsswa-n norwall-ənna yämmiläkäw "so it is her that he was sending [i.e. he said that he would send]!" (Balambaras Mahtämä-Səllase W.-M. *ənqəlf läməne?* 119:pu-u). The "so" [*OED* **so** 10b (IX 345a top)] is intended to convey what Leslau *Concise Dict.* 10b means by "particle indicating surprise of discovery"; cf. *Käsate Bərhan Täsämma* 21b bottom: *nägärun kätäräddaw bähwala* "läkka əndäzzih nuroallənə?" *bəlo bänägäru mäddämäm mankär, (as[räǧǧ:]) läkka əne nägärun salərädda qäräčče nurrealläh^w*; similarly Dässta Täklä-Wäld 720b. The same rendering suits the passage from Bl. Həruy *Dərsätočč* 163:12 quoted by Goldenberg art. cit. 18 under V: "so it was for Ṣ.-M.'s sake ...?!"; Ṣ.-M.'s parents had not realized —*nägärun sayərräddu qärtäw näbbär*—the purpose of the young man's visits.

SOURCE MATERIALS
FOR THE STUDY OF THE TIGRE LANGUAGE

S. RAZ

Tel-Aviv University

The purpose of this paper is to provide a survey of the published material that can be used as a basis for descriptive research on the Tigre language. The material discussed is not therefore the entire corpus of works connected with Tigre[1]. Certain works whose content has been summarized by other writers are not mentioned in every case.

The study of the language began with the appearance in Eritrea of missionaries, especially members of the Swedish Evangelical Mission, who laid the foundations of Tigre research and worked into it alone devotedly, until they were joined by European scholars. Most texts collected by missionaries saw light during the first half of this century. However, the actual work of collecting the material in the field took place during the second half of the nineteenth century. The present state of Tigre research is without doubt the result of those endeavours in the field by missionaries.

Owing to the fact that most European scholars used the same texts for their researches, it is necessary to clarify the questions of "who wrote what, when, and with whose help". The importance of throwing light on this matter lies in the need to establish the origin of the Tigre text or of the grammatical problem presented. Such clarification enables one to see if a certain problem is inherent in the language or results from previous writers' attempts at explanations.

The material surveyed is classified and presented in the following manner: A. texts, B. grammatical material, C. lexical material. A subdivision within each section is made by grouping together all works attributed to one person. In these subdivisions the names of other writers on Tigre are sometimes mentioned where relevant.

---

1 As regards bibliographies, two valuable works are available: E. Ullendorff, *The Semitic languages of Ethiopia*, London, 1955, xiv, 273pp., Bibliographical notes: pp. 233-239; W. Leslau, *The Semitic languages of Ethiopia*. An annotated bibliography of, The Hague, 1965, 336 pp., Tigre: pp. 145-164.

A. Texts

Texts collected by E. Littmann

The most distinguished scholar in the field of Tigre studies is Enno Littmann, whose *Publications of the Princeton expedition to Abyssinia*[2], the peak of his achievement in this field, is still the best available collection of Tigre texts. Littmann undertook an expedition to Eritrea in the autumn and winter of 1905/6. The material for *Publications of the Princeton expedition to Abyssinia* was collected with the help of the Revd. G. R. Sundström who spent many years in Eritrea, notably at the Swedish Mission in Galab, and was himself an accomplished student of the Tigre Language.

Sundström introduced Littmann, on the latter's arrival at Galab, to Naffa' wad 'Etmān, whose invaluable services, then and later, prompted Littmann to dedicate the first volume of his *Publications* to him. Naffa' travelled to Germany following the expedition and stayed there with Littmann for two years (1907-1909) while they worked together on the material collected in Eritrea[3].

In transcribing his texts, Littmann used Ethiopic characters together with a special sign to indicate the gemination of appropriate consonants. Throughout *Publications* all words which terminate with the vowel *a* have this vowel in the fourth order, including verbs in the perfect, third person, masculine singular[4]. In the preface to volume I Littmann gives an account of the manner in which the material was collected.

A more detailed account of his stay in Eritrea is given in "Preliminary Report"[5] (pp. 151-154), augmented by an account of the Tigre speaking people and a proposed outline (pp. 155-165) of what was later to be printed as *Publications*.

The contents of volume I of *Publications* may be classified under four headings: (a) — prose — consisting of anthropomorphic tales about animals,

---

2 E. Littmann, *Publications of the Princeton expedition to Abyssinia*, Leyden: late E. J. Brill, Ltd., 1910-15, 4v. in 5, 287, 344, 541, 1097 pp.

3 In 1909 Naffa', being en route from Naples to Sicily on his way back home, disappeared, never to be heard of again.

4 Littmann finally changed his mind about this, using the distinction between the first and the fourth orders to denote a morphological value, i.e.: the fourth order being used to denote a final radical which is a semivowel. Cf.: *Wörterbuch der Tigrē-Sprache* in section C. of this paper.

5 E. Littmann, "Preliminary report of Princeton University Expedition to Abyssinia", *ZA* 20, 1907, pp. 151-182.

stories from folklore, accounts of local historical events, stories about
the stars, descriptions of the Tigre speaking tribes, customs, riddles etc.;
(b) — a list of names — interpreted as fully as possible — of men (pp. 136-
156), of women (pp. 156-161), of *səqrāt*[6] (pp. 161-163), of swords and their
kinds (pp. 172-187); (c) — poetry — consisting mainly of songs and dirges
(pp. 203, 210-215, 229-250); (d) — idiomatic expressions such as salutations
(pp. 200-202) and curses (pp. 270-277).

Volume II of *Publications* consists of an English translation of volume I.
In the preface to volume II Littmann makes further remarks about the nature
of the material collected in volume I, e.g. an evaluation of the literary aspects
of the prose and poetry is given and a comparison made with similar material
from within the boundaries of Ethiopia and from outside it. He also comments
on the difficulties he encountered in the translation of Tigre names, suggesting
as possible for some of them the idiolectic interpretation of his "informant"
Naffaʿ. The translation of the poetry is supplemented by a commentary.

Volume III (published 1913) consists of a numbered sequence of seven
hundred and seventeen poems in the Tigre Language, in Ethiopic script. Each
poem is preceded by the poet's name. This poetry consists of (a) folk songs —
amounting to about two-thirds of the collection and (b) dirges — traditionally
sung by women. Some prose is also included in volume III. There is an
introduction of about thirteen pages, in the Tigre language, concerning
various aspects of the poetry of the Tigre people both in the past and at the
time at which this material was collected. There is also a description of the
origin of the Tigre speaking tribes, and an explanation of how certain rites
expressing clientship came into being. Apart from the introduction, many of
the poems are preceded by prose sections in which the background to the
poem related. At the end of the volume the poet's names are listed in Ethiopic
script, in Ethiopic alphabetical order.

Volume IV consists of a German translation of, and commentary on, the
poems of Volume III. It appears in two parts: A (published 1913) and B
(published 1915). Part A consists of a translation of, and commentary on
poems 1-391, part B of a translation of and commentary on the remainder. At
the end of part B there is a list of the poets in Latin alphabetical order.

In addition to *Publications*, two other prose texts published by Littmann
remain to be mentioned: (a) *The legend of the Queen of Sheba*[7] and (b) "Tigrē-

---

6 *səqrāt*: "The second name by which the mother and the other women call the child" (*LH*,
   181b). The use of these *səqrāt* names—in the majority of cases they are also battlecries—is
   found frequently in poetry.
7 E. Littmann, *The Legend of the Queen of Sheba in the tradition of Axum*, Leyden: E. J. Brill,
   1904, Bibliotheca Abessinica, no. 1, xi, 40 pp.

Erzählungen"[8]. Towards the end of 1902 G. R. Sundström sent Littmann the text of *The Legend of the Queen of Sheba*. The man who wrote the text down was "one of our evangelists of the Mensa tribe"[9]. Footnotes to the text preceded by the letter S are those of Sundström. The Tigre text appears on the left hand page with an English translation opposite. The text itself—about six pages—is in Ethiopic script, gemination not being marked and the final *a* of the verb in the perfect, third person, masculine singular, being represented by the first order[10]. These and other orthographic features found in this work are typical of the manner in which Tigre texts were transcribed by people of the Swedish Mission. Notwithstanding the generally consistent transcription and fairly accurate translation, the major part of the credit here due to Littmann derives from his editing of the material: he did not work on the material with an "informant" and thus had to rely entirely on Sundström in the case of passages that he did not understand or grammatical forms with which he was not acquainted.

"Tigrē-Erzählungen" is a collection of six Tigre tales rendered in Ethiopic script. The Ethiopic script is given on the right hand page followed by a free translation into German. On the left hand page the text is rendered in a narrow phonetic transcription with an interlinear translation into German. This collection of tales, both as to its nature and quality, resembles the prose material which appears in *Publications of the Princeton expedition to Abyssinia*, the symbol for gemination being omitted in the Ethiopic script owing to the presence of the coexisting transcription. No scholar has rendered better service to the cause of Tigre studies than E. Littmann. The translated and annotated texts of *Publications* have been a cornerstone of the work of the student of Tigre. Yet Littmann, especially in the earlier stages of his collection of texts and research, was heavily indebted to the endeavours in the field by members of the Swedish Evangelical Mission in Eritrea.

Texts published by Swedish Missionaries (and works connected with those texts)

Texts published by members of the Swedish Mission show two different levels of Tigre style: there are (a) folk tales, biblical tales, customs and rites, law, history of the Mansaʿ people, medicines and diseases, poetry, etc., and (b) Bible translations whose style is literary in the sense that it does not reflect the colloquial language in the manner that most of the prose texts of (a) do.

8 E. Littmann, "Tigrē-Erzählungen", *ZDMG* (1911), pp. 697-708.
9 In a letter from Sundström to Littmann, *The Legend of the Queen of Sheba*, x:16.
10 Cf. footnote 4 above.

Texts collected by K. G. Rodén

The most prominent text published in book form by the Swedish Mission is *Kəl'e Mansa'* - *The Two Mansa'*, or as it is better known among western scholars: *Le tribù dei Mensa*[11]. The text is in Ethiopic script. There is a preface in Italian (vii-x), for the benefit of the western reader, as well as a preface in Tigre (xi-xiii) which is directed at the indigenous Mansa' reader. K. G. Rodén, the head of the Missionary Station at Galab, devoted a considerable period— between his arrival in Galab in 1890[12] and the publication of *Kəl'e Mansa'* in 1913—to collecting material for the book, which is printed in two parts. The first part (pp. 1-87), entitled *Dəgəm Mansa'*—"The story of Mansa'", contains a description of genealogies of the Mansa', accounts of historical and of tribal traditions. Tables of genealogies (pp. 88-91) conclude part one. Part two, entitled *Fətəḥ Maḥāri wa'ādotāt*—"The law of Maḥāri and customs", consists of an account of the law and customs of the Mansa' tribes. Some of the tales and customs found in both parts of this book are also found in Littmann's *Publications of the Princeton expedition to Abyssinia*, volume I[13] in slightly different versions. A free translation by Rodén into Italian of *Kəl'e Mansa'* was published along with the Tigre version[14]. A much more accurate translation—which exists only for the second part of *Kəl'e Mansa'*— is the one into German, *Das Feteḥ Maḥārī*[15] made by M. Höfner. M. Höfner's translation incorporates a commentary with many references to Littmann's *Publication of the Princeton Expedition*. Critical observations on the translation of *Fətəḥ Maḥārī*, into Italian by Rodén and into German by Höfner, were later made by W. Leslau[16].

The credit for the only valuable[17] Tigre reader in existence —*Kətāb Fidel*—

---

11 K. G. Rodén, *Le tribù dei Mensa*. Storia, legge e costumi. A. Testo originale tigrè, Asmara, Evangeliska Fosterlands-Stiftelsens Förlags-expedition, 1913, xiii, 192 pp.

12 In 1900 Rodén handed over some material to C. Conti Rossini. Cf. section on Conti Rossini below. See *Tribù*, p. xi:10-13.

13 Cf. e.g.: *Tribù*, 3:18-4:6 with *PLI*, story no. 73; *Tribù*, 4:20-5:1 with *PLI*, story no. 74; *FM*, 102:23 et seq. with *PLI*, 112:5 et seq.

14 *Le tribù dei Mensa*, Storia, legge e costumi. B. Traduzione italiana, Stockholm, 1913, xi, 352 pp.

15 M. Höfner, *Das Feteḥ Maḥārī*. Sitten und Recht der Mänsa'. Nach dem Tigrē-Text K. G. Rodén's übersetzt. Verlag der: Akademie der Wissenschaften und Literatur in Mainz, Abhandlungen der Geistes- und sozialwissenschaftlichen Klasse, Jahrgang 1951, Nr. 8, pp. 647-746, off print, 102 pp.

16 W. Leslau, "Linguistic observations on a Tigre codex", *RSE* 11, 1952, pp. 33-46.

17 Two other readers exist: (a) *Fidel wəlād higa təgre lalətmaharobu*, Mukullo, 1889, 35 pp.; (b) *Fidel nāy higa təgre*, Asmara: Missione Cattolica, 1908, 32 pp., the first being a syllabary only, the second containing sentences, but not texts—being of doubtful value.

goes to K. G. Rodén. This reader—using Ethiopic script only—has gone through three editions, Rodén himself being the editor of the first two [18]. The third edition of the reader [19] is one revised by Musa Aron and published under the sponsorship of A. Berglund of the Swedish Mission. This third edition has been adapted to the needs of the young learner by means of a complete revision of the first part—entitled *'Ag'aẓot*—"spelling"—dealing with reading exercises, and by leaving out sections of the second part —entitled *Qər'ān*—"reading"—in the case of material thought by the reviser to be unsuitable for the young learner. The second part of the book (pp. 54-112) includes short phrases (pp. 54-55), salutations (p. 56), tales—some adapted from foreign languages—riddles and a few poems.

As well as participating in the translation of the New Testament into Tigre [20], Rodén translated into Tigre—in Ethiopic script—two theological works, based on Martin Luther's catechism [21]. Scriptural quotations in these works are taken from the Tigre translation of the New Testament [22] with some changes and omissions which simplify the literary style of that particular translation. Other texts in the publication of which K. G. Rodén participated are *Racconti biblici* — *'Adgāmāt qəddus kətāb* [23] and *Manuale di storia sacra* — *Dəgəm qəddus kətāb* [24]. Both publications, which are in Ethiopic script, consist of a selection of simplified versions of stories from the Bible translated from Swedish. *Racconti biblici* was originally translated by the Revd. A. Renlund

---

18 K. G. Rodén, *Sillabario della lingua tigré*. Per cura della Società evangelica nazionale svedese. Asmara: Tipografia della Missione Evangelica Svedese, 1904, 127 pp. K. G. Rodén, *Sillabario e comprimento per le scuole elementari inferiori in lingua tigré*. Seconda edizione, Asmara: Società Evangelica nazionale svedese, 1916, 173 pp.

19 K. G. Rodén, *Kətāb 'ag'aẓot waqər'ān*, 3rd edition, revised by Musa Aron, Printing and Stationery Directorate, Asmara, 1958, 112 p.

20 See the paragraph on Bible translations at the end of this section.

21 K. G. Rodén, transl., *Dottrina Cristiana, secondo il Piccolo Catechismo di Martino Lutero*, per opera del comitato catechistico (in Isvezia). Liberamente tradotta dallo svedese in tigré da K. G. Rodén. Asmara: Tipografia della Missione Evangelica Svedese, 1920, 128 pp. (pp. 117 et seq—the contents of the book). K. G. Rodén, transl., *Martino Lutero Piccolo Catechismo*. Tradotto in Tigrè da K. G. Rodén. Asmara: Missione Evangelica, 1926, 23 pp.

22 See the paragraph on Bible translations at the end of this section.

23 Norlén Wilh., and Fr. Lundgren, *Racconti biblici*. Illustrati, per le scuole elementari inferiori, di Wilh. Norlén e Fr. Lundgren, Rettori di scuole magistrali. Tradotti dallo svedese in tigrè da A. Renlund e K. G. Rodén. Asmara: Evangeliska-Fosterlands Förlags-expedition, 1916, 57 pp.

24 Norlén Wilh., and Fr. Lundgren, *Manuale di storia sacra* (versione tigré). Seconda edizione. Riveduta da K. G. Rodén e Giuseppe Hemmed. Asmara: Tipografia Evangelica, 1925, 200 pp.

with the help of an indigenous scholar[25], but was not then published. Years later Rodén undertook the work of revising the text which was finally published in 1916. The book contains stories from the Old (pp. 5-35) and New (37-58) Testaments.

Manuale di storia sacra which was published ten years later, in 1925, is an enlarged and revised version of *Racconti biblici*. At the end of the enlarged version there are four appendices consisting of: (a) the names of the books of the Bible (pp. 178-180); (b) a table of the most important events "from the time of the creation of the world until Christ and from Christ until our time"[26] (pp. 181-185); (c) a list of names appearing in the Bible with interpretations (pp. 186-193); (d) a list of abbreviations and symbols used in the book (p. 194). The above two publications supply the student of Tigre with excellent material as regards the syntactic structure of the language; all stories appearing in the shorter version of the work appear also in the enlarged edition, and comparisons of syntactic phenomena may thus be drawn. Furthermore, a comparison of three versions of certain texts is possible in the case of stories from the New Testament, owing to the existence of the Tigre translation of the latter.

To complete the list of publications by K. G. Rodén, it remains to mention a collection of songs: *Darus Ṣəyon — Cantici di Sion*[27] translated and edited by Rodén in collaboration with R. Sundström. This work, like all of Rodén's other texts, is in Ethiopic script and consists of three hundred and ten religious songs. An index to the songs, in Ethiopic alphabetical order and according to the first word of the opening verse, is found on pp. 423-435.

Texts collected by G. R. Sundström

The Revd. G. R. Sundström, a contemporary of K. G. Rodén, became known as Tigre scholar not only through the texts that he published but also by reason of the help that he offered to E. Littmann, in terms of both scholarly knowledge and the collection of material[28]. From a general point of view it

---

25 Yosef Ḥammad who helped Rodén and other members of the Swedish Mission with their translations into Tigre.

26 *Manuale di storia sacra*, 181:3. The first date given is that of the creation of the world, 4165 B.C., and the latest date—that of the translation of the Bible into Amharic, 1841 A.D.

27 K. G. Rodén and G. R. Sundström, transl., *Cantici di Sion*. In Tigrè. Tradotti ed ordinati da K. G. Rodén e R. Sundström. Seconda edizione. Asmara: Missione Evangelica Svedese, 1931, 437 pp.

28 See above, section on Littmann's collected texts.

can be said that Sundström presented his material in a more scholarly manner than his colleagues at the Swedish Mission, perhaps owing to his fruitful relation with E. Littmann. A few, relatively short, texts were published by Sundström.

One[29] was published in 1904 as an article in collaboration with E. Littmann, at a time when Sundström's experience of the Tigre language was limited to a couple of years. The text consists of two pages in Ethiopic script (pp. 11-12) out of the 34 pages of the whole article, one page of text being a Tigre tale, the other a song connected with it. The rest of the article is a translation (pp. 3-4) and commentary (pp. 4-10) in Swedish, with a translation of the Swedish into German (pp. 13-23) by E. Littmann. At the end of the article a phonetic transcription of the song is given (pp. 23-24), followed by a small glossary in phonetic transcription and a Swedish and German translation of this (pp. 25-34).

Another Sundström text published five years later, deals with (a) illnesses, injuries and their cure, (b) medicines, their preparation and use. The text is in Ethiopic script and a translation into Swedish is provided. Part A)[30] (pp. 127-151), entitled *'Amər 'ādār*—"The knowledge of illnesses", consists of a list of illnesses and injuries with, in each case, a description of symptoms and an outline of treatment. Part B)[31] (pp. 152-173), entitled *'Amər 'asəryat*—"The knowledge of remedies", consists of a list of medical trees and plants together with an account of the manner in which medicines are prepared, preserved and administered (i.e. dosages and frequencies).

The Sundström text[32] most enlightening from a linguistic point of view was published in 1914. Sundström wrote it, after a stay of twelve years among the Tigre-speaking peoples, with the stated aim of giving an idea of Tigre pronunciation and accent. In the preambule to the text an account is given of certain phonetic phenomena, the most interesting of which are the allophonic forms of the vowel *a*. Apart from his unclear statement that "the vowel of the first order is always short"[33], Sundström gives a striking description of the

---

29 G. R. Sundström, "En sång på tigrè-språket", upptecknad, öfversatt ock förklarad af R. Sundström. Utgifven och öfversatt till tyska af Enno Littmann. Uppsala: Akademiska bokhandeln, *SKVH*, vol. 8, no. 6, 1904, 34 pp.

30 G. R. Sundström, "Sjukdomar ock deras behandling av infödingar i Mänsa'", *MO* 3, 1909, pp. 127-151.

31 G. R. Sundström, "Kännedom om läkemedel ock deras användning bland infödingarne i Mänsa'", *MO* 3, 1909, pp. 152-173. Parts A) and B) appear as consecutive but separate articles.

32 G. R. Sundström, "Some Tigré texts with transliteration and translation", *MO* 8, 1914, pp. 1-15.

33 Ibid., page 1, A.

allophones of *a* though without relating them to their positional values. It is quite clear from this description that *a* may be open or close, front or centralized, and that the distinction between first and fourth order vowels cannot, thus, be a question of vowel-quality. Neither Sundström nor any other student of Tigre, for a long time afterwards, took pains to continue the analysis beyond this point; only in recent years has any advance been made as regards this aspect of Tigre phonology [34]. This third Sundström text contains four Tigre tales in Ethiopic script, each tale being followed by a narrow phonetic transcription with an interlinear translation; this in turn being followed by a free translation into English. The style of each tale is highly narrative, as if proceeding directly from the narrator's mouth.

A document of Sundström's concerning the "'Ad Šek" [35], a Tigre-speaking Muslim tribe [36], may be mentioned here. It was turned over by Sundström to Littmann and later published by M. Höfner. The text—in Ethiopic script—consists of a genealogy of the tribe and an account of its law, customs and songs together with a translation into German and a commentary.

Texts collected by C. Conti Rossini

A contribution to the corpus of Tigre texts was made by C. Conti Rossini, whose *Dəgəm Mansa'*—"Tradizioni storiche dei Mensa" [37] was, in fact, the first valuable text to be published in Tigre. The text, in Ethiopic script (pp. 45-68), gives an account of the history of the two branches of Mansa' and there follows a translation into Italian and a commentary (pp. 69-99). The Tigre text also contains (pp. 68-69) a short folktale, *Dəgəm walat ḥaṣay*—"The legend of the king's daughter". In a preambule Conti Rossini explains how and when his material was collected (pp. 41-44) and provides an ethnological introduction to the Tigre-speaking peoples. In his work Conti Rossini was helped by K. G. Rodén [38] and by Rodén's native assistant Tawalada Madḥən.

Indeed, a comparison of Rodén's 1913 text—bearing the same Tigre name *Dəgəm Mansa'*—*Le tribù dei Mensa*—with that of Conti Rossini's shows that the

34 See F. R. Palmer, "Openness in Tigre", *BSOAS* 18, fasc. 3, 1954, pp. 561-577. See also *The morphology of the Tigre noun* by the same author, §§ 1.2, 1.6 and 1.7. This work is dealt with at the beginning of section B of this paper.

35 M. Höfner, "Überlieferungen bei Tigrē-Stämmen (1). 'Ad Šek", *AE* 4, 1961, pp. 181-203.

36 Cf.: *PLi*, 285:5.

37 C. Conti Rossini, "Tradizioni storiche dei Mensa", *GSAI* 14, 1901, pp. 41-99.

38 Cf. ibid., p. 41:9-15.

same Tigre source underlies both[39]. Another text edited by C. Conti Rossini worth mentioning is "Documenti per lo studio della lingua tigré"[40]. This publication contains Tigre texts in phonetic transcription with an Italian translation. The transcription shows some peculiarities with regard to the phonetics and to the morphology of the Tigre language, e.g.: *y*, which is not geminated in the Tigre of Mansaʿ, is here geminated[41]; palatalization is marked as if it occurred regularly, when in fact it is non-existent in Tigre[42]; gemination appears in the consonants of certain words where gemination is in fact also non-existent[43]. The collection contains[44]: (a) fifty proverbs, (b) thirty-seven riddles, (c) two stories, a translation being given immediately after each proverb, tale and story.

Texts collected by W. Leslau

Leslau's "Tigre games"[45] consists of seven children's games in phonetic transcription, the Tigre text of each game being followed by an English translation. This material was recorded by Leslau during his stay in Keren in 1947, a stay which also yielded his "Supplementary observations on Tigre grammar"[46]. Some of the grammatical footnotes that appear in "Tigre games" appear also in the "Supplementary observations". However, further analysis was made of the material included in "Tigre games" since it was originally collected (1947) and commented on (1948). The phonetic transcription of the text shows some peculiarities: the gemination of semi-vowels[47] and the recurrence of the form *ʾəndä*—"while" instead of *ʾəndo*[48], other peculiarities occurring in either one of the works[49].

39 Cf. e.g., C. Ross. Trad., pp. 60-61 with *Tribù*, 46:27 et seq.; C. Ross. Trad., 63:13 et seq. with *Tribù*, 40:10 et seq.; C. Ross. Trad., 59:7 with *Tribù*, 8:8.

40 C. Conti Rossini, "Documenti per lo studio della lingua tigré", *GSAI* 16, 1903, pp. 1-32.

41 As e.g.: p. 6, no. 36; p. 7, no. 43; p. 18:21.

42 As e.g.: *teẓabbičko*—"I was sold (the slave cries [saying])", p. 8, no. 49 (phonetic transcription as in the original).

43 As e.g.: *ḥaqqobâ*—"after that", 14:8; *ellú*—"for him", 18:21 (phonetic transcription as in the original).

44 C. Ross. Doc. also contains a translation into Italian with a commentary (pp. 21-32), the text in Tigre appearing in *Ricordo di un soggiorno in Eritrea*, 1903, pp. 67-78.

45 W. Leslau, "Tigre games", *RSE* 17, 1961, pp. 61-68.

46 See section B) below.

47 As, e.g.: "Tigre games", p. 63, footnote 2; p. 64, footnote 7; "Supplementary observations", p. 128 §4; p. 131 §27a).

48 As, e.g.; "Tigre games", p. 62, footnote 2; "Supplementary observations", p. 137, §156a).

49 As, e.g.: "Tigre games", p. 64, footnote 3, where the form *ʾəllu*, instead of *ʾəlu*—"[which is] for him", is questioned by Leslau himself; "Supplementary observations", p. 127. §1, where examples of fricative [q] are given.

Bible translations

Only two parts of the Old Testament were translated into Tigre: *The Book of Psalms—Dərsān dāwəd*[50] and *The Book of Isaiah—Kətāb 'Esayās*[51]. G. R. Sundström is to be credited with the work, though its publication is posthumous. The names of the native speakers who helped him are not on record. As regards the New Testament, the first part to appear in print was the Gospel of St. Mark[52], from the Swedish Mission press at Monkullo—where there was at that time one of the two missionary stations among the Tigre speaking people (the other being at Galab). This translation into Tigre, in an Ethiopic script whose orthography is not consistent, was done by indigenous scholars under the supervision of Dr. C. Winqvist, a missionary physician, whose own scholarship was more in the domain of Tigrinya. The entire New Testament in Tigre was first published in 1902 by the Swedish Mission Press at Asmara. K. G. Rodén, the principal of the Mission station at Galab, supervised the work of translation which was carried out with the help of the native teachers at the Swedish Mission[53]. Books of the New Testament used now among Tigre speaking Christians are reprints of a second edition of the 1902 publication, produced in a revised and improved form at Asmara in 1931[54]. All Tigre Bible translations appear in Ethiopic script.

B. GRAMMATICAL MATERIAL

The scarcity of Tigre texts is paralleled by a scarcity of grammatical works. Practically all the grammatical works of the earlier period of Tigre studies are of no descriptive value to the student of Tigre, some of them now being linguistic curiosities of primarily historical value, while others were written by people who lacked the required skill or qualification for the task. Most

50 G. R. Sundström, transl., *I Salmi di Davide* in lingua tigré. Prima edizione. Pubblicato dalla Società Biblica britannica e forestiera, Asmara: Tipografia Evangelica, 1925.

51 G. R. Sundström, transl., *Il Libro di Isaia* in lingua tigré. Prima edizione. Pubblicato dalla Società Biblica britannica e forestiera, Asmara: Tipografia Evangelica, 1925.

52 *Evangelium enligt Markus på Tigre-Språket*, tryckt på Misssionspressen i Monkullo, 1889, 52 pp.

53 As for the sources from which the translation was made, see: E. Ullendorff, *Ethiopia and the Bible*, Oxford University Press for the British Academy, 1968, p. 71.

54 Ḥaddis Galad — 'əb ḥiga təgre, kālə' ḥətām 'ərrum — Il Nuovo Testamento in lingua tigré. Seconda edizione riveduta. Pubblicato a cura della Società Biblica britannica e forestiera, Asmara: Tipografia Evangelica, 1931.

of the credit for grammatical work on Tigre goes to E. Littmann, W. Leslau, and F. R. Palmer, the latter having made the strongest impact in his endeavours to bring Tigre studies into the domain of modern linguistic research.

Grammatical writings of E. Littmann, and connected works

E. Littmann published several monographs and articles concerning various aspects of Tigre grammar. The most comprehensive, "Das Verbum der Tigresprache" [55], is based on the published texts and grammatical works that were available at that time. A survey of such material is given at the beginning of the article (pp. 133-140), followed by an attempt at outlining distinctive dialectal features (pp. 140-152). General observations of a comparative and diachronic nature are made in part one (pp. 152-159).

Some of the gaps in *Das Verbum* were filled by M. Höfner in her article "Probleme der Verbalstammbildung im Tigrē" [56]. In this article M. Höfner attempts an analysis of the relationship of form and meaning between verb-moulds such as *qal* [57] (i.e. the invariable element of verb compounds whose second element is *bela*), *qalla* (i.e. triradicals with similar second and third radicals) and *qalqala* on the one hand; *qatla*, *qatlala* and *qataltala* on the other—with the preformatives *'an-* and *'as-* being examined in appropriate instances. Verbs of the form *qetala* and *qotala* are incorporated in the tables of examples. The data for this article appear in *Wörterbuch der Tigrē-Sprache* [58].

An article concerning the pronoun in Tigre, "Die Pronomina im Tigrē" [59], was published by Littmann prior to the publication of *Das Verbum*, utilizing the same corpus of material. This article—in two fascicles—includes a description of the personal pronoun, the pronominal suffixes with the noun and the verb, indirect suffixes (i.e. "Mittelbare suffixe", which are in fact the prepositions *'al*—"to, for", *'at*—"in, on, by, with"), the pronominal copula *tu*, the possessive *nāy*, the reflexive (as expressed by *nos*—"self", *ra'as*—"head, self"), the reciprocal (*nosnos*), the demonstrative, the definite article and the relative *la-*, the interrogative pronouns and, finally the indefinite pronoun (as expressed by the enclitic *-ma* with *gale*, *sema*—"some, any"). A short article by

---

55 E. Littmann, "Das Verbum der Tigresprache", *ZA* 13, 1898, pp. 133-178; *ZA* 14, 1899, pp. 1-102.
56 M. Höfner, "Probleme der Verbalstammbildung im Tigrē", *ZDMG* 101, 1951, pp. 89-106.
57 The graphemes q, t, l, stand for the radicals of the verbal root.
58 See section C) below.
59 E. Littmann, "Die Pronomina im Tigrē". Ein Beitrag zur aethiopischen Dialektkunde, *ZA* 12, 1897, pp. 188-230, 291-316.

Littmann, "Die Diminutivbildung im Tigrē"[60], deals with the formation of the diminutive in Tigre, mainly in proper names. The corpus of texts used is that of Littmann's *Publications of the Princeton expedition to Abyssinia*, where the lists of proper names and appellatives contain the equivalent diminutive forms[61]. Another short article by Littmann, "Bilitterale Verba im Tigrē"[62], deals with the morphology of irregular biradical verbs. The article is in the nature of a supplement to Littmann's *Das Verbum* (see section B above).

Grammatical writings of F. R. Palmer

F. R. Palmer has added a new dimension to reasearch work in Tigre by his attempts to put it on a purely descriptive plane. He has been able to do this because of the material he collected in field work during his stay in Eritrea in the early fifties. Palmer has written three grammatical essays on the Tigre language, the most comprehensive being *The morphology of the Tigre noun*[63]. In the first part of this book Palmer provides a brief discussion of the phonology of Tigre (pp. 1-10), emphasizing the principle of assimilation which is the most influential factor in phonetic variation in Tigre. In chapters two and three (pp. 10-15) the writer establishes an outline of those criteria, such as types of formation, noun and adjective, number and gender, etc., which form the basis of the classification in the following chapters. Chapters four (pp. 16-34) and five (pp. 35-39) deal with broken plurals and suffixed plurals respectively. Chapter six (pp. 40-64) deals with "derivatives", i.e.: diminutives, pejoratives and augmentatives, according to form and meaning; an analysis of problematic forms (i.e.: forms which raise problems of classification) being made at the end of the chapter (pp. 62-65). In chapter seven (pp. 66-69) and eight (70-73) respectively pronominal suffixes and adjectives are discussed. The grammatical part of the book is augmented by a list of nouns—arranged according to the different structural patterns of the singular form—and consists of material collected by the writer and selected by him for

60 E. Littmann, "Die Diminutivbildung im Tigrē". Estratto dagli Annali del R. Istituto Superiore Orientale di Napoli. Nuova Serie, volume II, Roma: Tipografia del Senato, 1942-XX, 89-103.

61 See *PLI*, p. 137 et seq.

62 E. Littmann, "Bilitterale Verba im. Tigrē". Donum natalicium H. S. Nyberg oblatum. Uppsala, 1954, p. 94-101.

63 F. R. Palmer, *The Morphology of the Tigre noun*. London: Oxford University Press, 1962, 96 pp. (London Oriental Series, vol. 13); The other two are: F. R. Palmer, "Openness in Tigre", *BSOAS*, 18, fasc. 3, 1954, pp. 561-577; F. R. Palmer, "Relative clauses in Tigre", *Word*, 17, 1961, pp. 24-33.

the purpose of this work. A glossary of the linguistic terms used in the book rounds off the work.

Grammars

Two attempts have been made to produce comprehensive works on Tigre grammar[64], the first in 1919, *Grammatica della lingua tigrè*[65], and the second, *Short grammar of Tigre*[66], in 1945. *Grammatica della lingua Tigrè* contains a description of grammatical data (pp. 10-71), texts with Italian translation (pp. 79-90) and vocabulary: Tigre-Italian (pp. 93-186) and Italian-Tigre (pp. 189-292) The Tigre material is in Ethiopic script. The grammatical data are not very helpful to the student of Tigre, since (a) the grammatical framework used is that of another language (probably Italian), and (b) many features of the data given are foreign to the Tigre language. Leslau's *Short grammar of Tigre* is the only valuable grammar of the language available. The book is a reprint of two articles which appeared in the same year[67], the dialect described being that of Mansa'. Leslau's treatise is mainly based on Littmann's *Publications of the Princeton expedition to Abyssinia*, volume I, and on certain of Littmann's articles. The Tigre material is given as a transliteration of the Ethiopic script of the sources used. The main problem which Leslau faced was his inability to check the material in the field. Consequently he left unsolved certain grammatical problems where he considered the evidence from existing material to be insufficient. Thus he made an attempt to supplement his work with fresh material which he collected while on a visit to Keren in Eritrea. The results were published as "Supplementary observations on Tigré grammar"[68]. The new material enabled him to throw further light on basic problems. However as he himself remarked, his time in the field had been too limited to carry out a systematic investigation.

---

64 The work on the Beni 'Amər dialect: A.C. Beaton and A. Paul, *A grammar and vocabulary of the Tigre language* (as spoken by the Beni Amer). Khartum: Publications Bureau, 1954, 88 pp., mimeographed, is not covered by the above statement. In any case, the worth of this book to the student of Tigre is not very great, mainly owing to the non-linguistic presentation of the data.

65 *Grammatica della lingua tigrè*, con annesso: Vocabolario tigrè-italiano e italiano-tigrè. Per cura della Missione Cattolica dell'Eritrea, Asmara: Tip. Francescana, 1919, 299 pp.

66 W. Leslau, *Short grammar of Tigré* (North Ethiopic), Dialect of Mensa. New Haven, 1945. Publications of the American Oriental Society. Offprint series, no. 18.

67 W. Leslau, "The verb in Tigré (North Ethiopic), Dialect of Mensa", *JAOS* 65, 1945, pp. 1-26; W. Leslau, "Grammatical Sketches in Tigré (North Ethiopic), Dialect of Mensa", *JAOS* 65, 1945, pp. 164-203.

68 W. Leslau, "Supplementary observations on Tigré grammar", *JAOS* 68, 1948, pp. 127-139.

C. LEXICAL MATERIAL

The only valuable dictionary of Tigre in existence—E. Littmann's *Wörterbuch der Tigrē-Sprache*[69]—incorporates most vocabularies and glossaries published previously. Littmann's *Publications of the Princeton expedition to Abyssinia* was the main text used, but almost all other published texts are represented as well. It also includes material produced by Sundström, Naffa' wad 'Etmān, and others, and thus saw light of publication for the first time in this Dictionary. M. Höfner who participated in the work of editing had the immense task of rounding it off. The Tigre entries are in Ethiopic script and in Ethiopic alphabetical order, with translations into German and English. The heading of a verb entry is usually given in the perfect, third person, singular masculine, the final consonant being put in the fourth order when it is a final semivowel. The heading of a verb entry is the verb form of the basic stem, other types of formation and their prefixed derivatives—with attested participles and infinitives—being given in each case. Each entry is usually attributed to several sources, and lexical, grammatical and dialectal notes accasionally given. Idiomatic expressions and compound words are included as well, full utterances being sometimes given as examples. At the end of many entries etymologies are adduced from Gə'əz, Tigrinya and Amharic, and the Arabic origin is given where the source of the Tigre word is Arabic. Proper names, names of tribes, names of animals, names of stars and geographical names appear in a list at the end of the book (pp. 678-738). An addendum which deals mainly with additional etymologies to previous entries rounds off the book (pp. 739-744). *Wörterbuch der Tigrē-Sprache* is an impressive work. Its range of entries covers almost all published texts of the language and the various sources attributed to each item of an entry make a fine collection of examples. The dictionary has, however, a weak point: too many entries are based on Littmann's poetry collection[70], where the meaning is frequently that of the contextual sense—specific to a certain verse—and not that of the general lexical content. Thus *balsa*[71], for example, has three meanings:I. "to turn (over)"; 2. "to cause to be"; 3. "to answer". Meaning no. 2 is practically non-existent in prose and would be unintelligible to the native speaker of Tigre outside the specific poetic context in which it occurs. From a general point of view it can be said that the dictionary is a compilation

---

69 E. Littmann und Maria Höfner, *Wörterbuch der Tigrē-Sprache.* Tigrē-Deutsch-Englisch, Wiesbaden: Franz Steiner Verlag, 1962, 744 pp.
70 *Publications of the Princeton expedition to Abyssinia*, vol. III.
71 *LH*, 269b.

of linguistic forms and their meanings as found in certain texts, rather than a reflection of the spoken language. The disadvantage of this is that the spoken Tigre of today is represented to a limited extent only.

Arabic loanwords in Tigre were analyzed by Wolf Leslau in "Arabic loanwords in Tigre", *Word* 12 (1956).125-141; and in "Additional Arabic loanwords in Tigre", *Al-Hudhud. Festschrift Maria Höfner zum 80 Geburtstag* (ed. Roswitha G. Stiegner, Graz, 1981), pp. 171-198. Suggestions for comparisons between Geez, Tigrinya, Amharic and Tigre using Enno Littmann and Maria Höfner's *Wörterbuch der Tigrē-Sprache* as a base were made by W. Leslau in *North Ethiopic and Amharic Cognates in Tigre* (Supplemento no. 31 *Annali. Istituto Orientale di Napoli*, 1982, vol. 42, 86 pages).

Abbreviations

AE	Annales d'Ethiopie.
'Ag'azot	K.G. Rodén, *Kətāb 'ag'azot waqər'ān*, 3rd ed., revised by Musa Aron, Asmara, 1958.
C. Ross. Doc.	C. Conti Rossini, "Documenti per lo studio della lingua tigré", *GSAI* 16, 1903, pp. 1-32.
C. Ross. Trad.	C. Conti Rossini, "Tradizioni storiche dei Mensa", *GSAI* 14, 1901, pp. 41-99.
Das Verbum	E. Littmann, "Das Verbum der Tigresprache", *ZA* 13, 1898, pp. 133-178; *ZA* 14, 1899, pp. 1-102.
FM	K.G. Rodén, *Fətaḥ Maḥāri wa'ādotāt* (Part two of *Le tribù dei Mensa*, pp. 95-187).
JAOS	Journal of the American Oriental Society.
LH	E. Littmann und M. Höfner, *Wörterbuch der Tigrē-Sprache*, Wiesbaden, 1962.
MO	Le Monde oriental.
Publications	E. Littmann, *Publications of the Princeton expedition to Abyssinia*. Leyden, 1910-1915, 4 vol. in 5.
PL	ditto.
RSE	Rassegna di studi etiopici.
SKVH	Skrifter utgifna af K. Humanistiska Vetenskaps-Samfundet i Uppsala.
ZA	Zeitschrift für Assyriologie.
ZDMG	Zeitschrift der deutschen morgenländischen Gesellschaft.

B. A. TURAEV'S CONTRIBUTION TO THE WORLD SCIENCE OF ETHIOPIAN STUDIES

Maria V. Right

Institute for African Studies, USSR

Among Turaev's numerous contributions to the field of Oriental studies, a great number of them contain works on history, philology and culture of Ethiopia. B. A. Turaev has left such a rich heritage in this field that it deserves without doubt thorough study. In this article we shall restrict ourselves to considering only his most important writings on different aspects of Ethiopian studies in order to show the versality and significance of his explorations.

Having learned by himself the basis of the ancient Ethiopian Geʿez (Geez), Turaev perfected his knowledge due to frequent contact with the great Russian scientist V. V. Bolotov to whose memory he later dedicated one of his most interesting works [1].

During his first foreign mission, Turaev took part in learning Ethiopic from Schrader. This gave him a more profound knowledge of Geʿez. Later on, with direct participation of B. A. Turaev, the teaching of Geʿez at the Petersburg University was brought up to a higher level. I would like to stress in particular the fact that Turaev always strove to have the students read texts in the language as soon as possible, thereby giving them the opportunity to use the ancient Ethiopian language in practice. It can be said that B. A. Turaev laid the foundation of Ethiopian linguistics in Russia, and was followed by a group of Soviet scientists, his closest pupils being I. Yu. Krachkovski, N. V. Yushmanov, T. L. Turumova and others.

His intimate knowledge of the ancient Ethiopian language has helped Turaev acquaint Russian and foreign readers with the monuments of Geʿez literature. Following B. A. Dorn, Turaev proceeded with a description of Ethiopian manuscripts in St. Petersburg. Having begun his work in 1897, he had already published the full catalogue of these manuscripts by 1906 [2].

For the first time in Russia, Turaev published a great number of Ethiopian manuscripts in Geʿez with a Russian translation and comments. Unfortunately

---

1 B. A. Turaev, *Investigations in the Field of Hagiological Sources on Ethiopian History*, St.Pb., 1902 (printed in Russian).

2 B. A. Turaev, "Ethiopian Manuscripts in Saint-Peterburg", *ZVORAO*. St. Pb., 1906, issue II-III, vol. XVII, p. 115-248 (printed in Russian).

not all of these translations have been drawn into scientific circulation though they represent a rich source for studying Ethiopian history.

In 1902, one of the most significant of Turaev's works on Ethiopian studies, *Investigations in the Field of Hagiological Sources on Ethiopian History*, was published. Academician I. Yu. Krachkovski said: "This monograph has definitely put Turaev in the forefront of European researchers of Ethiopia, and in the field of hagiological literature he has been indisputably recognized the greatest expert" [3].

Though Turaev was not the first to use this method [4], the importance of his work for the reconstruction of certain stages of Ethiopian history is hard to overestimate. Although Turaev himself in the preface to this work has emphasized that it would be impossible to write "almost the whole history of the Abyssinian (Ethiopian - M. R.) people only on the basis of hagiographical sources" [5], he noted the significance of these sources.

Turaev's research covers the period from the beginning of Axum to the end of the 17th century, that is, ancient and medieval Ethiopian history. He begins his work with a general characterization of the saints of the Ethiopian church. He dwells especially on the peculiarities of Ethiopian saints. The Ethiopian church is known not only to have been closely connected with the Coptic, but also fully subordinated to it. This explains why the Ethiopians worship Coptic saints as their own. But in the section "Saints of the Ethiopian church", Turaev points out local Ethiopian saints who occupy a notable place in the Ethiopian church calendar, and at the same time he examines the interplay between Coptic saints and those of Ethiopia. Here, in Ethiopia, one could see a concrete manifestation of the general historical process of the modification of world religion in a particular country. Turaev gives such examples of canonization. Thus some particular heroes often of mythical origin, enlighteners and even kings (Kaleb, Gebre Mesqel, Lalibela, Zera Ya'qob, Ba'eda Maryam, Lebna Dengel and others [6]) have been reckoned among the saints. Turaev draws an analogy with a similar process in Russia: "Abyssinian saints are local in the monophysite church exactly as the Russian

---

3 I. Yu. Krachkovski, *Introduction to Ethiopian Philology*, Leningrad, 1955, p. 106 (Printed in Russian).

4 Before Turaev, this method was applied by V. O. Kluchevski and Golubinski in their investigations on the history of Russia.

5 B. A. Turaev, *Investigations in the Field of Hagiological Sources on Ethiopian History*, p. VII.

6 B. A. Turaev, op. cit. p. 119, a transcription closer to the sound of the word has been used in the article, and in Turaev's quotations and works the transcription adopted by him has been kept.

saints are in the orthodox church"[7]. The remarkable thing is that the
Ethiopian church and the Ethiopian saint Takla Haymanot were worshipped
later on by the Copts[8]. In a separate chapter Turaev considers literary
peculiarities paying special attention to their origin and authorship. He
mentions that an answer to these questions can often be found in introduc-
tions, epilogues and notes, and sometimes directly in the main text. He
writes: "The authors of the 'Lives' generally were monks or clergymen, well-
read in the Holy Scriptures, who knew the Psalm-book and the Gospels by
heart, had studied the hagiological and apocryphal literature, and even were
acquainted with the Church Fathers"[9]. The establishment of the authorship
of this or that chronicle or 'Life' is of great importance for the dating of the
documents as well as for the elucidation of the authenticity of the events
reflected in the original sources. A careful literary analysis carried out by
Turaev helps to reveal borrowings in what are clearly original Ethiopian
texts[10].

The remaining parts of the book are mainly historical: they deal with the
Axum period, the transitional period, the time of persecution, Zera Ya'qob's
epoch, and the epoch of Franks. Special mention should be made of the
section on the transitional period. If, beginning with the 14th century,
historians have at their disposal different historical chronicles and travellers'
narrations, the sources used by Turaev for the period from late Axum until
'Amda Ṣeyon present themselves as almost unique and his research has not
lost its importance to this day. The sources used and cited by Turaev in this
section concern the lives of Lalibela, Neakuto Leab, Gebre Menfes Qiddus,
Takla Haymanot, Abbie Egzi' and Iraklid. The lives of Takla Haymanot and
of Gebre Menfes Qiddus are of special interest for the determination of the
southern boundaries of the Ethiopian empire of that time. Turaev identifies
Saint Abo about whom legends were spread not only among the Amharas,
but also among the Galla, Dawaro and Kafficho, with Gebre Menfes Qiddus
acting like Abe as "the master of fire and lightning"[11].

Turaev spends much more attention to the well-known Ethiopian saint
Takla Haymanot. Carefully analyzing different texts of this 'Life', he tried
to settle the question which still today intrigues researchers of Ethiopia,
namely the question of the time when Takla Haymanot lived. He came to

7 B. A. Turaev, op. cit. p. 9.
8 Ibid., p. 17.
9 Ibid., p. 27.
10 Ibid., p. 29.
11 Ibid., p. 81.

the conclusion that "the legend, placing Takla Haymanot at the period of Zagwe's rule and at the time of the so-called restauration of the Solomonic dynasty has been more convincing than that which made him a contemporary of Veniamin (Coptic patriarch - M.R.) and of Avva Ioann" [12].

The other descriptions of Lives containing material about the way of life of Northern Ethiopia are of equally great interest. As Turaev notes in his Conclusion, these Lives like the Lives of saints of the persecution epoch (15th-16th century) give important information about the history of Ethiopia after the decline of Axum's power when the cultural center had moved to the South in Amhara and Shoa. "Not being always accurate and authentic in relating facts, hagiological monuments", Turaev writes, "grasp more broadly, embrace more deeply and depict more vividly the historical life of its people than do chronicles" [13].

While recognizing the importance of the descriptions of the Lives of historical personalities and treating the Lives themselves as historical sources, we must note that B. A. Turaev undoubtedly has idealized these saints and has exaggerated their role in Ethiopian history. The decisive role in the preservation of the national integrity of Ethiopia has belonged not to them, but to the peoples of Ethiopia.

Due to I. Yu. Krachkovski's efforts, the various Ethiopian historical chronicles prepared by B. A. Turaev were published [14]. Turaev intended to publish all the chronicles of the 14th-16th century, but his premature death prevented him from doing so. As a result, only *The Legend of Amda Seyon's Crusade*, *The Chronicle of King Zera Ya'qob and His Successors*, and *The Cronicle of Lebna Dengel, Claudius and Minas* were published by him. There are prefaces to all the chronicles: two to the last two by Turaev, and those to the first chronicle as well as to the whole book by Krachkovski. The chronicles cited in this edition are written not only in ancient Ethiopic, but there are also Amharic words to be found, and this presented a great difficulty for translating. In fact the material used in the Ethiopian chronicles is both a direct continuation of and a supplement to those written sources which were used by Turaev in *Investigations in the Field of Hagiological Sources on Ethiopian History*.

The first of the chronicles, *The Legend of King Amda Seyon's Crusade*, is a valuable source for the restoration of Ethiopian history at the end of the

---

12 Ibid., p. 95.
13 Ibid., p. 288.
14 B. A. Turaev, *Abyssinian Chronicles of the 14th-16th century*, translated from Ethiopian, edited by I. Yu. Krachkovski, M.-L., 1936 (printed in Russian).

13th and the beginning of the 14th century; it gives a vivid picture of feudal wars of which the medieval history of Ethiopia is full. The author of the chronicle could reproduce in artistic form not only the battle of the Ethiopian ruler against the Muslims, but also acute conflicts between the ruler and the Christian clergy. It should be underlined that Turaev succeeded in substantially correcting J. Perruchon's translation. The material in the chronicle concerns feudal hierarchy, relations of vassals, and toponymic data still not elucidated at present; in comparison with later chronicles and travellers' narrations (Almeida, Zorzi and others), they can be a most valuable source for the restauration of the Ethiopian historical map of the 13th century, its feudal structure, and part of its political history.

The Chronicle of Zera Ya'qob and His Successors, as Turaev points out in his preface to it, is one of the most interesting documents informing us about an important epoch of cultural and political change in the history of the country, constant wars against Islam, and the beginning of relations with Western Europe[15]. At the same time Turaev stresses that the work has no "strict chronological basis, historical perspective, literary harmony, actual completeness"[16]. The chronicle is of special value because it contains most curious material on various customs and rites many of which were forgotten and again revived at the time of Zar'a Ya'qob.

The Chronicles of Lebna Dengel, Claudius and Minas deal with one of the most turbulent periods of Ethiopian history—an invasion of Ethiopia, on the one hand, by Turks-Osmans supported by the forces of the Muslim Sultanate Adal under the leadership of Ahmed ibn Ibrahim el Ghazi (nicknamed Grañ, i.e. the left-handed), and on the other hand an intrusion of the Galla. These are glorious pages in the historical past of the Ethiopian people when Ethiopia inspite of all these difficulties and complications managed to preserve the integrity of the state and did not fall under the opression of the Portuguese who, under the guise of "assistance", tried to strengthen their foothold in the country. We do not agree with B. A. Turaev who criticizes the authors of the chronicle for their telling little because of their "national feeling about the role of 'Franks', i.e. Portuguese, in saving Abyssinia"[17]. In our opinion, this is a merit of the chronicles and not a shortcoming. Of course, the Portuguese helped in the struggle against Ahmed ibn Ibrahim el Ghazi, but the decisive role in this belongs to the Ethiopian people; the Portuguese helped the Ethiopians in reality in order to strengthen their own position there, and the

---

15 B. A. Turaev, *Abyssinian Chronicles of the 14th-16th century*, p. 56 (printed in Russian).
16 Ibid.
17 Ibid., p. 116.

Ethiopians soon afterwards not only understood the essence of Portuguese "aid", but exerted every effort to drive the Portuguese out.

Having been engaged for a long time in various periods of Ethiopian history, Turaev also studied the ancient history of Ethiopia. In his two-volume work *The History of the Ancient East* he gives special consideration to the history of Axum. Using all the written and archeological sources in existence by 1913, as well as investigations of foreign researchers of Ethiopia such as Dillmann, Littmann, Conti Rossini, and Krencker, he has given a general picture of the Axumite kingdom. Of course, at present, scholarship has made great progress, but the chapter on Axum has not lost its importance[18]. Particularly interesting are the pages depicting the ethnic history of Axum which has been confirmed by the latest data.

Speaking about Turaev's contributions to Ethiopian studies, one must also mention certain articles, although small in size, on some questions of Ethiopian history published in encyclopedias and magazines. General articles such as "Abyssinia"[19], "Ethiopia"[20], "Ethiopian Literature"[21], "The Ethiopian Language" and others not only contain material on various questions of Ethiopian history, literature and linguistics, but also present a historiographic review of these questions.

Following Bolotov, Turaev gives great consideration to the history of the Ethiopian church, the peculiarities of the mode of life of monks and priests who played a significant role in the medieval history of Ethiopia.

Thanks to the versatility of Turaev's creative work and his endeavours, Russians as well as others at the very beginning of the 20th century could become acquainted with Ethiopian painting of the 19th century. Together with D. V. Ainalov, he published in *The Christian East* reproductions of Ethiopian paintings that were brought by Dr. A. I. Kokhanovski who had worked a long time in Ethiopia[22]. They are of great interest because they preserve the traditional art of Ethiopia with its peculiar features for posterity.

Turaev's merit was that he was aware of writings published abroad and responded to them quickly[23]. On the other hand, his scientific work attracted

---

18 See, for example: Yu. M. Kobitschanov, *Axum*, 1966 (in Russian).
19 *The Orthodox Theological Encyclopaedia*, 1900, columns 19-82 (in Russian).
20 *Byzantine Vremennik*, St.Pb., 1904, vol. XI, issue i/2, Sect. II, p. 365-379 (in Russian).
21 *Encyclopaedic Dictionary*, Brockhaus and Efron, vol. XLI, book 81, St.Pb., 1904, p. 261-266 (in Russian).
22 B. A. Turaev and D. V. Ainalov, "Abyssinian Paintings Collected by Dr. A. I. Kokhanovski", *The Christian East*, St.Pb., 1913, vol. II, issue II, p. 199-209 (in Russian).
23 See, for example: B. A. Turaev, "Dillmann", *Encyclopaedic Dictionary, Brockhaus and Efron*, vol. Xª, book 20, St.Pb., 1893, (in Russian); same, "Ludolf (Lodolf or Leutholf), Iov", *New*

the attention of scholars of his time dealing with Ethiopia in other countries. Indeed many of his works were immediately translated, after being published in Russia, into foreign languages such as Italian, French and German[24]. S. Zanutto, one of the greatest bibliographers on Ethiopia, gives a full list of B. A. Turaev's works in the second edition of his bibliography[25]. Another prominent Italian Ethiopist, C. Conti Rossini, in the Introduction to his work on Ethiopian History[26] also takes into consideration the works of Turaev.

One can hardly find a single historical source that was overlooked by B. A. Turaev. His investigations on Ethiopia have laid a solid foundation for Russian and Soviet Ethiopian studies.

Encyclopaedic Dictionary, Brockhaus and Efron, vol. XXV, 1915, col. 15-16 (in Russian); same, "Aethiopica for the years 1912-1914", *Christian East*, 1914, vol. III, issue II, p. 217-224 (in Russian).

24 B. A. Turaev, *Vitae Sanctorum Indigenarum* I. Acta S. Fere Mika'el et S. Zaria-Abreham, Rome, 1905; same, *Vitae Sanctorum Indigenarum* I. Acta S. Eustathii. Interpretatus est Boryssus Turaev, Rome, 1906; same, Testi etiopici in manuscritti di Leningrado, — *Rassegna di Studi Etiopici*, Rome, 1948, vol. VII, fasc. I.

25 S. Zanutto, *Bibliografia etiopica in continuazione alla "Bibliografia Etiopica" di G. Fumagalli.* Primo contributo: Bibliografia. Rome, 1936.

26 C. Conti Rossini, *Storia d'Etiopia*, Parte Prima. Dalle origini all'avvento della dinastia Salomonide. Bergami, 1928.

ÄTHIOPISCH UND HAMITISCH

O. RÖSSLER
Universität Marburg

Seit der Frühzeit äthiopischer Forschung und bis in unsere Tage ist die Frage nach den Beziehungen des Äthiopischen (eines fast schon im Lichte der Geschichte von Südarabien nach Ostafrika übergetretenen Zweiges des Semitischen) zu den hamitischen Sprachen gestellt worden[1]. Und da diese Frage stets auch das lebhaftes Interesse des hochgeschätzten Jubilars, des großen Semitisten und Erforschers äthiopischer Sprachen, gefunden hat, mag ein neuer Beitrag zu diesem Thema in seiner Festschrift nicht unpassend erscheinen.

Das Augenmerk soll dabei auf das Lexikon gerichtet werden. Und, anders als gewöhnlich, soll die lexikalische Vergleichung in zwei getrennten Listen erfolgen, einer 1. ausschließlich mit Vergleichungen zwischen äthiopischen und hamitischen Sprachen, und einer 2., in der semitisch-hamitische Vergleichungen — mit oder ohne Beteiligung äthiopischer Sprachen erscheinen. Die Unterscheidung der beiden Listen von Gleichungen erfolgt also nach einem einzigen, durchaus einseitigen Kriterium: danach ob die Vergleichung nur das Äthiopische nachweislich betrifft (1.), oder ob sie darüber hinaus »semito-hamitisch« ist (2.). Die 1. Liste wird vor allem Lehnbeziehungen aus der Zeit der Einwurzelung des Äthiopischen auf afrikanischem Boden erfassen, die 2. Liste altes gemeinsames semitohamitisches Wortgut, — ohne daß jedoch jeweils die andere Möglichkeit absolut ausgeschlossen werden könnte.

LISTE 1

1.01. *BGS*

Äth.: Tigré *bəgəs bélä* »aufbrechen lassen«, *täbgist* »Aufbruch« (H. 298).
Gem. Berber. (1.-4.)[2] *bgs* (3. Twâreg *gbs*, metathes.) »se ceindre« (La. 208).

---

1 Vgl. die heute noch wichtigen Artikel von F. Praetorius *ZDMG* 43 (1889) 317-326 und ZDMG 47 (1893) 385-394. In unseren Tagen insbes. W. Leslau *WORD* 1 (1945) 59-82; *LANGUAGE* 28 (1952) 63-81; *JAOS* 79 (1959) 1-7.

2 Die Ziffern 1. 2. 3. 4. im Berberischen beziehen sich auf die vier Dialektgruppen nach A. Willms, vgl. Literaturverz.

— (1.) Sûs *a-aggus* »ceinture« (Dest. 55).

Äg. (Neues Reich) *bgś* »Aufruhr« (Erm. I. 483). Kopt. *bekse* »Rebell« (We. 22).

Bedeutungsentwicklung: »sich gürten — sich bereit machen zum Aufbruch/ Kampf — aufbrechen/Kampf beginnen«. Entlehnung aus einem hamitischen Idiom wahrscheinlich, weil es sich um ein »starres«, indirekt mit Hilfsverb *bélä* »sagen« (nach kuschitischem Vorbild) flektiertes Verb handelt.

1.02. *BDD*

Äth.: Tigriñña *bädäd bälä* »sich rasch erhaben« (H. 298).

Gem. Berber. (1.-4.) *bdd* »être debout« (Ba. No. 9, p. 14-15); auch »veiller sur« gehört zum Bedeutungsfeld (Boul. 343), *a-nəbdad* »surveillant« (Boul. 338).

Auch dies ist ein indirekt flektiertes Verbum. Vgl. 1.08.

1.03. *GᵂZL*

Äth.:Geez *gᵂädälä* »mancus fuit, defecit« (Dill. 1201/1202).

Berber. (1.) Sûs *igzzul* »il est court« (Dest). 79. — (3.) Twâreg *gəzzul* »il est court« (F. I, 414). — (4.) Kabyl. *wəzzil* »il est court« (Dall. No. 2991).

Das Äthiopische hat typisch kuschitischen Lautstand: *gᵂ* und *z > d*. Im Berberischen gibt es ein Schwanken *g/w*, doch *z* bleibt erhalten.

1.04. *GMZ*

Äth.: Tigré *gundä-fälle, gənfəlle* »Daumen« (H. 590, 591).

Kusch./Agau: Bilin *gundä-fəllé-ra* »Daumen (= dicker Finger)« (Rei/Bi. 154); Somali *sūl-gumud* »Daumen(-Stumpf)« (Rei/So. 171.260).

Berber. (1.2.3.) *gməz* »pouce« (La. 281).

Herkunft des äth. Wortes aus dem Agau klar. Urspr. *z* (berber.) > kusch. *d*!

1.05. *WṬN*

Äth.: Geez, Tigriñña *wäṭṭänä* »coepit, incepit, incohavit« (Dill. 941).

Beǧa *din* (Wurzel *wḍn*, vgl. Kausativ *sōdin*!) »anfangen, beginnen« (Rei/ Be. 74).

Entlehnungsrichtung fraglich.

1.06. *WPI*

Äth.: Geez, Tigriñña, Tigré, Amhar. *'af* »Mund« (H. 388).

Kusch.: Saho, 'Afar, Somali *af* »Mund« (Rei/So. 16); Beǧa *yāf* »Mund« (Rei/Be. 241).

Äg. *wpy/ypy* »trennen, öffnen« (Erm. I, 298), *wp/yp* »eine Bezeichnung der Türen« (Erm. I, 302).

Im Äthiopischen wurde wohl die angestammte semitische Form des Wortes (*pû, pî, pâ*) durch die stammverwandte hamistische verdrängt.

1.07. *W T L*

Äth.: Geez, Tigriñña, Tigré *mäntälé* »Hase« (H. 128).

Kusch./Agau: Bilin *mäntälé-ra* »Hase« (Rei/Bi. 273), Kemant *bäntära* »lièvre« (vgl. Nubisch *widla, wudla* id.) (CR. 178).

Berber. (1.4.) *a-wtul, a-wtil* »lièvre« (La. 253).

Äth. aus Bilin, im Anlaut nach besonderen Gesetzen entwickelt, *n*-Infix bei Tiernamen.

1.08. *K R P*

Äth.: Tigré *käräf bélä* »schleppend gehen«, *käräfä* »krumm, lahm s.« (H. 405).

Kusch: Saho *kurúf ḍaḥ* »impotent s.«, wörtlich: »K. sagen« (Rei/Sa. 221).

Gem. Berber. (1.-4.) *k r f* »être engourdi, paralysé, entravé/entraver« (Ba. No. 3, p. 5. — F. II, 858. — Dall. No. 1433).

Indirekt flektiertes Verbum, vgl. 1.01. und 1.02.

1.09. *Q D N G L I*

Áth.: Amhar. *'ǝnqāqǝla* »Eidechse« (nach L. Reinisch).

Kusch./Agau: Kwara *'ǝnḥalḥala* id.; Beǧa *adangalāy* id. (Rei/Be. 8).

Hausa *ƙadángaṛe* id. (A. 442), vgl. Tubu *(k)adúnkuli* id. (Luk. 187).
        Hausa *ṛ < l.*

1.10. *Q L P*

Äth.: Geez *qäläpä, qäläbä* »hiante ore recepit« (Dill. 415-416); Tigré *qälbä* »wegnehmen, wegreißen« (H. 233).

Hausa *kaṛbáa* »to receive« (A. 483).

Es ist zu beachten, daß im Hausa der erste der beiden Emphatischen dissimiliert und daher einfacher Stimmloser ist. Vgl. 2.10. Hausa *ṛ < l.*

1.11. *S B K*

Äth.: Tigré *säbäkä* »to descend« (H. 184).

Hausa *sabkà > safkà > saukà* »to descend« (A. 757.760.788).

Die Wurzel scheint im übrigen Äthiopisch und Semitisch nicht belegt. — Im Hausa existieren alle angegebenen Entwicklungsstufen tatsächlich dialektisch nebeneinander.

LISTE 2

2.01. *D H R*

Äth.: Tigré *dähärä* »nieder s.« (H. 509).

Berber. (3.) Twâreg *e-dir* »bas d'une chose, fond« (F. I, 228).

Bemerkenswert der obligatorische Laryngalschwund im Berberischen, vgl. 2.08.

2.02. *W R Q*

Äth.: Geez *wärq* »aurum« (Dill. 898), Tigré *wärq* »Silber« (H. 434).

Akkad. *warāqu* »gelbgrün, fahl s./w.« (vS. III).

Gem. Berber. (1.-4.) *wərraq̇, əraq̇* »il est jaune« (Ba. No. 140, p. 109).

Äg. *wʒq̇* »grün, frisch s.« (Erm. I, 240).

Normale Entsprechung von äg. *ʒ* ist ursprachl. *r*; nach extremer Abschwächung dieses Lautes wurde das Graphem im Ägyptischen (über eine Stufe *r̯*) zum Vokalzeichen (die allgemein geglaubte Hamza-Funktion des Graphems wird mit einer isolierten Gleichung gestützt, ist exakt absolut unerweislich). Mit äg. *q̇* wird hier *d̠* der Ägyptologen umschrieben.

2.03. *D B B*

Äth.: Amhar. *zəmb* »Fliege«, vgl. Geez *zäbzäbä* »repulsit« (Dill. 1050).

Akkad. *zubbu, zumbu* »Fliege« (vS. III).

Berber. (2.) Rif *i-zəbb* »mouche (de cheval)« (Ren. 321); (3.) Twâreg *a-zəbb/a-həbb* »mouche (plate)« (F. II, 505).

2.04. *K N W*

Äth. car.

Akkad. *kanūtu* »Verehrte, Gehegte«, *kinītu* »Nebenfrau« (vS. I).

Berber. (1.3.4.) *knw* »être coépouse«, *te-kné, ta-kna* »coépouse« (Dest. 68. — F. II, 831. — Dall. No. 1412).

2.05. *K R I*

Äth. — (andere Bed.)

Akkad. *karû* (III. *w, y*) »kurz s.« (vS. I). — Gehört nicht wie von Soden meint zu aram. arab. *k r h*, sondern zu: Aram.: Syr. *karyā* »brevis« (Br. 342).

Berber. (1.) Sûs *k r y* »être court« (Dest. 79), (4.) Kabyl. *k r y* »être malingre, de petite taille« (Dall. No. 1448).

2.06. *K R M*

Äth.: Tigré *kärämä* »aufhalten, unterbrechen« (H. 397).

Akkad. *karāmu* »(zurück)halten«, *karmu* »verzögert« (vS. I).

Berber. (3.) Twâreg *k r m* »empêcher« (F. II, 876).

2.06[1]. *K R M*

Äth.: Geez, Tigriñña, Tigré *kärämä*, Amhar. *kärrämä* »hibernavit«, Geez,
   Amhar. *kərämt*, Tigré *käräm, kārəmät* »hiems« (Dillm. 834. — H. 397).
Berber. (1.) Sûs, Demnât *k r m* »être froid« (Dest. 135.-Boul. 347); (2.) Ṣanhâja
   k r m »se tapir« (Ren. 344); (3.) Twâreg *k r m* »(se) replier« (F. II, 876).

   Diese und die vorhergehende Wurzel sind offenbar ursprünglich identisch.

2.07. *K R Š*

Äth.: Tigré *käräsä* »aneinander befestigen«, *kərs* »Knopf« (H. 399).
Akkad. *karāsu* »zubinden« (vS. I).
Gem. Berber. (1.-4.) *k r s* »nouer« (Ba. No. 3, p. 5).
Äg. *čšs* »knoten, verknüpfen« (Erm. V, 396), *čšst* »Knoten« (Erm. V, 399).
Kopt. *čōs* »zusammenfügen« (We. 435).

Äg. *š* für ursprachl. *r*. Mit äg. *č* wird hier *ṯ* der Ägyptologen umschrieben,
   vgl. 2.02.

2.08. *M ʿ R*

Äth.: Geez *məʿr* »momentum v. ictus temporis« (Dill. 206).
Berber. (3.) Twâreg *e-mir* »moment«, *te-mirt* id. dimin. (F. III, 1225).
   Laryngalschwund im Berberischen wie im 2.01.

2.09. *N Z Q*

Äth. — car. —
Akkad. *nazāqu* »sich ärgern, Kummer haben«, *niziqtu* »Ärger, Kummer« (vS.
   I).
Bibl. Aram. *n z q* »Schaden erleiden«.
Berber. (4.) Kabyl. *n z q̇* »s'étouffer en pleurant« (Dall. No. 1974).

2.10. *Q Ṭ N*

Äth.: Geez, Tigré *qäṭin*, Amhar. *qäč̣č̣ən* »dünn, schmal« (H. 263).
Akkad. *qatānu* »dünn s./w.« (vS. II). Vgl. Hebr. Aram. *q ṭ n*.
Berber. (1.) Izayân *kəṭṭin* »être petit, court« (Loub. 555).
Hausa *kaδáŋ* (dial. *kaδána*) »a few, a little« (A. 442).

   Im Berberischen und im Hausa ist der erste der beiden Emphatischen
dissimiliert und daher einfacher Stimmloser wie in 1.10. Im Akkadischen
entsprechende Dissimilation des zweiten Emphatischen!

2.11. *Q R Š*

Äth. - car.
Akkad. *qarāšu* »zerschneiden« (vS. II).
Arab. *qaraša* »schneiden«.
Gem. Berber. (1.-4.) *q̇ r s* »couper« (c. dat. »égorger«) (Ba. No. 3, p. 5).

2.12. *RKS*

Äth. — (andere Bed.)

M. Hebr. *rikkes* »stampfen« (Dalm. 404).

Berber. (3.) Twâreg *rks* »piétiner« (F. IV, 1632).

2.13 *ŠRI*

Äth.: Geez *säräyä* »remisit, ignovit, condonavit (alicui peccatum)« (Dill. 346).

Aram.: Syr. *šrâ* »solvit, fregit, aperuit, liberavit, dimisit« (Br. 803).

Hebr. *šarâ* »loslassen«.

Berber. (1.) Demnât *sry* »dégager, faire passer, délivrer« (Boul. 350). (3.)
Twâreg *sry* »(faire) courir à bride rendue (cheval); pratiquer la liberté des
mœurs« (F. IV, 1854).

2.14. *TRK*

Äth. car.

Akkad. *tarāku* »schlagen, klopfen« (vS. III).

Berber. (3.) Twâreg *trk* »donner un/des coup/coups de poing«; (4.) Kabyl.
trk »battre, malmener« (F. IV, 1914. Dall. No. 2824).

Arabisch *taraka* ist wahrscheinlich eine ganz andere Wurzel.

Unsere beiden Listen dürften ein ziemlich genaues Bild von den zweierlei
»hamitischen Beziehungen« der äthiopischen Sprachen gegeben haben. Darüber hinaus bilden die in ihnen enthaltenen Vergleichungen einen Teil des
heute bereits rekonstruierbaren Netzes lexikalischer Beziehungen im gesamten
semitohamitischen Raum, — eines Netzes, das weiterhin noch engmaschiger
geknüpft werden kann und muß. Am eindrucksstärksten wird dabei vielleicht
die Regelmäßigkeit der Lautentsprechungen sein. Sie ist unabdingbare Vor-
aussetzung realistischer Ergebnisse.

Schließlich sei noch eine berühmte Gleichung erörtert, die hier in keiner der
beiden Listen Platz finden durfte. Sie geht auf W. F. Albright zurück (*AJSL*
34/1918, p. 216) und hat seither viele Anhänger gefunden. Sie wurde zuletzt
von G. Conti diskutiert.

Äth.: Geez *'əẓḫ* »silex, pyrites« (Dill. 791); Tigriñña *'azaḫit*, *qəzaḫit* »quarzo«
(Co. p. 4).

Äg. *šsḫ* »Korn mit der Sichel abmähen; Gemähtes: Ernte; Sichel« (Erm. I,
19).

Das *punctum saliens* dieser Gleichung ist die Tatsache, daß die
neolithischen Sicheln *Feuerstein*-Schneiden hatten.

Doch ist eine Wurzel »*'ẓ ḫ/ḥ*« weder semitisch, noch hamitisch, noch sonst
afrikanisch nachzuweisen (Co. p. 2), und sind die äthiopischen Formen

offenbar nur lautlich (dialektal bezw. unter Agau-Einfluß) veränderte und orthographisch verfremdete Erscheiningsformen eines $^+q\partial d\underbar{h}$, $^+q\partial da\underbar{h}it$ (von der bekannten semitischen Wurzel $QD\underbar{H}$), vgl. arab. $qad\underbar{h}$ »pierre à feu« (Do. II, 312). Der mittlere Radikal D aber wurde dabei — auf dem Hintergrund der bekannten Kuschitisierung von $\underbar{z} > d$ — fälschlich und überkorrekt als Z restituiert. Eine Beziehung zu äg. $\int s\underbar{h}$ kann daher nicht vorliegen, somit auch kein Beleg für irgendwelche ägyptisch-semitischen Lautentsprechungen (z.B. äg. $\int$ und sem. ').

Literatur

A. = R. C. Abraham, Dictionary of the Hausa language. London 1946.
Ba. = A. Basset, La langue Berbère — Morphologie — Le verbe — Étude des thèmes. Paris 1929.
Boul. = S. Boulifa, Textes Berbères en dialecte de l'Atlas Marocain. Paris 1908.
Br. = C. Brockelmann, Lexicon Syriacum. Halle 1928.
Co. = G. Conti, Egiziano $\int$S$\underbar{H}$ »tagliare col falcetto« — etiopico 'EZ$\underbar{H}$ »pietra focaia«. RSO 48 (1974), p. 29-35.
CR. = C. Conti Rossini, La langue des Kemant en Abyssinie. Wien, 1912.
Dall. = J. M. Dallet, Le verbe Kabyle I. Fort National 1953.
Dalm. = G. H. Dalman, Aramäisch-neuhebräisches Handwörterbuch zu Targum, Talmud und Midrash. (Neudruck) Hildesheim 1967.
Dest. = E. Destaing, Vocabulaire Français-Berbère. Paris 1938.
Do. = R. Dozy, Supplément aux dictionnaires Arabes². Leide-Paris 1927.
Dill. = A. Dillmann, Lexicon linguae Aethiopicae. (Neudruck) Osnabrück 1970.
Erm. = A. Erman - H. Grapow, Wörterbuch der Ägyptischen Sprache I-V. Berlin 1926ff.
F. = P. Ch. de Foucauld, Dictionnaire Touareg-Français I-IV. Paris 1951ff.
H. = E. Littmann - M. Höfner, Wörterbuch der Tigrē-Sprache. Wiesbaden 1962.
La. = E. Laoust, Siwa I, Son parler. Paris 1931.
Loub. = V. Loubignac, Étude sur le dialecte Berbère des Zaïan et Ait-Sgougou. Instit. des Hautes-Études Marocaines 14. Paris 1924.
Luk. = J. Lukas, Die Sprache der Tubu in der zentralen Sahara. Institut für Orientforschung 14. Berlin 1953.
Rei/Be. = L. Reinisch, Wörterbuch der Beḍauye-Sprache. Wien 1895.
Rei/Bi. = L. Reinisch, Wörterbuch der Bilin-Sprache. Wien 1887.
Rei/Sa. = L. Reinisch, Wörterbuch der Saho-Sprache. Wien 1890.
Rei/So. = L. Reinisch, Die Somali-Sprache II: Wörterbuch. Wien 1909.
Ren. = A. Renisio, Études sur les dialectes Berbères des Beni Iznassen, du Rif et des Sanhaja de Sraïr. Instit. des Hautes-Études Marocaines 22. Paris 1932.
vS. = W. von Soden, Akkadisches Handwörterbuch I-III. Wiesbaden 1965-1981.
We. = W. Westendorf, Koptisches Handwörterbuch. Heidelberg 1965-1977.
Wi. = A. Willms, Die dialektale Differenzierung des Berberischen. Afrika und Übersee (Beiheft 31) Berlin 1980.

ETHIOPIAN AND HEBREW PROSODY:
SOME PRELIMINARY OBSERVATIONS

STANISLAV SEGERT
University of California, Los Angeles

The relationship between Ethiopian languages and Hebrew was studied by Wolf Leslau in several publications (cf. pp. 1ff., nos. 149, 235, 256). His concentration on lexical matters brought reliable and commonly accepted results.

Some similarities between the forms of Ethiopian poetry and biblical Hebrew poetry were brought to the attention of scholars in both fields by Enno Littmann (1925:1-2; 1930:207-225, esp. 223-224; 1924: 272-273; 1949:3-4).

In his book on Ethiopia and the Bible, Edward Ullendorff (1968:90) quoted Littmann's observations (1949:3-4), but no subsequent work in this direction is mentioned. Ullendorff has added his own observations on the Ethiopic liturgical chants: the names of Ethiopic musical signs are similar to those of the Hebrew liturgical reading system in not less than five such pairs (1968:96).

Littmann's suggestions were not followed up in the study of Hebrew biblical poetry. In a thorough survey by Otto Eissfeldt (1965:57-64), provided with rich bibliographical data, there is no mention of such comparative study (cf. also Kaiser 1975: 319-326).

The present author considered in an article dedicated to Rudolf Meyer the possibility of using Ethiopian poetry as a parallel to the accentuating system of Hebrew biblical poetry, accepted by most scholars for all its periods (Segert 1969:316).

The correspondence of the prosodical system and phonological structure of the Hebrew language may recommend that the accentuation system be limited to the middle period of Hebrew biblical poetry, about 1000-500 B.C. in terms of absolute chronology. The oldest stage of Hebrew biblical poetry, at the end of the second millenium B.C., can be compared to Ugaritic poetry preserved from the 14th and 13th centuries B.C. The reliably reconstructed vocalic structure of Ugaritic words can help in the reconstruction of the oldest biblical Hebrew. For post-exilic biblical poetry after about 500 B.C., a time when the Hebrew language and prosody were exposed to the impact of Aramaic, the study of prosodical systems used in Aramaic and Syriac poetry can provide useful analogies (cf. Segert 1969: 315-317, 320). An analogy to Hebrew biblical poetry of the middle period, during which the accentuation prosody prevailed, would be welcome. Ethiopic languages and poetic traditions deserve to be taken into consideration in the search for such an analogy, in spite of their genealogical, chronological and geographical distance.

Already Iob Ludolf, who studied traditional Ethiopic poetry in Geez in the 17th century, observed that it is not composed according to a regular meter (cf. 1702:165). Later scholars confirmed this statement on the basis of their own analyses (cf. Littmann 1914:33; Grohmann 1919:36).

Among the various principles which were applied to both traditional and recent Ethiopic prosody, the syllable count seems to be most frequently represented (cf. Chaîne 1923:20; Cohen 1924:22; 1936:414; Littmann 1925:54; Kamil 1957:3-23; 1968:106-118; Schall 1961:291-194). Marcel Cohen also considered (1924:22) division into hemistichs; in 1936 he mentioned rhyme in the first place and syllable count second among the principles governing recent Amharic poetry. For Geez poetry, Cohen (1924:22) assumed a fixed number of accents for each verse (cf. also Schall 1961:3). The accent was acknowledged as a prosodic principle of recent Amharic poetry by August Klingenheben (1959:7-10).

The importance of rhyme in the structuring of Ethiopic poetry was recognized already by Enno Littmann (1909:229). Conti Rossini (1941:161) did not see any metrical principle in Ethiopic poetry in which verse ends were marked by rhyme or rather end assonance. A great part of Ethiopic poetry, traditional and recent, is sung, its rhythm determined by the music. The presentation of Ethiopic songs by native singers has been described by several observers (for references see pp. 345-346).

The following survey of some distinctive features of Ethiopic prosody is admittedly based on a very narrow corpus of material. Texts available in Roman letters are preferred. From poetry in the traditional language Geez which ceased to be commonly spoken in the Middle ages, short poems from the Synaxarion (Lambdin 1978: cf. 237-275) and short selections from the Hymns to the Virgin Mary (Grohmann 1919:398, 400) were used. The old Amharic poetry is represented by the Emperor songs from the 15th century (Praetorius 1879:499-502: cf. Littmann 1914).

For modern Amharic poetry the publications by August Klingenheben (1959) and Murad Kamil (1957; 1968; also apud Schall 1961) were used. The texts in Čaha, a dialect of the Central Ethiopic language Gurage, were taken from publications by Wolf Leslau (1950; 1964; 1982). The funeral songs and lamentations in Tigre as published by Enno Littmann (1949) represent a northern, rather conservative, language and poetry.

Special attention perhaps should be devoted to the poems which were composed or adapted by the Ethiopian poets as an expression of friendship to Western scholars since their date, author and circumstances of composition are exactly known. Such are the poems for Iob Ludolf (cf. 1702:169-171), August Klingenheben (1959:19) and Wolf Leslau (1950:125-126); cf. also the close cooperation of Murad Kamil with Amharic poets in the 1940's (Schall 1961:5).

Prosodical systems are bound to phonological characteristics of languages, especially to the structure of syllables and the kind and position of the word stress (cf. Lotz 1960:138-139). The traditional Ethiopic alphabet, used for the classical language, Geez, and also used with a few additional signs for Amharic, indicates fully the consonants and—by graphic modification of consonant letters—the vowels with one major exception: one series of signs indicates both consonants without a following vowel and consonants followed by the short vowel ǝ. There are no special signs for the double consonant. No information about the position of word stress is given (cf. Ludolf 1702:13; Cohen 1921:220; Leslau 1970:469-470). The data from written Geez texts have to be supplemented from traditional pronunciation (Cohen, 1921:247-267; Mittwoch 1926; Brockelmann 1929; Leslau 1970:468-470). Recent poetry in various Ethiopic languages is accessible mostly in texts in the Roman alphabet; some of them indicate word stress.

Open syllables with short (CV) and long (CV̄) vowels as well as closed syllables with short vowels (CVC) are frequent in the traditional pronunciation of Geez, while closed syllables with long vowels (CV̄C), appearing mostly at the end of words, are relatively rare. End syllables with short vowels do occur (-CV). Marcel Cohen (1921:267) has observed the shortening of short and long vowels due to accentuation.

In some modern Ethiopic dialects no long vowels have been recorded; only two types of syllables, CV and CVC, are attested.

The character and position of word stress are indicated differently by different scholars. In his work on the traditional pronunciation of Geez, Eugen Mittwoch (1926:32-40) understands the word stress as expiratory and emphatic (1926:33), i.e. dynamic, while he ascribes to the musical or tonic accent a subordinated role. The position of the word stress according to Mittwoch (1926:37) depends on the character of the word: it is set on the last but one syllable in verbs, on the last syllable in nouns, while prepositions and conjunctions have no stress (cf. Ludolf 1702:13-15). Edward Ullendorff (1955:189-197) emphasizes that in the traditional recitation of Geez the "musical" accent, tone and pitch, is decisive; it falls on the final syllable

(1955:192). The sentence accent is far more significant than the stress of
individual words (1955:193).

In the pronunciation of liturgical texts in Geez by Abba Mikael N. Taffese,
during a church service on Saturday, May, 15, 1982, in Los Angeles, stress of a
rather dynamic type on the end of verses was more audible than the relatively
weak word stress. The same could be observed in the reading of Biblical
pericopes in Amharic, performed by his assistants at the same service. These
observations agree in principle with those made by Iob Ludolf (1702:15, end
of c. VII) on Geez poetry three hundred years ago.

The most prominent feature of Ethiopic poetry in all languages is rhyme.
There is no monograph devoted to the kinds of rhyme and its function in the
poetic structure.

A detailed treatment of rhyme has been provided by Wolf Leslau in the
introductory sections of his publications of Čaha songs (1964:231) and
proverbs (1982:185-186). Nearly all of his observations can be applied to
rhyme in other Ethiopic languages.

Most of the rhymes in the Čaha songs end with a vowel: -V, -CV, -VCV,
-CCV. Rhymes ending with a consonant (-C, -CVC) are rare; final consonants
can be only -m and -r (1964:231). The rhyming consonants are not always
identical, homorganic sounds can rhyme, e. g. -täm, -däm, -ṭäm. A peculiar
feature in Čaha songs is rhyming of a form with final -m with a form without
it, e. g. -ša and -šam (1964:231). In Čaha proverbs identical or corresponding
verbal or nominal forms serve as the basis of rhyme, often because of the
parallelistic structure of verses (Leslau 1982:186, nos. 44, 15, 132, 65). Some
rhyming words are derived from the same roots but do not exhibit the same
form (1982:186, nos. 141, 72). Even rhyming words derived from different
roots do appear (1982:186, no. 131). In some Čaha songs more than one
rhyming pattern is used (Leslau 1964:231).

In an older, unpublished article "Abyssinian Folk-Poetry", Wolf Leslau
studied rhymes in 72 Amharic couplets, mostly love- songs, which were given
to him orally and in writing by Mr. Mangestu Mamača in the late 1930's.
Rhymes of one syllable prevail, but rhymes of two syllables are well
represented. In seven couplets whole words, of 2-6 syllables, do rhyme.

Some additional observations from other Ethiopic poems can be added.
The rhymes in the Hymns to the Virgin Mary, in the late Middle ages, were
characterized by Adolf Grohmann in the introduction of his edition (1919:38).
They are of two types, consonant + vowel, and end consonant only. This last
observation probably has to be modified on the basis of personal observations
by Murad Kamil (apud Schall 1961:127): after the last rhyme consonant a

short vowel is pronounced, indicated by Kamil as *a* but rendered in his transliterations as *e*—here the sign *ə* is used—, and compared to the Arabic *rawm*. (As an analogy the short e pronounced after a rhyming consonant in French religious songs can be adduced).

The rhymes in the Old Amharic Emperor songs (Praetorius 1879:499-501) are also short, of the -CV type. In the New Amharic Emperor songs (Kamil 1957:2-30) the rhymes are longer, mostly of the -VCV type. In some poems even the third vowel from the end is used for ("deep") rhyme. Rhyming patterns with at least two vowels and one end consonant, -VCVC are also frequent. Similar patterns also appear in various kinds of Amharic poetry presented by Murad Kamil (1968:106-118).

The rhymes in short poems consisting of five verses added at the end of the Lives of the Saints taken from the Synaxarion (Lambdin 1978:237-275, from Dillmann 1866:16-39) are mostly of the -CVCV type. But in the song for Yared, the patron saint of Ethiopic church music (cf. Lambdin 1978:268), the rhyme is enhanced by identical or corresponding vowels in the preceding syllable: -V(C)VCV.

The rhyme patterns in the lamentations, mostly composed in the 19th century (Littmann 1949:58-75) are also of a longer type: -VCV, -VCVC, -V(C)VCV, -V(C)VCVC.

It can be supposed that the old short rhyming patterns, attested from the 15th century, were gradually extended.

In those types of poetry where the differentiation of vowel length can be observed, it is also respected in the structuring of the rhyme: usually vowels correspond mutually according to their quantity.

The word stress is indicated consistently in the Tigre poetry presented by Enno Littmann (1949). In general, stress patterns are respected in rhymes. Stress is placed most frequently on the paenultima, often on the ante-paenultima, but on the ultima only when it is long and closed, -CV̆C, e.g. IV:f; 2:1-4; 7:3-9. Rare exceptions to the general agreement of stress patterns in rhymes can be observed, e. g. 4:7; 38:3; 43:5.

The considerable margin of freedom in Ethiopic rhyme can be explained by the phonological rather than phonetic character of rhyme in general, as defined by Roman Jakobson (cf. Worth 1977:516-517).

This approach corresponds to that of Conti Rossini who preferred to characterize this dominant feature of Ethiopic poetry as assonance rather than as rhyme (1941:161) Jakobson's concept of "deep" rhyme (cf. Worth 517-518) can be applied to the supporting of rhymes by the identical vowels in the preceding syllables.

The rhymes in Ethiopic poetry are in general arranged in straight sequence, their number varying between two in proverbs and short poems and several decades (54 in the first Old Amharic Emperor song, cf. Praetorius 1879:499-501). More than one sequence of different rhymes can be used in the same poem.

The grammatical or non-grammatical character of rhyme (cf. Jakobson 1960:368; Worth 1979:519-520) can be conveniently observed in Leslau's edition of Čaha songs, presented in Roman letters and provided with an interlinear English translation (1950:112-126). Out of ten songs three exhibit mostly grammatical rhymes: nos. 1, 6 and 8—with repeated suffixed pronouns. In three songs the non-grammatical rhymes are very strongly represented: e.g. no. 2, p. 114: $q^u ato$ "the mountains" — *yatšakato* "they were (very) proud" — *moto* "(they) died" — *yoto* "(to the) ants" — *moto* "O death!".

Grammatical rhymes appear with high frequency in Čaha proverbs which are often expressed in parallelistic verses; the patterns of rhyme and parallelistic structures are listed in their edition by Leslau (1982:184-186).

The proportion and function of grammatical rhymes in other Ethiopic poems deserves a closer scrutiny. Here only a few preliminary and general observations can be given. If very long poems with only one rhyme had to be composed, such as the first Old Amharic Emperor song containing 54 verses with the same number of identical rhymes (Praetorius 1879:499-500; cf. Littmann 1914:9-11), it was not possible to preserve grammatical rhymes throughout the entire poem. The use of non-grammatical rhyme can be considered poetic license. Non-grammatical rhymes appear, especially in more recent poetry, even in combinations of two verses (cf. for Tigre Littmann 1949: no. IVd; no. 10:7+8; for Amharic Kamil 1968:115 *'antṣār*).

(Similar use of grammatical and non-grammatical rhymes can be observed in Arabic folk poetry, e.g. in children poems published and discussed by Wiebke Walther, Altarabische Kindertanzreime, pp. 217-233 in *Studia Orientalia*; for bibliographical reference cf. Kamil 1968.)

Even if other poetic features on a phonological level similar to rhyme are not as important in Ethiopic poetry, they deserve to be briefly mentioned. Their use is quite different in various types and languages.

The inner rhyme, the correspondence of the end of the first half verse and the end of the verse, is consistently avoided in poetry in Geez and in older Amharic poetry as well as in songs in Tigre.

The inner rhyme is very frequent in short Čaha proverbs; it corresponds to their parallelistic structure (Leslau 1982:185). It is also represented, for the same reason, in Čaha songs (Leslau 1950:112, 116). In the song no. 1 three rhymes are exhibited in the first verse: *-šəm, -žəm, -səm*. Some other rhymes are corollary to the inner parallelism within the verse, e.g. no. 3, verse 23: *anqäpäräm andäpäräm* "he did not diminish, he did not add".

The use and frequency of epanaphoras and epiphoras corresponds to that of inner rhyme: they do not appear in Geez poetry and in older Amharic poetry. In recent Amharic poetry they are quite rare (cf. Kamil 1968:113 below, 115 below; epiphora in Kamil 1959:IV:1:1-3).

Both the epanaphora and epiphora are common features in Tigre poetry (Littmann 1949). Short poems are connected by identical words in the beginning of verses (e.g. 1 b, e), with even three or four such verses appearing in these poems (e.g. IV d, e, f; VI b, c). In longer Lamentations the epanaphoras are frequent, up to five verses (e.g. 48:1-5). Epiphoras appear at the end of half-verses in Tigre lamentations (e.g. 5:1a+2a+3a; 14:5-8). Both these features appear in 12:2a+3a+4a.

In some poems in Tigre and also in some recent Amharic poems, the corresponding ends of first half-verses serve to add cohesion to the poetic structure if they appear in the immediately following verses or shortly afterwards (cf. e.g. Kamil 1968: p. 108:1, second strophe, verses 2a+5a+6a+8a; p. 113, poem by Joftahe Negus from 1935: 7a+8a; p. 115, third poem: 1a+2a).

The rhyme is regularly used in nearly all types of older and recent Ethiopic poetry. The only type of non-rhymed poems is listed by Kamil in his survey of Amharic poetry (1968:110-111); it is called *həggä watt bet*, i.e. "exceptional", and is considered as archaic and unusual. In all eight distichs presented by Kamil there are two verses consisting of 5+5 or 6+6 syllables.

The overwhelming frequency and regularity of rhyme in nearly all types of Ethiopic poetry leads to the conclusion that the rhyme is its dominant principle. Since the end of the verse is so clearly marked by rhyme, a regular arrangement of the preceding parts of the verse is probably not essential. The only other feature is the not always obligatory ceasure (Cohen 1924:82) between the first and the second part of the verse marked by a short pause in recitation or singing (Grohmann 1919:41; cf. Schall 1961:291). In most of the Ethiopic poems this pause divides the verse into equal or at least symmetrical halves. In some types of poetry, especially in Tigre, asymmetrical verses are frequent (cf. Littmann 1924: 272-273; 1930:223).

Although many scholars since Ludolf (cf. 1702:165) supposed that the rhyme is the only principle recognizable in Ethiopic verse (cf. Littmann 1914:33; Grohmann 1919:36), some other structuring principles were considered: syllable count, accent and musical rhythm. The very rare occurrence of parallelism of members excludes it as a possible structuring principle, but because of its importance in older Semitic poetry it deserves to be mentioned.

In the Old Amharic Emperor songs parallelism of members appears with relatively high frequency. In the first of these poems (Praetorius 1879:499-501; Littmann 1914:9-11) the second and third verses in most strophes are bound by parallelism. Also in the second and tenth poems (Littmann 1914:12-16 and 29-31), parallelism is used frequently. In most of these instances it is synonymous, but complementary (no. 3:6+7) and antithetic (no. 2:96+97, 100+101) parallelism are also attested as well as a longer series of parallelistic verses (no. 4:45-49) (cf. Littmann 1914:17, 15, 19). In the Hymns to Mary parallelistic features are also represented.

But the parallelism of members is extremely rare in more recent Amharic poetry, in qǝnē (cf. Schall 1961: no. 31; no. 47:4+5), in various kinds described and presented in samples by Kamil (1968: p. 113 [1935]:9+10; p. 115 [1943] 1+2; [1915]:2+3) and in the New Emperor songs (Kamil 1959: I:2:3+4; IV:1:1+2; XI:55+56; XII:26+27).

Parallelism of members appears frequently in Čaha songs (Leslau 1950). In song no. 8 the majority of verses are connected by parallelism. There was a special reason for frequent use of parallelistic verses in poems no. 4 and 5 which describe the murder of two brothers by a cruel burglar: all the words in such verses correspond, only the names of the brothers are different.

In Tigre lamentations (Littmann 1949) parallelistic features are relatively less frequent, but they are of a different kind: inner parallelism with correspondence of the first and second half-verse (e.g. 2:9), two subsequent parallel verses (e.g. 3:2+3), and groups of more parallel verses (e.g. 14:5-8). Even repetitions of verses and half verses can be observed (e.g. 18:1-6; 46:5+7+9).

Parallelistic verses appear most frequently in comparisons and poetic descriptions. They probably reflect the old formulae of oral poetry which survived in the relatively remote area of Tigre and Čaha until recently, while in Amharic the use of this poetic device is rare in comparison to older Amharic poetry. Still the parallelism is attested in poems published by August Klingenheben (1959:13), and even in the third and fourth verse of the national anthem of Ethiopia (cf. ib.:19-20).

Many recent Amharic poems are composed in symmetrical verses of an identical number of syllables in each half-verse. Such verses continue in stichic arrangement through the longer poems. In other types of Amharic poetry cola with different number of syllables are combined into complex verse structures, as in the religious songs called qǝnē in Geez (cf. Schall 1961, esp. 291-294) and in Amharic (cf. Kamil 1968:116-118).

In older poetry in Geez and Amharic and in more recent poetry in Čaha and

Tigre such an exact regularity of syllables within verses and their parts does not appear, but the number of syllables oscillates within relatively small limits.

Also the exceptional verses with no rhyme (Kamil 1968:110-111) show the same regularity of syllable count as those with rhyme.

Syllable count itself is a limiting principle, which provides only the numeric regularity of metre, while the real rhythm has to be provided by other phonological features, such as word stress, regular patterns of long and short syllables, pauses between the words, or by non-phonological means, which together can form the parallelistic structures (cf. Lotz 1960:140).

Since rhyme is a regular feature of Ethiopic verse it can serve as a sufficient structuring principle clearly indicating the verse end, while the syllable count can be considered as facultative supporting feature.

In those verses in which the number of syllables varies and the length of half-verses within one verse often differs, the possibility of rhythm provided by word stress deserves to be considered. The number of stresses serves as a dominant rhythmic principle in Tigre according to Enno Littmann (1949:57). The lack of regularity between verses, even within one and the same poem, does not seem to support this rhythmical pattern.

The asymmetrical verses (3+2, 2+3, 2+1, 1+2) do not appear with such regularity, as the asymmetric qīnā verses in Hebrew biblical poetry, to which they are compared by Littmann (1924:272-273).

For other Ethiopic poetry, that in Geez according to traditional pronunciation and that in modern dialects, word stress is not appropriate as a prosodic principle as it is relatively weak and not easily perceptible.

August Klingeheben observed the dynamic accent in the recitation or singing of Amharic poetry (1959:7-8). But the position of the accent is not the same in the same word in its different positions, and also this accent does not coincide often enough with the word stress. Such an accent in songs has to be characterized rather as an ictus. In most of Klingenheben's (1959:8-19) analyses the syllables with and without ictus alternate regularly. Such a metrical system corresponds to the alternation prosody of Aramaic, especially Syriac poetry.

Neither syllable count nor word stress or any other prosodical system can explain the structure of poetry based on musical rhythm without knowledge of the rhythm of the individual poems. The importance of music for Ethiopic poetry, both traditional and modern, was observed and rightly evaluated by many scholars, i.a. Giusto di Urbino (quoted by C. Conti Rossini 1915: 223-224), Enno Littmann (1933:211-218; 1949:8-12, 17), Marcel Cohen (cf. 1921:222), Carlo Conti Rossini (1945; quoted by Schall 1961:297), August Klingenheben (1959:7-10), Murad Kamil (1968:105-107) and Edward Ullendorff (1968:90, 93-96, 98-99). Cf. also Schall 1961:3-4, 295-297. Some of them have observed and recorded how the Ethiopic poetry had been recited and sung with musical accompaniment. Murad Kamil also gave basic data about musical signs and kinds of melodies as well as the Ethiopic terms for various melodies and parts of verses (1968:105-107). The role of dance rhythm was taken into consideration by Adolf Grohmann (1919:37 and n. 3 there).

Knowledge of appropriate rhythms and melodies leads the performers in their recitation and singing of the poems. The authors of the poems are bound by these traditional patterns determined by the genre of the poem. (Cf. Giusto di Urbino, quoted by C. Conti Rossini 1915:223-224 and Schall 1961:4, n. 1; cf. also C. Conti Rossini [1945] and E. Cerulli [1956], quoted by Schall 1961:297, nn. 2 and 3). Without knowledge of a particular rhythm—the melody may be of somewhat lesser importance—any attempt to analyse the real verse structure remains hypothetical (cf. Schall 1961:295-296).

Since the dominant feature of Ethiopic poetry, both traditional and modern, is the rhyme, it can be compared to the stage of Hebrew poetry in which rhyme was used. Murad Kamil has already pointed to the rhymed poetry of the Hebrew poet Kallir (apud Schall 1961:134).

It is possible to trace the rhyme in Hebrew poetry farther back than to this poet, who was formerly supposed to have been active in the 10th century A.D.; but now, after new discoveries of his works, is dated into the pre-islamic period, perhaps to the 6th century A.D. A passage with many rhymes can be found already in the Book of Ben Sira (Ecclesiasticus) composed in Hebrew about 180 B.C. At the beginning of chapter 44, there are according to the Genizah manuscripts not less than nine rhymes in six verses. In two of these verses there are internal rhymes, the first half-verse rhyming with the second one. Most of the rhymes are grammatical, -tām, expressing suffixed plural pronouns attached to feminine nouns, but one of these rhymes is non-grammatical, 'ōlām "world/eternity". (Cf. Segert 1953:538-539). The prosody used in this section and apparently in most of this book is based on the principle of alternation, as stressed syllables alternate with unstressed syllables, while the word stress is often disregarded (cf. Segert 1953:538-539; Hrushovski 1981:61).

This use of rhyme did not find immediate adherence. The composer of piyuṭim Yannai is reputed to be the first Hebrew poet to introduce the rhyme; he lived probably in the 6th century A.D. (cf. Carmi 1981:87-88, 215-220). The rhymes in his poems are mostly grammatical: the suffixed pronoun can be repeated many times (cf. Carmi 215), but he also occasionally used non-grammatical rhymes. Most of his verses consist of two half-verses with four words each; the word stress probably played some role in this kind of prosody.

Eleazar ben Kallir was a follower of Yannai (cf. Carmi 1981:89, 221-232). The forms of his poetry correspond to those of Yannai, his rhymes are also mostly grammatical, but non-grammatical rhymes appear more frequently. A verbal form rhymes with a noun: ᵘ'ašen "I shall envelop" — haššen "(of) the tooth/ivory". Because of his stay in Old Cairo in Egypt, the poet Samuel Hashelishi, who died after 1012 (Carmi 1981:93, 254-256), deserves to be mentioned. In comparison with his predecessors, his use of non-grammatical rhymes is more frequent.

It would be interesting to compare the rhyme technique of Hebrew mediaeval poetry to that of Ethiopic poetry in more detail. The rhyme is mostly formed by the final syllables (-CV or -CVC) or by the two last syllables. It is sometimes supported by identical vowels in the preceding syllables, with different consonants after them (-VXVCV(C)). This "deep" rhyme, as it is defined by Jakobson (cf. Worth 1977:517:518), corresponds to that used in various kinds of Ethiopic poetry. (Cf. Hrushovski's term "discontinous-terminal", 1981:62). It would also be interesting to compare the arrangement of rhymes in the structure of strophes in both Hebrew and Ethiopic poetry.

While there are significant correspondences between early medieval Hebrew poetry and late medieval and later Ethiopic poetry, they are probably not the result of parallel spontaneous development. Hebrew poetry of late Antiquity and Aramaic poetry of that time influenced each other within the general symbiosis of these two cultures in Palestine, Syria and Mesopotamia. The literature of the Christian Aramaeans in the Syriac language was brought to Ethiopia by their first Christian missionaries in the 4th century A.D. Some contacts through Coptic, Greek and later Arabic intermediation can also be traced. (Cf. to these contacts Grohmann 1919:4-5, 37, 39, 46; Kamil apud Schall 1961:129-137; Schall 1961:295-296; Ullendorff 1968:89-100; and the references there; cf. also Littmann 1925:51-55).

If any relationship between Ethiopic poetry and the Hebrew poetry of the biblical period should be found, the investigation should concentrate on tracing parallel trends or tendencies rather than on a comparison of entire prosodic systems. The parallelism of members apparently served as a domi-nant principle of early Hebrew biblical poetry, and remained its frequent feature throughout the biblical period, whether the prosody was based on word stress or—later—on alternation of stressed and unstressed syllables. In Ethiopic poetry parallelistic structures were used rarely, rather as poetic ornaments, while the dominant principles were rhyme and musical rhythm.

Even if the structure of the language, especially the frequency and distribution of vowels in words, was very similar between Hebrew of the period of the Israelite and Judaean kingdoms in the first half of the first millenium B. C., and between classical and modern Ethiopic languages, considerable difference in the strength (cf. especially Ullendorff 1955:189-190) and consequently prosodical function of word stress distinguishes the respective prosodical systems.

The commonly accepted theory of Hebrew biblical poetry based on the rhythm provided by word stress is therefore not supported by the analogy of the Ethiopic poetry. Since this accentuation theory corresponds to our knowledge—although to a considerable extent hypothetical—of the phonological character of the Hebrew language of the period of the Kingdoms (cf. Harris 1941) it deserves this general acceptance, at least for that period.

These preliminary observations are presented to Ethiopists with the hope that further research in Ethiopic poetics will bring better documented results, to be gratefully acknowledged and used by Semitists and by those interested in general poetics.

Bibliographical References

1. Ethiopian poetry

Brockelmann, Carl
1929 "Zur Kritik der traditionellen Aussprache des Äthiopischen". *Zeitschrift für Semistik* 7:205-213.
Cerulli, Enrico
1916 "La poesia popolare amarica". *L'Africa Italiana* 35:172-179.
Chaine, Marius
1920-21 "La poésie chez les Éthiopiens. Poésie amharique". *Revue de l'Orient Chrétien*, 3/2/22: 306-326, 401-425. Reprint 1923.
Cohen, Marcel
1921 "La prononciation traditionelle du guèze (éthiopien classique)". *Journal Asiatique*, sér, 11, vol. 17:217-269.
1924 "Couplets amhariques du Choa". *Journal Asiatique* 205:1-100.
1936 *Traité de langue amharique (Abyssinie)*. Paris.
Conti Rossini, Carlo
1915 "Notice sur les manuscrits éthiopiens de la collection d'Abbadie". *Journal Asiatique*, sér. 11, vol. 6:223-224.
1941 *Grammatica elementare della lingua etiopica*. Roma.
Dillmann, August
1866 *Chrestomathia Aethiopica*, Leipzig. 2nd. ed., Littmann, Enno, ed., Berlin, 1950.
Grébaut, Sylvain
1919 "Note sur la poésie éthiopienne". *Revue de l'Orient Chrétien* 2/4:90-98.

Grohmann, Adolph

1919 *Äthiopische Marienhymnen*. Abhandlungen der Sächsischen Gesellschaft der Wissenschaften, Phil.-Hist. Kl. 33/4. Leipzig.

Kamil, Murad

1957 *Amharische Kaiserlieder*: Aufgezeichnet, umschrieben und übersetzt, Wiesbaden.

1968 "Die amharische Dicht- und Verskunst", in *Studia Orientalia in memoriam C. Brockelmann* (Fleischhammer, Manfred, ed., Halle [2nd ed. 1970]), pp. 105-119.

Klingenheben, August

1959 "Zur amharischen Poesie", *Rassegna di studi etiopici* 15:5-20.

Lambdin, Thomas O.

1978 *Introduction to Classical Ethiopic (Ge'ez)* (Harvard Semitic Studies 24). Missoula, Montana.

Leslau, Wolf

1945 *Short Grammar of Tigre* (North Ethiopic). New Haven.

1950 *Ethiopic Documents: Gurage*. New York.

1964 "The Farmer in Chaha Song". *Africa* 34:230-242.

1965 *An Annotated Bibliography of the Semitic Languages of Ethiopia*. The Hague.

1970 "Ethiopic and South Arabian", in: *Current Trends in Linguistics*, Sebeok, Thomas A., ed., Vol. 6. The Hague/Paris, pp. 467-527.

1982 *Gurage Folklore*, Wiesbaden: Franz Steiner Verlag.

Littmann, Enno

1909 "Geschichte der äthiopischen Literatur", in *Geschichte der christlichen Literaturen des Orients*. 2nd ed. Leipzig, pp. 185-270.

1914 *Die altamharischen Königslieder*. Strassburg.

1924 see section 2.

1925 *Galla-Verskunst*. Tübingen.

1930 "Abessinische und semitische Poesie". *Zeitschrift der Deutschen Morgenländischen Gesellschaft* 84:207-225.

1949 *Abessinische Klagelieder*. Tübingen.

1954 "Die äthiopische Sprache", in *Semitistik*, ed. Spuler, Berthold (Handbuch der Orientalistik 3/2-3). Leiden/Köln, pp. 359-275.

Ludolf, Iob

1698 *Grammatica linguae Amharicae ...* Francofurti ad Moenum.

1702 *Grammatica Aethiopica ...* Editio secunda. Accedit Prosodia ... Francofurti ad Moenum. (1st ed. 1661).

Mittwoch, Eugen

1926 *Die traditionelle Aussprache des Äthiopischen*. Berlin/Leipzig.

Praetorius, Franz

1879 *Die amharische Sprache*. Halle.

Schall, Anton

1961 *Zur äthiopischen Verskunst*. Eine Studie über die Metra des Qenē auf Grund der Abhandlung "Al-Qenē laun min aš-šiʿr al-ḥabašī" von Dr. Murad Kamil. Wiesbaden.

Trumpp, Ernst

1874 "Über den Accent im Aethiopischen". *Zeitschrift der Deutschen Morgenländischen Gesellschaft* 28:515-561.

Ullendorff, Edward

1955 *The Semitic languages of Ethiopia: A comparative phonology*. London.

1968 *Ethiopia and the Bible* (Schweich Lectures 1967). London.

2. Hebrew poetry and general poetics

Carmi T.
1981   *The Penguin Book of Hebrew Verse*. Harmondsworth.
Eissfeldt, Otto
1965   *The Old Testament: An Introduction*. New York (1976).
Harris, Zellig S.
1941   "Linguistic Structure of Hebrew". *JAOS* 61:143-167.
Hrushovski, Benjamin
1981   "Notes on the Systems of Hebrew Versification", in Carmi 1981, pp. 57-72.
Jakobson, Roman
1960   "Closing Statement: Linguistics and Poetics", in Sebeok 1960, pp. 350-377.
Kaiser, Otto
1975   *Introduction to the Old Testament*. Minneapolis (1977).
Littmann, Enno
1924   "Zum wechselnden Rhythmus in der hebräischen Poesie". *Zeitschrift für Semitistik* 2:272-273.
Lotz, John
1960   "Metric Typology", in Sebeok Thomas E., ed., 1960, pp. 135-148.
Sebeok, Thomas E., ed.
1960   *Style in Language*. Cambridge, Massachusetts (1966).
Segert, Stanislav
1953   "Vorarbeiten zur hebräischen Metrik, I-II", *Archiv Orientální* 21:482-540.
1960   "Problems of Hebrew Prosody", in *Congress Volume Oxford 1959* (= Supplements to Vetus Testamentum VII). Leiden, pp. 283-291.
1969   "Versbau und Sprachbau in der althebräischen Poesie". *Mitteilungen des Instituts für Orientforschung* 15:312-321.
1983   "Parallelism in Ugaritic Poetry". *JAOS* 103:295-306.
Worth, Dean
1977   "Roman Jakobson and the Study of Rhyme", in *Roman Jakobson: Echoes of his Scholarship*. Armstrong, Daniel, and van Schooneveld, C. H., eds. Lisse, pp. 515-533.

EMPEROR YOHANNES IV OF ETHIOPIA
AND THE BUILDING OF THE ETHIOPIAN CHURCH
OF DÄBRÄ GÄNNÄT AT JERUSALEM

Edward Ullendorff
London University (SOAS)

Professor R. Macuch of the Freie Universität Berlin has been kind enough to send me (on June 24, 1981) the Amharic letter whose text is here reproduced. It was "found among some old letters of Emmanuel Mountaki from Crete who now lives in Berlin". As we shall see in the following, the Greek provenance of this missive may well be significant.

I am grateful to Professor Macuch for making this document available to me, and to Dr. Richard Pankhurst for some very helpful observations.

Seal of Emperor Yohannes IV in Ethiopic and Arabic [1]:

ንጉሠ ፡ ነገሥት ፡ ዮሐንስ ፡ ዘኢትዮጵያ ፡

يوحنا ملك ملوك الحبشة

Translation of Amharic Text

Letter of the Elect of God, Yohannes, King of Zion, King of Kings of Ethiopia. May it reach the Greek [2] Consul of Jerusalem. How are you? (I

---

1 Cf. Pankhurst, "Royal & Imperial seals in Ethiopia", *JES*, XI, 1, 1973, especially p. 191 (where, however, يوهنا should read يوحنا) and 7th page of unnumbered illustration. See also Edward Ullendorff & Abraham Demoz in *BSOAS* 1969/1, pp. 135-142.

2 The Amharic *romawi* "Roman" and later *nəgusä rom* "King of Rome" present one of the ostensible difficulties in this document. The arguments in favour of interpreting this as Eastern Roman, Byzantine, Greek orthodox (rather than = Italian) seem wellnigh overwhelming. I have already referred to the Greek provenance of this document.
For the interpretation of *rom, romawi* as "Greece" and "Greek", cf. also Wright, *Catalogue of Ethiopic MSS in the British Museum*, Orient. 816, No. 13; *rum* is, of course, the traditional appellation for "Greece, Greek", i.e. "Byzantine" (cf. Dillmann, *Lexicon Ling. Aeth.*, col. 1412; Isenberg, *Dict. of the Amh. Lang.*, p. 45). Dr. R. Pankhurst has kindly drawn my attention to *Ṭəbyaros qesar romawi* "Tiberius Caesar, the Greek" in E. A. W. Budge, *Life & Exploits of Alexander the Great*, text p. 32, transl. p. 59; and many similar instances.
Furthermore, when Emperor Yohannes alludes to the Italians he normally uses *(i)ṭalya(n)*. The Greek king at the operative time (1883) was George I (as stated in line 9—though he

ask) repeatedly. By God's goodness, by the intercession of the true Ark of the Covenant[3]—may the God of the holy ones be honoured and praised—I, together with my army, am well. Your honoured letter with its seal[4] has reached me; I was very pleased about the message which I found in the letter. Please look after (for my sake) the monks who are at Jerusalem, those with Abba Wäldä Säma'ət[5], so that they may quickly build the church[6] without being disturbed. When you receive from Abba Wäldä Säma'ət the

is scarcely "new", some 20 years after his accession), while the King of Italy was Umberto I. Since Yohannes corresponded with Umberto (cf. C. Giglio, *L'Italia in Africa*, vol. I, Rome 1958, p. 173), he was well aware of the Italian king's name.

Moreover, we know that the Greek Consul at Suez (as such easily believed to be at Jerusalem = Palestine), Mitzakis, and his compatriot, the physician Dr. Parisis, were in the Emperor's confidence (Zewde Gabre-Sellassie, *Yohannes IV of Ethiopia*, Oxford 1975, pp. 137, 286, 288; M. de Coppet, *Chronique du règne de Ménélik II*, vol. I. p. 190, note 11; *Chi è dell'Eritrea*, 1952, p. 207; S. Rubenson, *Survival of Ethiopian Independence*, pp. 345, 350). Mitzakis visited the Emperor on several occasions and acted, according to *Chi è dell'Eritrea*, as his "consigliere". He took letters from the Emperor to various European heads of state, and he and Dr. Parisis maintained contact between George I, King of the Hellenes, and Emperor Yohannes.

It seems to me, therefore, that it is virtually certain that the Consul in question here was Mitzakis. It does indeed seem infinitely more probable that the Ethiopian Emperor would commend the Ethiopian monks at Jerusalem to the care of a Greek orthodox official rather than to that of a Roman Catholic functionary. Also, Mitzakis's dates fit those of the colophon admirably.

Dr. Pankhurst has furthermore drawn my attention to an article on Mitzakis and his 1879 mission by T. Natsoulas, "The Hellenic presence in Ethiopia", published in *Abba Salama*, VIII (1977), pp. 101-115 (at the time of writing I do not have access to this particular issue of *Abba Salama*).

In a more general context see also R. Pankhurst, "Greeks and other orthodox foreigners in traditional Ethiopia", Ἐκκλησιαστικὸς φάρος, 60, 1978;and "The role of foreigners in 19th century Ethiopia", *Boston Univ. Papers on Africa*, II, 1966.

3 Cf. Ullendorff, *Ethiopia and the Bible*, pp. 82-89, and esp. p. 83.

4 For the significance of seals, cf. footnote (1), particularly pp. 184ff.; also *The Amharic Letters of Emperor Theodore to Queen Victoria* (British Academy: Oriental Documents II), pp. 4b and 34b.

5 Abba Wäldä Säma'ət was before and during the reign of Emperor Yohannes the chief of the Ethiopian monks at Jerusalem. It was to him that the Emperor sent the considerable funds for the maintenance of the Ethiopian monastic community at Jerusalem and for the construction of the fine church of Däbrä Gännät ("hill of paradise") in new Jerusalem. See Abuna Philippos, *Know Jerusalem* (in Amharic and English, Addis Ababa 1972, pp. 187-8 and 161-2, respectively); also, Həruy Wäldä Səllase, *Biographie* (in Amharic), pp. 68-9; Bairu Tafla, *A Chronicle of Emperor Yohannes IV* (Wiesbaden 1977), pp. 163-189.

6 *Däbrä Gännät* (see previous footnote). Cf. in particular J. B. Coulbeaux, *Histoire politique et religieuse d'Abyssinie*, II, 476-81.

letter which I have written to the new King of Greece[2], George I, please send it on (for my sake) immediately by your own hand.

Written at the city of Sämära[7] on the 23rd of Gənbot in the Year of Grace 1875 (= 30th May, 1883).

---

7 Part of Däbrä Tabor, capital of Emperor Yohannes, some 30 miles east of Lake Tana. See *Guida dell' Africa orientale*, p. 391 and map p. 368. For details of Sämära and Däbrä Tabor see Pankhurst's admirable study in *BSOAS* 1977/2, pp. 235-266 (esp. pp. 257-8).

THE VOWEL SYSTEM OF GƏʿZ

RAINER M. VOIGT

Eberhard-Karls-Universität Tübingen

1.   The numerous kinds of vowel neutralization, especially in the neighbourhood of laryngals, represent one of the main features of Classical Ethiopic. Although this has been treated several times by Ludolf[1], Hupfeld[2], Dillmann[3], König[4], Praetorius[5], Marcel Cohen[6], Ullendorff[7], and others, I should like to take up this topic again in order to contribute to a system into which the rules in question can be incorporated.

2.   The vowel system that provides the context for treating vowel rules can be described in terms of the Protosemitic system as well as of the Modern Ethiopian one.

A derivation of the Gəʿz vowels from Protosemitic can be characterized conveniently by the systematic reduction of vowel length. Thus, the three-term opposition "short: long vowel: diphthong" yields the new opposition "centralized: short: long vowel" being represented briefly as follows[8]:

Sem.   s : l : d

Eth.   c : s : l

---

1 Iobi Ludolfi *Grammatica aethiopica*, ed. sec., Francofurti ad Moenum 1702. It seems that Ludolf does not know rule no. 2 (s. below) since he writes: "prima gutturalis nullam inflexioni mutationem offert" (p. 53).

2 H. Hupfeld, *Exercitationes aethiopicae* ..., Lipsiae 1825.

3 A. Dillmann, *Ethiopic grammar* (2. ed. by C. Bezold), transl. by J. A. Crichton, London 1907.

4 E. König, *Neue Studien über Schrift, Aussprache und allgemeine Formenlehre des Äthiopischen*, Leipzig 1877.

5 F. Praetorius, *Äthiopische Grammatik*, Karlsruhe (etc.) 1886.

6 M. Cohen, "Consonnes laryngales et voyelles en éthiopien". *Journal asiatique*, 210 (1927) 19-57.

7 E. Ullendorff, *The Semitic languages of Ethiopia*, London 1955.

8 The basic facts are well-known, s. K. Petráček, "Zur Entwicklung des phonologischen Systems des Altäthiopischen". *Rassegna di studi etiopici*, 20 (1964) 129-132.

As usual[9], the vowel shortening is accompanied by a modification of vowel quality. The step marked d→l implies monophthongization; s→c implies centralization:

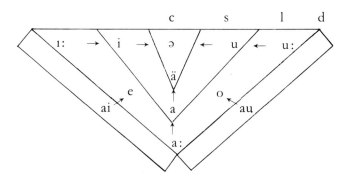

In addition to this diachronically based presentation, we can use the synchronic system of vowel evaluation as derived from the structure of Modern Ethiopic[10]:

	[front]	[central]	[back]
[high]	*i*	*ə*	*u*
[mid]	*e*	*ä*	*o*
[low]		*a*	

Which of the two systems is to be considered more appropriate for serving as a basis, if we want to describe the relevant vowel rules? It appears to me that in some cases the diachronically based system provides a more suitable and convenient way to formulate the rules, whereas in other cases the modern system appears more appropriate.

The enumeration of Praetorius, which has been adopted by other authors[11], presents the relevant vowel rules in the following manner:

(1) The vowel *ä* is lengthened before a syllable-closing laryngal, e.g. *yəmsä'* → *yəmsa'*, *bäṣäḥnä* → *bäṣaḥnä*, *mä'käl* → *ma'käl*, *'astäḥqärä* → *'astaḥqärä*.

---

9 Cf. in English the likewise non-phonetic distinction of vowel quality in quantity oppositions as bit: beat [ɪ]: [iː]) or bother: bought ([ɐ]: [ɔː]), s. P. Ladefoged, *A course in phonetics*, New York (etc.) 1975, p. 64, the short vowels being lower.

10 As Ullendorff would like to see it. The scheme is taken from J. Tubiana, "Système vocalique du guèze", *Comptes rendus du GLECS, 7* (1954-57) 81-82, s. M.L. Bender, H. Fulass, R. Cowley, "Two Ethio-Semitic languages". *Language in Ethiopia*, London 1976, pp. 99-119.

11 e.g. Cohen.

It was Ullendorff[12] who combined this rule with the pronunciation of *ä* as *a* after laryngal by using the syllable concept. Thus it is better to state that *ä* becomes *a* beside a laryngal belonging to the same syllable. This rule can also be formulated according to the mirror-image convention:

$$\ddot{a} \,/\!/ \,\_\_\, \mathrm{L\S} \to a \;(\text{i.e., } \ddot{a} \,/ \left\{ \begin{array}{c} \mathrm{L\S} \\ \mathrm{\S L\_\_} \end{array} \right\} \to a)$$

It seems that laryngals have a "marked preference for the *a*-sound"[13].

But if we added the rather marginal lengthening of *ə* before syllable-closing laryngal (as in *gəʿz*[14] [gɔ̄z]), we could extend the application of this rule to all centralized vowels:

$$\begin{array}{c} \mathrm{V} \\ [+\mathrm{centr}] \end{array} \,/\!/ \,\_\_\, \mathrm{L\S} \to \begin{array}{c} \mathrm{V} \\ [+\mathrm{long}] \end{array}$$

covering *ä→a* as well as *ə → ɔ̄*[15].

(2) *ə* before a laryngal followed by *ä* (which becomes *a* by dint of (1)) is replaced by *ä*, e.g. *məḥär →mäḥär →mäḥar, yəʿäqqəb →yäʿäqqəb →yäʿaqqəb*:

$$\text{əLä} \to \text{äLä}$$

(3) *ä* before a laryngal followed by a high vowel becomes *ə*, e.g. *ʾäxud → ʾəxud, ʾäxəw → ʾəx(ə)w, räḥib → rəḥib, (näḥnä →) näḥənä → nəḥənä*[16], *räʾyä* (sic) *→ rəʾyä*.

The rule application in *näśäʾä → näśəʾä* which contradicts the given rule could be derived by analogy from other forms of the paradigm, e.g. *näśäʾu → näśəʾu*[17], or by assuming another suffix (*näśäʾe?*).

$$\ddot{a} \,/\_\_\mathrm{L} \begin{array}{c} \mathrm{V} \\ [+\mathrm{high}] \end{array} \to \text{ə}$$

---

12 O.c. p. 212, cp. Praetorius o.c. p. 17.

13 Dillmann o.c. p. 85.

14 Usually rendered as *gəʿəz*.

15 The lengthening of postlaryngeal *ə* would be a disadvantage; up to the present time, there has been no substantial hint of such an instance. Cf., however, the remarks of Hupfeld (p. 12): "in principio vocis since vocali positae pro schevate plenam vocalem sibi assumunt e, quasi fortiorem sonum requirentes, ut ... *ērakkeb*".

16 The traditional explanation of this form being read *nəḥnä* refers to an underlying *niḥnä/ū* (s. C. Brockelmann, *Grundriß der vergleichenden Grammatik der semitischen Sprachen*, P. 1, Berlin 1908, p. 299).

17 s. Cohen o.c. p. 48.

The last two rules conspire in order to harmonize [18] two vowels separated by a non-geminated laryngal. In (3), *ä* actually becomes phonetically identical with the following vowel without leaving its vowel class (i.e. centralized):

> *'äxud* → [*'úxud*] |*'əxud*|
> *rähib* → [*rîhib*] |*rəhib*|

(4) Another rule hitherto not recognized should be added in this context. It is about a rule that feeds (3) and exhibits the same input as (1):

> *äLC* → *äLəC*

It is by the conflict with (1) that such doublets as *rahb/rəhəb* (sic), or *'ahzab/'əhəzab* (sic) arise:

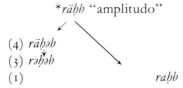

> **rähb* "amplitudo"
>
> (4) *rähəb*
> (3) *rəhəb*
> (1)   *rahb*

Rule (1) is regarded as a late and superficial rule bringing about no further consequences, contrary to rule (4) which changes the syllable structure and leads to the application of another rule.

If we object to accepting a perfect med. lar. *rä'əyä* as primary, we can derive this form from *rä'yä* by means of (4).

Two other well-known rules are relevant in this context:
(5) Short vowels are centralized in non-final, closed syllables, e.g. *säyyaṭ* — (f.) *säyyaṭ-t* → *säyyäṭṭ*, *nəgus* — (f.) *nəgus-t* → *nəgəst*, *ləhiq* — (f.) *ləhiq-t* → *ləhəqt*. The fact that final closed syllables are not affected by the rule proves the theory [19] of the original nominal suffix which represents the last remnant of the nominative and genitive suffix. Thus, *nəgus* (← *nəgusə*) remains unaffected.

$$\begin{matrix} \text{V} & \text{V} \\ [+ \text{ short}] \,/\underline{\quad}\text{CC} \to [+ \text{ central}], \text{ i.e.} \begin{cases} [\ddot{u}\bar{\imath}] \; /\partial/ \\ [\ddot{a}] \; /\ddot{a}/ \end{cases} \\ [+ \text{ high}] \qquad\qquad\quad [+ \quad \text{high}] \end{matrix}$$

A short vowel can resist to being reduced in that way if the preceding consonant is palatalizable, e.g. *rəkus* = *rək^wəs* — (f.) *rək^wəst* [*rŭkust*].

18 s. Ullendorff o.c. p. 215.
19 s. A. Dillmann, "Bemerkungen zur Grammatik des Geez ...", *Sitzungsberichte der Königlichen Preußischen Akademie der Wissenschaften zu Berlin*, Jg. 1890, pp. 3-17.

(6) The centralized vowels and their short counterparts of the same height are neutralized in the neighbourhood of semivowels and labialized (and palatalized?) consonants [20], e.g. *kul/kʷəl, moʿalt/(mʷäʿalt →) mäʿalt*.
On recording these rules in the given vowel scheme [21] we obtain:

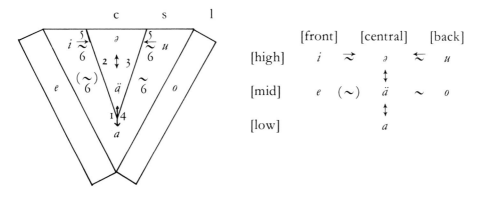

It is evident that *o* and *e* should be regarded as "long" since they cannot be reduced in closed syllables. In most Modern Ethiopic languages, *o* and *e* can cause labialization and palatalization—a remnant of their former diphthongic nature [22]. In terms of the distinctive-feature system, we could say that only [-mid] vowels become [+central] in closed syllables. It appears that in this case the first formulation is more revealing and instructive than the second one. In other cases, however, the df notation is more useful, cf. for

20 As for details, s. J. Tubiana, "Double neutralisation phonologique en amharique". *Revue de l'École nationale des langues orientales*, 5 (1968) 85-96.
21 Since the distinctive feature [rounded] for front vowels is unmarkedly minus, but for back vowels unmarkedly plus (s. N. Chomsky and M. Halle, *The sound pattern of English*. New York-London 1968, p. 409), the phonetically most realistic model is a three-dimensional vowel diagram as proposed by P. Ladefoged, "The classification of vowels". *Lingua*, 5 (1955-56), p. 121:

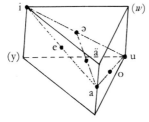

22 In the same way, labialization (and palatalization) of consonants followed by *u* (and *i*) shows the former length of these vowels. Cp. the two reduction steps d → l and l → s explained above.

instance the harmony tendency of some vowels to other vowels as well as to consonants. Roughly speaking, one can state the following affinity of consonants to vowels that is based on feature similarity:

$$w, C^w \; - \; u, o \; \Big\}$$
$$y\,(, C) - i, e \; \Big\}(6)$$
$$\text{L} \quad\quad - a \quad\quad (\text{1, first version})$$

Another harmony process is shown in the neutralized opposition between the two centralized vowels when separated by a laryngal:

$$\partial \sim \ddot{a} \,//\,\underline{\quad\text{L}\quad}$$

Thus, the three general principles underlying the given rules are:

vowel centralization (*shortening) in closed syllable
affinity of V and C sharing similar features
harmony of centralized vowels across a laryngal [23]

3.   It has long been observed that not all rules can be regarded as having been valid from the very beginning of the Geʿz language history, cf. the various doublets (e.g. *məhar* beside standard *mähar*) [24].

The laryngal sensitive rules (1-4) are arranged in the following chronological order:

$$
\left.
\begin{array}{c}
(4) \\
(3) \\
(2) \\
(1)
\end{array}
\right.
$$

(1-2) are younger than (3-4) since they show remarkably more exceptions. (4) can be regarded as the oldest vowel rule that reminds us of the former noun declension system (*kəburə* → *kəbur*). Furthermore (4) stands to (3) in a feeding order. (1) seems to be the latest rule.

The forming of laryngal-sensitive vowel rules emerges from the reduction process of these consonants that started in Gəʿz and led eventually to their loss (or morphological near-by loss) in Amharic.

The delaryngalization of the relevant consonants has been gradual. Its graphic representation could be as follows:

23 In this context, even Hupfeld speaks of vowel assimilation (p. 13).
24 s. Dillmann o.c. p. 85.

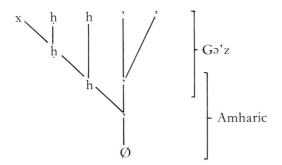

Some doublets can successfully be explained by taking into account the relationship between the vowel rules and the different stages of the laryngal development. It appears that we can distinguish three stages which represent two steps of delaryngalization:

(I)   L:LL, i.e., L is treated just like any other consonant
(II) L/LL, i.e., L can no longer be lengthened
(III) L′   , i.e., L is weakened to ʾ resp. h

The following model demonstrates the interaction between vowel rules and the degree of laryngality:

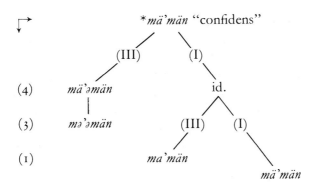

The arrows indicate the historical dimension. The underlying form is, of course, *mä'män* which yields regularly *mǝ'ǝmän*; the forms *mä'män* and *ma'män* owe their existence to the renewed use of the nominal pattern mägbär.

To provide further instances of how to demonstrate the interaction between vowel rules and degree of laryngality, I should like to present another two models:

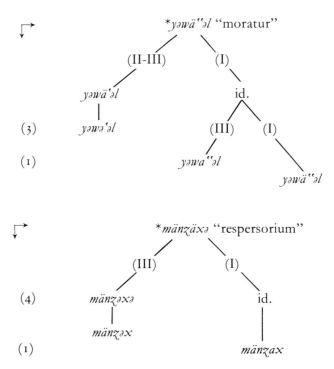

It appears worthwhile noting that the lengthening of the second radical is a prerequisit to the derivation of the *yəwa''əl* form. Otherwise, the rule that changes *ä* to *a* would not apply.

The observations made in this essay may be of some help in trying to reconstruct important features in the pronunciation of Old Ethiopic without having to rely solely on the oral tradition, which has, to some extent, become a controversial method. Through internal reconstruction, we may be able to arrive at results which can be discussed in a more systematic manner.

Note. df of page 359 = distinctive feature.

SELT'I-VERSE IN ARABISCHER SCHRIFT
AUS DEM SCHLOBIES-NACHLASS

EWALD WAGNER
Justus-Liebig-Universität, Gießen

Die Akademie des Wissenschaften und der Literatur in Mainz (BRD) verwahrt den Nachlaß des früh verstorbenen deutschen Orientalisten und Diplomaten Hans Martin Schlobies (1904-1950), der sich in den Zwanzigerjahren längere Zeit in Äthiopien aufhielt. Der Nachlaß enthält neben altsüdarabischen Materialien und arabischen und äthiopischen Handschriften auch Aufzeichnungen zu den modernen Sprachen Äthiopiens. Diese bestehen einmal aus Paradigmata für verschiedene Gurage-Sprachen wie Soddo (bei Schlobies »Dialekt von Dámo«[1]), Gogot (bei Schlobies »Dialekt von Dubi«[2]), Selt'i und Mask'an. Während die ersten beiden von Schlobies in Lateinschrift aufgezeichnet wurden, wurden die letzten beiden offensichtlich von einem einheimischen Schreiber in arab. Schrift hinter amh. Formenlisten gesetzt, die von Schlobies Hand stammen (leider alles über Kopf, was die Benutzung nicht gerade erleichtert). Daneben hat Schlobies acht Schreibhefte mit Texten in arab. Schrift hinterlassen, von denen die ersten vier die Aufschrift »Gurage-Lieder I-IV« und die weiteren Aufschriften »Silṭē, Maskan«, »Sänger Said Kebato« und die Daten VI. 26 und VII. 26 tragen. Die Texte sind sehr klar und voll vokalisiert von einem einheimischen Schreiber geschrieben worden[3]. Da aber sowohl eine Transliteration als auch eine Übersetzung fehlen, werden diese Texte nach meinen Erfahrungen mit arab. geschrieben Texten in dem sehr viel besser erforschten Harari kaum ohne Hilfe einheimischer Sprecher bearbeitet werden können. Etwas besser

---

[1] Zu Dámo vgl. Marcel Cohen: *Études d'éthiopien méridional*. Paris 1931 (im folgenden EEM abgekürzt), S. 91, wo es (*dammo*) zusammen mit *aymalläl* (alter Name für Soddo) und *nurənna* als linguistische Einheit genannt wird. Vgl. auch die Karte EEM 98.

[2] Auf der Karte bei Ulrich Braukämper: *Geschichte der Hadiya Süd-Äthiopiens von den Anfängen bis zu Revolution 1974*. Wiesbaden 1980. (Studien zur Kulturkunde. 50.) (im folgenden GH abgekürzt), S. 425 als ethnische Gruppe (Dobi) nördlich der Mask'an eingetragen, also in einem Gebiet, in dem nach der Karte von Wolf Leslau: *Etymological Dictionary of Gurage (Ethiopic)*. Wiesbaden 1979 (im folgenden EDG abgekürzt), Vol. 1, S. XXIX wirklich Gogot gesprochen wird.

[3] Es handelt sich wohl um die gleichen Texte, die bereits EEM 96, Anm. 1 erwähnt werden. Demnach war der Schreiber Muḥammad 'Arab.

steht es mit einem weiteren Heft mit der Aufschrift »Silṭē I. Poetische Texte«.
Es enthält elf kurze Gedichte, die von Schlobies in arab. Schrift offensichtlich
von einer einheimischen Vorlage abgeschrieben und mit einer Transkription,
einer amh. Übersetzung und Anmerkungen zu den Eigennamen versehen
wurden. Die amh. Übersetzung stammt anscheinend von einem Selt'i-
Informanten, der das Amh. nur sehr mangelhaft beherrschte. Sie gibt die
Selt'i-Texte oft nicht nur falsch wieder, sondern enthält auch viele Wörter
und Formen, die im Amh. nicht existieren, sowie falsche Konstruktionen.
Trotzdem bietet sie gewisse Anhaltspunkte für die Interpretation der Selt'i-
Verse.

Das Selt'i gehört zusammen mit dem Wolane und Zway zu dem Ost-
Gurage, das wiederum mit dem Harari eng verwandt ist[4]. Während das
Harari verhältnismäßig gut erschlossen ist, kann man das von dem Ost-
Gurage nicht sagen. Die ersten Vokabellisten im Selt'i-Wolane wurden
von Seetzen und Lefebvre in der ersten Hälfte des vorigen Jahrhunderts
gesammelt, allerdings für Argobba gehalten[5]. Anfang dieses Jahrhunderts
veröffentlichte dann Casimir Mondon-Vidailhet einige Paradigmata zum
Ulbarag (Dialekt des Selt'i) und Wolane, die jedoch für das Verb sehr mager
sind, und ein Vokabular des Ulbarag[6]. Eine recht ausführliche Darstellung
des Wolane bringt dann Marcel Cohen auf Grund eigener und älterer
Materialien (vor allem von d'Abbadie)[7]. Nach dem Zweiten Weltkriege
sammelten Leslau (Selt'i, Wolane und Zway), Drewes (Azärnät-Mugo [ein
Selt'i-Dialekt]) und Hetzron (Selt'i, Ennäk'or [ein Selt'i-Dialekt] und
Wolane) neues Material zum Ost-Gurage[8], von dem allerdings nur Leslau

---

4 Auf die Verwandtschaft machte zuerst Cohen in EEM 42 aufmerksam. Sie wurde dann
   von Wolf Leslau u. a. in: *Classification of the Semitic Languages of Ethiopia.* In: Proceedings
   of the Third International Conference of Ethiopian Studies, Addis Ababa 1966. 2.
   Addis Ababa 1970, S. 5-22, speziell S. 18-20 näher begründet. Auch Robert Hetzron:
   Ethiopian Semitic. Studies in classification. Manchester 1972. (Journal of Semitic Studies.
   Monograph. 2.), S. 42-44 stellt Ost-Gurage und Harari zusammen. Das Werk wird im
   folgenden ES abgekürzt.
5 Vgl. Wolf Leslau: *Examen du supposé Argobba de Seetzen et de Lefebvre.* In: Word 5 (1949),
   S. 46-54.
6 C. Mondon-Vidailhet: *La Langue Harari et les dialectes éthiopiens du Gouraghê.* Paris 1902.
   (Extraits du Journal asiatique et de la Revue sémitique), S. 77-119 und ders., *Études sur le*
   Guragiē. Publ. par Erich Weinzinger. Vienne 1913. (Kais. Akademie der Wissenschaften.
   Schriften der Sprachkommission. 5.).
7 EEM 55-241.
8 Vgl. A. J. Drewes: *Le Type verbal k'ätala en Gurage oriental.* In: Bibliotheca orientalis 17
   (1960), S. 5-10, speziell S. 6 mit Anm. 3, und Robert Hetzron: *Two Notes on Semitic*
   Laryngals in East Gurage. In: Phonetica 19 (1969), S. 69-81, speziell S. 69 mit Anm. 1.

den lexikalischen Teil seiner Sammlungen in seinem monumentalen *Etymological Dictionary of Gurage* veröffentlicht hat. Angaben zur Morphologie und Syntax der Ost-Gurage-Sprachen finden sich in den Werken der drei Autoren nur en passant zumeist in vergleichendem Zusammenhang. Textpublikationen fehlen praktisch ganz. Die wenigen im folgenden publizierten Selt'i-Verse aus dem Schlobies-Nachlaß sollen dafür keinen Ersatz bieten. Angesichts der Tatsache, daß andere Forscher umfangreiche Sammlungen zu dieser Sprache besitzen, wäre es vermessen, ohne eigene Aufzeichnungen und ohne einheimischen Informanten ein umfangreicheres Textkorpus interpretieren zu wollen. Der sprachliche Kommentar zu den Versen bringt deshalb auch keine neuen Erkenntnisse, sondern weist nur, soweit möglich, die im Text vorkommenden Erscheinungen in der Literatur nach. Vieles muß ungeklärt bleiben[9]. Mir geht es im Gefolge meiner Studien zu den *Harari-Texten in arabischer Schrift*[10] in erster Linie darum, eine Probe für die Anwendungen de arab. Schrift auf eine weitere semitische Sprache Äthiopiens vorzuführen[11].

Ich bringe die einzelnen Gedichte zunächst unverändert im arab. geschriebenen Text und in der Umschrift von Schlobies[12], dann folgt ein Übersetzungsversuch und ein Kommentar. Die amh. Übersetzung habe ich fortgelassen, da sie wegen ihrer Fehlerhaftigkeit eines eigenen Kommentars bedürfte. Ich verweise aber gelegentlich auf sie.

1   اِلْمْ اِلُ ٭ اِلْمْ اِلُ ٭ دِيْلَّانْشُنْ تَابَاشُّ ٭ سِلْطِنْ اَنُيَانْ وِيُشُّ

1. *ilä̆m ilù, ilä̆m ilù, dīllä̆nčòn tābä̆ččo silṭén ănuiän u̯ĕ̆ččo.*

Er sagt und sie sagen, er sagt und sie sagen. Dīllänčo und Abāččo machten Silt'ē angenehm(?).

> Nach Schlobies ist *ilä̆m ilù, ilä̆m ilù* die Eingangsformel für jedes zu dem Saiteninstrument *kərār* gesungene Lied. Zu dem Impf. *yəl* von *bāla* »sagen«

(EDG I 974b) vgl. das zusammengesetzte Impf. *yəlan* AFSE[13] 224a. Eine
2. Pers. sing. m. hinter der Konditionalpartikel *bə-* findet sich AFSE 218a in
bətlə. -u ist die Endung der 3. pl. Impf., vgl. *idäblun* = amh. *yəč'ämmərallu* und
ilädäblu = amh. *ayč'ämmərum* aus Schlobies' Paradigmata. *-m* »und« (EDG I
999b) koordiniert Sätze, vgl. auch ES 97. Vielleicht liegt aber auch ein altes
Gerundium *-äm* vor, das heute zumeist *-ä* heißt, nach ES 94 aber aus *-ä*
(Übertragung der alten gerundialen Akkusativendung auf das finite Verb) +
-m(a) entstanden sein soll. Das würde den Übergangsvokal *-ä-* erklären. —
Dīllänčo war nach Schlobies ein *šəfta* in Tōrā (Silṭē) und Abāčco ein *šəfta* in
Būzē (Silṭē). Zu *-n* »und« vgl. EDG I 1005a. Es ist hier mit *tä-* »mit«
(EDG 1020a) kombiniert. — Der Akkusativ lautet im Selt'i normalerweise *-ä*
(AFSE 217-18); bei Eigennamen wie hier *silṭén* scheint aber auch das amh.
-n vorzukommen, vgl. z. B. den von Schlobies notierten Satz *ṭěrāi iusúfĕn* »ruf
Yūsuf!«. — *ánuián* (richtiger *aňuyān*) ist 3. pl. des Präsens-Perfekts von *aňe*
»machen« (EDG I 969a) mit infigiertem Objektsuffix *-y-* (amh. Übers. *adärrägut*).
Zur Bildung des Präsens-Perfekt mittels des Hilfsverbs *-an* (< *hlw*) vgl. ES 40.
Zu dem im folgenden noch öfter vorkommenden Objektsuffix 3. sg. m. *-y* vgl.
aus den Schlobies'schen Paradigmata z. B. *ĭlenzui* = amh. *ayyəzutəm* »sie nehmen
ihn nicht« und AFSE 216b *yokäbku-y* »ich kaufte ihn«. — *u̯éččo* (so nicht in EDG)
wird durch das mir unbekannte amh. *mač250u* wiedergegeben. Vielleicht ist es
Fehler für *məčču* »passend, angenehm«. Die Wurzel kommt aber als *tämēčče*
»passend sein« (EDG I 999b) auch im Selt'i vor und ein Übergang *m > w* ist
eigentlich nur bei der Vorsilbe *mä-* der Verbalnomina belegt, vgl. EDG III,
XXXIII, so daß sich *u̯éččo* nicht recht erklären läßt.

2   يَكِيْبِىْ حَمِيْدْ ٭ أَرُوْتَيْ تِبَادْ ٭ مَالْتَيْ تَجِّهَادْ

2. *jakíbē hamíd̯*, *arótai tibád̯*, *máltai taǧíhádĕ*.

Ḥamīd b. Kībē (verbrachte) die Nacht mit Gebet und den Tag mit Glaubens-
krieg.

Ḥamīd und Kībē waren nach Schlobies *k'alləčča* (Magier) in Sōgārē (Silṭē). *yä-* ist
Genitivpartikel (EDG I 1028b). — *arōt* »Nacht« (EDG I 970a) und *mält* »Tag«
(EDG I 1001b) stehen im adverbiellen Akkus. auf *-ä* (AFSE 218) mit folgendem
Artikel *-y*, vgl. AFSE 218b *bučo-y* »der Hund«. — Den arab. Lehnwörtern *ibād*
»Gebet« (EDG I 961a) und *ǧihād* ist die Präposition *t(ä)-* (EDG I 1020a)
vorgesetzt.

---

13 Hiermit wird Wolf Leslau: *Archaic Features in South Ethiopic*. In: Journal of the American
    Oriental Society 71 (1951), S. 212-30 abgekürzt.

3 يَكِيبِي حَمِيْدْ ٭ بُجُفْلَلَ مِيْدِ ٭ تَمَارَقُوي چِدِ

3. *ja k̲ībē hàmīdḗ, bagṓflala mīdḗ, tamárak̲òi gidḗ.*

Ḥamīd b. Kībē (hatte) am Fluß Goflala mit den Mārak'o einen Kampf(?).

Goflala ist nach Schlobies eine Ebene, auf der Silṭē und Marak̲o Krieg führten. Da aber sowohl *mīde* (EDG I 1000a) als auch die amh. Entsprechung *wänz̧* »Fluß« heißen, habe ich so übersetzt. — Zu dem östlich der Selt'i wohnenden Marak'o vgl. GH 425-26 und EEM 69; 94; 98. Das *-i* am Ende des Namens kann ich nur als Artikel erklären. — *gid(ḗ)* muß nach der geographischen Anm. von Schlobies und nach der amh. Übers. soviel wie »Kampf, Krieg« heißen. Vielleicht ist es eine indirekte Entlehnung von *ǧihād*. Vielleicht hängt es auch mit der Wurzel *gdl* »töten« oder mit *gəd* »Gewalt« (EDG III 262) zusammen.

4 لَكِيبِي حَمِيْدْ ٭ قَلْبِمِ تَايُدْ ٭ اِجَبَاوُ بَجِدْ

4. *lak̲ībē Hamīdḗ, k̲álbĭmḗ tāiṓdd, igabáu bagĭdd̲ᵉ.*

Obwohl mein Herz den Ḥamīd b. Kībē nicht liebt, gehe ich doch gezwungenermaßen (zu ihm) ein.

Nach Schlobies handelt es sich um einen Gesang der Frauen. — Zur Einführung des direkten Objekts durch *lä-* vgl. AFSE 218b. — An arab. *qalb* »Herz« (EDG 1080a) ist zunächst *-m* »und, auch« (EDG 999b) (vielleicht handelt es sich auch um das von Verb getrennte *-m* verneinter Verbalformen wie *taykäflǝm* »ohne zu zahlen« [AFSE 218a]) und dann das Possessivsuffix 1. sg. *-e* (vgl. AFSE 218b *färäz-e* »mein Pferd« und das Paradigma der Possessivsuffixe an *gār* »Haus« bei Schlobies: *gārē, gārāʰ, gārāš, gārkä, gāršᵊ, gārǝna, gārāmu, gārnīmu*). Zur Infigierung des *-m-* zwischen Nomen und Possessivsuffix vgl. PG [14] 168 *abbo-m-kä* »und sein Vater«. Ähnlich steht das Possessivsuffix erst hinter der Kopula, z. B. AFSE 216b *uhä abbo-t-ah* »er ist dein Vater«. — *wädädä* »lieben« (EDG I 1025a) steht hier hinter der Konjunktion *tǝ-* »während« (PG 168) in der 3. sg. m. des verneinten Impf. im untergeordneten Satz (*aysäbǝr* gegenüber *ǝläsäbǝr* [oder *ǝläsäbǝr*, vgl. Ged. 9] im Hauptsatz, vgl. ES 95), vgl. auch das oben zitierte *taykäflǝm*. — *gäba* »hineingehen« (EDG I 986b) steht in der 1. sg. des zusammengesetzten Impf., dessen Konjugation ES 39 gegeben wird. — Zu *bägǝd* »zwangsweise« vgl. EDG I 987a.

---

14 Hiermit wird Wolf Leslau: *Is there a Proto-Gurage?* In: Proceedings of the International Conference on Semitic Studies held in Jerusalem, 19-23 July 1965. Jerusalem 1969, S. 152-71 abgekürzt.

5 يَكِبِى حَمِيدْ ⋆ اللهُ اَوَطَانْ جِزْ ⋆ يَارَقْ سُمَهَ ⋆ تَنَقْلُبُيْ اِلَانْ بِزْبِزْ

5. jakībē hàmīdʿ, allāʰ auaṭán gizʿ, jämárako sŭmahá, tinăḳlubúi ilán bĭzʾbĭzʾ.

Ḥamīd b. Kībē ist etwas, das Gott hervorgebracht hat (ein Geschenk Gottes). Sobald sie ihm gegenüber deinen Namen Marak'o erwähnen, steht er ganz aufrecht da.

> Das Kausativ awät'a »herausbringen« (EDG I 1027b) steht im Präsens-Perfekt, vgl. Ged. 1. Der Relativsatz wird wohl nur durch die Stellung zum Ausdruck gebracht. — Zu gǝzz »Sache« vgl. EDG I 991b. — Auf sum »Name« (EDG I 1015b) folgt das Akkusativsuffix -ä- und das Possessivsuffix 2. sg. m. -h, hier anscheinend in einer älteren Form -ha. Angeredet ist offensichtlich der feindliche Stamm Marak'o. — näk'älä »aufheben« (EDG I 1006a) hat wohl gleich dem synonymen amh. anässa auch die Bed. »(einen Namen) erwähnen« (vgl. Wolf Leslau: Concise Amharic Dictionary. Wiesbaden 1976, S. 111). Die Form setzt sich zusammen aus der Konjunktion tǝ + yǝnäk'lu (3. pl. Impf.) + Präposition b + Suffix 3. sg. m. -y. Der Übergangsvokal -u- ist wohl durch das b bedingt. — bǝzz bälä »aufrecht stehen« (EDG I 977b) ist hier redupliziert. Zu der 3. sg. m. des zusammengesetzten Impf. yǝlan von bälä s. AFSE 224a.

6 طِيَمُونْ تَحَتِ ⋆ اَطِيْدُونْ تَمَلْتِيْ ⋆ اَسَنُنْ تَبَالِّ ⋆ الْبُورْنْ تَكُورِيْ ⋆ اَجَاتِنْ تَمَلِّ ⋆ اِيتَامْ اَلِّفَرِ

6. ṭibamōn tagatē, aṭīdōn tamaltē, ásanún tabāllē, ilborón tákorē, ágatēn támallē, ētāmu állifari.

Ṭibamo und Gatē, Aṭido und Maltē, Asan und Bāllē, Ilboro und Korē, Agate und Mallē, ihren Ort will ich nicht fürchten!

> Nach Schlobies war Gatē balabbat (Stammesführer) in Ḳarriso; Ṭibamo war sein Freund; beide waren zu Schlobies' Zeit bereits tot. Aṭido und Malte waren Brüder. — Auf ēt »Ort« (EDG I 971b) folgt das Possessivsuffix 3. pl., vgl. Ged. 4. — färe »fürchten« (EDG I 985a) steht wohl im verneinten Jussiv 1. sg. Die Form entspricht bezüglich der Präfixe etwa Čaha anǝnkǝs <al+l+ǝnkǝs mit ll > n, vgl. Wolf Leslau: Ethiopic Documents: Gurage. New York 1950. (Viking Fund Publications in Anthropology. 14.), S. 29 und 13. Nach Wolf Leslau: Le Type verbal qatälä en éthiopien méridional. Beyrouth 1954. (Mélanges de l'Université Saint Joseph. 31, 2.), S. 56 lautet der Jussiv von dem Verb III inf. gäže (C-Stamm) yägaž, so daß man von färe allǝfär erwarten würde. Ich nehme deshalb an, daß das -i am Ende auf ēt rückbezügliches Objektsuffix 3. sg. m. ist.

$$7 \quad \text{مِنْ نَّادِنْ اَلۡاَبَا ∗ اَدُّمۡجِنَ تَايۡقَابَ ∗ بَسَتٍ جَبَابَا}$$

7. *Min nnādén ālābā, addä́mgĭn tāiḵába, básačé gabába.*

Wieso pries man Ālābā, nachdem er (der Stamm Ālābā), ohne sich einmal
umzudrehen, nach Gagāba geflohen war?

> Zu *mən* »was?« vgl. EDG I 1001b. — Ich nehme an, daß das doppelte *n* in
> *nnādén* nur das *šadda* der arab. Schrift wiedergibt, das seinerseits nur bedeuten
> soll, daß das auslautende *n* von *mən* und das anlautende *n* von *nādén* zusammen
> als ein gelängtes *nn* zu sprechen sind. Man wird also wohl *nādén* anzusetzen
> haben, das Grundverb von dem EDG I 1005a genannten Reflexiv *tänädä* »stolz,
> arrogant sein« in der Bed. »preisen« in der unpersönlichen Form (deutsch mit
> »man« zu übers.) des Präsens-Perfekt auf -*n*. Zu unpersönlichen Formen auf -*e*
> vgl. ES 108 und Beispiele wie *biče näqäle* »one lifted the mourning« von *näqälä*
> (EDG I 973b). — Die Ālābā wohnen südlich der Ulbarag, die wiederum südlich
> der Selt'i leben, vgl. GH 425-6 und EEM 98. — Zu *addä gən* »einmal«, hier mit
> eigefügtem -*m* »und, auch«, vgl. EDG I 989a. — *k'äbä* heißt nach EDG I 1007a
> »falten, aufrollen«; nach EDG III 332a bed. das Wort in den verwandten
> Sprachen aber auch »curve, turn the cattle in another direction«. Da es zudem
> mit amh. *tämälläsä* wiedergegeben wird, habe ich es mit dem reflexiven »sich
> umdrehen« zu übersetzen gewagt. Die Form ist wieder 3. sg. m. verneintes
> Impf. des untergeordneten Satzes hinter der Konjunktion *tə*-, vgl. Ged. 4. —
> Vor *sače* »fliehen« (EDG I 1014a) steht hier die Konjunktion *bä*-, die mit
> folgendem Perfekt und *rér* »since, as, after« heißt (EDG 973b). In dem
> poetischen Text fehlt das *rér* entweder oder *bä*- leitet hier nicht einen Nebensatz,
> sondern den Nachsatz ein, wie offensichtlich auch in Ged. 8. Dann wäre zu
> übersetzen: »Wieso pries man Ālābā? Ohne sich einmal umzudrehen, floh er
> nach Gabāba«. — Gabāba liegt nach Schlobies zwischen Silṭe und Ālābā.

$$8 \quad \text{يَفَرَزْ دَابَنَ ∗ بَالۡمَطَبِيَانْ دِيۡنَا ∗ بَسَتٍ وَنۡدَبَن}$$

8. *jafáraz dábana, bálmaṭabiján dínā, básačé u̯ándabana.*

Er floh zum Abhang hin, selbst wenn der Kriegsfeind nicht in der Wolke der
Pferde (von den Pferden aufgewühlten Staubwolke) kam.

> Schlobies bemerkt dazu: »Ulbarak u. Alaba flohen, die Silṭē waren die einzigen,
> die mit den Arussis und Marako kämpften«. — Zu *färäz* »Pferd« vgl. EDG I
> 985b, zu *däbäna* »Wolke« EDG I 980b. — *mät'a* »kommen« (EDG I 1004a) steht
> im mit *al*- verneinten Präsens-Perfekt auf -*an* mit eingeschobener Präposition -*b*-
> und auf die Wolke rückbezogenem Suffix 3. sg. m. -*y*. Vorangestellt ist die
> Konjunktion *ba*- »selbst wenn, obwohl«, die nach EDG I 973b allerdings nur

vor dem Impf. steht. — Zu *dīna* »Kriegsfeind« vgl. EDG I 982a. — Zu *bä-säče* vgl. Ged. 7. — Auf *wändäbän* »Abhang« (EDG I 1026b) folgt der Akkusativ der Richtung *-ä*, vgl. AFSE 218.

و يَدُورِ تَسَمَّا ٭ يَبَالِ اِلَسَمَا ٭ تَسَمَّا يَدُورِ ٭ بَفُولَا بَفُولِ ٭ اِزْلَزْلَاُوْ بَامُولِ ٭ اِلَوْجِبْرَيْ شُوْلِ

9. *ja dōrē tasammā, ja bāli ilasamā, tasammā jadōrē, bafōlā bafōli, ízlazláu bāmōlē, ilaᴜgēbräi čūlē.*

Tasammā b. Dōrē hörte nicht auf das, was man sagte. Oh Tasammā b. Dōrē, um dein Leben oder mein Leben (geht es)! Ich handle (zwar) mit Salzbarren, mein Kind will ich (dir aber) nicht als Steuer zahlen.

Nach Schlobies hat Tasammā Gangul, Sohn des Dōrē, z. Zt. Meneliks II im Jahre 1311 H. (1893) Silṭē tributpflichtig gemacht (mit dem GH 269 genannten *fitawrari* Tasammā Guči identisch?) — *bāli* steht vielleicht für *bāle*, dem unpersönlichen Perfekt von *bālä* »sagen«. Den bisherigen adjektivischen Relativsätzen fehlte das Relativpronomen *yä-*. Vielleicht muß es bei substantivischen Relativsätzen stehen. — *ᵊläsäma* ist 3. sg. m. des verneinten Impf. im Hauptsatz, das nach Schlobies' Paradigmata folgendermaßen konjugiert wird: *iläwdäbᵊl, ittᵊdäbᵊl, ittᵊdäbᵊl, ilädäbᵊl, ittᵊdäbᵊl, ilädäblᵊna, ittᵊdäblu, ilädäblu.* Da Schlobies mit *iläsäku* = amh. *ayšäšum* oder *ilämät'u* = amh. *aymät'um* weitere Formen mit *ä* hinter dem *l* anführt, ist das *ᵊ* in ES 95 *ᵊläsäbᵊr* vielleicht nicht richtig. Die Form *ᵊlak' atᵊl* »er kann nicht« (AFSE 218a) gibt über diese Frage keine Auskunft, da ihr das Kausativ eines C-Verbs *ak'atäla* (EDG I 1011a) zugrundeliegt. — Auf *fōl* »Atem« (EDG I 984a) folgt einmal das Possessivsuffix 2. m. sg. *-āh*, für das Schlobies' Gewährsmann Yūsuf eine Nebenform *-ā́* angab, und einmal das der 1. sg. *-ē̇*. Das *-i* ist sicher ein Fehler, da auch der Reim ein *-ē* verlangt. — *ẓiläẓälä* »kleinen Handel betreiben« (EDG I 1030a) steht hier in der 1. sg. des zusammengesetzten Impf., vgl. Ged. 4. — Zu *amōle* »Salzbarren« (früher als Zahlungsmittel verwendet) vgl. EDG I 965b. — *gēbärä* »Steuern zahlen« (EDG I 987a) steht in der 1. sg. des verneinten Impf. im Hauptsatz, vgl. neben dem obigen Paradigma auch AFSE 218 *ᵊläwsäma* »ich werde nicht hören«, *ᵊläwbälä* (zu lesen *ᵊläwbäla?*) »ich esse nicht«. Das seltsame *-äw* im Präfix ist vielleicht aus der Endung *-aw* (< *-alläh^w*) des positiven zusammengesetzten Impf. transponiert worden. Das *-i* an *ilaᴜgēbräi* ist auf *čūlē* bezügliches Objektsuffix 3. sg. m. — Auf *čūlo* »Baby« (EDG I 979a) folgt das Possessivsuffix 1. sg. *-ē*, vor dem das *-o* offensichtlich ausfällt. Das Wort ist im arab. mit *sīn* mit vier Punkten geschrieben, was Schlobies mit *č* umschreibt. *sīn* mit vier Punkten kann aber auch *č'* wiedergeben, vgl. z. B. in Schlobies' Paradigmata *ilämäč'č'ᵊnä* = amh.

anmät'am »wir kommen nicht« (von *mät'a* »kommen«), wo das *t'* gesichert ist, da es sich um eine Palatalisierung des *t'* handelt. Ich möchte deshalb einen Fehler in Schlobies' Umschrift annehmen und *t'ūlē* lesen.

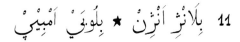

11. [15]. *bilāṇ̌zi aṇ̌z̆éñ, bilobái ambeñ.*

Wenn ich ihn sehen wollte, sah er mich. Wenn ich (mich) ihm aber (hin)geben wollte, lehnte er ab.

> Schlobies bemerkt dazu: »eine Frau an einen Helden, der sie nicht heiraten will«. — *anž̆e* »sehen« (EDG I 968b) steht hier wohl in der 1. sg. Jussiv mit vorgesetzter Konjugation *bə-* und folgendem Objektsuffix 3. sg. m. *bə-* steht nach EDG I 973b allerdings nur vor dem Impf. Man könnte sich deshalb fragen, ob in dem *l* nicht eine Verneinung steckt. Das verneinte Impf. 1. sg. mit Objektsuffix heißt nach den Schlobies'schen Paradigmata aber *ilaṇ̣ṇ̣âṇ̌zi* = amh. *alayäwəm.* Für das verneinte Impf. im abhängigen Satz sollte man nach der 3. sg. m. *aysäbər* (ES 95) für die 1. sg. eher *balāṇ̌zi* erwarten. — *anž̆éñ* ist 3. sg. m. des gleichen Verbs mit Objektsuffix 1. sg. *-ñ*, vgl. z. B. in den Schlobies'schen Paradigmata *aläñ* »ich habe«. — *bilobái* ist die *bilāṇ̌zí* entsprechende Form von *wäbä* »geben« (EDG I 1024b), für das Schlobies in den Paradigmata u. a. die Form *jōbáimäṇ* = amh. *əsät'atč̆äwallähʷ* zitiert. — Auf *ambe* »ablehnen« (EDG I 965a) folgt wieder das Objektsuffix 1. sg.

Das arab. Alphabet besitzt folgende Buchstaben, denen im Selt'i keine Laute entsprechen: ' (außerhalb des Anlauts), ', *ḍ, ḏ, ġ, ḥ, ḫ, ṣ, ṭ, ẓ.* Im Gegensatz zum Harari, bei dem archaisierende und hyperkorrekte Schreibungen vor allem bei den Laryngalen und *ḏ* in Mengen vorkommen [16], fehlen diese Buchstaben im Selt'i praktisch ganz. Nur der arab. Eigenname *Ḥamīd* wird mit *ḥ* geschrieben.

Bei den beiden glottalisierten Lauten *t'* und *k'* des Selt'i werden wie im Harari die Buchstaben für die arab. velarisierten Entsprechungen *ṭ* und *q* eingesetzt, vgl. z. B. *tamárakòi* (Ged. 3), *aṇaṭân* (Ged. 5), *tāikába* (Ged. 7), *bálmaṭabiján* (Ged. 8).

---

15 Ged. 10 habe ich übergangen, da bei Schlobies der Text in arab. Schrift fehlt.

16 Vgl. zunächst einmal Enrico Cerulli: *Studi etiopici.* 1: *La Lingua e la storia di Harar.* Roma 1936 (Im folgenden LSH abgekürzt), S. 346-49. Das Problem wird auch in der Einleitung zu HTAS angesprochen werden.

Darüber hinaus kennt das Selt'i die Laute *č*, *č'*, *g*, *ñ*, *ẓ*[17], die im Arab. fehlen. Außer *ẓ* finden sich diese Laute auch im Harari. Wird Harari in arab. Schrift geschrieben, so gibt es zwei Möglichkeiten: Entweder werden die Buchstaben *t* für *č*, *t'* für *č'*, *ǧ* für *g* und *n* für *ñ* mitverwendet, so z. B. im *K. al-Farā'iḍ* (LSH 344-46). Daneben kommt in HTAS mindestens ebenso häufig wie *t* ein *š* für *č* vor, eine Erscheinung, die im *K. al-Farā'iḍ* auf das Wort *däči* »Land« beschränkt ist (LSH 345). Die Folge dieser Möglichkeit der Schriftadaption ist, daß die Schrift nicht mehr eindeutig ist und einem Buchstaben zwei Laute entsprechen.

Die andere Möglichkeit besteht darin, durch die Setzung zusätzlicher Punkte neue Buchstaben zu erfinden. In HTAS finden sich folgende Zusatzbuchstaben, die jedoch nie konsequent, sondern offensichtlich nur, wenn Mißverständnisse befürchtet wurden, gesetzt sind:

č wird durch ein *t* mit zwei Punkten über und drei Punkten unter dem Buchstaben (in der Anordnung wie bei pers. *p*) ausgedrückt, z. B. in HTAS *awač ayač* »Väter und Mütter« (A 18[18] Hs. A); *asčäna* »laß uns trinken!« (A 32 Hs. A)[19].

č' wird durch *t* mit drei Punkten unter dem Buchstaben (in der Anordnung wie bei pers. *p*) ausgedrückt, z.B. in HTAS *č'aya* »Schatten« (A 31); *ač'uyu* »er (Respektform) wurde fortgeholt« (B 80).

g wird durch *ǧ* mit drei untergesetzten Punkten (wie pers. *č*) ausgedrückt, z. B. in HTAS *gir* »mal« (A 2); *uga* »Weg« (A 28)[20].

ñ wird durch *n* mit einem Punkt über und drei Punkten unter dem Buchstaben (in der Anordnung wie bei pers. *p*) ausgedrückt, z. B. in HTAS *uñäna* »mach uns!« (A 20 Hs. A); *mäñit* »Schlafen« (A 21 Hs. A)[21].

Das Selt'i verwendet nur in einem Falle die gleiche Wiedergabe wie das Harari: auch hier wird *g* durch *ǧ* mit drei Punkten ausgedrückt, vgl. *gōflala* und *gidē* in Ged. 3, *igabāu* und *bagĭddē* in Ged. 4 usw.

In allen anderen Fällen beschreitet das Selt'i eigene Wege. Am einfachsten ist der Fall bei *ñ*. Hier verwendet das Selt'i ein *y* mit drei Punkten darunter,

---

17 Die Selt'i-Laute *p* und *ṗ* (EDG III, XXXII) kommen in den Gedichten nicht vor.
18 Die Majuskel bezeichnet den Text und die Ziffer den Abschnitt von HTAS.
19 B 179 kommen ein einziges Mal Varianten mit *ǧ* (mit einem untergesetzten Punkt) und *ǧ* mit drei untergesetzten Punkten für *č* in *däči* vor. Es handelt sich wohl um Fehler.
20 D 9 werden die Wörter *ge* »Land«, *girgara* »Hilfe«, *gar* »Haus« und *gälgeb* »Unterhaltung« mit *kāf* geschrieben. Ebenso vereinzelt ist die Schreibung von *g* durch *kāf* mit drei Punkten unter dem Buchstaben in A 32 Hs. A.
21 E 25/26 wird in *ḫaneñ* »er ist für mich da« und einigen anderen Wörtern *ñ* vereinzelt durch eine dritte Methode, nämlich der Buchstabenkombination, ausgedrückt. Für *ñ* steht *ny*.

vgl. *ambéñ* in Ged. 11. Diese Schreibung des *ñ* findet sich in den übrigen Texten von Schlobies überaus häufig, z.B. *z̧it'äññe* »neun« (S. 19, Z. 15 [22]). So stellt es sicherlich nicht das richtige Verhältnis dar, wenn in unseren Gedichten das *ñ* gleich zweimal durch einfaches *n* wiedergegeben wird (*ănuiấn* in Ged. 1 und *anz̧éñ* in Ged. 11).

Das *č* wird durch *s* mit vier Punkten über dem Buchstaben ausgedrückt, vgl. *dīllắnčòn*, *tābắččo* und *ụ̄ěččo* in Ged. 1 und *básačē* in Ged. 7 und 8.

s mit vier Punkten wird gelegentlich aber auch zum Ausdruck des *č'* verwendet, vgl. *č'ūlē* in Ged. 9 und die im dortigen Kommentar genannte Form aus den Paradigmata. Viel häufiger ist in den sonstigen Schlobies'schen Texten aber für *č'* das in den Gedichten nicht belegte *t* mit drei Punkten darüber (in der Anordnung wie bei arab. *t̤*). Während das Harari also die Punkte unter das *t* setzt, setzt das Selt'i sie darüber. Beispiele: *č'unč'e* »Mücke« (S. 16, Z. 2; S. 18, Z. 8 u. 9); *anč'ǝr* »kurz« (S. 19, Z. 6); *č'ǝk'a* »Schlamm« (S. 7, Z. 7).

Darüber hinaus benutzt das Selt'i das *t* mit drei Punkten aber auch, um das *z̧* auszudrücken, das in den hier veröffentlichten Gedichten wie im Pers. durch *z* mit drei Punkten geschrieben wird, vgl. *bilānz̧í* und *anz̧éñ* in Ged. 11. In den Paradigmata, die für Schlobies aufgezeichnet wurden, wird das gleiche Verb *anz̧e* »sehen« durchgängig mit *t* mit drei Punkten geschrieben. In den übrigen Texten kommen beide Schreibungen vor: *bǝz̧z̧i* »viel« S. 4, Z. 8 mit *z* und drei Punkten, S. 13, Z. 2 dagegen mit *t* und drei Punkten. Im ganzen überwiegt wohl die Schreibung mit *t* und drei Punkten. Weitere Beispiele dafür sind: *kälbäz̧o* »Stern« (S. 8, Z. 9) und *z̧ubo* »Ding, Angelegenheit« (S. 8, Z. 6).

Bezüglich des Vokalausdrucks hat das Harari gar keine Versuche gemacht, die Schrift an die im Harari gegenüber dem Arabischen sehr viel größere Zahl der Vokalqualitäten anzupassen. Ja, es hat sogar die in der arab. Schrift gegebene Möglichkeit durch Defektiv- und Pleneschreibung die im Harari ebenfalls vorhandenen Vokalquantitäten auszudrücken, nicht genutzt. Plene- und Defektivschreibung gehen durcheinander [23].

Das Selt'i geht hier etwas weiter, vor allem durch die Nutzung des doppelten *ḍamma* (im Arab. Nūnation) zum Ausdruck des *o* und des doppelten *kasra* (im Arab. ebenfalls Nūnation [24]) zum Ausdruck des *e*, vgl. Ged. 1,

---

22 Alle im folgenden aus den übrigen Texten von Schlobies stammenden Beispiele sind einem einzigen der unbezeichneten Hefte entnommen. Ich zitiere nur nach Seite und Zeile.

23 Hierauf bin ich ausführlicher in der Einleitung zu HTAS eingegangen.

24 Im Harari wird das doppelte *kasra* wie im Arab. für die Endung *-in* gebraucht, vgl. LSH 351. In HTAS wird sogar die Kopula *intä-* gelegentlich so geschrieben, daß das vorhergehende Wort *tanwīn* erhält und man dann bei der Kopula mit dem *t* beginnt (A 30).

3, 4, 6, 7, 9. Die Gedichte zeigen aber ebenso deutlich, daß die Erfindung nicht konsequent angewendet wird. Wie im Harari hat sich auch keine konsequente Bezeichnung der Längen durch Pleneschreibung durchgesetzt. Mit der äthiop. Schrift teilt die Selt'i-Orthographie die crux, daß sie ǝ nicht eindeutig ausdrücken kann. Sie verwendet entweder *kasra* (dann von Schlobies auch meist mit *i* umschrieben) oder *sukūn*. In den Paradigmata wird z. B. eine Form wie ǝttǝdäbǝl = attǝčʼämmǝrǝm mit *kasra* unter dem *alif*, *šadda* und *sukūn* über dem *t*, *fatḥa* über dem *d* und *sukūn* über *b* und *l* geschrieben.

Zusammenfassend kann man sagen, daß die Selt'i zwar durch Erfindung von Zusatzbuchstaben mittels Abwandlung vorhandener arab. Zeichen (zusätzliche Punkte) und durch Umfunktionieren vorhandener orthographischer Mittel (Nūnation) einen Zeichenvorrat geschaffen haben, der dem Lautstand ihrer Sprache in etwa gerecht wird, daß sie aber durch inkonsequente Anwendung der neuen Zeichen einen großen Teil des Erfolgs wieder zunichte machen.

[*Korrekturzusatz*: Der Schlobiesnachlaß ist inzwischen an die Staatsbibliothek Preußischer Kulturbesitz, Berlin, überführt worden.]

BASIC NUMERALS IN THE OMOTIC LANGUAGES

ANDRZEJ ZABORSKI
Jagellonian University, Cracow

Although probably the majority of linguists are inclined to consider the Omotic languages of Ethiopia, formerly classified as a branch of Cushitic and hence called "West Cushitic", as an independent group of the Afroasiatic family, the problem of the genetic classification of these languages is not clear. There are even some (e.g. P. Newman, 1980) who deny that Omotic languages belong to Afroasiatic at all. The existing classification of Omotic as a separate and in fact the most distant group of Afroasiatic is actually only a hypothesis elaborated by H. C. Fleming and M. L. Bender. There were also some earlier attempts at a definitive separation of at least a part of Omotic from Cushitic by H. Plazikowsky-Brauner. This hypothesis is based mainly on lexicostatistics and on a very general synopsis of some basic grammatical features but not on regular comparison and reconstruction of proto-Omotic. Of course proto-Omotic should be compared with Cushitic and eventually also with other groups of Afroasiatic. Since at least in a number of cases lexicostatistic results do not contradict the genetic classification based on internal and comparative reconstruction of both phonology and morphology, I do not agree with those linguists who totally neglect the validity of lexicostatistics for genetic classification. Nevertheless, comparative and historical linguistics cannot be limited to lexicostatics, i.e. lexicostatics can be used only as an auxiliary, and not a basic method. It is possible to say, without being accused of hypercriticism, that before we finally accept the hypothesis about Omotic as an independent group within Afroasiatic we need a lot of elementary data on many Omotic languages and their dialects which are still practically unknown. Unfortunately there was a long standstill in Omotic studies between 1952 (and practically even since the II World War) till the mid 1970s. For a rather long period we had fresh data only thanks to Professor Leslau, who provided us with the pioneer grammatical sketch and a vocabulary of Mocha. Now we need data on the little known "South Omotic" languages since their affinity to the rest of Omotic is still provisional, and even more so, we need more data on a number of totally unknown North Omotic languages, since in general North Omotic languages are more conservative or archaic than "South Omotic" and hence more important for a comparison with Cushitic etc. As I have emphasized else-

where (Zaborski, forthcoming), we have to look for the most conservative
or archaic Omotic languages in order to explain the genetic classification of
the whole group within Afroasiatic (or even outside Afroasiatic) on the basis
of relative chronology.

It seems that basic Omotic numerals (the numbers from one to ten)
provide rather clear hints at the internal classification of these languages,
though obviously the evidence of the numerals alone cannot be decisive
but should be used only in conjunction with the evidence of the more
important parts of the system like e.g. verbal morphology. This pertains
even more to the question of the relevance of the evidence of the numerals
for any claim about the relationship of Omotic with Cushitic. Since we
lack so much data on the Omotic numerals, no attempt has been made here
to reconstruct proto-Gonga, proto-Ometo etc., or proto-Omotic numerals.
The transcription of the numerals has to be unified and in the course of the
transliteration of different systems used by different authors some problems
remain unsolved. Many linguists have not an adequate explanation of their
transcription or have used contradictory methods. This is particularly true of
the older authors (e.g. quoted by Conti Rossini), but also of some
contemporary linguists who use sometimes phonemic but sometimes rather
phonetic principles. Fleming-Bender's internal classification of the Omotic
languages has been taken as a basis and it has to be said at the very
beginning that this classification is confirmed in general terms by the
evidence of the basic numerals.

Let us deal first with North Omotic. The numerals "three" and "five" are
the same everywhere except in Anfillo where "five" is loan from Ethiosemitic,
probably through Highland East Cushitic. The number "ten" is the same
everywhere, with the exceptoion of Anfillo and Kafa (here also a loanword
from Ethiosemitic), Boro (Shinasha)[1] and Chara.

The Dizi (or "Dizoid") subbranch is clearly a unit, since only in Nao is
"one" different, though it agrees with Janjero, Chara and Central Ometo
(except Oyda). The Gonga subbranch differs from other subbranches in the
numerals "one" and "two"[2], and also in the series from "six" to "ten" (with
the exception of Boro "ten") which has been borrowed from Ethiosemitic
(on Anfillo "five", see below). It has to be emphasized that Gonga and all
other Omotic languages (including South Omotic) with the exception of

---

1 Plazikowsky-Brauner 1963, 470-471, explained Boro "ten" as a contraction of *gíttĕ úṣṣa
  "two fives". Cf. note 4.
2 This is a loanword from Southern Ethiosemitic, most probably Gurage, e.g. Soddo kitt.
  Cf. Cerulli 1951, 308.

Dizoid have the same numeral "four". Since Dizoid differs from the rest also in "one", "two", "six", "seven" and "eight", there is a good reason to consider Dizoid languages as a clearly separate branch. Janjero shows several cognates with Gimira, Chara and Ometo — or "Gimojan" languages — but at the same time differs in the number "two" from all other Omotic languages though the older numeral "two" survives, as pointed out already by Cerulli (1938, p. 57) in the compounds "eight" and "seven" which are "10-2" and "5+2" respectively. "Ten" has been borrowed from Ethiosemitic and the older form that survives in "eight" and "nine" (= 10 − 1) as *giḍin/girin* and *gin* is also a loanword — cf. Oromo *kuḍān* (Cerulli, 1938, p. 58). The Gimira subbranch, including Bencho and She also looks like a unit though we know too little about Bencho numerals to be sure. It is strange, however, that Gimira "seven" differs from all Omotic languages (Toselli, 1939, p. 35) and also from She and "Dizu" Gimirra (ibid., quoted from Conti Rossini and Montadon), the latter two coinciding with Janjero, Chara and Central Ometo. The number "one" separates "Gimojan" from the rest of Omotic and is most probably a loan from Highland East Cushitic (cf. Bender [ed.], 1976, p. 261, and cf. Cerulli 1934, pp. 89-92). The number "eight" also seems rather isolated, though it may be related perhaps to Chara and has also an original *na/nam* "two" as the first component. The number "nine" (= 10-1) which is related structurally to "eight" (both contain the final *-rs* which may be a remnant of the older "ten") is totally isolated. Chara differs from all other Omotic languages in the number "nine". Here it may be, perhaps, related to North Ometo "one"[3] and also "ten"[4]. The number "eight" may be related, perhaps, to Gimira and there is only a typological ("two" substracted from "ten" principle) parallel in Janjero; cf. also Cerulli 1938, p. 155. West Omotic, including Doko and Dollo, is separated from all other North Omotic languages by its cognates with South Omotic, namely "six" and "eight" (10-2?, cf. Cerulli, 1938, p. 110) as well the phonemic shape of "ten", in which /b/ corresponds to /b/ and /p/ in Hamer and Karo respectively. Also the number "seven" has cognates in South Omotic, but we find other cognates in North Omotic Sheko, Nao and Dizi. Cerulli's hypothesis that Basketo *tabẓā* may be related to Cushitic, i.e. Somali *todoba*, Oromo *torbā* (Cerulli 1938, p. 110) has to be verified since it is more probable that this is a loan. Another isogloss connecting West Ometo both with South Omotic and Dizoid is the number

---

3 Cerulli 1938, 155, explains it as "one subtracted from ten".

4 Cerulli 1938, 155, relates it to *tam* existing in other languages and connects its final *-sā/-tsā* with the hypothetical morph *-sa* in number "eight" but Chara *tantsā/tansā* bears some resemblance to Boro *taṣṣe*. Both similarities may be accidental.

"nine" which is also probably a loan from Cushitic (cf. Somali *sagaal*, Oromo *sagal*, Arbore *ẓagal* [Cerulli 1942, p. 267]). It is found probably as a loan from the neighbouring Dizoid or other Omotic languages in Me'en of the East Sudanic family (cf. Toselli 1939, p. 37, quoting Conti Rossini). Another interesting isogloss, the number "one" connects Basketo, Dollo and Doko with Male (South Ometo) and Oyda (Central Ometo)[5]. The Central Ometo languages have the same numerals with the exception of "one" in Oyda and the number "two". For the number "two" we shall have to search in the future for phonetically possible sound correspondences (Lautgesetze) to account for the existing divergencies. The numerals from "six" to "ten" in the alleged Dokko materials collected by d'Abbadie and published by Conti Rossini differ from those collected presumably by Sacchi (Conti Rossini 1927, p. 248) but obviously coincide with the respective numerals in Central Ometo. It is impossible to say whether this is due simply to dialect differences or to faulty identification. In general, the numerals "six" to "nine" provide a good isogloss connecting the Central Ometo languages. They are connected with East Ometo Koyra numerals and also with Zayse, but the forms found in the latter (only "six" and "seven") are already abbreviated. These numerals etymologically go back to "1 + 5", "2 + 5", "3 + 5" and "4 + 5" where the final *-punā* means "five"[6]. East Ometo languages (Zayse, Zergulla, Gidicho and Koyra) are well linked by the numeral "one". Koyra coincides in all other numerals with Central Ometo, but Zayse differs in the number "nine" from all other Omotic languages[7]. Furthermore in Zayse number "eight" we have initial *la-* going back to "two" but the second morpheme, meaning most probably "ten", remains without an etymology[8]. Kachama has been classified so far as a North Omotic, and more precisely East Ometo language, but strangely only the numeral "one" has cognates in East Ometo while all the other numerals have nothing in common with Omotic. Therefore we can ask the question whether d'Abbadie's data published by Conti Rossini really pertain to Kachama.

5 Cerulli's hypothesis (1938, 109) that *fättän/pettanĕ* etc. may be related to *mat* "one" in Gimira is quite improbable.

6 Cerulli 1938, 58, says that it may be, perhaps, related to East Cushitic "five" e.g. Afar *kōn* but this cannot be accepted, since it would be difficult to find an adequate sound correspondence. Also Dolgopolskiy's (1966, 62) hypothesis connecting **punā* explained as "above five" with the Chadic verb "to be superior" e.g. Hausa *fī*, Logone *fana* is hardly probable. Also a relation with Dullay *xupin*, Tsamay *kubin* is uncertain.

7 Cerulli 1938, 196, derives *tsingo* hypothetically from *sagn* (cf. Sheko and Nao) and this hypothesis merits attention.

8 Cerulli 1938, 196, explains the final *-uč* hypothetically as going back to a "negative" verb *kay* but this can hardly be accepted. Cf. n. 10.

Let us turn now to South Omotic. The numerals "one", "three" and "five" separate South Omotic from North Omotic and at the same time prove that South Omotic may be considered an independent subbranch. The numbers "one" and "two" also provide an isogloss that confirms the division of South Omotic into Hamer-Karo-Banna and Ari-Bako groups, while the third group i.e. Dime, is related to the former by "one" but to Ari-Bako by "two". Related to North Omotic is the number "four" (except Dizoid) while numerals "six" to "ten" show a relationship to West Ometo (Basketo etc.) which coincides also in "four". The number "two" of Hamer-Karo-Banna has the most evident cognate in Male which is spoken north of this group, but most probably Male /l/ corresponds to /n/ in West and Central Ometo, Chara and Gimira. Bako differs from Hamer and Karo in the number "nine" which is etymologically "one subtracted from ten". Common South Omotic "four" is the strongest link with North Omotic.

And now a synopsis of the basic forms:

1. — *k'oy* etc.: Dizi, Sheko
   — *ikko* etc.: Gonga languages
   — *issino* etc.: Janjero, Chara, Central Ometo, Nao
   — *matti* etc.: Gimira, She, Kachama; Chara in "nine" /ʔ/
   — *pettane* etc.: West Ometo, South Ometo, Oyda
   — *bizzo* etc.: East Ometo, Kachama; and Chara in 'nine'
   — *kala* etc.: Hamer, Karo, Banna; cf. *wallaqa*; cf. Beja *gāl* (!)
   — *wallaqa* etc.: Ari, Bako, Dime
2. — *tāgn* etc.: Dizoid languages
   — *gutto/gitto*: South Gonga and Anfillo versus North Gonga (cf. Fleming, 1976b, p. 370).
   — *hep*: Janjero
   — *lamma* and (?) *nama* etc.: Gimira, Bencho She; Ometo, South Omotic.
   — *makan* etc.: South Omotic
3. — *kadu* etc.: all North Omotic languages
   — *makam* etc.: all South Omotic languages
4. — *kubm* etc.: Dizoid languages
   — *obda/audo* etc.: all other languages
5. — *uččū* etc.: all North Omotic languages except Anfillo; cf. Hozo *k'witsi*, Sezo *uwisse*, Bambeshi *wusi* (Fleming MS)
   — *amitto*: Anfillo
   — *donk* etc.: all South Omotic languages and Male
   — **puna* etc.: preserved in 6-9 in Central Ometo, Koyra, Chara

6. — *yaku* etc.: Dizoid languages
   — *sapm* etc.: Janjero (?), Gimira, She, Chara, Central and East Ometo
   — *lehe* etc.: West Ometo and South Omotic
   — *širitto* etc.: Gonga
7. — *tubsu* etc.: Dizoid languages, West Ometo, South Omotic
   — *oddu*: Gimira
   — *napm* etc.: Janjero, She, Chara, Central and East Ometo
   — *šabáttō* etc.: Kefoid languages
8. — *zyed* etc.: Dizoid languages
   — *nangiḍin/nangirin*: Janjero
   — *nandirsa*: Chara
   — *nyartu*: She, Gimira(?)
   — *lamakoy* etc.: West Ometo, Hamer, Karo; cf. Male 'seven'
   — *hospuna* etc.: Central Ometo, Koyra
   — *lakkuč*: Zayse
   — *šimittō* etc.: Kefoid languages and Anfillo
   — *qastā'ntamers* etc.: Ari, Bako
9. — *sagil* etc.: Dizoid languages, West Ometo, Hamer, Karo; cf. Male 'eight'
   — *izgin* — Janjero
   — *irste, hirs* etc.: Gimira, She
   — *bizā*: Chara
   — *uddupuna* etc.: Central Ometo, Koyra
   — *tsingō*: Zayse
   — *žēdiye* etc.: Kefoid languages
   — *wolqāntamers* etc.: Ari, Bako
10. — *temma* etc.: all Omotic languages except Gonga; cf. Hamer, Karo and Male
   — *áširō*: Kefa including Mocha; Janjero
   — *tantsā* etc.: Boro, Chara
   — **giḍin*: Janjero

Coming back to the problem of the internal genetic classification of the Omotic languages, I can say that the basic numerals confirm the "genealogical tree" presented by Fleming (Fleming 1976, p. 300) in which Janjero is related to the group consisting of Gimira, Chara, Ometo rather than the tree presented by Bender (Bender 1976, p. 4) in which Janjero, Gimira, Ometo and rather enigmatic Mao languages are presented as coordinate branches of "Gimojan" with Chara not indicated at all.

The problem of contact and so-called borrowing is rather clear as far as the Ethiosemitic languages are concerned. As indicated already by Cerulli, Plazikowsky-Brauner and Leslau, Gonga "two" and "six" to "ten" (in Anfillo also "five") are loanwords from Ethiosemitic and in particular from Gurage. The contacts with Nilo-Saharan languages are rather clear: Gonga *ikko* "one" has been hypothetically connected by Cerulli with e.g. Mekan or Me'en *kon*; cf. also Mursi *raman* "two", *kadu* "three' etc. has been connected by Conti Rossini with NS *dek* (Conti Rossini 1925, p. 3), and Fleming (1976, p. 312) has linked "common" Mao *sīze* "three" with *twasan* in Koman rejecting an East Cushitic tie and apparently not taking into consideration a possible link with Omotic *kazu*, *heza* etc. If a sound correspondence /h/ to /s/ is finally detected, Southern Koman "one" *aseni* (Bender 1971, 275) may be accidental since geographically so distant. In Surma languages "two", "three" and "five" to "ten" are borrowed either from Omotic or Cushitic (cf. Haberland 1966, 95). This contact with Nilo-Saharan, even considering that a number of Omotic numerals do not have etymologies so far, is not surprising in view of the interference between Omotic and Nilo-Saharan, e.g. in pronouns and a part of the verbal morphology. At the same time, it provides some (though not very strong) argument for the much disputed Omotic-Cushitic relationship.

Some Omotic numerals have obviously been borrowed from the neighbouring East Cushitic languages. The number "one" *matti* comes from Highland East Cushitic languages (cf. Conti Rossini, 1925, p. 633; Cerulli 1934, 89-92) though now Gimira has no geographical contact with the speakers of Highland East Cushitic languages. There is also the numeral "one" *əmmāt* in Ennemor Gurage which is most probably a loan from Cushitic (on Highland East Cushitic numerals, see Grover Hudson in Bender /ed./ 1976, p. 261; Moreno, 1938, p. 290ff.; Cerulli 1938a, p. 149). It is quite probable that the number "nine" *sagal* etc. and "ten" *tamma* are also loans from East Cushitic (cf. Dolgopolskiy, 1973, p. 52). It is possible that they

---

9 In Mursi and some other Nilo-Saharan languages "three" is *sizzi* and this is related by Bender (1976, 472) hypothetically to Highland East Cushitic *sase* for example. In any case the position of southern Mao is, at least as I can judge on the basis of the data published by Grottanelli, rather outside Omotic, i.e. it is possible that Southern Mao is not Omotic and certainly not Cushitic at all. There could also be borrowing by Nilo-Saharan from Omotic and this may explain the occurence of *rama* "two" probably connected rather with Omotic *lama/nama* and not with Cushitic in the Nilo-Saharan Surma (see Bender, 1976, 483 and 542 quoting L. Ricci).

10 Conti Rossini's (1927, 250; cf. Cerulli 1938, 196) hypothesis that *lamakay* may go back to *lama-k-ayd* "twice four" merits some attention.

passed to Nilo-Saharan (e.g. Suri, Me'en etc.; Bender 1976, p. 542; Toselli 1939, p. 37, 141 "*sagen*") from Omotic. But still the possibility that at least "nine" is of common Omotic-Cushitic heritage cannot be totally rejected especially since "nine" occurs in several subbranches of Omotic. The number "eight" *zyed* etc. is a loan from East Cushitic (cf. Arbore *ze*, Tsamay *sezze*, Konso *settē'*, Sidamo *sette*, Hadiyya *sadēnto*, Oromo *saddēt*) as well as "seven" *tabza* etc. (cf. Oromo *torba*, Arbore *tuzba*, Somali *todoba* etc.). The problem of the number "six" *leh* etc. is similar to "nine" so that the decision as to whether it is a loanword or of common heritage may be rather a matter of intuition (cf. Dolgopolskiy 1966, p. 62, id., 1973, p. 165; Sasse 1979, p. 22). However since this numeral exists only in neighbouring Basketo and South Omotic, it is most likely a loanword. The common Omotic numeral "four" *aboda/audo* etc. has been given even an Afroasiatic genealogy by Dolgopolskiy 1973, p. 231-2; the same author evidently considers also "ten" and "six" proto-Omoto-Cushitic following Cerulli, 1938, p. 153, but this is rather uncertain though not impossible. Finally there is "two" *lamma/nama* which may be rather of common Omotic-Cushitic heritage. It is interesting that while most East Cushitic languages have initial /l/ like Central Cushitic (Agaw), Dullay (Werizoid), Arbore and Dahalo, but Dasenech has /n/ i.e. *nāma* (see H.-J. Sasse in Bender, ed., 1976, 218), and so also a part of Omotic has /l/ while another part has /n/. Of course the change of /l/ to /n/ may be secondary in both Omotic and in Dasenech. It is significant, perhaps, that the South Omotic languages and East Cushitic Arbore which border on Dasenech have /l/. A similar phonemic repartition is in the number "ten" where both some Omotic and some Cushitic languages have /m/ while other Omotic and Cushitic languages have /b/ — cf. Sasse 1979, p. 25 and 10.

Thus the genetic links with Cushitic numerals (e.g. "two" and less probably "three" and "four") are possible while borrowing from Cushitic (from Highland East Cushitic, Oromo, Dullay and Arbore) is rather certain, at least in some cases as far as numerals "six" to "ten" are concerned. Of course borrowing of some numerals does not exclude the possibility that some others are of common Omotic-Cushitic heritage. It is possible that more will be clear when we have a study of the comparative phonology of Omotic and Cushitic loanwords and when we have more data on Omotic in general. Internal Omotic borrowing between South Omotic and North Omotic is also possible in the case of the numerals "six" to "ten".

As far as the typology of the numeral system is concerned, South Omotic Hamer, Karo, Ari, Bako and North Omotic Chara, Zayse and West Ometo (but without d'Abbadie's Doko) as well as Janjero have "eight" going back to "two subtracted from ten", but only Ari, Bako, Chara and Janjero have "nine" going back hypothetically to "one subtracted from ten". On the other hand Koyra, Central Ometo and d'Abbadie's Doko have a system based on "five" i.e. "six" going back to "one plus five", "seven" going back to "two plus five", and so on up to "nine". Zayse, Janjero and She have an intermediate position with "nine" and "eight" according to the former system and "six" and "seven" according to the latter system. Male "seven" to "nine" have to be verified. Other languages i.e. Dizoid apparently do not follow any system, the relation of "six" with "one" and "five" being quite uncertain. Actually it is possible that in Dizoid all numerals from "seven" to "ten" are loans from Cushitic and Dolgopolskiy connects even Dizoid "six" *yaku* etc. (see above) genetically with Cushitic, though this is not clear. All this points out to is that, as expected, the numerals "one" to "five" in Omotic are older.

In closing this note I should like to say that numerals are quite important for the internal classification of the Omotic languages while they contribute less to the elucidation of the problem of the external genetic relationship of Omotic, though in light of them a genetic link with Cushitic is much stronger than a suspected link with Nilo-Saharan. Conti Rossini's Kachama (Haruro) and Grottanelli's Northern Mao are quite divergent.

NORTH OMOTIC

	Dizoid			*Gonga*				
	Dizi Allan 1976, 381; Toselli 1938, 13	Sheko Conti Rossini 1925; Bender 1971, 262	Nao Conti Rossini 1925; Bender 1971, 262	Anfillo Grottanelli 1940, 103; Bender 1971, 258	Kefa Cerulli 1951, 307; Bender 1971, 259	Mocha Leslau 1959; Bender 1971, 260	Shinasha Schuver (in Grottanelli 1940, 103; 1941, 266	Boro Brauner 1950, 70; Bender 1971, 259
1	kᵉ'öy; qoy	keoy; kʷoy	isin; isn; išn¹	ikeko	ikēō; ikeko	ikeko; ikeko	yega, ikeka	ieke, ikka
2	tȧgn; tag	t'agen; tȧgn	tagen; tagn	guto; guto	guttō; gūto	guto; gūto	gieta, gita	gitte; gittã
3	kȧdu; kȧdu; kaddu²	kaddu; kȧdu; kȧdem³	kaddn; kȧdu, kaddō	keg̃go; kēᵈjo |?|	kemō; kēᵼmo; kag̃ā⁴	kaig̃go, keg̃o	keza, keg̃a	kēze; kēᶎᶎa
4	kaibᵐ; kum	kaubᵐ	kaibm	auddo	áuddō	awuddo	anda, awźa	áuddē
5	učú; uču; ućŧō⁵	uču, učem	ućum; uču	amitto	ućō	ućo; ūg̃ā	ułsa, uła	wáṣṣē, úṣṣē
6	yȧku; yaku	yaku	yakeo	širto	širittō	širitto	šírta, šírta	širittē
7	tĥsú, tusu	tubsu	tessen, tešen	šabattó	šabattó	šabo	sawaíte, šawata	šawaíē
8	zyél; zyed	zyed	zyad	šimittó	šimittō	šimitto	šimíta, šimata	šimittē
9	sȧgúl; sȧgani, sageni	sagen	sagn	yiringo	yútiyō	yútiyo	źedia, g̃ādiyā⁶	źēdiyē
10	tȧmú; tamu	tam	tamu	ašíró	ášíró	ašíro	teša, tała	tasšē

¹ Cerulli 1938, 57.   ² Cerulli 1951, 309.   ³ Cerulli 1951, 309.   ⁴ Reinisch 1888.   ⁵ Cerulli 1951, 309.   ⁶ After d'Abbadie.

West Ometo

	Janjero Cerulli 1938, 57	Gimira Toselli 1939, 35	She Conti Rossini 1925	Bencho Bender 1971, 260	Chara Cerulli 1938, 151	Basketo Cerulli 1938, 108	Doko Conti Rossini 1927, 248	Doko d'Abbadie /Conti Rossini 1927, 248/	Dollo Conti Rossini 1927, 250
1	issō; isson[1]	matti	mat	māt[1]	issā	fáttän	pettanē	póṭṭo	pēttān
2	hep	nam	nam	nam	nantā	nam'a	nammē	lāmmā	nām
3	kēẓ	kaẓu	kaẓ	kəẓ	keẓā	hayẓẓā; bay/d/ẓī[2]	oyẓē	bāyẓā	aẓ
4	ačči	ottu	od		obdā	oydda	oydē	oydā	oyd
5	ūč	učču, učču	uč, uč		učča	išin	issinē	ečinā	eššen
6	issun	sap	sapm		sāfun, sapma	lebe	lebē	eẓepenā	leb
7	nāfun	oddu	nap		lāpun, lāfun	tabẓā	tabsā	lāpunā	tabeẓā
8	nangerin nangidim	nars	nyartu		nandirsa, landersa	lamakay	lamabē	bospunā	lāmākāy
9	iẓgin	birs	irste, irssen		biẓā[3]	sagāl	sabakalē	undapunā	sākeal
10	assir	tama	tam, tām		tantsā, tansā	taba	tabbā	tammā	tā'ba

[1] Bender, 1971, 258, Fleming, MS, isar.   [2] Bender 1971, 254.   [3] Fleming, MS, biẓa.

Central Ometo

	Male Bender 1971, 255; Da Trento 1941, 206	Oyda Bender 1971, 254	Welamo Moreno 1938, 37; Bender 1971, 252	Welamo Chiomio 1938, 4; Da Trento 1941, 206	Gofa Moreno 1938, 37	Zala Moreno 1938, 37	Malo Moreno 1938, 38	Kullo Allan 1976, 330; Bender 1976, 252	Konta Moreno 1938, 38
1	pete	pēto	issō, istā, issinō, esinō	ista; essua	issi, issino	istā	istá	ita, itu; itta	
2	lem'o; lam'o	nām'i	na'ā; na'a	na'a; nabū	náma	na'ā	lámma	naa, laa [na'a, la'a?]; la'a	na'a
3	baytso	hāydzi, oyddi	beẓā; bēẓa	esa, eẓa, beẓa	bedẓa	beẓā	beẓa	beẓa; bēẓa	
4	oydo		oidda	oidda, oyda	óyda	oidda	oyda	oyda	
5	dongo		ittasa	ittasa	ittata	iteša	ittetta	ites	ittēte
6	labo		usappunā, usaffunā	sappuna, saffuna, usuf	usáppuna	usaffunā	usúppuna	osap^b una	
7	lankay[1] (?)		láppunā	láppuna, láffuna	láppuma	láffunā	láppuna	lap^b una	
8	salli[1] (?)		hospunā, hofunā	hospuna, ospuna	hóspuna	hospunā	ospuna	hosp^b una	
9	tazuba[1] (?)		uddufunā, uddupunā	uddufuna, urtúfuna	uddúfuna	uddufun	uddúfunia	uDap^b una	
10	tapo		tammā	tamma	támma	tammā	támma	tamma	

[1] Da Trento, 1941, 206. This must be verified since in the neighbouring Hamer and Karo this is "eight" respectively. Also Male "nine" is suspected (cf. East Cushitic "seven").

East Ometo

	Dache Bender 1971, 253	Dorze Bender 1971, 253; Fleming MS	Zayse Cerulli 1938, 194	Zergulla Bender 1971, 257	Gidicho Bender 1971, 256	Koyra Hayward, MS Bender 1971, 256	Mezo Chiomio 1938, 255	Kachama Conti Rossini 1936, 631
1	isiɣno	isino; ista	biʐʐō	biʐo	bīʐe	biʐʐo; bidʐo	biʐo	biʐʐo
2	nəmə	nam'a	nām	namᵃ	namᵃ	lām'a; lamᵗ	lambe	fololo
3	hedʐa	hēdʐa; beiʐa	hayts	hayts	hāydʐi	haydʐe	haydʐi	mīrʐo
4		oyt; oyDa				ōyde; oittā[1]	woydi	sagānē
5			isit			ittitte, isit	itit	aysuma
6			iʐup			iʐʐuppe	iʐup	qēb'ē
7			lap			lappe	lap	walā
8			lakkut			haʐʐuppe	aʐup	hārnuʐā
9			tsingō			oddippe	oddip	māydonārā
10			tām			tamme	tamm	gaʿo, gongulā

[1] Cerulli 1938, 109.   [2] Cerulli 1951, 309.

SOUTH OMOTIC

	Hamer Cerulli 1942, 262	Karo Conti Rossini 1927, 252	Banna Bender 1971, 264	Ari Bender 1971, 263; Bliese, 1982;	Bako Da Trento 1941, 206	Dime Bender 1971, 263; Fleming MS
1	kalo	kailà, kala	kɔʔla	wɔlleka	wollaqá, ullaq, ellagá	wokɛl, ʃkɛl
2	lama	lammà, lama	lamma	kasten	k'astèn	k'àsten
3	makan	makàmm	mɔkəm	māken	makken	mekɛm
4	oydi	oydi	oydi	oyddi	oydi	uddu
5	don [1]	dònn [1]		donq	donk	ʃinne
6	lab	lhā, lab	lab	lā	la	
7	tobba	tsōbà		tabʐa	tabʐɛ	
8	lankày	lonkày		qastāntamers	kastatameʐ	
9	sal	sall		wolqántamers	alkeatameʐ	
10	teppi	tabi		tamma	tommà	

[1] Fleming, MS, donkʼ.

References

Allan E. J., 1976a, Kullo, in: Bender (ed.), 1976, 324-350.

——, 1976b, Dizi, ibid., 324-350.

Bender M. L., 1971, "The Languages of Ethiopia", *Anthropological Linguistics* 13, fasc. 5, 165-203.

——, 1975, *Omotic: a New Afroasiatic Language Family*, Carbondale, University Museum Studies 3.

——, (ed.), 1976, *The Non-Semitic Languages of Ethiopia*, Carbondale.

Brockelmann C., 1950, "Zur Grammatik der Kafa-Sprache", in: *Abessinische Studien*, Berichte über die Verhandlungen der Sächsischen Akademie der Wissenschaften in Leipzig, Phil.-hist. Klasse 97, Heft 4, 40-60.

Bliese L., 1982, personal letter.

Cerulli E., 1929, "Note su alcune popolazioni Sidama dell'Abissinia Meridionale II: I Sidama dell'Omo", *RSO* 12, 1-69.

——, 1934, "I numerali uno e due nel cuscitico", *Orientalia* 3, 88-97.

——, 1938a, *La lingua e la storia dei Sidamo*, Roma.

——, 1938b, *Il linguaggio dei Giangerò ed alcune lingue sidama dell'Omo*, Roma.

——, 1942, "Il linguaggio degli Amar Cocche e quello degli Arbore", *RSE* 2, 260-272.

——, 1951, *La lingua caffina*, Roma.

Chiomio Gm., 1938, *Brevi appunti di lingua wollamo*, Torino.

——, 1939, *Notizie sulla tribù Ghimirra dei Magi*, Torino.

Conti Rossini C., 1925, "Sui linguaggi dei Naa e dei Ghimirra Sce nell'Ethiopia meridionale", *RRAL*, Classe di sc. mor., Ser. VI, vol. 1, fasc. 7-8.

——, 1927, "Sui linguaggi parlati a nord dei laghi Rodolfo e Stefania", in: *Festschrift Meinhof*, Hamburg, 247-255.

——, 1936, "Contributi alla conoscenza della lingua Haruro", *RRAL*, Classe di sc. mor., Ser. VI, vol. 12, 621-671.

Dolgopolskiy A.B., 1966, "Materiali po sravnitelno-istoricheskoy fonetike kushitskikh yazykov: gubnye i dentalnye smychnye v nachalnom polozhenii", in: *Yazyki Afriki — voprosy struktury, istorii i tipologii*, Moskva, 35-88.

——, 1973, *Sravnitelno-istoricheskaya fonetika kushitskikh yazykov*, Moskva.

Fleming H. C., 1976a, "Omotic Overview", in: Bender, (ed.), 1976, 299-323.

——, 1976b, "Kefa (Gonga) Languages", ibid., 351-376.

——, MS word list.

Grottanelli V. L., 1940, *I Mao*, Roma.

——, 1941, "Gli Scinascia del Nilo Azzurro ed alcuni lessici poco noti della loro lingua", *RSE* 1, 234-270.

Haberland E., 1966, "Zur Sprache der Bodi, Mursi und Yidenič", in: ed. J. Lukas, *Neue Afrikanistische Studien*, Hamburg, 87-99.

Hayward R., MS, Notes on the Koyra Language.

Hetzron R., 1977, *The Gunnän-Gurage Languages*, Napoli.

Hohenberger J., 1975, *The Nominal and Verbal Afformatives of Nilo-Hamitic and Hamito-Semitic*, Wiesbaden.

Leslau W., 1959, *A Dictionary of Moča*, Berkeley.

Lydall J., "Hamer", in: Bender (ed.), 1976, 393-438.

Moreno M. M., 1938, *Introduzione alla lingua Ometo*, Milano.

——, 1940, *Manuale di Sidamo*, Milano.

Newman P., 1980, *The Classification of Chadic within Afroasiatic*, Leiden.

Plazikowsky-Brauner H., 1950, "Schizzo morfologico dello šinaša", *RSE* 9, 65-83.

——, 1963, "Zahlen und Zahlsysteme in den sogenannten Kuschitischen Sprachen", *MIO* 8, 466-483.

Praetorius F., 1870, "Die Zählmethode in der äthiopischen Gruppe der hamitischen Sprachen", *ZDMG* 24, 415-424.

Reinisch L., 1888, *Die Kafa-Sprache in Nordost-Afrika*, SBWAW, Phil.-hist. Klasse, 116.

——, 1890, *Das Zahlwort vier und neun in den chamito-semitischen Sprachen*, SBWAW, Phil.-hist. Klasse 121, Abh. 2, 1-40.

Sasse H.-J., 1979, "The Consonant Phonemes of Proto-East-Cushitic", *Afroasiatic Linguistics* 7, issue 1, 1-67.

Toselli G., 1939, *Elementi di lingua magi*, Torino.

Trento Da G., 1941, "Vocaboli in lingue dell'Etiopia meridionale", *RSE* 1, 203-207.

Zaborski A., forthcoming, "Can Omotic Be Reclassified as West Cushitic?", *Proceedings of the Sixth International Conference of Ethiopian Studies*.

ALPHABET

AMHARIC SCRIPT REFORM EFFORTS

ABRAHAM DEMOZ
Northwestern University

Amharic uses a script inherited from Geʻez. The Geʻez script itself was most probably derived from the cursive version of the South Semitic alphabet (Grohmann, 1918; Ryckmans, 1955; Drewes, 1955) though this theory is disputed by some (Ullendorff, 1955). Sometime in the second half of the fourth century the Geʻez script underwent an important and lasting reform. This was the introduction of special signs for vocalization of the consonantal script. The authorship and circumstances of this significant reform still remain shrouded in mystery. A fair case has however been made for a possible influence of the Indian Kharoṣṭī system of vocalization (J. Friedrich, 1935; Gelb, 1952). Since the early reform falls within the domain of Geʻez we will say no more about it here. Suffice it so say that the script which Amharic and some other Ethiopian languages, notably Tigrigna [1], inherited from Geʻez was already fully vocalized. It had however some important shortcomings for the rendering of Amharic. The periodical efforts, some successful and some not, to weed out these inadequacies, sometimes carried to the point of needless perfectionism, constitute the history of Amharic script reform.

Historical Survey of Reform Efforts

The earliest script reform during the Amharic period dates back to the fourteenth or possibly fifteenth century—that is to say, a century or two after the ascendancy of Amharic as a court language in the reign of Emperor Yekunno Amlak (1270-1285), the first ruler of the "restored Solomonic dynasty". We know little or nothing of the precise authorship of this reform but there can be no doubt that it came from the clergy who were then as for many centuries afterwards the sole custodians of the written word. The reform consisted of the invention of new symbols chiefly for the palatal

---

1 In Romanizing Ethiopian words and names in this article I have been guided by common usage and practicality where the precise form of the word is not germane to the issue at hand. Otherwise I have used Professor Leslau's system which should be familiar to readers of this volume.

sounds of Amharic which were not provided for in the Ge'ez script. Ge'ez itself did not have these sounds. The new symbols were devised in principle by the addition of small horizontal lines to the top of the symbols for the corresponding non-palatal sound. We shall have more to say about this below.

The next reform effort comes several centuries later during the reign of Emperor Menelik II (1889-1913). This was the new alphabet ascribed to personal invention by Emperor Menelik. The Amharic original of the Emperor's chronicle (Gebre-Sellasié, 1967) includes a table of the new alphabet (which, incidentally, the two copies of the French translation I have seen do not) but has no information whatsoever on why the Emperor decided to reform the script, what principles he followed in doing so, whether he had help from any *literati*, or even whether he took any steps to have the new script implemented. Maurice de Coppet in his annotation to the French translation of the Menelik Chronicle, which was published nearly three decades before the Amharic original (Guebre-Sellasié, 1930-32), writes "on nous a du reste affirmé que ce chiffre avait été établi, non par Ménélik, mais par Mèchècha Worqié ...". This same Meshesha Worke is referred to by Emperor Yohannes IV, in a manuscript brought to my attention by Dr. Getatchew Haile (1981), as one "who, after having studied all the languages of the world, is now diligent in learning the language of Satan". It would seem likely then that Meshesha Worke devised the new script and that Emperor Menelik lent his name to the effort perhaps because he saw some need for reform. The fact that the Emperor did not push on with the implementation of the script could conceivably have been due to opposition from the clergy, many of whom, as we shall see below, even now regard the Ethiopian script as a special gift from God not to be tampered with by mere mortals, at least not by the laiety.

Following the Menelik effort there was some sporadic discussion of the question of script reform in the early Amharic newspapers such as A'emero and Berhanenna Selam, concerned chiefly with the possible elimination of the "superfluous" letters (letters inherited from Ge'ez but having no distinctive sounds in Amharic) and with the adoption of a special sign for gemination. An Ethiopian scholar of the time, Abba Tekle-Maryam Semharay, who was conversant with both traditional and Western learning, has actually utilized symbols for accent, gemination and the sixth order vowel in his publication (Tekle-Maryam, 1911). His example, as indeed a similar example by Addis Alemayehu many decades later (see below) was never taken up by others.

A strong impetus for script reform came with the introduction of the typewriter into Ethiopia in the early nineteen twenties. The Ethiopian script had proved unsuitable for use in a typewriter because of the excessive number of symbols. A number of attempts were made to adapt it to that purpose (Anonymous, 1970). In 1924 (Eth. Calendar 1916), Ato Alemu Habtemichael prepared an Amharic typewriter and presented it to Emperor Haile Sellasie (then crown prince). In 1931 (E.C. 1923) Ato Ayyana Birru prepared a prototype Amharic typewriter. The same year Dr. Aleme Work had one made in England. The well-known scholar Aleka Kidane-wold Kifle published a system for the adaptation of the Amharic script to the typewriter. One of the reform proposals of the pre-war period, that of Ato Abbebe Retta, concerned itself more with simplifying the script for new learners than with adapting it to the typewriter. Except for the work of the last two scholars mentioned, which we shall discuss below, we do not have sufficient information of the efforts of these early script reformers to be able to describe their proposals in any detail or to discuss them at any length.

The first truly articulate effort on the reform of the Amharic script appeared in 1948 with the publication of *Fidälən maššašal* ("Improving the Script") by a group that called itself *yätəmhərt wädagočč* ("Lovers of Learning"). The group consisted of Ras Immeru Haile Sellasie, Ato Abbebe Retta and Blatta Merse'e Hazen Wolde Kirkos. The American educator Dr. Frank Laubach who happened to be on a visit to Ethiopia at the time also contributed a few suggestions to the publication. At a later time Professor Wolf Leslau made an extensive commentary on the proposals and added some suggestions of his own in a review article (Leslau, 1953). The reform proposals of the "Lovers of Learning" which, by and large, sought to eliminate superfluous symbols and to regularize the system of vocalization will be discussed in some detail below. None of them ever came close to implementation chiefly because of lack of any enthusiasm for reform on the part of the general public at the time. There was also some active opposition to reform on the part of the clergy.

Thirteen years after the publication of *Fidälən maššašal*, in March of 1961, a new committee was established by order of the Imperial Ministry of Pen which included two of the original "Lovers of Learning" and four other members. The immediate impetus for the establishment of this study committee was the submission of yet another reform proposal by a civil servant named Zewde Gebremedhin. In actual fact the discussions of the group as reflected in their published minutes (Anonymous, 1970) ranged beyond the mere evaluation of Zewde's proposals. The group finally agreed on a system that had an entirely regular system of vocalization and that rejected some of the superfluous letters (see below). The work of this committee too was destined to remain a more or less academic exercise.

Following the dissolution of the Ministry of Pen Committee no new committee was established to deal with the matter of script reform. A number of individuals however contributed proposals and studies dealing with aspects of the problem of script. These include Zeev Raz, a UNESCO expert at the Ministry of Education, who proposed a cursive script for use in speedy handwriting (Raz, undated), and Tekle-maryam Fantaye and Lulsegged Alemayyehu, who concerned themselves with the ever-present question of regularizing the system of vocalization. Yiggezu Bisrat, a professional calligrapher who has done much work on ornamental lettering, has also dealt with the question of script reform. Terrefe Raswork, an engineer in what was then the Imperial Board of Telecommunications of Ethiopia has adapted the Amharic script to the telex machine (Terrefe 1966). Ato Addis Alemayyehu, a high government official and a writer, actually implemented some of his own reform proposals in his well-known novel *Fəqər 'əskä mäqabər* ("Love unto the Grave", Alemayyehu, 1966). Roger Cowley has pointed out inconsistencies in Amharic and has pleaded for orthographic standardization (Cowley, 1967). Many of the established scholars on Ethiopian languages have at one time or another had their say on the question of Amharic script reform. In addition to specific references elsewhere in this article we might mention the individually solicited statements from a number of scholars (among them Leslau, Ullendorff, Gankin and Kassa Gabrehiwot) that are now in the files of the Amharic Language Academy in Addis Ababa. One minor reform gradually took root late in the post-war period without any public discussion. This was the elimination of the two dots (:) formerly used to separate words. It appears that with the spread of printing and typing the standardized and automatic spacing between words made the two dots superfluous.

Description and analysis of reform efforts

The only truly successful and significant reforms of the Ethiopic script so far have been two. The first was the introduction of a system of vocalization and the second the introduction of special symbols for the Amharic palatals[2].

---

2 The symbol for *hä* with all it vocalic variants (i.e. **ሽ**, **ሹ** etc.) and the one for *'ä* (the isolated **አ**) are of course not palatals but are usually grouped with the palatal symbols in discussions of script reform because of the time of their appearance. The set is sometime known as the *arabi* ("Arabic") letters (Leslau, 1961; Ullendorf, 1951). Other less significant but certainly successful reforms have been the addition of the letter **ፐ** *p* and **ጰ** *p* early in the Geʿez period (perhaps to accommodate Greek or Hellenized words and names).

The first took place during the Geʿez period and therefore does not fall in our purview. The second we consider hereunder.

Geʿez has no palatal sounds (see however, Leslau, 1961). As long as Geʿez was the literary language of Ethiopia no symbols were required to represent such sounds. With the emergence of Amharic as the court language in the thirteenth century a need presumably developed to render Amharic titles and names in the royal chronicles and local hagiographies which continued to be written in Geʿez. It was during this period that the new signs for the Amharic palatals made their first appearance. The earliest occurrence of a palatal sign so far attested seems to be in a manuscript dated 1434-1468. (Getatchew Haile, 1979)[3]. The occurrence in question is in the personal name *šiḫ mängäsa*. It is interesting to compare this name with a similar one in an earlier manuscript, EMML no. 1832, which contains the name *"siḫ debaba"* (i.e. ሲሕ ፡ ደባባ). Could we deduce from this that the palatal signs were still not invented as late as 1280, the date of the manuscript in question? The evidence is not compelling but it is not unreasonable to hypothesize on the basis of the evidence from the two manuscripts cited that the invention of the palatal signs of Amharic may have taken place roughly between 1300 and 1450. The earliest examples of Amharic known to us are the popular songs in praise of Emperor Amda Sion (1314-1344) (Guidi 1889). Though no extant copy of the songs is definitely datable to the Emperor's reign it is known that his reign was one of great literary activity. We may therefore hazard the further tentative guess that the Amharic palatal letters may have originated in the reign of Amda Sion.

The palatal signs, traditionally referred to as the *arabi* letters, a word of uncertain etymology (Leslau, 1961), are made rather uniformly by the addition of a small horizontal line to the top of the symbol for the corresponding non-palatal sound. For a possible precursor of the horizontal line see Ullendorff, 1955. Aside from minor concessions to the shape of the basic letters, the only exception to this general rule is the formation of the symbol for the glottalized palatal stop *č̣*, which calls for the addition of small rings to the legs of the basic symbol (see table I).

The complete success of this early reform is not surprising; for without it the writing of Amharic would have been highly unsatisfactory, if not well nigh impossible. It is also worth noting that this reform required the addition of new symbols rather than the elimination or modification of existing ones

---

3 I am grateful to Dr. Getatchew for bringing this occurrence to my attention. He also informs me that E. Ullendorff has noted this occurrence in his review of Getatchew's catalogue.

De Literis.

Literæ Habeſſinorum in Amharica lingua eædem ſunt ac in Æthiopica, eodemque modo per *ſeptem ordines* ſecundum vocalium ſonos variantur; niſi quod viginti ſex characteribus *ſeptem* alios addant, figura & poteſtate Æthiopicis affines, quos in hac tabella cognoſcere poteris.

Tabula literarum Amharicarum.

ă	u	i	ā	ē	ĕ	ō
Sha	Shu	Shi	Shā	Shē	Shĕ	Shō
Tja	Tju	Tji	Tjā	Tjē	Tjĕ	Tjo
Nja	Nju	Nji	Njā	Njē	Njĕ	Njo
Cha	Chu	Chi	Chā	Chē	Chĕ	Cho
Ja	Ja	Ji	Jā	Jē	Jĕ	Jo
Dja	Dju	Dji	Ijā	Djē	Djĕ	Djo.
Tsha	Tshu	Tshi	Tshā	Tshē	Tshĕ	Tsho

Table I
Amharic additions to the syllabary in an early form (*top*, Ludolf, 1698) and in a modern form (*bottom*, Habte-Maryam, 1970).

as did nearly all subsequent reform efforts. This may, in part at least, account for the failure of the latter. Other successful cases of "addition" (rather than "modification" or "elimination" of letters) have been the introduction of a series for "consonant plus -*wa*" (e.g. ቧ ቷ ጧ. etc.) and the letters ኸ *ä*, ኽ *hä* with its vowel variants, and ኻ (Ital. *gl*) and ኗ *vä* to accommodate European words (Ludolfo, H. 1698).

With the additional symbols for palatals the Ethiopic syllabary had become quite an adequate medium for the writing of Amharic. The reforms that followed were therefore merely concerned with some further refinements. They aimed at making the script:

a) *simpler to learn* — by regularizing the vocalization system, rejecting "superfluous" symbols and marking gemination;

b) *simpler to write* — by making it more of a cursive script; and

c) *simpler to mechanize* — by reducing the number of independent symbols to fit the standard keyboard of a typewriter or a telex machine.

We might examine the earliest of the modern reform efforts, namely the one attributed to Emperor Menelik, in light of the aims cited above. In the absence of any recorded discussion or commentary on the Menelik syllabary we have to rely mainly on internal evidence from the proposed syllabary to learn what the aim of the author might have been in designing it (see table II). The author has sought to make the syllabary easier to learn by making the vocalization affixes completely uniform and by reducing the number of basic symbols. He achieved this reduction in a number of ways. Firstly he eliminated the "superfluous" symbols inherited from Ge'ez (ሐነሠዐ) and the symbols for labialized consonants (ኰጐቈቈ) which he apparently believed, and not without reason, not to be strictly necessary for the writing of Amharic. Secondly, he derived the palatal symbols from their non-palatal counterparts by the mere addition of a diacritic (in this case an apostrophe at the top left of the base letter). He thus reduced the number of basic symbols from thirty-five to twenty—a reduction of over forty percent. The author also sought to make the letters easier and faster to write by making them truly cursive. Each of the letters can be written with one stroke without lifting the pen and generally without retracing any part of the letter. Not surprisingly, the similarity in shape between the Menelik script and the script proposed more than three quarters of a century later by Zeev Raz (which script is avowedly cursive) is a striking one.

There is no record that Menelik ever attempted to have this ingenious new script implemented on any scale. Had he done so the chances of success would probably have been slim not only for the sociological reasons mentioned earlier (opposition from the conservative and then much more powerful clergy) but also for some important structural shortcomings of the script itself. One of such shortcomings is the serious lack of distinctiveness between several pairs of symbols. Note particularly the great similarity between the symbols for * መ* and *ሠ* (nos. 3 and 4 on table), for *ተ* and *ደ* (nos. 8 and 15) and for *ገ* and *ፈ* (nos. 16 and 19). The minor and sometimes hardly perceptible differences between symbols are bound to disappear in freehand writing leading to serious ambiguity. Another important short-coming is that the symbols proposed are in many cases so unnecessarily divergent in shape from the existing symbols (e.g. nos. 10, 11 and 17 through 20) that the totality looks more like a newly invented script than the reform of an existing one. Not only does this detract from the visual and psycho-logical acceptability of the proposal but it also forgoes the important advantage of the transfer of previously acquired skills and knowledge for the already literate sector of the population. Menelik's proposal was never-theless an important step in the history of reform efforts in that it reflects an awareness of many of the problems that latter would-be reformers have tackled. It attempted the regularization of the system of vocalization; it proposed the elimination of the superfluous letters and attempted to make the symbols cursive. Although it tampered more than was necessary with the shape of the letter and perhaps overdid itself in relegating the all-too-important palatals to a minor diacritic, it did on the whole deal with the problem of reform in a manner that is rational in principle.

Among the group of reformers whose primary aim was to adapt the Amharic script to the typewriter, the only one on whose proposals we have some information is Aleka Kidane-Wold Kifle (Kidane-Wold 1956). His proposal was to retain all the basic symbols (the first orders) of the Ethiopic script including the symbols for the palatals and the labiovelars and the superfluous symbols. Vocalization would then be effected by using the six variants of *አ* and by *ዋ*. He would also retain the numerals "one" *፩* to "nine" *፱*, eliminating the top and bottom bars and using the symbol for ten as a cipher thus adapting the numerals to the so-called "arabic" system. This would result in thirty-seven consonant symbols, seven vowel symbols and ten numerals. With the addition of sixteen partly Ethiopian and partly Western punctuation marks the total comes to seventy symbols—about the number that can be accomodated on the double-shift keyboard of a standard typewriter. Although this may appear to be a satisfactory solution on the surface it is beset by a number of difficulties. The first-order symbol for instance is given in this system two distinct values which are not always disambiguated by context. Thus *በ* would stand for both *bä* and *b*. To remedy

፶፪   ዳንጋዊ ፡ ምኅለክ ።

ከዚያም ፡ አንኮበር ፡ ወርደው ፡ ክረምቱን ፡ ከተማዎን ፡ ሲያድሱ ፡
ከረሙ ። በዚያም ፡ ጊዜ ፡ ክልቡናዎ ፡ አንቅተው ፡ እንግዳ ፡ ፊደል ፡
ጻፉ ። ፊደሉም ፡ ይህ ፡ ነው * ።

1.	h									
2.	l									
3.	m									
4.	s								ሸ :	
5.	r									
6.	q									
7.	b									
8.	t								ቸ :	
9.	n								ኘ :	
10.	ʾ									
11.	k									
12.	w									
13.	z								ዠ :	
14.	y									
15.	d								ጀ :	
16.	g									
17.	ṭ								ጨ :	
18.	ṣ									
19.	f									
20.	p									

* ይህ ፡ ፊደል ፡ የተቀዳው ፡ መጼ ፡ ደኮቴ ፡ ከዋናው ፡ የታሪክ ፡ መጽሐፍ ፡ ላይ ፡ አገ
ኝተው ፡ በፈረንሳዊኛ ፡ ከፉት ፡ መጽሐፍ ፡ ላይ ፡ ነው ።

Table II: The Menelik Syllabary

this the author had to add a special symbol (¨) to mark any vowel sign that is meant to be read independently rather than with the preceding first order symbol which would now be read with its proper *ä* vowel. For example ለኢጠእ would be *liṭ* but ለእየአበእ would be *läiyyob*; ሀኤደዋለእ would be *hedwal* while ሀኤደፇለእ would be *hedäwal*. A corollary of this rule is that the sixth order vowel (እ) represents not only the high central vowel but also the absence of any vowel—leading to the anomalous and confusing situation of sometimes adding a vowel symbol to mark the *absence* of a vowel. This system retains all the symbols that are superfluous to Amharic. No justification is given for this unless it is to be understood that the proposed typewriter is meant to serve for the writing of Ge'ez as well as Amharic. If so, it can only be countered that this is an unnecessary burden as the typewriting needs for Ge'ez are now few and getting fewer all the time. Furthermore Kidane-Wold's system shares the problems of all systems that propose separate vowel signs rather than affixes for vocalization. They nearly double the amount of space required for any piece of writing. Besides, because of the radical change from a syllabic to an alphabetic system they reduce the entire literate population to a merely quasi-literate status—at least for a short period. On the whole, it is not a matter of regret that the Kidane Wold system did not gain acceptance.

The next major effort at reforming the Ethiopian alphabet was that of the "Lovers of Learning" (henceforth LL). The LL group was made up of individuals who had previously concerned themselves in one way or another with the question of script reform. The group was assembled at the initiative of Abbebe Retta in 1946 (Eth. Cal. 1938) with the purpose of discussing each other's ideas and perhaps arriving at some common ground. Though this purpose was never realized, a tentative agreement was reached by the group that the idea of using Latin characters in an auxiliary capacity to the unreformed Ethiopian script should be seriously considered for implementation (Lovers of Learning, 1948). Nevertheless, all the recommendations discussed by the group were published for further public discussion. These recommendations are briefly discussed below as LL-I through LL-V.

LL-I is a recommendation of Ras Imru Haile Sellasie as submitted to the study group through Ato Abbebe Retta. The features of LL-I are as follows:

1) Thirty-one of the first order symbols of the syllabary are to be retained.
2 The superfluous letters (ሐነሠዐፀ) are to be dropped.
3) The first order symbols are to signify both consonant with vowel *ä* and consonant without any vowel.
4) The second through the seventh orders of letter አ are to serve as discreet vowel symbols for the six remaining vowel phonemes of Amharic.

LL-II is a recommendation of Abbebe Retta himself and has the following features:

1) Only twenty-one of the first order symbols are to be retained.
2) The "superfluous" symbols, the palatal symbols and the labialized consonant symbols are to be dropped.
3) The palatals are to be indicated by the addition of a diacritic to the symbols of the non-palatal sounds [4]. The labialized consonants are to be indicated by the addition of **ወ** to the appropriate non-labialized letter.
4) The first symbols are to represent vowelless consonants with the high central vowel.
5) Six out of the seven orders of **አ** (the sixth **አ** being dropped) are to serve as the discreet vowel symbols of the system; the first order **አ** is to stand for the mid-central vowel *ä* and not for the low central vowel *a* as in the traditional system.
6 Gemination is to be indicated by doubling of the consonant symbol.

LL-III is an alternative recommendation submitted by Abbebe Retta and shares the same features as LL-II except for the following important differences:

1) The first order symbols retain the value they have in the traditional system. That is, they represent consonant with vowel *ä*.
2) The other six vowels are indicated by diacritic affixes uniformly applied to all the basic symbols as follows:

ሀ   ሁ   ሂ   ሃ   ሄ   ህ   ሆ

LL-IV, submitted by Blatta Merse'e Hazen Wolde Kirkos, recommends the retention of the unaltered Ethiopic alphabet for general purposes and the adoption of the Latin script for certain "modern" uses. Sounds peculiar to Amharic would generally be indicated as follows in the Latin script.

1) Glottalized consonants by a superscript "v"; e.g. *ṭ* for **ጠ**
2) Palatals by a circumflex; e.g. *ŝ* for **ሽ**
3) Labiovelars by the insertion of "u"; e.g. gue for **ጐ**
4) Gemination by doubling of the consonant symbol.
5) The seven vowel phonemes according to the following example: **በ** (be), **ቡ** (bu), **ቢ** (bi), **ባ** (ba), **ቤ** (bé), **ብ** (b or bê) and **ቦ** (bo).

---

4 Possibily due to some typographical difficulties the nature of the diacritic is not indicated in the publication. It is obvious however from the chart given that some diacritic was intended.

LL-V, submitted by Dr. Laubach, is the same as LL-III, the second recommendation of Abbebe Retta except that it retains all the thirty-six first order symbols and uses slightly different diacritic affixes all attached on the left. Thus:

$$\text{ᰰ}\qquad\text{ᰰ}\qquad\text{ᰰ}\qquad\text{ᰰ}\qquad\text{ᰰ}\qquad\text{ᰰ}\qquad\text{ᰰ}$$

Professor W. Leslau has later suggested a modification of this system using ᰰ for the fifth order and ᰰ for the sixth order (Leslau, W. 1953).

Following the publication of the *Fidälən maššašal* by the LL group there was a hiatus of about thirteen years in the formal discussion of the question of script reform.

The reform question was formally taken up again in March 1961 when a new committee was set up by order of the Ministry of Pen under the chairmanship of Ato Abbebe Retta, a one-time member of the now defunct LL group. The express aim of this committee was to consider a reform proposal submitted by Zewde Gebremedhin. There was little that was new in his proposal. In its vocalization system it differed from Abbebe Retta's earlier proposal (LL-III) only in using a small sublineal vertical line on the right for the fourth order instead of his horizontal line on the left. Nevertheless, the committee held five lengthy meetings and used the occasion to examine in detail all reform proposals made until then (except for the Menelik script which they did not mention) and to agree finally on what they believed to be the best way to reform the Ethiopian script. Their final choice coincides with Abbebe Retta's LL-III except that the symbols for palatals were retained. The minutes of their meetings were published in the Journal of Ethiopian Studies (Anonymous, 1970) with a lenthy introduction and a summary of their final decision. According to the proponents, the benefits that would supposedly accrue to the nation with the acceptance of the proposed reform are of millenial dimensions (see below). However, no official action was ever taken to implement their proposals.

Of the later reform proposals we need comment perhaps only about those made by Addis Alemayehu, Tekle-Maryam Fantaye and Zeev Raz. Addis Alemayehu (1966) dropped the "superfluous" letters and those for the labialized sounds, substituting for the latter a combination of the symbol for the non-labialized sound and the appropriate order of "ᰰ". He also used a superscript dot to mark gemination though he did not apply this consistently. His initiative was commended in the daily papers but his example was never followed. Tekle-Maryam Fantaye proposed a system with discreet vowels. For consonants he used the first order symbols and for vowels the "ᰰ"-series without the cross bar. Zeev Raz (undated, *circa* 1964) proposed a cursive system strangely similar to the Menelik script (see above) to which however he does not refer at all. He has not attempted to reduce the number of letters (except for making the palatal symbols uniformly derivative) or to regularize the vocalization. His proposals have not found acceptance anywhere.

Why reform the Amharic Script

Although expressed in different ways by different authors the criticism of the existing Amharic script can be reduced to five principal points.

1. *Overabundance of symbols.* The existence of about 270 symbols is said to be a major drawback because this makes the script difficult to learn and too cumbersome to use in machines such as the typewriter and telex. The fact that many of the symbols inherited from Ge'ez do not have a distinct phonetic value in Amharic is believed to add to the learning difficulty and to inflate the number of symbols unnecessarily.

2. *Irregular vocalization.* Although vocalization is indicated by the addition of fairly regular signs to the basic symbols there are nevertheless very many exceptions some of which are imposed by the shape of the basic symbol itself. This is believed to make the script more difficult to learn and more unwieldy for use in machines.

3. *The absence of a sign for gemination* is believed by some of the critics to lead to serious confusion for the reader.

4. *The double value of the sixth order.* The sign of the sixth order indicates both a voweless consonant and a consonant with the high central vowel. Not many even notice this shortcoming but some of those who do believe that it creates serious difficulties in reading.

5. *The non-cursive nature of the script* has appeared to some to be an important defect because it leads to slow freehand writing in an age when speed is essential.

The would-be reformers have held that the removal of these deficiencies of the script will lead to untold benefits for the country. Some of the claims as to these benefits have been obviously overstated. As an example of the more ardent claims I quote at some length in my own translation from the report of the last Alphabet Reform Committee (Anonymous, 1970).

1.   – The number of symbols in the present Amharic script is not less
     than 271. In the reformed script however there are only 27 consonants
     and 2 vowel symbols [5] giving a total of only 29.
2.   This means that a man who would need nine months to learn the older
     script would now need only one month – and would thus save eightfold
     or 89% of his time and use it for other purposes.
4.   The time needed for composing plates at printing presses, for learning to
     type, and for manufacturing type would be cut by 89% and thus provide
     a shortcut for the objectives of work and education.
6.   – It is obvious that the time needed for consulting dictionaries and
     telephone directories will be cut by 89% and thus lead to greater
     efficientcy.
7.   The time needed to teach students to read or to typewrite will be cut by
     89% – and lead to a saving of 89% in teacher salaries (sic!)
9.   In the political sphere – the Ethiopian script as the only script native to
     Africa will, if simplified and regularized, find acceptance in other African
     countries and thus promote the modern concept of Pan-Africanism.

The belief that once you reduce the number of symbols by 89%, if that
indeed is what the proposed system does, then everything from learning time
to teacher salaries will benefit at a pro-rata saving of 89% is too naive to
require any refutation here.

In sharp contrast to those who have seen script reform as a panacea to all
ills there are those who have viewed reform as an insidious tool of the devil
designed to rob Mother Ethiopia of her God-given gift. A noted old guard
literatus with strong clerical affiliations has expressed his unqualified opposition to any reform thus:

> "Each country has a symbol and an alphabet. Whenever a powerful
> enemy comes from outside and destroys the government and violates
> the boundary, the first sign of the victor is to destroy the symbol and
> the alphabet and thereby the language of the conquered nation". (Asress
> Yeniesew, 1959, p. 63).

> "Unless the system of the Ethiopic alphabet is preserved it will mean the
> destruction of the symbol of Ethiopian freedom" (Ibid p. 241).

---

[5] It is misleading to say that there are only two vowel symbols (i.e. a small dash and a ring)
because such a claim ignores the fact that each of these symbols is attached to different
parts of the basic symbols to signify different vowels.

"God drew Enos into a vision as he did Moses and gave him the alphabet to clarify and magnify the law and the commandments as glasses for the eye of understanding" (Ibid p. 257).

The last quotation refers to the Ethiopian Church tradition based on pseudoepigraphic literature, that the alphabet first appeared displayed on the surface of the firmament in a revelation to Enos, son of Seth and grandson of Adam (Habte-Maryam, 1970, p. 17).

Script reform in Ethiopia as indeed in most other countries is thus not a merely technical question to be settled by experts but a question with broad social implications that sometimes fall beyond the pale of rational discourse (Berry 1958, 1977 and Fishman 1977)[6]. Not all the opposition to reform has however been of the crankish variety. Dr. Getatchew Haile has expressed his reasoned opposition to script reform on the ground mainly that available resources are better invested in developing better teaching methods for the existing script than in attempting to eliminate whatever minor deficiencies there might be (Getatchew Haile, 1966-7).

A Critique of Reform Efforts

How serious indeed are the deficiencies ascribed to the present Amharic script? The overabundance of symbols is presented in a misleading fashion by those who claim that there are about 270 symbols. Although this is true in the trivial sense that there are that many discreet symbols in the syllabary it ignores the very important fact that there is a high degree of regular patterning. The script consists of a limited number of basic symbols each with generally six rather regularly derived variants to indicate various consonant-vowel combinations. To get the true number of symbols therefore we should count the basic symbols and the various formatives. On this basis we have 26 basic symbols and 3 formatives for the first order, 3 formatives for the second, 4 for the third, 5 for the fourth, 4 for the fifth, 15 for the sixth, and 6 for the seventh, giving us a total number of 66 distinct symbols for the Amharic script. The number may vary a little depending on which formative you count as same and which as different. However you may count, the number cannot be considered excessive by any standards. In a syllabic script any number significantly less than this would either leave too many important features unsignified or make it necessary to attach several

6 The first version of this article was prepared for the Fishman volume cited here. Ethiopian circumstances of the time made it impossible for me to complete the manuscript on time. I am nevertheless grateful to professor Fishman for giving the initial impetus for this article.

phonetic values to certain symbols. It is doubtful in any case whether the number of symbols in itself constitutes a serious learning problem even if we accept the inflated figure of 270. Yuen Ren Chao has estimated that the optimum number of symbols for a script may be "probably about 200 monosyllabic symbols, such that a string of 'seven plus or minus two of them can be easily grasped in one span of attention'" (Chao, 1968). The claim that an overabundance of symbols in the Amharic script makes it especially difficult to learn seems to be without any firm basis. As to the claim that this renders it unsuitable for use in machines there is no better refutation than that both a serviceable typewriter and a reasonably satisfactory telex machine are now in existence and in use. In any case, where it is at all possible to adapt the machines to the script it is certainly less socially disruptive to do that than to try to adapt a long entrenched script to the machines.

The irregularity of the vocalization signs is no doubt an impediment to the learning of the script but the case must not be overstated. The number of signs is truly excessive only in the case of the sixth order vowels where there are fifteen different signs. All the other orders have signs that range between three and six signs each, some of which are only slightly different from each other. All things considered the irregularity in the vocalization of Amharic pales into insignificance when compared to the irregularities in the spelling of languages like English and French. This is not to say that some rationalization of the vocalization could not improve the Ethiopic script but to restore a sense of perspective to the often exaggerated portrayals of its mild shorthcomings.

The absence of a sign for gemination is hardly ever a source of confusion for anyone who speaks the language. Where there are two possible readings for a word resulting from the absence of a sign of gemination then the context in which they occur nearly always disambiguates the issue. In real situations few and far between are the cases where even context fails to resolve the ambiguity. The addition of a special sign for gemination would therefore only create more practical problems that it would solve. For non-speakers of Amharic however, the addition of a gemination sign in primers and lexicons could be of some help at the initial stages of learning.

The fact that the sixth order stands for both a voweless consonant and a consonant with the high central vowel (the *shewa na'* and *shewa naḥ* of Hebrew) is also of no pratical concern to the speaker of Amharic because it results in no ambiguity that context cannot resolve. In Amharic as in Hebrew a number of rules govern most of the occurrences of the two forms limiting even further the possible areas of confusion. This is true of initial, final and geminate medial consonants.

Conclusion

Most efforts in script reform in Ethiopia seem to have tackled problems that were largely imaginary or were not compelling enough to justify the social cost of script reform. It is therefore not hard to understand why most of them failed. The two that did succeed, namely the introduction of vocalization signs in the pre-Amharic period and the introduction of derived symbols for the Amharic palatal sounds in the fourteenth century seem to have answered real and pressing needs. Furthermore they did not involve drastic reshaping of existing symbols. Sociological factors have played an important role in determining success and failures in Ethiopian script reform. The two successful reforms of the past were initiated and implemented by the church at a time when it had a monopolistic control of learning and the written word. Modern reform efforts have emanated from non-clerical sources and have at times assumed a posture of confrontation vis-à-vis the church establishment which, while no longer in a monopolistic position, nevertheless still exercises a decisive influence in such matters. With the establishment of the Amharic Language Academy under governmental authority a third important factor has come into play.

A conclusion that emerges from our investigation is that a radical script reform is *not* an imperative necessity for Amharic. A mere "streamlining" of the script could make it significantly easier to use if it could have behind it a legitimacy conferred by a broad consensus that includes the Language Academy, the Church, and the Ministry of Education. The streamlining would involve the rejection of the "superfluous" letters inherited from Geez, the regularization of some of the vocalization signs (primarily those of the sixth order vowel) and the restricted use of a gemination sign in Amharic primers for non-speakers of the language. The syllabic nature of the script should by all means be retained and the obsession with perfect regularity in vocalization should be tempered by practicality. A gemination sign has no place in normal writing for literate Amharic speakers as it would only serve to clutter up the page. A sign to distinguish between a quiescent and mobile *shewa* would definitely be superfluous in normal writing. To make the script more suitable for machines it would seem to be far less disruptive to tamper with the machines than to tamper with the script. Greater attention to machines could perhaps also lead to the development of a more economical typeface than the one now normally used. Imagine the cost in paper and printer's ink if everything in, say English, including newspapers and magazines were printed in boldface as Amharic now in effect is. The efforts at cursivization of the script have so far not yielded any viable system. This problem is perhaps one that is best left to spontaneous developments in calligraphic style. These developments have already given rise to some cursive styles that are gaining greater acceptance.

The Ethiopian case provides one more illustration if such were needed, that script reform calls not only for a competent professional assessment of the technical aspects of the script but also for a careful weighing of these against the psychological and socio-political factors that have a bearing on the written word and all that it stands for.

Bibliography

Addis Alemayyehu 1966. *Fəqər əskä mäqabər.* ፍቅር ፡ እስከ ፡ መቃብር (Love unto the grave). Addis Ababa.

Addis Alemayyehu 1981. *Wängäläññaw daňňa.* ወንጀለኛው ፡ ዳኛ (The criminal judge). Addis Ababa.

Anonymous 1970. "*Amarəñña fidäl həggən ənditäbbəq lämadräg*" (To make the Amharic syllabary observe rules.), *Journal of Ethiopian Studies* 3: 119-134.

Asress Yeniesew 1959. *Təbe aksum männu antä* ትቢ ፡ አኵሱም ፡ መኑ ፡ አንተ ("Who art thou?" sayeth Axum.) Addis Ababa.

Bender, L. M.; Head, S.; and Cowley R. 1976. "The Ethiopian Writing System", in *Language in Ethiopia.* M. S. Bender et al. eds. London: Oxford University Press.

Bemnet Gebre-Amlak 1955. *Yand qʷanqʷa ədgät* ያንድ ፡ ቋንቋ ፡ እድገት (The growth of a language.) Addis Ababa.

Berry, Jack 1958. "The Making of Alphabets", in *Proceedings of the VIII International Congress of Linguists,* Oslo: University Press.

Berry, Jack 1977. "'The Making of Alphabets' Revisited", in *Advances in the Creation and Revision of Writing Systems,* J. Fishman ed. The Hague: Mouton.

Chao, Yuen Ren 1968. *Language and Symbolic Systems.* Cambridge University Press.

Cohen, Marcel 1958. *La grande invention de l'écriture et son évolution.* Paris: Librairie Klincsieck.

Cowley, Roger 1967. "The Standardization of Amharic Spelling", *Journal of Ethiopian Studies* 2:1-8.

Deecke, W. 1877. "Über das indische Alphabet in seinem Zusammenhange mit den übrigen südsemitischen Alphabeten", in *Zeitschrift der deutschen morgenländischen Gesellschaft* 31:598-612.

Diringer, D. 1937. "Le origini della scrittura etiopica", in *Atti del terzo congresso di studi coloniali.* Firenze-Roma.

Diringer, D. 1949. *The Alphabet: a Key to the History of Mankind.* London, New York: Hutchinsons Scientific and Technical Publications. 2nd ed.

Drewes, A. M. 1955. "Problèmes de paleographie éthiopienne", *Annales d'Éthiopie* 1:121-126.

Driver, G. R. 1954. *Semitic Writing from Pictograph to Alphabet.* London: Oxford University Press. Revised edition.

Février, J. G. 1959. *Histoire de l'écriture.* Paris: Payot.

Fishman, J., ed. 1977. *Advances in the Creation and Revision of Writing Systems.* The Hague: Mouton.

Friedrich, J. 1935. "Einige Kapitel aus der inneren Geschichte der Schrift", *Archive für Schreib-und Buchwesen*, n. F. II, 8-18 (reference from Gelb, below).

Gebre-Sellassie 1967. *Tarikä zämän zädagəmawi mənilək* ታሪክ ፡ ዘመን ፡ ዘዳግማዊ ፡ ምኒልክ (Chronicle of Menelik II ...). Addis Ababa: Berhanenna Selam Press. (Also see Guèbre-Sellassié, below).

Gelb, I. J. 1952. *A Study of Writing*. Chicago: University of Chicago Press.

Getatchew Haile 1967. "The Problems of the Amharic Writing System", paper presented at the *Seminar of Arts and Education Faculties, Haile Sellassie I University*. Addis Ababa.

Getatchew Haile 1979. *A Catalogue of Ethiopian Manuscripts ...* Vol. IV. Collegeville: Hill Monastic Manuscript Library.

Getatchew Haile 1981. *A Catalogue of Ethiopian Manuscripts ...* Vol. V. Collegevill: Hill Monastic Manuscript Library.

Grohmann, A. 1915. "Über den Ursprung und die Entwicklung der äthiopischen Schrift", *Archiv für Schriftkunde* 1:57-87.

Guèbre-Sellassié 1930 (vol. I), 1932 (vol. II). *Chronique du règne de Ménélik II, roi des rois d'Éthiopie*. Maurice de Coppet (ed.) Paris: Librairie Orientale et Américaine. (See also Gebre-Selassie above).

Guidi, I. 1889. "Le canzoni ge'ez amarigna in onore dei re abissini", in *Rendiconti della Reale Accademia dei Lincei* ser. IV, vol. V, p. 53.

Habte-Maryam Workneh, *Liqä Səltanat* 1970. *Ṭəntawi yä'ityoppya təmhərt* ጥንታዊ ፡ የኢትዮጵያ ፡ ትምህርት (Traditional Ethiopian learning.) Addis Ababa.

Honeyman A. M. 1952. "The letter order of the Semitic Alphabets in Africa and the Near East", *Africa* 22: 136-147.

Kidane-Wold Kifle 1956. *Mäṣhafä Säwasəw wägəss wämäzgäbä qalat haddis* መጽሐፈ ፡ ሰዋስው ፡ ወግሥ ፡ ወመዝገበ ፡ ቃላት ፡ ሐዲስ (A grammar and a new dictionary). Addis Ababa.

Leslau, Wolf 1953 (1954). "La réforme de l'alphabet éthiopien", *Rassegna di studi etiopici* 12:96-106.

Leslau, Wolf 1961. "Sur les lettres 'arabes' de l'alphabet éthiopien", *Bulletin de la Société de Linguistique* 56:18-21.

Leslau, Wolf 1965. *An Annotated Bibliography of the Semitic Languages of Ethiopia*, pp. 62-72. The Hague: Mouton.

Lovers of Learning. See *Yätəmhərt wädaǧočč* የትምህርት ፡ ወዳጆች below.

Ludolfo, Iobo (Ludolf, Hiob) 1698. *Grammatica Linguae Amharicae*. Frankfurt: J. David Zunner.

Raz, Zeev 1964 (?) "Amharic Running-band Letters", Addis Ababa (undated mimeo).

Ryckmans, J. 1955. "L'origine et l'ordre des lettres de l'alphabet éthiopien", *Bibliotheca Orientalis* 12:2-8.

Tekle-Maryam Wolde Semharay 1911. *Mämhärä ləssanä gə'əz* መምህረ ፡ ልሳነ ፡ ግዕዝ (Instruction book for the Ge'ez language). Rome: Casa editrice Italiana.

Terrefe Raswork 1966. "Introduction of Amharic Teleprinters". Internal memorandum of the Telecommunications Board, Addis Ababa.

Ullendorff, E. 1951. "The Origin of the Ethiopic Alphabet", *Bibliotheca Orientalis* 12:217-218.

Yätəmhərt Wädaǧočč 1948. *Fidälən maššašal* ፊደልን ፡ ማሻሻል (Improving the script). Addis Ababa.

Yiggezu Bisrat 1958. *Fidäl* ፊደል (The Syllabary). Addis Ababa.

Zewde Gebre-Medhin 1968. *Bä'addis sər'at yätäzägaǧǧä fidäl* በአዲስ ፡ ሥርዓት ፡ የተዘጋጀ ፡ ፊደል (A Syllabary on new principles). Addis Ababa.

LES ORIGINES DE L'ÉCRITURE ÉTHIOPIENNE

ROGER SCHNEIDER
Institut Français d'Archéologie, Addis Ababa

Si on excepte les peuples riverains de la Méditerranée, l'Éthiopie est le seul pays africain à avoir connu l'écriture depuis l'Antiquité, probablement depuis la seconde moitié du cinquième siècle avant J.C.

L'écriture éthiopienne fait partie de la vaste famille des écritures sud-sémitiques qui étaient jadis en usage en Arabie (thamoudéen, sudarabique, lihyanite etc.) toutes remplacées par un alphabet nordsémitique, l'arabe; la seule exception est l'écriture éthiopienne, qui a survécu jusqu'à nos jours.

L'alphabet éthiopien est originaire de l'Arabie du Sud. Vers le milieu du Ve siècle avant notre ère deux variétés d'alphabets étaient en usage en Arabie du Sud, une qu'on appelle «cursive», l'autre «monumentale». L'écriture cursive est la forme primitive et ordinaire. De nombreux graffites ont été trouvés en Arabie du Sud, mais peu ont été publiés jusqu'à maintenant, de sorte qu'il n'est pas encore possible de se faire une idée nette de l'évolution de l'écriture cursive en Arabie méridionale.

L'alphabet monumental est une écriture créée à partir du cursif, régularisée suivant des normes strictes pour la forme, la symétrie et la composition, soigneusement gravée par des artisans, utilisée comme monument et sur des monuments, et destinée à être exposée en public.

Ces deux écritures, cursive et monumentale, se rencontrent aussi en Éthiopie. La paléographie montre que l'écriture monumentale a dû être introduite en Ethiopie peu de temps après sa création en Arabie du Sud, durant la seconde moitié du Ve siècle avant notre ère, selon la chronologie la plus communément admise actuellement. Déjà en 1956 A. J. Drewes a constaté que nous avons affaire à deux groupes d'inscriptions. La langue du premier groupe est du sabéen, et les auteurs sont des Sabéens; par leurs inscriptions nous savons que certains étaient originaires de Marib, d'autres de Hadaqan au nord de Sana'a.

La langue du second groupe d'inscriptions présente un certain nombre de différences avec le sabéen, qui font pressentir des faits qu'on trouve plus tard en guèze. Il est clair que les auteurs n'étaient pas des Sabéens, mais sans doute des autochtones. Notons que les inscriptions des quatre rois «éthiopiens» connus sont toutes rédigées dans cette langue.

À côté de ces inscriptions monumentales nous trouvons aussi de nombreux textes en cursive. Les premières inscriptions sudarabiques découvertes en Éthiopie étaient en écriture monumentale. Au temps de Littmann on en connaissait une dizaine, presque toutes fragmentaires. Littmann releva aussi quelques graffites en cursive sudarabique. Depuis une trentaine d'années environ, d'autres inscriptions monumentales furent découvertes, mais aussi de nombreux textes en cursive. Au début on pensait que ces textes cursifs éthiopiens représentaient une espèce de monumental dégénéré et étaient à peu près tous postérieurs aux inscriptions monumentales. Cette opinion est à modifier. Certains de ces textes sont sans doute au moins aussi anciens que les premières inscriptions monumentales; et cette écriture cursive, qui se rencontre dans des graffites rupestres, sur de la poterie, sur des objets en bronze, ne dérive pas du monumental; entre autres indices, on constate que certaines lettres ont des formes archaïques qui n'existent pas dans le monumental et n'en peuvent pas dériver.

Quand et comment cet alphabet cursif a-t-il été introduit en Éthiopie, nous l'ignorons encore. Même s'il n'est pas à dériver de l'alphabet monumental, on pourrait supposer que les mêmes Sabéens qui amenèrent le monumental introduisirent également le cursif. Mais ce n'est pas certain. D'abord ces immigrants sabéens semblent bien avoir été en nombre réduit; et avec leur disparition l'écriture monumentale, elle, disparaît, tandis que l'écriture cursive se maintient. Ensuite, ces graffites sont concentrés dans l'Akkele-Guzay, en Erythrée orientale, en des endroits où, à l'exception de Matara, la présence des Sabéens n'est pas documentée, tandis que dans les régions plus à l'ouest où la présence de Sabéens est bien attestée, rien, ou presque rien, n'a encore été découvert. Enfin, ni la langue, ni l'onomastique de ces textes n'est spécifiquement sabéenne. L'explication nous échappe encore. Est-ce que cette écriture cursive fut introduite en Éthiopie par des immigrants venus de l'Arabie à une époque antérieure, ou est-elle le résultat de contacts des Éthiopiens avec la rive est de la Mer Rouge? En d'autres mots, s'agit-il d'une importation ou d'un emprunt? Pour l'alphabet monumental nous savons qu'il fut importé par des immigrants venus du royaume de Saba; nous savons maintenant que certains au-moins étaient des maçons ou des sculpteurs, et il est possible qu'ils étaient surtout au service du roi.

De toute façon, à partir du milieu du Vᵉ siècle avant J.-C. ou peu après nous trouvons, à côté de l'écriture cursive, des exemples sporadiques d'inscriptions monumentales; celles-ci disparaissent quand disparaissent les Sabéens, après une centaine d'années au plus, mais l'écriture cursive continue. L'alphabet monumental n'avait apparemment que des emplois limités. Des quelques 50 ou 60 inscriptions monumentales connues, une quinzaine ont des Sabéens

comme auteurs; au moins 13 sont des inscriptions royales, et 7 autres
s'y rattachent probablement. Les auteurs d'une dizaine d'autres sont des
»Éthiopiens«; le reste est constitué par des fragments inclassables. Il semble
bien que l'alphabet monumental était une espèce d'écriture de prestige,
réservée pour certains usages et à certaines gens, et cet impact limité était
sans doute une des causes pour sa rapide disparition, une fois que les Sabéens
avaient disparu.

Durant la seconde moitié du IIe siècle de notre ère, l'écriture éthiopienne commence à émerger de l'écriture cursive. D. H. Müller en 1893, et
E. Littmann en 1913[1], ont affirmé que l'écriture éthiopienne dérive de
l'écriture monumentale sudarabique par une réforme intentionelle. Il est
vrai qu'à cette époque, peu d'exemples de textes cursifs étaient connus, et
en plus Littmann était peut-être influencé par le fait que le roi Ezana, au
IVe siècle, a laissé quelques inscriptions doublées d'une version écrite en
caractères sudarabiques, bien que la langue soit du guèze. Cependant en 1915
Grohmann[2] était arrivé à la conclusion que l'origine de l'écriture éthiopienne
était à chercher dans une écriture cursive; mais d'une façon générale c'est
l'opinion de Littmann qui prévalut.

À l'époque où Littmann situe la création de l'écriture éthiopienne, il y avait
au moins 500 ans que l'alphabet monumental sudarabique avait disparu en
Éthiopie. Le modèle qu'auraient choisi les Ethiopiens aurait donc été
l'alphabet sudarabique contemporain. Mais il est difficile d'expliquer la forme
de certaines lettres éthiopiennes à partir de ce modèle, tandis qu'on peut les
rapprocher sans difficulté des formes cursives.

Depuis le milieu du IIe siècle de notre ère, quand les lettres commencent à
évoluer dans le sens des formes éthiopiennes, jusque vers le milieu du IVe
siècle, où sont introduites les marques vocaliques, nous pouvons maintenant
suivre l'évolution suffisamment pour établir une séquence. Avec l'introduction
des marques vocaliques la forme définitive des lettres éthiopiennes est atteinte;
par la suite ce qui va changer, c'est le style de l'écriture, non la forme des
lettres.

Les voyelles n'ont pas été notées comme des lettres indépendantes. Le
signe, qui auparavant valait une consonne, à prononcer avec la voyelle requise
par le contexte, a été pris comme forme de base et notait une consonne suivie

---

1 D. H. Müller, *Epigraphische Denkmäler aus Abessinien*, Denkschriften der Kais. Akademie der
Wissenschaften, Phil. Hist. Kl., Wien, 1894.
Deutsche Aksum-Expedition, vol. IV, E. Littmann, *Sabäische, Griechische und Altabessinische
Inschriften*, Berlin, 1913.
2 A. Grohmann, *Über den Ursprung und die Entwicklung der äthiopischen Schrift*, Archiv für
Schriftkunde, I, 1915.

d'une voyelle *a*; les autres voyelles sont indiquées soit par une modification de la forme de la lettre, soit par l'adjonction d'une marque diacritique: l'alphabet consonantique est ainsi devenu un syllabaire, chaque signe notant une consonne suivie d'une voyelle ou de zéro. Évidemment ceci a amené une multiplication des formes; mais cette difficulté est quand-même considérablement réduite du fait que les changements sont systématiques, justement parce que la base du syllabaire est un alphabet consonnantique. En plus, l'écriture syllabique éthiopienne est capable de noter les sons de la langue avec une précision très grande.

Au moment où l'écriture éthiopienne est déjà constituée, il y a quelques exemples où une graphie monumentale sudarabique est employée pour écrire du guèze; mais cet usage semble restreint à la cour royale. Nous en connaissons quelques exemples pour Ezana, au IVe siècle, et pour Kaleb et son fils W'ZB au VIe.

Une inscription trouvée en Erythrée, dans le Qohayn, une région du Seraé oriental, reste mystérieuse. Elle est écrite en un alphabet sudarabique assez similaire à celui employé au IVe siècle à la cour d'Aksum, ce qui est déjà surprenant. Plus surprenant est le fait que la langue est inconnue. Ce n'est ni du sudarabique, ni du guèze, ni en fait du sémitique.

Quelques mots sur l'ordre des lettres. Pour le nordsémitique il est connu; notre «alphabet» ou ABC en dérive. Pour le sudsémitique on ne connaissait que l'ordre éthiopien, qui est différent, et qui n'était pas attesté avant le Moyen-Age. Il y a une trentaine d'années, les fouilles à Beihan, au Yémen du Sud, ont révélé un alphabet sudarabique incomplet; d'autres exemples ont été découvert depuis, de sorte que l'ordre sudarabique est maintenant assez bien connu. Il est intéressant de noter que les quatre premières lettres sont les mêmes que dans l'ordre éthiopien, *h l ḫ m*; mais la suite est différente. Il y a deux ans il fut découvert qu'un graffite trouvé à Dakhanomo, en Erythrée, publié en 1959, mais resté incompréhensible, représente un alphabet sudarabique presque complet, semblable à ceux trouvés en Arabie[3]. Quelques mois après il s'est avéré qu'un autre graffite de Dakhanomo, également publié en 1959 et resté incompréhensible, fournit, dans ses parties conservées, une partie de l'alphabet éthiopien. Dans la première ligne on lit la séquence *h l ḫ m š r s q b t*; la seconde ligne est en grande partie détruite, mais il subsiste un groupe: *y*, puis une lettre maintenant disparue, ensuite *g* et *ṭ*. Ceci correspondrait à la séquence *y [d] g ṭ*. Même si dans les parties maintenant disparues il a pu y avoir

---

3 L. Ricci, *Iscrizioni rupestri dell'Eritrea*, Rassegna di Studi Etiopici, vol. XV, 1959; N° 7.
   A. J. Drewes et R. Schneider, *L'alphabet sudarabique du Dakhanomo*, Raydān, III, 1980, p. 31 ss.

l'une ou l'autre divergence, ceci correspond à l'ordre des lettres de l'alphabet éthiopien, et prouve que cet ordre est ancien, remontant peut-être à la fin du IIIe, début du IVe siècle.

HISTORY

KING FĀSILIDAS, ABUNA MARQOS AND ABĒTO GALĀWDĒWOS

E. van Donzel

Netherlands Institute for the Near East, Leiden

The long reign of king Fāsiladas (1632-1667) is undoubtedly crucial for the Ethiopian history of the XVIIth and also the XVIIIth centuries. Yet, a monograph of this important period has not yet been written and, it would seem, for good reasons. First, the contemporary sources are limited. Apart from the indispensable—although often biased—reports of the Western Roman Catholic missionaries [1], we have at our disposal only the archives of the Dutch East India Company [2], al-Ḥaymī's *Sīrat al-Ḥabasha* [3] and the few data provided by Ethiopian sources [4]. Secondly, and more important, these sources have not as yet been compared with each other.

In order to make a first step towards a critical study of Fāsiladas's time, it seems useful to draw attention to the stories of abuna Marqos and Abēto Galāwdēwos as told by al-Ḥaymī and by the Catholic missionaries, respectively. This small contribution to our knowledge of Ethiopian history after 1632 is offered to Professor Leslau as a token of the author's esteem for his achievements in the whole range of Ethiopian Studies.

Neither of the two sources mentioned above is objective. The attitude of the Catholic missionaries is well-known. In their eyes, Fāsiladas was the great enemy who had put an end to Roman Catholic influence in the country. They could not but interpret anything he did, or was said to have done, as being directed against the Roman Catholic faith and its missionaries. Their writings therefore have to be used with great care. This does not however mean that everything they say is a priori to be rejected. A number of details may be

---

1 C. Beccari, *Rerum Aethiopicarum Scriptores Occidentales Inediti a Saeculo XVI ad XIX.* 15 vols., Rome 1903-1913. Photomechanical reimpr. Brussels 1969. In the following quoted as *Rerum*.

2 E. van Donzel, *Foreign Relations of Ethiopia 1642-1700.* Leiden 1979.

3 F. E. Peiser (ed.), *Der Gesandtschaftsbericht des Ḥasan ben Aḥmed El-Ḥaymī* (sic). Berlin 1894. In the following quoted as *Sīra*. A new translation by the present author is in preparation.

4 René Basset, *Études sur l'histoire d'Éthiopie* in *Journal Asiatique*, série 7 (1881), tome 17 (1881), 315-434, tome 18 (1881), 93-183, 285-389; Fr. Béguinot, *La Cronaca Abbreviata d'Abissinia.* Rome 1904; I. Guidi, *Le liste dei Metropoliti d'Abissinia.* Rome 1899; J. Perruchon, *Le règne de Fasiladas (Alam-Sagad), de 1632 à 1667*, in: *Revue Sémitique d'Épigraphie et d'Histoire Ancienne*, v (1897), 360-72; vi (1898), 84-92.

very correct, but it is hard to discover the truth in a context which reveals a mentality fiercely opposed to the king, and, for that matter, to the abuna and the Ethiopian orthodox church as a whole.

Al-Ḥaymī's case was different, but he could not be objective either. He left the Yemen with great expectations, intentionally caused by Fāsiladas himself, that the Ethiopian king was interested in Islam. The king's intentions were however of quite a different nature[5]. He did not want to become a Muslim, but wished to open a trading-route at Baylūl, the small port on the Red Sea ca. 50 km. north of Asab, which was free from Turkish control. In order to achieve this, he needed fire-arms which could be obtained from the Imām of Yemen. The latter however would only be interested in Ethiopian internal affairs if he was approached on a religious basis. And so Fāsiladas made him believe that he was interested in Islam[6]. This so-called "secret of the king" caused the Imām to send a mission to Ethiopia, headed by al-Ḥaymī. Before reaching Gondar, the Yemenite ambassador heard the stories about abuna Marqos and abēto Galāwdēwos and he saw in the king's behaviour towards them a sign "that the king would embrace Islam"[7]. Later he was to discover that "the thunderous cloud", i.e. the prospect of Fāsiladas becoming a Muslim, turned out to be "a rainless one", i.e. an empty promise[8]. It is quite understandable that al-Ḥaymī "lowered a curtain before the king and closed himself off from him"[9]. His disappointment was no less than that of the Western missionaries. The latter, notwithstanding their strong feelings against the king, could not complain about any deceit on his part, his attitude toward them having been very clear from 1632 onwards. Al-Ḥaymī, however, must have felt cheated. The king had used Islam, most sacred to him and the Imām, as a decoy, which was a severe blow to the faithful Yemenite ḳāḍī. No wonder that he remarks: "These Amharas are well-known for their determined cunning and for being sagacious in planning ways of strategems"[10].

Yet one has the impression that al-Ḥaymī, in his Sīra, was less taken away by his disappointment than the Roman Catholic missionaries. He seems to have been able to write in a more detached way than the Westerners.

---

5 *Foreign Relations*, 9-12.
6 *Ibid.* 5-6.
7 *Sīra*, 61.
8 *Sīra*, 63.
9 *Sīra*, 44.
10 *Sīra*, 62.

Abuna Marqos

The story of abuna Marqos is told by al-Ḥaymī as follows[11]. During his twelve years in office, the abuna had gathered great wealth and had become self-assured. He had also won the esteem of the nobles and was liked by the soldiers and the people. Consequently, Fāsiladas had become jealous and wanted to put him out of the way. An opportunity was found when Marqos assaulted a Muslim who was his personal servant, robbed him of his possessions and even "ripped away his coverings" i.e. seduced his wife. The Muslim, after some difficulty, brought his case before the king. Fāsiladas, who had been looking for such an occasion, summoned his ministers one by one and informed the ěčägē. At a court meeting it was decided that accusations against the abuna could be brought forward by the inhabitants of Gondar at a public gathering. Many men and women stood up to testify against the abuna, and some of the king's women declared in public that they had taken part with him in "debauchery" and, on Easter Sunday, in "shameful abominations". These accusations were noted down by monks and, in order to be carried to the Patriarch in Alexandria, translated into Arabic by al-Sharīf Muḥammad ibn Mūsā from Bukhāra, an apostate from Islam who had served as al-Ḥaymī's interpreter during his audiences with the king. The majority of the ministers and notables wanted the abuna to be killed, but the king imprisoned him "on an island in the Nile". The Patriarch then appointed a new abuna. Al-Ḥaymī learned these details from a certain Khāṭirūs, the Arabic-speaking superior of a religious community, established on the "recreation grounds" outside Gondar where the Abuna used to go. Although a pupil of Marqos, Khāṭirūs censured the latter scathingly for his actions.

The Western authors have some more details about the abuna's conduct. Bernardus Nogueira[12] writes: "The Abuna led groups of dancing girls, who are skilled in the performance of Herodias's daughter and have no shame, and is even said to take delight in "vino, in Sodomae proelis expresso". When this was divulged by those whom he used to violate petulantly, he became execrable to everybody, whereas before he had been respected by his people. According to Alphonso Mendez[13], Christian and Muslim merchants from Ethiopia arriving at Mokha and a Greek from Istanbul who was a domestic of the abuna, related that the latter "because of his abnormal and

---

11 *Sīra*, 57-9.
12 *Rerum*, IX, 382. On Bernardus Nogueira, see *Rerum*, Index (vol. xv), s.v. Nogueira.
13 *Rerum*, IX, 428-30.

manifest infamous deeds" had been deposed and that another abuna had been asked for in Egypt. Marqos had been "playing his own zither together with the tambourine players and the dancing girls, regularly singing and playing with them promiscuously, and acting as a priest of Venus, not of God". Prince Galāwdēwos, comparing his behaviour with that of the Roman "praesules", had spoken out against him, thus provoking the abuna's and the king's wrath.

From Mendez's remark that the abuna's sense of shame was lulled after Galāwdēwos's fall, it would seem that the prince was banished—or killed—before the deposition of Marqos. On the other hand, it was Galāwdēwos who had sent for abuna Yohannes as the successor to abuna Marqos, while the king wanted abuna Mikael [14]. Since both Mendez and Torquato Parisiani (see below) state explicitly that Galāwdēwos was murdered in 1646, we must assume that the deposition of the abuna and the fall of the prince took place in this year.

Mendez then goes on: "Apart from the large group of common (*vulgarium*) women whom he used to entertain, the abuna extended his libido to married women and to catamites (*pueros cinaedulos et catamitos*), of whom he kept a very great (*ingentem*) number. Passing his entire day and the nights with them, he disregarded his office and did not deign to look at or to address word to the dignitaries and governors who came to his house, in order not to interrupt that depraved intercourse". The rumour of the abuna's dissolute life spread everywhere and the *ĕč̣ägē*, calling about one hundred of his servant boys, forced them to tell him what they knew about their master and the women. The boys named "about three hundred married and as many unmarried women to whom they served as errand-boys (*nuntii*). Many of these women, when summoned, confessed his turpitude openly ... The same boys and other youngsters bore witness to the abuna's sodomy (*posticam procaciam*)". Marqos was then sent into exile on a mountain opposite to that where Sela Kristos had been banished [15]. Mendez does not mention abuna Yohannes, and names abuna Mikael as the successor to Marqos.

The deposition of Abuna Marqos is confirmed by other sources. Khodja Murād related in Batavia [16] that abuna Marqos, the patron of Petrus Heyling of Lübeck, "fell into disgrace with the emperor, was attacked by the

---

14 Basset, *Études*, in *JA* 18 (1881), 288 and note 291; Guidi, *Liste*, 12; James Bruce, *Travels to discover the Source of the Nile, in the years 1768, 1769, 1770, 1771, 1772 and 1773*. 5 vols. Edinburgh 1790, ii, 346.

15 See *Rerum*, Index s.v. Sella Christôs (p. 313a).

16 *Foreign Relations*, 99.

common people and put into prison". Consecrated by the Patriarch of Alexandria towards the middle of 1634, he had set out for Ethiopia before the end of the year, accompanied by Heyling [17]. He arrived in the fourth year of the reign of Fāsiladas [18], i.e. between June 1635 and June 1636, and was deposed before al-Ḥaymī's arrival in Gondar on March 20, 1648. Thus the latter's information that the abuna had been in office for about twelve years is correct, Ludolf's date of 1651 [19] being wrong. The news of the deposition reached the Portuguese in Mokha in August 1649 [20].

Abēto Galāwdēwos

Abēto Galāwdēwos, whose story is somehow linked to that of abuna Marqos, was the youngest son of king Susneyos and queen Wäld-Sehlä (Selṭān Mogasā), and the only full brother of Fāsiladas. Born ca. 1608 [21], he had been present at the solemn reception of Alphonso Mendez at the Ethiopian court [22], had became a Roman Catholic and was friendly to the Jesuit fathers [23]. His tendency towards the religion of the Westerners must not have been very strong for, after Ethiopia had returned to the orthodox faith, he took possession of Mendez's house in Depsan (near Anfraz) [24] and sentenced three Catholic priests to death [25]. On the other hand, Mendez relates [26] that he and his mother, although "durissimi sanctae fidei Romanae insectatores", requested Fāsiladas to restore the Roman faith after the devastating invasion of Tigre by the Gallas in 1641.

According to al-Ḥaymī [27], Susneyos before his death recommended to

---

17 J. Ludolf, *Ad suam historiam Aethiopicam antehac editam Commentarius.* Frankfurt a.M. 1691, 554; Mich. Le Quien, *Oriens Christianus in quatuor patriarchatus digestus; quo exhibentur ecclesiae patriarchae caeterique praesules totius Orientis.* 3 vols, Paris 1740, ii, 658; *Rerum.* Index s.v. Marqos, abuna.

18 Basset, *Études*, in JA 18 (1881), 287.

19 J. Ludolf, *Historia Aethiopica*, Frankfurt a.M. 1681, L. III, C. 7[25].

20 Lobo-Legrand, *Voyage = Voyage historique d'Abyssinie du R.P. Jerome Lobo, de la Compagnie de Jésus, Traduite* (sic) *du Portugais, continuée et augmentée de plusieurs Dissertations, Lettres et Mémoires,* par M. Le Grand, Paris-La Haye 1728, 153.

21 *Rerum*, XII, 70.

22 *Rerum*, VIII, 143.

23 *Rerum*, XII, 70.

24 *Rerum*, IX, 156; cp. *ibid.* Index s.v. Depsan.

25 *Rerum*, VII, 405.

26 *Rerum*, IX, 321.

27 *Sīra*, 61-3.

Fāsiladas not to confine Galāwdēwos to the *amba nagast*[28], but to keep him at the court as a minister. Fāsiladas complied with this rather unusual request and put his brother in charge of military affairs. The prince gradually became arrogant and independent, and it was reported to the king that he wanted to dethrone him. So Fāsiladas tried to lay hands on Galāwdēwos, but succeeded only after a long time. "At dead of night, a group of intrepid, brave and strong men" imprisoned him. At the pleading of their mother, the king spared his brother's life and banished him to "an island of the Nile". Nobody heard any more about him, and so people thought that the king had murdered his brother.

The reports of the Western authors, who give more details about Galāwdēwos's fate, suggest that the latter's rebellion was directly connected with the religious question which still hovered over the country.

In his *Relatio de statu Aethiopiae ann. 1647-1649*[29], the Jesuit Torquato Parisiani, who wrote in 1649, related that in 1646 (*trè anni sono*) Fāsiladas's youngest brother and other chiefs "moved by the zeal of public good and of Christianity", decided to depose the emperor, to put his brother (Galāwdēwos) on the throne and to recall the Roman Catholic priests. The king, informed by the abuna "heretico scismatico", summoned his brother "che subito, senza essamine di testimonii et atti giudiciarii, in presenza sua commandò alli suoi schiavi suffocarlo con una tovaglia, di che morì". Then, "per sviare ogni speranza alli Porthoghesi e maestri della fede romana d'entrare in Etiopia, et alli nativi in Etiopia di chiamarli", Fāsiladas decided that he and his whole empire would become Muslim. So one day he called a servant of his "di costumi depravati e di setta moro" and informed him in secret about his intention to ask the Imām for "un maestro di auttorità e dotto nella setta di Maffamede" who should instruct his people in Islam. With slaves, eunuchs, gold and other matters of great value, the Muslim servant left Ethiopia in August 1647 without telling anyone why and where he was going. He was accompanied by an Ethiopian Christian with whom he quarrelled whether presents should be given to the governor of Mokha. The Christian, who maintained that the presents were destined for the Imām only, was put into prison for three days by the Muslim ambassador and afterwards looked for an occasion to revenge himself. In Mokha the ambassador made it public that the Ethiopian king wished to become a Muslim and revealed the aim of his mission. In Ṣanʿāʾ he was received with great honour by Imām

---

28 Possibly Ambasal, for Gēšēn had been destroyed by Grāñ in 1539, and Waḥnī was established by Fāsiladas only in 1647, see *Foreign Relations*, 193 n. 22, 224 n. 32.

29 *Rerum*, XIII, 333-45.

Ismāʿīl. Accompanied by the "maestro che domandava della setta di Maffamede", and with rich presents, he went back to Mokha. For fear of the Turks he left, not for Masawwaʿ, but for "Asab" where he arrived in October 1647. From there the Christian went ahead and informed the monks and notables about the king's intentions. "The monks and through them the whole people" said to the king that he would not be recognized any more as sovereign if he persisted in his plans. The "maestro della setta di Maffamede" was received with great honour by the king but "the people, on the contrary, did not rest day and night to affront him in every possible way, setting fire twice to his house and all his books and trying to kill him, but they did not succeed since the "maestro" was very much on the alert". The king had the Ethiopian ambassador imprisoned for a couple of days, under the pretext that he had brought "quel maestro" without his order, and declared that he had not taken such a resolution (as to become a Muslim), that on the contrary he abhorred Islam. The situation calmed down and the king sent "il maestro" back to Arabia where he arrived in February 1649. Torquato then adds "In order that "il maestro" might understand that he (the king), notwithstanding this (departure), would not fail to embrace the sect of Muḥammad, he honoured him greatly when he left Ethiopia and presented him with much gold and many slaves"[30]. The mother of the king "fece anco gran carezze al maestro donandogli fra l'altre cose un ricco vestimento".

The death of Galāwdēwos

Whereas al-Ḥaymī says that prince Galāwdēwos was banished and heard of no more, the sources collected by Beccari state that he was murdered. According to Torquato, he was suffocated with a napkin. Mendez relates[31] that Fāsiladas had him beheaded (*obtruncavit*) or, according to others, suffocated (*fauces linteo elisit*). This information is based on a letter of Bernard Nogueira, dated 11 March 1647[32]. Mendez later adds that the story of the murder of Galāwdēwos, as told by "a plebeian but honest woman who had fled from Ethiopia" and by Bernard Nogueira, was "rather obscure and confused". He therefore asked Bernhard, his vicar-general in Ethiopia, to

---

30 "Acciò che vedesse non mancar per esso d'abbracciar la setta di Maffamede, all'uscir di Etiopia gli fece molti honori et diede molto oro e molti schiavi". (*Rerum*, XIII, 340).

31 *Rerum*, VIII, 333.

32 *Rerum*, IX, 381.

relate Galāwdēwos's story and the way he died (*causam et modum*) shortly and clearly (*strictim et diserte*). Bernard then sent the following information[33].

Galāwdēwos was beloved by everybody, except the monks, who hated him because of a rumour according to which he was about to take over the reign from his brother Fāsiladas. The Portuguese would then come back, the Alexandrian creed buried and the Roman faith restored, like in the days of his father Susneyos. Galāwdēwos did not think much of the monks "often disclosing and expanding before many people their infamous deeds and execrable manners and those of the abuna". And so they excited the king against him. Nogueira had heard this from a certain "Ludovicus", an Agau who was a Catholic at the time, brother of a Johannes Anbessa who was a great friend of the emperor and also known to Mendez[34]. Later, Ludovicus turned orthodox and told the emperor everything prince Galāwdēwos had said to him in secret. The king then summoned the prince to the court under the pretext of discussing a public matter (*publici negotii specie*). Suspecting no harm, Galāwdēwos arrived and was received by the king "with the blandishments of simulated love". He was invited to a separate room "so that, away from witnesses, we might talk there about the matter for which I have made you come". There the king had kept ready "some brawny and intrepid young men" (*iuvenes aliquot torosos et audaces*), who put the prince's hands and feet in irons and threw him into a tower. Within three days, all the children of Galāwdēwos were imprisoned. Then the prince was shown to the people of the royal camp, and the herald cried: "Look at Claudius (Galāwdēwos), the manifest conspirator of treason and enormous crimes against the legitimate faith of Alexandria and Our crown. For he tried to send envoys to Rome, India and Portugal in order to invite the Portuguese whose faith We have condemned and whom We have expelled from Our territory. Give your opinion about what must be done with him". The people cried that he should be put to death. The following night Galāwdēwos was beheaded and his head sent to Ganata Iyasus[35], to be buried in the tomb of his father Susneyos.

According to Bernard Nogueira, many people thought that Galāwdēwos was a true Roman Catholic. He relates that he had expelled from his house Adrianus Andradius and Petrus Oina, two Portuguese in his service, when they had turned orthodox. Another Portuguese, Emmanuel Nogueira from Gambela, a son of Damianus Nogueira, had been flogged and forbidden access to the prince's house after he had become orthodox.

33 *Rerum*, IX, 373.
34 Cp. *Rerum*, XIII, 101.
35 See *Foreign Relations*, 193 n. 23.

After mentioning the names of Galāwdēwos's friends who suffered from the king's wrath, Bernard Nogueira relates the mission to "Imam Ismael, Felicis Arabiae regem, iura dantem in urbe Senaar (sic = Ṣanʿāʾ)", as it is told by Torquato.

If we compare Torquato's *Relatio* with the information provided by the letters exchanged between Fāsiladas and the Imāms of Yemen before al-Ḥaymī's journey[36], and by the latter's *Sīra*, the following remarks can be made.

The first letter of Fāsiladas to the Imām dates from Shawwāl 1051/January 1642, and the first Ethiopian mission, led by al-Ḥādjdj Sālim b. ʿAbd al-Raḥīm, arrived at Shahāra in Ramaḍān 1052/1643. The king's decision to enter into contact with the Imām can therefore not be brought in direct connection with Galāwdēwos's rebellion which, as Torquato himself states, came to a head only in 1646. In his letter of 1642, Fāsiladas "requested a man from among the notables of the Imām to come to him"[37], not in order to become a Muslim but to enter into negotiations about opening a trading-route at the port of Baylūl. In 1057/1647 Sālim arrived again in the Yemen. The latter was indeed a Muslim[38], but there is no indication whatsoever that he was "di cosumi depravati" as Torquato has it. The Roman Catholic priest must have given the envoy this epithet for the simple reason that he was a Muslim. Sālim—if indeed he is meant by Torquato—cannot have left Ethiopia in August 1647, for, according to al-Ḥaymī, the second Ethiopian mission arrived at Shahāra in Muḥarram or Ṣafar 1057/February or March 1647[39]. Besides, al-Ḥaymī, apparently the "maestro di auttorità et dotto nella setta di Maffamede", left Shahāra, in the company of Sālim, on 1st Djumāda al-ukhrā 1057/4 July 1647[40]. Sālim thus must have left Ethiopia sometime in 1646. Since in 1642 the journey from Gondar to Shahāra took him eleven months[41], it seems that we should correct "August 1647" to "August 1646" at the very least.

Lobo-Legrand[42] confirms that al-Ḥādjdj Sālim was accompanied by a Christian and that the latter suffered a bad treatment at the hands of the

36 To be published in my forthcoming translation of al-Ḥaymī's *Sīra*.

37 *Sīra*, 3.

38 *Sīra*, 2, 4.

39 *Foreign Relations*, 5 and n. 19.

40 *Sīra*, 10.

41 Ambrosiana ms. ar. 115, fol. 118ᵛ = al-Djarmūzī, *al-Djawhara al-munīra fī djumal min ʿuyūn al-sīra*, containing the *Sīra* of Imām al-Muʾayyad billāh Muḥammad b. al-Manṣūr billāh al-Kāsim (reigned 1029/1620 - 1054/1644).

42 *Voyage*, 148.

Muslims in Yemen. The same source also says that it was the Christian envoy
who spread the word that Fāsiladas wished to islamicize Ethiopia. Al-Ḥaymī
too refers to this in his *Sīra*[43]. The rumour about Fāsiladas's pretended
intentions of becoming a Muslim, which, according to Torquato, was started
by Sālim in Mokha, was in any case strengthened by the latter's remark to
Imām al-Mutawakkil ʿalā Allāh Ismāʿīl b. al-Manṣūr billāh al-Ḳāsim
(1054/1644 - 1079/ 1668): "I think that the king wants to embrace Islam"[44].
Sālim was indeed well received by the Imām, not in Ṣanʿāʾ however but in
Shahāra. Al-Ḥaymī confirms that the mission left Mokha not for Masawwaʿ
but for Baylūl, for fear of the Turks[45], but they arrived there on 17 Shaʿbān
1057/17 September 1647.

The Yemenite author does not mention any quarrel between the king and
his people about the royal intentions to become a Muslim. He knew the
king's plans much better than the people did. The enmity of the Gondarese
towards the mission from Yemen, which reflects perhaps the feelings of the
people about the rumour, is however quite clear from al-Ḥaymī's account,
and the two fire-incidents are fully related in his *Sīra*[46]. On the other hand, if
we believe al-Ḥaymī—and why should we not—it is not true that he left
Ethiopia in the way described by Torquato. The king certainly did not show
any interest in Islam and no present, whether for the Yemenite ambassador
or for the Imām, is mentioned in the *Sīra*, let alone "much gold and many
slaves". Nor does al-Ḥaymī refer to any contact with the queen-mother who,
according to Lobo-Legrand[47], was a grand-daughter of a Muslim woman
and had a great penchant for Islam. If this had taken place, he would
certainly have talked about it, for a better case in point could hardly be
imagined. Finally, al-Ḥaymī returned to Shahāra not in February but on
19 March 1649.

Conclusion

The story of abuna Marqos is clear enough. Although the accusation of
sodomy is not found in al-Ḥaymī's *Sīra*, there seems little doubt that the
abuna was deposed because of his dissolute conduct. Al-Ḥaymī's remark that
Fāsiladas acted against him also out of jealousy can not be confirmed from

43 *Sīra*, 35.
44 *Sīra*, 6.
45 *Sīra*, 11.
46 *Sīra*, 51, 55.
47 *Voyage*, 148.

other sources. The abuna's opposition to Galāwdēwos, who had criticized his conduct, apparently had not made him an ally of the king, who was opposed to his brother for quite different reasons.

The position of Galāwdēwos seems to have been more complex. His rebellion against the king probably originated in his strong position at the court. It was quite exceptional that such a close relative of the king and potential rebel was not banished to the *amba nagast*, and, on top of that, was put in charge of military affairs. Susneyos's recommendation can hardly have been the only reason for this quite uncommon royal behaviour, but the sources do not provide us with another one. In any case, his great influence on affairs may well have led Galāwdēwos to arrogance and independence, as al-Ḥaymī remarks. The prince's hatred of abuna Marqos and the monks may have been another incentive for him to consider the possibility of using the Portuguese and, by implication, the Roman Catholic faith to arrive at his political aims. If so, his calculations were ill-inspired for the court as a whole, the monks and the majority of the people, were too strongly opposed to the foreigners and their faith to go along with him in that scheme. Moreover, by acting in that way, he gave Fāsiladas every possible opportunity to make full use of the strong anti-Catholic feelings of the people in order to get rid of his brother, as he indeed did by exposing him in the royal camp. The question of how to deal with the invading Gallas may have been a third reason for serious discrepancy between the two brothers.

On the other hand, the Jesuit thesis according to which the rebellion of Galāwdēwos was directly connected with Fāsiladas's contacts with the Imāms of the Yemen—explained as a wish to become a Muslim—, must be rejected. Al-Ḥaymī's *Sīra* does not leave any doubt that the king's intentions were completely different from those which Torquato Parisiani, Mendez and Bernard Nogueira ascribe to him. The Western priests were led more by their feelings against the king and their dislike for Islam[48] than by a sincere endeavour to discover the truth behind the king's actions. The fact that they were no impartial historians but greatly disappointed missionaries is no excuse. It must however be remarked that Fāsiladas had caused an imbroglio, misleading even the Imām of the Yemen.

48 Cp. Torquato Parisiani: "questa mala razza (= Muslims) non manca in Etiopia", *Rerum*, XIII, 337.

FRANCE'S ABANDONMENT OF ETHIOPIA TO ITALY, 1928-1935

HAROLD G. MARCUS
Michigan State University

In *La Décadence* (Paris, 1979), Jean-Baptiste Duroselle claims that during a conversation *"seul à seul"* with Mussolini from midnight to 1:00 AM on 7 January 1935, Pierre Laval agreed to French economic disinterest in Ethiopia but not to any Italian military adventure. According to Duroselle, Mussolini invented the "free hand" as part of the etiological charter for the restored Roman Empire[1]. Yet, Duroselle's rendering of the 1935-1936 crisis certainly reveals that "From France, the Emperor [Haile Sellasie I, r. 1930-1974] had little to hope for after the Laval-Mussolini accords of January 1935", to use the words of Gontran de Juniac, the monarch's recent biographer and Paris's ambassador in Ethiopia from 1960-1965[2]. One witness outside the door of the French Embassy's White Room, where the mysterious *tête à tête* transpired, credits Laval with then conceding economic primacy to be followed by an Italian protectorate[3]. Pierre Laval's biographer and private secretary for fifteen years, Alfred Mallet, emphasizes the premier's often repeated assertion that he abandoned Ethiopia to Italy's lire but not to its legions[4]. Laval himself claimed that he "urged Mussolini not to resort to force .... He committed the blunder of going to war. He started war against my will and my solemn protest"[5]. Nevertheless, if the premier advised peace, his behavior on 7 January 1935, led to the Italo-Ethiopian war[6].

Laval's abdication of Ethiopia stemmed from his deep concern for France's security and not, as Vansittart would like us to believe, from perverse criminality and opportunism[7]. The Englishman was malicious to assert that "when Laval sold Abyssinia to Italy he must have known that he was thereby

---

1 Jean Baptiste Duroselle, *La Décadence* (Paris, 1979), pp. 132-33.

2 Gontran de Juniac, *Le Dernier Roi des Rois: l'Éthiopie de Hailé Selassié* (Paris, 1979), p. 125.

3 Jean-Paul Garnier, "Autour d'un Accord", *La Revue de Paris*, 68 (1961), p. 112.

4 Alfred Mallet, *Pierre Laval*, 2 vols. (Paris, 1954), I, p. 102-03.

5 Pierre Laval, *The Unpublished Diary of Pierre Laval*, (London, 1948), p. 34.

6 Most scholarly writers agree. For a characteristic treatment, see Charles O. Richardson, "The Rome Accords of January 1935 and the Coming of the Italian-Ethiopia War", *The Historian*, Vol. 41 (Nov. 1978), pp. 41 ff.; cf. Paul Reynaud, *La France a sauvé l'Europe*, Vol. 1 (Paris, 1947), p. 157.

7 Lord Vansittart, *Lessons of My Life* (New York, 1943), pp. 37-39.

selling Austria to Germany", and inevitably pushing Mussolini and Hitler toward the Axis. The British bureaucrat underestimated the impact of London's subsequent policy as forcing an alignment of black and brown shirt and ignored Laval's reasonable view that a Franco-Italian military alliance, a major part of the 1935-agreement, was necessary "to defend Italy and France against a German invasion of Austria. This was of paramount importance; as long as Italy was France's ally we had a bridge leading to all those countries of western and eastern Europe which were then our allies" [8]. When viewed this way, and with the Nazi threat increasingly evident, France's national interest in 1935 demanded the sacrifice of Ethiopia, a possibility first raised in the Quai d'Orsay in 1928, even if some Frenchmen privately had considered the option earlier [9].

Throughout the twenties, France's position of predominance in Ethiopia had eroded as Ras Tafari's (regent, 1916-28; king, 1928-30; and as Haile Sellassie I, emperor, 1930-74) internal policies greatly increased cash-cropping, and Ethiopia joined the world economy. The country's ruling classes became a profit-conscious oligarchy which demanded greater internal security and more efficient communications. Addis Ababa had been unable to acquire enough capital in London, Paris, and Rome to build a modern infrastructure and could not evade Europe's post-war arms embargo. In line with the developing economy and the growing need for arms, Tafari broadened Ethiopia's international relations, particularly in the direction of Japan and the United States [10]. Merchants in Addis Ababa also diversified international purchases in line with external developments and the availability of foreign exchange, and even the country's students were parcelled out to various European countries and the United States, as were government jobs [11]. By 1928, France was losing its primacy in Ethiopian trade; Gallic culture was not so dominant; and fewer Frenchmen were being hired for expatriate positions in the central administration. Paris reacted by undertaking a

---

8 Laval, *Diary*, 34.

9 General Maurice Gamelin, *Servir*, Vol. 2 (Paris, 1946), p. 163.

10 Southard to SS, Addis Ababa, 2 June 1928, United States National Archives, Records of the Departments of State Relating to the Internal Affairs of Ethiopia (Abyssinia), 1910-29, Microcopy, roll 2; "L'Éthiopie et le Japon", *Correspondence d'Éthiopie*", 5 (21 July 1927), 2. Given superficial similarities between the two countries, Ethiopians were fascinated by Japan's economic success and progress. Blattengeta Herui, Ethiopia's long-time foreign minister, visited the country and wrote a glowing account of his expriences, *Mahdärä barhan hagärä Ǧapan (The Case of Light, the Country of Japan)* (Addis Ababa, 1924, Eth. Calendar).

11 H.G. Marcus, "The Infrastructure of the Italo-Ethiopian Crisis: Haile Sellassie, the Solomonic Empire, and the World Economy, 1935-36", *Proceedings of the Fifth International Conference on Ethiopian Studies*, (Chicago, 1980).

reevaluation which uncovered attitudes that underlay subsequent French decisions about Ethiopia.

One might indeed characterize such thinking as the official mind of the Quai d'Orsay, although some scholars might rejoin that during the twenties and thirties, ministerial leadership changed so frequently that there could be no consistency of policy. They fail to appreciate, however, that the Quai's permanent staff developed and recommended policies to transient political appointees who gratefully adopted them. In the Ethiopian case, officialdom sustained a strikingly uniform set of ideas, which dominated thinking about Haile Sellassie's empire from at least 1928 through the *dénouement* of 1935-36. When Laval proferred Italy a "free hand" in Ethiopia, he was not acting in any opportunistic or extraordinary fashion, but fulfilling a policy evolved by permanent officials.

In January 1928, an internal Quai d'Orsay memorandum had investigated the possibility of trading France's interests in Ethiopia for Italy's rights in Tunisia. Its author commented rhetorically that: "It might be objected that in thus allowing Italy *a free hand* [my italics] ... we renounce ... our traditional policy which has always been to support Abyssinia against the avarice of the two other limitrophe powers, notably the Italians". In self-rebuttal, he explained that:

> all the marks of sympathy which we have shown these last years toward Abyssinia, all the efforts we have expanded in its favor ... have not received for us any gesture of recognition. To the contrary, it seems that at no time have our interests been more maltreated than at the present. Might we not therefore be justified in ceasing to compromise ourselves, without benefits, for this country, and, if we can obtain from Italy other areas of certain advantage ... benefit from the position we possess in Ethiopia from the international point of view [12].

France's alienation grew stronger in early 1931, when depression-ridden Ethiopia sensibly raised import duties on luxury goods, on which a hefty 30% sales tax was also levied. Since most of the items were French-produced, Paris's plenipotentiary was irate. Hitherto a staunch proponent of France's putative role as Ethiopia's protector, M. Reffye dolefully reasoned that Haile Sellassie's policies would drive Rome and Paris together; he believed the emperor assumed Gallic amity "an axiom, and that, thanks to this sentiment, our country is obliged to always give, without getting anything in return";

---

12 "Au sujet des relations Franco-Italiennes en Abyssinie", 12 Jan. 1928, Archives of the Quai d'Orsay, K-Série, Afrique, 1918-1940, Ethiopie, Affaires générales, 1928, vol. 19.

but he hoped that the monarch could be taught that Ethiopia is not "the center of the world, that it only plays a peripheral role in the relations between great powers and that it is above all France which up to now has been the principal safeguarder of its independence"[13]. Significantly, the 1928-memo, word-for-word, shows up again, this time masquerading as a "Note pour le ministre"[14]. The French were moving toward a new policy, and on 20 April 1931, the Quai d'Orsay cabled its ambassador in Rome seeking his advice on the Ethiopian question.

Count Beaumarchais responded that he did not believe that Haile Sellassie would be able, by himself and using only Ethiopia's resources, to develop the country to the point of civilization. He also considered that Italy's nationalistic energies would be dissipated more harmlessly in building an Ethiopian colony than by entering into the intrigues and uncertainties of European great-power politics. If Mussolini would not be satisfied with one-third of Ethiopia, as stipulated in the (Anglo-Franco-Italian) Tripartite Treaty of 1906[15], then "we must hold out the bright prospect of an exceptionable situation in the whole Empire ... [and] we should disinterest ourselves in Ethiopia's future". Beaumarchais realized that abandonment of France's involvement, except for the profitable railway, would upset public opinion, but he reckoned that Rome's friendship "is worth a sacrifice and I would be disposed to think that it is in Ethiopia where the sacrifice would be the least costly as much for our self-respect as for our [European] interests". Tactically, he realized that Paris could not raise the matter, since a *volte-face* would be embarrassing politically; it was up to the Italians to "ask us to let them have *a free hand* in Abyssinia"[16].

Meanwhile, the French legation fought a losing battle to preserve Paris's position in Haile Sellassie's Empire. Minister Reffye continued to grumble about the failure of French goods to retain their markets in Ethiopia; he was positively acid about Addis Ababa's arbitrary efforts to reduce the salaries of his compatriots to the levels of Russian emigrés; and he was indignant that an increasing number of positions fell to non-Frenchmen[17]. The diplomat

---

13 Reffye to Minister, Addia Ababa, 2 April 1931, d42, AQO, K-Afrique, Ethiopie, Relations et Conventions Commerciales, tarifs douaniers, Vol. 135.
14 Note pour le ministre, 10 March 1931, AQO, K-Afrique, Projet d'alliance entre la France et l'Ethiopie, Vol. 62.
15 H. G. Marcus, "A Preliminary History of the Tripartite Treaty of December 12, 1906", *Journal of Ethiopian Studies*, 2 (1964).
16 Beaumarchais to Briand, Rome, 25 April 1931, AQO, K-Afrique, Projet d'alliance entre la France et l'Ethiopie, Vol. 62. Italics mine.
17 Reffye to Minister, Addis Ababa, 8 Jan. 1932, d6, ibid.

nevertheless argued strongly that France's position ought to be maintained as
a bargaining chip in any future negotiations with Italy, so that Paris would
not "meet with a response from our neighbor that what we pretend to give
them in exchange [for their rights in Tunisia] no longer has value". He
foresaw negotiations because the Italians were implementing a hard line in
Ethiopia, and he knew the Quai would not counter "to the point of
compromising the peaceful relations between our two countries"[18].

Haile Sellassie and his close associates, most of them French-educated or
French-speaking, were made aware of Paris's alienation by the increasingly
melancholic and aloof Minister Reffye. They gradually came to realize that
French abandonment would leave the country open to Italian aggression, and
they therefore sought to restore the *status quo ante* by negotiating a Franco-
Ethiopian treaty of alliance, the provisions of which would resolve the
nagging economic questions. The legation received the *démarche* positively,
pleased that Haile Sellassie wanted to restore French primacy; but the Quai
d'Orsay spurned the offer, instructing Reffye to explain that it had abandoned
the idea of alliances in favor of arbitration and conciliation pacts under the
auspices of the League of Nations[19].

The minister was advised confidentially that France would undertake no
action in Ethiopia which would disrupt "the equilibrium of our general
policies and disturb England and Italy"; neither did it seek another entangling
alliance; nor did it want to invest scarce resources in a country governed "so
capriciously by a self-serving oligarchy"[20]. When Reffye attempted to marshal
a loan for Ethiopia to purchase weapons and to pursue Haile Sellassie's
ambitious road-building scheme and to arrange a duty-free-zone in Jibuti,
neither Paris nor the protectorate government were willing to cooperate.
Finally, when the emperor desperately asked for a secret treaty guaranteeing
Ethiopia's independence, the Quai d'Orsay flatly refused[21]. Thus, mid-1932
is the time when France really abandoned Ethiopia to the Italians, a fact
which when sensed, sent Addis Ababa scrambling for support in London,

---

18 Reffye to Minister, Addis Ababa, 9 Nov., 1932, d222, AQO, K-Afrique, Correspondance
Générale politique, Vol. 59.

19 Reffye to Minister, Addis Ababa, 9 March, 1932, c38-41; 16 March 1932, d65; 14 April
1932, c70; and Military attaché, "Étude sommaire du refus ou de l'acceptation des offres
d'alliance faites par l'Ethiopie à la France, Addis Ababa, 5 April 1932, AQO, K-Afrique",
Projet d'alliance entre la France et l'Ethiopie, Vol. 62.

20 Tardieu to Reffye, Paris, 2 May 1932, c55-60, ibid.

21 Reffye to Minister, Addis Ababa, 13 May 1932, d111; Reffye to minister, 24 May 1932,
c108-09; and Tardieu to Reffye, Paris, 26 May 1932, c76, ibid. Also AQO, K-Afrique,
France-Ethiopie, Projet d'alliance entre la France et l'Etiopie Vol. 63.

Washington, and Tokyo, and which stimulated Rome to undertake the forward policy which led to the Italo-Ethiopian War of 1935-36.

There were, of course, other reasons for the Italian shift. Since 1914, when Addis Ababa had massed troops on the Eritrean border, to exploit Italy's presumed entry into the war as one of the Central Powers, Rome had developed a paranoic fear of an Ethiopian attack on its colonies[22]. Consequently, when in 1931-32, the emperor moved into the Ogaden in force—to establish garrisons, to assert Addis Ababa's sovereignty, and to counter infiltration from Italian Somaliland—Rome's latent fears revived and authorities became hypersensitive about colonial security. Besides, Italian policy in Ethiopia was in disarray: the vaunted Dessie-Assab route, as previewed in the 1928 Italo-Ethiopian Treaty of Friendship and Arbitration[23], was real only on surveyors' maps; and instead of paramountcy in the Ethiopian economy, another object of the 1928-agreement, Italians were becoming less important and were even being excluded from participating in development projects. Since profits and primacy were lacking, the Italian plenipotentiary, Marquise Gaetano Paterno, sought new instructions in light of his warning that Haile Sellassie's policies were succeeding in creating a strong Ethiopian state.

However limited Ethiopian development was between 1928, when Tafari became king, and 1935, when the crisis intervened, it was impressive to Italians in Ethiopia, Eritrea, and Somaliland, who knew and understood African problems. They watched the Solomonic state begin to establish a national highway system radiating from Addis Ababa, where the emperor was paving roads, building the city's first electoral plant, and improving tele-communications to the provinces and the world. They observed the promotion of modern fiscal and administrative practices in the central government by an increasing number of educated young returnees. The onlookers also beheld the arrival of European military and police officers who were to train a modern army and constabulary. And in 1931, they read with interest Ethiopia's liberal-bourgeois, Japanese-style constitution which established a two-house consultative legislature.

These strong assertions of centralized power were capped in 1931-32, by Addis Ababa's categorical assumption of power over hitherto semi-autonomous Gojjam and Jimma. In other provinces, Haile Sellassie degraded

---

22 For an excellent example, see Roberto Cimmaruta, *Ual Ual* (Milan, 1936), 48; Esmonde M. Robertson also makes this point in *Mussolini as Empire-Builder* (London, 1977), p. 28.

23 Giuseppe Vedovato, "Gli Accordi Italo-Etiopici dell'agosto 1828", *Rivista di Studi Politici Internazionali*, XXII (1955).

traditional authority by interjecting crown officials into the process of administration, nowhere more marked than in the frontier province of Tigre, where Ras Seyoum lost control over customs revenues. Finally, Addis Ababa began to establish government schools, post offices, and hospitals in the provinces, although often he used missionaries, even Italians, to finance and staff them [24]. Thus, in Rome, on 21 January 1932, Paterno, the ministers of foreign affairs and colonies, and other high functionaries could warn Mussolini that:

> The progressive strengthening of the [Ethiopian] Empire as a unitary state and the able foreign policy of the Emperor, which aims *inter alia* to establish economic relations with the Americans and the Japanese, not only dismisses the possibility by the shaping of an internal situation which would permit us to benefit ultimately from ... our policy in Ethiopia, but also represents the establishment of a threat, today only potential, tomorrow perhaps developed, towards our East African Colonies, territories which are considered by the Ethiopians as *terrae irridentae*.

The co-authors were also quick to point out that Ethiopia had abandoned its reliance upon France, a change which might make Paris more receptive to overtures from Rome [25].

In a subsequent memorandum, Paterno observed that only strong measures would stop the erosion of the Italian position. Such a course of action:

> necessarily presupposes the preparation of an Italo-European diplomatic situation such as to permit us at the right time to create or provoke the *casus* which might allow us also to confront the Abyssinian question internationally .... A program, which presupposes a strong policy, while today an essentially political program, inevitably becomes in its execution an essentially military program [26].

The arch-imperialist Raffaele Guariglia, undersecretary in the foreign ministry, agreed, since he considered that all great nations needed colonies and that obtaining them was unfortunately bloody but necessary business [27]. Developing his ideas, the undersecretary stressed that "Ethiopia was being civilized, armed, and united through the exceptional ability of the present

24 Marcus, "Infrastructure", passim.
25 Relazione per sua eccelenza il Capo del Governo, Rome, 12 Jan 1932, Archivio Storico of the Ministero degli Affari Esteri, Serie Affari Politici, 1931-35, busta 21.
26 Paterno, Schematico Riassunto della Situazione Etiopica, 19 Aug. 1932, ibid., busta 6.
27 Relazione Guariglia, 19 Feb. 1932, ibid, busta 13. After World War II, he wrote that, even in light of subsequent events, he would not change one comma of the memo, and, to his death, he remained an unrepentent imperialist. See R. Guariglia *Riccordi, 1922-1946* (Naples, 1950), p. 50.

emperor ... [Thus] for us he represents an increasingly grave obstacle and a threat to our colonies". He observed that even if colonial expansion were not a consideration, the menace of Haile Sellassie had to be eliminated. Realistically, however, he cautioned that the Ethiopian question could not be resolved without France's agreement; while London's acquiescence was important, an abortive 1925-agreement already had demonstrated Britain's willingness at least to concede economic primacy in return for guarantees concerning Nile sources and affluents in Ethiopia [28].

As for Paris, alienation from Ethiopia and the paramountcy of France's security in Europe already were working in Italy's favor. In July 1931, conversations in France between Foreign Ministers Dino Grandi and Pierre Laval convinced Guariglia that the Quai d'Orsay was leaning toward the idea of permitting Rome "a free hand" over most of Ethiopia, in return for Italy's special rights in Tunisia [29]. Thus, the logic of the identical memoranda of 1928 and 1931 dominated the course of events in the Horn of Africa. Ironically, Ethiopia was largely responsible for helping to bring its own house down, although Haile Sellassie could never have foreseen that his efforts to modernize his nation and to broaden its international and economic relations would cause France drastically to alter its policy toward Addis Ababa.

In light of the proceeding analysis, it is reasonable to argue that between midnight and 1:00 AM on 7 January 1935, Pierre Laval implemented a new but cleverly calculated French policy in regard to Rome's aspirations in Ethiopia. In return for relatively unimportant Italian concessions in Tunisia and strategic cooperation in Europe—the real aim of Laval's machinations— the Frenchman sacrificed inconsequential interests in Ethiopia to the point of abandoning the Solomonic state to fascism. Subsequent protestations that he had merely conceded economic primacy to Italy boil down to sophistry; primary responsibility for Ethiopia's abandonment must be given to anonymous officials in the Quai d'Orsay, who, after 1928, considered France's diminishing interests in Ethiopia logically expendable, a hostage to European national and geo-political needs.

---

28 Relazione Guariglia sull'Etiopia, 27 Aug. 1932, ASEA, Serie Affari politici, busta 13. Concerning the 1925 Anglo-Italian Agreement, See Antoinette Ladgarola, "The Anglo-Italian Agreement of 1925: Mussolini's 'carte blanche' for War Against Ethiopia", *Northeast African Studies*, 1, 1, (1979).

29 Renzo de Felice, *Mussolini, il Duce, Gli Anni del Consenso*, (Turin, 1974), p. 397-98. Grandi to Mussolini; 25 July 1931, Archivo Centrale de stato, Rome, Grandi Papers, F3/SF2; Tyrrell to Henderson, Paris, 1 Aug. 1931, FO371/15255. I want to express my thanks to Peter C. Kent of the University of New Brunswick for having made these items available to me.

OBI: AN HEROIC GURAGE PRAISE CHANT

William A. Shack
University of California, Berkeley

This praise-chant, known as *wäyäg*, is typical of secular chants composed about chiefs, famous warriors, and other prominent tribesmen, whose heroic deeds have become legendary in the history of the tribe. *Wäyäg* compositions are intended to glorify the clan or tribe through its warrior-heroes, whose collective achievements have assured the group's independence, or enabled it to extend hegemony over other clans or tribes. This style of *wäyäg* is to evoke imagery of warriors ambling astride their favorite war-horses, galloping into battle, then attacking the enemy, and finally retreating and celebrating victory.

> Obi, gəbarahä sänäfwim!
> le yäšäraem alläfwim;
> eyasra yäḴwäṭäre alläfwim;
> Ḵwäṭär täḴwänčače alläfwim;
> 5 Yabḵəl täDesänä alläfwim;
> ahäm badäghwän žäng tänäfwim;
>   Zəme Čäha čanom alläfwim;
> ahäm badäghwän žäng tänäfwim.
>   Həme Ənor wawəm alläfwim;
> 10 Ənor yaməst wärär gälläfwim!
>   Näne Gwäməyä kwänäm alläfwim;
> Gwäməyä bira ṭäfər gälläfwim!
>   Ġəma Kella wärəm alläfwim;
> Kella bira ṭäfər gälläfwim!
> 15   Obi, gəmbarahä sänäfwim!
> häče Mwähər wärəm alläfwim;
> Mwähər bira ṭäfər gälläfwim!
>   Obi, gəmbarahä sänäfwim!
> oy, səma gänä!
> 20 səma säbat gänä:
> Mäṭär bäDesanä,
> kəra däDäbanä,
> bahä mwan ammwanä?

mwanäm säbat gänä!
25 Čäha Mwägämänä;
Ġəgär Tärgus dänä.
Gwəra, Danfwa mwanä;
Amya, Gäma mwanä.
Nəgwəs Naǧi mwanä;
30 Ato Šəkur mwanä.
 əšta mər yəbräma?
bahuš angäbanä!
 Zärma bokyär käta,
ete nəgäbanä?
35 kätam məzämäzäm,
ete nəgäbanä?
 Säbo billatänä!
yägaz billatänä!
yarəb ṭäbätänä!
40 säfär tigäwe,
yäsrat billatänä!
bägän yəzräkwi ḳar,
zəkka yayo dänä!
 Wəbra be täčänä?
45 Žäp be täčänä?
borba bagaz dänä!

Obi: An Heroic Gurage Praise Chant

Oh Obi[1], your face inspired fear!
Thanks to you, they passed through[2] Šärar[3];
they passed through Ḳwäṭär[4];
they passed through Ḳwäṭär and Ḳwänčača[5];
5 they passed through Abḳəl and Desänä[6];

---

1 Obi, the principal hero of this praise chant.
2 The impersonal phrase "they passed through" refers to the soldiers under Obi's command who, according to legend, are said to have pillaged village after village in war campaigns.
3 Šärar, the dominant political clan in Äža. Here the clan's name is used to refer to the entire tribal district.
4-5 Two major clans of the Čäha tribe.
6 I am unable to identify these place names.

they were saved by the bridge[7] you built.
  Here in Čäha they also passed through;
they were saved by the bridge you built.
  There in Ǝnor they also passed through;
10 Ǝnor was whipped[8] five times!
  Up there in Gwämära[9] they also passed through;
Gwämära was whipped with raw leather!
  They passed through Kella in Ǧǝmma[10];
Kella was whipped with raw leather!
15 Oh Obi, your face inspired fear!
They passed through, way up there in Mwähǝr[11];
Mwähǝr was whipped with raw leather!
  Oh Obi, your face inspired fear!
Yes, listen oh country[12]!
20 Listen all the seven countries:
In Mäṭär, in Desänä[13];
up there in Däbanä;
was there anyone not jealous of thee?
The seven countries were jealous of thee!
25 Čäha and Mwägämänä[14];
  Ǧǝgär and Yärgusdan[15].

---

7 The praising of Obi in lines 1-6 as a great military strategist is underscored in the phrase "saved by the bridge", *badäghwän*, lit. "by the passage which you cleared". This alludes to the fighting manœuvre of deploying soldiers to form a phalanx to break through the enemy's defence, i.e., to build a bridge over which the army can pass.

8 "whipped" here means "subdued", not military defeat.

9 Gwämärä, one of the politically autonomous clans of Čäha, has often been mistakenly listed by writers as a "tribe", perhaps because Gwämärä forms a distinct dialect group of the Western Gurage languages. See W. Leslau, *Ethiopic Documents: Gurage* (1950), p. 11.

10 This line is perhaps a gross exaggeration of Obi's military exploits, implying that he led an army against the Kella, of the Ǧǝmma Galla (Oromo) kingdom in southwestern Ethiopia. Kella is not identified as one of the clans of Ǧǝmma in G. W. B. Huntingford, *The Galla of Ethiopia* (1955), E. Haberland, *Galla Süd-Athiopiens* (1963), or H. S. Lewis, *A Galla Monarchy* (1965).

11 Mwähǝr is the northernmost of the Western Gurage grouping.

12 Lines 19-20: the common oratorical form used when addressing one's self to a tribal body; thus "seven countries" (*säbat gänä*) here means the "seven houses of Gurage".

13 The place names in line 21 cannot be identified; Däbana (line 22) perhaps refers to a district in eastern Äža.

14 Mwägämänä: a politically dominant clan in Čäha.

15 Major lineages of the Mwägämänä clan. See W. Shack, *The Gurage: A People of the Ensete Culture* (1966); W. Shack and H-M. Marcos, *Gods and Heroes: Oral Traditions of the Gurage of Ethiopia* (1974).

In Gwəra, Danfwa was envious[16];
in Aməya, Gäma was envious[17].
King Naǧi was envious[18];
30 Ato Šəkur was envious.
    What do women say?
We do not want you to marry us!
    Men trembled in their wəkyär[19],
saying where shall we hide?
35 They were trembling and trembling,
saying where shall we hide?
    Oh was he knowledgeable!
What a war tactician!
What a wager of battle!
40 And when in towns[20],
what knowledge of law!
and in tribal assemblies,
what a wise judge!
    Who begot this brave?
45 Who begot this lion?
The brave *Agaz*[21]!

16 Gwəra: a maximal lineage district of the Mwägämänä.

17 Aməya: the same as n. 15, 16 above. Gäma is not identified.

18 Lines 29-30: Naǧi of Gwəra died in Eyand, a village near Yäbrite, during the Italian occupation of Ethiopia. His son, Zägra, a guerilla fighter noted for his bravery and heroics, led the raid which sacked the Italian Catholic mission in Əmdəbər. He was subsequently captured and executed. Ato Šəkur (line 30) perhaps refers to *Balambaras* Šəkur of Aməya.

19 Customarily, men of the village congregate nightly in small groups, meeting in each homestead in turn, for discussion of common concerns. These informal gatherings are called *wəkyär*. See Shack, 1966, op. cit., pp. 43-4.

20 *säfär*, an Amharic loan word, is here translated as "towns". The specific meaning, "military camp", fails to convey the essence of the word's usage in this and the next line - 41.

21 *Agaz*: the highest military title a warrior could earn signified that the enemies killed numbered at least one hundred. When warfare was rife most Gurage chiefs had this honorific title bestowed upon them for conspicuous bravery. However, the *Agaz* referred to in this line is the father of the hero, Obi. On political status associated with military titles see Shack, 1966, *op. cit.*, pp. 155-7; Shack and Marcos, 1974.

LE MARIAGE ÉTHIOPIEN D'ARNAULD D'ABBADIE

Joseph Tubiana
Laboratoire Peiresc, CNRS

Préparant en 1955 la publication du «Journal de voyage» d'Antoine d'Abbadie [1] j'y découvrais la note suivante:

«La dot d'une dame veuve de rang wäyzäro qu'on proposa à mon frère dans le Gojam comprenait: terres patrimoniales donnant 50 tchan (40 hectolitres) de blé; 2. bestiaux; 3. une mule; 4. selle ornée de cuir rouge; 4. [sic] 3 ou 4 esclaves; 5. 10 filles et 5 à 6 domestiques mâles; 6. un eunuque; 7. parasol; 8. bourriques de charge; 9. alga et son cuir; 10. bagues et bracelets en argent et en corne; 11. mäntaves; 12. quelques wantcha; 13. corne pour le tädj; 14. qöl pour id.; 15. faucille; 16. 2 chemises, 3 kwaré, une paire de pantalons pour la mule, qu'on ne lave jamais; 17. vase travaillé en paille pour le beurre à oindre la tête tous les matins; 18. rasoir pour l'öms; 19. bournous blanc; 20. paire de souliers qui durent 6 à 7 ans; 20 [sic] peigne en argent à trois dents; 21. sait faire le chero, du vulnéraire, guérit des malades, et fait engraisser n'importe quel homme en moins de deux mois» [2].

Je n'ai jusqu'ici retrouvé nulle part ailleurs d'allusion à ce projet de mariage et ignore s'il fut suivi d'effet; mais la pudeur de mise à l'époque fait que nous ne sommes guère informés sur la vie amoureuse d'Arnauld d'Abbadie en Éthiopie, pas plus d'ailleurs que sur celle de James Bruce avant lui par exemple. Or l'édition des papiers inédits d'Arnauld d'Abbadie à laquelle se consacre Madame Jeanne-Marie Allier [3] lui a permis d'entrer en relations avec les descendants du voyageur français, dont elle reçut des informations intéressantes qu'elle a eu l'obligeance de me communiquer.

---

1 Laquelle publication ne put avoir lieu, l'éditeur s'étant dérobé sans préavis.

2 Cf. Fragments du *Journal de Voyage* d'Antoine d'Abbadie, présentés et annotés par Joseph Tubiana, *Cahiers de l'Afrique et l'Asie*, V, 1959, p. 319. «Wäyzäro» signifie noble; ce terme s'appliquait aussi bien aux hommes qu'aux femmes à l'époque. Un «alga» est un lit; le «cuir» est une peau de bœuf tannée tenant lieu de matelas. Les «mäntaves» sont des tapis. Un «wantcha» est un gobelet de corne. Le «tädj», c'est l'hydromel, transporté dans des grandes cornes de bœuf ou de buffle. Une «qöl» est un récipient fait d'une gourde évidée. Le «kwaré» est une toge de coton blanche à bande rouge. «öms» désigne le sexe féminin. Le «chero» est une bouillie de farines mêlées de légumineuses diverses.

3 Arnauld d'Abbadie, *Douze ans de séjour dans la Haute-Éthiopie (Abyssinie)*. Réédition anastatique du t. I et première édition du t. II. Città del Vaticano, Biblioteca Apostolica Vaticana, 1980. Le t. III est actuellement en cours d'impression.

Selon la tradition familiale Arnauld d'Abbadie aurait contracté mariage en Éthiopie avec une femme de l'aristocratie du nom de Wålättä-Rufa'el, parente (peut-être une cousine) du däǧazmač Gʷošu qui, on s'en souvient, régnait sur le Godjam à l'époque[4]. Était-ce cette veuve dont Antoine décrit quelque peu malicieusement la dot et les talents?

Toujours selon la tradition familiale, Arnauld aurait eu deux enfants de ce mariage éthiopien: un garçon et une fille. Cette dernière, Maïten de Kaizowane, aurait été emmenée par son père à Beyrouth, pour y être éduquée par des religieuses. Elle y mourut prématurément et y est enterrée. Pourquoi au Liban? Arnauld y avait, semble-t-il, des relations qui mériteraient d'être éclaircies[5]. Il y a, parmi les papiers déposés à la Bibliothèque Vaticane, quelques feuillets consacrés aux grandes familles du Liban, qui contiennent peut-être des informations intéressantes pour le spécialiste.

Quant au garçon, prénommé Mikaël (comme son père), il fut laissé à sa mère éthiopienne. Arnauld, ou Mikaël, comme il se faisait appeler en

---

4 «Pendant son long séjour là-bas il s'était marié avec une indigène, parente de Dedjatz Guocho et qui se nommait Welleta-Rafael.», Mémoires inédits de Madame Angèle de Lasteyrie du Saillant, fille d'Arnauld.

5 Lorsqu'il rentre en France en compagnie de son frère Charles, fin 1848, Arnauld emmène avec lui sa fille. Il s'arrête à Beyrouth et y confie l'enfant aux Sœurs de Saint Vincent de Paul pour qu'elle soit élevée «en catholique et en française». La date de 1853, retenue par la tradition familiale pour la remise de la petite fille au couvent de Beyrouth, contredit cette information. Elle est vraisemblable, en ce sens qu'on voit mal le couvent recevoir un bébé d'un an ou deux à peine, tandis qu'en 1853 la petite fille doit avoir environ six ans. Mais alors on doit se demander ce qui s'est passé entre temps: depuis la sortie d'Éthiopie cinq ans s'étaient écoulés. L'année suivante, en décembre 1864, Arnauld épouse Elisabeth West Young.
Arnauld avait dû mettre sa future femme au courant, puisque leur fille Angèle écrit dans ses Mémoires inédits: «Ma mère serait aussi heureuse qu'une petite Maïten lui serait confiée un jour, mais elle ne l'a jamais connue. Très vite après leur mariage la jeune fille mourut et mes parents s'occupèrent ensemble de la tombe qui fut commandée et existe encore à Beyrouth. Deux de mes frères ont eu l'occasion de se la faire indiquer par une religieuse qui avait connue l'enfant Éthiopienne et l'inscription portait: Maïten de Kaizowane». (Faut-il supposer Kesrouan?) Pourquoi la jeune fille ne portait-elle pas le nom de son père? Toujours selon sa fille, à partir de 1855, après son second voyage en Éthiopie, Arnauld était plus attiré par l'Orient que par Paris: «il séjourna plusieurs fois au Caire ou à Beyrouth chez les frères Riskallah et Dominique Khadra. C'est là qu'il se lia avec un célèbre maronite, Joseph Kharam. Celui-ci était l'âme de la révolte qui eut lieu dans le Liban contre les Druses en 1860». La jeune Maïten mourut, dit la tradition familiale, à l'âge de dix-huit ans, peu après le second mariage de son père, alors que la nouvelle Madame Arnauld d'Abbadie avait l'intention de la faire venir en France pour s'occuper d'elle. Si son décès remonte à 1865 elle serait née vers 1847, et c'est ainsi que nous avons supputé qu'elle avait dû quitter l'Éthiopie à l'âge d'un ou deux ans au plus.

Éthiopie, ayant conçu de sérieux doutes sur la fidélité de sa femme, était convaincu que cet enfant n'était pas son fils et ne voulut jamais le reconnaître. Il ne s'en occupa pas [6]. La fille était l'aînée des deux.

La réalité de ce mariage éthiopien ne peut faire de doute. En effet, lorsqu'Arnauld voulut épouser la jeune américaine Elizabeth West Young, il prit soin de s'assurer de la nullité de son premier mariage [7]. Cela suffit à prouver l'importance juridique et religieuse qu'il attachait à ce mariage, dont on ignore dans quelles formes il fut contracté [8].

[6] La fille d'Arnauld écrit: «Il arriva qu'au retour d'une de ses campagnes certains confidents, ou malveillants ou avertis, lui révélèrent que le fils de Welleta-Rafael n'était pas le sien. Cette délation devait se terminer par une rupture. Welleta eut beau se défendre contre ce qu'elle jurait être une calomnie, mon père refusa d'accepter le petit Mikaël comme son fils. Il le laisserait à sa mère et emporterait au loin sa fille. Ayant juré avec solennité qu'elle n'était pas coupable, Welleta-Rafael mit toute sa maison en deuil et se fit raser ses cheveux, comme font seules les veuves suivant l'usage du pays».

[7] C'est du moins ce qui a été dit à Madame Allier. Mais peut-être n'est-on pas allé jusqu'à Rome. En effet Angèle d'Abbadie a écrit: «Mon père avait lui-même pensé qu'un sérieux obstacle l'empêchait de faire une demande en mariage puisqu'il s'estimait marié. C'est le père Olivaint qui décida à ce sujet et lui enleva toute hésitation». Il s'agit du jésuite qui fut fusillé par la Commune.

[8] Monsieur Salvatore Tedeschi, qui a bien voulu relire cet article me communique les observations suivantes: «Ce mariage devait être, sauf erreur, un mariage *mixta religio* et non pas *disparitas cultus*». En droit canon actuel, le mariage est assujetti à des «conditions», ou «obstacles», ou «empêchements». On distingue des conditions *dirimentes* («dirimantes») et des conditions *impedientes* («empêchantes»). Les premières sont plus graves. a) Les *dirimentes* sont celles qui enlèvent ou annulent à la racine toute volonté au mariage et le rendent *invalidus* (non valide, nul depuis le début). Parmi ces *dirimentes* il y a la *cultus disparitas* (différence de religion) c'est-à-dire le mariage entre une personne baptisée dans l'église catholique et une personne non baptisée. b) Les *impedientes* sont celles qui, tout en s'opposant en principe au mariage, ne le rendent pas *invalidus* si elles sont violées (le mariage est *illicitus*, mais pas nul); parmi ces conditions il y a la *mixta religio* c'est-à-dire le mariage entre une personne catholique et une personne appartenant à une secte hérétique ou schismatique (une personne non catholique mais chrétienne). On peut donc aisément obtenir (sous certaines conditions) une dispense de respecter une condition *impediens*; en l'absence de la dispense, le mariage n'est pas *invalidus* mais simplement *illicitus*; il peut donc être *sanatus* par la suite, c'est-à-dire régularisé; la *sanatio*, «régularisation», le rend parfait avec effet rétroactif *ab initio*, c'est-à-dire depuis le jour de la célébration. Quand le droit canon parle d'un mariage *illicitus* à cause de *mixta religio* il se réfère en principe à un mariage célébré par un prêtre catholique. Cette règle cependant souffre plusieurs exceptions; en particulier le droit canon reconnait comme étant simplement *illicitus* le mariage *mixta religio* d'un catholique célébré dans certains pays d'Orient par un ministre d'un culte chrétien; le cas le plus fréquent et le plus connu est celui du mariage d'un catholique célébré en Orient par un prêtre orthodoxe (Grèce, Turquie, etc.) mais il y en a d'autres (il existe une jurisprudence ample, touffue et ... souvent variable). Ce mariage n'est donc pas *invalidus*.

Pour en venir à notre cas, j'ignore quelle était la jurisprudence vers le milieu du XIXe

Retrouver la trace en Éthiopie de ce fils réel ou supposé d'Arnauld d'Abbadie apparait comme quasiment impossible, compte-tenu de l'usage éthiopien de désigner une personne par son prénom suivi (parfois précédé) de celui de son père. À la troisième génération on ne sait plus qui est qui. Le nom du grand-père a disparu.

Je n'avais aucun espoir de découvrir de nouvelles informations sur ce garçon lorsque le hasard, plus d'un an après ces révélations, me favorisa. Mon savant ami Salvatore Tedeschi attirait mon attention sur l'ouvrage assez rare d'un voyageur français, le capitaine Alexandre Girard, qui voyagea au Tigré dans les années 1868-1869[9], et me montrait à Rome l'exemplaire qui était entre ses mains, lorsque le feuilletant je tombais sur le récit d'un repas offert à Girard par le botaniste Schimper, qui s'était fixé en Éthiopie:

«Parmi les convives se trouvait un jeune homme de seize à dix-huit ans, dont le teint était presque blanc; c'était le fils d'un Européen dont le nom est célèbre parmi les explorateurs de l'Abyssinie. Ce jeune homme, nommé Ouold-Mikael, avait de très bonnes manières; il se ressentait de son origine; il me semblait que j'allais l'entendre me parler français, tellement sa pensée se peignait lisiblement dans ses yeux. Pauvre jeune homme! son père est rentré en Europe, et ne s'occupe plus de lui».

Reprenons l'information: le père de ce jeune métis est un Français, d'excellente famille, explorateur de l'Éthiopie *célèbre en 1868*. Il a abandonné son fils lorsqu'il est reparti pour l'Europe, *avant 1868*. Le garçon se nomme Wäldä Mikael, ce qui est plus normal en Éthiopie que Mikael tout court, mais Mikael peut s'employer seul (cf. le fameux Ras Mikael du Tigré); l'expression guèze signifie «fils de Saint Michel» mais littéralement peut se comprendre, par jeu de mots, «fils de Michel».

Est-ce le fils d'Arnauld d'Abbadie? Cela est bien possible, mais son âge fait problème. En effet Arnauld-Mikael a quitté l'Éthiopie vers la fin de 1848; son fils devrait avoir une vingtaine d'années. Peut-être Girard n'a-t-il pas évalué correctement l'âge du jeune homme: plutôt 18 à 20 ans que 16 à 18? Il

siècle et nous ignorons dans quelles formes a été célébré le mariage éthiopien d'Arnauld. Dès lors surgit une question: Arnauld a-t-il vraiment fait valoir à Rome l'argument de la *mixta religio* (mariage d'un catholique avec une schismatique éthiopienne)? N'est-il pas plus probable qu'il a demandé une véritable déclaration de nullité de son mariage éthiopien en invoquant la violation d'un des très nombreux (il y en a une quinzaine) empêchements connus par le droit canon?».

9 Capitaine Alexandre Girard, *Souvenirs d'un voyage en Abyssinie (1868-1869)*, Le Caire, Librairie Nouvelle Ebner, 1873. Cf. Fumagalli, n. 316. Le passage cité se trouve p. 235. La Bibliothèque de l'École des Langues Orientales, 4 rue de Lille, à Paris, possède un exemplaire de l'ouvrage.

est toujours très difficile d'évaluer l'âge de quelqu'un et en particulier des jeunes Éthiopiens qui paraissent souvent plus jeunes que leur âge.

Arnauld est revenu en Éthiopie vers 1850 ou 1851, la date est imprécise [10]. A-t-il franchi le Täkkäze? Sa fille Angèle dit que oui, mais Arnauld semble bien dire que non (cf. *carte* 15, f. 810-811): «Les miens — dit Arnauld — avaient exigé de moi au moment de mon départ de France une promesse de ne pas traverser volontairement le fleuve du Tacazzé». Est-il allé seulement jusqu'au bord du fleuve, sans le traverser? Il a pu de toute façon se rendre chez Schimper à Adoua à l'aller ou sur le chemin du retour. C'est la route. A-t-il revu sa femme au cours de ce voyage? celle-ci pouvait se trouver au Tigré, ou s'y être rendue spécialement.

Parlons un peu de Schimper. Le naturaliste allemand est entré en Éthiopie en 1837. Il y est mort, à Adoua, en octobre 1874. Il a eu largement le temps de connaître les frères d'Abbadie, arrivés peu de temps après; leurs relations ont pu se resserrer lorsque Schimper se convertit au catholicisme en 1843. Il épousa ensuite une Éthiopienne, catholique elle aussi [11]. Son foyer était donc un foyer mixte. On lui attribue quinze enfants, métis, comme les enfants d'Arnauld. Après le départ de son mari, la femme d'Arnauld était-elle allée attendre son retour auprès des Schimper? Lorsque le refus d'Arnauld de reconnaître son fils lui fut signifié, n'a-t-elle pas préféré confier l'éducation du jeune métis aux Schimper, catholiques, chez qui il se trouvait moins isolé, que de s'en occuper elle-même?

Autant de questions qui risquent de rester à jamais sans réponse, mais qu'il faut bien se poser. Un autre aspect intéressant des choses, qui, lui, pourra sans doute être élucidé, c'est le rapport de Schimper avec les Saint-Simoniens. Il était venu en aide aux médecins français Petit et Quartin-Dillon, qui faisaient partie de la mission dirigée par Théophile Lefèbvre. Ce

---

10 Les Mémoires de Madame A. de Lasteyrie du Saillant situent ce retour en Éthiopie en l'année 1853. Arnauld a franchi le Täkkäze lorsqu'il apprend que G^wošu vient de périr dans la bataille qu'il livrait à Gur Amba au futur Théodore. Ce combat eu lieu le 27 novembre 1852, sauf erreur.

11 Au début du tome I^e des *Douze ans*, Arnauld parle de Schimper sans le nommer. Il y a six Européens à Adoua: un tailleur grec, un officier allemand, trois missionnaires protestants également allemands, entretenus par la Société biblique anglaise, et un naturaliste allemand, envoyé par une société scientifique de son pays (p. 6). Après l'ordre d'expulsion des missionnaires protestants, l'officier et le naturaliste sont également chassés. Cependant «à force d'instances, ce dernier obtint un sursis; il abjura ensuite le protestantisme, pour adopter la croyance eutychienne, et il vit encore dans le pays, où il s'est marié.» (p. 19). Wilhelm Schimper, si l'on en croit Arnauld, serait donc passé par l'orthodoxie avant d'être converti au catholicisme par Mgr De Jacobis. Schimper et Arnauld avaient en commun d'avoir vécu en Algérie.

dernier était selon toute vraisemblance adepte des thèses saint-simoniennes et les frères d'Abbadie, ardents catholiques, ne le portaient pas dans leur cœur. Alexandre Girard aussi devait être dans la mouvance saint-simonienne [12].

Toutes ces recherches de détail n'en constitueront pas moins des contributions utiles à l'histoire de l'exploration — et donc de la connaissance — de l'Éthiopie. Peut-être l'attention attirée sur le jeune Wäldä-Mikael permettra-t-elle de repérer des informations passées jusqu'ici inaperçues [13].

[12] Sur les Saints-Simoniens en Afrique du Nord on se reportera aux savants travaux de l'historien Marcel Emerit et, pour le sujet qui nous intéresse, à ses articles «Les explorations saint-simoniennes en Afrique Orientale et sur la route des Indes», (*Revue Africaine*, Alger, 1943, p. 93-116) et «Le premier projet d'établissement français sur la Côte des Somalis» (*Revue Française d'Histoire d'Outre-Mer*, 1963, p. 179-196). La faible compilation de Richard Pankhurst: «The Saint Simonians and Ethiopia», *Proceedings of the IIId International Conference of Ethiopian Studies*, t. I, Addis Ababa, 1969, p. 169-223, traite surtout des activités des voyageurs français Combes et Tamisier, dont elle résume longuement le récit de voyage. Madame Allier a découvert récemment qu'Arnauld avait des Saint-Simoniens dans ses relations. Algérie, Égypte, Levant, Éthiopie: autant de pays où Arnauld a vécu et où les Saint-Simoniens étaient actifs. Rappelons enfin que des lettres des frères d'Abbadie à des Saint-Simoniens se trouvent à la Bibliothèque de l'Arsenal et signalons encore l'article de M. Emerit «Diplomates et explorateurs saint-simoniens», (*Revue d'Histoire Moderne et Contemporaine*, 1975, p. 397-415).

[13] Les Saint-Simoniens, qui cherchaient la *Mère* en Orient, s'intéressaient donc aux femmes. Et si on essaie de préciser le regard qu'Arnauld posait sur les femmes, il est constant que les portraits qu'il en fait sont aussi détaillés que ceux qu'il a faits des hommes, mais son attention ne néglige jamais leur beauté. Par exemple: «Les femmes [de Moussawa], strictement voilées, sont souvent d'une rare beauté et d'une très grande élégance de formes.», *Douze ans*, t. I, p. 9-10. «Mon hôte, qui parlait un peu l'arabe, me pria de visiter sa femme malade. (...) Je ne pus rien comprendre à la maladie de mon hôtesse; je vis seulement qu'elle était jeune et remarquablement jolie ...», *ibid.*, t. I, p. 30-31. «... sur ces hauts plateaux l'on trouve plus fréquemment les femmes du teint clair, mat, légèrement doré, se rapprochant, comme il a été dit, du teint européen.», *ibid.*, t. I, p. 97. «Les femmes des kouallas passent pour être les plus jolies, les plus attrayantes et savoir se draper avec le plus de coquetterie dans la toge; leur éclat est précoce, mais peu durable; leur accortise, la beauté de leur regard, la gracieuse souplesse de leur démarche, la perfection de leurs formes et la mobilité de leur caractère justifient, du reste, la jalousie proverbiale de leurs maris. Les femmes des deugas, plus grandes, plus fortes, sont moins avenantes, moins gracieuses, moins fécondes, dit-on, mais plus laborieuses, plus économes, moins fantasques et plus soumises; belles plutôt que jolies, elles passent pour exercer des séductions moins entraînantes que les femmes des kouallas, mais elles conquièrent dans la famille une prépondérance plus durable». *ibid.*, t. I, p. 99-100. «Ailleurs, apparait à mule, une femme tout enveloppée de sa toge: on ne voit d'elle que ses grands et beaux yeux; des suivants à pied l'entourent et pressent la marche, tant ils craignent la rencontre de quelque cavalier trop curieux.», *ibid.*, t. I, p. 107-108.

On pourrait multiplier les citations de ce genre (toujours dans le t. I: p. 193-194; 204-205; 273; 325; 412-419; 422; 435; 527; 556; 588; etc. etc.).

On a peine à se refuser d'admettre qu'Arnauld avait du goût pour les femmes. C'est lui-même qui note, en parlant de Bərru: «Il parlait religion, philosophie, guerre, poésie, chasse, médecine; d'amour fort peu.» (*ibid.*, I, p. 485).

C'est lui-même qui rapporte que lorsqu'il se présente au Ras Ali à Däbrä Tabor, celui-ci essaie de le retenir auprès de lui en lui disant: «Arrête-toi ici, vis avec moi; tu auras des chevaux, une femme, des pays à gouverner ...» (*ibid.*, t. I, p. 196). Même discours quelques années plus tard, tenu à Arnauld par le Däǧač Yasu: «Nous sommes moins beaux diseurs qu'en Godjam, mais tu trouveras parmi nous de fiers cavaliers capables d'amitié sincère, des hommes pleins de prud'homie, des femmes belles et de riants pays à gouverner.» (*id.*, t. III, inédit, ch. I).

Voilà ce qui pouvait séduire Arnauld.

ANTHROPOLOGY

GAMBO'S STORY — A MYTHICAL TRADITION
FROM MALE (S-W ETHIOPIA)

EIKE HABERLAND
Frobenius-Institut, Universität Frankfurt

Members of the Frobenius Institute travelled to visit the Male in 1950/51. Short reports have already appeared by Ad. E. Jensen on the social life and religion, by Elisabeth Pauli on the material culture and economy and by Willy Schulz-Weidner on the physical anthropology [1]. The results of Donald Donham's longer studies (he spent almost one year there in 1974/75) have unfortunately not been published yet.

The Male live on the southwestern edge of Ethiopia, where the cool, moist high plateaus finally plunge into the hot, dry savannas. Their general culture contains many elements that they share with other peoples to the west and northwest (Ari, Dime, Dizi etc.) which Ad. E. Jensen has designated "ancient peoples" [2]. This applies particularly to material property, with political structures strongly influenced by the Ometo peoples living to the east (e.g. the Kamba). In 1951 religious beliefs were still characterized by older ideas and traditions, of which the myth presented here is a vivid example.

The Male grow their crops on terraces and small fields hacked out of the bush. Their main crops are sorghum bicolor (mä'y), Zea maize (gombutso) and Eleusine coracana (barči), and include the cabbage tree (Moringa steneopetala, halako), typical of southern Ethiopian terrace cultivation. The climate is too dry for most of the other plants endemic to Ethiopia. Animal husbandry (cattle, fat-tailed sheeps and goats) also plays an important role.

In 1950/51 I tried over a short period of weeks to record the main features of the Male language in an unpublished study. The Male language belongs to the Ometo family of languages, but is—like the languages of the Tṣara, the Basketto group or the Oyda—far removed from Common Ometo, which is understood without difficulty by speakers from the Dauro people in the north to the Kamba in the south, and from the Dorze in the east to the Gofa in the west [3]. I cannot say with certainty whether the Marta, directly to the east of

---

[1] Ad. E. Jensen 1959, Elisabeth Pauli 1959, Willy Schulz-Weidner 1952.
[2] "Altvölker", cf. Haberland 1981, p. 123.
[3] Cf. Moreno 1938.

the Male, speak the same language, or whether their language resembles that of the Kamba.

The text reproduced here was dictated and explained to me in January, 1951 by Digga Eroka, a priest and wise man. (It was included in abridged form by Ad. E. Jensen in his Male report)[4]. I am giving it here in its original form because it is source material for a virtually unknown language[5]. It also provides interesting evidence that the religious beliefs of these "ancient peoples" also differ considerably from the common Ethiopian culture. Unfortunately, such examples of genuine "ancient" myths—Digga Eroka dictated a series of others to us—were already rare in south Ethiopia by the beginning of the Fifties, surviving only in stories of the supernatural origins and fates of the first priest-kings and dynastic founders[6]. This narration is, however, also extremely important because it presents a piece of mythical "reality" from another context; and because of the immediacy of its language, with its direct speech, unadorned view of right and wrong, and depth of feeling, giving us a marvelous insight into the character of this people.

The story is centered around a force which is seen by southern Ethiopian farmers as a supernatural power: the life-giving rain, on which men, animals and plants depend for their very existence. Rain sacrifices are accordingly the most important of all ceremonies. The hero of the myth is Gambo, a charismatic personality. Terribly humiliated and wronged by the chief, who should have been maintaining order but instead perpetrates a grave injustice, Gambo leaves his home in Male which, through his supernatural power, he brings to the brink of destruction by preventing rain. Famines, loss of livestock and harvest failures resulting from drought were not infrequent events in Ethiopia, extending up to the great famine in Wollo, which was a contributory cause in the overthrow of the last emperor. Such disasters were often attributed to the moral incapacity of the rulers to maintain a proper balance in the world. Gambo also demonstrates his charisma by his gift of the miraculous increase of grain and water to his friend Šade, and by his power over the snakes, the embodiments of fertility, the phallic principle, rain and sperm. When his secret is penetrated and the Male—represented by the elders and wise men—beg his forgiveness, he returns to his ruined farm and saves his people—again in a miraculous way. Then he retreats into private life and lives out his days as a normal man. It would seem that

---

4 In Jensen 1959, pp. 300 et seq.
5 Some vocabulary of the Male language can be found in Trento 1941.
6 So for example in Jensen 1959, pp. 35, 169 et seq, 297 et seq, 317.

Gambo belonged to a family that had lived in the region before the advent
of the usurping dynasty. Miraculous deeds, such as the increase of water,
preventing or causing rain, creating new springs by striking the ground or
rock with a stick (like Moses) figure frequently in southern Ethiopian
tradition[7]. However, such acts almost always represent the revelation of the
charisma of previously concealed miracle-workers, who are then generally
acclaimed and become rulers and founders of dynasties. In this way, the
myths serve to legitimate these rulers. Here, however, possession of charisma
does not affect political power. These are ideas—also met with among
neighbouring peoples—which do not link priesthood and power over nature
and the elements with political rule. Here we see the dominance of moral
and religious categories which are unknown to this exclusive degree in the
structures of the secular state, late arrivals in southern Ethiopia.

Text and Translation

Gambo-ko	tārik-kē[8]		Məna	kāti[9]	gaḍe[10]
Gambo's	story-is [this].		In old times	a chief	a ceremony

maǧäne.	Gaḍe	maǧao	iya-ko	wudurnay
he performed.	The ceremony	performing	him-with	girls

mizābi	lam'o	āni[11]	Lam'ontsi	kāti	kalallo
beautiful	two	were.	These two	[for] the chief's	tribute

maḍo	āni.	Iya	maḍo-ro	izata	ēkäne[12].
labour	were.	He	work-for	them	he employed.

Ēkazā			wola	hanti	maḍo		maḍäne.
After	he	employed [them]	together	going	[to the]	work	they worked.

7 Haberland 1975, pp. 30 et seq, Haberland 1983.

8 Here the Amharic word *tarik* has been taken over. Story is *haysi* in Male.

9 *Kāti* is the title given by the Ometo peoples to a chief, head of a people or king. Sago was
   the eighth *kāti* in a series of 17 chiefs which reaches up to the present day and begins with
   the mythical Maläka, who is supposed to have come from Bussa near Gidole and took the
   chieftainship from the Simari who had previously ruled in Male.

10 *Gaḍe* is a special sacrificial ceremony, about which nothing else was known.

11 I.e. Gambo had two very beautiful daughters.

12 Apparently they were helping erect a special fence around a holy place.

Maḍanti   kāti   na'ontsi   fugäne.[12a]
While they were working   the chief   [with] the girls   slept.

Fugazā   gobadäne.   Gobadazā,
After he slept [with them]   they became pregnant.   After they became

              kāti   gobasazā:
pregnant,   the chief   after he made them pregnant [he said[:

"Ači-gəda   šowuāse,   bāzi-da   kērwuāte!"[13]   Izi
"Country-in   they should not give birth,   river-into   throw!"   He

itṣi: "Ta na'o   kayka   kēra'a!"
refusing: "My children   [in] the wilderness   I don't throw!"

Hizi gē'y   nāto   harḳi   Banni[14]   dändäne.   Banni
thus saying   the children   taking   to Banna   he went.   To Banna

dändazā   ačo-da   ābi   ēḳäne[15].   Ābi   ēḳao
after he went   the country-over   the sun   stood.   The sun   after it

        ačo   kursäne: mä'y   baykäne,   ḳolmo
stood   the country   perished: sorghum   perished,   domestic animals

mäläne.   "Woytanday?"   gē'y,   nanganti.   Iya
died of thirst.   "What shall we do?"   saying,   they sat.   He

bēzo-do   watsi   āni[16].   Ḳolma   izasi   dändi
residence-at   water   was.   Domestic animals   his   since he went away

šoyntäne   kumäne.   Ḳolma   hayḳi
brought forth   [and] multiplied.   The animals [of the Male]   dying

---

12a f is always bilabial.

13 On the one hand illegitimate children are regarded as particularly shameful among a people which prizes virginity as highly as the Male do. These children were, however, doubly cursed as they had been begotten in a holy sacrificial place where all sexual acts were forbidden. Indeed, men who had very recently engaged in sexual acts could not stay in such places. Pregnant or menstruating women were also forbidden to come near a holy place. (The same tabu applied, incidentally, to chiefs and other "holy" men.) This is why the chief himself ordered that the children should be exposed.

14 The Banna are a people of livestock farmers living directly to the south of the Male in the Savanna. Gambo withdrew to the no-man's-land between Male and Banna.

15 I.e. it no longer rained.

16 Gambo was a rain-priest who had power over rain and could increase water.

kudäne.   Kudazā   bay   fätte   Šāde-ko [17]   āni.   Šāde-ko
perished.   While they perished   cow   one   Šāde-from   was.   Šāde-of

mara-fa   bay   dändäne   gūte.   Dändi   watsi   uški
house-from   the cow   went   in the morning.   Going   water   having

          mukäne.   Watso   uški   mukao,
drunk   it returned.   Water   having drunk [and]   having come back,

šeškäne.   Šežo   zagao: "Hanna   bay   aygo
it urinated.   The urine   having seen [Šade said]:   "This   cow   what

uški   šeḳay?"   Hatsa   lam'o   worḳao
having drunk   it urinates?"   Then   two [days]   having passed

dändäne.   Dändao   watsi   uškäne   mukäne   gəntsa.
it went [again].   Having gone   water   it drank [and]   it came   back.

Mukao   gūte   šeḳäne.   "Hanna   ba   aygo
Having come   in the mourning   it urinated.   "This   cow   which

watsi   wo-fa   deynḳi   uški   mukay?"   Hizi   gazā
water   where-from   finding [and]   drinking   it came?"   Thus   saying

gūte   fuḳa   uṅka   tukäne.
in the morning   a bunch [of straw]   [at] the tail [of the cow]   he bound.

Uṅka   tukao   gūte   kēskäne.   Dändäne
[At] the tail   after he bound   in the morning   he started.   He went

dändi gafao   fuḳo   kērao,   fuḳo
after he went a while   the straws   [the cow] after it let fall,   the straws

sa'a   kērazā   iza   zagi,   zagi,   dändi,
on the ground   after they fell   he   seeing,   seeing,   going,

hantante   hantante   Banni   gēläne.   Banni   gēlanto
he went [and]   he went   in Banna   he entered.   In Banna   after he

          izi   gəntso   bay'əlo   kobəsao   mukäne.
entered   he   behind   this cow   which had made tracks   he came.

Watso-woro [18]   gēläne.   Bay   uškante   gēläne.
Water-river   it entered.   The cow   while it drank   he entered [in the

17 Šade was an old friend of Gambo's.

18 *Woro* is the dry bed of a river, which becomes *watso*-("water") *woro* when it fills up in the rainy season. Even after the rainy season, pools remain in the river bed, forming important water-holes.

Ahari   ba'a   watsa   āni.   "Watso   tāna-fero
water too]. Then   the cow in the water   was.   "Water   myself-for

uške,   uške!"   Miškao   ahari   kēskäne.
I will drink, I will drink!" After being satisfied   then   he went out.

Boko-da   Gambo-ko   wāra   kumäne.   Gambo-ko   wāra   biya
Pasture-in Gambo's   goats   many were. Gambo's   goats   all

särkokē[19],   wāro   zagao: "Hay   Gambo
ear-marks [they had],   the goats   after he saw: "These   Gambo's

wāro   aygo   musē?"   Šauki   dē'äne: Gambo
goats   what   made them come [to here]?" A little   he rested: Gambo

mukäne! Mukazā   Šāde: "Nēna   ayge   musay?"
came   ! After he came [he asked] Šāde: "You   who   had brought?"

"Tṣosi   tāna   musäne."   Hizi   gene.   Äkki   fē-mārē
"God   me   brought [here]." Thus   he said. Now   to-the house

dändäne.   Fē-māra   dända'a,   āla   ušäne,
they went. To-the house after he went,   beer   he caused him to drink,

dagatsia ušäne.   Ziro   fēškäne,
mead[19a] he caused him to drink. The next day   he remained,

hinto   fēškäne,   haytso   iza   workäne.
the day after tomorrow   he remained,   three [days] he   he stayed.

Iza   hatsi   bälämo   naškäne   yekao[20]:
He   now   [to] the friend [whom] he loved   weeping [he said]:

"Ta   nātē   kudäne   ta aygo muzanday?"   Hizi   gene,
"My   children   perish   I what shall let them eat?" Thus   he said,

hizi gazao: mä'y   kōbōna   uçao   ingäne:
thus after he said: sorghum   a handful   scooping   he gave:

"ēki dändao,   tāna   kēzife!   Nē,   kēzeto,
"Taking [it] away,   of myself   don't tell! You,   if you will tell,

---

19 The Male clip their animals' ears as marks of ownership and as signs of sacrifice (cf. Pauli
   1959, ill. 45,2 et seq).
19a Mead is drunk only on very special occasions.
20 Gambo and Šade wept with emotion when they met and when they parted.

haykandane!"[21] Hizi gene.   Watso   gusi   nay
you will die!"   Thus he said.   Water   [in] a little gourd   [for] the

              ingäne[22],   ingao: "Hanno   watsälo   çoro
children   he gave,   after he gave [he said]:   "This   water   cistern

gədda   wahe!   Çoro   äto-da   wahe!   Çoro
in the middle   pour!   [In] the cistern   hole-in   pour!   [In] the cistern

wahao,   mä'ontsi   ōtō   fūfō   kolotsi-da
after you poured,   these sorghum [-grains]   a pot   big [and]   wide-in

wahe!   Haytso   workao   ōtō   karo   buli   zage!"   Hizi
pour!   Three [days]   waiting   pot   lid   opening   see!"   Thus

gene[23].   Mä'əla   kobono   wuçi   kolotsi-da   wahäne.
he said.   This sorghum   a handful   taking   wide-in [pot]   he poured.

Haytso   workäne.   Haytso   workazā: karo
Three [days]   he waited.   Three [days]   having waited: the lid

buläne,   karo   bulazā: ōtō   kumäne.   Ōtō
he opened,   the lid   after having opened: the pot   full was.   The pot

kumazā   watso   gusi   eki mukätsi
after it was full   water   [from] the gourd   [which] he had brought

çoro   wahäne: watsäla   šauko   guso
[in] the cistern   he poured: this water   [this] little   [from] the gourd

wahazā   watso   çoro   kumäne.   Ahari   watso
after he poured [it]   [this] water   the cistern   filled.   Now   water

uškäne.   Uški   nanganti.[24]   Mä'əlo   katsi
they drank.   Having drunk   they recovered.   Sorghum   cooked

muäne.   Ba'a   watso   uškäne.   Izata   atsi-ko   māra
they ate.   The cows   water   drank.   They   [in] the men's   house

uški   nanganti.   Kāti   māra   äläne: "Šade
drinking   they rested.   [In] the chief's   house   they called: "Šade

21 Curse.
22 The Male have cisterns in their farms of various sizes, often tidily lined and edged with
    stones (cf Jensen 1959, table 26,5).
23 Šade then returned home.
24 "They recovered, they gained new strength".

mä'y   muane!   mä'y   muane!" Izi kāti   māra-fa
sorghum   eats!   sorghum   he eats!" Him chief's   house-from

älätsi   atsi   musäne.   Mukäne.   Mukazā:
calling a man   caused [him] to come.   He came.   After he came [the

          "Šāde,   nē   mä'y   muane!"   "Ta   kāti,   mä'y
chief said]: "Šāde,   you   sorghum   eat!"   "My   chief,   sorghum

muwāsē!"   "Nē   mä'y   muane!"   "Ē'e kātiyo   muwāse;
I did not eat!" "You   sorghum   eat!"   "No o chief I did not eat;

mä'y   ayga-fa   deynḳi   muanday?"   Hizi   gene.
sorghum   where-from   finding   should I eat?"   Thus   he said.

"Čaḳe!"   "Ēy'e,   ta   muwuāse   kāti   hayḳo!"[25] gene.
"Swear!"   "No,   I   did not eat [by] the chief's   death!"   he said.

Hizi   gazā   bay   šukäne.   Aško   iza
Thus   after he said   a cow   he [the chief] slaughtered. The meat   him

muzäne[26].   Aško   muzi gafao,   kafäne[27]:
he made eat.   The meat   after having made [him] eat,   he watched:

"Manni[28]   kafuwāte!"   hizi gene.   Hatsa   rori   gǝntsa
"Potters   watch [him]!" thus he said. Now   the day   following

lam'i   muzäne.   Šio   arḳäne.
twice   he made [him] eat. [The urge to] defecate   seized [him].

Šio   arḳazā   kayzi-da   aḍäne.
After [the urge] to defecate   had seized [him]   bush-in   he went.

Aḍazā   gǝntso   kafäne.   Kafanti
After he went   again   they watched [him].   During they watched [him]

ši'äne.   Ši'aza,   šio   kološo-do
he defecated.   After he defecated,   the excrement   a piece of a broken

---

25 The Male swore—like most Ethiopians—by the death of an important person: "May the
    chief die (if I do not speak the truth)!".
26 He gave him meat to eat in order to expedite the passing of sorghum. Sorghum on its own
    leads to sluggish bowel movements, but fat meat speeds up digestion.
27 The chief had Šade watched.
28 The potters in Male—as throughout Ethiopia—are members of a particular ("despised")
    caste. (The same was true of hunters, tanners and smiths.) They were under the special
    command of the kings and chiefs and provided their bodyguard, "police" and executioners.

	ekäne,	eki	kāti-bärto	mukäne[29].
gourd-in	they put,	taking [it]	the chief-in front of	they came.

Mukazā	šio	zagao:	"Mä'y	tuway?	Nē
After they came	the excrement	seeing:	"Sorghum	is [this] not?	You

muwatsi?	Mä'y	tuway?"	Hizi	gene.
[what] did you eat?	Sorghum is [this]	not?"	Thus	he said.

"Ta	nē	bodandane!"	gene.	"Nē	mä'o	eki	bēzo-fa
"I	you	will kill!"	he said.	"You	sorghum	taking	place-from

tam	kēze!	Kēza'a,	tāni	nē wodandane!"	Hizi	gene.
me	tell!	If you don't tell,	I	you will kill!"	Thus	he said.

"Ta	wozigē	kēzanday?	Nē	tāna	wodandane,	hangotsia
"I	what	should I tell?	You	me	will kill,	the other one

tāna	wodandane!	Tam	ayge	koškanday?"[30]	"Ayga-fa
me	will kill!	For me	what	I should do well?"	"Where-from

nē	mä'y	ekay?"	hizi gene.	"Ta gōda,	Gambo
you	sorghum	did take?"	thus he said.	"My lord,	Gambo's

māreka-fa	ekäne."	Hizi gene.	"Gambo?	Wokazay?"
house-from	I took."	Thus he said.	"Gambo?	Where is he?"

"Banka[31]	āni."	"Dänduāte	čīmi![32]	Dändao
"In Banka	he is".	"Go	[you] old men!	After you have gone

	samuāte[33]	ḳayšuāte!"	Hizi gene.
[to Gambo]	[the ground] kiss	[and] plead with him!"	Thus he said.

Hizi	gazao,	čima	dändäne.	Dändao
Thus	after he said,	the old men	went.	After they went

ḳayšäne.	Ḳayšazā	iskäne[34].
they pleaded [with him].	After they pleaded	he refused [to hear them].

---

29 "they brought".
30 "What should I do for the best?"
31 This is a locality in Banna.
32 "Old men", i.e. old, experienced men were sent as intermediaries.
33 Surprisingly the Amharic word for kissing (samä) is used here. The Male word is ulint.
34 Or itsäne.

Iskazā   may   gəntsa   mukäne,   gəntsa   mukazā
After he refused   now   again   they came,   again   after they came,

may   gəntsa   dakäne.   Gəntsa   dakao
now   again   he sent [them back].   Again   having sent [them back]

may   ḳayšäne   ḳayšäne.   "Bakkali
now   they pleaded [and]   pleaded. [Gambo asked:]   "Is it true [that]

kāti   əntsi   dakīya?"   "Nuna   kāti   dakäne."   "Kāti   ənti
the chief   you   did send?"   "Us   the chief   sent."   "Kāti   you

tṣilo dakīya?"   Nay   tuko[35]   faḳäne.
truly did he send?"   The son [of Gambo]   coffee   poured [in a gourd].

"Faḳi   gura   yewuāte!"[36]
"During you pour   for the [ringshaped] stand   call [the snakes]!"

Hizi gene.   Kaiya-fe   šošihatsi   buki   mukäne.
Thus he said.   Bush-from   these snake[s]   assembling   they came.

Hizi   buki,   guri   māhi   dēäne.   Tuko-ando[37]
Thus   assembling,   a stand   forming   they sat.   Coffee-gourd

šarile   izo-ko   tuko   faḳäne.   Faḳazā   šoyäle
this new one   him-of   coffee   he poured.   After he poured   the snakes

guri   māhi   getsäne.
a stand   forming   he put [the gourd in the middle of the stand].

Getsazā   toko   ando-ko   gula   getsäne.
After he put   the head [of a snake]   the gourd-of   the handle   he put.

"Tṣilo   ənti   mukiátato   eki   uškuāte!"[38]   "Nū
"[If] truly   you   came [as messengers]   [then] taking   drink!"   "We

---

35 Among the Male—as among other peoples in southwest Ethiopia—the liquor from
   infused, dried coffee leaves was an old ritual drink.
36 Gambo, like many priests (cf. Haberland 1963, pp. 158, 163) in southern Ethiopia, had
   power over snakes and could call them:—"Here, boys"—and they would come. Here they
   form the ring, otherwise made from grass or strips of bark, in which the gourds and other
   round vessels were placed to stop them tipping over.
37 *Anda* is a gourd halved lengthways, a popular drinking vessel (cf. Pauli 1959, ill. 17,1).
38 After the snakes had formed the ring, one of them coiled itself round the stem and reared
   its head over the edge of the vessel. Gambo said: "If you are really genuine ambassadors,
   you must have the confidence to drink!" If they had been liars, the snakes would have
   bitten them.

ekandane" gazā   tṣilo   gazā   tuko-ande
shall take" if [somebody] said [and if] the truth he said coffee-gourd

gədafa toko   šišäne.   Šišao   uškäne
from   the head   [the snake] raised. After it raised [the messenger]

       Uškao: "Hanno   salowoytsi [39]
drank.   After they drank [Gambo said]: "From today on the eighth day

ta mukandane.   Mä'y   tāna   bayḳäto,
I will come [to forgive].   [If] the sorghum through me   spoils,

ba'a   tāna   kudäto, tāni   hanno   salowoytsi-da
the cattle through me perishes, [then] I from today the eighth [day]-on

mukandane Ɇnti asa   buki   gafao   tāko
I will come. You the people   collecting   have finished of me

ba'o   gēli   fətsuäte! Tamia   dändeana
compound   entering   clean [it]! The fire [which as] I went away

gāra   āni,   tamo   ätswäte!
in the interior of the house   was,   [this] fire [newly] kindle!

Ta dändanti   lä'y   lam'o mä'äne [40], tāni   tamo
I when I will come   years   two   have been, [since] I   fire

nāba   gatsäne; ätswäte!   Gāra
[on] the hearth left;   kindle [it again]! The interior of the house

tāko   kaysi   mä'ätsi."   Hizi   gene.   Salowoytso
of me   wilderness   it became." Thus   he said.   The eighth [day]

gafäne. Gafazā   himābo   gūte   ami
came.   After it came on this date in the morning early [41]

čaränča   žibare gumäne   faränǧa-ko   nēroflan.
in the heaven wind made noise [like] Europeans-of aeroplane.

Čaränča   gumao: bay,   wāri,   maray, asi
[In] the heaven after it made noise: cows,   goats, sheep, men

---

39 This eighth day, i.e. after a week, is a "recent" element in Male culture.
40 "It is two years since I left".
41 *Ami* is the night, *gūte ami* the very early morning.

čaränči-na   gumi   mārē   ardäne.
heaven-from   noise making [they came] [42]   [in] the house[s]   they entered.

Ardazā   ače   dakäne.   Bay   šoyäne,
After they entered   the land   was saved.   The cows   brought forth,

ərzi   warkäne.   Ҙrzi   warkia,   āhari   hidi
the rain   rained.   The rain   had rained,   now   like this

gafao   ača   dakäne.   Yēmao   Gambo
[all this] had happened   the land   was saved.   Such was   Gambo's

haysi.   Tāriki [43]   nū-ko   haysi.   Gafäne.
story.   "Tariki"   us-with   "haysi" [is].   It is finished.

Digga Eroka later added another ending to this story, which I was unfortunately not able to record in the Male-language.

"When Gambo returned, he took a staff of Juniperus procera wood (hiziki) in his hand and stuck it into the earth on his farm, where it began to sprout. Until then there had been no Juniperus in Male. Gambo gave the land that he had formerly owned to the ancestor of the Irbo goda [44], who had imigrated from Gamu. He did this because it would have brought him no blessing after his exile to live there again as a great man and landowner. It would have only caused sorrow and aggravation. So he ended his days as a poor man on the land of the Irbo goda".

Free translation

This is Gambo's story. In ancient times a chief was performing the gaḍe ceremony. Two beautiful maidens were helping in the preparations for this ceremony. They were performing their tribute-work for the chief. He set them to work for him. The two worked together. When the work was done, the chief lay with both maidens, and they became pregnant. When they had become pregnant, the chief said: "They shall not give birth in this land, throw the children into the river!" Gambo, the father of the two maidens, refused: "I shall not cast my grandchildren into the wilderness!" He took the children and went to Banna (where he settled).

---

42 They fell from heaven to earth as God's gift to the wasted land.
43 Cf. fn. 8.
44 The Irbo goda is one of the twelve subchiefs in Male, whose district is the southernmost, bordering on Banna. This region originally belonged to Gambo.

After he had moved to Banna, there was a time of drought in Male, and the land was destroyed. Sorghum withered, the livestock died of thirst. The people sat and said: "What should we do?" Where Gambo lived, there was enough water, his animals multiplied, but the animals of the Male died of thirst. While they were dying of thirst, there was a cow of Šade (a friend of Gambo). One morning, it left Šade's house and went to Gambo's property. There it drank water, and came back. When it came back, it pissed. When he saw the piss, Šade said: "Where has the cow drunk water to be able to piss?" Two days later, the cow went away again, drank and came back. After it had returned, it pissed again. "Where has this cow found water?" Šade asked. The next morning he tied a bundle of straw to the cow's tail and tracked her by following the straws that fell. He went on and on until he came to Banna. He followed the cow's spoor. The cow came to a river bed where there was water and went in. While the cow was drinking, he went to the river bed too. "I want to drink too, I want to drink!" When he had slaked his thirst, he went further. In the meadow were Gambo's goats. They carried Gambo's ear-mark. When Šade saw the goats, he said: "Who brought Gambo's goats here?" He rested for a while, and then Gambo came. He asked Šade: "Who brought you here?" "God brought me here," said Šade. They went to Gambo's house, and Gambo gave him sorghum beer and mead to drink. Šade stayed there the next day and the next, he stayed for three nights. Then, weeping, he said to his beloved friend: "My children are dying, what can I give them to eat?" When he said this, Gambo gave him a handful of sorghum: "Take this with you, but do not tell anyone about it! If you tell anyone, you will die!" That is what Gambo said. He poured water for Šade's children into a gourd and said: "When you come home, pour this water into the middle of your well. Then put the sorghum grains into a large, broad pot. Wait for three days, then remove the lid from the pot and see what is there!" This is what Gambo said.

(Šade went back home.) He took the handful of sorghum grains and put them in a large pot. After he had waited for three days, he took off the lid. The pot was full of sorghum. When the pot was full, he poured the water that he had brought in the gourd into the middle of the well. The small quantity of water that he had brought with him in the gourd filled the well. Then they drank the water. After they had drunk, they recovered their strength. They boiled the sorghum and ate it. The cows drank. They sat in the men's lodge, drank and rested.

In the chief's house, the people said: "Šade is eating sorghum, Šade is eating sorghum!" They called him to the chief's house. When he had come, the chief said: "Šade, you are eating sorghum!" "My chief, I have not eaten any sorghum!" "You are eating sorghum!" "No, no, my chief, I have not eaten any sorghum—where should I get sorghum?" "Swear!" said the chief. "No, I have not eaten any sorghum, by the chief's death!" he said. When he had said this, the chief had a cow slaughtered. He made him eat the meat. After he had made him eat, he had him watched: "Potters, watch him!" he said. On the next day again he made him eat meat twice. Šade was seized by the urge to defecate. He went into the wood, the potters followed and kept watch on him. He defecated. They gathered the stools in the pieces of a gourd and brought them to the chief. When he saw the stools, he said: "Is not this sorghum? What have you eaten, and what have you passed? I will kill you!" he said. "Tell me where you got the sorghum? If you do not tell me, I will kill you!" he said. (Šade thought:) "What am I to say? You want to kill me, and the other one will kill me! What should I do for the best?" "Where did you get the sorghum?" he asked. "Lord, I got the sorghum in Gambo's house," he said at last. "Gambo? Where is he?" "He is in Banka". (The chief then began to organise an attempt at a reconciliation with Gambo).

"Go, elders and wise men. When you come to Gambo, kiss the ground and beg him for forgiveness!" said the chief. When he had said this, the elders went to Gambo. They begged him, but he refused to listen to them. When he had refused, they came again, and again he sent them back. After he had sent them back, they came again and begged him repeatedly. (Finally Gambo said:) "Is it really true, that the chief sent you?" "The chief has really sent us." "Did the chief really send you?" "Yes, the chief really sent us!" Gambo's son poured coffee into half of a gourd. "While you are pouring, call the snakes to form a ring to set the gourd in!" he said. The snakes came from the bush and assembled, and formed a ring to set the gourd in. Then he poured the coffee into the new gourd. After he had poured it, he set the gourd in the ring formed by the snakes. He laid the head of a snake on the handle of the gourd. "If you have really come as ambassadors, then take the gourd and drink!" If anyone said: "I shall take the gourd", and spoke the truth, the snake raised its head, (looked at him and did nothing). After all the ambassadors had drunk, Gambo said: "In eight days from now I shall come to forgive. If the sorghum has withered on my account and the livestock have died of thirst on my account, then I shall come eight days from now. Gather the people, go to my farm and make it tidy. When I went away, there was fire in the house, light it again! It is two years since there was fire in my house, light it again. My house has become a wilderness in this time". That is what he said.

When he came on the eighth day, early in the morning there was a rushing noise of wind in the sky. Early in the morning, the wind made a noise in the sky like a European's aeroplane: cows, goats, sheep, people, they all made a noise in the sky and fell to the earth. They entered into the houses (and filled the wasted land). The land was saved. Cows dropped calves, the rain rained. After it had rained again, after all this had happened, the land was saved. That is Gambo's story. The word "tariki" ("story" in the Amharic language) we call "haysi". That is the end.

Bibliography

Haberland, Eike 1963 *Galla Süd-Äthiopiens*. Stuttgart.

Haberland, Eike 1975 "Mündliche Überlieferungen über die Geschichte von Gofa (Süd-Äthiopien) bis 1889". In: *ZfE* 100:27-37.

Haberland, Eike 1981 "Die materielle Kultur der Dizi und ihr kulturhistorischer Kontext". In: *Paideuma* 27:121-172.

Haberland, Eike 1983 "An Amharic Manuscript on the Mythical History of the Adi kyaz (Dizi, Southwest Ethiopia)." In: *BSOAS* forthcoming.

Jensen, Ad. E. 1959 "Die Male." In: Jensen, Ad. E. (Ed.), *Altvölker Süd-Äthiopiens*: 263-302. Stuttgart.

Moreno, Martino Mario 1938. *Introduzione alla lingua Ometo*. Roma.

Pauli, E. Ch. 1959 "Materielle Kultur der Male." In: Jensen 1959: 303-312.

Schulz-Weidner, Willy 1952 "Vorläufiger Bericht über die anthropologischen Ergebnisse der Frobenius-Expedition nach Südwest-Äthiopien 1950/1951". In *Homo* 3:162-167.

Trento, P. Gabriele da 1941 "Vocaboli in lingue dell'Etiopia meridionale." In: *RSE* 1:203-207.

SPIRIT POSSESSION IN ETHIOPIA:
AN ESSAY IN INTERPRETATION [1]

HERBERT S. LEWIS
University of Wisconsin

An early paper by Wolf Leslau concerned the phenomenon of spirit possession in Ethiopia (Leslau 1949). The article was based on his own experiences among the Falasha near Gondar in 1947 and dealt primarily with the argot utilized by those possessed by *zar* spirits. In it Leslau recounted a "rationalistic explanation of the zar institution" which was given to him by an educated Ethiopian in Paris. That explanation attributed the phenomenon to the frustrations and restrictions upon women who, in reaction, "invented the existence of the zar" (1949: 205).

In view of the relative frequency with which women are possessed by spirits in Ethiopia and elsewhere it is not unreasonable that some variation of this "folk explanation", involving deprivation and low status, has come to be the preferred one in social science as well. I. M. Lewis has made it the central point in his writings on spirit possession in the Horn of Africa and elsewhere (1966; 1969; 1971), and it has even become "text book wisdom". For example, Cohen and Eames (1982: 248-250) cite a case from Trinidad, described by Mischel and Mischel (1958), which sounds strikingly like *zar* possession in Ethiopia. They use this case to illustrate I. M. Lewis's contention that such spirit possession represents "oblique social protest" by women and low status men.

In this paper I shall attempt to broaden the discussion to deal with a wider range of manifestations of spirit possession in Ethiopia. Although *zar* possession is surely the best known and reported form of spirit possession in Ethiopia, there are a good many other types, and the importance of possession goes well beyond protest by unhappy individuals.

Spirit possession is found throughout Ethiopia, among many, if not most, of its peoples. It was reported, during the 1960's and 1970's, among the: Amhara (Gondar, Menz), Qemant, Oromo (Shoa, Wellega, Arsi, Guji,

---

1 This paper was originally delivered in a slightly different form at the Seventh International Conference of Ethiopian Studies in Lund, Sweden, April 27, 1982. I wish to thank Sidney Greenfield, Arnold Strickon, and my wife, Marcia, for reading and criticizing the paper.

Jimma, Borana of Isiolo [Dahl]), Sidamo, Konso, Kafa, Gurage, Somali, and others. Although belief in spirits and their ability to possess humans is ancient, there is good evidence indicating that, contrary to the expectations of evolutionist or "modernization" theory, it was spreading and becoming more significant throughout the twentieth century. Haberland (1963), Knutsson (1967), H. S. Lewis (1970a), Hallpike (1972), Hinnant (n.d.), Hamer (n.d.) all report an increase in frequency and importance in the areas they studied. (There is evidence that it is spreading also in the Sudan, Kenya, Tanzania, Uganda, and elsewhere—not to mention Brazil and other parts of the New World).

A number of explanations have been suggested to account for these manifestations of "ecstatic religion" in Ethiopia. Most of them cite deprivation of one sort or another as the basis of most kinds of possession. These are psycho-social explanations, which hold that socially induced deprivation, low status, or feelings of inadequacy or inferiority produce psychological reactions in individuals which become manifest in the odd, but socially acceptable, behaviors which accompany spirit possession. Aside from the psychological effects of this behavior, it is argued that there are rewards to be received from society, in terms of attention, improved treatment, the company of fellow sufferers ("group therapy"), perhaps enhanced status, or the opportunity to earn money and prestige as a *bala-zar*, or other practitioner of the spirit religion.

Most prominent of the explanations in the literature are those by Messing and I. M. Lewis, which point to situations in which women who are socially disenfranchised, or men of "downtrodden categories" (I. M. Lewis 1971: 32), or men with "frustrated status ambition" (Messing 1958: 1125) are possessed by spirits. Similarly, William Shack has argued that one form of Gurage spirit possession involves men suffering from anxiety related to hunger, due to the institutionalized deprivation of food (1971).

John Hamer (n.d.) accounts for one form of spirit possessing among the Sidamo by *group* deprivation, and he considers that type (which Knutsson and I would call the "*k'allu* institution") to be millenarian in nature. Hamer also reports individual possession, involving women and low status men, which he relates to individual deprivation. On the other hand, Jan Brøgger who also worked among the Sidamo disagrees, for he found that it occurred among well-off men with high prestige. He prefers a different psychological explanation, seeing spirit possession as an outlet for "aggressive impulses" which may not otherwise be released within Sidamo society (1975: 289). (Gamst suggests a similar functional explanation for possession among the Qemant. He calls it a "social and psychological mechanism for maintenance of social cohesion and preservation of the group" through the release from frustrations and the redirection of hostilities [1969: 48]).

The other major attempt at explanation is also basically "functional", but more descriptive than "causal". I. M. Lewis considers that the types of possession which he calls "central possession cults" present systems of morality, especially in "highly atomized societies" (1971: 34). Having come to the fore as "mainline religions", they "become the mystical idiom in terms of which men of substance compete for positions of power and authority in society at large. (33)". Knutsson, whose study of the *k'allu* institution among the Mech'a Oromo Lewis uses, argues that this spirit possession complex offers the Mech'a social system a "final authority" to replace earlier ones which were lost.

Discussion and analysis of spirit possession, in short, has centered primarily around the problem of cause and of individual participation, due to deprivation of one sort or another. To a lesser extent writers have considered the classification, or typology, of spirit possession manifestations. (Cf. Todd, 1979-80; Torrey 1970). With few exceptions most discussions have been societally specific rather than comparative, and largely functionalist, seeking explanations in terms of "need"—either individual or societal.

In this paper I want to suggest some alternative perspectives which may offer complementary or different insights. I shall do this (a) by viewing spirit possession as a widespread areal phenomenon, and not from the vantage point of any single society or culture; (b) by stressing, *instead* of "function" and "need": ideas, belief, imagination, invention, imitation, action, and ambition.

Spirit possession rests on an idea and a belief, the idea and the belief that there are incorporeal beings in the universe which are capable of, and interested in, seizing the bodies of human beings and using them for their own purposes. The spirits can do make themselves manifest to humans in various ways, and interact with them. Because they are "super-natural" and invisible they are, however, mysterious and not really knowable, and thus the idea can be elaborated in an extraordinary number of ways. The idea is susceptible to many interpretations, elaborations, and uses, and it, and all that pertains to the spirits can spread from one group to another.

In the beginning was the idea. It may be quite true that possession by the spirits can serve the needs of a victimized wife, or an individual "of uncertain gender", or an ambitious man or woman trying to improve his or her economic or political situation, but it is not justifiable to seize upon these as "the cause" of the institution. The idea must pre-exist. And in this case the idea of the spirits, and of their powers and their concern with humankind is clearly one which has the ability to inspire concern and perhaps hope or dread in humans, and leads them to spend considerable energy and ingenuity in their attempts to deal with them. (This is recognized by the Mischels, who wrote [1958: 258], "Even though our approach has been to infer reinforcements [for spirit possession] on a rational and primarily external basis, it is important to keep in mind that for the participants, 'possession by the god [is] the supreme religious experience' [Herskovits 1941: 215]").

In twentieth century Ethiopia the idea of spirit possession was clearly a *productive* idea (in the linguists' sense, as a "productive derivation")—one capable of remarkable spread and elaboration, of many uses and variations.

"Types" of possession. It is not possible to isolate just a few types of spirit possession, even in Ethiopia, so subtle and many are the variations and combinations. I want to suggest a few *variations*, but not a "typology", in order to give some sense of the range of possibilities, as these are revealed in the literature and in my fieldwork.

(a) Possession of an individual man or woman by an evil or troublesome spirit, perhaps called some variant of *setana* (shaytan, zitana, shetana, [Shetani among the Segeju of Tanzania (Gray 1969)] or *jinn*, seems to be encountered almost everywhere. The spirits are usually considered evil and must be exorcised, anathematized (Morton 1976, Messing 1958, Hinnant n.d.), for they cannot be otherwise controlled, and they cause disruption, physical and mental illness, and misery. They are uncontrollable and unpredictable.

(b) In *zar* possession, in theory, an individual is possessed by a spirit which cannot or should not or need not be exorcized but may be and must be appeased, bribed, perhaps reasoned with, to give temporary respite. Spirits like the *zar* may return regularly, at possession ceremonies, perhaps annually, and extract promises and material rewards from their human "horses". The spirit is not usually considered to be evil, but may not be too good, either. In some cases of *zar* possession the spirit behaves badly; in others, the spirit may be protesting wrong behavior on the part of the human "horse" or some other member of the immediate community.

(In a further complication, sometimes an individual may show symptoms of possession which are not, in fact, due to actual possession by *set'ana* or *zar*, but to punishment, being "caught", for wrong behavior, by a spirit. That is, there is no actual possession [Morton 1975: 75]).

(c) Apparently this form of spirit can sometimes pass to the status of a guardian spirit, a *wuk'abi*, as some groups call it. (Morton, Messing, Reminick). Such a guardian spirit may protect an individual, or a family, lineage, a community. (Cf. Reminick on Menz Amhara *adbar*). In some Oromo areas there are *ayan-abba*, "the spirit of the father", who act as guardian spirits of lineage groups. Orent (1969) reports a similar phenomenon in Kafa. There are many variations here, too, in how these spirits are envisioned, how they are inherited, and what they do, and often these shade into "seer" or *k'allu*-like phenomenon.

In these cases we have moved from evil, troublesome, capricious spirits in the first "types" to ones which, though fierce when aroused, are basically good, helpful to humans, and concerned with morality and right conduct.

(d) "Seer", or *k'allu* type. (Torrey 1970, cf.). In this kind of possession basically good spirits (*ayana* among the Oromo) periodically possess particular men and women, not just anyone, as is the case with *set'ana* and *zar*, and aid the *k'allu* or *k'alliti* or *bale wuqabi* (Morton) to act as a medium, to help other human beings. People in trouble come to the seer at a time when she or he is possessed by a spirit in order to seek information and diagnosis of their ills; to speak to the spirits directly and beg forgiveness for the evil deeds for which they are being punished; to plead for help in all manner of affairs: court cases, conflicts with more powerful opponents (including landowners), the recovery of lost or stolen livestock, the birth of children, illness.

These spirits are basically good and are concerned with right conduct (as I. M. Lewis has suggested). They may be helpers of the oppressed and the unfortunate, avengers of wrongs, and guardians of morality. They may be "seen as operating as agents for men vis-à-vis (God)" ... (Morton 1975: 76), while the *k'allu*, *k'alliti* is the intermediary who makes direct contact with the spirits possible.

"Seer" or *k'allu* institutions depend upon the presence of a medium who is possessed by one or more spirits from this category of beings. These mediums, once they develop a reputation, have the means to gain some wealth and prominence. Thus there are men and women offering their services to those in need, usually for a fee throughout the countryside and towns of Ethiopia. Some have gained considerable fame and power through their impressive and apparently successful "mediation".

There are some, in addition, who have become the center of major, multifunctional institutions, such as those described by Knutsson, Morton, and myself, among Shoan Oromo. Hinnant and the Hamers have reported something similar among the Guji (currently) and the Sidamo (some years ago), and an analogous institution exists among the Kafa, with the cult of *ek'o* and Doche (Orent). The "mystical sanctions" (Morton 1975) which have developed from the belief in and attendance upon the *ayana* have become significant in conflict resolution, political leadership, and community organization. In some cases the *ayana* have become the basis of much individual and group religious belief and practice, serving everyone and not merely the "down-trodden". We have in these cases the development, the "invention", within several generations apparently, of a whole new series of institutions and ideas based on the concept of spirit possession—a far cry from the *set'ana* possession we began with. (We shall discuss this further below).

(e) Group possession. Among the Gurage and the Mech'a Oromo it is women, and among the Sidamo, young men, who are seized by spirits and made to run in packs throughout the countryside, behaving in an aggressive and hostile manner towards those who get in their way or deride them. The possession is contagious, and spreads as the affected people leave their homes and responsibilities and roam the countryside under the leadership of individuals, often transvestite men who can calm and control them when necessary. The *moata* (Mech'a) or *mweyet* (Gurage) represent yet another manifestation of the presence and power of the spirits. Although more restricted in its distribution than the other forms, it, too, is capable of spread—or of contraction.

Having presented these 5 varieties of possession I realize that those who know spirit possession in Ethiopia might object at any point to the specifics of these descriptions. And that is part of my point. There can be no "right" classification because we are dealing with phenomena which are truly protean, exceedingly variable, capable of all manner of elaboration and recombination[2].

At any particular time a group of people may believe in and be involved with more than one of these forms of spirits. For example, the Mech'a Oromo, as Knutsson has pointed out, can be said to be involved with all of the above, except for *zar* (1975). Knutsson also suggests that possession by Atete is another distinct form, while Baxter claims that, for the Arsi Oromo, Atete isn't a spirit at all, but the name of a particular type of ceremonial engaged in by women (Baxter 1979). My own material from Mech'a agrees with Knutsson, but Baxter's evidence for Arsi is equally consistent with my argument, to whit: anything is possible.

While the Mech'a Oromo are particularly richly endowed with forms of spirit possession, Hallpike reported that possession was fairly new in Konso,

---

2 The *Guji Waka* spirits reported by Hinnant may represent still another variation, different from others previously reported. In addition, their *ayana* include some spirits considered *shetana*! (Hinnant n.d.).

and in the 1960's they had only (a) and (d). The Hamers report that they found
(b), (d), and (e) among the Sidamo. Hamer gives the impression that the
development of powerful seers occurred several times, but declined or died
out, while Hinnant reports that the Guji were making increasing use of this
form in the 1970's. In addition, if I read Alice Morton's material correctly,
it appears that possession by "seers" (*k'allu*, *k'allicha*) was gaining greater
acceptance among people of all sorts of backgrounds around Bishoftu, that is,
in the small towns and countryside within the orbit of Addis Ababa.

The spread of spirit possession in the past decades has been such that it
should be no surprise to find any manifestation among any people, in any
area. Nor should it be surprising that some gain popularity for a while and
then seem to die out. This is precisely what we should expect, as the idea that
supernatural beings can take hold of humans goes through a particularly
active period of growth, spread, and elaboration[3].

Not only do the various forms of possession spread; so do the names,
statuses, behaviors, symbols, paraphernalia, ceremonies and activities associated with them. One person, one group, borrows from another, and adds
innovations of its own. We are not dealing here only with "distress", or
reactions to conquest, but with innovation and creation, emulation, and
ambition.

Again and again we encounter the same elements being used in different
combinations: words and names (for particular spirits and categories of
spirits; for religious specialities, [the "caught", the diviners, the assistants,
agafari, and interpreters]; the placement of the medium behind a curtain; the
use of such symbols as fresh cut grass on the floor, branches with green leaves,
flowers; butter, coffee, porridge, and blood; standing stones, bells, rings,
miniature metal tools, mirrors, cloth, and thread; speaking in tongues, or the
use of separate argots (which Wolf Leslau described 35 years ago); food
taboos; the concept of ritual pollution, and the barring of menstruating
women, those who have recently had sexual intercourse or been near a dead
person, from the presence of the medium or the spirits; the similarities in
calling the spirits, the drumming, and the dance and trance and jerking (*gurri*)
which indicates the spirits' presence; the dreams which foretell the coming of
a spirit and call for the building of temples; the idea that a person is

---

[3] It is worthwhile emphasizing that this same spread seems to be occurring in many parts of
the world, including the Americas, and that there has apparently been an increase in
Pentacostalism and ecstatic religious manifestations in some American Protestant churches
as well (cf. Shack n.d.). Possession in African Christian churches, by the Holy Spirit,
Jesus, or angels, has been extensively reported on by Sundkler (1961) and others.

"caught" by the spirits; the enlistment of servants pledged to the service of the spirits.

All of these elements, and others, occur over and over in different combinations, among different peoples, with different types of spirits, with different individual spirits and mediums.

We also encounter a range of social groups formed about the various spirits. There are some spirits which are associated explicitly with descent groups (Guji, Mech'a Oromo; Menz Amhara [Reminick], Kafa [Orent]); some with *communities*. Others form as the congregations and followings of *k'allus*, seers, or other practitioners. (See, e.g., Morton 1976, n.d.; Leiris 1939: 108).

In all these ways the peoples of Ethiopia have taken ideas, beliefs, practices, esthetic expression (poetry, language, music, costume), symbols (both verbal and physiscal), social relations, etc., and developed complex institutions and behaviors centered about, but not restricted to, these spirits which possess human beings. At this point it will be worthwhile to take a brief look at the development of one such complex institutition among one group of people, the Mech'a Oromo of western Shoa province.

The Spirits Among the Mech'a Oromo

At the heart of much of the social, political and religious life of the western Shoa Oromo are seers, spirit mediums called *k'allu*, who are regularly possessed by spirits known collectively as *ayana*.

Whereas the Oromo long had individuals with the title of *k'allu* it seems clear that these were originally ritual experts and leaders whose position was *not* based upon spirit possession, (See, e.g., Asmarom Legesse 1973, Knutsson 1967: 135 ff., and esp. 142 ff.; Haberland; Hinnant). On the other hand, while there is evidence that the term *ayana*, spirit, is old, it does not seem to have been related to possession, either, until relatively recently. Azaïs and Chambard (1931: 108) report that *ayana* was a "good spirit" for the Oromo, and Tutschek referred to "spirits of the father"—*ayan-abba* (Tutschek cited in Knutsson 1967: 139-140), as guardian spirits, but there seems to be no connection with possession—which is so clear today. Knutsson (1969) and I (H. S. Lewis 1970a [1966]) independently came to the conclusion that the complex combining the *k'allu* with possession by the *ayana* is a relatively new development, a product of the 20th century, about three generations old, among the Mech'a Oromo of Shoa province.

While the Mech'a Oromo also believe in guardian spirits associated with lineages (*ayan-abba*), and individual troublesome idiosyncratic possession by wicked spirits, and in *moata*, group possession (cf. Knutsson 1975), the key to the very important *k'allu* institution is the *ayana*, numberless named spirits who possess the bodies of particular individuals, *k'allu*. These spirits are capable of affecting the lives of humans directly and powerfully, aiding them or punishing them. They care about right behavior, about good and evil, truth and justice, peace and harmony. They become involved in the everyday affairs of humans as guardians of right conduct. They punish wrong-doers in a myriad of ways, but especially through illness, madness, bad luck, and death. On the other hand they can protect and aid men and women in any conceivable manner.

When an *ayana* possesses a *k'allu* it is possible for mortals to communicate with the spirit world. People can tell their troubles, ask what is wrong and why they are being punished, request aid in some human endeavor, or ask for forgiveness so that they may no longer be tormented. While it is true, as I. M. Lewis contends, that the *ayana* are guardians of morality (1971: 150) they also stand at the core of a system which permits humans to believe that they can learn the cause of their troubles. They believe, therefore, that they are not powerless but can try to either change their behavior, or beg, reason, pledge, bribe (through sacrifice) their way to better fortune, to end their woes. In this way the *ayana* are not only guardians of the social system and morality, but serve to aid human beings in their lives.

If Knutsson and I are correct in our reconstruction, the conception of the *ayana* as possessors of humans, and the *k'allu* as mediums through whom the *ayana* communicate with mankind, has come together in this form and risen to such prominence only since the Amhara conquest and incorporation of these Oromo groups, and since the demise of both the *gada* system [4] and the "big-men" war leaders who were formerly politically prominent in western Shoan Oromo life. (Knutsson 1967: 207; Lewis n.d.) During this period the *k'allu* institution has become deeply imbedded in Oromo life, and has become enormously elaborated through the adaptation of older ideas and customs, the borrowing of some symbols and practices and ideas from other groups, and the invention of new ones. (Knutsson offers a rich description of the concepts, rituals, symbols, and "ritual topography" of one such group).

The great *k'allus* hold annual ceremonials attended by thousands of congregants. More importantly, they also host activities lasting several days, as often as every two weeks, that are attended by hundreds of people each day.

---

4 *Gada* is a highly elaborated social, political, ritual, and religious system found among many Oromo groups, and, presumably, among all of them several hundred years ago. It is, in essence, an age-set and age-grade organization, but as Asmarom Legesse points out, it "represents an extreme development" of this type of institution (Asmarom Legesse 1973: 50).

On these occasions the *k'allu* and his attendants call upon the *ayana* to possess them. When the spirit is upon the *k'allu* scores of people approach and tell their troubles, ask for aid, plead for release, and so on. Such sessions may last for many hours, perhaps from sundown to sunup the next morning. And the whole process involves special personnel, music, patterns of speech, taboos, symbols (in the architecture, the paraphernalia, the compound [*galma*], and so on).

The court of the *k'allu*, or, more correctly, the *ayana*, is also the site of conflict resolution, litigation, the hearing of court cases. The *galma* areas are sacred ground, consecrated to and watched over by the spirits. They thus serve as the place for the settlement of disputes. Respected elders are chosen by their neighbors and installed formally in these positions by the *k'allu*. The judges listen to cases and pass judgments in an attempt to bring about justice and reconciliation. At some major *galmas* there will be a half dozen such courts operating concurrently. They provide a very important component of order in the rural areas in western Shoa (or did before the revolution). (See Knutsson 1967; Morton 1975; Lewis 1970a, b).

The *k'allu* of the Mech'a Oromo became, within several generations, the center of an enormous *new* complex, built around the idea of spirit possession but going far beyond it in certain respects. As the spiritual leaders of 10s of 1000s of Oromo, some of the *k'allu* became powerful and prominent figures able to act in the political arena as well (H. S. Lewis n.d.). These developments fit neither the view of spirit possession as the "religion of the dispossessed" nor a "central morality cult" (I. M. Lewis 1971). They are multi-functional, and a historical development created by human actors with a variety of motivations, aims, talents, opportunities, and a stock of ideas derived both from their own tradition and those of their neighbors.

In another Oromo area, that of the Guji, John Hinnant was able to witness the more recent development of a rather similar series of institutions. Among the Guji it is primarily women, known as *k'alliti*, who have taken the lead in developing "courts" (*madaba*), in which *abba sera* (father of the law) interpret the words of the spirits and apply "law" to the cases that come before them. With their own rules, personnel, terminology, and customs these "courts" resemble in some respects those of the *k'allu*s of the Oromo further north and west, but they also differ in important ways. Most importantly, the followers of the *k'alliti* become lifelong members of the group who cannot abandon it under the threat of madness or death. "Once in the group they become as kinsmen, compelled to aid each other in all aspects of daily life. The house of the *k'alliti* is a center for visiting and forming groups to carry out various tasks. Members of the group draw together in a society writ small, bound by their own laws and protected from problems with non-members by their spirits, which settle on any who offend the possessed. These in turn are incoporated into the group" (Hinant n.d. 21-22). According to Hinnant (personal communication) they work their fields cooperatively and participate in weddings and funerals of all members. (Cf. Mech'a Oromo *iddir* and *debo*. Lewis 1970).

Hinnant's evidence indicates that this form of spirit possession by *ayana*, is new. "Ayana trance is clearly a product of the outside world (24)", but in a very short time the Guji made it very much part of their own world. "The ability of Guji to assert their own understanding through a great proliferation of ritual systems was truly amazing (22)". And they were developing a new social organization as well, using spirit possession as the basis.

As a final example we may cite the observations of Gudrun Dahl (n.d.) in a small urban community in Kenya, involving members of Boran and other Oromo groups and Somalis. As she reports the situation in Isiolo, "The position of the cult at the crossroads of cultures has implications ... for the position of the *ayana* specialist as a kind of cultural entrepreneur". Because people of different cultures are joined in the same sects, and may interpret the same symbols in differing ways, and because these symbols may be ambiguous in any case, "The specialist is left room to work out his own exegesis while trying to bring order into the system ... (3)".

Conclusions

The evidence seems clear that spirit possession in Ethiopia was in a remarkable process of proliferation and elaboration during the past few decades. Without wishing to deny that this was also a time of cultural change due to the increasing impact of "the modern world" and the loss of autonomy for many groups, I would argue that, with its many manifestations and permutations, spirit possession in Ethiopia was not *merely* a response to deprivation, change and conflict. The phenomena are too varied, multi-functional and multi-faceted to be attributed to such causes alone. (Nor, I would argue, is deprivation always evident. Cf. Todd; Brøgger).

To use a metaphor from biological evolution, we might say that spirit possession has been undergoing "adaptive radiation" in Ethiopia. That is, that the phenomenon has found an unoccupied "niche" and been able to move into it in all sorts of forms. As a productive idea, capable of wide variation, manipulation, and many uses, it has taken many forms in its dispersion throughout the niche. We must not push the metaphor too far, however, but must remember that it is human actors who account for this radiation, who seize upon its possibilities and make them manifest in ideas and action.

Perhaps we might hypothesize that the conquest and subsequent occupation of the non-Amahara populations of the south created fertile conditions for someting new. On the one hand the conquest may have lessened the importance of, or even destroyed, earlier authorities, and perhaps religious and ritual figures as well, thus leaving the niche unoccupied (cf. Orent 1969, Knutsson 1967, Lewis n.d.). On the other, it introduced increased communications and movement, enabling ideas to spread even more rapidly and easily.

It is not necessarily my intention to deny any specific attribution of function or cause which has been suggested for any given case[5]. It seems entirely reasonable (and my own experience in the field bears out) that wives may use possession a weapon in the "battle of the sexes", that possession offers a role for the "sexually indeterminate male", that it relieves anxiety over food deprivation among men in Gurage, and that it offers a release from the tensions of enforced peaceableness among the Sidamo. But it may also be a route to a livelihood for a divorced woman in a town, the basis for a career and power for a *k'allu* or *k'alliti* who can build a following of believers. It could perhaps serve as a basis for a prophetic or political movement (Shack n.d.: 10). It offers access to the spirits that are believed to control human fates. It can also offer excellent entertainment to participants. At base, however, it rests upon a *belief* in these supernatural beings and in their involvement with humankind. This elementary fact makes all other manifestations and elaborations possible. What I object to is attempts to reduce the phenomenon to a few "types" or a few "causes" because I think this can only be misleading and unnecessarily restricting.

In addition, the "functionalism" which attributes spirit possession either to the psychological needs of individuals with problems, or sees "central morality cults" as a reflection of social systems, tends to distort our view of process and of the richness and complexity of the real world. These phenomena are not mere reflexes or reflections but are the products of mind involving creativity and imagination as well as action: attempts to persuade, to organize, to build (socially and materially/physically), to lead, to profit, to understand, to help, etc. To return to the metaphor of evolution, we have actors undertaking actions, some of which fail, but others of which seem to

---

[5] For some criticism of I. M. Lewis's claims regarding "peripheral cults" and status-seeking see Todd (1979-80).

succeed and are then adopted by others—both other individuals in the same society, and members of other societies or cultures.

This view of spirit possession does not deny that any given group of people may use the idea for their own personal or social, psychological, ideological, political, or economic purposes. On the contrary, it accepts all this as a given. Indeed, the uses to which spirit possession is put may very well be a good indication of the conditions and problems of that society at a given time. However, the many manifestations and permutations which these phenomena can take leads to the conclusion that no simple typology or the attribution of a few causes can adequately account for, or capture, the rich and complex reality of spirit possession in Ethiopia.

Bibliography

Asmarom Legesse
    1973 Gada: *Three Approaches to the Study of African Society.* New York: The Free Press.
Azaïs, F. & Chambard, R.
    1931 *Cinq Années de Recherches Archéologiques en Éthiopie.* Paris: Paul Geuthner.
Baxter, Paul
    1979 "*Atete* in a Highland Arssi Neighborhood". *Northeast African Studies,* 1:1-22.
Brøgger, Jan
    1975 "Spirit Possession and the Management of Aggression Among the Sidamo". *Ethnos,*
        40:285-290.
Cohen, Eugene N. and Edwin Eames
    1982 *Cultural Anthropology.* Boston: Little, Brown.
Dahl, Gudrun
    n.d. "Possession among the Waso Borana". (Abstract of conference paper—Seventh
        International Conference of Ethiopian Studies).
Gamst, Frederick C.
    1969 *The Qemant: A Pagan-Hebraic Peasantry of Ethiopia.* New York: Holt, Rinehart and
        Winston.
Gray, Robert F.
    1969 "The Shetani Cult Among the Segeju of Tanzania". In John Beattie and John
        Middleton (eds.), *Spirit Mediumship and Society in Africa.* London: Routledge and
        Kegan Paul.
Haberland, Eike
    1963 *Galla Süd-Äthiopiens.* Stuttgart: W. Kohlhammer.
Hallpike, C. R.
    1972 *The Konso of Ethiopia.* Oxford: Oxford University Press.
Hamer, John
    n.d. "Quasi-Millenial Possession States and Adaptation to Social Stratification in an
        Equalitarian Society: The Sidamo as a Case Study". (Paper presented at 1972 —
        annual meetings of American Athropological Assn.).

Hamer, John and Irene
: 1966 "Spirit Possession and Its Socio-Psychological Implications Among the Sidamo of Southwest Ethiopia". *Ethnology*, 4:392-408.

Herskovits, Melville J.
: 1941 *The Myth of the Negro Past*. New York: Alfred Knopf.

Hinnant, John
: n.d. "Guji Trance and Social Change: Symbolic Response to Domination". (Paper presented, March 1982, to the Conference on Society and History in Imperial Ethiopia: The South, ca. 1880-1974).

Knutsson, Karl Eric
: 1967 *Authority and Change: A Study of the Kallu Institution Among the Macha Galla of Ethiopia*. Goteborg: Etnografiska Museet.
: 1975 "Possession and Extra-institutional Behaviour: An Essay on Anthropological Micro-Analysis". *Ethnos*, 40:244-272.

Leiris, Michel
: 1938 "La Croyance aux Génies 'Zar' en Éthiopie du Nord". *Journal de Psychologie*, 1-2:108-126.

Leslau, Wolf
: 1949 "An Ethiopian Argot of People Possessed by a Spirit". *Africa*, 19:204-212.

Lewis, Herbert S.
: 1970a "Kud'arfan: A Multi-functional Institution Among the Western Galla". *Proceedings of the Third International Conference of Ethiopian Studies*, Addis Ababa 1966. Vol. III. Addis Ababa: Haile Sellasie I University.
: 1970b "Wealth, Influence and Prestige Among the Shoa Galla". In Arthur Tuden and Leonard Plotnicov (eds.), *Social Stratification in Africa*. New York: Macmillan.
: n.d. "Gada, Big Man, K'allu: Political Succession Among the Eastern Mech'a". Paper contributed to the Conference on Society and History of Imperial Ethiopia: The South, ca. 1880-1974. 1982.

Lewis, I. M.
: 1966 "Spirit Possession and Deprivation Cults". *Man*, 1: 307-329.
: 1969 "Spirit Possession in Northern Somaliland". In Beattie & Middleton (see Gray, above).
: 1971 *Ecstatic Religion*, New York: Penguin.

Messing, Simon D.
: 1958 "Group Therapy and Social Status in the Zar Cult of Ethiopia". *American Anthropologist*, 60:1120-1125.

Mischel, Walter & Frances Mischel
: 1958 "Psychological Aspects of Spirit Possession". *American Anthropologist*, 60:249-260.

Morton, Alice L.
: 1975 "Mystical Advocates: Explanation and Spirit-Sanctioned Adjudication in the Shoa Galla Ayana Cult". *Proceedings of the First United States Conference on Ethiopian Studies*, 1973. East Lansing, Michigan: Michigan State University.
: 1976 "*Dawit*: Competition and Integration in an Ethiopian Wuqabi Cult Group". In V. Crapanzano (ed.), *Case Studies in Spirit Possession*. New York: John Wiley.
: n.d. "Political Isssues in the Ada Galla Ayana Cult". Paper contributed to the conference on Regional Cults and Oracles, Association of Social Anthropologists, 1976.

Orent, Amnon
> 1969 *Lineage Structure and the Supernatural: the Kafa of Southwest Ethiopia*. Unpublished Ph.D. Dissertation, Boston University, 1969.

Reminick, Ronald A.
> 1975 "The Structure and Functions of Religious Belief Among the Amhara of Ethiopia". *Proceedings of the First United States Conference on Ethiopian Studies*, 1973. East Lansing, Michigan: Michigan State University.

Shack, William A.
> 1971 "Hunger, Anxiety, and Ritual: Deprivation and Spirit Possession Among the Gurage of Ethiopia". *Man*, 6:30-43.
> n.d. "Social Anthropological Problems in the Study of Spirit Possession in Ethiopia". (Unpublished paper read at 1972 meetings of American Anthropological Association).

Sundkler, B. G. M.
> 1961 *Bantu Prophets in South Africa*. London: Oxford University Press. (Second edition. First 1948).

Todd, Dave
> 1979-80 "Problems of Comparative Ecstasy". *Northeast African Studies*, 1:49-57.

Torrey, E. Fuller
> 1970 "The Zar Cult in Ethiopia". *Proceedings of the Third International Conference of Ethiopian Studies*, Addis Ababa, 1966. Addis Ababa: Haile Sellassie I University.

SOME NAMES FOR FOREIGNERS IN MENILEK'S ETHIOPIA: FÄRÄNJ, ṬALEYAN AND 'ALĪ — AND THE GREEK WHO BECAME A FÄRÄNJ

RICHARD PANKHURST
Royal Asiatic Society, London

The founding of Addis Ababa, in 1887, marked the inauguration of a new era in Ethiopian history. It was a time of unprecedented innovation which witnessed the opening of diplomatic relations with the principal European powers, the United States and Turkey, as well as the arrival of a hitherto inconceivable number of Europeans and other foreigners in many walks of life. These developments had significant linguistic consequences. The object of this paper is to examine the history of some of the principal terms used to describe or address foreigners in the age of Menilek.

Afrenj or Färänj

Considerable use was made in Menilek's day, as previously, of various forms of the Amharic *Afrenj* or *Färänj*, an Arabic loanword which had been used in Ge'ez for centuries [1]. The word had long been synonymous with Frank, or Roman Catholic. This was clearly explained in the seventeenth century by Hiob Ludolf, founder of Ethiopian studies in Germany, who in his Ge'ez lexicon of 1661 equates an *Afrongi*, as he calls him, with "a Frank or man of the Latin or Roman religion", but notes that the term was also popularly used for "all Europeans (except Greeks)" [2]. Orthodox Christian foreigners were spoken of, on the other hand, as *Gebṣ*, an epithet which was originally associated with Egypt, but had acquired a wider meaning [3]. It denoted Greeks and Armenians, hence Ludolf's caveat that the former were not considered as *Afreng*. The term *Gebṣ* thus had an essentially religious connotation in that it

---

1 R. Basset, "Études sur l'histoire d'Éthiopie", *Journal Asiatique* (1881), XVII, Avril-Mai-Juin, p. 326; Août-Septembre, p. 96; S. Grébaut, *Supplément au Lexicon Linguae Aethiopicae de August Dillmann* (Paris, 1952), p. 253.

2 J. Ludolf, *Lexicon Aethiopico-Latinum* (Frankfurt, 1699), col. 383.

3 C. F. Beckingham and G. W. B. Huntingford, *The Prester John of the Indies* (Cambridge, 1961), I, 227, II, 349.

distinguished Orthodox Christians from Catholics or Franks[4]. The latter had
been hated since the seventeenth century when they had been expelled, by
Emperor Fasilädäs.

The meaning of the term *Afrenj* or *Färänj* underwent a significant
modification in the nineteenth century, particularly during the reign of
Menilek. The principal reason for this was apparently the steady decline in
religious animosities, exemplified by Menilek's secular interests and the
increasing toleration of foreign missionaries, which reduced the need to
identify foreigners on a sectarian basis. Another factor was the coming of
Protestant missionaries and other travellers of that faith who were indis-
tinguishable from Catholics in their physical appearance, dress and behaviour,
and therefore tended to be taken for, and referred to, as *Afreng* or *Färänj*. This
usage was reinforced by the fact that the English loanword *Perotästant*[5], listed
by the Protestant missionary Karl Isenberg in his Amharic-English dictionary
of 1841, does not seem to have gained much popular acceptance.

As a result of these developments the religious significance of the term
Färänj began to change. Ludolf's old statement that an *Afrongi*, i.e. *Färänj*,
was "a Frank or man of the Latin or Roman religion" was broadly accepted in
the early nineteenth century by Isenberg who nevertheless introduced the
word "European" into the definition, asserting that the word designated, "a
Frank, i.e. European; esp. a *Roman* Catholic"[6]. That the missionary
considered the term to some extent applicable to Protestants is apparent from
an Amharic Geography in which he referred to the West Europeans, including
the British, in the plural, as *Ferenjoč*[7].

By the second half of the century the sectarian implication of the word had
significantly weakened. The Italian Catholic missionary Guglielmo Massaia
asserted that the term should simply be equated with European[8], i.e. without
any religious inference, while the distinguished French traveller and lexicographer Antoine d'Abbadie wrote in his dictionary of 1881 that the word was
by then employed for a European "without distinction of religious belief". He

---

4 E. Cerulli, *Il libro etiopico dei miracoli di Maria* (Roma, 1943), pp. 136-7, 139, 145, 196-7;
   E. A. Wallis Budge, *The Contendings of the Apostles* (London, 1899-1901), text, p. 22,
   translation, p. 25; idem, *The Life and Exploits of Alexander the Great* (London, 1896), text,
   p. 1, translation, p. 2.

5 C. W. Isenberg, *Dictionary of the Amharic Language* (London, 1841), I, 137, 187.

6 *Ibid.*, I, 137, II, 89.

7 *Idem, Géwografiya malät yämeder temhert* (London, 1841), p. 72.

8 G. Massaia, *Lectiones Grammaticales pro Missionariis qui addiscere volunt Linguam Amaricam*
   (Paris, 1867), p. 352.

nevertheless added, significantly, that is was "always used in an injurious sense"[9].

The secularisation of the concept of *Färänj*, which was to continue during the Menilek period, had coincided with a gradual modification in the manner in which the word was pronounced. A variety of forms had been in vogue in the early nineteenth century, as evident from contemporary dictionaries. D'Abbadie thus reported two variants, both with an initial A, namely *Afrenj* and *Aferanj*[10], and Isenberg two, one with and one without it, *Afrenj* and *Frenji*[11]. Massaia, on the other hand, later recorded only one form, *Franji*[12]. By Menilek's time the initial A had largely been abandoned. The noted Italian linguist Ignazio Guidi thus declared in his *Vocabulario* of 1901 that *Feränj* or *Färenj* were then more widely employed than the earlier *Afrenj*[13].

The term *Färänj* was extensively used in Menilek's reign, notably in the early 1890's at the time of the Italian invasion, and the subsequent Ethiopian victory at Adwa in 1896. The enemy, though on occasion referred to as Italians, were no less frequently spoken of merely as *Färänj*. The use of the generic rather than the specific term was scarcely surprising in that many Ethiopians at this time had only a limited knowledge of the geography and the culture of Europe, and found little need to distinguish too precisely between foreigners from various parts of that far-off continent. An Amharic poem composed immediately after the battle recalled that the enemy had been defeated with weapons they had themselves supplied to Menilek in the period preceding the hostilities. It declared[14]:

> *Meneñña moñň näw käFäränj agär säw*
> *Endét mämäččawen särto yesäṭal säw*
> *Bamäṭṭaw Wäčäfo hamäṭṭaw ersas*
> *Qolla andägäddägäw yan yäbaher gäbso*

"What kind of fools are these in the country of the *Färänj*?"
"How? They themselves made the instruments of their destruction, and
gave them to us".

9 A. d'Abbadie, *Dictionnaire de la langue amariñña* (Paris, 1881), col. 590.

10 *Ibid.*, col. 590.

11 Isenberg, *Dictionary of the Amharic Language*, II, 89.

12 Massaia, *op. cit.*, p. 352.

13 I. Guidi, *Vocabolario amarico-italiano* (Roma, 1901), cols. 514, 874. See also G. J. Afevork, *Grammatica della lingua amarica* (Roma, 1905), p. 37; C. H. Armbuster, *English-Amharic Vocabulary* (Cambridge, 1910), II, 96; J. I. Eadie, *An Amharic Reader* (Cambridge, 1924), pp. 114, 119.

14 E. Cerulli, "Canti popolari amarici", *Rendiconti della Reale Accademia dei Lincei. Classe di Scienze Morali, Storiche e Filologiche*, Serie V (1916), XXV, 569.

"With the Wetterly which they brought, with the bullets which they
brought",

"[Menilek] roasted and burst this overseas barley".

Most of the 1,865 Italian prisoners captured in the campaign were taken to
Addis Ababa prior to repatriation. Their captors, and the Ethiopian public in
general, often addressed them, in many cases with derision or abuse, by the
appellation *Färänj* as recalled by one of their number Major Giovanni
Gamerra[15].

The Italians are likewise frequently referred to as *Färänj* in Gäbrä Sellasé's
great chronicle of the reign of Menilek[16].

The term *Färänj*, though used for the enemy, had by then apparently lost
most of its early religious and derogatory connotation, and was tending more
and more to approximate to European or even "white man".

The phrase "country of the *Färänj*" used in the poem also finds frequent
expression in Gäbrä Sellasé's chronicle. This work states for example that the
pipes installed to bring water to Menilek's palace in 1894 came from the
country of the *Färänj*[17], an obvious reference to Europe rather than to any
Catholic country as such; that the postal system, in fact established by the
French, was the work of *Färänjoč*[18]; and that the first steam-engine, which
was actually sent by the Austrian state, had been brought from the land of
the *Färänj*[19]. Also illustrative of the width of application of the term was
the assertion that the foreign bridge-builders, whom we know to have been
Greeks introduced early in the twentieth century, had arrived from the
country of the *Färänj*[20]. Still more remarkable is the statement that Harar at
the time of its seizure by Menilek in 1887 was occupied by many *Färänj*[21]—an
apparent allusion to the Turkish forces in the city.

The concept *Färänj* was similarly applied to the European colonial powers,
Protestant Britain as well as Catholic France and Italy, by which Ethiopia was

---

15 G. Gamerra, *Ricordi di un prigioniero di guerra nello Scioa* (Firenze, 1897), p. 81. On the prisoners
    see also G. F.-H. Berkeley, *The Campaign of Adowa and the Rise of Menelik* (London, 1935),
    pp. 346-8.
16 Guèbrè Sellassié, *Chronique du règne de Ménélik II* (Paris, 1930-1), I, 372; Gäbrä Sellasé, *Tarikä
    Zämän zä Dagmawi Menilek Negusä Nägäst zältyopya* (Addis Ababa, 1959 E.C.), p. 224.
17 Guèbrè Sellassié, *op. cit.*, I, 341; Gäbrä Sellasé, *op. cit.*, p. 205. See also Guèbrè Sellassié, *op.
    cit.*, II, 485, 499; Gäbrä Sellasé, *op. cit.*, p. 293, 304.
18 Guèbrè Sellassié, *op. cit.*, II, 472; Gäbrä Sellasé, *op. cit.*, p. 286.
19 Guèbrè Sellassié, *op. cit.*, II, 509; Gäbrä Sellasé, *op. cit.*, p. 312.
20 Guèbrè Sellassié, *op. cit.*, II, 529; Gäbrä Sellasé, *op. cit.*, p. 334.
21 Guèbrè Sellassié, *op. cit.*, II, 239; Gäbrä Sellasé, *op. cit.*, p. 141.

encompassed, and which tended to be regarded with popular suspicion, and fear. A common Amharic saying declared[22]:

Färänjoč endä märfé fätel yegäbu
Endä wärqa yesäfu

"The *Färänjoč* enter like thread through the eye of a needle,
"[and then] expand like the *wärqa* [i.e. sycamore tree]".

The advent of increasing numbers of *Färänj* was meanwhile giving rise in Addis Ababa to new employment opportunities, mainly for servants, who, it may be noted, tended to be poorly regarded in Ethiopian society. A contemporary Amharic couplet ran as follows[23]:

YäFäränj aškär näčč läbaš,
Kälay wädä tačč yäsähän ammälalaš

"The *Färänj's* servant dressed in white,
"Carries plates up and down [i.e. does nothing worthwhile]".

Growing familiarity with *Färänj* also found expression in the adoption of the word *näčč*, or "white", for a European. This term, which probably followed European usage , was included by the Swiss- and Italian-educated Ethiopian intellectual Afäwärq Gäbrä Iyasus in a grammar of 1905[24] and by the Italian missionary Angelo da Ronciglione in a primer of 1912[26]. The word is also found in an early twentieth century Amharic poem which speaks of servants of the Europeans as *yänäčč aškär*, or "servant of the whites"[26].

The widened significance of the term *Färänj*, it may be concluded, is evident in the Amharic vocabularies of the British officer Major J. P. H. M. Alone and of the Italian Amleto Bevilacqua, published in 1906 and 1917 respectively, both of which translate the term as "European" without any of its former religious connotation[27].

22 Guidi, *op. cit.*, col. 874. See also J. Baeteman, *Dictionnaire amarigna-français* (Dire Daoua, 1929), col. 1225.

23 Guidi, *op. cit.*, col. 874. See also Baetman, *op. cit.*, col. 1225.

24 Afevork, *op. cit.*, p. 35.

25 Angelo da Ronciglione, *Manuale amarico-italiano-francese* (Roma, 1912), p. 162.

26 Eadie, *op. cit.*, pp. 248, 250. See also W. Leslau, *English-Amharic Context Dictionary* (Wiesbaden, 1973), p. 1470.

27 J. P. H. M. Alone, *Short Manual (with Vocabulary) of the Amharic Language* (London, 1909), p. 169; A. Bevilacqua, *Vocabolario italiano-amarico* (Roma, 1917), col. 125.

Ṭaleyan

Though the word *Färänj* had served since the Middle Ages in a general way
when referring to Catholic Europeans, other specific terms, among them as
we have seen *Gebṣ*, were also used. This practice became more common in the
nineteenth century as a result of closer contacts with Europe, and the need to
differentiate between the various European powers.

Italy, the first European country with which Menilek developed relations,
seems to have been originally known in its Italian form, *Iṭaliya*, which is
embodied in the ill-fated Italo-Ethiopian treaty of Weçalé which Menilek
signed in 1889 [28]. Italian nationals, though often spoken of, as we have seen,
as *Färänj*, were also called *Ṭaleyan* (plural *Ṭaleyanoč*) [29]. This word, which was
pronounced, and written, in a variety of ways, gained extensive circulation at
the time of the 1895-6 war with the Italians, and appears for example in a
poem in praise of one of Menilek's nobles, Fitawrari Gäbäyyähu, who had
died at Adwa. Of him it was said [30]:

> *Engedih Ṭalyanoč käman yewwaggallu*
> *Yabba Daññäw gašša täsäggʷädäčč alu*

"And now with whom shall the Italians fight?"
"They say that the shield of Abba Daññäw [i.e. Menilek] is crushed".

Italians captured in the campaign were often directly addressed, not only as
Färänj, but also with the epithet *Ṭaleyan*, as noted in the memoirs of one of
their number, Sergeant Giovanni Tedone [31].

Many Italians were subsequently employed in construction work in Addis
Ababa and elsewhere [32].

Variations of the word for Italian in this period included *Ṭaleyan*, *Ṭaliyan*,
Ṭeleyan, or, as Angelo da Ronciglione states, even *Iṭalyan*, with such plurals
as *Ṭaleyanoč*, *Ṭaliyanoč*, or *Ṭeleyanoč* [33]. At least one other variant was heard

---

28 Italy, Archivio Storico, Ministero degli Affari Esteri, Series V *Trattati, Etiopia*,No. 3. See
    also S. Rubenson, *Wichale XVII* (Addis Ababa, 1964), Appendix.

29 M. Cohen, "Couplets amhariques du Choa", *Journal Asiatique* (1924) CCV, Juillet-
    Septembre, pp. 23, 34; Bevilacqua, *op. cit.*, cols. 33-4; C.H. Walker, *English-Amharic
    Dictionary* (London, n.d.), p. 88.

30 E. Cerulli, "Una raccolta amarica di canti funebri", *Rivista degli Studi Orientali* (1924), X, 272.

31 G. Tedone, *I ricordi di un prigionero di Menelik dopo il disastro di Adua* (Roma, 1915), pp. 40, 92.

32 R. Pankhurst, "Menilek and the Utilisation of Foreign Skills in Ethiopia", *Journal of
    Ethiopian Studies* (1967), V, No. 1, pp. 44-7.

38 Cerulli, "Canti popolari amarici", p. 272; Cohen, *op. cit.*, p. 67; Bevilacqua, *op. cit.*, col. 190;
    Eadie, *op. cit.*, pp. 248, 250, 260-1, 269; Angelo di Ronciglione, *op. cit.*, p. 162.

by the British linguist Armbruster who records the curious singular form *Ṭalinyani*, apparently derived from the Italian plural "Italiani"[34].

'Alī

Italians taken prisoner at Adwa, and by extension all Europeans, were also known, and addressed, by another, and at first sight unlikely epithet: 'Alī. This common Muslim name was used as a term of abuse when the local populace flung at the captives such insults as[35]:

> *'Alī šärmuṭa!*

> i.e. " 'Alī, prostitute!"

a saying heard by Tedone, the use of which was also reported at about the same time by two other Italians, Vannutelli and Citerni[36].

The prisoners, according to Tedone, might similarly be assailed, in a mixture of Amharic and Italian, with cries of[37]:

> *'Alī, Ṭaleyan forza yälläm?*

> " 'Alī, the Italians, have they no power?"

and:

> *'Alī, gininnär forza yälläm?*

> " 'Alī, [your] generals, have they no power?"

Many Ethiopians in the aftermath of the Adwa war seem to have extended their disapproval from the Italians to other Europeans. A French resident, M. Stévenin, was subsequently quoted, possibly with exaggeration, as stating that there was a "terrible" upsurge of hostility against all "whites". Any European leaving his house without an escort of four or five servants was in consequence, he claims, liable to be insulted[38]. Though he does not specify any particular form of abuse it would appear probable that it would include the term 'Alī which was soon applied, not only to Italians, but to all

34 Armbuster, *op. cit.*, II, 153.
35 Tedone, *op. cit.*, p. 82.
36 L. Vannutelli and C. Citerni, *L'Omo* (Milano, 1899), p. 474.
37 Tedone, *op. cit.*, p. 56.
38 D. Pariset, *Al tempo di Menelik* (Roma, 1937), pp. 61, 128. On similar attitudes in the Somali area see Count Potocki, *Sport in Somaliland* (London, 1900), p. 88.

Europeans, for, as Herbert Vivian, a British traveller of this period, recalls, "the Abyssinians ... realise very little difference between an Italian and any other European [39].

An indication of the degree of irritation which this practice aroused among racially proud Englishmen of the day is provided by Count Gleichen, a member of a British diplomatic mission which arrived in Addis Ababa in 1897, the year after the battle. In his autobiographical work, *With the Mission to Menilek*, he recalls that during his first days in the Ethiopian capital whenever he and his colleagues went for a walk "some Abyssinian or other was certain to murmur, or even to shout, at them the word Ali", and he continues:

> "Not knowing what this meant, or imagining that it was perhaps only an Ethiopian abbreviation of the word alien, we took no notice of it, till one day it came out in conversation with some other Europeans that this was an abusive epithet" [40].

'Alī, the British envoys learnt, had in fact been "the generic name for an Abyssinian, according to the Italian idiom", and after Adwa the victors had "retaliated" on their enemies "by calling *them* Ali". (The Italians, we may interpolate, had acquired their first contacts with the local population while still at the coast inhabited predominantly by Muslims). Gleichen, unhappy at the discomfiture of fellow Europeans, dubbed this "a poor form of repartee", but notes that it had become "universal in the country" and had "stuck". What irritated him most was, however, that "all white men are now included in the same category, and the common people cry 'Ali' at any European stranger" [41].

Realisation of the origin of the term greatly angered the envoys, so that, Gleichen reports:

> "The next time we heard the word, we turned round and raised our sticks in a threatening way; this was generally sufficient, and in nearly every case the utterer of the word curled up and ran away" [42].

One member of the mission particularly incensed at being addressed as 'Alī was Lieutenant-Colonel Wingate, who, on hearing the word, bristled, Gleichen says, "like a gamecock" [43]. In his own report on the incident,

39 H. Vivian, *Abyssinia* (London, 1901), pp. 213-14.
40 Count Gleichen, *With the Mission to Menelik 1897* (London, 1898), p. 216.
41 *Ibid.*, pp. 216-17.
42 *Ibid.*, p. 217.
43 *Ibid.*, p. 218.

embodied in an angry letter of May 12 to Rennell Rodd, the leader of the
mission, Wingate speaks of the "righteous fury" which he felt, and states that
he and his party had accordingly raised their sticks in a "threatening way".
This action doubtless only exacerbated matters, for, subsequently, he says:

> "Whilst walking this evening in the vicinity of Ras Mikhael's camp [i.e.
> that of Ras Mika'él the governor of Wällo], in company with Lord
> Edward Cecil we were assailed by cries of 'Ali' from several Abyssinians,
> one or two of whom began picking up stones as if to throw at us. We at
> once made for the aggressors, and they fled. Feeling that some steps
> should be taken to prevent the reoccurrence of these insults, we proceeded
> directly to Ras Mikhael's inclosure, and whilst passing through the tent by
> which it is surrounded, 'Ali' was shouted at us from all sides. Noting one
> tent in particular, the occupants of which were more aggressively
> insulting than the rest, we entered the Ras' inclosure and demanded that
> the guard should at once conduct us into his presence ...".

On gaining access to the chief, Wingate continues, "the Ras, appeared
much put out, apologized profusively, and , summoning one of his Headmen,
gave orders that the entire camp should be punished. We at once begged him
not to inflict such wholesale punishment on our account, but offered to point
out to his officer the tent from which the specially abusive cries had been
issued, and to this arrangement he agreed. We then went on to explain that
we had reported the conduct of the men rather with the object of calling
attention to the behaviour of the Abyssinians in general towards the officers
of the British Mission, of which he was no doubt in ignorance; but he replied
that he was aware the Abyssinians were in the habit of shouting out 'Ali'
when they saw Europeans, and this had become a term of reproach only since
the Italian prisoners had been with them; he explained that formerly it was
the habit of the Italians to address all Abyssinians as 'Ali', but when the
tables were turned by the Italian defeat, they had fastened on the name 'Ali'
for their captives; he also said that the Emperor had given very strict orders
that this civil practice should be discontinued, but his own men, having just
arrived in camp, and being perhaps ignorant of the presence of the British
Mission, had commited this serious fault, which he deeply regretted"[44].

Wingate's complaint received the full support of Rennell Rodd, who three
days later wrote to the British Foreign Secretary to say that his two

---

44 Great Britain, Foreign Office, 403/255, *Further Correspondence respecting the Red Sea and Somali
   Coast* (1897), No. 183, Wingate to Rodd, 12 May 1897. See also Gleichen, *op. cit.*, pp. 217-18;
   P. H. G. Powell-Cotton, *A Sporting Trip Through Abyssinia* (London, 1902), p. 209.

subordinates had "showed considerable presence of mind", and that their "energetic action was wholly successful", for they were "conducted back to their quarters by a guard of honour", and there had been "no repetition of the offence". Elaborating on the use of the appellation *'Alī* he declared:

> "The cry of 'Ali, Ali!' is universally recognised as a slighting form addressed to Europeans, who are now all confounded by the ignorant populace with Italians, and even the oldest foreign inhabitants here have to submit to having it called after them when they go abroad"[45].

The practice which the aristocrats from Britain found so distressing was but a short-lived one in Addis Ababa. By 1899 the British big-game-hunter and ethnographer Powell-Cotton reported that it had "quite died out". Whether this was because of British representations, and the Emperor's intervention, or the subsiding of the excitement engendered by the war with Italy we do not know. In the countryside, on the other hand, the custom continued for several more years. Alfred Pease, another hunter from Britain, stated in 1900 that on crossing the Awaš river on the journey inland he and his party were "well jostled by a rabble", among whom, he claims, some "insolent ruffians ... shouted 'Ali' at us as we went by"[46]. The continuing use of the word was corroborated by Vivian who noted in 1900 that in the countryside around the capital the inhabitants would "indulge ... in impertinent chaff", repeating "in unmistakingly insulting tones 'Ali, Ali, Ali'". Like the British diplomats he had initially been "unaware" of the significance of the epithet, and adds: "I daresay many people have called me Ali on the way up, but if they did I should not have minded what I did not understand". After reading Gleichen's book, in Addis Ababa, however, he realised the "insulting" aspect of the word. Describing his consequent indignant reaction, he declares:

> "On the way down I heard the expression twice, once from a group of women, for whom there was no answer except to comment upon their surprising ugliness in languages which they did not understand. The other time was near the end of my last march back to Harrar. In a narrow path between high hedges of candelabra cactus I encountered several men in charge of some fifty donkeys ... They made no sign of moving aside to let me pass. Indeed one of them danced about in front of my mule, and shouted 'Ali, Ali, Ali'. I raised my whip as though to

45 *Ibid.*, Rodd to Salisbury, 15 May, 1897.
46 A. E. Pease, *Travel and Sport in Africa* (London, 1902), II, 63.

strike him, imagining he would at once move aside, but instead of doing that he raised his hand to mock my gesture, and went on repeating with increasing insolence, 'Ali, Ali, Ali'. I lashed him three times across each side of his face with the thong of my whip" [47].

Despite this incident, it is clear that the word *'Alī* was by no means always uttered with hostile intent. Powell-Cotton, an essentially saner traveller, relates that before leaving Addis Ababa for the north he had been told, doubtless by some of his more apprehensive compatriots, that he would "probably have to put up with derisive shouts of 'Ali'", and that as he got further from Šäwa he "might even be greeted with mud and stones". With such warnings in mind he was "rather surprised", he relates, that the crowds of buyers and sellers at Däbrä Marqos in Gojam province received him "so well", and adds:

"One man came up, and bowing, said, 'Salaam Ali'; I glanced strongly at him, to see if it was meant as an insult, but it was evident from the man's expression and manner that he intended it as quite the reverse" [48].

The term *'Alī*, we may conclude, had thus lost its deprecatory connotation, and was indeed no more than a short-lived form of address, a synonym for *Färänj*, and then disappeared altogether.

The Grék who became a Färänj

The era of Menilek witnessed the arrival of many other foreigners besides the Italians, in particular numerous Greeks, Armenians and Indians [49].

The Greeks, with whom we are here alone concerned, were a people known in Ethiopia since ancient times. Sometimes referred to, as we have seen, because of their Orthodox faith, as *Gebṣ*, they and their country were traditionally known by a variety of terms, among them the Biblical names *Ṣer'e* [50] and *Yonanawiyan* [51], as well as *Rum*, *Rumi*, *Rom* and *Romeya*, names

---

47 Vivian, *op. cit.*, pp. 214-15.

48 Powell-Cotton, *op. cit.*, pp. 209-10.

49 Pankhurst, *op. cit.*, pp. 29-86.

50 Cerulli, *Il libro etiopico dei miracoli di Maria*, pp. 130, 132, 196-7; Wallis Budge, *The Life and Exploits of Alexander the Great*, text, pp. 361, 381, translation, pp. 564, 589; *idem*, *The Contendings of the Apostles*, text, pp. 101, 162, 226, translation, pp. 111, 190, 269; Ludolf, *op. cit.*, col. 582.

51 Wallis Budge, *The Life and Exploits of Alexander the Great*, text, pp. 32, 36, 60, 71, 107, 252, translation, pp. 60, 67, 108, 128, 189, 426; *idem*, *The Contendings of the Apostles*, text, pp. 391, 448, 454, translation, pp. 476, 541, 548.

which had their origin in the identification of the Greeks with Constantinople or the second Rome [52].

Greek immigration in Ethiopia increased rapidly in the first part of the twentieth century. The number of Greeks, estimated at over three hundred in the capital in 1910, grew to over ten times that figure in the country as a whole by 1935 [53]. Their coming introduced the Ethiopians to a new class of foreigners who, because of their distinct, and in the popular mind inferior, occupational pattern, were considered a group apart as was emphasized by contemporary observers, among them the French educated scholar Faitlovitch and his compatriots F. F. Kulmer and E. G. Pick [54].

The immigrants from Greece were referred to in Ethiopia by a new loanword, *Grék*. This largely superseded the older terms by which Greeks had formerly been designated. However, the earlier names were retained in scholarly circles. *Şer'e* was used for the Greeks of the past [55], and for their language [56], but also for Greeks of conteporary times. Gäbrä Sellasé thus referred to the Greek clergy at Jerusalem as *Şer'aweyan* [57] while Raad and Ghaleb designated modern Greece by another of its old names in their vocabulary of 1910 as *YäYonan agär*, or land of *Yonan* [58]. The new name *Grék* served both for Greece and the Greeks, as instanced by Afäwärq Gäbrä Iyasus as early as 1905 [59], and half a decade later by the French linguist Marcel Cohen (who states that in Šäwa it was often pronounced *Gréh*, or, in the plural, *Grehoč*) [60].

The preponderance of Greeks as masons and road-builders, small-scale restauranteurs and retail traders, had the effect of causing this entire occupational group to be spoken of as *Grék*, irrespective of the fact that some of its members were actually Armenians or Italians [61]. This category tended to

52 Isenberg, *Dictionary of the Amharic Language*, I, 45, II, 96, 172; *idem, Géwografiya malät yämeder temhert*, pp. 63, 72-3.

53 P. Mérab, *Impressions d'Éthiopie* (Paris, 1921-9), II, 204; A. Zervos, *L'empire d'Éthiopie* (Alexandria, 1936). See also Zervos, *op. cit.*, pp. 458-69.

54 J. Faïtlovitch, *Quer durch Abessinien* (Berlin, 1910), p. 122; F.F. Kulmer, *Im Reiche Kaiser Meneliks* (Leipzig, n.d.), p. 181; E. G. Pick, *Reisenbriefe* (Wien, n.d.), pp. 160-1.

55 Leslau, *op. cit.*, p. 534.

56 Eadie, *op. cit.*, pp. 79, 81.

57 Guèbrè Sellassié, *op. cit.*, II, 515; Gäbrä Sellasé, *op. cit.*, p. 319.

58 A. Raad and B. Ghaleb, *La clé de la conversation abyssine* (Beyrouth, 1910), p. 67.

59 Afevork, *op. cit.*, pp. 37, 245. See also Armbruster, *op. cit.*, II, 125; Bevilacqua, *op. cit.*, col. 152; Angelo da Ronciglione, *op. cit.*, pp. 160, 162; Baeteman, *op. cit.*, col. 1042; I. Guidi, *Supplemento al vocabolario amarico-italiano* (Roma, 1940), col. 212.

60 Cohen, *op. cit.*, p. 30.

61 *Ibid.*, p. 30.

be despised as noted by Cohen who remarks: "The Abyssinians distinguish them by their mode of life and their appearance from other Europeans, diplomats, officials, travellers and merchants" whom they called *Färänj*. The two categories, *Grék* and *Färänj*, thus designated "classes rather than different nationalities"[62].

Corroboration of the poor regard in which the Greeks were held is provided by Faitlovitch who remarked that "if a European is seen on foot the native looks down upon him, and designates him as Greek, a name which the European does not like to hear, for a large part of the Greeks who have immigrated into Abyssinia, mostly the worst elements from their homeland, have acclimatised themselves to the low social status of the lowest strata of the Abyssinians and individually stand even lower, and are therefore called *YäFäränj bareya*, slaves of the Europeans. The marked contrast between the way of life and the whole manner of the other Europeans living there and these Greeks causes the Abyssinians to imagine that the latter serve as slaves in Europe[63]".

The result of such thinking was that the Greeks, who had once been differentiated from *Färänj* on account of their Orthodox faith, now tended to be regarded as distinct from them by reason of their occupation or socio-economic class. That this was the case is confirmed by the story, told by Cohen, of a Greek who had succeeded in life, and of whom it was therefore said that having been a *Grék* he had become a *Färänj*[64].

*   *   *

The rôle of Greek artisans subsequently decreased in importance, with the result that the word *Grék* came to be used exclusively to designate Greek nationals. As a derogatory term with connotation of class it thus died out as *'Alī* had done a generation or so earlier. The term *Färänj*, the oldest of the four names under discussion, alone survived as a generic term for foreigners.

The practice of addressing foreigners with the word *Färänj* has remained to the present day. On occasion instead of repeating the word several times children, may shout out the rhyme[65]:

Färänj
Qiṭu renj

62 Ibid., p. 30.
63 Faïtlovitch, *op. cit.*, p. 122.
64 Cohen, *op. cit.*, pp. 30-1. See also pp. 27, 33.
65 I am endebted to Alula Pankhurst for this poem.

"*Färänj*
"His bottom [is] tar".

Though this may seem uncomplimentary the second line is added merely for the rhyme, as evident from its absurd meaning, and the good-humoured self-mocking following couplet:

Abäša
Qiṭu mädoša.

"Abyssinian
"His bottom [is] a hammer".

Though the term *Färänj* has always been the principal term used in addressing Europeans, i.e. Caucasians, whenever contacts with a particular nationality prevail other foreigners tend to be subsumed under the same designation. Just as most Europeans in Menilek's day had been called *'Alī*, a term initially conceived for Italians, so after the Italian fascist occupation of 1935-41, Europeans of many nationalities were popularly called *Ṭaleyan*. A few years ago to his surprise the present author was addressed as *Čäyna* near Däbrä Tabor where Chinese workers were building a road, while European travellers to Socialist Ethiopia have on occasion been hailed as *Kuba*[66].

66 Heard for example by Alula Pankhurst in the Spring of 1981.

A FOURTEENTH-CENTURY REPORT ON ETHIOPIA

Franz Rosenthal
Yale University

In the early summer of the year 1330, the Syrian historian (Ibn) al-Jazari, then seventy years old, asked a Syrian merchant about the observations made by him during a trip to Ethiopia and incorporated the information thus obtained in his great historical work. During my stay in Cairo in 1947-48, while working on my *History of Muslim Historiography*, I copied the passage containing that information from a photostat of the Istanbul manuscript of al-Jazari preserved in the Egyptian Library[1]. No doubt already at that time, I had in mind to show it to the great Ethiopic scholar who has been my friend since the early days of our coming to the United States. It is as a token of this friendship that I am presenting a brief treatment of it in the volume published in his honor. My contribution is clearly not meant to be in any way definitive; others better qualified than I am will, I hope, correct and add to my presentation.

The report on Ethiopia is a good example of the efforts often made by Arabic historians to obtain information of historical or cultural interest on remote countries and civilizations. It never was easy for them to obtain such information. Although merchants traveled far and wide in rather large numbers, they had no particular training or incentive for collecting local data. The combination of observant traveler and learned scholar did indeed exist, and quite a few famous examples are known to us. Most historians, however, were of necessity restricted in the extent of their knowledge of remote countries. They had neither the time nor the opportunity to acquire such knowledge independently. It is to their credit that they did as much as they did to widen their horizon. The sum total of their efforts added up to a considerable amount of knowledge that is most valuable and indispensable for us. The results achieved by individuals may often seem to us somewhat disappointing[2]. But in al-Jazari, we encounter information that appears to be

---

[1] Cf. p. 415, n. 1 (Leiden 1952), 2nd ed., p. 493, n. 1 (Leiden 1968).

[2] Cf. H. Horst, "Berichte frühmamlûkischer Historiker über Äthiopien", in *Wort und Wirklichkeit* (Festschrift Eugen Ludwig Rapp, ed. B. Benzing, O. Böcher, G. Mayer), 170-185 (Meisenheim am Glan, 1976). Horst concludes that historical information on Ethiopia is found in Mamlûk historians as a matter of chance rather than as the result of real interest and effort on their part, as the history of the Muslims of Ethiopia was no

unusually factual for its kind. His informant seems to have recalled what he
was told—rather than what he had observed himself—as accurately as could
be expected, and any misunderstandings may be blamed on his sources. He
does not seem to have relied on the writings of others. The report thus adds to
our store of knowledge. Its very existence should be appreciated as a
noteworthy accomplishment.

Al-Jazari's *History*, which is preserved only in part as far as we know at
this time, has been much studied in recent years. A thorough analysis of it
and its author has been provided by Ulrich Haarmann in his *Quellenstudien zur
frühen Mamlukenzeit* (Freiburg 1969). At the same time, Donald P. Little made
intensive use of al-Jazari's work in his *Introduction to Mamlûk Historiography*
(Montreal 1970, also published as Vol. II of *Freiburger Islamstudien*). For the
year 730/1330, only one manuscript seems to be known to scholarship at
present[3]. Professor Haarmann kindly sent me a xerox copy of the folio
containing our passage (Ms. Köprülü, I, 1037, pp. 183f.) for comparison with
my original handcopy. I was also informed by Professor Haarmann that
Dr. Manfred Kropp had expressed interest in the report. I am grateful to
Dr. Kropp for not objecting to my publishing it on this occasion.

Translation

On Wednesday, Ramaḍân 9, (730)/Tuesday (evening), June 26, 1330, I had
an opportunity to be together with *al-mawlâ* Burhân-ad-dîn Ibrâhîm b. ash-
Shaykh Shams-ad-dîn Muḥammad b. 'Îsâ at-Tadmurî, then a merchant and
traveler[4]. He had made a journey from Mecca—May God Most-High honor

---

matter of concern to them. This is basically correct but does not consider the very obvious
difficulty of obtaining such information. Professor Haarmann has referred me to Horst's
article, which does not include the Jazari passage.

3 I may be permitted to mention here that I provided a regrettable piece of misinformation
in the second edition of my *History of Muslim Historiography* when I referred to a manuscript
in Rabat as containing an earlier portion of al-Jazari's work. C. Cahen has pointed out
that the Rabat manuscript contains a portion of the historical section of the encyclopaedia
of an-Nuwayri (d. 732/1332), cf. *Israel Oriental Studies*, 2 (1972), 144-147, and 3 (1973), 293.
As far as I know that portion of an-Nuwayri has not yet been published. I was misled by
the indication of author and title on the first and last pages of the Rabat manuscript, clearly
pointing to al-Jazari (*Hawâdith az-zamân* by Shams-ad-dîn Muḥammad b. Ibrâhîm al-Ḥariri
[al-Jaziri?] ad-Dimashqi). Those pages were, however, written by a hand different from
the rest of the manuscript.

4 I have not succeeded in finding any information on this Burhân-ad-dîn. According to his
nisbah, his family originally came from Palmyra, and it would seem that both he and his
father had scholarly training.

it!—to Ethiopia and had come to Damascus in this year with the pilgrims. I asked him about the remarkable things he had seen in Ethiopia, and he said:

They eat the meat raw[5]. I ate some with them. They assume that they gain from it strength which they do not from cooked meat.

He said: They have leaves they call *čât*[6]. They cut them from a tree there and eat them. They use (*čât*) as a gift to give to one another, and it enjoys great esteem among them. When the king wants to honor one of the amîrs or dignitaries of his dynasty, he takes some of those leaves and gives them to him. During that (presentation, the recipient) stands with his hands tied behind his back[7] and kisses the ground. He said: This is considered by them a greater gift than gold and silver[8].

I say: This is similar (to) and resembles the betel leaves[9] in India and the way their kings and dignitaries give betel leaves to their inner circle. (Betel

---

5 This observation, repeated later on and apparently considered very noteworthy, was also mentioned by al-Maqrizi in his *Historia Regum islamiticorum in Abyssinia*, ed. Fridericus Theodorus Rinck (Leiden 1790), text, p. 5, trans., p. 5, of the section in Rinck's publication that deals with Ethiopia. Cf. also E. van Donzel, *Foreign Relations of Ethiopia 1642-1700*, 14, 17 (Istanbul 1979).

6 Spelled *jât*, but no doubt intended to be pronounced čât, cf. Amharic *čât* (W. Leslau, *Concise Amharic Dictionary*, 239b [Berkeley-Los Angeles-Wiesbaden 1976]). It is the famous *qât* of the Yemen, about which very much has been written and is still being written, cf. the comprehensive study by Armin Schopen, *Das Qât* (Wiesbaden 1978, *Arbeiten aus dem Seminar für Völkerkunde der Johann Wolfgang Goethe-Universität Frankfurt am Main*, 8), and Maxime Rodinson, *Esquisse d'une monographie du Qât*, in *JA*, 265 (1977), 70-96 (as W. Leslau informs me). Both authors maintain that the use of the mild narcotic probably spread from Ethiopia to the Yemen. For the notion that it was the other way round, cf., for instance, Enrico Cerulli, *Studi Etiopici*, II, 16 (Rome 1938). But there is our early testimony for the use of *čât* in Ethiopia and the much quoted reference to it from the Chronicle of 'Amda Şeyôn, dating from about the same time as al-Jazari's work, cf. Schopen, 46; trans. G. W. B. Huntingford, 56 (Oxford 1965). But see n. 17, and the problem of earlier references to "*qât*" in the East.

7 The *Wörterbuch der klassischen arabischen Sprache*, letter *K*, does not indicate the use of the fifth conjugation of *k-t-f*, but only the seventh. Dozy, *Supplément*, lists the fifth conjugation as referring to the crossing of one's arms in front of the body.

8 Betel is thus described by Ibn Baṭṭûṭah, ed. C. Defrémery and B. R. Sanguinetti, II, 205 (Paris 1854, reprinted Paris, n. y. [1969?]), trans. H. A. R. Gibb, II, 387 (Cambridge 1958-1971).

9 Piper betle, in Arabic, following various Indic forms, transcribed as *tanbul* (with *n* representing *m*), *tanbûl*, *tânbûl*, *tâmûl*. Betel leaves are usually chewed together with the so-called betel nut (areca). Cf. the highly informative work by Solange Thierry, *Le Bétel, I. Inde et Asie du Sud-Est* (Paris 1969, *Supplément au tome IX,3, d'Objets et Mondes, Revue du Musée de l'Homme*). Entries on betel from Arabic pharmacopoeias published in recent years are ar-Râzî, *Ḥâwî*, XX, 188 (Hyderabad 1374-1390/1955-1971), with excerpts from other

leaves) are like the leaves of the orange[10]. They possess the property of speeding digestion. Much eating of them colors the teeth red. (The Indians) are fond of them and have many statements on them[11]. I have seen imported (betel leaves) in Alexandria, which had been placed in bee honey in (clay) pots. I bought three leaves for three quarters, each for a quarter[12], and I, as well as my brother Taqî-ad-dîn 'Abdallâh[13], each ate one of them. I did not find that they tasted good; they were hot[14] like ginger and pepper. It has been mentioned that their effect is noticeable only after eating ...teen[15] individual (leaves). God knows best what is correct.

I further asked the aforementioned Burhân-ad-dîn about the properties of the Ethiopian *čât* leaves. He said: They decrease (the desire and ability for) sleep, sexual intercourse, and eating. They clear the mind and increase the

sources in the editor's footnote, and al-Bîrûnî, *Kitâb aṣ-Ṣaydalah*, ed. Hakim Mohammed Said, text, 109, trans., 87 (Karachi 1973). Cf. also Abû Ḥanîfah ad-Dinawarî, *Kitâb an-Nabât*, ed. Bernhard Lewin, 221, 230 (Wiesbaden 1974, *Bibliotheca Islamica*, 26).

    Al-Jazari's comparison of *čât* and betel chewing is apt in many ways. Such a comparison was also made by Ibn Faḍlallâh al-'Umarî (700-749/1301-1349), who, though much younger than al-Jazari, wrote his *Masâlik al-abṣâr* at about the same time, cf. the translation by M. Gaudefroy-Demombynes, I, 11f. (Paris 1927). Ibn Faḍlallâh, however, states correctly that as such *čât* and betel are not similar.

10 *Čât*, and not betel, is compared with the leaves of the orange tree in al-Maqrizi, *op. cit.*, text, 11, trans., 12; Schopen, 46f.

11 The effect of betel as a laxative is also mentioned by Ibn Baṭṭûṭah, II, 206, trans. Gibb, II, 387. Red coloring of the teeth as a result of betel chewing is mentioned by al-Mas'ûdi, *Murûj*, ed. C. A. C. Barbier de Meynard and B. M. M. Pavet de Courteille, II, 84 (Paris 1861-77), ed. C. Pellat, I, 247f. (Beirut 1965-74). In fact, betel is known for giving a red color to gums and spittle; the often mentioned black coloration of the teeth is said not to be an effect of betel chewing. The "statements" apparently refer to literary and poetical discussions of betel, which were indeed numerous. With al-Jazari's remark that he obtained betel leaves in Alexandria, one may compare Ibn Baṭṭûṭah's statement that he was given betel leaves in Mogadishu, cf. II, 184, trans. Gibb, II, 375.

12 Apparently referring to fourth parts of the dirham. As compared to the Ethiopic prices mentioned later on, betel in Alexandria would appear to have been expensive. This would not be surprising for an imported luxury item.

13 Al-Jazari is said to have been very close to his younger brothers, but no reference to this 'Abdallâh seems to have been traced so far. "Brother" could also refer to friend or colleague, but a real brother is perhaps more likely to be meant here. Cf. also Haarmann, "Ein Damaszener Reisender des 13. Jahrhunderts an der Wolga", in *Festschrift für Wilhelm Lettenbauer*, 29-38 (Freiburg 1982), correcting my misunderstanding of *akh* as "brother" in *History of Muslim Historiography* (above, n. 1).

14 The *ḥiddah* "sharpness" of betel is also mentioned by ar-Râzi.

15 Here, as well as nn. 21 and 26, numbers seem to be meant, possibly *khams sittah 'ashrah* «fifteen, sixteen». Numerals are carefully written out elsewhere in the passage.

memory [16]. I say: This is an excellent summary of the properties of those *čât* leaves [17].

He also told me that (the Ethiopians) have a large valley (*wâdî*) surrounded by a mountain, on top of which there are trees called *dâdî* [18]. (The trees) have flowers, which are washed down (the mountain) when there is rain, and fall into caves. Those caves contain honey in which bees nest. The honey melts [19] and descends to the deepest part of the valley. It becomes a good, sweet wine which people drink. It is permitted to everybody; no restrictions are placed by the government on it, but (it is) like permitted water [20].

He said: Among them, the price of the dînâr is ... [21]. Exports from that country are skins, slaves, gold, civet, ivory, and other commodities. Ethiopia is reached from the Yemen via Aden and the land of az-Zayla' [22] where Ethiopia begins.

---

16 Cf. the analogous description in al-Maqrizi, *op. cit.*, text, p. 5, trans., p. 5. Al-Maqrizi adds *tufarriḥ* "causes joy", the common word for indicating the pleasurable effects of narcotics.

17 This statement would seem to suggest that al-Jazari had information about *čât* also from other sources. If that information came from Arabia, it would have bearing upon the problem mentioned in n. 6.

18 For *dâd(h)î*, cf. F. Rosenthal, *The Herb*, 124, n. 6 (Leiden 1971). In this context, it is of interest to note that there circulated a legend which linked the discovery of the «intoxicating» property of the shrub to the accidental dropping of its leaves into the water of a pond, cf. al-Birûni, *Ṣaydalah*, text, 188, trans., 155. And we are told that in the 'Irâq, its flowers were added to wine in order to increase the wine's potency, cf. M. Meyerhof and G. P. Sobhy, *The abridged version of "The Book of Simple Drugs" of ... al-Ghâfiqî ...*, I, 3, 488 ff. (Cairo 1938). Here, *dâdî* may have been substituted for *gešo* which is used in the preparation of the celebrated *ṭäǧǧ* "hydromel" (also of *ṭälla* "beer") of Ethiopia, cf. W. Leslau, *Etymological Dictionary of Gurage*, vol. 3, p. 616; J. Doresse, *La vie quotidienne des Éthiopiens chrétiens aux XVIIe et XVIIIe siècle*, 262 (Paris 1972); E. Ullendorff, *The Ethiopians*, 178 (Oxford University Press 1960). I do not know whether the legend told here is known from Ethiopic sources.

19 It might be "(the flowers) melt the honey", but the above translation seems preferable.

20 According to Muslim law, water (here in the plural) is res nullius, not privately owned but "permitted" to every member of the community, although there are exceptions under certain circumstances. Cf., for instance, D. Santillana, *Istituzioni di diritto musulmano malichita*, I, 318, 373, 408 (Rome, n. y.).
For the plural *amyâh*, see J. Blau, *A Grammar of Christian Arabic*, 228, para. 116 (Louvain 1966-67, *CSCO, Subsidia*, 28-29).

21 Read "fourteen"?? The price seems to indicate that gold coins were unusually cheap in Ethiopia, just as the prices for meat and cereals also appear to be cheap in comparison to prices in Syria.

22 Zayla' appears ordinarily without the definitive article, but cf. Yâqût, *Mu'jam, s.v.* In his article on Zayla', Yâqût also refers to marriage customs somewhat analogous to those mentioned here later.

He said: Fowl, monkeys, gazelles, water buffaloes, elephants, and other (animals), all of them wild, (live there and) are hunted by (the Ethiopians). They catch them when they are young, in order to raise and domesticate them. Others are slaughtered at the time they are caught, and eaten fresh, while the meat of others is cut and dried and eaten at some later time.

Again, on Friday, Ramaḍân 18, 730/Thursday (evening), July 5, 1330, (Burhân-ad-dîn) told me that on the day of the festival [23], the king of the Ethiopians fills a large vessel with honey wine. All who present themselves at court—amîrs, wazîrs, and soldiers, also the retainers and inner circle of (the king) as well as the dignitaries of his country—have their hands tied behind their backs and sip that wine with the mouth until they get drunk. Whenever the vessel gets empty, it is replenished. The king and his inner circle remain all that day at the gate of his palace and drink. Nobody who presents himself is prevented from obtaining some of that wine and drinking it.

When I asked (Burhân-ad-dîn) whether they have a table(cloth) [24] spread for eating, he replied: No, there is something else to take the place of our table(cloth) among them for eating [25] and other things.

When I asked him about the things they ate, he replied: They mostly eat raw beef. A head of beef costs from ten to ... [26] dirhams, a head of sheep from two dirhams to one dirham. Three *mudd*s of wheat (flour) cost a dirham, and each *kayl* of durrah costs a dirham [27].

They have bedouins who are Berbers, but not racially (identical with true Berbers) [28]. When one of them wants to get married, they do not let him get married until he brings them a man's penis with its skin and testicles intact. This is part of the dowry. Some bring three, four, or five. They boast of that. God knows best about that.

23 The Arabic could indicate the singular or the plural.

24 *Simâṭ* may also refer to the meal or banquet itself, but here it is more likely to refer to the way in which meals were set up on a low table, cf. J. Sadan, *Le mobilier au Proche Orient médiéval*, 55, n. 198, and 80, n. 296 (Leiden 1976).

25 Read *bi-akl*, or correct to *li-akl*?

26 "Fifteen"? "Head" does not seem to be meant literally but to refer to the whole animal. This makes it very cheap, although prices are notoriously difficult to evaluate even with the help of a work such as E. Ashtor's *Histoire des prix et des salaires dans l'Orient médiéval* (Paris 1969).

27 The fluctuations in the size of the *mudd* and the *kayl* are very great, but on the basis of the indications in W. Hinz, *Islamische Masse und Gewichte*, 46 and 40 (Leiden 1955, *Handbuch der Orientalistik, Ergänzungsband*, 1), a *mudd* in contemporary Syria may have represented about two pounds, and a *kayl* about thirty to forty pounds.

28 *Al-jins* seems to be clearly indicated in the manuscript. A correction to *al-Ḥabash*, yielding the sense "Berbers but not Ethiopians", must be ruled out. According to W. Leslau, there can be no doubt that the Danākil are meant here.

Text [29]

وفى يوم الاربعا التاسع من شهر رمضان حصل الاجتماع بالمولى

برهان الدين ابرهيم بن الشيخ شمس الدين محمد بن عيسى التدمرى

التاجر السفار يومئذ وكان قد سافر من مكة شرفها الله تعالى

الى بلاد الحبشة وقدم الي دمشق فى هذه السنة مع الحجاج

سالته عن عجائب ما راه في بلاد الحبشة فقال

ياكلون اللحم نيّا واكلت معهم منه وهم يزعمون انهم يتقووا به

بخلاف المطبوخ

قال ولهم ورق يسمونه جات يقطعونه من شجر هناك ياكلونه وهم

يكارمون به بعضهم بعضا وله عندهم مزيّة عظيمة واذا اراد الملك

اكرام احدًا من امرا دولته او كبيرًا منهم ياخذ من ذلك الورق

يناوله منه فعند ذلك يقوم يتكتف ويقبل الارض قال وهذا

عندهم اعظم من اعطايهم الذهب او الفضة

قلت وهذا نظير ويشبه ورق التنبل الذى فى بلاد الهند

وملوكهم وكبرايهم واعطاهم لخواصهم ورق التنبل وهو ورق مثل

ورق النارنج ومن خواصه انه يهضم الطعام والاكل سريعا

واذا كثر من اكله حمّر الاسنان ولهم فيه غرام وافاويل

كثيرة رايته فى ثغر الاسكندرية وقد جلبوه اليها ووضعوه

فى برانى فى عسل النحل فاشتريت منه ثلاثة اوراق بنصف

29 This is as accurate a copy of the text as I have been able to provide, but diacritical dots are usually supplied as needed, whether or not they are found in the manuscript. The reader may rest assured that the many strange things he will observe are not copying mistakes. The numerous offenses against the classical language are left just as they are found in the manuscript. We are dealing with a rough draft. Moreover, our passage reflects the spoken words of the reporter. Yet, it is somewhat surprising that an educated man would put such things on paper, even if there was time for later polishing and editing by the author or his amanuenses.

وربع كل واحد بربع اكلت منهم واحدة واخى تقى الدين عبد الله

واحدة فما وجدتها طيبة الا فيها حدّة مثل الزنجبيل والفلفل

وذكروا ان ما يحصل للانسان تاثيرا الا اذا اكل او/تم عشرة

واحدة من الورق والله اعلم بالصواب

وسالت ايضا لبرهان الدين المذكور عن خواص ورق الجات

الذى بالحبشة فقال انه يقلل النوم والجماع والاكل ويصفى الذهن

ويكثر الذكر قلت وهذا مجموع حسن مليح فى خواص هذا

الورق الجات المذكور

وقال لى ايضا ان لهم وادى كبير وفى اعالى الجبل المحيط

بالوادى شجر يقال له دادى وله زهر فاذا جا المطر رمى الزهر

فيسقط الزهر على كهوف وفى تلك الكهوف عسل يعشعش فيه

النحل فيذيب العسل وينحدر الى اسفل الوادى فيصير منه خمرا

طيبا مليحا فيشربون الناس منه وهو مباح للعالم ولا عليه احتجار

من جهة السلطان الا مثل الامياه المباحة

قال وعندهم سعر الدينار ارعما والذى يجلب من تلك البلاد

الاديم والرقيق والذهب والزباد والعاج وغير ذلك من الاصناف

والسفر اليها من اليمن من عدن ومنها الى بلاد الزيلع وهى

اول اقليم بلاد الحبشة

قال والدجاج والقرود والغزلان والجاموس والافيلة وغيرهم الجميع

وحوش فيصطادوهم فمنهم من يصطادوه صغيرا فيربوه ويولفوه ومنه ما

يذبح فى وقت الصيد ويوكل طرا ومنه ما يقدد لحمه الى وقت

اخر فياكلونه

واخبرني ايضا في يوم الجمعة ثامن عشر شهر رمضان المعظم
سنة ثلاثين وسبعماية قال ان ملك الحبشة يعلي يوم العيد مركب
كبير خمر من خمر العسل وكل من حضر الى الخدمة من الامرا
والوزرا والجند ومن اعوانه وخواصه واكابر اهل بلده يتكتف ويضع
يديه خلف ظهره ويغب بفمه من ذلك الخمر حتى يسكر وكلما
نقص المركب زادوه ويبقى الملك هو وخواصه طول ذلك النهار
على باب داره يشربون وكل من حضر لا يمنع من التناول من
ذلك الخمر وشربه

وسالته هل يمد لهم سماط ياكلون منه قال ما ثم شى
غير ذلك وهو عندهم بمعنى السماط عندنا ناكل الطعام وغيره
وسالته عن ماكلهم ما هى قال اكثر اكلهم لحم البقر نيًّا
وراس البقر يسوى من عشرة دراهم الى ﮒﻉ وراس الغنم من
درهمين والى درهم واحد والقمح كل ثلاثة امداد بدرهم
والذرة كل كيل بدرهم

ولهم عربان وهم برابر غير الجنس اذا اراد احدهم ان
يتزوج لا يزوجوه حتى يجيب لهم ذكر ابن ادم يكون مسكه
وخصاه فيكون ذلك من جملة النقد وبعضهم يجيب ثلاثة واربع
وخمسة يفتخرون بذلك والله اعلم بذلك

ARCHAEOLOGY

TUMULUS, PIERRES LEVÉES ET AUTRES VESTIGES DANS LE MENZ EN ÉTHIOPIE

Francis Anfray

Institut Français d'archéologie, Addis Ababa

Sur ses hauts plateaux entaillés de profondes vallées, le Menz conserve des souvenirs anciens. On rapporte que le dernier roi d'Axoum, Anbasa Wedem, s'y réfugia au dixième siècle. Baeda-Maryam au quinzième siècle y établit sa résidence. L'imâm Ahmed ben Ibrahim el-Ghâzi, plus connu sous le nom de Grañ, le dévasta en 1531 [1].

Il possède nombre de monastères et de vieilles églises.

Trois régions le divisent, traditionnellement : Mama-Meder, Lalo-Meder et Gera-Meder.

C'est un district au nord-est du Shoa, avec Mehal-Meda pour ville principale et siège de l'administration, à 260 kilomètres d'Addis Abeba par la route.

Peu d'étrangers l'ont parcouru dans le passé ; rares sont ceux qui ont laissé des récits de leur visite. Il n'y a guère à mentionner que les brefs passages du missionnaire Krapf en 1842 et de Paul Soleillet qui en 1882 y resta deux jours en compagnie de Chefneux et d'Alfieri [2].

Il faut cependant préciser qu'il n'est pas fait état ici de plusieurs renseignements que fournit la chronique éthiopienne, de manière sporadique [3]. Cela étant, l'abondance des faits n'est pas ce qui caractérise la documentation historique relative au Menz. Quant à l'information archéologique, elle est quasiment nulle. La précieuse nomenclature des églises rupestres que R. Sauter a dressée, enregistre Alobar (un lac de vallée entouré de légendes, près de Zemmero), Ghebre-Krestos-Aragawi et Yeghem-Washa, sans description [4].

L'objet de cette note est de livrer quelques indications sur des sites observés à l'occasion d'un voyage effectué dans la région de Gera-Meder, à l'ouest de Mehal-Meda, en novembre 1980 [5].

---

1 D.N. Levine, *Wax and Gold*. 1967, p. 28-54.

2 P. Soleillet, *Voyages en Éthiopie*, p. 87-90.

3 Guèbrè-Sellassié, *Chronique du Règne de Ménélik II*. Paris. 1931. Notamment p. 28 note 2. Etc.

4 R. Sauter, «Où en est notre connaissance des églises rupestres d'Éthiopie», *Annales d'Éthiopie*. 1963, vol. V, p. 276.

5 Ato Kostantinos Tesfaye-Tsyon et M. Yves Baudouin étaient du voyage. M.Y. Baudouin a dessiné la carte.

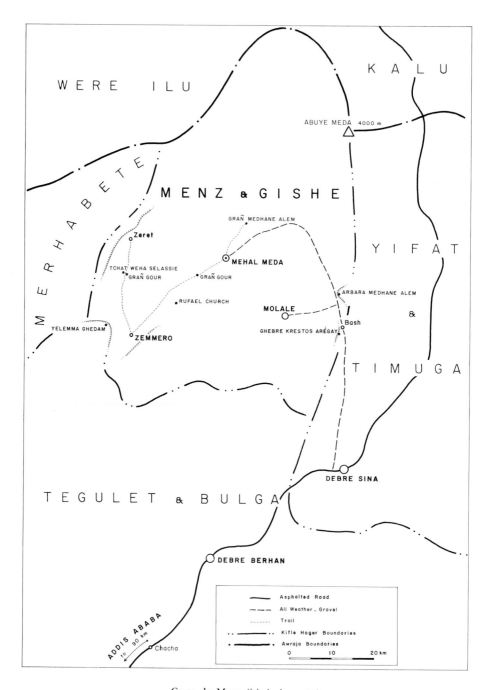

Carte du Menz (itinéraire 1980)

TUMULUS

Ils sont assez nombreux en Éthiopie. On en connaît aux parages de Ham, en Erythrée, ainsi qu'au sud d'Assab, à Eyilou[6].

Ceux du Harar ont été signalés il y a une cinquantaine d'années par Azaïs et Chambard[7].

Dans le Arsi, Amara est un site à tumulus[8].

Plusieurs ont été repérés dans le Shoa: à Ilalu-Maskal dans la contrée de Balli-Abbo du canton de Loumé, à une soixantaine de kilomètres au sud d'Addis Abeba; dans le Soddo, à Harmuffo-Dildilla, Waraddi, Osole, Dimbo-Der, notamment[9].

Le Sidamo peut également figurer dans la liste avec ses sites de Gobatcho(?), Tuto-Fela et Ghinno, dans les districts de Sidama et de Gedeo, à l'est du lac Abaya.

L'inventaire général n'a pas été fait, tant s'en faut.

Tous ces tumulus sont anciens. Il est difficile d'en spécifier la date; plus encore d'indiquer le nom du peuple qui les a construits.

A ce jour une seule étude apporte des données précises à leur sujet, et tente de les situer dans un cadre chronologique: celle de Roger Joussaume. Elle concerne des recherches entreprises autour de plusieurs tumulus du Tchertcher, dans le Harar[10]. Certains tumulus de cette région seraient à dater approximativement des environs du dixième siècle après J.-C. Des ossements humains et des poteries y ont été trouvés.

Les tumulus sont particulièrement nombreux dans les monts du Tchertcher. La carte complète demeure à établir.

Un point réclame quelque éclaircissement: tumulus désigne ici des amas anciens de pierres aux dimensions notables et dont on présume qu'ils recouvrent des sépultures.

---

6 Fr. Anfray, *Annales d'Éthiopie*, vol. VI 1965, p. 8. Chronique archéologique, et vol. VIII, 1970, p. 41. Notes archéologiques.

7 Azaïs et Chambard, *Cinq années de recherches archéologiques en Éthiopie*. Paris. 1932. En 1980, des tumulus ont été observés par Fr. Anfray et Ato Kostantinos dans les collines au sud de Mieso, à Debiti. Il y en aurait aussi à Bio, sur les hauteurs à l'est de Debiti.

8 Fr. Anfray, «Notes archéologiques», *Annales d'Éthiopie*, vol. VIII, 1970, p. 32.

9 Ces tumulus ont des dimensions moyennes: environ un mètre d'élévation; cinq ou six mètres de diamètre; parfois moins.

10 R. Joussaume, *Le Mégalithisme en Éthiopie. Monuments funéraires protohistoriques du Harar*. 1974, pages 11 et 12, 51 à 59, 109 à 112. Des cistes mégalithiques dateraient des environs du milieu du deuxième millénaire avant l'ère. Recouvertes de pierres et de terre au temps de leur aménagement, elles formaient alors des tumulus.

1. Grañ Gour à dix kilomètres de Mehal-Meda.

Leur hauteur est comprise entre trois et huit mètres. À la base, leur diamètre peut atteindre une dizaine de mètres, et davantage.

Selon Roger Joussaume, à Watcho dans le Tchertcher des tumulus «dépassent cinquante mètres de diamètre et une douzaine de mètres en hauteur» [11].

Azaïs et Chambard, à propos des investigations qu'ils entreprirent au cours des années vingt, mentionnent des tumulus de pierres observés dans l'Arsi, dont ils disent qu'ils sont «entourés de pierres atteignant 1 m 50 de hauteur sur 0 m 80 de large» [12]; en pays Amarro, dans le Sidamo «un peu avant Alga … une centaine de petits tumulus, d'un mètre et demi de diamètre, surmontés de pierres basaltiques»; à Chama, dans le Gamo-Gofa, «une vingtaine de tumulus» dont la hauteur varie de 0 m 50 à 0 m 75. Il est certain que les petits monticules de terre et de pierre abondent dans tout le pays éthiopien, certains d'une ancienneté presque impossible à apprécier, d'autres d'une époque récente. Dans le Sidamo on en élève toujours, sur les tombes. En quelques endroits, des tas de pierres ne marquent pas l'emplacement de sépultures; ce sont de simples monuments commémoratifs d'évènements particuliers, d'intérêt local. Il y a lieu de distinguer ces monticules des grands tumulus, dans une première approche de la question en tout cas.

GRAÑ GOUR

À dix kilomètres au sud-ouest de Mehal-Meda, en bordure du chemin qui conduit à Zemmero un gros entassement de pierres basaltiques signale très vraisemblablement une sépulture ancienne (voir la carte et la photo n° 1).

Sa hauteur dépasse cinq mètres. À la base, son diamètre est d'une vingtaine de mètres. La tradition locale y voit un tombeau. Elle y accroche le nom de Grañ, comme d'ailleurs à plusieurs sites historiques de la région [13].

Au dire des habitants du voisinage, plusieurs tumulus du même type se rencontrent dans le pays. De fait, un autre a été remarqué à TCHAT-WEHA-SELLASSIE, localité qui se trouve à une quinzaine de kilomètres en direction

---

11 R. Joussaume, *Le Mégalithisme*, p. 55.

12 Azaïs et Chambard, *Cinq années de recherches archéologiques en Éthiopie*. Paris. 1932, pages 215, 246, 264. Les auteurs font état de tumulus observés à Matara, Wenni, Gayet-Gareno; il semble que ç'ait été par erreur.

13 Ainsi l'église de Grañ-Medhane-Alem, à huit kilomètres au nord de Mehal-Meda, bizarrement.

2. Grañ Gour près de Tchat-Weha-Sellassie.

de l'ouest, à vol d'oiseau ; à quelque trente-cinq kilomètres par le chemin qui mène à Zeret. (Photo n° 2).

Ce tumulus offre les mêmes caractéristiques que le premier : entassement de grosses pierres basaltiques, dimensions sensiblement égales. Il est aussi appelé Grañ Gour. (Ce dernier mot, en amharique, signifie d'ailleurs tertre artificiel).

PIERRES LEVÉES À TCHAT-WEHA-SELLASSIE

Près du deuxième Grañ Gour, entre Zemmero et Teret, à proximité d'une église, trois pierres sont dressées en alignement. Ce sont des pierres laissées à l'état brut, et hautes de 1 m 70. Selon les gens du lieu, elles ne seraient pas à leur emplacement d'origine. Elles se trouvaient jadis non loin du tumulus [14]. Photo n° 3.

PIERRES SCULPTÉES À L'ÉGLISE DE RUFAEL
DANS LA RÉGION DE MESAHALE-MARYAM

Au sud-ouest de Mehal-Meda, on atteint par la route, à quinze kilomètres, le village de Tsehay-Sina, puis, de là, après une heure de marche une colline ombragée d'oliviers et de genévriers où est une église dédiée à Rufael — anciennement Lidetta-Maryam. Autour de cette église on discerne les vestiges, dispersés et très effacés d'un ancien établissement. Photo n° 4. Ici et là des élévations de terrain semblent indiquer la présence d'un mur d'enceinte.

Selon la tradition, le roi Baeda-Maryam qui régna de 1468 à 1478 fixa un temps sa résidence en cet endroit.

Les habitants du pays racontent qu'ils y ont découvert des blocs de pierre ouvrés en creusant le sol. Dans les murs du porche (dedje selam) sont remployées des pierres sculptées. L'une d'elles (photo n° 5) montre deux rouelles encadrant un motif hélicoïdal, en champlevé. Longueur : 77 cm. Largeur : 55 cm.

Trois blocs de facture semblable sont encastrés dans les murs, à l'intérieur du porche.

Que de tels éléments de décoration architecturale remontent au quinzième siècle, l'attribution n'est rien de moins que plausible. Au nord du Menz, la

---

14 Des pierres semblables, au nombre de trois, ont été observées sur le tertre de l'église Ghiorghis, à Dankaz, non loin des ruines du château de Gomenghê, au sud de Gondar. 1980.

3. Pierres levées près de l'église de Tchat-Weha-Sellassie.

4. Mesahale-Maryam. Vestiges anciens près de l'église de Rufael.

5. Mesahale-Maryam (Rufael). Pierre sculptée dans le mur du porche.

région voisine de Wera-Ilu conserve des vestiges sculptés de cette époque. Ainsi à l'église de Mekane-Sellassie [15].

Dans la chronique de Haylu, il est dit que Baeda-Maryam bâtit une église à Meshale-Maryam qui est le nom de la contrée environnant la colline de Rufael [16].

ARBARA-MEDHANE-ALEM

Peu après l'embranchement de Molale, sur la route de Mehal-Meda, en contrebas vers l'est (dix minutes à pied), une grotte naturelle a été aménagée en sanctuaire chrétien. Au fond de la grotte sont entassés des corps momifiés — de façon naturelle — dont la plupart ont été enveloppés dans des peaux. Squelettes de moines, dit-on, vieux de plusieurs siècles. On en dénombre une bonne centaine.

GHEBRE-KRESTOS-AREGAY

Non loin de la bourgade de Bash (une heure de marche, en direction du sud-ouest), une autre grotte naturelle, très profonde est elle aussi aménagée en sanctuaire. (Cette église de caverne est signalée dans l'article de R. Sauter, *Annales d'Ethiopie*, V, p. 276, n° 88). La rivière Ghebre-Ghiorghis coule en contrebas de la grotte.

Il y aurait des églises rupestres à l'ouest de la route qui de Zemmero conduit à Zeret. Les noms de Taghero-Balewold et de Kolakwo-Maryam ont été indiqués par des personnes rencontrées sur le chemin.

Bien qu'à proprement parler se situant hors du domaine de l'archéologie, il vaut la peine de signaler à l'attention de l'historien l'existence d'une communauté monastique depuis longtemps à demeure dans la profonde vallée que creuse la rivière Yelemma-Djirat, dans le canton de Qahia-Gabriel.

L'endroit se nomme YELEMMA-GHEDAM. Il s'atteint en partant de Zemmero. À huit kilomètres de cette bourgade on trouve le hameau de Siter. De là, deux heures de marche sur le plateau, une descente abrupte, et on arrive à Yelemma-Ghedam où vit cette communauté composée — au dire du supérieur — d'environ 175 cénobites — hommes et femmes. L'espace qu'occupe le monastère est exigü: une corniche au pied d'une haute falaise.

---

15 E. Cerulli, *Africa italiana.* 1933. XI-XII, p. 57-112. L'Etiopia del secolo XV.
16 E. A. Wallis Budge, *A History of Ethiopia.* 1928, vol. I, p. 314.

Habitant des huttes de caractère sommaire, ces cénobites semblent mener une vie très ascétique: jeûnes des plus rigoureux, maigre nourriture, prières nocturnes prolongées jusqu'au matin. Ils n'ont pas d'église mais une salle de prière dans une maison ronde. Aucune image religieuse ne se remarque. On ne porte pas l'insigne de la croix. On affirme ne pas savoir le nom du fondateur. Ces moines pratiquent le tissage, la poterie (de belle qualité), la meunerie [17].

Anciens Falasha? Témoins d'une antique communauté chrétienne sise à l'écart de l'orthodoxie éthiopienne?

[17] Cf. D.N. Levine. On the History and Culture of Manz. *Journal of Ethiopian Studies*. Vol. IX n° 1. p. 204, note 3.

ART

A NOTE ON THE COSTUMES
IN 15TH AND EARLY 16TH-CENTURY PAINTINGS: PORTRAITS OF THE NOBLES AND THEIR RELATION TO THE IMAGES OF SAINTS ON HORSEBACK

STANISŁAW CHOJNACKI
University of Sudbury

The following note is the fortuitous outcome of the writer's research in Ethiopian painting and an attempt to explore it as a possible source for the study of Ethiopian dress in the past [1].

The subject matter of Ethiopian paintings is almost exclusively religious. The painters depicted biblical stories, the Virgin Mary as well as the saints and martyrs, usually following the iconography either of the East or the West. They rarely ventured to create their own compositions. Nevertheless, the imported models had to be adapted to the local cultural environment and this was achieved by transforming these models according to the local idiom as well as by adding details taken directly from Ethiopian life. The transformations and additions are important for the study of the material culture of the Ethiopians, including their way of dress. Although on the whole the Ethiopian painters preferred to follow convention in depicting the human figure and objects, they occasionally became realistic in depicting such details as crosses, house implements as well as costumes and weapons. This was particularly true whenever the painter did not refer to the already established model and composed the painting by himself. Moreover, we occasionally find scenes of daily life depicted among the sets of religious images and thematically related to them. Such scenes are exceptional in paintings prior to the 18th century when they became more frequent. These genre scenes mostly show people on horseback, boys playing lawn hockey, and a farmer plowing his field.

---

1 The study of Ethiopian costumes is much neglected. One has the feeling that the description of costumes in Jean Doresse, *La vie quotidienne des éthiopiens chrétiens aux XVIIe et XVIIIe siècles* (Paris, 1972; passim and p. 255-58) is based rather on the author's knowledge of the 20th-century Ethiopian countryside than the study of travellers' narratives and paintings. Pankhurst in his *Economic history of Ethiopia*, 1800-1939 (Addis Ababa, 1968), p. 263-66, gives a glimpse of 19th-century clothing = Pankhurst 1968.

Similar to Christian art in other countries, the religious themes are occasionally put entirely into local settings. Such is the case of the Flight into Egypt, which in painting evokes travelling in Ethiopia, including the manner of dress.

The other source for the study of the past is the so-called portraits of the donors. Following the practice common in the Christian world, the donations were attested by including the donors in pictures. Until the 18th century, there are few of these instances, but afterwards they became a popular and permanent feature of Ethiopian painting. The donors' images are not their portraits in a strict sense. The painters do not strive after the likeness of the donors, but individualize them by way of presenting their attire, weapons and ornaments.

Starting with the 15th century, the more gifted painters depicted the religious themes by combining a vigour of observation with a strong sense of ornamentation. They created the images of Saint George and the other saints on horseback in which the painter's imagination was well-rooted in Ethiopian culture. To depict the saints they took the forms which originally were developed in Eastern iconography, but transformed these entirely into the Ethiopian idiom. The Paleologian image of St. George with an adolescent face and in a coat of arms reached Ethiopia as late as the second half of the 15th century. That image brought with it the change from the mature and bearded faces of the equestrian saints to the youthful, as well as the change from the snake to the dragon, but it did not affect their costumes, the horse trappings as well as several minor details. Ethiopian painters virtually never depicted saints wearing a coat of arms. Their attire differs from those of similar saints in Byzantine and related art. Moreover, the attire of equestrian saints in Ethiopian painting varies from one period to another as if the artists followed the changes in fashions. However, these changes do not recall any European costumes that we know of. Would the saints be wearing local costumes? According to the hagiography of St. George as well as of other equestrian saints, they are either of royal or noble blood; we may assume therefore that the costumes in the paintings correspond to their high rank. If the costumes are Ethiopian, they indeed must be those of the nobility. The purpose of this note is to investigate selected 15th and early 16th-century paintings in order to substantiate that hypothesis.

The main pieces of evidence are three miniatures, two Ethiopian noblemen on horseback and one a noble lady travelling, persons who ordered the manuscripts to be produced and their portraits depicted.

The evidence thus obtained is compared with the information on the Ethiopian manner of dress obtained from written records. The narratives of

Father Francisco Alvarez, referring to the period 1520-1526[2], and those of Miguel de Castanhoso, referring to 1541-1543[3], are the main sources of information. The writings of Francesco Suriano[4], Alessandro Zorzi and two 17th-century writers, Manuel Barradas and Job Ludolf are also quoted in the course of the discussion.

Although the narratives do not give a full description of Ethiopian costumes, they contain a great deal of valuable information. The narratives and the paintings seem to complement each other. The paintings give life to some laconic statements of the travellers whereas the writings provide additional information on the costumes and weapons which are not shown in the paintings.

The present investigation is the first of its kind and the conclusions should therefore be considered as tentative; some additions and perhaps corrections are to be expected as the result of further discoveries in monasteries and old churches of Ethiopia. Indeed, the inventory of Ethiopia's pictorial heritage is not complete as yet. Nevertheless, it is hoped that this study will initiate a systematic investigation of the history of Ethiopian costumes and will help to change some current misconceptions.

It is a commonplace that in recreating an aspect of past material life such as costume, one good painting or drawing can be more telling than a long description. The travellers' remarks about the costumes are mostly casual, at times lacking precision and when they describe the particular part of the costume, use expressions which by themselves need a glossary, whereas the costumes depicted in the painting can be "seen", provided of course that they are well-delinated, as is the case with the works described below.

Description of paintings

Let us start with the equestrian portraits of two 15th-century Ethiopian nobles. Belin Saggad, *aqanṣana* of Sarāwē[5], is shown in the Book of Psalms and

---

2 Francisco Alvarez, *The Prester John of the Indies; a true relation of the lands of the Prester John, being the narrative of the Portuguese embassy to Ethiopia in 1520 written by Father Francisco Alvares*; ed. with additional material by C.F. Beckingham and G.W.B. Huntingford (Cambridge, 1961) = Alvarez 1961.

3 Miguel de Castanhoso, *The Portuguese expedition to Abyssinia in 1541-42, as narrated by Castanhoso*; ed. by R.S. Whiteway (London, 1902) = Castanhoso.

4 Francesco Suriano, *Treatise on the Holy Land*; tr. by Th. Bellorini and E. Hoade (Jerusalem, 1949) = Suriano 1949. Suriano recorded the information on Ethiopia brought by Giovanni Battista da Imola (G.B. de Brocchi) who visited the country in 1481-82.

5 According to the inscription he was the son of Bagada Sayun. *Aqanṣana* is a title of the

Prayers produced for him in 1476-77[6], and prince (*masfen*)[7] Yemḥarana Egzi'e, probably local governor in Tegrē province or its Eritrean part is depicted in the *Lives of the Martyrs* produced for him in 1451-53[8]. In the latter manuscript there is a miniature facing his portrait which shows his wife Lady Amata Le'ul with her retinue.

Both manuscripts are enlivened with numerous miniatures representing the life of Christ as well as various saints including those on horseback. The miniatures are executed in the style which developed during the second half of the 15th century in the scriptoria of Tegrē and Eritrea. Unfortunately we know neither the names of the scriptoria nor those of the artists. The book of Yemḥarana Egzi'e was kept a long time in the Eritrean monastery, Dabra Māryām (Qoḥāyen) which is reputed to have been in the past a great centre for manuscript production. It is possible that both manuscripts originate from that monastery and perhaps were illuminated by the same artist.

The portrait of Belin Saggad (fig. 1) is very stylized but the details the artist thought essential for the donor's identification are drawn from life and well delineated. The ornamented bandlet on his head, the sword and spear, the bare foot inserted into the stirrup iron as well as the colorful saddle cloth and horse trappings mirror the way of life of 15th-century noblemen. Short broad-bladed swords with ornamented handles occasionally appear in 15th-century paintings, which corresponds to the statement by Alvarez that "the great lords have a few swords". Perhaps they were made locally. The spear is certainly Ethiopian; its spearhead is fixed either on a bamboo cane,

feudal lord. C. Conti Rossini, *Studi su popolazioni dell'Etiopia* (Roma, 1914), p. 92-95 uses the forms *āqaṣen* and Bagadā Ṣeyon. The writer is indebted to Dott. S. Tedeschi for checking this point and other suggestions.

6 At present in the Bibliothèque nationale, Paris (Fonds d'Abbadie No. 105). Described by Carlo Conti Rossini, "Un codice illustrato eritreo nel secolo XV (Ms Abb. N. 105 della Bibl. Nat. di Parigi)", *Africa Italiana* 5 (1927) p. 83-97; "Notice sur les manuscrits éthiopiens de la collection d'Abbadie", *Journal asiatique* 19 (1912) p. 551-78, 20 (1914) p. 5-72, 449-494; Antoine d'Abbadie, *Catalogue raisonné des manuscrits éthiopiens* (Paris, 1859) p. 114-18; Ewa Balicka, Miniatury piętnastowiecznego psałterza etiopskiego (studium ikonograficzne), *Biuletyn historii sztuki* (1975) p. 89-113 = Balicka 1975.

7 Title of the feudal lord. According to Beckingham "Litt. 'governor', undoubtedly old title for sub-king". Alvarez 1961, 21.

8 Discovered and photographed by David R. Buxton at Dabra Māryām in Qoḥayen, Eritrea. Mentioned *passim* by Beatrice Playne in her *St. George for Ethiopia* (London, 1954) and "In search of Early Christian paintings in Ethiopia", *The Geographic magazine* XXII 10 (1950) 400-11; the latter include two hand made copies of the miniatures in the manuscript. One miniature is reproduced in David Buxton, *The Abyssinians* (London, 1970), fig. 80. The writer is indebted to Mr. Buxton for the permission to reproduce the miniatures.

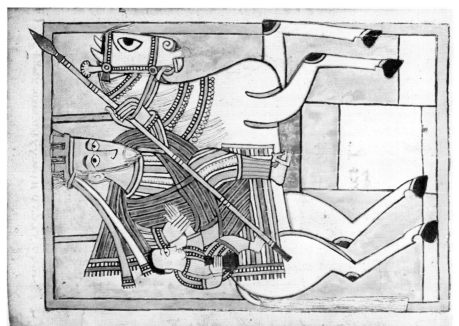

Fig. 2

Fig. 1

or on a shaft decorated with rings. Spears, or javelins, according to Alvarez, were the main pieces of Ethiopian armament[9].

Particularly striking is Belin Saggad's head attire. It is composed of two parts, the bandlet and the trinket attached to it. Ewa Balicka who studied the miniature thought that "he has on his head a crown with ribbons which recalls the *kamelaukion*, called in Ethiopia *zeud*"[10]. It is doubtful that the 15th-century Ethiopians called this kind of head decoration *zewd*; it corresponds rather to the one used at the ceremonial investiture by the king of the high officials in former times and called *rās warq*, literally "head gold"[11]. Perhaps Balicka took the sharply delineated noble's hair as the form of the crown. In fact, the miniature shows his hair cut and dressed in the fashion characteristic of 15th- and early 16th-century Ethiopia. We have a description of that fashion in the notes of the erudite Italian Alessandro Zorzi of Venice. He wrote down all information on Ethiopia as given to him by Ethiopian monks who passed through his town during the years 1519 to 1524. One of these, brother Thomas of Ganget told him the following: "The hair of the men is long, but they cut it in the shape of a hat; the hair is drawn out and oiled with a certain mixture of herbs so that when dry it stands on end, and with a long and rather twisted iron they comb it so that it stands out like a hat"[12]. This description is well illustrated in a number of 15th-century miniatures including the portraits of Belin Saggad and Yemḥarana Egzi'e as well as that of the page who attends the wife of the latter. Such a hair arrangement is usually combined with an ornamental bandlet bound over the front, but the arrangement without the bandlet is also known[13].

Bandlets were worn in Ethiopia to single out an office or distinction and were bestowed upon warriors by the rulers to express their appreciation for bravery during battle. Bandlets were probably also worn by the 15th-century rulers and were common among the nobles, if one considers the number of bandlets in the paintings of the period. Alvarez noted that a high official presenting tribute at the Ethiopian court was wearing "a crown [or cord in another version of the narrative] round his head like the little cap of a

---

9 Alvarez 1961, 129; Suriano 1949, 100.

10 Balicka 1975, 107.

11 Alvarez 1961, 114 footnote 1.

12 O. G. S. Crawford, *Ethiopian itineraries circa 1400-1524 including those collected by Alessandro Zorzi at Venice in the years 1519-24* = Haklyut Society, second series No. 109 (Cambridge, 1955) p. 171.

13 Four soldiers plaiting the crown of thorns on Christ's head in the 15th-century manuscript which was kept until 1974 at the Palace Library, Maqalē in Tegrē.

Castilian muleteer" [14]. At another occasion Alvarez recorded that the chiefs of Tegrē "all had small red caps with big points, which fluttered in the wind" [15]. The expressions "crown", "cord" or "cap" would vaguely correspond to Belin Saggad's and Yemḥarana Egzi'e's head attires, which undoubtedly are a faithful illustration of how the nobles ornamented their heads.

The bandlet of Belin Saggad is fastened with a knot on his right temple with the extremities of the bandlet waving to the back. A similar ornamental knot with swelling fillets appears in the portraits of Yemḥarana Egzi'e as well as in many portraits of 15th-century equestrian saints.

Over the front, three short round trinkets are affixed. They seem to have a phallic form. If indeed that form was intended, it must have had a special significance for Belin Saggad. Moreover, this would be the only known instance of such head ornamentation depicted in early Ethiopian art.

The phallic ornamentation is well known in Ethiopia and was mainly worn by the Boranā and Guği people in the South, either as the decoration for men (*kallaĉā*) or for married women (*banaĉo*) who wore it attached to the back of their capes [16]. The ritual head cover of the kings of Kafā, at present at the Institute of Ethiopian Studies collection, Addis Ababa, is ornamented in the front with three phalli. So, there is a reason to believe that, indeed, Belin Saggad's head attire was ornamented with phallic trinkets, perhaps made of silver or gilt and studded with semi-precious stones. The painter did not know how to draw the trinkets at an angle as they are usually attached and has given the impression that they were placed upright.

Let us now turn to the horse trappings. Three collars are ornamented with small balls, while the brow and nose bands have colorful leather straps; a plume is affixed over the bridle. All these in addition to the rich saddle cloth evidence the lavishness of the Ethiopians in decorating the trappings as well as their love of horses.

Belin Saggad has his foot supported by the stirrup irons. The latter is of the type used in Europe as well as in the Near East, i.e. a U shaped clamp or piece of iron flat at the bottom. Belin Saggad's stirrup iron as well as those of the subsequently described riders are virtually always of that type and not of the simple ring which is also used in Ethiopia.

The foot of the noble is bare. It is a well-known fact that until the 20th century the Ethiopians as a rule did not use footwear. Suriano states tersely

14 Alvarez 1961, 426.
15 Alvarez 1961, 429.
16 Ad. E. Jensen ed., *Altvölker Süd-Äthiopiens* (Stuttgart, 1959), I pl. 29; Eike Haberland, *Galla Süd-Äthiopiens* (Stuttgart, 1963), II 46.

Fig. 3

that Ethiopians are "bare footed"[17] which is attested by all subsequent travellers' descriptions; the same is evidenced in virtually all paintings from the 13th century onwards.

What about Belin Saggad's costume? If we assume that in his portrait all the above described details are drawn from life, the costume he is wearing must also be Ethiopian. It is composed of three pieces: a striped tunic (*qamis*) reaching to the knees and having a round braided collar; trousers (*surri*) also striped and large at the knees but narrowing towards the ankle; and a loose cloak thrown over the shoulders. The identification of the latter is not certain, Is it a *šammā*, a loose white outer garment usually light and made of cotton? Our cloak seems to be of a heavier type and perhaps made of silk. Alvarez describes how the Portuguese met the Ethiopian Captain of Arqiqo, a locality on the coast of the Red Sea, who wore "a *bedem* a wide Moorish cape over a rich Moorish shirt"[18]. In another instance the courtiers were "clothed in [white] shirts and good silk cloths"[19].

St. George (fig. 2) and St. Theodore (fig. 3) on horseback are depicted in the same manuscript; they wear costumes which are very similar to that of Belin Saggad and they are also armed with a spear. The trappings of their horses are identical to those of the nobleman's horse. Moreover, St. George's ornamented bandlet closely recalls those of the warriors accompanying Yemḥarana Egzi'e and his wife described subsequently which proves that this detail is certainly drawn from life. If Belin Saggad's portrait mirrors the costume and the weapons of 15th-century nobles as well as the trappings of their horses, we must conclude that St. George and St. Theodore are depicted in Ethiopian costumes. This is also the opinion of Balicka[20].

Let us now verify our finding and analyse the miniatures in the manuscript which belonged to Yemḥarana Egzi'e and his wife. The miniatures offer a glimpse of 15th-century Ethiopia, his portrait and that of his spouse being part of a genre scene whose force comes entirely from its life-likeness due to a sense of observation and care for details.

In pictorial plan, the portraits of Yemḥarana Egzi'e and Lady (*Etteyyē*) Amata Le'ul should be considered as one image although they are arranged in two miniatures facing each other[21]. They show the noble couple travelling

---

17 Suriano 1949, 100.
18 Alvarez 1961, 56.
19 Alvarez 1961, 269.
20 Balicka 1975 p. 106 writes: "In the miniature, the indigenous elements [are] the costume of the Saint, the horse-trappings (particularly the saddle-cloth and the stirrup irons) and the youth".
21 The inscription over the miniature runs: "Picture of *Etteyyē* Amata Le'ul, wife of

and accompanied by two pages, four warriors, two porters as well as one maid servant. In life, this highly reduced train must have been one of several tens, perhaps hundreds, of people.

Yemḥarana Egzi'e leads the party (fig. 4). Not surprisingly the features of his face are almost identical to those of Belin Saggad. Ethiopian painters did not endeavour to individualize the facial characteristics of the people portrayed. Everyone has a stereotyped face. This anonymity is partly due to the technical limitations of the painters, but also refers to a deeper level of people's attitudes. The face, the part of the body most exposed to others' scrutiny, should not reveal our inner and true feelings and thoughts; the reluctance to display these was one of the characteristics of traditional ways of life in Ethiopia. The face in this context plays the role of a mask, behind which the true face is hidden, and consequently it was not important what the mask looked like. We may assume, nevertheless, that the painter rendered Yemḥarana Egzi'e with all the attributes of his social position. He depicted his hair combed in an elaborate manner as already explained; and indeed, more conspicuously than Belin Saggad's. Also he depicted the former's beard neatly trimmed and his moustache shaved. Does this detail mirror Ethiopian fashion? In both manuscripts the beards and moustaches are depicted in varied ways; Christ and the saints, except those on horseback, are mostly but not exclusively bearded and with moustache, whereas the equestrian saints are either beardless or with the beard but without moustache. We suggest that the painter truly depicted the mode of shaving of the period though king Zar'a Yā'qob in his writings exhorted the Ethiopians not to shave their beards which he justified by quoting the text of the Didiscalia [22].

The quality of Yemḥarana Egzi'e's raiment corresponds to his high rank. His dress is composed of three pieces, that is the striped tunic, blue trousers pulled at the ankle and the ample cloak surrounding his body. Both shoulders are covered with the cloak, the extremities of which are billowing on his back. The cloak is made of a colorful textile, beautifully embroidered at its extremities. We suggest that all three pieces are made of silk which according to Alvarez was the material used for the costumes of the nobles.

Yemḥarana Egzi'e's hair is fastened with a bandlet which has unusually long extremities; his forehead is adorned with a piece of silver work which

Yemḥarana Egzi'e, may God grant them love and peace until the day of their death and cause [them] to inherit the kingdom of heaven". The writer is indebted to Rev. R.W. Cowley for the translation. *Etteyyē* can be a name as well as a title.

[22] C. Conti Rossini, *Il libro della Luce del Negus Zar'a Yā'qob (Maṣḥafa Berhān)* = CSCO 251 (Louvain, 1965), 90.

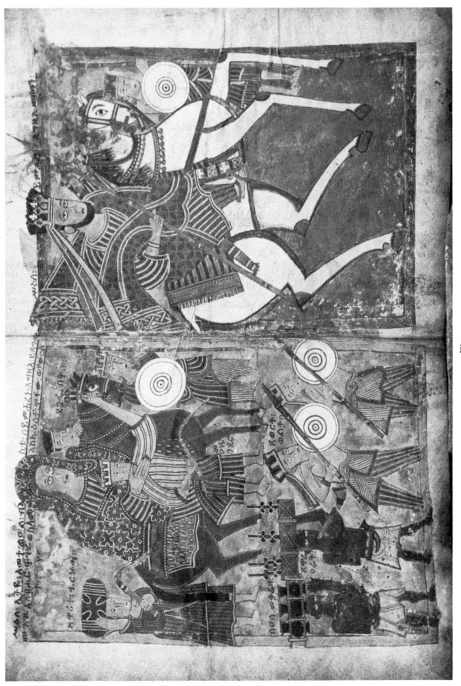

Fig. 4

seems to be a combination of fleurons and crosses. He also wears on his right wrist a bracelet which may be an ornamentation as well as a sign of distinction, for in the past successful hunters used to receive ivory bracelets from rulers. One of the warriors accompanying Amata Le'ul also wears a bracelet on his right wrist, and we presume that he also got it as a reward.

The surprising detail is the spur. It is not clear how it is fastened to Yemharana Egzi'e's bare foot. Fortunately this detail is better defined in the portrait of St. Theodore depicted in the same manuscript; we suggest that the spur was fastened with a leather strap running over the tarsus and below the feet.

The spurs depicted in our miniatures are virtually unique in Ethiopian art. Did Yemharana Egzi'e really wear spurs? More study is required before we venture upon a hypothesis, as to why and how these appeared in 15th-century miniatures.

Another detail of some importance is the sheath, emerging from the folds of Yemharana Egzi'e's cloak; the sheath does not appear in other miniatures of the manuscript, but nevertheless it is certainly drawn from life.

The horse trappings are elaborate and lavishly ornamented. The large girth is made either of colorful textile or coloured leather, and ornamented with metal plates, rows of bells are attached to the collars and a plume or cockade is attached to the bridle. The saddle cloth entirely covers the crupper. Indeed, the horse trappings are gorgeous.

The attendant walks in front of the noble; he is stripped naked from the waist up, looking like the warriors depicted with Amata Le'ul, except that his trousers are much shorter and only reach to his knees.

Let us turn now to the scene in the second miniature. Amata Le'ul rides a horse or perhaps a mule and she is supported by two pages who walk on either side of the mount. One page holds its bridle with one hand and its lash with the other. This corresponds to the Alvarez description of the pages at the Ethiopian court; they wear, he writes, short silk shirts and carry "whips (made) of a short stick and a long leather thong" [23].

The function of the pages in our miniature is corroborated by the description of the royal procession of Queen Sabla Wangēl in 1541, then widow of King Lebna Dengel. She came down from the monastery of Dabra Dammo to receive the Portuguese Christavao da Gama and his small army. On this occasion, writes Miguel de Castanhoso who witnessed the moment, the *Bāhr nagāš*, governor of the province adjacent to the Red Sea, "walked on foot naked to the waist, with a lion or tiger skin on his shoulders as a covering,

23 Alvarez 1961, 269.

with the right arm exposed, and he led her [that is her horse or mule] by the bridle". Alvarez describes a similar mode of traveling by King Lebna Dengel. Two pages, he writes, "lead the mule" holding "thick tassels" attached to the halter, and two other pages "go, one on each side, with their hands on the neck of the mule, and two others behind them in a similar manner, with their hands on the mule's haunches, on the hinder pommel" [24]. The train of Amata Le'ul is simpler than that of the royal couple but still her two pages combine the role of attending the Lady with that of holding the bridle of her mount.

Behind the horse a maid transports goods on her head, as well as a whisk which obviously belongs to her mistress. In Ethiopia, the whisk serves primarly for chasing flies but it is also carried as a sign of social status. Amata Le'ul's whisk is therefore large and its handle is ornamented. Warriors protect the noble lady; they are armed with spears and shields. One guard walks in front of her and keeps his spear vertically upwards. His task is probably to guide the horse. Two guards at the bottom of the miniature hold a shield in their left hand and a spear in their right. Their outstretched legs express the fast pace at which they march. Their bodies as well as their spears are slanted menacingly towards anyone who would interfere with Yemḥarana Egzi'e or Amata Le'ul's travelling. Inside of this area defended by the guards, the slaves transport the goods necessary for their masters' comfort. One slave carries earthenware containers with *maqārēẓā* according to the inscription which probably means mead or beer, while the other slave carries a bed. One slave holds in addition a mace whereas another blows a trumpet. The latter has a curved knife attached to his belt. Such knives are usually carried by the Nilotic people living in the lowlands situated north and west of Ethiopia's heartland. We presume that the slaves depicted here originated from these areas; the painter has indicated this by making their complexion dark. Until recent times the Ethiopians did not consider themselves as belonging to the Black People, the *šanqallā*; they differentiated themselves as being "red". The miniature dramatically illustrates this belief and proves that it was then already well-rooted. The slaves wear a simple loin cloth fastened with a belt probably made of leather. The loin cloth is either made of tanned skin or more probably of coarse cotton cloth which due to prolonged use and washing became greyish yellow. Similar loin cloths are still in use among the people of the Ethiopian lowlands.

Amata Le'ul wears a loose robe striped with white and covered with a colorful mantle, no doubt following the fashion of the court. Miguel de

---

24 Castanhoso 1902, 19; Alvarez 1961, 336.

Castanhoso describes as follows the dress of Sabla Wangēl riding a horse:
"The Queen", he writes, "was all covered to the ground with silk, with a
large flowing cloak (oparlandas)". The cloak (bedem) was made "of black
satin, with flowers and fringes of a very fine gold"[25]. It is clear that
Castanhoso, as well as Alvarez, used the term bedem or even burnous for
describing the outer garment worn by men as well as women. For her
travelling, Amata Leʿul probably put on a similar cloak made of precious
material. A somewhat surprising detail is her exposed face. According to
Alvarez "the wives of gentlemen and lords go about wholly covered";
Castanhoso describes Queen Sabla Wangēl "so muffled in a very fine cloth
that only her eyes could be seen"[26]. Probably Amata Leʿul's head was also
muffled, but the painter has changed this detail because of his intention of
making her "portrait".

The gorgeous trappings of the Lady's horse evidence her high breeding.
The horse is covered with a large ornamented saddle-cloth; the collars of the
trappings are large, painted red and ornamented with tiny silver or copper
plates; two cockades adorn the bridle.

The attendants and the guards are dressed according to their function. Two
pages wear shirts and trousers reaching their calves; the large belts are wound
around their waist. They carry no arms. The scout walking in front of the
Lady wears a shirt and trousers which are wide at the waist but tapered at the
ankle. He also wears a large belt. Two guards are stripped naked from the
waist upwards and because of the shields carried on their left arm, their right
arm exposed; perhaps this is to express their respect for their mistress. The
guards wear blue trousers similar to those of Yemḥarana Egzi'e. Their girdles
have unusually large extremities.

The Ethiopian habit of keeping the upper half of the body naked on
certain occasions is well attested by the travellers. Giovanni Battista da Imola
told Suriano that "men and women are naked from the navel upwards"[27].
Alvarez was struck by the particular form of respect used by Ethiopians, that
of being "stripped from the waist upwards" whenever someone made a call at
the court[28]. He mentions the "honourable men, who were not clothed except
from the waist downwards, with many thin white cotton cloths ..."[29]. On
another occasion, the high official of the realm presented himself half-naked

---

25 Castanhoso 1902, 18.
26 Castanhoso 1902, 18; Alvarez 1961, 144-171.
27 Suriano 1949, 100.
28 Alvarez 1961, 431-446.
29 Alvarez 1961, 269.

at the royal gate when bringing the tribute and later on his sons were also half-naked when asking justice[30]. When the *Baḥr nagāś* received the messenger from the court, he "went out of the town to receive him at a small hill near the houses ... and he was naked from the waist upwards"[31].

This custom persisted until the present but in changed form. "When someone, let us say a man of a lower rank", writes the modern scholar Tilahun Paulos, "wishes to enter the house of a superior to greet him or to make some private appeal, he must first of all take off his shoes ... Then on entering the hall he must twist his *šammā* round his waist and holding the end in one hand he approaches the host"[32]. He thus symbolically strips himself, though he still wears his shirt.

It seems that the oldest, though indirect, indication of this custom is a miniature in an Arabic manuscript dated AD 1306. The miniature shows the reception of a Muslim delegation at the Ethiopian court. Although the miniature is not a true illustration of the event, it certainly contains details which the painter must have learned from someone who had knowledge of Ethiopia. The Ethiopian king is sitting on his throne with a high foot-stool and is attended by six courtiers all stripped to the waist. Also, the painter had no prejudices about skin complexion and therefore depicted the Ethiopians with dark colours[33].

The pages and the warriors have their heads adorned with bandlets and their hair is dressed to stand erect. One page has a simple narrow bandlet to hold his hair, while all the others wear more elborate head-gear, with or without a long ribbon attached in the back. The head-gear seems to be a metal ring ornamented with either a lion's or baboon's mane similar to the *gofar* used nowadays. The identification is not certain, but there is no doubt that this detail also is depicted from life.

In conclusion, the two miniatures faithfully reproduce the travelling habits of 15th-century nobles including costumes, ornaments and weapons. Let us now see how this conclusion relates to the equestrian saints depicted in the same manuscript.

Saint Mercury (*Marqoryos*) (fig. 5) is shown in the composition illustrating the reading in the Ethiopian Synaxary for the 10th day of *Ḥedār*. Emperor

---

30 Alvarez 1961, 426.
31 Alvarez 1961, 122.
32 Tilahoun Paulos, "Forms of greetings and other signs of respect in Ethiopia", University College of Addis Ababa Ethnological Society. *Bulletin* 5 (1956), 27-8.
33 Universal story (*Jāmiʿ al-Tawārīkh*) of Rashīd al-Dîn. At present in the University of Edinburgh Library (Ms 20, fol. 52r). Miniature reproduced in David Rice, *Islamic art* (New York, 1965), 115.

Fig. 6

Fig. 5

Julian, runs the reading, has ordered fifty "pure and holy" Christian virgins killed together with their Abbess Sophia. "And because of this thing the Lord took vengeance upon him with the vengeance of his wrath, that is to say, Saint Mercurius the martyr speared him with his spear ... and he cast him down from his horse, and killed him" [34]. The miniature shows that very moment which is rendered with a sense of drama rare in Ethiopian painting. Especially impressive is the difficult pose of Julian who has just fallen from his saddle; he is already transfixed by the spear thrust by Mercury but still holds the reins, the usual behaviour of riders when falling from a horse. The fall of Julian is made emphatic by the two extremities of his cloak which seem to fly in the air. Undoubtedly the composition was conceived locally, perhaps by the painter of the miniature himself, the usual representation of Mercury in Christian iconography being either his trampling the emperor underfoot or piercing him with the lance, but not actually fighting the emperor.

If it is so, the details in our composition must also be taken from Ethiopian life; indeed, the raiments of Mercury and Julian, their hair style and head gear as well as their weapons and horse trappings are all similar to those in the travelling scene just described. Nevertheless, the figure of Julian brings a new element for our investigation; his raiment seems to be composed of four pieces instead of three. He wears a tunic with wide short sleeves which reaches to his knees, and a skin-tight shirt underneath. The latter is not shown in the portrait of Yemḥarana Egzi'e. Also, we have a glimpse of the kind of saddles then used. The realistically drawn saddle from which Julian fell, has a straight high pommel, flat at the top, and a pointed cantle, gently curved in the back.

The representation of St. Theodore (*Tēwodros*) (fig. 6) follows the snake-slayer type which appeared already in Ethiopia around the 14th century, but it is translated entirely into the Ethiopian idiom. Indeed, the image of the saint is modelled on the portrait of Yemḥarana Egzi'e, except of course, for the snake, the hand of the angel leading the spear as well as the cross in the saint's hand. In the Ethiopian Synaxary, Theodore the Egyptian, son of John, is commemorated on the 20th day of *Hamlē*. He is supposed to have killed the snake which devastated the city of Eukitos, whereas according to another Eastern Christian tradition, Theodore Stratelates, commemorated on February 7, is credited with slaying the dragon armed only with a holy cross and his faith. Our miniature combines both, the spear and the cross. The latter is clearly of the type which was popular in the 15th and 16th centuries. The cross has a particularly long lower arm which was convenient whenever

34 E. A. W. Budge, *The Book of the Saints of the Ethiopian Church* (London, 1928) p. 228-29.

the priest sitting on a horse offered the cross to the faithful for kissing. Therefore, the cross in our miniature is also drawn from life.

St. Marbehenām's hair is dressed in the "hat" fashion and his clothing is on the whole similar to those in the two previous miniatures. His head is adorned with an object which vaguely recalls the "crown" worn by Josue in the miniature discussed subsequently. The ornament consists of two finials filled with the acanthus motif, common in 15th-century art, and probably joined with the pattern of small crosses.

St. Gabra Krestos (fig. 7), son of emperor Theodosius[35], is dressed differently; he wears a tunic half-way down his calf and wide-striped trousers; his body is enveloped in a white or yellow cloak, which can be easily identified as the Ethiopian *šammā*, an outer garment made of cotton which is widely used even nowadays by all classes of society. The way of wearing the *šammā* vaguely recalls that of the Roman toga. Gabra Krestos's *šammā* is thrown over his left arm, but leaves his right arm exposed. One of its extremities falls over his right arm while the other extremity falls over his back. In fact, there are many ways of draping the *šammā*, each one having a special meaning in social etiquette. The *šammā* of Gabra Krestos has a large embroidered band at its extremities; such conspicuous ornamentation is used as the mark of distinction reserved for people of the upper classes.

Alvarez describes as follows a high official who was "covered with a hairy cotton cloth which they name besutos [*bezzet*, piece of cotton cloth]. They are good for the country, and there are some here of a high price"[36]. Alvarez probably meant the *šammā* or the other, heavier type of cloak, *bullukko*, used also as a bed cover.

The Ethiopian origin of Gabra Krestos's raiment is thus obvious. Moreover, he holds a whisk. The spur on his bare foot recalls that of Yemḥarana Egzi'e, but the rowel is delineated more clearly.

The Saint's elegantly dressed hair covers his neck and rises high in the form of a top hat. The beauty of the arrangement is enhanced with a delicate bandlet and an ornament composed of three dainty lozenges and crosses. The ribbon hangs down instead of flying in his back; perhaps the painter's intention was to depict the horse in a gentle trot instead of a gallop as in previous miniatures.

The trappings of the horse include a short ribbon and a small cockade attached to the brow band, all three collars garnished with large bells and breast and belly girths joined with a buckle-ring. Moreover, the horse's full

---

35 St. Alexis in Greek hagiography.
36 Alvarez 1961, 127.

Fig. 8

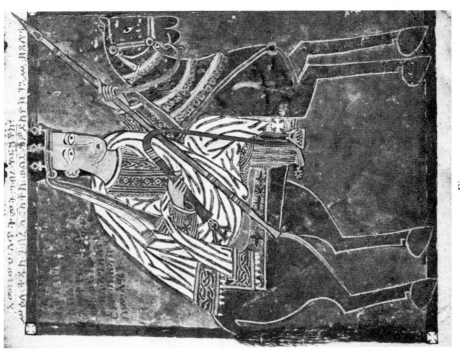

Fig. 7

anatomy is in accordance with the painter's endeavour to depict the things observed accurately.

Let us now briefly analyse a few other 15th and early 16th-century paintings in which, we believe, the personages are dressed in the Ethiopian manner.

The miniature, folio of the lost manuscript, Institute of Ethiopian Studies Coll. No. 4501 (fig. 8) is painted in a style similar to that of the miniatures just described. It shows three biblical heroes, Josue seated in the middle and flanked by Caleb and Samson standing. The latter wear tunics which extend below the knee, tight trousers and short loose cloaks, perhaps *šammā*, partly covering their shoulders and arms. They also wear large waist-bands which are first twisted and then wound around their loins. Their extremities are embroidered. Alvarez seems to have seen such waist-bands which he calls "girdles of coloured silk, in width and weaving like horse-girths", and he notes that "they were long and had long fringes reaching to the ground" [37]. The guards of Amata Le'ul seem to wear similar "girdles". Bands of cotton wound many times around the waist were used in 19th-century Ethiopia as ornaments as well as for the protection of vital organs during battle [38]. It is possible therefore that the waist-bands of Caleb and Samson, as well as those of the guards served that double purpose.

Josue's princely rank (he is called *masfen* in the inscription) is expressed by the crown on his head and the raised sword in his hand. He also wears a robe reaching his ankles and a large cloak over it, both obviously made out of precious material. Moreover, he holds a big handkerchief in his hand. In 17th-century paintings and those of the following centuries, Christ, Mary and the saints as well as personages of some mark are usually depicted with handkerchiefs in their hands. Our miniature is the earliest example of the ceremonial use of the handkerchief known to this writer.

All three personages wear either sandals or shoes which are drawn realistically; this is an exception since people are generally depicted barefoot.

Caleb and Samson each hold a spear in one hand and a shield in the other. All arms in the miniature are delineated with precision and are identical to those carried by Bilen Saggad, Yemḥarana Egzi'e, and the guards of Amata Le'ul as well as by the equestrian saints. It can be inferred from the pictures that iron was used for making spearheads. As to round medium-size shields, ornamented with embossed circles, they were in use until recent times by the Ethiopians. This precision of representing arms gives the impression that the costumes of the personages well evoke the life of 15th-century nobles.

---

37 Alvarez 1961, 143, 269.
38 Pankhurst 1968, p. 263.

Fig. 10

Fig. 9

The large diptych, IES Coll. No. 4053, is attributed to the 15th century. It shows equestrian saints who are called "martyrs" in the inscriptions. They are Aboli, George, Claude, Theodore, Basil and Mercury. Additionally there are king Lālibalā on horseback and St. Stephen holding a chalice and a sacramental spoon in the gesture of offering Holy Communion—the same gesture as observed nowadays in the churches of Ethiopia. We presume, therefore, that other details, including the costumes, are also depicted from life.

Although the costumes of the saints, for example that of Claude (fig. 9) as well as that of Lālibalā, are composed of the same three pieces as those previously described, they differ in details. The tunics reach the knees, but they are always in plain colours, either yellow or red. The trousers taper towards the feet, but they are rolled into a band at the ankles. The trousers are made of colorful materials and ornamented with patterns which recall Indian textiles. Over the tunic the saints wear a long piece of light material resembling a stole; it is either red or white, and tied across the chest but loose in the back. Could it be the Ethiopian *šammā* draped in the manner which seems to be characteristic of the 15th and early 16th-century paintings? The other novelty is an apparently full robe under the tunic; the robe is beautifully draped in flowing folds. Could it be the piece of official attire of the "Azayes" which Castanhoso observed in 1541, but worn on horseback? A similar full robe under the tunic appears in a number of 15th-century paintings.

The hair of the saints is cut round and smooth, but some wear it larger and covering the neck. The others have bandlets tied in a knot over their foreheads and a more elaborate flowing knot at the back of their heads. All hold realistically drawn spears in one hand and reins in the other. The way of holding the reins with the thumb is used widely nowadays by riders in the Ethiopian countryside and therefore certainly drawn from life.

Both the gorgeous horse trappings and saddle-clothes mirror the sophisticated taste of the nobility. The bridle is ornamented with a metal ball at the top, the collar with a cockade and the breast girth with bells.

The bare feet of the saints are deeply inserted into the stirrup irons.

The image of Lālibalā (fig. 10) is the earliest portrait of the 12th-century king known to this writer. Lālibalā is venerated as a saint and therefore has a nimbus depicted around his head. His raiments are similar to those of other saints in the diptych and probably do not correspond to his way of dressing during his life time. We believe, nevertheless, that the painter has depicted him clad in the Ethiopian manner, and consequently other saints in the diptych wear the costumes used by 15th-century Ethiopian kings and nobles.

Fig. 11

The following paintings provide additional information to the already described costumes and horse trappings.

St. Theodore and St. George depicted in the 15th-century diptych, IES Coll. No. 3980 (fig. 11), wear tunics reaching their knees. A full robe reaches their calves and is so large that it is folded three times. Underneath the robe the blown-out trousers are pulled in at the ankle; they are clearly tailored in the Moorish fashion. The *šammā* is tied across the saints' chests; its loose end billows in Theodore's back, whereas one end of George's *šammā* is twisted around his arm, which evidences the varied manner of its draping. Tunic and robe as well as *šammā* are plain blue, red and yellow, whereas the trousers are either striped or ornamented with dot-and-line pattern.

A large plume in yellow, red and green is affixed to the ornamental leather strap which runs from the bits to the crest of the horse. Alvarez probably referred to the same detail in the horse trappings of the royal mount when he wrote about "the great diadems which came down to the bits and big plume in the diadems"[39]. On another occasion Alvarez notes that the horses "had diadems high above their ears: they came down to the bits of the bridle, with large plumes on them"[40].

In the early 16th-century triptych, IES Coll. No. 5093, the elegance of the raiments is matched by the lavishnes in the horse trappings. The robe of St. Theodore as well as of St. George (fig. 12) reaches his feet and is unusually large at the bottom. An embroidered or bejewelled collar binds the neck to the robes. Alvarez notes that men "like courtier" wore "collars of gold badly wrought, and other jewels and false stones, and rich pieces round their necks"[41]. The trousers are equally wide and give the impression of being blown up like balloons, then sharply pulled in at the ankle and having many folds. The *šammā* is arranged crosswise on the chest and covers both arms.

The saddle-cloth is made out of precious material, ornamented either with tassels or with embroidered edging; long fringes are affixed to the crupper; a tasseled cord hangs behind the saddle and other tassels embelish the reins held by St. George; large bells are attached to the collars; moreover, either jewels or the plates of copper, silver or gold are affixed all along the pommel and the cantle. Alvarez described a saddle "all worked with carnelians"[42] and a caparison of "metal plates"[43] as well as a mule which "carries a rich halter

39 Alvarez 1961, 402.
40 Alvarez 1961, 269.
41 Alvarez 1961, 269.
42 Alvarez 1961, 299.
43 Alvarez 1961, 300.

Fig. 13

Fig. 12

over the bridle, and this carries or has at the lower jaw two ends with thick tassels of silk" [44]. All these embellishments are depicted in our painting.

The stirrup irons are probably of Moorish type; they are wider at the bottom than all stirrup irons previously described.

The saint killing two naked figures in the early 16th-century painting, IES Collection, is probably George because of the white colour of his horse (fig. 13). His raiment is elaborate and comprises a long tunic with braided collar and either trousers or more possibly a full robe which emerges from below the tunic. The other piece seems to be the extremity of a colorful belt similar to that of Samson and Caleb.

The embellishments of the horse trappings include a plume affixed to the bridle, a colorful collar with bells and a breast girth doubled with precious material. The stirrup irons are in the form of a large ring inserted between the big and the second toe. Rings were used in Ethiopia in the past. They appear occasionally in 17th-century paintings and more frequently in the following centuries, though never entirely replacing the standard stirrup irons. Our picture is the earliest record of the use of rings.

On the occasion of the Conference on Ethiopian feudalism at the Institute of Ethiopian Studies, Addis Ababa, in 1975, Merid Wolde Aregay, an Ethiopian scholar, put forward a theory explaining the lack of technological development in "Mediaeval Ethiopia"; he relates it to the use of the stirrup irons. He believes the Ethiopians in the past were exclusively using the "big toe stirrup" that is a ring into which they inserted the big toe while riding their horses. The "wide stirrups", he asserts, "never made any headway in Ethiopia", with the exception of Emperor Menilek's court in the late 19th century. Yet, he thinks, the adoption of the wide stirrups would "have made the mounted soldiers more mobile" and also "sparked off a shoe industry" [45]. One would infer from the above theory that the main reason why the Ethiopians walked barefoot in the past was the "big toe stirrup". However he acknowledged himself that he had "stretched the hypothesis beyond what would maybe he considered scholarly sound" [46]. Unfortunately for this exciting theory, the Ethiopians in the past were indeed familiar with the standard "large" stirrup irons, and have used them since time immemorial. Evidence for this is found in a great number of Ethiopian paintings from the 15th century onwards.

44 Alvarez 1961, 336.
45 *Technology in Medieval Ethiopia*, mimeographed paper presented at the Conference on Ethiopian feudalism, Addis Ababa, 1975, f. 8.
46 Ibid. f. 1.

Fig. 14

Let us conclude this survey with the portraits of St. Theodore and of king Lālibalā, both depicted in the wall paintings of the rock-hewn church of Yediba Māryām, dedicated to Abuna Musē, Dāwent in Wallo. The paintings are ascribed either to the first half or the middle of the 16th century.

The raiment of St. Theodore (fig. 14) follows the fashion as already described and shows the same lavishness in ornamentation. The novelty is his shirt with braided sleeves and the large turban on his head. According to the Portuguese chronicler the *Bāḥr nagāś* was dressed in Arab fashion and wore the turban when he first met Dom Rodrigo de Lima and his companions[47], which was obviously the result of Ethiopia's contacts with her Islamic neighbours. Ethiopian priests wear turbans though of different shape than those of the Muslims. It is possible that, occasionnally, the nobles living close to the coast of the Red Sea used turbans, and thus their usage found its way into paintings.

King Lālibalā (fig. 15) is accompanied by two attendants; one attendant holds an open umbrella, whereas the second attendant blows a horn, similar to Amata Le'ul's trumpeter. The scene then is inspired by the custom still prevalent in 15th-century Ethiopia. Lālibalā wears a shirt with a "V"-shaped collar and braided with colorful lace. His hair is fastened over his forehead with a bandlet; three trinkets vaguely recalling the fleur-de-lis crown seem to be attached to the bandlet the extremities of which are floating on his back. The King wears an ornament which is either a short thick piece of wood or a round metal trinket inserted into the lobe of his left ear. Such an ornament, made of wood, is still occasionally worn by the males of the Ethiopian highlands, but it is more common in the hot lowlands.

Lālibalā's *śammā*, one extremity of which is thrown over his right shoulder and the second extremity over his left arm, along with his large striped robe as well as his blown-up trousers and bare feet in a Moorish stirrup iron, all faithfully illustrate the style of dressing of the 16th-century Ethiopian nobleman.

Conclusion

In the 15th- and early 16th-century paintings selected, it was found that the costumes of the equestrian saints as well as their weapons and horse trappings are similar to those in the portraits of two Ethiopian noblemen and a noblelady of the same period. We suggested therefore that the painter has depicted the saints wearing the costumes of Ethiopian nobles provided that

47 Alvarez 1961, 62.

Fig. 15

the above portraits truly mirror Ethiopian life. The analysis of the portraits has demonstrated this. On the one hand the costumes of nobles, their weapons and other details as well as the costumes of guards, attendants and slaves are drawn with remarkable realism and accuracy, and on the other hand, they correspond to the information gathered from written records as well as to our knowledge of Ethiopian life in the past. The conclusion is that the costumes of the equestrian saints in the discussed paintings and, by analogy, the costumes of similar saints in other paintings of the period evoke indeed the state of dressing of Ethiopian nobles. However, usually the Ethiopian painter is not interested in realistic accuracy in depicting objects and persons. He prefers to follow convention in representing these. It is the exception to find an illustration of a particular costume worn by an individualized person. Most often we find a schematic representation of the types of costumes. Another factor is the painter's tendency to enhance the decorative value of paintings. Hence there is abundance of ornamentation. In our miniatures the personnages wear mostly bright and colorful costumes made of materials with intricate linear design whereas most Ethiopians probably used plain white cotton clothing in their everyday life and on the whole their costumes were rather simple. This plainness was striking for the travellers.

Suriano laconically states that "men and women are badly dressed ..."[48]. A century and a half later the German scholar, Job Ludolf who did not visit the country but gathered reliable information from an Ethiopian priest, made a similar remark: "Their Apparel", he writes, "is no less mean and poor, only the Princes wear Silk, the Clergy and richer sort make use of Cotton; the poorer sort half-naked, cover themselves with Skins, that hardly hide their privy Parts, which is also common among some Nobility and Priesthood ..."[49]. Suriano and Ludolf meant, of course, the general conditions and the manner of dress of the common people, whereas Alvarez and Castanhoso recorded what they had seen at the royal court. Indeed, they marvelled about the dazzling colours and the beauty of royal raiments as well as the dress of the courtiers. There is no doubt about their truthfulness. The Ethiopian painters depicted Belin Saggad and Yemharana Egzi'e clad in their best apparel thus expressing their high social position, but they also depicted their slaves having their loins merely covered, thus dramatically illustrating their low social status. The statements of Suriano and Ludolf as well as those of Alvarez and Castanhoso evidence the differences in social conditions in Ethiopian society.

---

48 Suriano 1949, 90.
49 Hiob Ludolf, *A New History of Ethiopia, being a full and accurate description of the kingdom of Abessinia* (London, 1682), 388; also Alvarez 1961, 143.

The way of depicting slaves in our miniatures is as true as that of their masters; all are equally drawn from life. It is also obvious that the painters would not depict the equestrian saints dressed as common people, but as the highest nobles, and indeed only in the costumes they used for grand occasions.

The garment of the nobles as well as of the equestrian saints in the paintings is composed of three basic pieces, a tunic which at times perhaps should be called a robe; trousers and a kind of loose cloak variously draped. In some paintings, the latter is clearly the Ethiopian *šammā*. Occasionally a large belt is wound around the waist and a full robe added under the tunic. The bandlet on the head is adorned with trinkets. No footwear seems to be used.

The form of these pieces is not static; during the short period under review, from the second half of the 15th century to the middle of the 16th century, we note changes in their length, volume and even shape. For example there are at least three types of trousers. They may be short, reaching the knees and widely open at the bottom. Two other kinds of trousers are clearly influenced by the Islamic world. One kind is large at the knees, tapered towards the feet and rolled into a band at the ankle. This form seems to be worn with a tunic reaching the knees. The other form is rather striking in its "Moorish" character; the trousers are very large all the way down, they seem to be blown-up and then sharply pulled in at the ankle. The trousers are worn with either a tunic, or a robe reaching the calf. Similarly varied are the bandlets. The ornamental cockade is either affixed to the forehead or over the temple and the knot in the back may be either small or quite elaborate. We may infer from the above that in portraits of the saints the painters followed the changes in fashions of the day.

How did these changes come about? It seems that one of the main causes was that 15th-century Ethiopian nobles not unlike those in subsequent centuries as well as the upper classes of 20th-century Ethiopia used on special occasions either imported costumes or costumes made out of imported materials, though a very fine cotton cloth was also available in the country. Alvarez explains in a number of passages that the costumes of the dignitaries and pages at the court were made of a "good silk cloth"[50], whereas the king himself was dressed "in a rich mantle of [gold] brocade and silk shirts ...»[51]. Since Ethiopians did not know how to produce silk, all these gorgeous materials must have been imported. Throughout the centuries Ethiopia's main source of supply of luxury goods was partly the Near East and predominantly India. The Indian trade in Meṣewwā is well documented in

---

50 Alvarez 1961, 269.
51 Alvarez 1961, 304.

Alvarez narratives [52]. Moreover, the Portuguese traveller and missionary, Manuel Barradas in his detailed description of Tegrē in the beginning of the 17th century lists imported "brocades, velvets, damasks, satin and similar" [53], most of these very probably imported from India. Barradas explains also the Islamic character of the Ethiopian costumes in the 17th century. These textiles, he writes, were usually not imported in pieces 'but already tailored, even in Moorish style" [54]. The pattern of Ethiopian trade was the same from the 15th through the 18th century. It is therefore possible that Belin Saggad as well as Yemḥarana Egzi'e were depicted in costumes which were either made locally but out of imported material, or were already tailored abroad and bought from the Indian or Arab traders on the Coast of the Red Sea. Indeed, the surprisingly constant influence of Islamic culture on the Christian art of the Ethiopians in the 16th and 17th centuries should be explained by the dress habit of the nobility which in turn was strongly influenced by trade with the Near East and particularly India.

The ease with which the Ethiopians used to accept foreign clothing is illustrated by Alvarez's description of the Portuguese Embassy's intercourse with King Lebna Dengel. While messages were exchanged, writes the traveller "they came on the part of the Prester John [Lebna Dengel] to beg for some breeches, and the Ambassador sent him some of his own and others of Lopo de Gama's" [55]. The courtiers who liked the Portuguese "breeches" would probably not hesitate to put on the Indian wide trousers drawn up and gathered into folds round the ankles, called churidar [56].

As already explained the paintings give an incomplete view of the costumes, weapons and other details of 15th-century material life. For example Alvarez mentions the use of animal skins by Ethiopians for ornamentation and for covering. He lists sheep as well as lion skins which, he writes, are "very shaggy" [57]. Skins neither appear in our miniatures nor in 16th-century paintings. They are first worn by the servants of St. George in 17th-century paintings but are never part of the attire of equestrian saints.

The same with bows and arrows. They are listed by Alvarez and Suriano as the usual equipment of "men of war" [58]. The guards of Amata Le'ul carry neither bows nor arrows which are also lacking in the portraits of equestrian

52 Alvarez 1961, 117-18, 359, 417, 429.
53 Camillo Beccari, Il Tigrè descritto da un missionario gesuita del secolo XVII (Roma, 1909), 109.
54 Ibid.
55 Alvarez 1961, 297.
56 S. N. Dar, Costumes of India and Pakistan (Bombay, 1969), 46.
57 Alvarez 1961, 116, 128, 269, 429, 446.
58 Alvarez 1961, 129, 516; Suriano 1949, 100.

saints. Thus the narratives complete the information gathered from the pictures. Similarly the paintings provide the details which have escaped the travellers' attention. Alvarez writes time and again about the splendour of the Ethiopian horse trappings, but he fails to give exact information as to the kind of stirrup irons: were they of a conventional type or that of a ring? The paintings provide exact information about this detail which as we have seen is considered by young Ethiopian scholars as having some importance for their country's development.

Acknowledgements

Fig. 1, 2, 3 Bibliothèque Nationale, Paris.
Fig. 4, 5, 6, 7 David R. Buxton.
Fig. 14, 15 Walter Krafft
The other photographs have either been made by S. Chojnacki or are his property.

AN ETHIOPIAN MINIATURE OF THE HEAD OF ST. MARK:
EGYPTIAN INFLUENCE
AT THE MONASTERY OF ST. STEPHEN, HAYQ

MARILYN E. HELDMAN
Washington University, St. Louis

The Ethiopic manuscript of the Four Gospels presented by Abbot Iyasus Mo'a in 1280 A.D. to the monastery of Ḥayq Esṭifānos (St. Stepehn at Lake Hayq, Wollo Province, Ethiopia), a monastery which he himself had founded some thirty years before, continues today to be the prized possession of the monastery [1]. While the monks of Ḥayq Esṭifānos primarily treasure the Four Gospels as a precious gift from their founder, the manuscript is also an especially valuable artistic and historic treasure. Its provenance is known. It is securely dated. Historic notes are recorded within it. Furthermore, at present, it is the earliest dated example of an Ethiopian Gospel book illustrated with an extensive multiple frontispiece, a class of Gospel decoration favored by Ethiopian painters during the fourteenth and fifteenth centuries [2]. In addition to richly illuminated Canon tables and portraits of Evangelists which introduce the respective Gospel texts, there is a multiple frontispiece of miniatures with scenes of the life of Christ. The multiple frontispiece in the Gospels of Iyasus Mo'a [3] is introduced by a picture of the head of St. Mark.

---

1 The manuscript is described in, Getatchew Haile, *A Catalogue of Ethiopian Manuscripts Microfilmed for the Ethiopian Manuscript Microfilm Library, Addis Ababa and for the Hill Monastic Manuscript Library, Collegeville*, V, Collegeville, Minnesota, 1981, EMML Pr. No. 1832, 293-301, note especially varia 16 (hereafter, *EMML Catalogue*). First note of the manuscript was published by Taddesse Tamrat, "The Abbots of Dabra Hayq, 1248-1535", *Journal of Ethiopian Studies*. VIII/1, 1970, 87-117 (hereafter, "The Abbots").

2 The extensive multiple frontispiece of the Ethiopian *de luxe* Gospels may include nineteen or more miniatures of scenes from the life of Christ; for further discussion and bibliography, see M. E. Heldman, "The Miniatures of the Gospels of Princess Zir Gānēlā, an Ethiopic Manuscript dated 1400/01 A.D.", unpublished Ph. D. diss., Washington University, St. Louis, Mo., 1972; for the Ethiopian limited multiple frontispiece with the Crucifixion, Resurrection and Ascension: M. E. Heldman, "An Early Gospel Frontispiece in Ethiopia", *Konsthistorisk Tidskrift*, XLVIII, 1979, 107-121.

3 Photographs of these miniatures have not been published, but their subjects are listed in Getatchew, *EMML Catalogue*, V, 300-301. Microfilm of the manuscript is available at the Hill Monastic Microfilm Library of St. John's Abbey and University, Collegeville, Minnesota. For the gracious assistance extended to me during and after my visit to the library, I wish to thank the director and staff, in particular Dr. Getatchew Haile and Mrs. Marianne Hansen.

This unique miniature of the head (rəʾs in Ethiopic or Geʿez) of St. Mark Evangelist, author and teacher, is the subject of this paper dedicated to Professor Wolf Leslau, teacher and author, and for many years virtual head (rəʾs) of Ethiopian studies in the United States.

The image (fig. 1) is a visually compelling one. Within a rectangular frame is a series of concentric circles, the outer two painted red and yellow, surrounding the head of a bearded saint ringed by a yellow halo. The eyes of the saint gravely stare out beyond the beholder. While the enframing device of concentric circles resembles the medaillion frame of a bust portrait [4], this image is not a portrait, for the head has neither neck nor shoulders. Moreover, the Hand of God reaches down from above to maintain, indeed to assist, the cosmic hypostasis of this majestic apparition. The inscription above its frame reads: "Head of [St.] Mark" [5]. Questions arise immediately. Why is only the head and no other part of the body of St. Mark depicted? Why does the Hand of God present the apparition of the rəʾs so boldly? And what special meaning could this picture have had for Abbot Iyasus Moʾa and his spiritual sons, the monks of Ḥayq Esṭifānos? The answers to these questions are disclosed in the history of the relics of St. Mark.

The facts of St. Mark's historical life are recorded in the *Acts of St. Mark*. He was the first apostle to go to Africa to teach the Gospel. He went to Alexandria, converted the cobbler Anianus, baptized many, and established the patriarchal See of Alexandria. Alexandria was the city of his martyrdom and burial. He was tied by the neck and dragged through the streets until he died; his body was saved miraculously from burning and was buried by the faithful in a cave [6].

---

4 The bust portrait framed by a circular medaillion, the *imago clipeata*, a formula commonly employed in Early Christian art for portraits of Christ, the Apostles, prophets and martyrs, continued to be used in Byzantine art, as on the ivory relief of St. John the Baptist with busts of Sts. Philip, Stephen, Andrew, and Thomas in the Victoria and Albert Museum (A. Goldschmidt and K. Weitzmann, *Die byzantinischen Elfenbeinskulpturen*, II, Berlin, 1934, No. 68, Pl. XXVII).

5 The writing in the lower portion of the miniature is a later monastic note in a nonscribal hand.

6 Getatchew Haile, "A New Ethiopic Version of the Acts of St. Mark (EMML 1763)", *Analecta Bollandiana*, IC/1-2, 1981, 117-134 (hereafter, "A New Ethiopic Version"); Migne, *PG*, 115, cols. 163-170; F. Halkin, "Actes inédits de Saint Marc", *Analecta Bollandiana*, LXXXVII/3-4, 1969, 343-371. The Acts of St. Mark are retold in the Apocryphal Acts of the Apostles, the Synaxarium of the Egyptian Church, etc. According to the *History of the Patriarchs*, he was buried within the church in which the Christians of the city celebrated the liturgy. Sawirus, bishop of al-Asmunin, et al., *History of the Patriarchs of the Egyptian Church*, I, i, tr. and ed. B.T.A. Evetts, in *Patrologia Orientalis*, I, 147-148 [49-50] (hereafter, *HPEC*).

1. "Head of [St.] Mark". Gospels of Iyasus Mo'a (EMML 1832), fol. 13r
(photo: Ethiopian Manuscript Microfilm Library, Addis Ababa/Collegeville, Minnesota).

The text of the *Acts of St. Mark*, however, sheds no light on the meaning of the miniature of the head of St. Mark. For this, one must turn to the complicated history of the church in Egypt and the veneration of the body of St. Mark. The *History of the Patriarchs of the Egyptian Church* is a most important source for both these subjects. The first note of the burial place of St. Mark appears in the *History of the Patriarchs* in the biography of Patriarch Peter I, Martyr (300-311). Before his death, Peter was allowed to visit the place where the body of St. Mark lay and he prayed and received a blessing from the relic. "When the holy father [Peter] had finished his invocation, he kissed the Apostle's tomb and the tombs of the fathers which were there also"[7]. No church is mentioned in the account of Peter's visit to St. Mark's tomb, yet the quoted passage demonstrates that by the time of the composition of this biography, later incorporated into the *History of the Patriarchs*[8], the custom of patriarchal burial at the tomb of St. Mark had been firmly established. It is assumed that soon after the conversion of Emperor Constantine a church or martyrium was built to mark the site of St. Mark's tomb.

Two events which most affected the See of St. Mark after the peace of the church were the doctrinal disputes at the Council of Chalcedon and the Arab conquest of Egypt. At the Council of Chalcedon (451 A.D.), the patriarch of Alexandria, adhering to a monophysite definition of the nature of Christ, refused to accept the dyophysite dogma proposed by the Church of Constantinople. With both parties claiming to hold the orthodox position while condemning the other's definition as heretical, the Monophysite Egyptian Church came into being. Persecution of the Egyptian Monophysites soon followed and their patriarchs Dioscorus (444-458) and Timothy II (458-480) were forced into exile[9], while the pro-Chalcedon or Dyophysite party named their candidates to the throne of St. Mark. The final schism did not occur until the reign of Justinian, who seems to have instituted the custom of ordaining a Dyophysite patriarch for Alexandria in Constantinople[10]. By Justinian's

---

7 *HPEC* I, ii, in *P.O.* I, 397-399 [133-135]. See also page 153 [55] for reference to the burial place of Patriarch Celadion.

8 Sawirus, Bishop of al-Asmunin, began compilation and composition of the *History of the Patriarchs of the Egyptian Church* in Arabic in the tenth century, an undertaking which marks the beginning of Arabic literature of the Egyptian Church. G. Graf, *Geschichte der christlichen arabischen Literatur*, II (Studi e testi 133), Vatican City, 1947, 295 (hereafter, *Geschichte*). Subsequent biographies were composed in the following centuries. After the thirteenth century, the biographies decline in both richness and length and generally become a mere listing of those who held the patriarchal office.

9 *HPEC*, I, ii, in *P.O.* I, 443-445 [179-181].

10 *HPEC*, I, ii, in *P.O.* I, 469 [205].

decree, the churches of Alexandria were closed to the Monophysites and given
to the Dyophysites. The Monophysites of Alexandria countered by building
the church of Sts. Cosmas and Damian (finished 561/62) and the Angelion,
which served in the early century as the cathedral of the Monophysite
Egyptian patriarch [11]. The Monophysites were denied access to the church of
St. Mark in which his tomb was situated, for it was now under the
administrative control of the Greek or Dyophysite party.

As the cult of relics and the institution of pilgrimage developed, the tomb
of St. Mark became an object of veneration throughout the Christian world.
The so-called Pilgrim from Piacenza, who wrote c. 570 A.D., is the first
of the pilgrims to the Holy Land to mention the tomb of St. Mark at
Alexandria [12].

The first half of the seventh century was a period of trial for the Egyptian
or Monophysite Church. The Persians invaded Egypt, took Alexandria, and
by 618 gained control of all Egypt, which they held until 627. Although
many monasteries were destroyed, the city of Alexandria was unharmed.
During the patriarchate of the Monophysite Benjamin (622-661), Egypt was
regained by the Emperor Heraclius, then taken by the Arabs, recaptured by
Roman troops, and retaken, this time permanently, by the Arabs. Also during
Benjamin's patriarchate, God granted to the Monophysite or Egyptian Church
the miraculous recovery of the relic of St. Mark.

Extant historical sources, Egyptian, Greek and Arab, offer no complete
account nor precise chronology of the Arab conquest of Egypt. The *History of
the Patriarchs* tells vividly of the persecutions of the Monophysites between 631
and 641 under Cyrus, the Dyophysite patriarch and civil governor appointed
by Heraclius, during which time Benjamin endured a difficult exile in Upper
Egypt until his return to Alexandria probably in the last months of 644
A.D. [13]. According to Butler's careful reconstruction of the Arab conquest,
the Arabs took Alexandria a second time from the Roman troops in 646, not
peacefully as during the first capture in 642, but by force. After the second
capture, they plundered and burned the city [14].

According to the *History of the Patriarchs*, the Muslims "destroyed its
[Alexandria's] walls, and burnt many churches with fire. And they burnt the
church of St. Mark, which was built by the sea, where his body was laid; and

---

11 *HPEC*, I, ii, in *P.O.* I, 467 [203], 484 [220].
12 "Travels from Piacenza", Sec. 45 in J. Wilkinson, *Jerusalem Pilgrims before the Crusades*,
    Warminster, 1977, 89 and 6 (hereafter, *Pilgrims*).
13 *HPEC*, I, ii, in *P.O.* I, 489-493 [225-229]
14 A. J. Butler, *The Arab Conquest of Egypt and the Last Thirty Years of Roman Dominion*
    (Oxford, 1902), 1973 reprint, 439-441, 336-367, 474-475 (hereafter, *Arab Conquest*).

this was the place to which the father and patriarch, Peter the Martyr, went before his martyrdom and blessed St. Mark ... And at the burning of the said church a miracle took place which the Lord performed ..." [15].

A ship captain stole the head from the plundered tomb of St. Mark and hid it in his ship. Meanwhile Patriarch Benjamin returned from his exile to Alexandria. When the fleet set sail, the ship in which the stolen head was hidden could not be moved toward open sea. Simultaneously, Benjamin had a dream in which a man in shining garments appeared and commanded Benjamin to prepare a place for him that he might abide with Benjamin. When the ship could not be moved, the owner ordered that the cargo be searched and the captain confessed his theft. Benjamin was summoned to the scene, at which time he recognized the import of his dream and identified the head as the relic of St. Mark. The owner of the ship, a Christian, gave Benjamin money for the rebuilding of the church of St. Mark, but instead Benjamin had a wooden chest made as a resting place for the head and "he waited for a time in which he might find means to build a church" [16]. The time did not come to Benjamin. During the remainder of his patriarchate he encouraged the rebuilding of the monasteries [17], a decision that seems to reflect the mutual dependency that developed between the Egyptian monasteries and the patriarchate.

The miraculous recovery of the head of St. Mark follows the *topos* of an attempted relic theft which is thwarted by the saint who does not wish to be translated [18]. Within this stereotyped plot are two significant points: the rescue of the head of St. Mark before his church is burned [19] and the donation of the head to Benjamin, Monophysite patriarch of Alexandria, by the will of St. Mark.

According to the *History of the Patriarchs*, the church of St. Mark at Alexandria was rebuilt during the patriarchate of John III (677-686) [20]. After the Arab conquest, the Dyophysite patriarchs no longer enjoyed the rights and privileges once conferred them by the civil government. Claim to the church of

---

15 *HPEC*, I, ii, in *P.O.* I, 494-495 [230-231].

16 *HPEC*, I, ii, in *P.O.* I, 495-500 [231-236].

17 *HPEC*, I, ii, in *P.O.* I, 504 [240] ff.

18 P. J. Geary, *Furta Sacra, Thefts of Relics in the Middle Ages*, Princeton, N.J., 1978, 137-139 and 11-16 (hereafter, *Furta Sacra*).

19 *The History of the Patriarchs* (*P.O.* I, ii, 494 [230]) is the only source that specifically says that the church of St. Mark was burned by the Arabs. Butler contradicts himself, saying both that the church burned and that it survived the Arab conquest. Butler, *Arab conquest*, 115, note 1 and 475.

20 *HPEC*, I, iii, in *P.O.* V, 18 [272].

St. Mark reverted to the Monophysite or Egyptian Church. The tradition of patriarchal interment at the church of St. Mark was re-established and continued until the ninth century[21].

The tradition of Alexandria as the site of the tomb of St. Mark continued to appear in pilgrims' literature postdating the Arab conquest of Egypt. Abbot Adomnan of Iona, recording Bishop Arculf's account of his visit to the Holy Land, wrote between the years 679 and 688 that the tomb of St. Mark lay before the altar in a great church in Alexandria[22]. St. Mark's tomb is also mentioned in a guide book for Greek pilgrims compiled during the mid-seventh and eighth centuries[23]. Bernard the Monk, who visited Alexandria in c. 870, wrote that St. Mark "has a monastery outside the east gate, and at the church there where he used to be buried there are monks. But the Venetians came by sea, stole his body from its guardians, and took it away to their island"[24].

Venetian tradition places the date of their theft of the body of St. Mark in the year 827 A.D.[25]. The Venetians made no note of a missing head. Of the translation of the body of St. Mark to Venice, the *History of the Patriarchs* is silent. Obviously there exists two conflicting traditions concerning the relics of St. Mark, the authenticity or priority of which I shall not attempt to establish. The Republic of Venice claimed the relic of St. Mark for reasons of ecclesiastic independence and prestige. The Egyptian Church claimed the head of St. Mark as symbol of rightful succession from the Apostolic throne of St. Mark. That the tomb of St. Mark and the body therein survived the Arab conquest of Alexandria is essential to the Venetian claim to his body. The Egyptian tradition posits the destruction of the church of St. Mark during the Arab conquest and proposes the recovery of the head of St. Mark by miraculous means.

Mawhub ibn Mufarriǧ, compiler of the biographies of Patriarchs Christodoulus (1046-1077) and Cyril II (1078-1092), inserted three items in the *History of the Patriarchs* that reassert Egypt's claim to the authentic relic of the head

---

21 *HPEC*, I, iii, in *P.O.* V, 21 [275], 25 [279], 215 [469] and *HPEC* I, iv, in *P.O.* X, 360-361 [474-475], 544 [658].

22 Adomnan, "The Holy Places", II, 30, in Wilkinson, *Pilgrims*, 110 and 9-10.

23 Epiphanius the Monk, "The Holy City and the Holy Places", VI, in Wilkinson, *Pilgrims*, 119 and 11.

24 Bernard the Monk, "A Journey to the Holy Places and Babylon", Sec. 6, in Wilkinson, *Pilgrims*, 141-142 and 13. This passage could be an interpolation.

25 O. Demus, *The Church of San Marco in Venice: History, Architecture, Sculpture* (Dumbarton Oaks Studies, VI), Washington, D.C., 1960, 7-19 (hereafter, *San Marco*). The earliest manuscript account of the theft dates from the tenth century; for a summary of evidence concerning the acquisition of the relics see, Geary, *Furta Sacra*, 112-114.

of St. Mark. First, he named the head of "the illustrious saint, my lord Mark, the Evangelist, at Alexandria" in a list of holy places and relics that he had personally seen[26]. Secondly, he told of the hardship that befell his own father Abu-l-Fath ibn Mufarriğ because he, fearing reprisal from the civil government, had refused to receive the head of St. Mark in his house in Alexandria. Following his refusal of the head, he was seized by Muslim authorities and taken to Miṣr (Cairo) where he was jailed. After a period of imprisonment, St. Mark appeared to the Muslim jailer, saying that Abu-l-Fath had profited from his endurance of this trial and that he would be released from prison in three days. And he was free three days later. Abu-l-Fath ibn Mufarriğ returned to Alexandria and kissed the head of St. Mark[27]. Thirdly, Mawhub ibn Mufarriğ wrote of St. Mark's visit to him in a dream. St. Mark revealed to Mawhub that his brother doubted the authenticity of the relic of the head of St. Mark. When Mawhub told his brother of the dream, the brother repented of his lack of faith[28]. Mawhub ibn Mufarriğ may have included these assurances of the authenticity of the head of St. Mark in the *History of the Patriarchs* to counter the claim of Venice to the relics of St. Mark. The rebuilding[29], which began in 1063, of the church of San Marco at Venice, in which the relics of St. Mark were deposited in 1094, dramatically symbolized the presence of St. Mark in Venice. The renown of the great church and the growing number of Venetian legends of St. Mark[30] may have continued to inspire some doubts. Abu-l-Barakat ibn Kabar, the famous Egyptian scholar (died 1324), attempted to reconcile the conflicting claims of the two cities to the relic of St. Mark in his encyclopaedic *Lamp of Darkness*: he wrote that the body of St. Mark was buried in the eastern church on the shore of Alexandria up to the time when it was taken by some Venetians who stole the body and left the head. They took the body to Venice, "where it is now, and the head was transferred to a house in Alexandria known as Ibn as-Sukkari where it is until now"[31].

---

26 *HPEC*, II, iii, tr. and annot. Aziz Suryal Atiya, Yassa Abd Al-Masih and O. H. E. Burmester, Cairo, 1959, 358-362.
27 *HPEC*, II, iii, 265-267.
28 *HPEC*, II, iii, 275-276.
29 For what is known of the ninth-century church of San Marco in Venice see, Demus, *San Marco*, 64-70.
30 Demus, *San Marco*, 12-15.
31 Abu-l-Barakat Ibn Kabat, *The Lamp of Darkness for the Intelligence of the Service* (in Arabic), Cairo, 1950, 67, cited by, O. F. A. Meinardus, "An Examination of the Traditions pertaining to the Relics of St. Mark", *Orientalia Christiana Periodica*, XXXVI, 1970, 361. The head of St. Mark is believed today to repose in Alexandria: Meinardus, "An Examination", 348-350.

The Synaxarium of the Egyptian Church commemorates on 8 Tubah
Patriarch Benjamin (622-661) and his consecration of the church at the
monastery of St. Macarius[32]. The readings for this primary commemoration
are followed by secondary commemorations including Patriarch Zacharias
(1003-1031/32) which are in turn followed by a commemoration of the death
of Benjamin and the story of the miraculous recovery of the head of St. Mark.
When the story of the recovery of the head was added to the Synaxarium is
not clear[33], but it certainly had been added by the late fourteenth century,
when the Synaxarium was translated into Ge'ez or Ethiopic by Simeon, a
monk from the monastery of St. Anthony who had come to Ethiopia with the
metropolitan of Ethiopia[34]. The story is included in the readings for 8 Ṭer in
the Ethiopian Synaxarium[35]. From the time of its addition to the Synaxarium,
Egypt's claim to the head of St. Mark was vindicated, as the story of the
miracle of the recovery of the head was declaimed annually in the churches
of Egypt.

For the Egyptian Church, Alexandria continued to be the city of the throne
of St. Mark, although the patriarchal residence had been transferred to other
locations, notably the monastery of St. Macarius at Wadi Habib, finally to
Miṣr (Cairo), and the last patriarch to be buried in Alexandria "with the
holy fathers" was Joseph (830-849)[36]. Nevertheless, Alexandria retained its
prerogative as the site of the primary consecration of each new patriarch.
The church of St. Mark, apparently badly damaged or destroyed during
the persecutions ordered by al-Hakim during the second decade of the
eleventh century, was rebuilt and consecrated anew during the patriarchate
of Christodoulus (1046-1077)[37].

And what of the relic of the head of St. Mark that Benjamin in the mid-
seventh century had placed in a specially-made wooden box? The next

---

32 R. Basset, ed. and tr., "Le synaxaire arabe-jacobite: les mois de Toubah et Amchir",
    Patrologia Orientalis, XI, 556-664.
33 Egyptian menologia of the thirteenth and fourteenth centuries reflect stages of development
    of the church calendar; these as well as the calendar of Abu-l-Barakat Ibn Kabar list only
    Benjamin and the consecration of the church at St. Macarius for 8 Tubah. F. Nau, ed. and
    tr., "Les ménologes des évangéliaires coptes-arabes", *Patrologia Orientalis*, X, 167-224;
    E. Tisserant, "Le calendrier d'Abou'l-Barakat", *Patrologia Orientalis*, X, 262.
34 E. Cerulli, *La letteratura etiopica*, 3rd ed., Florence/Milan, 1968, 55-56.
35 E. A. W. Budge, ed. and tr., *The Book of the Saints of the Ethiopian Church*, 4 vols., (Cambridge,
    1928), 1976 reprint, I/II, 467-474.
36 *HPEC*, I, iv, in *P.O.* X, 544 [658].
37 *HPEC* II, i, tr. and annot. Yassa Abd al-Masih and O. H. E. Burmester, Cairo, 1943, 59;
    HPEC II, ii, tr. and annot. Aziz Suryal Atiya, Yassa Abd Al-Masih, O. H. E. Burmester,
    Cairo, 1948, 103, 208-209; *HPEC* II, iii, 249.

reference to the relic in the *History of the Patriarchs* is not until the eleventh
century when, during the persecutions of al-Hakim, an amir acquired the relic
and ransomed it to a Christian who took the head of St. Mark to Patriarch
Zacharias, then living in safety at the monastery of St. Macarius, Wadi
Habib [38]. By the second half of the eleventh century, it was custom to conceal
the head of St. Mark for safe-keeping at Alexandria in a private residence of
a prominent Christian. Among those who stored the relic were one Simon,
priest of the church of St. Mark, and Mawhub ibn Mufarriǧ, compiler of
several biographies in the *History of the Patriarchs* [39]. In 1235, it was kept in the
house of Ibn as-Sukkari, the same house where, according to Abu-l-Barakat
ibn Kabar, it was kept in the early fourteenth century.

Although the tomb of St. Mark in Alexandria had once been a focus of
international pilgrimage as well as local veneration, the relic of the head of St.
Mark, when deposited for safe-keeping in a private residence, could not
function as an object of popular devotion. Nevertheless, it represented the
person of the founder of the patriarchate, the possession of which validated
the Monophysites' claim to the throne of St. Mark. Indeed, this was its
function.

The consecration of Patriarch Cyril III is described in some detail. In 1235
A.D., he was consecrated on a Sunday at the church of the Saviour and
"Monday ... he rode and went to the house of Ibn as-Sukkari in which was
the head of St. Mark ... And it was brought out for him according to the
custom ... And it was placed in a room and he enveloped it in a new covering
according to the custom" [40]. This ritual is prescribed in the *Rite of Consecration
of the Patriarch of Alexandria* in a manuscript dating to 1364, the earliest extant
copy of the text. On the first day following his consecration, the new patriarch
is to proceed to the Angelion church, the second day to the church of Michael
Archangel, the third day to the church of St. Mark where "he celebrates the
Anaphora and takes the Apostolic Head of the divinely-inspired Mark into
his bosom, for whom he had become a successor prepared to walk in his
foot-steps unto the glory of the Lord" [41].

---

38 *HPEC* II, ii, 201. Was the amir's acquisition of the head of St. Mark related to the general
    confiscation of treasures of the Church ordered by al-Hakim? For the confiscation decree,
    see *HPEC* II, ii, 194 and D. L. E. O'Leary, *A Short History of the Fatimid Khalifate*, London,
    1923, 155-160.

39 *HPEC*, II, iii, 248, 265, 275-276, 279-280.

40 *HPEC*, IV, i, tr. and annot. A. Khater and O. H. E. Burmester, Cairo, 1974, 138-139.

41 O. H. E. Burmester, tr. and annot., *The Rite of Consecration of the Patriarch of Alexandria*,
    Cairo, 1960, 83. Evidently the text was composed before the head had been moved to a
    private residence.

The miniature of the head of St. Mark in the Gospels of Iyasus Mo'a obviously represents the relic which had been delivered to the Monophysite patriarchs of Alexandria by divine intervention. There is no evidence of a special devotion to St. Mark himself at Ḥayq Esṭifānos, a devotion that might have inspired the inclusion of this miniature. The miniature of the head of St. Mark in the Gospels which the Ethiopian abbot donated to his monastery suggests an allegiance to the Monophysite patriarch of Egypt and to his Church which proceeded from the Apostle St. Mark. The chief prelate of the national Ethiopian Church, the metropolitan, was an Egyptian monk appointed and consecrated by the Monophysite patriarch of Alexandria [42]. However, the miniature suggests, I believe, not simple allegiance, but a wish for spiritual and intellectual affiliation with the Egyptian Church which, at this time, was undergoing a great literary revival [43]. According to hagiographic tradition, Iyasus Mo'a was renowned as a teacher. He was a scholar and writer of biblical commentary [44]. Such reputation suggests that he would have welcomed introduction to Christian Arabic literature in contacts with the Egyptian metropolitan and his court. It is said also that Iyasus Mo'a refused to leave his island monastery [45]. If this tradition is correct, he would have been isolated from informal or chance contacts with Egyptian monks. Nevertheless, the abbot may have learned of Christian Arabic literature during more formal visits with the metropolitan or members of his court for whom a visit to Ḥayq Esṭifānos would have been politic, considering the regard with which Abbot Iaysus Mo'a and his monastery were held by the Ethiopian royal court. King Yekunno Amlāk (1270-1285), the founder of the so-called Solomonic dynasty, had been, according to tradition, a student of Iyasus Mo'a. He is said to have acquired the throne with the blessings of his monastic teacher and, in gratitude, gave lands to the monastery and bestowed in perpetuity the title of monastic chief, 'Aqqābe sa'āt, upon its abbot [46].

---

42 It is by no means certain when the Monophysite patriarch of Alexandria acquired the right to ordain the metropolitan of the Ethiopian Church. The earliest reference in the *History of the Patriarchs* to the ordination of Ethiopia's metropolitan by the Monophysite patriarch appears in the life of Michael I (744-767). *HPEC* I, iii in *P.O.* V, 146· [400]. For evidence of a pro-Chalcedonian or Dyophysite bias in the Ethiopian or Axumite Church during the sixth century see, Getatchew Haile, "A New Ethiopian Version", 119-123.

43 Graf, *Geschichte*, II, 294-295.

44 S. Kur, *Actes de Iyasus Mo'a*, Corpus Scriptorum Christianorum Orientalium, vol. 260, Script. Aeth., t. 50 (tr.), 1965, 28-29.

45 Kur, *Actes*, 26.

46 Kur, *Actes*, 20-26.

2. "St. Mark Evangelist". Gospels of Iyasus Mo'a (EMML 1832), fol 132v (photo: EMML).

3. "Portrait of Abbot Iyasus Mo'a". Gospels of Iyasus Mo'a (EMML 1832), fol. 5v
(photo: EMML).

Subsequent history of the monastery vindicates this tradition of imperial support and its accompanying prestige[47].

Activity of Egyptian monks at Ḥayq Esṭifānos can be documented from 1375 A.D. until at least the mid-fifteenth century[48]. Evidence of familiarity with Arabic Christian literature at Ḥayq Esṭifānos during the abbacy of Iyasus Mo'a (died 1291/92) is scant, but, of course, the miniature of the head of St. Mark offers demonstrable proof of some familiarity with the customs of the Egyptian church, i.e. of the veneration of the relic of St. Mark.

A note in the Gospels of Iyasus Mo'a lists seven books left to the monastery by one Baḥayla Krestos (a monk at Ḥayq?) at his death in 1292[49]. Among these is the title *Qwesqwām*. It is safe to assume that the title refers to the story of the rest of the Holy Family in Egypt at Qusqam. Abu Saliḥ, in Egypt at the beginning of the thirteenth century, wrote of the monastery at Al-Muḥarrakah near Qusqam and of the church there dedicated to Mary that marks where the Holy Family lived when they had fled from Herod. He added that a homily of Patriarch Theophilus commemorates the foundation of the church there[50]. Perhaps the title *Qwesqwām* refers to the homily attributed to Theophilus, Patriarch of Alexandria, on the Virgin Mary and the place where the Holy Family stayed during their flight to Egypt, which was translated from Arabic (no Greek or Coptic versions are known) into Ge'ez[51]. It has been assumed that the translation was undertaken in the fourteenth century, perhaps during

---

47 Taddesse Tamrat, "The Abbots", 87-117.

48 A deed in Arabic, dated 1375 A.D., from the metropolitan court was added to the Gospels of Krestos Tasfāna; no longer at Ḥayq, the manuscript is Ms. 5 of the National Library, Addis Ababa. Pawlos Sadwa, "Un manoscritto etiopico degli evangeli", *Rassegna di studi etiopici*, XI, 1952, 23-24. For the significance of this land grant see, Taddesse Tamrat, "The Abbots", 102-103. *Acts of Saints and Martyrs* (EMML 1824), copied at the order of Yosēf, abbot of Ḥayq Esṭifānos during the reign of Emperor Yeshaq (1414-1429), includes two hagiographies translated into Ge'ez from "Coptic" by the Egyptian priest Sem'on in 1396/97 A.D. According to Getatchew Haile, this manuscript is most probably the original copy of the translations which it includes. Getatchew, *EMML Catalogue*, V, 267-270. See also EMML 1480, fol. 49r, a reference, dating to the reign of Emperor Zar'a Yā'eqob (1434-1468), to the Egyptian Yoḥannes of Barārā of St. Stephen's monastery: Getatchew, *EMML Catalogue*, IV, Collegeville, Minn., 1979, 600, lines 37-39.

49 EMML 1832, ff. 24v-25r. Getatchew, *EMML Catalogue*, V, varia 17, 296.

50 Abu Salih, *The Churches and Monasteries of Egypt and some Neighbouring Countries*, ed. and tr. B. T. A. Evetts, notes by A. J. Butler, Oxford, 1895, 224-226.

51 C. Conti Rossini, "Il discorso sul monte Coscam attribuito a Teofilo di Alessandria, nella versione etiopica", *Rendiconti della Reale Accademia dei Lincei*, sc. mor., ser. 5, XXI, 1912, 395-471 (hereafter, "Il discorso"); M. Guidi, "La omilia di Teofilo di Alessandria sul Monte Coscam nelle letterature orientali", *Rendiconti della Reale Accademia dei Lincei*, sc. mor., ser. 5, XXVI, 1917, 381-469.

the metropolitanate of Abbā Salāmā, surnamed the Translator (1348-1388)[52].
Nevertheless, even if the title *Qwesqwam* does not refer specifically to the
homily attributed to Theophilus, it certainly refers to a literary composition on
the resting place of the Holy Family in Egypt, a work inspired by the Arab
Christian literature of the Egyptian Church[53] which may have been at Ḥayq
Esṭifānos in the possession of Baḥayla Krestos before his death in 1292.

Of the Evangelists whose portraits introduce their respective Gospel texts
in the Gospels of Iyasus Mo'a, only St. Mark (fig. 2) wears a pointed cap,
similar to the *qob* or monastic headpiece worn by Iyasus Mo'a as he appears
in his donor portrait (fig. 3). (The others, following the usual iconography
of Evangelist portraits, wear the chiton and himation and are bare-headed.)
St. Mark, wearing the monk's pointed headpiece, is presented as a monastic
scholar[54], the spiritual father of the scholars of the Egyptian Church, a figure
with whom Iyasus Mo'a and his successor abbots at Ḥayq Esṭifānos could
identify. Iyasus Mo'a's actual spiritual father was Abbā Yoḥanni, his teacher
and mentor at the renowed ancient monastery in northern Ethiopia, Dabra
Dāmo[55], the importance of which as a center of learning was eclipsed by the
school established at Ḥayq Esṭifānos by Iyasus Mo'a[56].

Both the miniature of the head of St. Mark and the portrait of St. Mark as
monastic scholar in the Gospels which Iyasus Mo'a presented to his monastery
in 1280 suggest his interest in Egyptian Christian literature and learning and
his wish to expand the scope of Ethiopian learning and literature in his
monastic school at Ḥayq Esṭifānos. The impact of his professed interest upon
later generations at Ḥayq Esṭifānos is a subject for future scholarship.

52 C. Conti Rossini, "Notice sur les manuscrits éthiopiens de la collection d'Abbadie", *Journal
   Asiatique*, CLXXXI, 1912, 452. He also suggested that the translation was undertaken at
   the monastery near Qusqam, where a group of Ethiopian monks was living by the mid-
   fourteenth century. Conti Rossini, "Il discorso", 399. On the activities of Abbā Salāmā:
   A. van Lantschoot, "Abbā Salāmā, métropolite d'Éthiopie (1348-1388) et son rôle de
   traducteur", *Atti del convegno internazionale di studi etiopici* (Roma 1959), Rome, 1960, 397-401.
53 For writings inspired by the Flight to Egypt, see: G. Graf, *Geschichte*, I (Studi e testi 118),
   Vatican, 1944, 227-234.
54 Patriarch Mark (1167-1189) wears a similar monastic hood and cape in his portrait in the
   Four Gospels dated 1179/80 (Paris, Bibl. nat., Copte 13): J. Leroy, *Les manuscrits coptes et
   coptes-arabes illustrés*, Paris, 1974, Pl. 41 and 113-148.
55 Kur, *Actes*, 7-12.
56 Taddesse Tamrat, *Church and State in Ethiopia, 1270-1527*, Oxford, 1972, 158-59, 163-64.

MUSIC

A NEW SYSTEM OF MUSICAL NOTATION IN ETHIOPIA

Kay Kaufman Shelemay
Columbia University

Ethiopian music has been transmitted and performed primarily as an oral tradition. The relatively late development of a notational system for Ethiopian Christian liturgical music (*zema*)[1] has not substantially changed the role of oral tradition in the perpetuation of the Church music tradition. The first indigenous attempts to notate Ethiopian secular music (*zäfän*) took place in 1974. This brief discussion of the transition from oral to written tradition in a musical domain is dedicated to Wolf Leslau, whose studies of the spoken and written word in Ethiopia are an invaluable resource for scholars of many disciplines.

The new notational system was "presented to the public" on July 20, 1974 at the Creative Arts Centre of the then Haile Selassie I University[2]. Tesfaye Lemma, assisted by Nigussu Retta and Abebe Wolde, created the notation for use by Orchestra Ethiopia. The purpose of the notation was threefold. The system was intended to aid "those who know the instruments to play ... by number". A second, descriptive function was "to aid people who want to know about Ethiopian instruments". Finally, the system was seen as a way "to preserve compositions so that they are not forgotten"[3]. Orchestra

---

[1] A. Dillmann quotes a manuscript attributing invention of the Christian notational system (*mǝlǝkkǝt*) to two Church musicians who lived during the reign of Emperor Galāwdewos (1533-1552). See *Lexicon Linguae Aethiopicae* (reprint ed., Osnabrück: Biblio Verlag, 1970), p. 1130. Ethiopian oral tradition credits invention of the notational system to Saint Yared, said to have lived during the sixth century reign of Emperor Gabra Masqal, while the Ethiopian Synaxarium simply credits Yared with inspiration of the Church modal system. Sir E. A. Wallis Budge, *The Book of the Saints of the Ethiopian Church*, Vol. III (Cambridge: At the University Press, 1928), pp. 875-877. Some contemporary Ethiopian sources try to reconcile the two traditions by crediting the sixteenth-century musicians with "fresh notations on the model of those invented by Yared". See *Patterns of Progress, Music, Dance and Drama* (Addis Ababa: Ministry of Information, 1968), p. 25.

[2] I attended this session, where an explanation of the numerical signs and the musical example reproduced here were distributed. Abebe Wolde later discussed the system with me in detail and provided the complete list of signs found in Figure 1. Although the notation was said to be "in progress" when I collected this information, I have been unable to gather any further details since my departure from Ethiopia in late 1975.

[3] Private interview with Abebe Wolde, July 27, 1974.

Ethiopia leadership planned to publish an Amharic booklet about their new notation and to distribute it for wider use.

Why is this notational system of interest? First, it provides an example of the manner in which changes in the context of performance directly affect methods of musical transmission. Second, an understanding of this notational system provides information concerning the nature of the creative process in urban Ethiopian musical life. Finally, it provides an instructive example of the role of both adaptation and synthesis in the creation of new cultural forms in modern Africa.

The development of notation by Orchestra Ethiopia

Orchestra Ethiopia was founded in 1963, two years after the estrablishment of the Creative Arts Centre. A speech by Emperor Haile Selassie at a University Convocation set the stage for the University's role in artistic "development":

> Music, dance and other forms of art are rooted in the ancient history of our Empire, and their development to an even higher peak of perfection will be possible in the atmosphere of a University[4].

The new Creative Arts Centre housed musical, dance, and dramatic activity. Orchestra Ethiopia was conceived as a forum for "modern presentation of orchestral songs through the traditional musical modes and instruments of Ethiopia", as well as an opportunity "to create a taste for Ethiopian music and dance among the younger generation"[5]. However, this new "orchestra" of local musicians playing traditional instruments raised complex problems:

> Used to giving solo recitals, the instrumentalists had to work long and hard to play in symphony and adhere to set tunes and melodies[6].

Musicians from different Ethiopian provinces were chosen through open auditions and joined in a single musical context. Accustomed to solo performance in different provincial styles, they now performed as an ensemble. Soloistic variation in taking repeats, elaborating instrumental interludes between vocal verses, and adding ornamentation, could no longer be accommodated. Instruments such as the *mäläkät*, a long, end-blown trumpet once used to proclaim public gatherings, now had to assume

4 *Patterns of Progress*, p. 59.
5 *Ibid.*, pp. 60-61.
6 *Ibid.*, p. 60.

unfamiliar "musical" roles. Instrumental tone quality and volume had to be standardized[7] for a busy concert schedule. Some instruments were modified and rebuilt to new specifications to better fulfill acoustic requirements for commercial performances and recordings. Perhaps predicatbly, this diverse group of individuals and styles could only be welded together through use of new musical materials and a new method of musical transmission.

The notational system

The three men responsible for the notational innovations drew upon their experience with both Ethiopian and western music. Nigussu Retta and Abebe Wolde studied at the Yared Music School in Addis Ababa, where traditional and Western music were combined in a joint curriculum. Both joined Orchestra Ethiopia in 1972 with the stated aim of "experimenting and developing Ethiopian musical instruments, dances, and songs"[8].

In addition to a traditional music education and study at the Yared School, Tesfaye Lemma studied music, dance, and choreography with the Alvin Ailey Dance Company in the United States in 1970, as well as musical composition at Indiana University during 1971-1972[9]. By 1973, he was playing an increasingly active role as arranger and composer of Orchestra Ethiopia's musical repertoire.

Knowledge of western notation certainly influenced both the genesis and general concept of the new notational system. However, a more direct model is found in Ethiopian sacred music. A conscious nod to Ethiopian Church notation is found in the title *maləkkət* (signs), and the statement that "the signs are not musical notations but guides for the fingers and the instrument playing particular music"[10].

---

7 Musicians from different locales generally prefer different tone quality. Ashenafi Kebede writes that rural *krar* players often prefer a more subtle, subdued tone generated by a clay or wood resonator, while urban *krar* players are accustomed to the louder volume resulting from metal resonators. "The Bowl-Lyre of Northeast Africa. *Krar*: The Devil's Instrument, *Ethnomusicology*, XXI (September, 1977), p. 383.

8 "Signs Developed for Musical Instrument", *Ethiopian Herald*, July 5, 1974, p. 1.

9 Tesfaye Lemma, *Ethiopian Musical Instruments*, I issue, 1975, p. 6. Tesfaye became director of Orchestra Ethiopia in 1966.

10 *Ethiopian Herald*, July 5, 1974. The Orchestra Ethiopia musicians do not use the term *nota* (note) in referring to the notational system. They tend to use *maləkkət* (signs) when discussing the system in Amharic and either "signs" or "notation" when speaking English.

Figure I: Signs (ምልክ ት) of the Orchestra Ethiopia Notational System

	Sign	Name	Meaning		Sign	Name	Meaning
Alphabetical Signs							
1	⸦	ትዝ ታ	Təzzəta mode	18	▬	አንፅ	Quarter rest
2	∩	በt	Bati mode	19	▣	ገማ ሽ	Eighth rest
3	ኢ.ህ.	አን ፄ ህይ	Anči hoy mode	20	✚	አፈብ	Sixteenth rest
4	ኽ	አም በስል	Ambasəl mode	21	∠	ጣማ ራ	Add half to rest
5	⸌	ዝዝ	Faster	22	——	መ ገ ራ	Continuous playing
6	∩	በ.ር	Quiet	20	←→	ቀስ ት	Repeat
7	⚤	ፙማ ት	Pluck string hard	24	✕	ስረዝ	Stop
8	ፖ	ጉዥም	Gojjam rhythm	25	⌣	ኮፍ ት	Loud
9	ፖገ	ጉንራር	Gondar rhythm	26	•– ——	ቀስ ቀስ	Soft
10	ୟ	ዶርዝ	Dorze rhythm	27	——┤	አፕር	Short cutoff
11	∞	ወ ላም	Wollamo rhythm	28	– – –	ጉርራ	Staccato
12	ፐ ∾	ትግሬ	Tigre rhythm	29	• • • • •	ነጥብ	Walking pace
13	୫	ራበ.ብ	Doubled rhythm	30	∩ ∩	ምስሌ	Imitate
14	∞ ፖገ	መ ሃለ ገ ንንራር	Middle rhythm Gondar				
15	∞ ፖ	መ ሃለ ገ ጉዥም	Middle rhythm Gojjam		**Pictographic Signs**		
				31	⧸⧹	ጣ ት	Pluck mildly (mäsənqo)
	Diagrammatic Signs			32	➤	ወ ፍር	Scrum string (mäsənqo)
19	▭	አራት	Whole rest	33	⟱	ክራር	Krar
17	▰	ሁለ ት	Half rest	34	✝⬦	መ ስነ ቀ	Mäsənqo

	Sign	Name	Meaning
35		ዋሽንት	Wašənt
36		በገና	Bäqäna
37		እጅ	Clap
38		ጣት	Snap fingers
39		ሞላስ	Ullulate
40		ጭር	Pluck string (mäsənqo)
41		ትኩሽ	Dance (əskəsta)
42		ሞላ	Vibrato
43		መስላሶ	Lengthen
44		ስንስላት	Close in time
45		እላ	Slower
46		ንስ	Ornament
47		ሞዙጋ	End of composition
Composite Signs			
48		ጠርፍ	Hit drum frame
49		መሃል	Hit drum center
50		መስንቀ ገስት	Hit mäsənqo sound-board
51		ክራር ገስት	Hit krar sound-board

NUMERICAL SIGNS

Krar

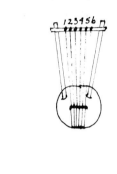

1   2   3   4   5   6

1	፯
2	፪
3	፫
4	፬
5	፭
6	፮

The signs developed for Orchestra Ethiopia are set forth in Figure 1 [11]. For purposes of discussion and analysis, they are divided into four classes: alphabetic, diagrammatic, pictographic, and numerical [12]. Figure 1 presents alphabetic, diagrammatic, and pictographic signs with their Amharic names and musical meanings. The figure also contains numerical signs which indicate melody pitches by specifying the strings (for *krar*, *bägäna*) or fingering (for *mäsənqo*, *waŝənt*). Only numbers for *krar* in *təʐʐəta* mode are provided in Figure 1.

The alphabetic signs (1-15) borrow members of the Amharic syllabary to represent complex musical phenomena. Signs 1-4 are the initial syllables of the Ethiopian modes (or tuning systems) they represent. Signs 8-15 derive from Amharic phrases describing provincial rhythms. Signs 5-7 indicate a tempo, dynamic level, or articulation, respectively. The alphabetical signs are therefore abbreviations for aspects of regional musical style or indicators of performance practice [13].

The diagrammatic signs (16-30) are freely created from various geometric forms and designate aspects of duration, dynamics, texture, and articulation. Diagrammatic signs are named either according to their diagrammatic equivalents (sign 24 is named "cross", but indicates "stop") or according to the musical concept they represent (sign 25 is both named and indicates "loud"). All are mnemonic devices which help recall a specific musical activity.

Some of the pictographic signs (31-47) signify the actual object and/or musical activity pictured; other play a mnemonic role. Signs 33-37 indicate the solo instruments pictured, while sign 32 represents the plectrum with which stringed instruments are strummed. Signs 37-47 are more diverse in their naming and in relationship to the musical event. Several portray the body part performing the musical function: sign 37 ("hand") indicates "clap"; sign 38 ("collision") indicates "snap fingers"; sign 39 ("tongue") indicates "ullulation"; and sign 41 ("shoulders") indicates "dance *askəsta*". Other pictographs do not relate directly to the musical event. For example,

---

11 Abebe Wolde provided a list of the signs in random order. I have preserved his drawings of the signs, as well as the names and meanings he supplied.

12 Two sources were particularly useful in arriving at this division: Sir Alan Gardiner, *Egyptian Grammar. Being An Introduction to The Study of Hieroglyphs* (3rd. ed. rev; London: Oxford University Press, 1969); and René Labat, *Manuel d'Épigraphie akkadienne* (5th ed.; Paris: Librairie Orientaliste Paul Geuthner, S.A., 1976).

13 Although two alphabetic signs are spelled ቢ (2 and 6), an indication of *Bati* mode would occur only at the beginning of a composition, while the sign indicating "quiet" would be placed within an instrumental part.

sign 40 ("tail") indicates "pluck (*mäsanqo*) string", sign 42 ("spring") indicates "vibrato", and sign 44 ("chain") indicates "close in time". Two pictographic signs draw upon zoological associations: sign 45 ("turtle") indicates "slower", and sign 46 ("bee") indicates "ornament".

Four signs overlap categories and are classified as composite signs. Signs 48 and 49 are both pictographic and diagrammatic, indicating the part of the drum head to be struck. Signs 50 and 51 apply the shape of the *mäsanqo* and *krar* sound-boards diagrammatically to indicate percussive striking of that part of the instruments.

Ethiopian Church *malakkat* clearly inspired signs 1-15. The leaders of Orchestra Ethiopia have borrowed the alphabetic system as a convenient way to represent rhythmic and melodic patterning, although their system differs from the Ethiopian Church's in its relationship to the musical materials [14]. A small number of diagrammatic signs are also found in Ethiopian Church notation to indicate aspects of tempo and articulation [15]. Both Ethiopian Church and Orchestra Ethiopia notations are closed systems dependent upon knowledge of the oral tradition for their realization.

Figure 2: Rest Symbols in Western Musical Notation

14 Within the Church notational system, alphabetic signs are derived from the text with which a melodic phrase is commonly associated. These signs would then be placed above a new text which should be sung to the same melody.

15 There is some confusion concerning the names of diagrammatic signs within Ethiopian Christian notation. In some sources, both the alphabetic and diagrammatic signs are termed *malakkat*. Abba Tito Lepisa, "The Three Modes and the Signs of the Songs in the Ethiopian Liturgy", *Proceedings of the Third International Conference of Ethiopian Studies*, II (Addis Ababa, 1966), pp. 166-169. In others, the syllabic signs are termed *malakkat* and the diagrammatic signs *sarayu* (*Patterns of Progress*, p. 25) The Ethiopian Church musician with whom I studied said that *sarayu* is a word written out in full instead of abbreviated in *malakkat*. Tito Lepisa defines *sarayu* as a duplication of signs (p. 167). My informant, Aleqa Berhanu Makonnen, defined ten diagrammatic signs in Ethiopian Christian notation, which he termed *fidäl malakkat*. Interview with Berhanu Makonnen, June 2, 1975.

Musical example I: Orchestra Ethiopia Notation and its Western Equivalent

Western notation probably served as a model for some diagrammatic signs. The rests (16-20) are similar in design to the western whole and half rests and are organized according to the same binary system (Figure 2). The mixed symbolic-linear system [16] also has clear precedents in western staff notation. Although there is no indication that Orchestra Ethiopia musicians drew upon it, Chinese *ch'in* notation uses numbers to represent the string to be played [17].

A Musical Example sets forth the Orchestra Ethiopia notation with equivalent western notation below each staff. The pictographic and alphabetic signs above the first system indicate a composition for solo *krar*, played with mild plucking in *təzzəta* mode. The alphabetic signs at the beginning of the first musical system are not explained in Orchestra Ethiopia materials, although they probably pertain to the rhythmic content "translated" as quadruple meter. The *təzzəta* mode is represented in western notation as an E^b key signature, althoug no A^b is present in the *təzzəta* pitch system.

Other than the above signs at the beginning, only the diagrammatic sign for repetition (23) is found in the body of the notated selection. Pitch is specified through numerical signs deployed along one horizontal line, while rhythmic values are set forth around a lower line. The notation of rhythmic values, not explained in Orchestra Ethiopia materials, resembles diastematic notation used to indicate pitch relationships in early medieval western notation [18]. Whole (◻) and quarter (△) notes are deployed below the line, while eighth (⬠) and sixteenth (▲) notes intersect the line. Beaming (connecting several notes in groups) is indicated by a line between the signs (△▲▲). Triplet rhythms are notated in a western manner with the number 3 (𝟥) written over beamed note values.

This notational system codifies changes in traditional style. All rhythmic and pitch content is prescribed with no latitude for ornamentation. Rhythmic and melodic content are simplified, leaving little to the discretion of the performer.

Evidence from the musical example indicates that Orchestra Ethiopia musicians may be altering traditional *krar* tunings. A *krar* is customarily tuned with the primary tone (*mällas*) at the sixth string and the same pitch

---

16 Charles Seeger, "Prescriptive and Descriptive Music Writing", *Studies in Musicology* 1935-1975 (Berkeley: University of California Press, 1977), pp. 168-169.

17 William P. Malm, *Japanese Music and Musical Instruments* (Rutland, Vermont and Tokyo: Charles E. Tuttle, 1959), p. 264.

18 Diastematic notations employ signs grouped above a line in a pattern corresponding to the size of the desired interval. Curt Sachs, *The Rise of Music in the Ancient World East and West* (New York: W. W. Norton & Company, 1940), p. 138.

an octave higher at the fifth string[19] (See Figure 1). There is considerable confusion in the musical notation between the pitch E (*mällas̆*) and E¹, its octave equivalent. According to traditional tuning, the sixth string should represent E and be notated as $\frac{z}{4}$, while E¹ should be notated as $\frac{z}{4}$. Ambiguity concerning the identity of E and E¹ either reflects a different *krar* tuning or disregard of notational constraints.

Conclusion

Orchestra Ethiopia is itself a creation and reflection of urban Ethiopian society and the dream of a multi-ethnic, yet unified culture. The new notational system was a device through which musicians of diverse ethnic and regional backgrounds could perform together in a new context, and through which a new repertory of music could be taught and transmitted.

The development of the notational system provides a glimpse into musical changes in the Ethiopian capital. Orchestra Ethiopia was not the first folklore orchestra in Addis Ababa—both the National Patriotic Folklore Orchestra and the cultural troupe of the Haile Selassie I Theatre were founded much earlier[20]. However, these groups learned and performed musical arrangements orally. Western musical notation was used only by the Imperial Court Orchestra, which played a strictly "western" repertoire[21]. By the early 1970's, Orchestra Ethiopia's musical needs were no longer met by oral transmission. Their activities had shifted from preservation of provincial musical traditions to innovation in a traditional style. This new creative

---

19 Ashenafi Kebede, "The Bowl-Lyre of North-East Africa", p. 386.

20 The National Patriotic Association was founded in around 1935 by Makonnen Habte Wold. *Ethiopian National Patriotic Association, Oldest & Popular Cultural Institution in Ethiopia* (Addis Ababa: Publication of the Ethiopian National Patriotic Association, 1970), p. 3. The Haile Selassie I Theatre band was recruited in 1946 by the municipality of Addis Ababa, and incorporated into activities of the Haile Selassie I Theatre after its inauguration in 1955. *Haile Selassie I Theatre, The Storehouse of Ethiopian Music, Dance & Drama* (Addis Ababa: Publication of the Haile Selassie I Theatre, 1970), p. 8.

21 Members of the Imperial Court Orchestra learned western notation from their conductors as early as 1930. This information was supplied by Gustav Meier, conductor at the University of Michigan School of Music, Ann Arbor, who conducted the Imperial Court Orchestra in Addis Ababa during 1955. Meier recalls that some Orchestra members had studied in Europe or at the Yared School. Orchestra repertory was almost exclusively western "classics" and one favorite was Stravinsky's "L'histoire du soldat". Occasionally, members of the Orchestra would play an Ethiopian melody in unison with percussion accompaniment, but these arrangements were never notated.

activity demanded adjustment in the process of transmission, and the musicians chose to develop a system of musical notation.

Recent studies of aspects of urban musical culture in Africa have cautioned against classifying as "imitative" traditions which apparently copy western culture. In a study of dance societies in East Africa, T. O. Ranger concludes that

> Beni (*ngoma*), with its overwhelmingly imitative character, turns out in the end to be deeply rooted in pre-colonial dance and competitive modes. In this it serves to remind us that judgements of derivation or creativity need to be more subtle than a mere assumption that everything "modern" comes from the whites [22].

Musical folklore groups in Addis Ababa have often been disparaged as flawed and westernized reflections of traditional musical practices. Yet this brief discussion shows that what might be casually attributed to the influence of western notation is solidly linked to precedents within Ethiopian culture. The leaders of Orchestra Ethiopia have not borrowed a notational system. Rather, they have fused Ethiopian and western elements as part of a dynamic musical process.

Acknowledgements

I thank the leaders of Orchestra Ethiopia for access to their new notational system. Charlotte Wright and Jack Shelemay made helpful suggestions concerning organization and analysis of the notational system. Thomas Kane provided guidance in the presentation of Amharic terms. This article was written during a 1981-1982 fellowship year supported by the American Council of Learned Societies.

Sources cited

Ashenafi Kebede. "The Bowl-Lyre of Northeast Africa. *Krar*: The Devil's Instrument". *Ethnomusicology*, XXI (September, 1977), 379-396.

Budge, Sir E. A. Wallis. *The Book of the Saints of the Ethiopian Church. A translation of the Ethiopic Synaxarium made from manuscripts 660 and 661 in the British Museum*. Vol. III. Cambridge: At the University Press, 1928.

Dillmann, Augustus. *Lexicon Linguae Aethiopicae*. Reprint ed. Osnabrück: Biblio Verlag, 1970.

22 T. O. Ranger, *Dance and Society in Eastern Africa 1890-1970* (Berkeley: University of California Press, 1975), pp. 6-7.

Gardiner, Sir Alan. *Egyptian Grammar. Being An Introduction to the Study of Hieroglyphs.* 3rd ed. London: Oxford University Press, 1969.

Haile Selassie I Theatre, The Storehouse of Ethiopian Music, Dance, & Drama. Addis Ababa: Publication of the Haile Selassie I Theatre, 1970.

Labat, René. *Manuel d'épigraphie akkadienne.* 5th ed. Paris: Librairie Orientaliste Paul Geuthner, S.A., 1976.

Lepisa, Abba Tito, "The Three Modes and the Signs of the Songs in the Ethiopian Liturgy". *Proceedings of the Third International Conference of Ethiopian Studies*, II. Addis Ababa, 1966, pp. 162-187.

Leslau, Wolf. *Concise Amharic Dictionary.* Wiesbaden: Otto Harrassowitz, 1976.

Malm, William P. *Japanese Music and Musical Instruments.* Rutland, Vermont and Tokyo: Charles E. Tuttle, 1959.

Patterns of Progress. Music, Dance and Drama. Addis Ababa: Ministry of Information, 1968.

Ranger, T. O. *Dance and Society in Eastern Africa 1890-1970.* Berkeley: University of California Press, 1975.

Sachs, Curt. *The Rise of Music in the Ancient World East and West.* New York: Norton & Company, 1940

Seeger, Charles. "Prescriptive and Descriptive Music Writing". *Studies in Musicology 1935-1975.* Berkeley: University of California Press, 1977.

"Signs Developed for Musical Instruments". *The Ethiopian Herald.* July 5, 1974.

Tesfaye Lemma, *Ethiopian Musical Instruments*, I issue. Addis Ababa: n.p., 1975.